Instructor's Manual to accompany

LITERATURE

STRUCTURE, SOUND, AND SENSE

SIXTH EDITION

LAURENCE PERRINE

THOMAS R. ARP

Southern Methodist University

G. R. H. S.
Desk Copy

Harcourt Brace College Publishers
Fort Worth   Philadelphia   San Diego
New York   Orlando   Austin   San Antonio
Toronto   Montreal   London   Sydney   Tokyo

ISBN: 0-15-500299-6

FOREWORD

This instructor's manual offers ideas for interpreting all of the stories, poems, and plays included in *Literature: Structure, Sound, and Sense,* Sixth Edition, and makes some suggestions for teaching them. It cannot answer all questions, however, nor can it replace the body of criticism that has grown up around many of these selections. Interpretation is a joint critical enterprise, and the good teacher will often consult the interpretations of other readers. For this purpose, basic bibliographical tools are essential. Among the most useful are the following:

1. For short stories: see Warren S. Walker, *Twentieth-Century Short Story Explication: Interpretations, 1900–1975, of Short Fiction Since 1800,* 3rd ed. (Hamden CT: Shoe String, 1977), with supplements published at frequent intervals. For interpretations published since 1975, you may also consult the annual bibliographies published in the summer issues of *Studies in Short Fiction.*

2. For poetry: very recently G. K. Hall and Company have begun publishing a new series of guides to poetry explications (e.g., *Guide to American Poetry Explication,* vols. 1 and 2), which list explications published through the 1980s. The annual bibliographical issues of *The Explicator* and *PMLA* may be checked for more recent explications.

3. For plays: see Helen H. Palmer, *European Drama Criticism 1900–1975,* 2nd ed. (Hamden CT: Shoe String, 1977) with supplements; Irving Adelman and Rita Dworkin, *Modern Drama: A Checklist of Critical Literature on 20th-Century Plays* (Metuchen NJ: Scarecrow, 1967); Charles A. Carpenter; *Modern Drama Scholarship and Criticism: An International Bibliography* (Toronto: U of Toronto P, 1980); and Philip C. Kolin, ed., *American Playwrights Since 1945: Guide to Scholarship, Criticism, and Performance* (New York: Greenwood, 1989). These may be supplemented by the annual bibliographies in *Modern Drama* (now published at the University of Toronto).

To the interpretations and judgments in this manual we should be foolish to expect universal consent; they will serve their purpose if they provoke a more careful scrutiny of the works in question, and an intelligent dissent. Indeed, we have not always agreed with each other, and for that reason, although we have checked and criticized each other's work, we have appended after each discussion the initials of its main author. Certainly, the approach taken here to any selection is only one of various possible approaches. Zeus does not speak in any of these comments, but in the works themselves. The oracles that report him here are neither priests nor prophets, but fallible human beings like yourselves.

Laurence Perrine and Thomas R. Arp

CONTENTS

POETRY   **The Elements of Poetry**   87

CHAPTER EIGHT   *Allusion*   161

CHAPTER NINE   *Meaning and Idea*   171

CHAPTER THIRTEEN   *Sound and Meaning*   213

CHAPTER FOURTEEN   *Pattern*   229

CHAPTER FIFTEEN   *Bad Poetry and Good*   245

CHAPTER SIXTEEN   *Good Poetry and Great*   255

Poems for Further Reading   257

DRAMA   The Elements of Drama   345

Plays for Further Reading   370

Thematic Table of Contents   383

The Elements of Fiction

CHAPTER ONE

Escape and Interpretation

Richard Connell **The Most Dangerous Game** (page 8)

"The Most Dangerous Game" is an exciting suspense story, and students will like it. The kinds of conflict it embodies and its chief devices for arousing and maintaining suspense are discussed on pages 42–44. Its use of name symbolism is briefly discussed on page 195, its point of view on page 143, and its irony on page 200. The trick in teaching it will be to draw from the students themselves, as subtly as possible, a perception of its limitations, for nothing turns students off faster than scoffing at something they like, or betraying a tendency to look down on it.

The improbabilities of the story are patent enough. There is, first of all, the implausibility of the "mystery" of Ship-Trap Island. In the opening conversation between Whitney and Rainsford we are given to believe that very little is known of this "God-forsaken place"—only vague superstitions and ominous legends. Yet when Rainsford visits the place, we find out that the island is equipped with electricity and that General Zaroff, in his immense, well-maintained château, serves soup with whipped cream, imports his clothes and his champagne from overseas, and smokes perfumed cigarettes. It clearly takes a community of thousands to run this place, and there must be constant commerce between it and the rest of the world. It is hard to fathom how there can be much of a secret about it. But the author disguises this implausibility from us by showing us no human beings there except Zaroff and Ivan. Unless we stop to think, we regard the island as isolated and virtually uninhabited. The problem of social control—of how Zaroff runs this place and pursues his inhuman pleasures without inspiring rebellion (it would take a small private army) — is not addressed. This basic unreality of social environment may be contrasted with the firm sense of a community that we get in "The Child by Tiger."

The character of Zaroff is equally implausible. Manufactured by the conjunction of contradictory traits — extreme savagery (he says that Ivan is "like all his race, a bit of a savage," and then adds, "He is a Cossack. . . . So am I") and extreme civility, Zaroff is an effective character for a story of this kind — that is, he is blood-chilling. But he adds nothing to our knowledge of human nature. Boredom with the tameness of hunting grizzlies, jaguars, and Cape buffalo (and, after all, a Cape buffalo did lay him up for six months) is hardly enough to explain his psychological aberration, nor is it probable that his psychological aberration should have no other symptom but scorn for "romantic ideas about the value of human life." Calm rationality marks everything that Zaroff does. Even so, his character is inconsistent. A gambler plays to win his bet, a hunter hunts to kill. There is no plausible reason why Zaroff should thrice turn back from the hunt after tracking down his game, except that the author arbitrarily wants to prolong the excitement. In short, Zaroff is not believable (contrast him with the delinquents in "The Destructors" and Dick Prosser in "The Child by Tiger"). He *is*, however, vivid. The little details of characterization ("Then he sat down, took a drink of brandy from a silver flask, lit a perfumed cigaret, and hummed a bit from *Madame Butterfly*") make him a much more memorable and substantial character than Rainsford. Rainsford is merely a stock adventure-story hero: tall, brave, strong, resourceful, virtuous (he is quick to condemn manhunts as "cold-blooded murder"). His one individualizing trait — the touch of unimaginativeness betrayed in his opening conversation with Whitney — is made no more of. The main conflict of the story is good versus evil, hero versus villain.

But the basic evidence that "The Most Dangerous Game" is an escape story is its absence of organic unity and therefore of theme. This is discussed on page 316.

Should we care? It has been a good story — perhaps that is enough. But it is not enough if we never ask for anything more. LP

A British film based on this story is entitled *The Hounds of Zaroff*; an older full-length feature version using the original title fabricates a "love interest" for Rainsford.

Thomas Wolfe **The Child by Tiger** (page 24)

Originally published in *The Saturday Evening Post* for September 11, 1937, and reprinted in *Post Stories of 1937* (Boston: Little, Brown, 1938), "The Child by Tiger" was afterward slightly altered and expanded by Wolfe for inclusion as Chapter 8 in his novel *The Web and the Rock* (New York: Harper, 1939). The earlier version is used here because, written to be a short story rather than part of a novel, it has a self-contained self-sufficiency that the later version lacks. The chief change between the two versions is an alteration in the point of view. The short story is told from the first-person point of view with the boy (named Spangler) as narrator. The novel uses the limited omniscient point of view. The reason for the change is that

2

the boy, who is only a minor character in the short story, becomes the central character of the novel (though, re-named "Monk" Webber, he remains an observer in this episode). For a story told from the angle of vision of an observer rather than a participant, first-person point of view is ideally adapted, for it has greater naturalness and immediacy than other points of view, and there is seldom need for the author to tell us more about the narrator than he can tell us about himself. Use of the limited omniscient point of view, as pointed out in Chapter 5, is extremely rare when the viewpoint is that of a minor character. Wolfe shifted to the limited omniscient point of view for his novel probably for two reasons: first, with the minor character now his major character, he did need to tell us more about him than the protagonist could believably tell us; second, he wished as much as possible to avoid identification of the protagonist with himself, for which he had been criticized in his earlier novels.

Like "The Most Dangerous Game," "The Child by Tiger" is the story of a manhunt, complete with the use of hounds; but in setting, plot, character—in almost all respects—it is more credible, more complex, and more significant.

The most significant fact about the town that furnishes the setting of the story (in the novel it is called Libya Hill and is clearly a fictional version of Asheville, North Carolina, where Wolfe grew up) is that its social and economic structure is based on white dominance over blacks. It is a town where blacks work as chauffeurs, handymen, cooks, and Pullman porters, and where the mayor, the police, the professional men, and most of the shopowners are white. Blacks have a choice of living in basement rooms or in "Niggertown"; the best parts of town are reserved for whites. The spectrum of white inhabitants of the town extends from decent people like the Sheppertons, who are kindly to their colored help, to vicious types like Lon Everett, the sot who smashes Dick in the face after drunkenly running into him, and Ben Pounders, the ferret-faced, mongrel-mouthed "collector of usurious lendings to the blacks," who boasts of putting the first shot into Dick.

The conflicts of the story, however, do not just involve blacks against whites. Dick's maniacal outburst is triggered by conflict with a black man over possession of a black woman, and, when he goes berserk, he kills indiscriminately, black or white. The whites are also in conflict with one another. Mayor Will Hendershot, Hugh McNair, and one or two others make a heroic effort to protect Cash Eager's hardware shop and to keep the mob from lynch law.

Yet the origins of Dick's craziness, insofar as they are not part of the mystery of all human nature, lie clearly in the racial situation of the town and region. A man of superior abilities and gifts, Dick must take work tending the furnace and driving a car. A grown man of over thirty, he has learned to flatter the children of the white race by addressing them as "Cap'n" and "Mr." A highly religious man, he waits for his white employers on Sundays standing at the side door of the white church, "holding his chauffeur's hat respectfully in his hand." Unjustly struck in the face by a drunken white man, he knows that, to keep out of trouble, he must keep his hands at his sides and let himself be struck again. Discovered with a rifle in his room by the white boys, he knows that it may be taken away from him unless he gives an acceptable explanation for possessing it, and he does so by inventing a falsehood. In short, Dick functions constantly in situations that are an affront to

3

his human dignity and abilities, and he constantly suppresses his instinctive reactions to such situations until suppression itself has become a kind of second instinct. The strain of these suppressions, shown only occasionally in a narrowing and reddening of his eyes, is what leads to Dick's homicidal outburst. Yet Dick is not conscious of being oppressed by a white society; he has merely adjusted, subconsciously, to what seems to him the natural order of things. His outbreak, therefore, does not take the form of turning against whites. He goes truly crazy: he turns against everybody.

The theme of the story has to do with the mysterious presence of violence, savagery, and evil in the human soul. Dick is a symbol of that destructive violence, as is the tiger in Blake's poem. From the beginning of the story, Dick is identified with that tiger or with the offspring of that tiger. He gathers up the football ''in his great black paw,'' at boxing he is ''as cunning and crafty as a cat,'' he moves softly and swiftly and is on one ''sometimes like a cat.'' At the end he is identified explicitly as ''a tiger and a child.'' But Dick is not the symbol of black violence; he is the symbol of *human* violence. His savage outbreak is matched by the savage outbreak of the whites. There is a ''blood note'' in the ugly growl of the crowd that gathers in the square. In the sound of the baying hounds, there is ''the savagery of blood'' and ''the savagery of man's guilty doom.'' It is significant that this savage excitement touches even the boys, who are Dick's friends and champions. Nebraska Crane's eyes, as he summons his friend, shine ''with a savage sparkle.'' The whites, when they riddle Dick's body with bullets, have gone berserk just as Dick went berserk. Dick is ''night's child and partner, a token of the other side of man's dark soul . . . a symbol of men's evil innocence.''

''The Child by Tiger'' is not a suspense story like ''The Most Dangerous Game,'' yet there is plenty of suspense in it. At first there is the mystery of Dick's character. Dick is declared by Mr. Shepperton to be ''the best man he'd ever had.'' ''And yet?'' the narrator asks. ''He went too softly, at too swift a pace . . . there was something moving in the night. . . .'' The reader's curiosity is aroused by this mystery and by the sense of something to come. Then, as soon as the boys see the rifle in Dick's room, ''blue-dull, deadly in its murderous efficiency,'' and especially when they hear the ringing of the fire bell in the city hall, the reader wants to know what will happen next. The excitement continues unabated until Dick's death.

What is the meaning of Dick's final gesture of removing his shoes and facing the mob, erect, on bare bleeding feet? It is something, the narrator says, ''that no one ever wholly understood.'' It may be an act of humility as Dick prepares to meet his Maker (see Exodus 3.5 and Acts 7.33). Or it may be equally a gesture of human dignity, an assertion of manhood. Dick will no longer flee like a hunted animal. He is a man, and will face his death like a man.

Dick, in fact, is not only a man; he is ourselves.

There are further brief references to this story in the text on pages 46, 70, 98, 145, 198, and 199. LP

4

CHAPTER TWO

Plot

Graham Greene **The Destructors** (page 49)

"Destruction after all is a form of creation," the narrator tells us in what might well serve as a compact statement of the theme of the story. The creative instinct, unable to find a constructive outlet, turns to destruction and derives artistic and imaginative satisfactions from it. The protagonists of this story—the gang—work hard at destruction. They reject opportunities for personal gain that accompany it. Absorbed in their work, they forget personal rivalries. Blackie and Trevor cooperate fully. "The question of leadership no longer concerned the gang."

But the story has a social setting, which expands the theme. The members of the gang live in a blitzed world. Unconsciously they are taking revenge on a society that has betrayed them. This society is a class society, and all the values associated with it are fitly symbolized in the two-hundred-year-old house, built by a titled architect, Sir Christopher Wren. Partly these are snob values, as evidenced by Trevor's mother, who "considered herself better than her neighbors" though her husband has "come down in the world." Partly they are money values, as represented by the bank notes that Trevor and Blackie burn. But they are also such values as beauty, courtesy, love. "It's a beautiful house," says Trevor, who is later ridiculed when he says "Please." Trevor has turned against these values himself: "All this hate and love," he tells Blackie, "it's soft, it's hooey. There's only things." The symbolic identification of the house with the old social order and its values is established by the link between Blackie's meditation on the word "beautiful" and the lorry-driver's vision of the house at the end of the story. Blackie worries over the word "beautiful": it "belonged to a class world that you could still see parodied at the Wormsley Common Empire by *a man wearing a top hat* and a monocle, with a haw-haw accent" (italics LP). The lorry-driver cannot constrain his laughter: "One moment the house had stood there with such dignity between the bomb-sites like *a man in a top hat*, and then, bang, crash, there wasn't anything left—not anything" (italics LP).

There are additional brief comments on this story on pages 67–68, 97, 143, 195, and 200.   LP

Alice Munro **Prue** (page 61)

The ending of this story is indeterminate, for as Prue says, "'nobody knows what can happen in a few years' time,'" so there is no way of predicting whether Prue and Gordon will marry, or in fact if they will still continue to see each other after his strange announcements — "'The problem is that I think I would like to marry you,'" and "'I think I'm in love with this person'" (the unseen woman who presumably expected to be spending the night with him).

The absence of a resolution of the conflicts is central to the theme of the story, for it is concerned with the personal complications that arise in the lives of people who have failed to mature beyond a kind of emotional adolescence. Neither Gordon nor Prue has been able to achieve emotional stability and selflessness in love. This is most easily seen in Gordon, for he is the simpler case (perhaps because he is filtered through Prue's point of view).

"Gordon is rich," a neurologist whose behavior suggests an inability to restrain his sexual impulses, or at least a lack of respect and insight into his sexual partners. Prue's relationship with him apparently began when he stayed at the resort hotel on Vancouver where she worked, an affair that resulted in her moving to Toronto to be near him. The opening two paragraphs sketch in Gordon's sexual morality: an affair with a dining-room hostess who moves to a location near his home, where the affair continues while he lives with his wife; then during a separation from his wife, "a year and four months" of living with Prue, a return to his wife, a divorce, and then "a period of indecision, of living together off and on" until "the wife" (as she is called) leaves the country, and finally the present arrangement in which he sleeps with Prue as well as with other women. The ambiguity of the statement about the "period of indecision" is functional — it is unclear whether he was "living together off and on" with Prue or with the wife, and one may safely assume that *both* women continued to have his attention during this post-divorce time.

Prue's summary definition of Gordon is that "there is a helpless, baffled soul squirming around inside" his bulky body, an apt phrase for a man who cannot find in himself the certainties of love and commitment.

Prue herself is more complicated. Divorced after a "marriage she calls a cosmic disaster" in the "lighthearted way" she expresses her cynical view of her experiences, she has apparently taken on that tone as a way of avoiding a serious self-examination. She amuses and baffles others by making herself the butt of jokes and wisecracks, and seems to regard life without seriousness but with amused detachment. She has become "like a flighty daughter" to her own children, regressing into childlike ir-responsibility. Once when they tried to joke her out of smoking (because they were seriously worried, but wanted to meet her on her own terms), they presented her with a tobacco tin full of candy, "with a note saying, 'Please get fat instead.'" This box has become the repository for symbolic tokens of her disappointing emotional relationship with Gordon, aptly so since like a child she has a secret cache of useless treasures taken from him that she refuses to think symbolic or meaningful, for that would invest them with importance and require her to analyze herself. So, into the tobacco tin/candybox she lightheartedly deposits serious reminders of her emotional life. Early in the story we learn that Prue has a way of talking about her life in anec-dotes: "it is the point of most of her anecdotes that hopes are dashed, dreams ridi-culed, things never turn out as expected, [yet] everything is altered in a bizarre way and there is no explanation ever." This is true of the contents of the box — they are bizarre, unexplained evidence that in her relationship with Gordon she has had her hopes dashed, her dreams ridiculed, her expectations frustrated. But she willfully refuses to face the conflicts that exist within herself and with her antagonist.

"Prue is a schoolgirl . . . and Prudence is an old virgin," she complainingly says of her name. And these two extremes are sad definitions of this woman "in her late forties," still maintaining the happy-go-lucky flippancy of a schoolgirl, but facing a future not technically virginal, though most probably without a lasting, loving relationship.   TRA

CHAPTER THREE

Character

Sherwood Anderson   **I'm a Fool** (page 71)

There are brief remarks on the theme of this story on pages 95 and 99, on its point of view on pages 145–47, on its use of dramatic irony on page 200, and on its style on pages 315–16.

The swipe has a strong inferiority complex, deriving from the depressed social and economic status of his family, his lack of success in school, and his inability to get work though he is a "big lumbering fellow of nineteen." His behavior and his philosophy are largely explainable in terms of attempts to establish a sense of his own importance. His actions are unconsciously designed either to let himself feel superior or to retaliate against having been made to feel inferior. He enjoys having "a fine nigger like Burt for best friend," for instance, because, although Burt is clearly superior to him in knowledge and talents, Burt's color allows the swipe to associate with him as an equal. Being on the inside of the race track world also gives him pleasure, for it enables him to feel superior to those on the outside, whom he contemptuously refers to as "yaps" or "common cattle." Appearing in front of the grandstand in his "dirty horsy pants" gives him a sense of importance, and so does sitting in good clothes in good seats in the grandstand. His declaration, "You can stick your colleges up your nose for all me," is rationalization. He is aware that the world in general respects education; deep down he has respect for it too, derived from his family; and he must protect himself from self-condemnation because of his failure at it. His statement that "a fellow, just because he has been a swipe with a race horse, and works taking care of horses for a man in the teaming, delivery, and storage business isn't any better or worse than anyone else" is also a rationalization. A person who's always thinking and saying that he's just as good as anyone else is obviously afraid that he isn't, and must constantly reassure himself. The boy's mother and sister both think it "something disgraceful" that one of their family "should take a place as a swipe with race horses." The swipe has himself partly internalized their judgment, or he wouldn't have to fight so hard against it. The swipe's central principle for action, "Put up a good front," is clearly designed to make himself feel important. It works until he meets someone who puts up a better front than he does. Such behavior stirs up his feelings of inferiority again. He resents it, refers to it as "putting on airs," and retaliates against it. On the other hand, when he meets people superior to himself who treat him as an equal, he is deeply grateful. Wilbur Wessen is "the kind that goes to college and then comes to be a lawyer or maybe a newspaper editor or something like that, but he wasn't stuck on himself . . . he didn't talk big and noisy and let everyone around know he was a sport, as some do'' (including the swipe himself, though he doesn't realize it). The swipe's acceptance by the Wessens and Miss Woodberry, with their good families and "swell names," gives him a sense of importance. Even so, he feels the need to continue putting up "a good front" and establish equality with them, and so he invents the story that he is Walter Mathers. The drink of whiskey and the man in the Windsor tie have nothing to do with this. It is the culmination of his normal pattern of behavior.

Morally the swipe is of little account. He accepts going through a house in its owner's absence and the "fixing" of horse races (pages 74–75) as a matter of course, and he regards stealing, getting drunk, and swearing as signs of manliness (page 72). He isn't positively mean (though he would like seriously to "injure" the lad who took his lawn-mowing jobs away from him), but he passively accepts the morals of the race-track world he finds himself in and the values of those who have been successful in it. Because the story is told from the first-person point of view, however, the reader identifies with the swipe and shares his feelings. The reader sees him as a human being capable of joy and hope, subject to hurt and disappointment, and deserving of compassion. The end of the story brings genuine heartbreak. The reader feels *with* the swipe, not just *for* him, let alone *against* him.   LP

A dramatized version of this story starring Ron Howard was produced for the PBS television series "The American Short Story." The objective point of view created for filming blunts the irony of the imperceptive narrator, and some alterations in the plot serve to make the swipe a more charming and ingenuous character (he has apparently never been with a girl, for example, so his knowledge of what "some Janes" are willing to do is excised). Because of these changes, the videotape can be a valuable contrast for the classroom teacher even while it is less than faithful to the meaning of the story.   TRA

Alice Walker **Everyday Use** (page 80)

The theme of "Everyday Use" is mentioned on page 97, and its symbolism and use of irony on pages 195, 197, and 199.

The story presents its theme ironically by contrasting ideas of "heritage." Dee (self-named "Wangero"), dressed in African costume and scornfully bullying her mother and sister for their backwardness even while she plunders their house, has artificially, fictitiously created for herself a past that includes pride in an African origin and a nostalgia for the simplicity of her downtrodden kinfolk; the narrator has as her past what she can remember having lived and heard (Wangero's attempts to make her mother acknowledge that the name Dee originated with the white oppressors fails—for though the mother believes she *could* trace the name back to the days of slavery if she wanted to, she reacts to the bullying by saying she will go no further back than her own and her sister's time). Hakim, Wangero's companion (husband? wonders the mother), has his version of a past, captured in committing himself to Islam. Maggie's past is not only memory (she wouldn't need a quilt to

9

remember Grandma Dee) but also a vital and active part of her present—for she can in fact make quilts herself, having been taught by her authentic ancestors the arts and crafts of making things for "everyday use" that her sophisticated sister considers artifacts of a quaint past.

The contrast between Maggie and Wangero is the battleground of the mother's spirit, and when the conflict focuses on the quilts that her educated daughter would snatch away and hang on the wall to display her heritage, the mother takes her stand: what has been promised to Maggie will be Maggie's, and Dee will not get her own way—for once. This climactic decision defines the dynamic characterization of the mother, not a temporary but a permanent change, for it has been working its way to the fore throughout the narration.

The preparation for this change has been embedded in the mother's continuing ambivalence about Dee, a woman both to be admired and to be feared, so headstrong as always to have managed "to stare down any disaster in her efforts," dangerous but strong. How dangerous she is may be indicated by the implication that she burnt down their house—and nearly burnt her sister to death—because of hatred for it (and perhaps, as the narrator once thought, hatred of her sister as well). The mother knows her well, knows that there should be limits on what she can get away with, yet until the climax has always found it better to yield. But she remembers, having been "hooked in the side in '49, [that] cows are soothing and slow and don't bother you, unless you try to milk them the wrong way." In this story, Dee finally tries "to milk" her mother "the wrong way," and discovers the limits of maternal indulgence.

Much can be taught about the subtleties of fiction with this story: the first-person narration, from the perspective of a woman who freely concedes lack of education and sophistication, lack of femininity and grace, displays an admirable economy in the selection of detail and meditation. Like the remark about cows, almost every reported thought has the double purpose of revealing character and advancing theme. For example, the mother's little "dream" of appearing on TV on "This Is Your Life" to greet her grateful, successful daughter discriminates between fiction and reality (she knows that all is rehearsed and prettified for the audience), but it also reveals a desire to be the glamorous, svelte, witty, and self-confident woman Dee would like her to be. The narrator is ignorant of the black movement and its varieties of expression—Wangero's allegiance to a tribal Africa in her name, her dress, her jewelry; Hakim's allegiance to a Muslim Africa and its Arabic traditions; and the "beef-cattle peoples down the road," apparently a black nationalist commune so unimaginable to her that the narrator "walked a mile and a half just to see the sight" of black men having rifles to protect themselves against racial assault. Yet her wonder at these things, and her simple naiveté in reporting them, comically reveal her balanced judiciousness in reacting to them. While it is not in her nature to judge outright (perhaps as a result of her religious faith), she is certainly a trustworthy observer of fads and fashions—and she remains honest about her feelings even when circumstances might elicit blanket condemnation: although she thinks Dee's dress outlandish, "so loud it hurts [her] eyes," when she sees her daughter walk in it she admits she likes its flowing looseness.

The central thematic contrast in the story pits the narrator's (and Maggie's) honesty and integrity against the posturing and artificiality of Dee, their self-sacrifice against her rapacity, their authentic relationship to a heritage of beautiful things made for "everyday use" against her ethnic pretentiousness. What is most remarkable about the mother, perhaps, is her patience and forbearance — how many of us would have sat through Dee's taking "picture after picture" of what she regards as squalid quaintness, photographing a tin-roofed duplicate of a house she may have destroyed out of hatred for it and what it stood for, but now to be recorded as evidence of her "heritage"? And all that before she puts her camera away for a condescending kiss of greeting! TRA

Katherine Mansfield **Miss Brill** (page 88)

The story's theme is briefly discussed on page 98, its plot on pages 47 and 316, its point of view on page 144, and its symbolism on pages 197–200.

Katherine Mansfield's little masterpiece presents us with the pathetic moment in the life of an elderly and lonely spinster when she realizes for the first time that she is old and lonely. The setting is a French resort town, probably on the Riviera. Miss Brill is an Englishwoman who supports herself by tutoring the children of English families in the town and by reading the papers to an old invalid gentleman. We know that she is getting old because of her methodical ways and set habits. She keeps her fur wrapped in moth powder and repairs it with sealing wax. Every Sunday, in season and out, she goes to the park, always starting from home at exactly the same time, always sitting in her "special seat," always on the way back buying an almond cake for her Sunday treat. We know that Miss Brill has no friends, for she goes to the park alone, eats her Sunday meal alone, has no one to confide in except her pupils, has to make up surprises for herself. (When there is an almond in her cake, Miss Brill strikes her match in "quite a dashing way.") We never learn her first name, for no one ever calls her by it. The fact that she is a spinster and in a foreign country underlines her isolation. The title suits this story perfectly: it tells us that the protagonist is English, unmarried, and friendless.

At the beginning of the story, however, Miss Brill does not realize her loneliness, for she has developed a knack for projecting herself into the lives of people around her. She dramatizes her fur: "Dear little thing! . . . 'What has been happening to me?' said the sad little eyes. . . . Little rogue biting its tail just by her left ear." She dramatizes the band: out of season it "was like someone playing with only the family to listen." Especially she dramatizes people: she has become an expert in eavesdropping on conversations, "sitting in other people's lives just for a minute." The fur, the band, its conductor with his new coat, the other people in the park, the children — all become persons in Miss Brill's life. She doesn't realize that she's living entirely in her own imagination, in a world of her creation. Neither does she think of herself as old. At one point she makes a significant observation.

Other people sat on the benches and green chairs, but they were nearly always the same, Sunday after Sunday, and — Miss Brill had often noticed — there was something funny

11

about nearly all of them. They were odd, silent, nearly all old, and from the way they stared they looked as though they'd just come from dark little rooms or even—even cupboards!

This description is ironic, for, without Miss Brill's realizing it, it fits her perfectly. At the end of the story she is called "a stupid old thing," and she returns to her dark little room "like a cupboard."

The moment of insight is shattering for Miss Brill and poignant for the reader. It is so, for two reasons. First, Miss Brill, however odd, old, and withdrawn she may appear on the outside, has been revealed as warm and gentle on the inside. There is nothing mean, cranky, or vindictive about her. She wants people to love one another. She would like to "shake" the English lady who keeps complaining to her sympathetic husband. She is distressed when a beautiful woman flings away her violets that a little boy has picked up for her. And she hears the drum beating "The Brute! The Brute!" when a man puffs smoke into the face of the lady in the ermine toque. (The "lady" in the ermine toque is clearly a prostitute soliciting trade, but Miss Brill, innocent and unworldly, does not realize this and sympathizes with her entirely.) Though Miss Brill's own need for love is frustrated and repressed, she desires love for other people. Second, the moment of disillusion contrasts sharply and ironically with the mood of joy which Miss Brill, and the reader, feel up until that shock. Joy rises steadily in the story from its opening sentence: "It was so brilliantly fine—the blue sky powdered with gold and great spots of light like white wine splashed over the Jardins Publiques," through Miss Brill's fancying that she is participating in a play, to the climax in which it seems to her that "in another moment all of them, all the whole company, would begin singing." Then come the cruel words, thrust like a dagger at her and her beloved fur.

What effect does the incident have on Miss Brill's life? Does she ever strike her match in "a dashing way" again? We know that she does not buy her usual almond cake that Sunday. And we know that an illusion has been destroyed for her. She will never be able to think of herself in quite the same way again. At the beginning of the story Miss Brill is in love with the world. At the end she has been rudely thrust out of it.

What are we to make of the last sentence? She puts her fur back in its box: "But when she put the lid on she thought she heard something crying." In one respect Miss Brill has not changed. She still dramatizes the things around her, and her poor little fur piece has been insulted. The fur piece, of course, is a symbol for Miss Brill herself. It too comes out of a dark box, and goes back into a dark box. It too has been ridiculed. At the end of the story Miss Brill and the fur piece merge. It is herself that she hears crying. LP

CHAPTER FOUR

Theme

Isaac Bashevis Singer **The Son from America** (page 99)

There is a brief reference on page 143 to the point of view used in this story.

The heart of the story centers on the conflict between the Old World values of peasants in a tiny Polish village and the New World values of most Americans. The theme (or one way of putting it) is that peasants in a small farming community in Europe may be perfectly content in their lives with only the simplest belongings, and with none of the sometimes fierce desire for possessions that motivates people in America.

Though Samuel is the antagonist, he is a very sympathetic antagonist. A dutiful and loving son and a generous giver, there is nothing greedy or grasping about him. Nevertheless he finds it hard to conceive that his mother and father have no needs or desires that can be satisfied by a gift of money. He has lived all his adult life in a country that guarantees a right to "the pursuit of happiness" to every citizen, and where, indeed, most individuals are in ardent pursuit of pleasure, power, wealth, or fame. Berl and Berlcha are not in pursuit of anything. They are simply content in their lives, reckoning on what they have rather than what they do not have. They are sustained by the stabilizing effects of religious ritual and tradition, by a community whose values are the same as their own, and by a simple religious faith that God will "provide for all their needs." There are no glaring extremes of rich and poor in Lentshin. The more prosperous members of the community have kerosene lamps rather than a wick in a dish of oil. The very poor (represented by the toothless old man whom Samuel encounters reciting psalms in the synagogue) do not understand the phrase "make a living" (that is, make money), but accept their lot in life: "If God gives health, one keeps on living." Samuel, in the final paragraph of the story, puts his hand into his jacket pocket and touches "his passport, his checkbook, his letters of credit." These things represent security for Samuel and a chance to make a better life for his parents and for the village of his birth. But "this village in the hinterland needed nothing." The synagogue is big enough. No one is ever without shelter for the night. Lentshin takes care of its own.

Singer does not present Berl and Berlcha as saintly. They are uneducated and ignorant. They are willing to believe that people in America walk "with their heads down and their feet up." With a little imagination they might have used some of their money to buy a hearing aid for Berlcha, eyeglasses for them both, and wheeled transportation for their thrice-yearly journey to Zakroczym. They might even have found a translator to read their mail from Samuel. Would these expenditures have made them happier? Who can tell? Berl insists that he and Berlcha "have everything" and "want for nothing." If so, how could they be more content than they are?

Most Americans would be unwilling to exchange their dwellings for Berl's and Berlcha's one-room hut, shared with a goat and chickens. But who would claim that the lives of the well-to-do families in John Cheever's "The Swimmer" or of the English parents in D. H. Lawrence's "The Rocking-Horse Winner" are more satisfying than Berl's and Berlcha's?

The storyteller regards Berl and Berlcha with humor and respect. His story is amusing and touching. LP

Neil Bissoondath **There Are a Lot of Ways to Die** (page 105)

The limited omniscient point of view is exploited in this story in the presentation of theme — for Joseph is in the midst of stating and restating the meanings of his life at this juncture. The title is an explicit though figurative statement of theme, since while there are literal deaths, the more meaningful are figurative. Joseph also pronounces on other changes that are deathlike — the loss of gratifying memories in the face of present realities, the disappointing sense of defeat in his return to the island when he had expected to be treated as a conquering hero, the sense that his native land is a second-rate "way-station . . . from which nothing important ever emerged," the death of his dream of helping his people out of their poverty, the growing animosity toward his wife and her pretentious friends, the failure of his friend Frankie, even the destruction of the mystery of Pacheco House. All of these, and many other examples, prove to Joseph that he is immersed in a dead and decaying world and that his own idealism is also now dead.

In a town in which he discovers crime and violence, indolence and pretentiousness, he must witness the uselessness of his plan to create jobs and help his people. He must keep his shop chained and padlocked against burglars, has a nightmare that one of his tools will be stolen and used in a murder, must keep firing his workers because they refuse to work. When he returns unexpectedly home, he faces the pretentiousness of his wife and her friends, further evidence of the pointlessness of trying to be of help to his people. Escaping his house, he wanders "without direction" through the town, stepping around "a common sight," a dead dog lying in the street, until, hungry, he enters a cheap restaurant where a chance meeting drives him away without lunch.

His encounter with Frankie is the climactic event in the plot, furnishing the story with its title as Frankie recites "the death roll" of their schoolhood friends that seems to Joseph "to snuff out a little bit of his own life." Frankie was the most intelligent of his friends, ambitiously dreaming of university and a professorship, a potential historian. But no one wanted to publish his history of their people, because it "doesn't lead anywhere [— it's] just a big, black hole." In his total disillusionment, Frankie has been drained of emotion, works in a bank (when he feels like it), drinks and smokes to excess — "a depleted man" who is "lost in the confusion of his mind."

Joseph's sense of dying vicariously in the deaths of his friends is forcefully brought to him as he witnesses the deterioration of the best of them all. His response is to try to purchase from the bar owner the travel poster with the pictorial representation of the words he has come to loathe—*tropical, verdant, lush, exotic*—so that he can rip it up and symbolically destroy "the necessary lie" about his people and his land.

The talk with Frankie also punctures the myth of the Pacheco House as Joseph learns that "Pacheco" was not a Venezuelan general who romantically exiled himself there but a "crazy old man from Argentina" who lived as a hermit and died in obscurity. When Joseph goes to explore the house, he finds it completely empty, with an "emptiness [that] engendered an atmosphere of uncommon despair." He concludes that the death of its owner might have been engendered by the house—"with rooms destined to no purpose, with a façade that promised mystery but an interior that took away all hope."

Joseph's situation is parallel: in the course of this day, he discovers over and over again the emptiness of his life as its mysteries are peeled away. His island was not as he remembered it, his idealism has borne nothing, his marriage is deteriorating, and he finds no hope in himself. "*I am going back,*" he writes to his wife—back to Toronto, we assume, but not back to being the ambitious idealist spurred by altruism, for that too has died in him. His note includes drawings of a circle, triangle, and square, reminiscent of an educational toy or a psychological test in which the right shaped blocks must be inserted: "Were not two dislocations enough in one man's lifetime? Would not yet a third prove him a fool?" Joseph no longer fits into any of the roles he has defined for himself.

There is a brief reference to the use of irony in this story on page 201.   TRA

Philip Roth **Defender of the Faith** (page 117)

The title and central ironies of the story are discussed on pages 199 and 201, and its point of view on pages 145–46.

The story, written by a Jewish author and concerned with conflicting loyalties, including racial and religious loyalties, is complex, and sometimes misunderstood. The charge has been made that it is anti-Semitic. It is not; but one must be prepared to meet the charge. Study question 9 is one means of getting at the problem. There may be legitimate disagreement as to how it should be answered, but the discrepancies should not be major ones. My own ranking would be (1) Marx, (2) Halpern, (3) Captain Barrett, (4) Fishbein, (5) Grossbart. If this ranking is accepted, the one non-Jewish character falls exactly in the middle, and the Jewish characters as a whole are depicted neither less favorably, nor more favorably, than their counterparts.

Surely there should be no disagreement that Sergeant Marx belongs at the top of any such listing. He is an admirable soldier, an admirable first sergeant, and an admirable human being, characterized by self-awareness, moral sensitivity, a commitment to humane values, and a determination to be fair in his position of responsibility. His self-awareness and essential decency are indicated in the first paragraph when he speaks of having developed "an infantryman's heart," which "finally grows horny enough for him to travel the weirdest paths without feeling a thing." Most people who have developed "infantryman's heart" are not aware that they have done so. Captain Barrett, we may guess, has grown up with such a heart. Though he, too, is basically committed to fairness, his commitment is a cruder one and he lacks Marx's sensitivity to moral complexities and to human feeling. But Marx *is* self-aware; he knows that in order to function as a soldier, or as a human being, in our world, it is necessary to develop a certain toughness—a hardness toward human suffering: not to do so would be to break down altogether as a functioning human being. But he knows also that to lose compassion and sensitivity to suffering is to lose an essential aspect of our humanity, to become less than fully human. To be compassionate without being weak, to be strong without being insensitive, these are the almost impossible demands made of human beings, and Marx has met them far more successfully than most. That he has not lost the capacity to feel (he overstates the horniness of his heart) is proved by his responses throughout the story. Whether justice and mercy can be perfectly combined, even by God, is a question that the Book of Job itself fails finally to answer convincingly. Sergeant Marx fully realizes the difficulty of the task, and does his human best, even in his final decision.

Though the idea of Jewishness seems central to the story, the basic theme is that the process of being fully human requires a difficult balance of conflicting values—particularly of justice and mercy. The idea of Jewishness comes in because one of the values involved is loyalty to members of one's own group. Sergeant Marx wants to be a good human being, a good sergeant, and a good Jew, in that order. As a human being he wants not to lose his capacity for human feeling and compassion, to be merciful as well as just. As a sergeant, he wants primarily to be just, to treat his men equally, not to grant special favors to some. As a Jew he wishes to be faithful to his religious beliefs and feelings and to keep in touch with his community. His problems arise because the pressures from Grossbart to grant special favors to his co-religionists involve him in dilemmas of justice and mercy. He wants to be righteous without being self-righteous, he wants to be just without being inhuman and hard of heart. The demands are well-nigh impossible to meet. (Grossbart, in contrast to Marx, consistently puts himself first, his Jewishness second, his integrity as a human being last.) Marx, in his final decision, acts from a variety of motives: he does what he thinks just as a first sergeant; he does what he thinks best for Jews as a whole; but primarily he reacts as a human being, and this time not so much out of mercy or compassion as out of anger, indignation, and vindictiveness. When he accepts his fate at the end of the story, the fate he accepts is that of being human, and therefore limited and imperfect.

"Defender of the Faith" exists in several versions, the difference being primarily in the kind of language used by Captain Barrett. In its first hardback publication in the volume *Goodbye Columbus and Other Stories*, Captain Barrett's speeches are rather colorful, and are embellished with four-letter words and barracks room terminology. The version included in the *Literature: Structure, Sound, and Sense* text is Mr. Roth's own choice as the final version of the story. He has explained that he toned down the speeches because he wanted to keep Captain Barrett from appearing overly gross or crude or stupid and because he wanted Marx's problem to reside entirely with Grossbart and not with a brutish superior officer as well.   LP

CHAPTER FIVE

Point of View

Willa Cather **Paul's Case** (page 148)

In the first ten paragraphs of the story we see Paul principally as other people see him, especially his teachers. His drawing master voices their common feeling when he says, "There is something wrong about the fellow" — something that none of them understands. At the beginning of paragraph 11 ("As for Paul, he ran down the hill . . .") we are taken into Paul's inner world. The author lets us understand what it is that is "wrong" about Paul, and why he commits suicide. But she does not trace the origins of his trouble (the fact that his mother is dead is almost the only clue) nor give us a psychiatric diagnosis. Instead she lets us share Paul's experience, his apprehension of life.

Throughout the story Paul moves between two worlds — a world of drab reality, as represented by school and his home on Cordelia Street; and a world of glamor, lights, music, color, and luxury, as represented by Carnegie Hall and the stock theater, and later by New York and Europe. The first world oppresses him; the second attracts and draws him: he dreams about it and invents fictions about it. An abnormally sensitive boy — he cannot stand the yellow wallpaper — he is nevertheless not creative or truly artistic. Symphonies as such mean nothing to him; a barrel-organ will touch him off as readily as an orchestra. He does not desire to be a musician or an actor. All he needs is "the spark," the stimulus, the release, that enables him to revel in daydreams. When he goes to the art gallery, paintings of Paris or Venice provide the "spark," allowing him to dream of luxurious, exotic worlds. Not the artistic merit of the paintings, but their subject matter, excites him. He does not stand and admire them, but sits before them and loses himself.

All of Paul's pleasures invoke an escape from the real world he lives in into a glittering unreal world of ease, style, fashion, and refinements. When one route of escape is cut off, he is forced to find another, more drastic and less rational. When the theater and the symphony hall are denied him, he embezzles money and goes to New York. When New York is threatened, he takes the ultimate escape in suicide.

Pittsburgh, known in Willa Cather's time as the "Smoky City," and New York, the modern Baghdad, have obvious symbolic value in terms of Paul's two worlds. LP

Eric Roberts stars in a dramatized version of the story in the PBS television series "The American Short Story." The film is generally faithful to the story, so that a discussion of the difference between the points of view displayed in the two different media of drama and fiction can be very useful. TRA

18

There are brief remarks about characterization in this story on page 68, and on its use of irony on page 200.

Much of the humor of this gentle story about a violent subject lies in the character and personality of the narrator, Estelle. As Darlene says of her, "She's a card" (page 166). *Card* is defined by three desk dictionaries as "an amusing or eccentric person," "a clownishly amusing person," and "an amusing or facetious person." The term is quite appropriate for Estelle, whose clownish behavior (doing a Cossack dance under a desk at an office party) and frequent witty interjections ("So who takes a bath in their clothes?") are always harmless, often expressive of good sense, and not infrequently self-directed.

Yet to characterize Estelle as a "card," though accurate enough, is hardly sufficient, for it suggests that she is a flat character, like the joker in a deck of playing cards, who can be summed up in a single word. She is, in fact, a round character, who reveals herself rather fully during her narration, and we can say a good deal about her.

She is first of all a talker. She loves conversation, and the whole story is in fact her part (by far the biggest part) of a conversation she is having with a new acquaintance, probably at a bar (page 170). It begins with her account of a conversation at the office and continues with what is virtually a monologue about herself. In the penultimate paragraph, Estelle half-apologizes for having talked at such great length about herself: "I don't know why I'm telling you all this, except I think it helps you to get to know a person, especially at first, hearing some of the things they think about." In the final paragraph she justifies conversation again: "How could a fellow" rape a girl "he's just had a long conversation with, once you let them know you're human, you have a life too . . . ?" So Estelle is a practicing and believing nonstop talker. But she's no bore. The story is entertaining because her talk is entertaining.

She is not an intellectual. She's probably not even college-educated, but came directly from her home town of Leamington and high school to Toronto and employment. Her culture is the popular culture of women's magazines, TV, and movies (especially reruns on the Late Show). Her speech is loaded with clichés ("It's a small world," "Life's too short," "the last straw") and with current speech mannerisms ("I mean," "you know," "right?"); and yet she's no dummy. From the middle of a thicket of clichés she will flush a startling new metaphor or turn of thought that happily confirms the "original mind" Darlene half-in-jest attributes to her—as when she says of Chrissy, "She's pretty but cool as a cucumber, like she's been painted all over with nail polish, if you know what I mean. Varnished."

She is shrewd in her perceptions of human nature, and, though her characterizations of the other women in the office are brief, they are sharp and revealing: Darlene—denouncing the whole idea of rape fantasies as "disgusting" and turning her back on the conversation, but later getting really interested; Chrissy—eager to tell about her own fantasy but not wanting to be first; Sondra—miffed because she never gets a chance to tell hers; Greta, wanting to be a receptionist like Chrissy and engaged in a contest to outdress her. Very briefly, Estelle gives us a sharp impression of each of them.

Estelle herself, we gather, is too tall and too plain to be much sought after by men; when she goes out in the evening for a drink or two in a nice place, she must go by herself (behavior of which Darlene disapproves, page 164). She admits quite frankly that she has fantasies about handsome strangers coming through the window, like "Mr. Clean," but she's realistic enough to know it's not likely to happen. She has no pretenses about herself. She freely confesses her moral peccadilloes to her new acquaintance, such as looking up confidential information about her associates in the employees' file. Though she's not sure it's "fair" of Darlene to tell everyone new in the office the story about her knocking herself out on the bottom of the desk, she doesn't really object: in fact, we hear her telling the story herself to her new acquaintance. She probably enjoys being known as something of a "card"; yet she's not irresponsible: she is also known at the office as the "worry wart." And with all her realism and pungent wit, she has a sentimental streak. She likes June Allyson movies; as a little girl she buried dead robins; she cries at the ends of movies, "even the ones that aren't that sad."

Her fantasies especially display her "original mind." They blend her humor and her sentiment into original and highly amusing creations: the inept rapist who gets his zipper stuck at the crucial moment and whose life she restores to normal by giving him the name of her dermatologist; the rapist with a terrible cold whom she comforts with Kleenex and a medicated drink and ends up watching the Late Show with; the polite rapist who holds her things for her while she digs out her plastic lemon and who then unscrews the top for her. Her "rape fantasies" have mostly happy endings, and none eventuates in rape. She feels guilty herself, however, about the one whose eyes she zaps. Undoubtedly she enjoys most the one in which she and the rapist discover they both are dying from leukemia and live happily together until death—it's so sad and sweet. Estelle sees clearly that the "rape fantasies" of Greta and Chrissy are really erotic fantasies: her own are humorous-sentimental-humanitarian fantasies.

The use of a first-person narrator, colloquial language, and digressive method (the speaker revealing her character through both her language and her digressions)—all evident in the very first paragraph—reminds one of "I'm a Fool," and comparisons and contrasts may be profitable (either for written assignments or class discussions). This story differs from Anderson's chiefly in two respects: (1) the narrator is not the victim of dramatic irony (this is not to say that none is present, but that what there is is muted and Estelle is not much injured by it); and (2) where "I'm a Fool" ends with a heartbreaking disappointment in love, the end of this story is indeterminate.

Is Estelle's new acquaintance male or female? Conclusive evidence is lacking, but her repetition of "But I guess it's different for a guy," "But maybe it's different for a guy," and her explanations in the last two paragraphs, seem to imply a male auditor. If so, she has laid her cards on the table, and "Mr. Clean" (if it is he) may pick them up if he chooses. Estelle's sense of humor should make her a good companion. If he does not pick them up, or if her auditor is a woman, Estelle's sense of humor is her armor against loneliness and the sorrows of the world. Even if she should spend the rest of her life working in a filing department, her humor—and her common sense—will keep her life in balance. LP

Ernest Hemingway **Hills Like White Elephants** (page 171)

The whole story takes place during a forty-minute wait between trains. What lies behind the couple is indicated by the labels on their bags and by a line or two of dialogue. What lies ahead of them is implied by the entire force and direction of the story. Within this forty-minute interval a decision is confirmed that will affect the whole quality of their future lives. The circumstances in which the decision is settled have symbolic force. The couple lose the chance to change directions. The man's refusal to accept the burden of parenthood, his wish to make the woman undergo an abortion so that they can be "just like we were before," represents a nonacceptance of change, a denial of growth and life, a movement toward sterility and emptiness, and this is what the future lives of the couple will hold. The child begun in the woman's womb is a "white elephant" for a man eternally unwilling to accept responsibility. The symbolic dimensions of the story are enlarged in Chapter 6, pages 195–99 passim.

With this story and others like it Ernest Hemingway revolutionized the style of modern prose fiction. The third study question is thus perhaps the most important for thorough class discussion. The main force of the story lies in the tone and the changes of tone in the dialogue of the two characters, all indicated by the words they use. The story is much like a small play with the stage directions incorporated in the dialogue itself. Oral reading of portions of the story by members of the class may help to emphasize this point. Three pairs of students might be asked to read the same passage, followed by class discussion of their readings. Hemingway's contribution to prose style is well discussed, with particular reference to this story, by H. E. Bates in *The Modern Short Story* (Boston: Writer, 1941) 167–73. LP

Ernest J. Gaines **Just Like a Tree** (page 175)

The narrative technique of the story—a sequence of internal monologues in the first-person point of view—has a direct antecedent in William Faulkner's *As I Lay Dying*, though counterparts of the device in English go back to Samuel Richardson's epistolary novels. For Gaines, the device is a means of capturing a variety of responses and reflections by friends and kin as an old woman is on the eve of being forced to leave her house and land. With one exception all the characters are black, and all of the blacks but one are local country folk. Anne-Marie, the only character that is not black, is a white woman whose family back to her great-grandfather has known and employed (perhaps, in the past, owned) these blacks. James is a northern black who has married the last kinswoman of old Aunt Fe and with his wife is planning to take the old woman north to safety.

21

The narration raises several unanswered questions, as such a fragmented series of monologues might be expected to do, but the factual haziness has an important emotional purpose. We cannot be precisely sure how the various people are related; while some definitions are given (Aunt Lou is the mother of Emile and the grandmother of both Chuckkie and Ben O; Adrieu is the goddaughter of Aunt Fe; Adrieu is Emile's sister-in-law, and so on), the blood- or marriage-links between many of the characters are left undefined, an omission emphasizing links of love that may have nothing to do with kinship (no one is more distressed over Aunt Fe's departure than Anne-Marie Duvall, for example). The sense of community, of mutual interdependence, is thus established by strength of feeling that overrides obligations of kinship. This plantation exhibits such bonds that any old woman is "Aunt" to all the younger folk, all of whom have a sense of care and responsibility for their elders.

The exception here, an important ironic contrast, is James the northerner, whose attitude toward these country people is sarcastically condescending. He derides their communal virtues, their sentiment, their graces, their small accomplishments. But his judgments are invalidated: his disrespect reveals his callousness, and he winds up in a drunken stupor. To him, Aunt Fe is "this ninety-nine-year-old chick" whom he must "haul away." His wife Louise is called "Baby" and subjected to intimate indignities in public, and he lustfully imagines what he might do to make another "little chick" cry for more than her loss of Aunt Fe. The "backwardness" of this community is obviously preferable to his modernity.

Another of the hazily presented facts provides the impetus for the plot: a local house has been bombed, killing a woman and her two children. The cause of the bombing has been some nonviolent activity by a young man named Emmanuel, and as Anne-Marie's monologue makes clear, the activity has had to do with racial equality. The astonishment of the blacks when Anne-Marie arrives is the result of newly polarized racial attitudes. The bombing is the reason for Louise's decision to move Aunt Fe north—to escape what more is likely to occur here. Despite what appears to be universal opposition to this uprooting, Louise invokes her blood kinship to have her benevolent way.

That solution, the story suggests, is no solution: from Aunt Clo's monologue comparing Aunt Fe's removal to tearing out a tree and dragging it north along the paved roads, to the boyish disrespect but obedience shown by Ben O, all the emotional links argue against escape and flight to safety. Aunt Fe's death comes as an act of will after she sings her "'termination song" (presumably meaning *de*termination, and probably to be identified as the epigraph song—and no doubt an unconscious pun, for her determination is for her soul to terminate in heaven, and her body to have its terminus in this plantation). All the emotional pointers suggest that she is right, that Emmanuel is right, and that the changes to come will cause hardship and loss, but that they must come. The undetermined question is whether the values embodied in the old "Aunts" can be maintained through those changes.   TRA

CHAPTER SIX

Symbol and Irony

Albert Camus **The Guest** (page 202)

"The Guest" reflects its author's existentialist philosophy that man's life is difficult and without ultimate meaning but that nevertheless a man defines himself during life by the quality of his moral decisions and his courage in acting on them.

The protagonist, Daru, a French Algerian who teaches Arab children in the middle of a bleak Algerian plateau where he was born and which he loves, is given the unwelcome "duty" of transmitting an Arab prisoner to police headquarters at a village some four hours' distant. It is not his job, but police shorthandedness in the face of an incipient Arab revolt has thrust it upon him. A sensitive, humane, and compassionate man, Daru treats his hostage as a human being rather than as a member of a subject race, as guest rather than as prisoner. Though he is a French civil servant, he is revolted by the notion of handing the Arab over to French authorities for trial.

The story centers on Daru's dilemma. Should he do what Balducci would consider his duty, obey orders and deliver the prisoner? Or should he follow his own human impulse and give the Arab his freedom? On the one hand, Daru is responsible for the prisoner. He has been given an order; he has signed a receipt. In addition, he is a Frenchman; he will fight against the Arabs if war is declared; for him, as for Balducci, the French are "us" and the Arabs are "they." Moreover, the Arab is a murderer; and Daru, a peaceable man, cannot repress his wrath against all men who wantonly kill, motivated by hate, spite, or blood lust. But on the other hand, the Arab is a human being, and it offends Daru's "honor" to treat him, however guilty, with anything less than human dignity. Such treatment demands that the Arab be judged by his own people, not by alien French masters.

The necessity of moral choice can be an almost intolerable burden, and Daru several times wishes he were free of it. He is filled with joy when, awakening from his nap, he thinks that "the Arab might have fled and that he would be alone with no decision to make." When the Arab gets up to urinate during the night, Daru at first thinks, "He is running away. . . . Good riddance!" In the morning he simultaneously curses "his own people who had sent him this Arab and the Arab who had dared to kill and not managed to get away." But the decision must be made.

Daru solves his dilemma by taking the Arab on a two-hour journey across the plateau to where two ways divide, by giving him money and food to last for two days, by pointing out the way to a prison, a two-hour walk, and the way to freedom, a day's journey to the pasturelands where the nomads will take him in and shelter him according to their law. When Daru looks back, later, he sees "with heavy heart"

23

the Arab walking slowly on the road to prison. Still later, back in the classroom, he finds clumsily chalked up on the blackboard the words, ''You handed over our brother. You will pay for this.''

Camus's story is about the difficulty, the agony, the complexity, the necessity, the worth, and the thanklessness of moral choice. It tells us that moral choice may be difficult and complex, with no clear distinction between good and evil, and with both rational and irrational, selfish and unselfish claims justifying each course of conduct. It tells us that moral choice is a burden that man would willingly avoid if he could, but also that it is part of the human condition that man cannot evade and remain man. It shows us that man defines himself by moral choice, for Daru makes the choice that the reader wants him to make, and establishes his moral worth thereby. But the story also shows that moral decision has no ultimate meaning, for the universe does not reward it. Not only does the Arab fail to take the freedom offered him but, ironically, the Arab's tribesmen misinterpret Daru's action and threaten revenge.

In large terms, Daru is representative of moral man, and his desert is representative of the world. He is essentially alone in this world, which is ''cruel to live in,'' and life has no overarching or transcendental meaning. ''This is the way it was: bare rock covered three quarters of the region. Towns sprang up, flourished, then disappeared; men came by, loved one another or fought bitterly, then died. No one in this desert, neither he nor his guest, mattered.'' In Camus's world man lives alone, makes his moral decision alone, suffers alone, and dies alone. At the end of the story, in consequence of the very action by which Daru has affirmed his selfhood, he has cut himself off from those he had tried to aid. ''In this vast landscape he had loved so much, he was alone.'' His aloneness is both literal and symbolic.

Four misconceptions of the story should be avoided:

1. The main conflict of the story is not between individual conscience and society or the state, between Daru and Balducci. Daru's own conscience and loyalties are divided. What is required of Daru is not simply the courage to resist the pressures of society and do what is right; it is the courage to make a moral decision between alternatives neither of which is entirely right.

2. The story does not concern the impossibility of isolating oneself from society and from human responsibility, as does, for instance, Conrad's *Victory*. Daru has fled neither responsibility nor mankind. He is an employee of the French government engaged in the responsible task of education. In times of drought he distributes wheat. If war comes, he will be a soldier. He has chosen this isolated region to live in because he loves it, not because he hates mankind.

3. Daru does not evade making a decision. True, by pointing out the two ways to the Arab he does shift some of the weight of decision from himself to the Arab — but only some. For Daru is not paralyzed by inaction. He does not simply wait in indecision till the authorities or the Arabs crash in on him. By putting the Arab two hours on his way and giving him money and food to last two days, Daru takes positive action. The decision to let the Arab make his own decision is itself a decision. In allowing the Arab to make his own choice, he has given the Arab the ultimate freedom — the only real freedom, Camus might say, that men have.

24

4. The Arab does not choose the road to prison because of Daru's kindness. From the beginning the Arab is pictured as passive, uncomprehending, a little stupid. He at no point makes any motion toward attempting to escape. Some prior attempt to escape, or an act of rebellion, would be necessary to establish a change of attitude on the Arab's part after Daru's decision. Instead, his passivity is stressed throughout. He is anxious about his fate but also resigned to it. He is warmed by Daru's humanity, but his response is to want Daru to accompany him and Balducci to police headquarters. His final attempt to communicate with Daru — "Listen" — is best interpreted as a repetition of this earlier request. He doesn't want to be left alone in a hostile world. He wants the man to come with him who has treated him as a human being.

The above discussion is a condensation of an article originally published in *Studies in Short Fiction* 1 (1963): 52–58. A reply by John K. Simon was published in 1 (1964): 289–91. LP

Flannery O'Connor **Greenleaf** (page 212)

Mrs. May's family is on its way down. Her deceased husband had been a businessman in town. She has had to go to the country. Her sons, who represent respectively decadent materialism and sterile intellectualism, are unmarried. She has no grandchildren. The Greenleafs are a family on the way up. Mr. and Mrs. Greenleaf, who represent the family's primitive beginnings, have seven children. Their sons have educated themselves, are practical and productive, and are advancing in the world. The Greenleafs have six grandchildren, three by each son. While one family is dying on the vine, the other is growing and thriving. Mrs. May, whose consuming mental preoccupation is social status and who has an acute need to maintain belief in her own innate superiority, is exasperated by her sons' failure to support their "position" and by the prospect that the low-born, vulgar Greenleafs will usurp it. "In twenty years do you know what those people will be?" she asks her sons. "*Society*," she says blackly.

The two families are contrasted in many ways, perhaps most significantly in religion. Mrs. May's nominal religion is Christianity; her real religion is respectability. She has no deep religious beliefs, but she believes in going to church. Mrs. Greenleaf's religion is primitive and grotesque, but springs from genuine conviction. Her "prayer healing," however naive or superstitious, is motivated by a desire to help people totally unknown to her. The self-righteous Mrs. May is recurrently motivated by a desire to hurt people whom she knows.

Mrs. May wonders how she has put up with Greenleaf for fifteen years. The reader is more disposed to wonder how Greenleaf has put up with Mrs. May for so long. The two figures seem almost embodiments of impatience and patience. But Greenleaf's patience has its limits. When Mrs. May insists on Greenleaf's killing a bull belonging to his own sons, he finally loses his temper, though he continues to obey her orders. Mrs. May's most characteristic emotion throughout the story is anger. At this point Greenleaf also becomes angry.

The story makes use of all three kinds of irony. Scofield uses verbal irony, for instance, when he displays Mrs. May's delicate blue-veined little hand dangling from her wrist and yells out, "Look at Mamma's iron hand!" Most consistently the story depends on dramatic irony that results largely from the use of the limited omniscient point of view with Mrs. May as the focal character. We continuously see the characters and the events of the story as reflected through Mrs. May's mind, but we see them in a quite different light than she does. When Mrs. May retires to bed thinking that "if the Greenleaf boys had risen in the world it was because she had given their father employment when no one else would have him," we see that she thinks of herself as deserving gratitude for her generosity, but when later we are told that "She had not fired him because she had always doubted she could do better," we plainly see that she has hired Greenleaf, and hung on to him, entirely from self-interest. When we are told of the Greenleaf boys that during the war they "had both managed to get wounded and now they both had pensions," we see that Mrs. May thinks of the wounds as something the boys had deliberately incurred from motives of self-interest, but we interpret them as evidences of bravery. Throughout the story the reader's judgments and Mrs. May's judgments are at variance, largely because Mrs. May is constantly reflecting on the shortcomings and deficiencies of other people, but is conscious of none in herself. When Mrs. May tells Mrs. Greenleaf, "Jesus would be *ashamed* of you," our chief response is to think that Jesus would be ashamed of *her*.

The story also makes repeated use of irony of situation. The most obvious example results from Mrs. May's imagining Greenleaf gored by the bull and thinking of it "almost with pleasure as if she had hit on the perfect ending for a story she was telling her friends." The actual ending of the story is perfect from a different point of view: it represents poetic justice for Mrs. May's fifteen years of persecuting Greenleaf and for trying to make him kill his sons' bull. Mrs. May's revenge boomerangs.

The symbolism of this story is complex, and the following discussion will attempt only a partial exploration of that complexity. The bull is a multiple symbol. It symbolizes, first of all, the Greenleafs. The bull is "gaunt and long-legged"; the Greenleaf boys are "long-legged and raw-boned and red-skinned." The bull is a scrub bull—of inferior stock—yet it is healthy and hardy; the Greenleafs, as Mrs. May sees them, are "scrub-human," yet also healthy and hardy. The bull eats Mrs. May's hedges; Mrs. May dreams of something eating her farm, feels that the Greenleafs have lived off her for fifteen years, and fears that they may eventually get the farm. The bull comes "like some patient god" to woo Mrs. May; Greenleaf has been patient, or enduring, for fifteen years. The bull finally becomes angry and gores Mrs. May; Greenleaf finally becomes angry, and the bull, which belongs to his sons, is in a sense the agent of his revenge. But the bull, besides being a symbol of the human Greenleafs, also represents something divine. At the beginning of the story it has a hedge-wreath on its horns "like a menacing prickly crown." Bull-worship, according to Frazer's *Golden Bough*, was common in several ancient lands: bulls were considered symbols of the sun, types of reproductive energy or generative force, and emblems of the Father God. In Mrs. May's second dream, the bull is identified with the sun: the sun charges her, as the bull actually charges her later. The bull, the sun, and the Greenleafs in this story may all be taken as symbols of natural and divine forces, of reproductive energy, and of life itself, which Mrs. May attempts to pen up, shut out, or destroy. These forces seek Mrs. May's regeneration. The bull is said to be "like some patient god come down to woo her," "like an uncouth country suitor," and finally "like a wild tormented lover." But when Mrs. May persistently denies these forces, they destroy her. At the end Mrs. May has "the look of a person whose sight has been suddenly restored but who finds the light unbearable," and in death she seems "to be bent over whispering some last discovery" into the bull's ear. Mrs. May's revelation has come too late to be of any use.

There is an excellent discussion of the mythic dimensions of this story by Frederick Asals in *Studies in Short Fiction* 5 (1968): 317–30. LP

Anton Chekhov **Gooseberries** (page 229)

In her penetrating and admiring essay "Reality in Chekhov's Stories," Eudora Welty states the central paradox of Ivan Ivanych's experience at Alyohin's farm: "he moves from the profundities of joy to the heights of despair" (*The Eye of the Story: Selected Essays and Reviews* [New York: Random, 1979] 76). The paradoxical phrasing is necessary in summarizing this story, for both in theme and in structure, Chekhov displays the complex self-contradictions of experience, a subject matter that any writer must approach with caution and with mastery of his art lest the result be merely self-contradictory.

Structurally, "Gooseberries" presents one example in this book of a "frame story," an extended narration by a character who is himself the subject of a narration (the other is Nadine Gordimer's "Once Upon a Time," page 253). This "story within a story" technique opens up numerous possibilities as it permits the interplay of the narrator's ideas and attitudes with the materials of the narrated frame. Quickly one notices that Ivan Ivanych's story about his brother's ambition and then success as a landowner with a gooseberry patch is paralleled by the setting and situation in which the story is told, Alyohin's prosperous but grimy farm that mixes the owner's filth, hard toil, and simple living habits with the luxury of his inherited surroundings—the white bath house, the elegance of the second-story rooms, the beauty of his young maidservant. As Welty puts it, "as Ivan talks, the farm, the day, the house with its encrustations of time, the seductive room with its beautiful attendant, its romantic portraits of ladies and generals around the walls, and the rain falling outside, all stand about the story he tells like screens of varying substance of reality and dream" (75). These materials provide a commentary on the values that Ivan Ivanych dismisses and on those he embraces.

From the very opening paragraph of the story, Chekhov indicates that we must recognize the possibility of self-contradiction and complexity in reactions to the scene. The day is "tedious . . . gray and dull . . . and you wait for the rain that does not come," yet by the end of the paragraph this oppressive setting is interpreted as "mild and pensive," evoking "love for this plain" and this "beautiful land." And then, within ten lines, the long-awaited and much desired rain begins to fall—and even the dogs perceive it as an ordeal to be avoided. The men take shelter at Alyohin's, which from a distance presents them with a beautiful, inviting vista (''the river gleamed, and the view opened on a broad expanse of water with a mill and a white bathing-cabin''). A little closer, and the mood reverses itself yet again: ''it was damp, muddy, dreary; and the water looked cold and unkind.''

But this is not merely a matter of appearance giving way to reality, of a closer view removing the attraction of the distant prospect—though that theme is part of the experience of the story. As a matter of fact, its opposite is equally present: what seems ugly in prospect may turn out to be beautiful, and what seems delightful may ultimately be a cause for despair. That is the complex paradox of Ivan Ivanych's story about his brother Nikolay, a story of a man whose obsession with possession and ownership (what he desires to own is a romanticized, self-gratifying notion of rural life) leads him morally downward as he gets closer and closer to his goal; and by the time he achieves that goal he and his household, servant, dog and all, have been transformed into pigs. The much-prized gooseberries are hard and tart—but not to him, for he has managed to crawl into his dream and refuses to perceive the reality. To Nikolay, this is beauty and perfection; to Ivan, the result is haunting, disgusting, and depressing.

In telling his tale, Ivan seems gradually to discover its ''moral'' in its contrast to Nikolay's counterpart, what Alyohin has and is. Nikolay—vicious, selfish, money-grubbing materialist, finally a deluded, lazy, self-satisfied pig among his pigs; Alyohin—generous, vigorous, unconcerned with appearances, unconscious of the bounty of inherited status, surrounded by delights and personally careless about himself. It is to him that Ivan addresses his discovery: ''There is no happiness and there should be none, and if life has a meaning and a purpose, that meaning and purpose is not our happiness but something greater and more rational. Do good!'' (page 236).

Ivan progresses from the joyous exhilaration of his swim (plunging over and over to the bottom as if to discover the ultimate dimensions of his world) to the anguish and despair of his final insight. What he sees is what the reality of the story has reiterated over and over: in happiness there lies pain, in agony the beauty of life may be felt, and in being alive each of us must be prepared to realize the immense complexity of life. Welty's paradox—''the profundities of joy . . . the heights of despair''—captures that theme, for joy may be found at the bottom of the darkest river, despair in the sweet and brilliant luxuriance of a drawing room.

Is Ivan Ivanych's outburst to Alyohin the ''moral'' of Chekhov's story? The answer must be ''neither yes nor no.'' It is what one human being has made of his observations and experience, and is therefore a true representation of a human truth. But this particular, realistic man is framed by Chekhov's story, the rain continues to fall, and for all his moralizing Ivan's story is disregarded by both Burkin and Alyohin, to whom it (like the gray, dull day that has preceded it) is ''tedious,'' having no direct bearing on *them* as individual human beings. And in an open-ended symbol, Ivan Ivanych's pipe reeks.

In addition to Welty's essay, the following provide valuable insights into this masterwork: Ronald Hingley, introduction to Anton Chekhov, *The Russian Master and Other Stories* (New York: Oxford UP, 1984) x–xi; Irina Kirk, *Chekhov* (Boston: Twayne, 1981) 107–10; Donald Rayfield, *Chekhov: The Evolution of His Art* (New York: Harper, 1975) 191–92; Mark Schorer, *The Story: A Critical Anthology* (New York: Prentice, 1950) 61–65; and the following articles collected in *A Chekhov Companion*, ed. Toby W. Clyman (Westport, CT: Greenwood, 1985): Andrew R. Durkin, ''Chekhov's Narrative Technique,'' 123–32; Ralph Lindheim, ''Chekhov's Major Themes,'' 55–69; Donald Rayfield, ''Chekhov and the Literary Tradition,'' 35–51. An invaluable research guide, for those wishing to go further, is K. A. Lantz, *Anton Chekhov: A Reference Guide to Literature* (Boston: Hall, 1985).   TRA

CHAPTER SEVEN

Emotion and Humor

McKnight Malmar **The Storm** (page 243)

This story is discussed briefly on pages 316–17. It is included in the book chiefly as a foil for "Once Upon a Time," to illustrate the difference between terror-for-its-own-sake and terror-for-illumination, or, in other words, between escape and interpretation. For what it attempts to do — namely, scare the reader — it is skillfully written. The first two sentences are particularly effective in rapidly establishing the tone of the story. This story and Gordimer's — like the other two pairs included in this chapter — may be substituted for the stories in Chapter 9 as exercises in evaluation. LP

Nadine Gordimer **Once Upon a Time** (page 253)

The sample analysis in the Appendix (page 1399) discusses the relationship of the "frame" to the body of this story.

The story is rife with ironies, the most obvious and appalling being the destruction of the little boy by the wire coils installed for protection. Many lesser ironies anticipate that effect: the alarm systems (whimsically compared to a flock of animals exchanging "bleats and wails") create enough din for burglars to saw through bars and gain access to houses, "under cover of the electronic harpies' discourse"; the boy uses the electronic gate receiver as a walkie-talkie to play "cops and robbers"; the installation of burglar bars to keep out intruders makes the family view "the trees and sky through bars," imprisoning them and leaving the burglars at large; the happy story of Sleeping Beauty leads the boy to emulate Prince Charming braving "the terrible thicket of thorns" — only to fall prey to the "DRAGON'S TEETH" of the wire coils.

In addition to these examples of situational irony, the point of view itself is ironic because of its resemblance to a children's story. The tone is created by the "once-upon-a-time" phrasing: "In a house, in a suburb, in a city, there were a man and his wife who loved each other very much and were living happily ever after." The man's mother is a "wise old witch" (the perspective here is no doubt the wife's) who bestows both gifts and advice, including the book of fairy stories that leads to the catastrophe and the warning against any dealings with the blacks in the streets. The simplifying tone reduces the emotional life of this family to two basic, complementary feelings: fear of the blacks outside their house, and loving protectiveness of the family. All the actions of the story rest on those paired impulses, just as characters in children's stories are simply motivated and easily explained. The plot, therefore, contains no interior conflicts of any kind—no self-examinations or doubts about these paramount motives, no moral questioning, no concern for justice or fairness.

In the brief space of the story, the motive of fear grows in a steady sequence of actions, each new fear leading to a new protective action. That the members of the family acknowledge this process and yet approve of the efforts made to protect them is reflected in the decision to install the wire coils: "It was the ugliest but the most honest in its suggestion of the pure concentration-camp style, no frills, all evident efficacy." Their growing fears have led them step by step and open-eyed into imprisoning iron bars and then the isolation of a "concentration camp." But they are not hysterical about their fear (that is left to the trustworthy housemaid); they are almost cool and smug as they act upon it. They are convinced that their way of coping with perceived danger is the correct way.

What they do *not* act upon or consider is the cause or source of the danger. The wife's charitable instinct, to feed the hungry beggars, is overruled by the housemaid and the protective husband, for the husband believes that charity will only "encourage them" and besides, "they are looking for their chance" to break in. The true needs and purposes of this intrusive crowd are covered over by fear of them. Trying to live in safety, the members of the family create for themselves an image of the nation they live in—a nation separated by extreme and cruel measures into islands of safety surrounded by need, want, and oppression. This "children's story" is a parable of the South African experience, and a warning about its consequences. From the white perspective, riots in the black quarters arouse no pity and bring no aid—"buses were being burned, cars stoned, and schoolchildren shot by the police in those quarters out of sight and hearing of the suburb," eliciting from the family only the response of fortifying *their* quarter, guarding *their* child.

The introductory frame defines the true issue, and reveals honest fear. The writer who awakens fearing some personal threat from an intruder (in a world where there are murdering housebreakers and vengeful victims of injustice) discovers that *that* fear, while reasonable and justifiable enough, is less disturbing than the fear and pity she feels for the victims of a racist nation. To think of the interment "in the most profound of tombs" of the wage-slave gold miners is far more distressing than the fear of personal danger, for it confesses guilt for the complicity of living in a structure of "brick, cement, wood and glass" literally built upon a foundation of cruelty and injustice.

The "children's story" ironically detaches itself from these realities, so that its fears seem wholly selfish and even unjustified. The horror with which it concludes ironically seals the theme of both story and frame: an unjust social system creates an environment of fear that can destroy both the oppressor and the oppressed.   TRA

"The Catbird Seat" is a deservedly famous story by one of America's foremost comic talents. It is nevertheless a story that manipulates its materials for the sake of humor, not one in which the humor flows consistently from life honestly observed.

The manipulation is first apparent in the author's handling of the limited omniscient point of view. Thurber presents the events of the story through the consciousness of Mr. Martin. We are taken fully into Martin's mind as he reviews his case against Mrs. Barrows, revealing his motivations for the murder. We are also taken fully into his mind as he makes preparations for the murder on the following evening. But then, after his failure to find a suitable murder weapon in her apartment, we are told, "Somewhere in the back of his mind a vague idea stirred, sprouted. . . . The idea began to bloom, strange and wonderful." We are not told what the idea is. At this point Thurber censors Martin's thoughts in order to set up his surprise ending. The ending, of course, is hilarious, and we are glad to see Mrs. Barrows get her "come-uppance," but it does not give us any new revelations about life.

The main conflict of the story is man-against-man, with Mr. Martin as protagonist and Mrs. Barrows as antagonist. There is some internal conflict in Martin as he reviews his case against Mrs. Barrows. He has difficulty keeping his mind "on her crimes as a special adviser, not on her peccadillos as a personality." Given the obnoxiousness of Mrs. Barrow's personality, this is understandable enough, and has the ring of truth. What we are not given is any moral conflict in Martin over the commission of murder. There is no struggle with conscience. And, indeed, the greatest improbability of the story is that a man of Martin's character and temperament could ever deliberately set out to murder anyone, even a Mrs. Barrows. But the idea of murder is given only facetious treatment in the story. From the time we are told that Mr. Martin has decided to "rub out" Mrs. Barrows and that the term "rub out" pleased him "because it suggested nothing more than the correction of an error," we cease to consider murder as the serious matter it really is.

Thurber omits internal moral conflict because he is mainly writing a humorous escape story. However, few good stories are without interpretive elements. "The Catbird Seat" gives us authentic insights into the politics of a business office and the kind of irritation and disruption that are caused by certain personalities, especially when they acquire power. The sentence in which Miss Paird, of whom we already know that she "seemed always able to find things out," gets up and walks "slowly past the closed door of Mr. Fitweiler's office" contains more interpretation than the whole paragraph that succeeds it. There is a Miss Paird in every business office. The succeeding paragraph, in which Mr. Martin confronts Mr. Fitweiler and calmly lies about what he had done the previous evening, is as incredible as that in which he deliberately sets out to commit murder. Mr. Martin is an authentic office type who acts out of character for almost half the story. When he remembers with pride the compliments his employers have paid him—"Man is fallible but Martin isn't" and "Our most efficient worker neither drinks nor smokes. The results speak for themsleves"—he is very much in character. When he reviews his grievances against Mrs. Barrows, he is very much in character. When he arrives at her apartment "unable to speak," his heart "wheezing in his throat," he is in character. But not when he calmly lies or coolly sets out to commit murder.

Thurber is at his best in this story in his use of language. The sustained metaphor of the trial for Martin's review of the case against Mrs. Barrows—with Martin acting as prosecuting attorney, defense attorney, and judge—is delicious. His reflection that if he runs into anybody on the way to Mrs. Barrows's apartment, he would simply "have to place the rubbing out of Ulgine Barrows in the inactive file forever" is beautifully appropriate. Thurber's characterization of Mrs. Barrows, through her outlandish collection of clichés, her quacking voice and braying laugh, and her name itself, is wonderfully completed by his choice of verbs to present her in action ("romped," "bounced," "yelled," "brayed," "bawled," "bragged," "shouted," "swept," "snorted," "catapulted," "glared," "screamed"). We can fully believe that Mr. Martin *wants* to kill her; but not that he ever deliberately sets out to do so.

This story is included as a foil to "The Drunkard," and this pair, like the other pairs in this chapter, may be substituted for the stories in Chapter 9 as an exercise in evaluation. The value of "The Catbird Seat" is discussed on page 317. LP

Frank O'Connor **The Drunkard** (page 265)

Frank O'Connor's enchanting and hilarious story is one in which human insight accompanies and gives rise to the humor from beginning to end. In its account of Father's reactions to Mr. Dooley's death; of his motivations for attending the funeral; of his spiritual pride over teetotalism and its consequences; of the progress of his drunkenness; of Mother's attempt to use the son as a brake; of Father's bribing the son with lemonade and telling him to go play in the road; of the son's motivations in drinking the beer; of the progress of the son's drunkenness; of Father's reactions to his missing drink, and to the boy's sickness; of Father's embarrassment and shame on the way home; of the final ironic reversal in which Mother calls the son an "angel" for having got drunk; the story is continuously funny and continuously true. Even such a small detail as the narrator's remark about "the lonesomeness of the kitchen without a clock" presents an insight of poignant and absolute authenticity.

O'Connor's shrewd observation of human nature is nowhere better manifested than in his depiction of the ambivalent and mixed motivations of human beings. The shallow writer oversimplifies human motivation. The good writer realizes its full complexity. In his desire to attend his friend's funeral, for instance, Mr. Delaney is prompted partly by the Christian motivation of "Do as you would be done by" ("We'd be glad," he says, "if it was our own turn"). But he is also acutely aware of what other people may think ("'Twould be expected. . . . I wouldn't give it to say to them"). In addition, he *enjoys* funerals for their show ("Five carriages and sixteen covered cars!" he exclaims afterwards. "There's one alderman, two councillors and 'tis unknown how many priests. I didn't see a funeral like this from the road since Willie Mack, the publican, died"). Finally, of course, he looks forward to the celebration in the pub afterwards—a regular holiday outing. Undoubtedly the first two reasons are partly rationalizations for the latter two, but there is no reason not to regard them as genuine at the same time, for Mr. Delaney is a man of decent human impulses and of normal awareness of social opinion.

Students with a moralistic turn of mind (and there are surprisingly many of them) misread this story as a story of the Drunkard Reformed. The father is so acutely ashamed when his little boy gets drunk and he recognizes his own behavior in his son's, they claim, that he discovers the folly of his drinking and his guilt in causing his family to suffer. Thereafter he never takes another drink. Such a reading is unfortunate, for it turns the story into a tract. O'Connor is not writing about the Evils of Drink; the neatest twist in the story, in fact, lies in the son's being congratulated for getting drunk. O'Connor's story is about numerous human vanities and foibles; it is not directed against the existence of pubs. The misinterpretation may be countered with at least five lines of argument: (1) The father already knows the folly of drunkenness, and during his periods of abstinence he laughs at the folly of men who waste their money on liquor. (2) He does not consider himself to blame for his son's drunkenness; rather, he indignantly strives to absolve himself: "I gave him no drink. . . . He took it while my back was turned." (3) The chief emotion he feels over his son's drunkenness is social embarrassment, not moral shame. What acutely distresses him is being made a spectacle for the neighbors. (4) His regret is not over having gone to the pub but over having been denied his fun there: "Not one drop of drink crossed my lips the whole day. How could it when he drank it all? I'm the one to be pitied, with my day ruined on me, and I after being made a show for the whole road." This is not the language of contrition. (5) Finally, there is the narrator's response to Father's "Never again, never again, not if I lived to be a thousand!" "To this day," says the narrator, " I don't know whether he was forswearing me or the drink." If Father had successfully forsworn either one, the narrator would have known about it.

The value of the story is discussed briefly on page 317.   LP

Truman Capote   **A Christmas Memory** (page 273)

"Imagine . . ." With this imperative command the narrator waves the magic wand by which he carries us back "more than twenty years" but keeps us in the present tense, so that his Christmas "memory" is no dim recollection from the past but an experience we live through with him. So complete is the illusion that we think of the narrator throughout as a seven-year-old boy, not as the twenty-seven-or-eight-year-old that he must be to possess the literary skills requisite for relating this story. Curiously, our first return to a sense of the pastness of this experience occurs when a past event is referred to in the *future* tense: the two friends run to a pasture "where Queenie has scooted to bury her bone (and where, a winter hence, Queenie will be buried, too)."

But use of the present tense is a minor part of the story's magic. The major part is its being so deeply imagined—by which is meant not that it takes us into an imaginary world, like Never-Never Land or the Kingdom of Oz (in that sense it is possibly the least imagined story in this volume)—but that it is fully "imaged":

presented through the language of the senses. Here is how the activity of hulling pecans is described: "Caarackle! A cheery crunch, scraps of miniature thunder sound as the shells collapse and the golden mound of sweet oily ivory meat mounts in the milk-glass bowl. Queenie begs to taste . . ." We see the golden mound mounting in the milk-glass bowl, we hear the hulls crackle and crunch, we smell the sweet odor of the "meat" and feel its "oily" texture, and along with Queenie we can almost taste it. Almost every item and action in the story is thus particularized and made unique—even the hoard of money poured from the bead purse taken from the secret hiding place (pages 275–76).

The protagonist, if we choose one person rather than a triumvirate, is over sixty years old. She and the narrator are "each other's best friend." They have lived together for as long as he can remember. That would be at least since he was four, for he can remember that they exchanged slingshots for Christmas three years ago. "She is still a child." She is a child in the sense that her most intense pleasures and excitements are those of a child's world: she "can get a kite aloft when there isn't enough breeze to carry clouds," on Christmas Eve she "can't sleep a hoot" for excitement, and on Christmas morning she is "so impatient to get at the presents" she can't eat a mouthful. But she is a child also in the sense of being "old and funny," as she puts it, or "loony," as a relative puts it: she won't get out of bed on the thirteenth of the month, she sends fruitcakes to total strangers, she has to be supported and taken care of by others. Nevertheless she has a deeper tap-line to wisdom than those who take care of her. She knows "There's never two of anything"—not of anything important. She knows that "it's bad enough in life to do without something *you* want" but it's worse "not being able to give somebody something you want *them* to have" ("It is more blessed to give than to receive"). Though her mind was touched perhaps by the youthful disease that hunched her shoulders, her heart is uncorrupted. (Was characterization ever more particularized or more delightfully conveyed than in the catalogues of things she has never done, and things "she has done, does do"?) But perhaps she is most like a child in her openness to wonder, her ability to see the world with fresh eyes, her capacity for pure happiness. It is probably too much to claim her as a developing character, but she does have, on the Christmas Day related, a new religious insight. She had always thought a person "would have to be sick and dying before they saw the Lord." But now she thinks that seeing things as they are (clouds, kites, grass, a dog burying a bone) is seeing Him. "As for me," she concludes, "I could leave the world with today in my eyes."

The theme of the story might be framed—though Capote wisely refrains from so framing it—in the words of Christ (Mark 10.15; Luke 18.17): "Verily I say unto you, Whosoever shall not receive the kingdom of God as a little child shall in no wise enter therein."

The antagonists, vaguely described, are "Those who Know Best," relatives with "eyes that scold, tongues that scald." "Though they have power over us," Buddy says, "and frequently make us cry, we are not . . . too much aware of them." They do indeed make Buddy's friend cry, after her distribution of two inches of whiskey, and it is the seven-year-old child who consoles and comforts the over-sixty-year-old. Since this is not the Kingdom of Oz, the antagonists triumph in any real conflict;

35

penultimately they separate Buddy and his friend. Then other antagonists appear—Jim Macy's horse; age, senility, death. These also triumph.   LP

Benjamin Capps   **The Night Old Santa Claus Came** (page 282)

This "Christmas memory" has many superficial resemblances to Truman Capote's. It also takes place in rural America during the Great Depression (the Ford Model-T was produced between 1920 and 1928, and there is nothing to suggest that Mama's is brand-new), it has a boy's perspective reflected in the mature man's recollections of his experience, its protagonist is an older woman loved and respected by the boy, and it situates itself at Christmastime. Furthermore, its central actions display a warmhearted and optimistic world contrasted to the relatively difficult economic condition of its characters, suggesting that there are resources in the human spirit that can overcome deprivation and distress.

The protagonist is Mama, a pious woman whose resources of cheerful goodwill, self-sacrifice, perception, and responsiveness certainly make her "rich" in ways the narrator did not realize when he considered her "hundred dollars a month" to be riches. She has been a widow for three or four years, and supports herself and her three school-age sons by teaching in a one-room rural schoolhouse which also serves as their home. In addition, she burns the midnight kerosene studying for junior college credits to "further her education," her teaching certificate having been granted by examination rather than by college course work. Her Christmas surprise for her boys is typical: the Peanut Pattie that she allowed little Roy to give her to assuage his guilt and grief at having no present for her she then divides between the three Christmas socks—she has given Roy the pleasure of showing his love through his gift, and then rewarded him and the others through her further generosity.

She knows children well. She can cow an unruly "big boy" by showing her disappointment in him, and leads all her pupils into regarding working for others as a reward for their good behavior and diligent study: "[I]f a big boy did good in Geography, Mama would let him bring in wood or stoke the fire or draw water for the water keg," bestowing on him her own attention and teaching him to feel the virtue of responsibility and service to the community. Her motto—and the theme of this story—is her paraphrase of Acts 20.35, " 'Remember, it's better to give than to receive.' "

To counteract the sentimentality of this stock portraiture, Capps creates a conflict out of the "dumb" behavior of five-year-old Roy who selfishly spends his gift allowance on himself and is careless enough to lose some of it. Roy is, in the eyes of the narrator, Mama's antagonist, living the opposite philosophy, that self-satisfaction comes first. Consequently, when Mama gives Roy another nickel to buy her a Christmas gift, the narrator feels resentful at the injustice of rewarding the miscreant who ought to be taught a lesson by being disappointed on Christmas morning—"he got a reward for being dumb," he silently objects. But this conflict is resolved in the best possible way when the narrator too gets rewarded not only

36

with a Christmas stocking but also with a conspiratorial wink from Mama as she enlists him and his elder brother in helping Roy to believe in Santa Claus.

The story is full of frank sentiment, blunting the hardship and difficulty with the pervasive sweetness and goodness of Mama. It may or may not be sentimental, depending upon how much sincerity the reader feels in the narrator's obvious love and admiration for his mother. The story does not at least manipulate its situation other than by stressing the good feelings that make the hardships seem inconsequential.

But when compared to Capote's "A Christmas Memory," its weaknesses are obvious, from its shallower characterization to its didactic purpose. Mama says " 'it's better to give than to receive' "; Capote's protagonist says " 'it's bad enough in life to do without something *you* want' " but it's worse " 'not being able to give somebody something you want *them* to have,' " a remark that seems to grow out of personal experience rather than to be a Sunday school lesson. In Capps's story, the inability to give just doesn't occur — in fact, the same gift can be multiplied and given again.

"Imagine a morning in late November," Capote begins. "Imagine a white schoolhouse sitting on a hill," Capps begins. Examining the quality of the imagination behind each story may be the most illuminating comparison. Capps has accurate and honest descriptive powers, and he helps us to see the scenes in the schoolroom, the living space, the dime store, and at the Christmas party. But these seem two-dimensional beside the vivid and colorful scenes of Capote, where the imagery is visual, auditory, olfactory, tactile — where scene after scene comes to life, and the feelings each contains grow naturally out of the action. As for human truth, a single paragraph in Capote's story, like that expressing Buddy's reaction to his Christmas presents, has more of it than the whole of Capps's story: "Well, I'm disappointed. Who wouldn't be? With socks, a Sunday school shirt, some handkerchiefs, a hand-me-down sweater and a year's subscription to a religious magazine for children. *The Little Shepherd*. It makes me boil. It really does." One might guess that Capps's narrator would have found those gifts heartwarming.   TRA

CHAPTER EIGHT

Fantasy

D. H. Lawrence **The Rocking-Horse Winner** (page 291)

The opening sentence of the story tells us that the mother "had no luck." The boy's last words are "I am lucky." The first use of the word exemplifies verbal irony; the final use, dramatic irony. Both uses are literally true in the restricted sense that the mother gives for the word: "It's what causes you to have money." The boy's mistake about "filthy lucker" is at the thematic heart of the story, for the confusion of luck with lucre causes all the unhappiness of the story. (Such confusion is not rare, but almost universal, as demonstrable from the history of our language. Though the similarity of "luck" and "lucre" is accidental, the near-synonyms "fortune" and "a fortune" link the two meanings in one word.)

It is an irony of situation that the woman who considers herself unlucky has been immensely lucky in a truer sense of the word. She is beautiful, she started with every advantage, she married for love, she has bonny children, and she has artistic talent. But all these gifts are negated by her inability to love, and by her need to live "in style," to "keep up" a social position, and to satisfy expensive tastes. Nevertheless, this mother is characterized differently from the greedy stepmothers of the fairy tales. She is not cruel. She is gentle and anxious for her children. Her heart is "curiously heavy" when she sees her son becoming tense and overwrought. At a big party in town, she feels such "rushes of anxiety" about him that she cannot suppress the impulse to leave the dance and to telephone home. But gentleness and anxiety are not love. Love puts love first always, and is willing to sacrifice for what it loves. Paul's mother subordinates love to social position and expensive tastes, which means that she doesn't love at all, for where is the willingness to sacrifice?

Paul feels the lack of the love he should be getting from his mother, he unconsciously realizes that the demands of the house for more money are connected with that lack, and he blindly tries to cure the condition by supplying the money. But the whispers of the house are only a symptom, not the cause, and Paul's remedy only makes things worse. Materialistic craving can never be satisfied. Paul's compulsive efforts to satisfy his mother's craving finally kill him. Riding the rocking-horse is an effective symbol for materialistic pursuits, for it is a furious activity that gets one nowhere.   LP

A film of this story was made in 1950 (91 minutes, British). It may be obtained from Janus Films, 745 Fifth Avenue, New York, New York 10022.

To the question "Had Goodman Brown fallen asleep in the forest, and only dreamed a wild dream of a witch-meeting?" critics have proposed four basic answers: (1) yes, the whole experience was a nightmare induced in him by his own and/or his society's preoccupation with evil and sin; (2) no, he was indeed guilty of keeping an appointment with the devil, who showed him the evil in himself, in his wife, and in apparently just and godly citizens and churchmen, including his own forebears; (3) no, he had seen and heard the evidences of evil reported in the story, but they were delusions produced by the devil; (4) no, he had not slept but had experienced hysterical hallucinations, the product of his own obsessive concern with sin and marital fidelity.

The necessity for answering the narrator's question rests on more than the fact that he asks it and then offers no answer but "Be it so, if you will." The nature of the question itself is implied throughout the story, for it asks "Is there a natural (as opposed to supernatural) explanation for what Brown underwent?" For Hawthorne not to resolve this issue is characteristic of a writer who often creates ambiguities out of such natural/supernatural conflicts (readers of *The Scarlet Letter* will recall the question of the flaming "A" in the night sky during Dimmesdale's crisis, and the unresolved question of whether Dimmesdale does in fact have a scarlet letter on his own naked breast).

The ambiguity in "Young Goodman Brown" is created at many points in the story. Technically, it is almost entirely told from the limited omniscient point of view—Brown's perception—and to the extent that it is so limited, it is impossible for a reader to discriminate between fact and Brown's imagination. But there are frequent moments in the course of the forest narration that expand the point of view to include an authorial voice even before the narrator poses his dream question. Such, for example, are the words and phrases *as it were, as if, perhaps, some affirm that, must have been an ocular deception,* and *doubted whether he had heard aught but the murmur of the old forest, whispering without a wind.* In addition, Hawthorne reports Brown's perceptions with *seem, appear, beheld,* and *fancied,* and the persons he sees are called *figure, form,* and *shape.* The cumulative effect of such language is to cast doubt on the literal reality of Brown's experience, to suggest that it might indeed have a natural explanation depending on the distortions of his imagination. The reader is not forced to believe literally in witchcraft and the devil, but may if he is so inclined accept any of the four major explanations.

The ending of the story is not indeterminate—the whole of Brown's future is presented—but the theme is indeterminate, for Hawthorne's ambiguous narrative creates an issue even larger than the question of Brown's personal experience; that is, is the diabolical figure right when he pronounces that evil is the nature of mankind? Has Brown's forest journey, whatever its reality, revealed to him a truth? Typically, Hawthorne refuses to answer explicitly, but he does show the effect of Brown's belief—a life darkened with suspicion, mistrust and gloom, a mind poisoned by doubt (yet as some critics point out, his misanthropy is sporadic, the result of doubt rather than conviction: though he "often" shrank from his wife, he was the progenitor of "a goodly procession" of children and grandchildren).

The structure of the tale has been much praised. It has an archetypal familiarity: the young man undertaking a journey into the unknown, possessed by a desire for knowledge but aware that the knowledge is forbidden, who draws back time and again, yet moves forward until the climactic revelation that thenceforward changes his life (parallels to Adam, and to his relations with Eve, have been drawn). That Brown's "evil purpose" has to do with forbidden knowledge rather than with power seems clear from the promises of the devil at the interrupted baptismal ceremony: if they join in the communion, Brown and Faith will "be partakers of the mystery of sin, more conscious of the secret guilt of others, both in deed and thought, than they could be now of their own." Brown goes into the forest to meet the devil, but he claims that his "covenant" with him is fulfilled simply by meeting him; his intention has been to keep the appointment and thus confirm the devil's existence, but to return the next day still a good Christian, clinging to Faith and following her to heaven. The evidence presented to him to prevent his turning back systematically reveals that there is no such thing as a good Christian. But at the climax, apparently to protect his Faith from such knowledge, he exhorts her to rely on God and resist the devil, and this exhortation forestalls his own baptism into evil knowledge. He is left with doubt, the suspicion of the truth of the devil's pronouncement, based on the evidence he has seen and heard.

Until the climax, Goodman Brown repeatedly plans to leave the forest, and is repeatedly dissuaded by deepening visions of evil — the information that his father and grandfather were in league with the devil in their unjust and inhumane behavior; the appearance of "his moral and spiritual adviser" Goody Cloyse chatting amiably with the devil; the audible but invisible minister and Deacon Gookin on their way to the meeting; and finally the voices in the dark cloud, including Faith's, and the apparently material evidence of one of her pink ribbons. The result of this last is his frenzied rush toward the meeting-place, with the declaration "My Faith is gone! . . . There is no good on earth, and sin is but a name. Come, devil! for to thee is this world given." The satanic parody of a communion service is dispelled when he recognizes in "the slender form of a veiled female" his wife Faith, and protectively stops her from joining.

The ambiguities of perception and theme focus the story not on theological truth but on the psychological consequences of belief and doubt. One of Hawthorne's recurring themes is that dwelling on moral absolutes — good or evil, virtue or sinfulness — is destructive and dehumanizing, as demonstrated by the long life of gloom that resulted from Brown's forest journey in quest of a moral absolute. Taking a clue from the technical fact of a manipulated point of view, we may leave the ambiguities where Hawthorne so carefully placed them, and recognize that ambiguity itself is part of the theme. We cannot know whether Brown had suffered a hallucination, or what might have induced it; there is evidence to support the devil's claim that mankind is devoted to evil, if we accept Brown's certainty that all apparent goodness is mere hypocrisy; but there is also evidence to suppose that he is wrong, if we judge the actions of the townspeople after his return. Judging by other works of Hawthorne, men are not inherently evil but are capable of evil actions, chiefly actions that spring from excessive pride and intellectuality, and that victimize or exploit other people. An evil act may be done by an otherwise good person, and good consequences may be the result of willfully evil actions. For Hawthorne, all men are potentially evil — and potentially good. Moral ambiguity is a pervasive fact of life.

This is Hawthorne's most widely analyzed short story, chiefly because of its ambiguities; certainly no single analysis will satisfy all readers. The foregoing should be regarded as *an* analysis, to be supplemented by the following: Thomas E. Connolly, ed., *Nathaniel Hawthorne: Young Goodman Brown* (Columbus, Ohio: Merrill, 1968), which anthologizes twelve critiques; Robert W. Cochran, ''Hawthorne's Choice: The Veil or the Jaundiced Eye,'' *College English* 23 (1962): 342–46. Consult also the extensive bibliography of articles about the story listed in *Twentieth-Century Short Story Explication, 1900–1975.* TRA

CHAPTER NINE

The Scale of Value

Exercise (page 320)

"A Municipal Report" and "A Jury of Her Peers" both present a situation in which a wife is oppressed by her husband. In each story the husband's tyranny eventuates in his being murdered. Each story directs the reader's sympathy toward rather than against the murderer. In each story the external sign of this is that the character from whose viewpoint the story is told conceals a crucial piece of incriminating evidence. These are the principal similarities between the two stories. The differences will be apparent from what follows. LP

O. Henry **A Municipal Report** (page 320)

"A Municipal Report" is one of the most celebrated stories of one of America's most celebrated writers. It has been reprinted in dozens of anthologies. It is nevertheless a contrived story. Written with O. Henry's usual verve, entertaining in its account of Nashville, it falsifies and sentimentalizes its human materials.

In plot the story is a tissue of coincidences. Hardly has the narrator arrived in Nashville—a city of over one hundred thousand people—than he independently encounters, quite by accident, first, the husband, and, second, the faithful former family retainer of the sequestered woman he has come to visit. In each encounter money changes hands. He observes Major Wentworth paying for the drinks with silver money. He himself pays his carriage driver with two dollar bills, one of which is easily identifiable. A second pair of coincidences lies in the fact that the crucial clues of the story—the patched dollar bill and the variegated coat with its single yellow horn button—are both uniquely identifiable. It is, of course, the patched dollar bill that Azalea Adair coincidentally draws forth to pay for tea, and that, coincidentally, the Major is on hand to intercept. That evening, back at his hotel, the narrator again coincidentally encounters the Major, who buys the drinks with the patched dollar bill. On his next visit to the house on Jessamine Street, the narrator is coincidentally present at Azalea Adair's hunger-faint (the narrator is always on hand for significant happenings), and leaves her a $50 advance. That evening he again encounters Uncle Caesar at his stand and notices the missing button (Caesar never has other customers when the story needs him). Coincidentally it is during the narrator's visit to Nashville that Caesar, after a long history of the Major's villainies, is finally moved to kill him. Coincidentally the narrator is present at the drug store where the Major's body is brought, and later, at the hotel, he coincidentally overhears a man who had been coincidentally present when the Major had displayed fifty dollars that afternoon to people in the hotel. Some of these coincidences are large, some are small; all together, they are incredible.

The characters who enact this plot are the paper-thin cutouts of sentimental fiction. The Major is pure villain, differing from the waxed-mustache variety mainly in being clean-shaven and failing to say "Aha!" He is fully characterized as a blabbing rat, but, lest we miss the point, we are later told that he is "despicable" and "a drunken, worthless loafer." Azalea Adair is the dignified heroine, frail, white-haired, long-suffering, brave in poverty, too proud to accept charity from her friends though dying of hunger. (She is like the Kitty Morgan that she tells about: "The boiling oil was sizzling as high as her heart; but I wish you could have seen the fine little smile that she carried from table to table.") Old Caesar, the carriage driver, is the picturesque Negro retainer, descended from kings, absolutely loyal to the daughter of the man who owned his father. Thus, there are two characters with hearts of gold and one with a heart as black as night. But the narrator, too, has a heart of gold. Though a commercial agent, he nevertheless arranges a contract for Azalea at eight cents a word rather than the authorized two. None of these characters is substantial enough to bear psychological probing. Azalea, after an altercation with her husband that results in his taking both of her dollars, returns to her guest without signs of discomposure. Uncle Caesar, after murdering the Major "in terrific battle," returns to his street corner and his trade without discomposure: "Step right in suh. Fifty cents to anywhere in the city. . . ." And the narrator thinks, after disposing of the evidence, "I wonder what's doing in Buffalo!"

The theme of the story is that romance can happen anywhere—even in Nashville. This theme is stated in a kind of essay placed around the narrative proper (and is repeated in the conversation of Azalea Adair), and the narrative proper is meant to illustrate it. Abstractly, of course, the theme is perfectly true, but the narrative proper is too contrived to give it a true embodiment. And, if the essay were removed from the narrative, the theme would disappear also, or be greatly altered. It *ought* to have something to do with the psychology and ethics of murder. But the characters are so unreal that the murder becomes unreal.

If we read the story purely for humor, it is entertaining. But insofar as it appeals to our moral sympathies, it oversimplifies complex issues and gives us a false and facile view of life.   LP

Susan Glaspell **A Jury of Her Peers** (page 332)

"A Jury of Her Peers," first published in 1917, was based on the original one-act play *Trifles*, which Miss Glaspell wrote for the Provincetown Players in 1916. Students interested in differences between dramatic and narrative techniques may wish to compare the two versions. [The play is reprinted in Laurence Perrine and Thomas R. Arp, *Literature: Structure, Sound, and Sense*, 6th ed. (Fort Worth: Harcourt, 1992) 870.]

Like "A Municipal Report," "A Jury of Her Peers" has a specific locale—the

American Midwest (knowing Miss Glaspell's life and other writings, we can place it in Iowa). The hard conditions and lonesomeness of life in this locale have everything to do with the story. The setting is an accessory to the murder.

Though the murder is under investigation by the sheriff and the county attorney, the story is not a who-dun-it. The murderer is already in jail, suspicion is cast on no other person. The story focuses not on *who*—but on *why*. Its interest is psychological.

The husband in this story is not a villain. He is known among his neighbors as "a good man": he doesn't drink, he keeps his word, he works hard, he pays his debts. But the exigencies of a difficult existence have made him "a hard man"—taciturn, "close" with money. Having eliminated all frivolous pleasures from his own life, he is infuriated when he finds that his wife has spent hard-earned money on a canary—and he breaks its neck. Though hardly likable, he is understandable and believable.

Unlike Old Caesar in "A Municipal Report," who kills Major Caswell for injury done not to himself but to his father's master's daughter, Mrs. Wright has not committed a disinterested murder. Her injury is personal, her motivation more believable. She kills her husband in a cold passion. Her behavior after the killing is also more believable. She looks "queer . . . as if she didn't know what she was going to do next. And kind of—done up." Yet out of long household habit she has resumed her household tasks. Her worrying about her fruit—after being taken to jail—has the touch of absolute authenticity. (It is matched by Mrs. Hale's worrying—at the scene of the murder—whether her son is dressed warmly enough.) The lonesomeness of a hard life—without children, without company, without conversation, without song—has shaped Mrs. Wright as it has shaped her husband. Less hard than he, she cannot bear it.

But the foreground conflicts in this story are more important than those of the unseen murderer and her victim (or should we say, the murdered man and his victim?). They concern Mrs. Hale *versus* Mrs. Peters, Mrs. Hale and Mrs. Peters *versus* themselves, and the women *versus* the men. The story contrasts the men's world and the women's. Concerned with "important" matters, the men feel superior to the smaller world in which, they think, the women live. They minimize the difficulties of running a kitchen and keeping towels clean. They laugh at "the insignificance of kitchen things," at worry over preserves, at concern with the difference between quilting it and knotting it. Mr. Hale explains that "women are used to worrying over trifles" and questions whether they would "know a clue if they did come upon it." For all the gallantry of the county attorney's "what would we do without the ladies?" the men unconsciously patronize them. Ironically, of course, their very familiarity with "the insignificance of kitchen things," and their recognition of the true importance of these things, enables the women to discover the evidence that the men cannot find. It is the men who would not "know a clue if they did come upon it."

But perhaps the true center of the story lies in what the women do with the evidence. Mrs. Wright is tried by "A Jury of Her Peers." The title has an ironic twist, for there is no formal trial in the story, and the "jury" consists not of twelve men but of two women—Mrs. Wright's "peers" in a stricter sense than usual (at the time of the story women were not called on for jury service nor were they allowed to vote). The implication of the story is that, if a motivation were supplied at the trial, Mrs. Wright would be found guilty and put to death. "The law is the law," and "the law has to punish crime," says Mrs. Peters before she makes her final decision; and the county attorney had said of Mrs. Wright, "I guess before we're through with her she may have something more serious than preserves to worry about." The central conflict of the story therefore comes to be between legalistic justice and the larger understanding and compassion of the women. Who killed John Wright? In the eyes of the law, Mrs. Wright. But the evidence of the strangled canary, which is a symbol of the former Minnie Foster as well as a piece of evidence, is that John Wright killed Minnie Foster. And was this just one person killing another? "I know what stillness is," says Mrs. Peters, a statement later echoed by Mrs. Hale. And Mrs. Hale breaks out, "Oh, I *wish* I'd come over here once in a while! That was a crime! That was a crime! Who's going to punish that?" In other words, Mrs. Hale sees even herself, shaped by the conditions of *her* life, as accessory to the murder. The law would only oversimplify.

So the final conflict of the story, an internal one, belongs to the two women—and especially to Mrs. Peters. *Is* she "married to the law"—in both senses of that phrase? She decides she is not and conceals the evidence. Whether she did right or not is an arguable question, but the story is on her side. The strangled canary has paradoxically both convicted and exonerated Mrs. Wright before "a jury of her peers."   LP

William Faulkner **Spotted Horses** (page 349)

Although he appears "on stage" only in the first and last and briefly in the third of the six sections of the story (and isn't even mentioned in the fourth), Flem Snopes is its protagonist. It is he who instigates the action ("Yes, sir. Flem Snopes has filled that whole country full of spotted horses"), who is constantly the object of the other characters' fascinated curiosity and attention, and who concludes the action by denying ownership of the horses and sending Mrs. Armstid away with a nickel's worth of candy. His relatively infrequent appearance "on stage" is appropriate, for his characteristic method of operation is to keep himself to himself, to confide in no one, to work behind the scenes. Flem is a man "on the make." His main if not his sole motivation is to acquire money (and power) as quickly as possible. The son of an impoverished sharecropper (he is the elder son in the story "Barn Burning"), he appears here first as a clerk in Varner's country store ("Uncle Billy" Varner, we learn elsewhere in Faulkner, is the biggest landowner and richest person in the rural hamlet known as Frenchman's Bend; he is also a farmer, a veterinarian, and owner of the country store managed by his son Jody). Those who know Flem predict that he will own the store within ten years, but Flem finds a quicker way to wealth: he marries Varner's daughter—not out of sentimental feelings but purely as a business arrangement. Eula has been made pregnant by one of the "young bucks" swarming around her "like bees around a honey pot," and

Flem offers the opportunity to "legitimize" the pregnancy. During their stay in Texas (long enough to conceal the progress of the pregnancy and the early birth of the child), Flem finds a Texas "partner" and returns with a string of wild horses. Though Flem is certainly their owner or part-owner, no one can prove it. Flem "trims" all his antagonists, but the story hardly has a happy ending, for the reader's sympathies lie with the antagonists (the victims).

As Flem's partner, the Texan must be considered a co-protagonist (though not coequal). An expert auctioneer (as unprincipled as Flem in selling off the useless horses), he earns our admiration for his utter fearlessness and skill in handling the horses and by his chivalry toward Mrs. Armstid. Though not a round character, he is made vividly memorable by his ivory-handled pistol and his habit of dropping gingersnaps into his mouth from a constantly renewed box in his hind pocket.

The narrator, a traveling sewing-machine salesman temporarily rooming at Mrs. Littlejohn's boarding house, is a born storyteller. A keen observer of human nature with a deep interest in human diversity, he has a rich sense of humor and is able to turn all kinds of material, including himself, into comedy. He confesses freely that he has been himself "skun" by Flem Snopes in two trades and one of the funniest parts of his story is his account of the invasion of Mrs. Littlejohn's by one of the horses, in which he hardly plays a heroic role ("I was in my room, in my underclothes, with one sock on and one sock in my hand when . . . I looked over my shoulder and see something that looked like a fourteen-foot pinwheel a-blaring its eyes at me. It had to blare them fast, because I was already done jumped out the window"). He has a rich gift for comic hyperbole and colorful simile (see the passage just quoted) and, uneducated but intelligent, he has a marvelous instinct for a creative misuse of language. (In the passage quoted, the correct word would be *glaring*, but his mistake, adding noise to light, is twice as expressive. "Swurging," in the opening paragraph, combines the sense of *surging, swirling, urging*, and *swerving*.) He also makes effective use of sardonic irony, as when he says that "it was considerate in Flem to get them started early" (page 359) or makes the remark "That Texas man told her to get that five dollars back from Flem next day. I reckon Flem's done already taken that money to Mrs. Littlejohn's and give it to Mrs. Armstid" (page 361). What is his attitude toward Flem? The irony in the remarks just quoted should warn us that his apparent admiration for Flem is severely qualified. Though he may praise Flem's cunning in a trade, he is not blind to the moral horror that Flem represents, and his admiration is largely a pretense that he uses to probe the depths of Flem's depravity. Of the men gathered on the porch in the final scene, he is the only one bold enough to ask Flem right out whether Flem had an interest in the horses. "Flem's done skun all of us so much . . . that we're proud of him. Come on, Flem, . . . how much did you and that Texas man make offen them horses?" In his next remarks he would seem to be voicing the same moral views as I. O. Snopes—"Well, if a man can't take care of himself in a trade, he can't blame the man that trims him . . . A fellow like Henry Armstid ain't got nobody but hisself to blame"—but, in reality, he has seen Mrs. Armstid approaching, is eager to see what will happen, and wishes to divert the others from noticing her for as long as possible. In a sense, he is "setting up" the confrontation. A student of human nature, he can tell a marvelously comic tale, but he is fully aware of the pathos, the brutality, the hypocrisy, and the ruthlessness involved in the story. He can make us bleed for Mrs. Armstid without ceasing to see her as a subject of humor. And yet, perhaps his greatest pleasure is telling a good tale. He is telling this one, probably, to a group of listeners in a neighboring hamlet gathered on a porch much like that of Varner's store. "I reckon you-all know that gal of Uncle Billy Varner's, the youngest one; Eula. . . . One of these here kind of big, soft-looking gals that could giggle richer than plowed new-ground" (page 350). "And what do you reckon Flem's com-ment was? . . . That's right. Nothing. Because he wasn't there" (page 359). Of all the antagonists, he suffers least, not only because he doesn't buy a horse, but because he is able to turn the episode into a tale.

The central antagonist, and the one who suffers most, is Mrs. Armstid. Brutally treated by her stupid and stubborn husband ("I bought that horse and I aim to have him if I have to shoot him"), Mrs. Armstid, though persistent in trying to protect her family from her husband's foolishness, accepts absolutely the authority of the husband in marriage. Patient as Job in her suffering (after her husband's purchase she sits all day in the wagon, looking at nothing, "like something carved outen wood"), she is exasperating in her vacillation (Mrs. Littlejohn gets so impatient with her that it finally sounds to the narrator as if she were throwing all the dishes at the cook-stove), heroic in her devotion to her family (she earns clothing-money for the five children weaving by firelight after Henry is asleep, and after Henry's accident she nurses him all night, works in Mrs. Littlejohn's kitchen in the morning, and drives home in the afternoon to cook and care for the children), pathetic and submissive in her victimization (she stands on the porch in her characteristic posture, "her hands rolled into her dress, not looking at nothing," and says "You're right kind" when Flem gives her the candy), but she is nevertheless not destroyed ("I reckon I better get on back and help with the dinner"). From the narrator's final image of her — "She looked like a old snag still standing up and moving along on a high water" — we are given the impression that she is the kind who, however often carried off on the floods of misfortune, "will endure."

There is further comment on this story on pages 48–50 of this manual.   LP

William Faulkner   **Mule in the Yard** (page 363)

The principal character, a widow of forty-odd years who wears a man's felt hat and a man's shoes and keeps her life savings in a fruit jar, is hardly the kind of protagonist you would find in commercial fiction. Mrs. Hait, whose first words are "Them sons of bitches," is grim-faced and untalkative through most of the story. Yet she is undoubtedly its heroine, if only because she outwits I. O. Snopes. Faulkner makes no attempt to draw sympathy toward her for her widowhood. She wears "an air of indomitable yet relieved bereavement" for her ten-years' dead husband, who was a scamp and in some ways a good riddance. Her best quality is her ability to make the best out of a bad situation. After her house burns down, she makes a pallet in the cowshed and cooks her supper in the open air. She is without pretension in dress, social status, or wealth, and she accepts the companionship of a black woman without any pose of superiority.

But if Mrs. Hait is the "heroine," Old Het, the secondary protagonist, is the most delightful character. A seventy-year-old inhabitant of the poorhouse, grotesquely dressed, she cheerfully sponges on the housewives in town whom she has nursed in infancy (or claims to have). But what delights us about her is her endless zest for life, despite her age and poverty. "Mule in de yard!" she shouts "with strong and childlike pleasure" as the action begins. She anticipates the chase with the eagerness of a ten-year-old and participates in the pursuit with unflagging energy, "panting happily" when the mule disappears down the street after its third circuit of the house. She is about to express her satisfaction when she smells the smoke of the fire and warns Mrs. Hait. In the evening she anticipates dinner with the innocent guile of a child (the same guile with which she exaggerates the number of housewives she has nursed in their infancy): "I ain't had no appetite in years now. A bird couldn't live on de vittles I eats. . . . Now, ef you jest had nudder little piece o dis ham." When Snopes wants to send Old Het away so he can talk privately with Mrs. Hait, Het says, "Lawd, honey, I done already had so much troubles myself dat I kin set en listen to udder folks' widout hit worrying me a-tall." Afterwards she guilefully asks Mrs. Hait, "Wuz hit me er you dat mentioned something erbout er nudder piece o dis ham?" And when the meal is concluded, she sighs with weary and happy relaxation the judgment she had begun to make before the fire broke out: "Gentlemen, hush! Ain't we had a day!"

The chase is described with all the comic verve we have learned to expect from our Nobel-Prize novelist. Before it is over, it involves not only the mule, Mrs. Hait, and Old Het, but a cow, a choleric-looking rooster and eight Rhode Island Red hens, and I. O. Snopes. Mrs. Hait's handerkerchief-sized yard is "as incredibly full of mad life as a drop of water beneath the microscope." The pursuit is furious, with the mule periodically vanishing in the fog, "its wake indicated by the tossing and dispersing shapes of the nine chickens like so many jagged scraps of paper in the dying air blast of an automobile." It continues till, "with brief demon thunder and a keen ammonia-sweet reek of sweat sudden and sharp as a jeering cry," the mule disappears down the street.

The two antagonists are the mule, which sets Mrs. Hait's house on fire and is ultimately shot by Mrs. Hait, and its owner, I. O. Snopes. In "Spotted Horses" I. O. appears in the final section as the new clerk in Varner's store, dressed in shirt sleeves with his hair parted in imitation of his cousin Flem. He is positively gleeful over Flem's financial cunning and is notable mainly for cackling like a hen and exclaiming, in a trance of admiration, "You can't git ahead of Flem." His business ethics are summed up in his statement, "Henry Armstid's a born fool. . . . If Flem hadn't a got his money, somebody else would." "Mule in the Yard" shows him with his business ethics unchanged. His primary motivation is to make money by fair means or foul. But he lacks Flem's shrewdness, he talks too much, and he is thus outmaneuvered by Mrs. Hait. Though as repellent as his cousin Flem, he is a figure of fun rather than of menace. One of the funniest parts of the story (if somewhat macabre) is his expression of aggrieved injustice that Mrs. Hait should profit so greatly from her husband's death while he, who took the risks, got almost nothing out of it (page 372).

The point of view and the tone differ sharply from those of "Spotted Horses." Here the story is told by an omniscient narrator commenting on and evaluating the action, privileged to be everywhere, giving us an account of the events sometimes as perceived by "the town," at other times by Mrs. Hait, Old Het, I. O. Snopes, and even (or almost) the cow (pages 364, 367) and Snopes's mules (page 366). The narrator displays gifts for simile and overstatement similar to those of the sewing-machine salesman in "Spotted Horses," but he has a much more extensive and sophisticated vocabulary. The tone of this story is burlesque, a heightening of diction and an elaboration of sentence structure that lend mock-dignity to the proceedings, as an ironic literary device of detachment and amusement. The elevated narrative style is juxtaposed with the colloquial dialogue, and deflates the events that seem so important to the actors. Faulkner's literary antecedents for this technique include Mark Twain and the American tradition of the tall tale, as well as Alexander Pope and his Roman models.

Within this framework, we are not tempted to read the story as a conflict of good and evil, or to read into I.O.'s defeat a victory for goodness, because the exaggerating tone makes us reduce rather than extend the significance of events. The loss of life, of money, and of home are balanced against the mere spiting of the antagonist, as if there were an equality of value between them. Mrs. Hait endures with a minor victory and a major loss, but the scale of value is so comically distorted by the narrative tone that we are not likely to extend the meaning of the events because the narrator has already extended them so far.

"Mule in the Yard" is a fine comic story, told with flair. It couldn't have been written by anyone other than William Faulkner; the hand of the master is evident in every line. It has three memorable characters, lively dialogue, and hilarious action. But it lacks the scale, the scope, and the resonance of "Spotted Horses." Partly this is the result of its burlesque technique, which reduces its significance by overstatement. Partly this lack of resonance is the result of its happy ending. At the end of the story everything has been wrapped up. The mule has been shot, evil (in the person of I. O. Snopes) has been defeated, poetic justice has been done, and we close the story with much the same feeling as Het closes it: "Gentlemen, hush! Ain't we had a day!"

"Spotted Horses" is a comic masterpiece with a major theme. Its tone derives from the great vernacular tradition (again epitomized, in his masterpiece *Huckleberry Finn*, by Mark Twain). The narrator's exaggeration and the originality of his language and imagery are imbedded in that tradition, and have an effect opposite that of "Mule in the Yard": there, burlesque exaggeration leads us to question the scale of value; here, colloquial vitality invites us to examine the deeper significance of events that have the ring of truth as they are told by a realistic storyteller.

"Spotted Horses" brings before us not just three characters but a whole community. It has two or three times as many memorable characters. It embraces a much fuller range of tones. And it continues to haunt the imagination after the story is over. The horses are still loose, leaping over roads, "running back and forth across them little bridges" (none of them has been caught, except that one that broke its neck). Poetic justice has not been done, and the world retains its "spotted" mixture of good and evil, with evil threatening to grow both in the increasing power of Flem and through the agency of his admiring "cousins."

Accepting Faulkner's invitation to universalize the theme, we might identify Flem with the course of a society in which unscrupulous, immoral grasping, and pride in evil (which can be indulged even in vanquishing such a defenseless opponent as Mrs. Armstid) predict a satanic conquest of the world. It is a story of a fallen race, pitting the guileful against the gullible, strong evil against weak good. In her simplicity, all that Mrs. Armstid has is her moral goodness, but *that*, Faulkner says, will endure even while the evil embodied in intellectual superiority rages all around her. LP/TRA

Stories for Further Reading

Alice Adams **Fog** (page 376)

QUESTIONS

1. Explore the relationships between the three couples in the story. What has brought each couple together? What now keeps them together? What private or unspoken thoughts does each person have about his or her companion? Is there an implied hierarchy in which the three couples can be ranked in terms of the quality of their relationship?
2. What ironies are created by the omniscient point of view in which the author describes actions and quotes speeches, and also reveals unspoken thoughts? How does this technique contribute to characterization?
3. The focus of all the characters (including Antonia herself) is Antonia Love. What attitudes and feelings does each of the characters (including Antonia herself) have about her? How does she figure in the way they interact with each other?
4. Define the symbolic meanings of the title, and use them in formulating the theme of the story.

The three couples in the story represent three different stages in the development of a relationship. Phyllis and Bynum are married, but both of them foretell the breakup of their marriage. Antonia and Reeve live together unmarried, and are "'free'" to see other people (though there's no evidence that Antonia exercises that freedom). At the story's end, their relationship has deepened to the extent that Antonia will allow the younger Reeve to supply their living and working quarters in his native Wyoming. Lisa and Perry are at the beginning of a relationship that is not yet sexual, though both of them expect that it will become so. Like her friend Antonia, Lisa is older than her companion.

This array of pairings might be ranked in terms of the emotional satisfactions shared by the couples with Antonia and Reeve at the top, looking to grow stronger; Phyllis and Bynum at the bottom, moving toward separation; and Lisa and Perry in between and following the lead of Antonia and Reeve. But all three couples are revealed, through the ironic contrast between their speeches and their thoughts, to be troubled by uncommunicated misgivings, most of them (including her own) focused on how they feel about Antonia. She is the protagonist of the story and the central character in their lives.

Lisa, her "old friend," explicitly feels both love and envy for Antonia, expressing herself in "bitchy" remarks that denigrate her friend's habits, her tastes, her relationship with Reeve, her artistic abilities. Some of her nastiness may be the result of superficial jealousy provoked by Perry's "babble," which keeps their conversation focused on Antonia when Lisa wants to be the object of his attention, but her envy of Antonia's accomplishments goes deeper and is of a much earlier origin. She is anxious that Perry may not really be interested in her, but her anxieties about Antonia spread beyond this immediate situation.

Perry's interest in Antonia is initially self-serving: he wants to meet her so as to write an article about her, and he has struck up his acquaintance with Lisa for just that purpose (she is susceptible to his approach because of her desire to be known as Antonia's close friend). Of all of the characters, Perry is the one who consciously and overtly wants to exploit Antonia for his own purposes. Perry also is drawn to Antonia in another way, as he fantasizes about similarities between himself and Reeve, and indulges in thinking of himself as an even younger "painter companion" of the famous artist. His age as well as the newness of his acquaintance with Lisa and her set place him at a disadvantage at the dinner party when he finds it difficult to compete for the attention he wants. But he luckily discovers what he needs for his article in Reeve's announcement that Antonia is moving with him to Wyoming—not only has he captured Antonia descriptively, he has "struck on the first sentence of his article: 'Antonia Love these days is a very happy woman.'" And in the bargain, he has come to the decision that Lisa is more than a means of access to Antonia and "plans to see her again." Lisa's interest in him—or at least in his type ("small, dark, trimly built men")—suggests that she will be responsive.

Bynum, Lisa's rival for "oldest friend," is like her in disparaging Antonia behind her back, and in part his motive seems to be like Lisa's, a desire to be the one who knows Antonia best and therefore is most aware of her flaws. His self-analysis, when he contemplates losing Phyllis and then marrying yet another younger woman, leads him to frame a new hope: "why not Antonia" as his next wife? He counts on her tiring of young Reeve, and believes that "despite [their] fights," Antonia would "be a perfect companion" for him. This train of thought reflects his smug self-assurance (a trait he detects in Perry when they meet) and adds to the growing impression that all of Antonia's friends prize her for the ways in which *she* can gratify them.

Phyllis focuses on Antonia in two ways: she too envies her, for her "larger, darker style" and for being "so emphatic" a contrast to herself, a feeling that ambivalently also "diminishes [Phyllis] to almost nothing." But in talking about Antonia with Bynum, Phyllis also finds that "she is aware of enjoying this conversation, perhaps because it is one, a conversation." That is, the topic of Antonia is one that excites a mutuality between this mismatched couple. Antonia is sufficiently interesting to both of them that through her they can momentarily find a link—until Bynum's superior attitude breaks the mood. For Phyllis, as for the others, then, Antonia is a means to an end.

Reeve at the outset is exercising his right to be " 'free' " of Antonia. He starts out for Oregon alone but doubles back to see an attractive young woman for whom he is beginning to feel desire. But what he wants to do with Sharon is talk—about Antonia! And when he recalls that Sharon is unlikely to "understand a single word of all that [he] would like to say," he decides to hold the conversation with Antonia herself, the only person who can make sense of his "ravings." His rescue of Antonia is a feather in his cap (though the guests at the dinner party refuse to let him wear it, as they repeatedly cut him off as he tries to describe his heroic deed), and is in fact a precursor to his adopting the role of Antonia's protector and supporter. There remains in him, of course, the need to be credited with what he can do for her, the need indeed to use her to create his identity.

And then there is Antonia herself—who in Bynum's glib remark is the only self-created character in the story, the only one who does not depend on others for her sense of self. Like the rest of them, of course, her focus is "Antonia," and like them her relationship to herself is self-serving. But despite the fact that she is physically impaired, she has wholeness and integrity, and a clear-sighted self-awareness that enables her to explore even her subconscious impulses ("if I didn't want people to dinner, I could just have not asked them," she thinks as she supposes her fall was purposeful and defensive). She understands her relationship with Reeve, and accepts his help in changing her life for the better.

The enveloping fog of San Francisco is physical and obtrusive, as it hinders Lisa's driving and obscures the view, the only remarkable thing about Antonia's apartment. It is also symbolic of the quality of human interrelationships, of the obscurity and confused self-definition of these characters. Each of them feels that he or she has achieved clarity in self-definition, yet each must live in a reflection of Antonia. The plot moves from the isolation of each character (well represented as the omniscient narrator moves successively into each separate mind) to the decisive move of Antonia and Reeve from "fogbound, dangerous San Francisco" to the "heady, pure, exhilarating air" of Wyoming (to use Perry's over-excited language).   TRA

Raymond Carver   **The Bridle**   (page 385)

QUESTIONS

1. Characterize Marge, the point-of-view character. What are her motives in such actions as waiting for a second ring of the doorbell and offering Betty a free manicure? What is she doing most of the time? What does she think of herself? What are her attitudes towards Spuds and Linda Cobb? Connie Nova and her men? Holits? Betty? Harley?

2. Discriminate between Marge's expressed opinions and those that are only implied. Would you call her opinionated? Do her judgments change or grow as a result of the events she witnesses? Is she a developing character?
3. Characterize Harley. What are his typical actions? How does his persistence in calling Holits a "Swede" indicate the quality of his perceptivity?
4. Describe the events in Holits's life, both those that are summarized and those that occur as actions in the story. Do they form a meaningful progression? Characterize Betty Holits and account for her remarks about her dreams.
5. What does the bridle symbolize? What is a "prayer plant" and what does it symbolize in the story?
6. This story exemplifies what has been called "neo-realism" or "minimalism" in fiction. Compare Carver's use of a first-person narrator to that of Wolfe ("The Child by Tiger"), Faulkner ("Spotted Horses"), and Anderson ("I'm a Fool"), examples of an older fictional technique. How are the author's evaluations of events and presentation of theme different in Carver's story?

With selective, described physical details and a short series of observed events, Carver suggests the pathos and hopelessness of a contemporary world. The attention of the first-person narrator, Marge, is on the sad situation of the Holits family—chiefly that of Betty, from whom she gleans a few facts about their life. It is indeed a pathetic sequence: Holits's desertion by the boys' mother, divorce, a promising second marriage that "had its ups and downs" but seemed to be "working toward something," and then Holits's new-found obsession with his hapless racehorse "Fast Betty," which apparently absorbed all his affection as well as destroying him financially. Now Betty has lost all hope, given up all dreams, and cannot even suppose that anyone would be interested enough in her to ask what her dreams might be. Holits, on the other hand, seems not to have been disillusioned by his experiences (he still carries with him the bridle of his horse and tries to re-live his more exuberant and dashing youth) until the foolish accident leaves him dazed and taciturn and then leads him to take the family back onto the road, possibly at Betty's insistence.

But the Holitses, though they preoccupy the narrator, are not in fact the only examples she observes of broken dreams and human inadequacies. She is in a perfect position to pick up on many passing lives; she works as an apartment manager whose windows overlook both the swimming pool and the parking area, and also as a hair "stylist," skilled at drawing life-stories out of her customers. The other two domestic situations she digressively describes in her narration tell similar stories: the widower whose second wife, with brittle zeal, pretends to enjoy his home movies of the first Mrs. Cobb; the cocktail waitress with her series of lovers (alcoholic lawyer "fiancé," long-haired college student). And then there is Marge's own situation, which is the author's focus: the nosy neighbor who vicariously lives in other people's lives, the pathetic wife of a man glued to his remote-control TV when he is not doing his handyman chores as the manager's husband, a man locked into cliché-ridden imperceptiveness about real people. Marge is the protagonist who finally sees that her husband "acts like nothing has happened or ever will happen," a man who unwittingly interrupts her when she is about to match Betty Holits story-for-story in telling "how it was" and "how it's still like that" — for Marge, a frustrating missed chance, perhaps, to reach a definition of what troubles her own life.

Marge's discovery of the symbolic bridle produces her dawning sense of the cruelty and control exercised over a wife by a shiftless, worthless husband. What she has been experiencing for some time, her equivocal but concealed dissatisfaction with her life, is finally focused for her in the contrast between Betty's carefully cleaned and shined bedroom and Holits's careless (or purposeful?) abandonment of the bridle.

Carver's technique typifies the "neo-realism" of some contemporary fiction: a narration flatly reporting actions (how coolly Holits's accident is presented — "I see him hit the deck. I hear him too"), paying most attention to the visual detail, and avoiding direct interpretation or evaluation. In this instance, the strict limitation of point of view in a narrator whose powers of analysis are undeveloped produces a story that at first reading appears to be no more than anecdotal reporting by an unimaginative observer. In such fiction the symbolic object or action may carry the thematic weight. In addition to the title object, which Marge finally perceives symbolically, both she and Betty pay sufficient attention to the "prayer plant" to suggest that it has a symbolic purpose as well, though they are not consciously aware of this. This tropical plant (botanically *Maranta*) thrives on moisture but is being gradually stripped of its foliage by neglect and by the Arizona climate; its nickname alludes to its nocturnal habit of raising up its flat, horizontal leaves as if raising hands in supplication. Like the two women, it is being destroyed by neglect and an alien environment; unlike the two of them, it at least displays a semblance of awareness of its plight through its natural tropism. Why is Marge not giving it the water it needs? Is she subconsciously aware that like herself it is a plant out of place, that not even prayer can help it or her now? These two objects, the bridle and the plant, embrace the symbolic breadth of the story and indicate the method employed by Carver: they radiate meanings, one of them impressing itself on the narrator's consciousness, the other remaining unanalyzed but essential to the author's evaluation. That Marge can at least recognize a meaning in the bridle is the mark of her growth as a developing character — though one would not predict that her insight can lead to any change of behavior.   TRA

John Cheever   **The Swimmer**   (page 398)

QUESTIONS

1. What is Neddy's reason for wanting to "swim across the county"? Is this presented as a plausible motivation? Is it more plausible in a man called "Neddy" than in a man named "Edward"?
2. The point of view of the story is omniscient, but is more or less limited to Neddy's consciousness. At what points in the story is it more strictly limited? How are those limitations related to the plot and theme?

3. Collect examples of Neddy's definitions and evaluations of himself, and of the social world around him. Is he consistent in his self-estimations? How do you account for his attitude toward (a) the Biswangers, (b) the Hallorans, (c) the crowd at the public pool?
4. What is the social structure of Neddy's world? What are its rituals and customs? How does it contrast with the life at the public pool? Are there stratifications within it? Is Neddy typical or untypical of his social set? What about this social world is appealing, and what is judged satirically?
5. Is there a particular place where the story clearly begins employing fantasy? What nonrealistic distortions of time and its effect on weather are manifested? How old is the protagonist at the end of the story? What truth about Neddy and about his social world is manifested in the fantasy?
6. What incidents in Neddy's life must be inferred from the words and actions of other characters, because they are not registered directly in Neddy's consciousness? What does the psychological suppression of these incidents add to the characterization of Neddy?
7. In the second paragraph of the story, the narrator reports of Neddy that "he might have been compared to a summer's day." Do you recognize the literary allusion here? (Consult Shakespeare's Sonnet 18, and consider the relevance of the poem to Neddy Merrill's estimation of himself and his youth.)
8. Define the conflicts presented in the story. Do they include man-against-himself? Is Neddy a developing character? What theme is expressed by the plot of the story?

Neddy or Ned Merrill (not Edward, but only the boyish nicknames) undertakes a whimsical pilgrimage, a journey of exploration and discovery intended to lend support to his semi-heroic, self-satisfied feeling about himself, the first man to swim across the county. But the realistic narration, the matter-of-fact tone, and the limited omniscient point of view creates a somber fantasy satirizing both Neddy and his social world. At what point does the fantasy begin? It is really difficult to say: certainly after the welcomed but destructive thunderstorm, the time races through the day and through seasons, the warm midsummer becomes a chill autumn, the vigorous and virile protagonist is debilitated and sapped of strength and dignity. But even before these overt signals, the story has given a sense of its allegorical framework, as Neddy leaves a poolside party of the hungover and visits, in order, a party at the Grahams' just getting underway, a party at the Bunkers' in full swing, and the eerily deserted site of a party at the Levys'. Neddy's pilgrimage is not only geographical but also social, across a landscape familiar in its customs and in "the rigid and undemocratic realities" of its society.

As Cheever is renowned as the fictional explorer of suburbia, so Neddy's trek displays the attractive and unattractive features of that social landscape. This is a world of leisure, parties, overindulgence in food and drink, and material accumulation; yet it also worships sport, youth, vitality, friendliness. In its artificiality it has created a "river" of swimming pools that allows the protagonist to go exploring, though its denizens display a broad range of attitudes towards naturalness (including the eccentric nudists). Its morality is easy, condoning adultery and snobbery. Success, as displayed in its possessions, seems its highest value.

Neddy's journey takes him not only across this social world but also through his own history, though there the landscape is less familiar, both to Neddy and to the reader. As Neddy asks himself, "Was his memory failing or had he so disciplined it in the repression of unpleasant facts that he had damaged his sense of the truth?" For Neddy has become so secure and confident in his relationships, so practiced in maintaining his youthful attitudes and outlook, and so incapable of self-examination, that he has been unable to comprehend what has happened to him: his loss of fortune, stability, family, and health. As naturally as day passes to night or summer to autumn, Neddy has descended from his apex — but without recognizing the signs of it, so that each change seems a fresh and inexplicable shock of loss. The naiveté of his boyish charm is also a barrier to self-knowledge. His "determinedly original" mind is one that has not been shaped by experience, so like an adolescent he has a "vague and modest idea of himself as a legendary figure . . . a man with a destiny."

Cheever takes Neddy from the fullness of his complacency to the emptiness of his reality — and then leaves him there, shivering outside his locked and deserted house, leaves him with the potentiality of self-discovery but without any implication that Neddy will proceed to know himself. Will he, like Goodman Brown, live on as a bitter, poisoned pessimist? Will he, like Sherwood Anderson's swipe, find ways of rationalizing and shifting the responsibility from himself? Will he, like Miss Brill, manage to put these experiences away in a box?

The allegory here moves symbolically from summer to chill, and from a fully supported social existence to desolation. In the second paragraph the narrator paraphrases Neddy's abundant good feeling about himself: "he might have been compared to a summer's day," alluding to Shakespeare's Sonnet 18, that lovely, extravagant proclamation of the triumph of youthful beauty over all the ravages of time. At the end Neddy is left in the condition of another Shakespeare creature, "unaccommodated man . . . a poor, bare, forked animal" suffering loneliness, desolation, and terror. Is Neddy Merrill ready now, finally, to explore the meaning of being human?

This story has received considerable critical attention. Among the most useful analyses are Robert M. Slabey's "John Cheever: The 'Swimming' of America," Eugene Chesnick's "The Domesticated Stroke of John Cheever," and Stephen C. Moore's "The Hero on the 5:42: John Cheever's Short Fiction," all collected in R. G. Collins, *Critical Essays on John Cheever* (Boston: Hall, 1982).

A Columbia Pictures adaption of this story starring Burt Lancaster (1968) is available on videocassette. Although it devises more elaborated scenes of Neddy's encounters on his journey, it is faithful to the tone and meaning of the story.
TRA

Stephen Crane **The Bride Comes to Yellow Sky** (page 407)

QUESTIONS

1. Like most western stories and movies, this one has the classical confrontation of town marshal and desperado. In what way does it differ from the expected stereotype? Where does the interest of the story lie?
2. The story is built around a number of ironic contrasts. Explore each of these for what it contributes to the theme:
   a. Jack Potter's behavior on the train, especially as it approaches Yellow Sky; the contrast between his thoughts and feelings, and his actions and speeches.
   b. Scratchy Wilson's sense of his role, and his costume and actions.
   c. Mrs. Potter's attitude toward her puff sleeves and her view of her new position in life.
   d. The décor of the parlor car and the appearance of the main street in Yellow Sky.
3. Although written in the omniscient third-person point of view, the story frequently presents visual details as they are perceived by one or another of the characters. Show how these moments of limited point of view are used to reveal character (include the barkeeper's dog).
4. What does the image in the last sentence of the story reveal about what has happened to Yellow Sky?

Time has run out for the old way of life in Yellow Sky. In the last sentence of the story, Scratchy Wilson's boot heels leave "funnel-shaped tracks in the heavy sand," the last vortex as the sands flow through the hourglass. But the story ironically and steadfastly refuses to sentimentalize either the rough masculinity of the old West or the domesticating femininity of the East, which is replacing it. Crane's comic irony consistently undercuts the expected stereotypes of both ways of life, providing detail after detail to demonstrate the shortcomings of both. "The dignity of motion" of "the great Pullman" in the first paragraph immediately sets up the central theme: as the train speeds westward the perspective of its passengers makes it seem that the "plains of Texas [are] pouring eastward"—not as one might have supposed, that eastern values are rushing west (as they certainly are) but that the West is rushing to easternize itself. This visual first impression is subsequently supported by the portraits of Jack Potter and his unnamed bride. He had traveled eastward, but not to the East, to fetch himself a wife from San Antonio. In the civilized sumptuousness of the parlor car, a glittering parody of elegance, surrounded by more worldly passengers and tyrannically highbrow railroad personnel, Potter is extremely ill at ease and yet proud of his transformation, and his bride, whose hands are probably as red as his (from cooking rather than from outdoor work), preens herself on her stylish "puff sleeves" at the same time that they embarrass her. These two self-conscious westerners have decked themselves out in eastern garb and are on their way to carry style into Yellow Sky country. To the blasé characters on the train they are a joke, two overdressed hicks posing as sophisticates; to themselves, although they are too shy to acknowledge it, they are terribly apprehensive about how Yellow Sky will react to the new roles they believe they have adopted.

The second section of the story backtracks chronologically, from 3:42 when the train arrives, to 3:21 when the action in Yellow Sky begins. Any expectations about the wildness of the Wild West are immediately overturned: the saloon is not the Golden Nugget or the Last Chance, but the "Weary Gentleman"; its patrons are not macho cowboys and gunslingers but a garrulous traveling salesman whose jokes fall flat, three taciturn locals, and two Mexican sheepherders; the rest of the town is dozing through the hot afternoon. While the townspeople may occasionally kick a dog on the boardwalk, showing the motiveless brutality associated with a frontier town, the processes of civilization have already taken root in "vivid green grassplots" carefully nurtured in the inhospitable natural climate.

Only Scratchy Wilson remains as a vestige of the stereotypical gunslinger (and the bachelor Marshal Potter was his law-and-order counterpart, the only man who could master him). "About the last one of the old gang that used to hang out along the river," Wilson has come to town on one of his regular drunken sprees to shoot up Yellow Sky. But how wild is this last representative of the West? Tricked out in his maroon-colored flannel shirt from the garment district of New York City and his garishly decorated boots, he displays his prowess by terrifying the barkeeper's dog. In the final confrontation with the marshal, Scratchy uncomprehendingly surrenders to the fact that his nemesis is not only unarmed but married—the game between them, playing out those old western roles, is "all off now."

What Crane demonstrates throughout the story are the false assumptions that the characters have about their roles and how other people see them. With relentless but good-humored irony, he punctures one after another—the manly hero, the blushing bride, the vicious desperado, the blasé sophisticate, the witty drummer—but most of all, the readers' own assumptions about frontier life. All are subjected to the test of reality, and all collapse in a comic heap. TRA

Louise Erdrich **A Wedge of Shade** (page 416)

QUESTIONS

1. What personal conflicts does the narrator anticipate from her marriage? How does she expect her mother to react to her? How fully are her expectations fulfilled?
2. In what ways are the mother and her sister Aunt Mary opposites? What does the narrator expect from Aunt Mary, and what does she find?
3. The narrator supposes that the central conflict of the situation will be between Gerry and her mother. Trace the development of their relationship and its ironic overturning of the narrator's expectation.
4. Throughout the story, and especially in the initial scene between mother and daughter, there are references to staged or theatrical actions. Explore these as an evidence of the state of mind of the narrator. How are the scenes of this story

dramatically developed? Is the drama of the first scene resolved? What resolution occurs at the end of scene 2 (in the butcher shop cooler)? At the end of the last scene? The end of the story is determinate: explain how all conflicts have been resolved.

5. What are the symbolic implications of the title and its identification with Gerry as he emerges from the distance? How is a wedge both positive and negative in its potential uses?

The unnamed narrator has returned from "cities" to her mother's rural house in North Dakota after more than six months. She has brought with her a surprise, her new husband, Gerry Nanapush, an agitator (presumably in the movement for Native-American rights). But she faces the problem of informing her mother of the fact of her marriage and of the identity of her bridegroom, for she anticipates conflict on both scores. In addition, the weather is unbearably hot and dry. For the protagonist, then, there seem to be three arenas of conflict: with herself, in the necessity to work up the courage to reveal her surprise, for she knows how her mother will react and she hates to face that; with her mother, in the fear of her awful anger; and with the environment, in the unforgiving and oppressive heat.

Her mother seems true to expectation in her response — a long, drawn-out silence, a "frighteningly neutral" voice when she does speak. But as they wait for Gerry to arrive, the narrator perceives that the situation is theatrical, artificial, and unnatural: both she and her mother gesture and speak "as if [they're] in a staged drama," and with the same sense of inadequacy that she feels toward her mother from the outset, she thinks herself "a bad actor."

Gerry's arrival augments the arranged, artificial nature of the scene. He appears as a dot at the end of the road, and then slowly, as if filmed with a long-distance lens, the dot grows, the silhouette of a man emerges and is lost in the heat shimmers, until "in that shining expanse he is a little wedge of moving shade." His appearance as he nears the yard is large and magnificent, the climax of the scene is about to occur — when "like a choreography design" the police arrive, snap handcuffs on Gerry, and carry him away for questioning. "This is terrible timing," says the narrator/theater-critic. The scene that she had imagined for herself, with its dramatic structure and dénouement, the powerful clash of opponents when her mother and her husband meet, all is undermined and falls away. The curtain drops on that stage.

The second scene of the story, at Aunt Mary's butcher shop, is also characterized by heightened, theatrical qualities. Aunt Mary is in every way the opposite of the narrator's mother, physically in her own person and temperamentally — "cold yellow eyes" like a hawk, inhabiting the coolness of the meat locker. There the narrator easily tells her news, for Aunt Mary is never surprised, and her heart goes "still and cool" inside her as she describes Gerry and his activities. Aunt Mary is utterly practical (and non-judgmental): when she learns that Gerry does not work, that the narrator expects that she will be their support, Aunt Mary determines to "fix that." Momentarily the narrator supposes she means that she will find a way of separating the married couple, but Aunt Mary's intention is again cool and practical: she will teach the couple how to practice her trade, and leave them the shop and go off to Arizona with her sister. This scene, too, has its theatrical conclusion, a tableau with the three women sitting in the cooler, "upright and still" with faces "blank as the gods' . . . dreaming the world up in [their] brains." The image conjured up by the narrator symbolically closes the episode: the conflicts between narrator and mother are resolved, the coolness has overcome the overheated emotion, and they are ready to move on from a position of total illumination and calm relief.

The final setting resolves the other imagined conflict, that between bridegroom and mother-in-law. As the women near the house, the narrator has the intuition that "there must be a close to this day," that more dramatic resolutions are in store. Surely enough, the mother finds in Gerry an equal—the same height, with eyes at the same level (and so looking over the head of the narrator), they discover their blood kinship. But the discovery does not bring them together: "they are like two opponents from the same divided country, staring across the border," two opposite ways of life as Native-Americans. Then they go to work together on the broken fans, clanking their tools "as if they are fighting a duel" and yet cooperating as they work to bring some cool into the stifling house.

Once again the scene ends in a motionless tableau. The narrator has brought ice and dark-colored sodas (to drink in the night) from the convenience store, and the now reconciled "opponents" have together furnished the cooling breeze of the fans. The three of them lie on cushions on the floor, the women on either side of Gerry, "huge as a hill between [them], solid in the beating wind." The "wedge of shade" that emerged out of the blinding sunlight now comfortably joins rather than separates the two women, a wedge that holds them steady and balanced rather than a wedge to rive them apart.   TRA

Richard Ford   **Great Falls** (page 424)

QUESTIONS

1. "This is not a happy story," the narrator Jackie begins. How much unhappiness is there in the events he reports and in his assessment of them?
2. Characterize Jack Russell, the father. What has made him happy in the past? How important to his characterization is his illegal sale of the fruits of his hunting and fishing? How does he treat his unfaithful wife? Why doesn't he shoot Woody?
3. Characterize Jackie's mother. How does her concluding conversation with her son explain her behavior?
4. Can you explain why Jackie's sympathies are drawn to Woody in the confrontation with Jack? Is Woody his brother?
5. The story ends with a direct statement of theme. Is there any reason to suppose that the theme of the story is different from the theme that Jackie defines for these events? What kind of a man has Jackie become in the time since the events took place?

61

The story concludes with the narrator directly stating a theme: there is

some coldness in us all, some helplessness that causes us to misunderstand life when it is pure and plain, makes our existence seem like a border between two nothings, and makes us no more or less than animals who meet on the road — watchful, unforgiving, without patience or desire.

It is a bleak and universalizing statement that seems almost too general for the incidents that make up the story, but as a conclusion casts its shadow backward to provide a definition of the experience of this unhappy man.

At fourteen, Jackie, as the stability of his family life is destroyed, has a glimpse into the private worlds of his parents and of the young stranger Woody. These events are not particularly mysterious: a faithless wife, caught with her lover by her husband, kicked out of their house, leaving the father to raise their boy by himself. But such a sequence, while unfortunately unremarkable, destroys the boy's life, and makes of him the nihilist revealed in the conclusion, a man who some years later is still puzzled by the unanswered questions, and is still refusing to ask them.

What occurs in the breakdown of this family is an emotional shock from which the boy cannot recover. In glimpsing the private lives of others he learns that there are mysteries, but reticence and the need to protect himself from further shock turn him from seeking out their meanings. This lesson is placed before him twice: first, when after asking his son what worries him, his father pledges to respect his "privacy," and second, when his mother begins her talk with him in the motel the next morning with the statement "Privacy can be a burden, sometimes." That is the burden that is laid on him: the knowledge that there are private feelings, reasons, motives, but that these must be left unexamined and undisclosed. Why do people do what they do? Jackie asks himself, but he doesn't put the question to anyone who might answer him. As his mother also says to him, "Your life's your own business, Jackie. . . . Sometimes it scares you to death it's so much your own business." Seeing his father's money clip in her purse, Jackie draws the same conclusion: "We were all of us on our own in this."

There are for the reader unanswered questions as well, with some implied answers that don't really come to Jackie's awareness. For example, how much does Jack know about his wife's affair? He breaks his habitual routine to return home early after the hunting trip with his son, then drives to the house from an unaccustomed direction after pausing to listen for the high-flying geese, "those boys" who are "long gone." His manner clearly suggests that he is expecting something to be happening in his house, and for reasons of his own doesn't comment on the Pontiac parked surreptitiously nearby. He shows no surprise at the sight of Woody in his kitchen, but sends him and Jackie outside so that he can confront his wife. As a consequence of these details, the reader may safely infer that Jack has purposely planned to catch his wife in her infidelity. Why has he staged it in this fashion? Why is he displaying it to Jackie? (These questions are not Jackie's — his curiosity turns rather to what this situation has done to Woody and to his mother.)

And what truth is there to Woody's claim that Jackie's mother had been married before and divorced? Jackie in his confusion of feelings claims to know that already, though of course he does not, and arouses his mother's anger (against her husband) when he asks her about it. Has there been something in her past that is clear to Woody but eludes Jackie? At any rate, Woody stands in a very strange relationship to this family: Jackie sees in him another self, or a brother, someone he wants to be like — possibly in fact a brother from his mother's first marriage. Woody may be hinting at such a relationship with his apparently irrelevant remark to Jackie about not recognizing *his* brother as they passed in the airport. Yet Woody is also another version of Jack the father — another man in the Air Force younger than the mother with whom she finds an opportunity to escape her too domestic life. To add these details in a way which Jackie cannot, we might even see a hint of oedipal incestuousness in the relationship between Woody and the mother — and, with Woody as his surrogate, between Jackie and his mother. Although this suggestion would seem to be undercut by Woody's information that he is from a suburb of Chicago, and that his parents are alive, the emotional force of Jackie's response remains valid:

> . . . I remember wondering if Woody's heart was broken and what any of this meant to him. Not to me, or my mother, or my father. But to him, since he seemed to be the one left out somehow, the one who would be lonely soon, the one who had done something he would someday wish he hadn't and would have no one to tell him that it was all right, that they forgave him, that these things happen in the world.

It is, finally, Jackie's story, long after Woody has disappeared, Jack has died, and his mother has drifted from man to man. Jackie is the one who needs to be told "that it [is] all right, that they forgave him, that these things happen in the world," and that the burdens of privacy can be shared. Without that knowledge, there is no happiness.   TRA

Shirley Jackson   **The Lottery** (page 436)

QUESTIONS

1. What is a scapegoat? Who is the scapegoat in this story? Look up other examples of scapegoats (Sir James Frazer's *The Golden Bough* is an excellent source).
2. What law of probability has the author suspended in writing the story? Granting this initial implausibility, does the story proceed naturally?
3. What is the fundamental irony of the story?
4. What is the significance of the fact that the original box has been lost and many parts of the ritual have been forgotten?
5. What different attitudes toward the ritual are represented by (a) Mr. Summers, (b) Old Man Warner, (c) Mr. and Mrs. Adams, (d) Mrs. Hutchinson, (e) the villagers in general? Which would you suppose most nearly represents the attitude of the author? Why?
6. By transporting a primitivistic ritual into a modern setting, the author is enabled to say something about human nature and human society. What?
7. "The Lottery" must obviously be interpreted symbolically or allegorically (as a

pattern of symbols corresponding to some pattern in the real world). How far is the meaning of its symbols fixed? How much is the meaning open to various interpretations? What specific interpretations can you suggest?

The theme of the story may be expressed in some such form as this: Essentially decent and kindly people may perform cruel, irrational actions through their unquestioning acceptance of traditions and customs that have lost their original meaning or ground for belief. The symbol of the lottery is obviously an open one and might accommodate a wide range of specific applications (social segregation? class distinction? racial and religious prejudice? hazing? capital punishment? nationalism? war?). The suggestion of specific applications is less important than the comment made on human nature. The main irony of the story lies in the discrepancy between the friendliness and good will of the community and the cruelty and meaninglessness of the practice it perpetuates.

Though Jackson has developed none of her characters, she has skillfully indicated a range of attitudes among them. Mr. Summers represents civic duty. He is reasonably progressive, has substituted slips of paper for chips of wood, would like to have a new box. But he doesn't question the ritual itself. He is a man of ignorant good will. Old Man Warner is the bigoted reactionary who complains that "People ain't the way they used to be" and is contemptuous of the younger generation. Ironically, he does not recognize his own inner contradictions. "Next," he says of the young folks, "they'll want to go back to living in caves," not realizing that he himself has never emerged from the cave. Mr. and Mrs. Adams are the liberals. They at least question the necessity of the lottery. "Some places have quit lotteries," they point out. But they do nothing to protest against the lottery or to change it. Mrs. Hutchinson is the self-centered individual, and perhaps the one in whom latent cruelty is most apparent. She accepts the lottery without concern until it falls on *her*; then she protests that it is unfair, and would eagerly shift her fate to someone else, even her own daughter. Mr. Summers becomes *her* scapegoat. The majority of the villagers simply accept the lottery without question.

Students who misread the story are likely to do so by overemphasizing the role of Mrs. Hutchinson or by seeing the story merely as a satire on the acceptance of tradition. The protagonist of the story is the whole community, not Mrs. Hutchinson. Mrs. Hutchinson, if she emerges as the central figure at the end of the story, is nevertheless only significant insofar as she is representative of the community. The chief antagonist of the story is probably the villagers' own blind acceptance of tradition, but the horror of the story arises from the fact that there is so little conflict. The antagonist wins without a struggle. Nevertheless, the story is not an attack against the acceptance of tradition as such. Many traditions (for example, the exchange of gifts at Christmas time as a symbol of love and concern) are beneficent and enrich our lives. The thrust of the story is against the unquestioning acceptance of cruel, irrational traditions.

As a final comment, I quote one of my students: "Had the author left the scapegoat custom in its primitive setting, the reader very likely would have dismissed the story with a few complacent reflections on man's glorious conquest of ignorance and superstition. On the other hand, if the story had dealt with an actual modern example of cruel traditional social custom, the tendency would have been to narrow the message of the story instead of suggesting by symbolism its many modern parallels.''

In *Come Along with Me* (New York: Viking, 1968) Miss Jackson has an amusing account of the to-do that followed the initial publication of this story in *The New Yorker*. It is instructive in its revelation of the many ways in which a writer's intentions may be misunderstood.

There are brief references to this story on pages 146 and 290. LP

A film of this story (1969) is available from Encyclopaedia Britannica Educational Corporation, 425 N. Michigan Avenue, Chicago, Illinois 60611.

James Joyce **Eveline** (page 443)

QUESTIONS

1. Construct the events of Eveline's life up to the time of the story. What has given her pleasure? What has given her pain?
2. What in her present circumstances makes it desirable for her to escape her home? Characterize her father and Miss Gavan, her supervisor. What does the memory of her mother contribute to her decision to leave?
3. At just about the middle of the story (end of paragraph 9), Eveline sums up her life in Dublin: "It was hard work—a hard life—but now that she was about to leave it she did not find it a wholly undesirable life." What about it makes it attractive to her?
4. What kind of man is Frank? Why does Eveline's father forbid her to see him? Is there any evidence to support her father's suspicion about Frank?
5. To what extent is Eveline's refusal to board the ship based on her judgment and will? Has she *decided* not to go?
6. Is her refusal to go a defeat, or is it a victory?

This story is put forward as an example of what Joyce called the "paralysis" of Dublin. It presents its protagonist at a crisis in her life, at the moment when she might take decisive action and (like Joyce himself) escape the constrictions of an ugly and dispiriting life.

The beginning scene, with Eveline sitting exhausted at the darkening window, breathing in the "odor of dusty cretonne," leads her to a nostalgic reminiscence of childhood where there was an open field for her to play in with her siblings and other children. Even though her father would beat them if he caught them at play, ". . . they seemed to have been rather happy then" (the phrasing suggests that it was not a carefree and joyous childhood—*seemed* and *rather* undercut that impression). This wistfulness for past pleasure is then abruptly stopped: childhood is gone, people have died, and Eveline herself is about to go away.

She then meditates on her present situation, on the dissatisfaction of her work,

65

the hardship and growing threat of living with her father, the loneliness of her life at home. Her rescuer has come into her life in the form of Frank the sailor. Their brief courtship had its excitements and then aroused the animosity of her father, who protectively (and jealously?) forbade her to see Frank—"'I know these sailor chaps.'" So they met furtively, and planned an elopement to Buenos Aires where Frank has "a home waiting for her."

In the growing darkness, as she sits, Eveline hears a street organ and flashes back to the death of her mother after a "life of commonplace sacrifices" (like Eveline's) that closes "in final craziness." Terror-stricken, she rushes to Frank as her savior from such a life.

The moment of departure arrives, Eveline meets Frank at the quay, and in "a maze of distress, she [prays] to God to direct her, to show her what [is] her duty." Whether by God's direction, or by her own helplessness to act, she remains while Frank boards the ship.

As critics have shown, it is possible to view these incidents from at least two quite different perspectives—and it is not really possible to decide between them. Eveline may in the end collapse into the creature of habit, the passive, defeated drudge, who "like a helpless animal" cannot break out of its captivity. Or her excited, frenzied state may be rescuing her from an unprincipled seducer, at the last moment leading her back to safety and respectability. Frank is, after all, a "sailor chap" about whom she knows nothing and who may or may not be telling her the truth about their future. If his purposes are marriage and a home with her, why should the marriage be postponed until they have departed? Is there really a home waiting in Buenos Aires? If this is the future he dreams about, why is he willing to leave her behind? Her father may be motivated by his need for a housekeeper and her small wages, but he may also sincerely be trying to protect her from a seducer.

Whichever perspective one chooses, Eveline's fate is pathetic, for she has not escaped the dreariness of her life in Dublin, and she has lost what seemed to her the promise of a new and happy life. The future promises little but the sameness of her stifled, lonely life, with the additional growing threat of violence from her father. If this is an escape from a possible danger, it is also a retreat into a known "life of commonplace sacrifices." TRA

Walter McDonald **The Track** (page 447)

QUESTIONS

1. Look up the history of Vietnam from its period as part of French Indochina to the end of the American Vietnamese War. At what time in that history does this story take place?
2. What symbolic values have the following: (a) the French mansion; (b) the Vietnamese shacks; (c) the dead yellow grass and rusting goalposts of the football field?
3. What are the individualizing personality traits of the American men in this story? How do they represent the variety of a military force?

4. What stated and implied physical distances does the story present? Where do the Americans want to go? What is the symbolic meaning of the American military men's running around the track?

"I knew . . . there was still a long, long way to go," says Moose in conclusion. Drawing on several references, the story locates itself in distances and motion through time and space. The longest "way to go" is the one that originated with Vietnam as part of French Indochina in the era of colonial exploitation, that proceeded through the long war of independence from France and then the American military involvement in the name of protecting the independence of an anti-communist nation. It is toward the end of that historical development that the story takes place, with the Americans now winding down their direct military activities and handing over the responsibility to the Vietnamese army. The dilapidation and deterioration of the football field and its grandstand and goalposts are witness to the historical movement that will finish with the total withdrawal in defeat of the American forces, their attempts to create an Americanized nation having fallen apart. By contrast, the continued existence of the French estate with its swimming pool and its sensual laughter and music "like Paris in springtime" is an anachronistic reminder of the heyday of colonial rule—for the "cats" behind their wall, their "Promised Land" of luxurious living is where time and distance have stopped.

The other "long way" in the temporal dimension is represented by the individual careers of the men who appear in the story, for they range from the newcomer Moose, who has just arrived from the States, to his guide Lebowitz, experienced and informative after spending some time in Bien Dien, to the old, white-haired sergeant or colonel who prudently avoids the potential danger of the Vietnamese shacks, counting his time until "it's over" and he can return home. All of them are keenly aware of their own DEROS—"Date of Earliest Return from Overseas: months, impossible months" in the future.

The vast space between this land and home is what these men all hope to live to be able to cross. In the meanwhile, they exist in two other spatial relations. The regular North Vietnamese Army, coming to the aid of the Viet Cong guerrillas, is rumored to be only forty kilometers to the north, advancing across the forbidden space of the demilitarized zone and coming toward Bien Dien. And to the Americans at the base, there is the track itself—six laps to the mile, four or five miles a day, run at varying speeds and with varying thoughts and feelings, they go around and around until they run even beyond their own fatigue. This is the most meaningful spatial movement in the story, for it images the others and symbolizes the war itself. Past decaying evidence of other times, other regimes, past the dangerous animosity of the people whose land they are occupying, past the dead idea of colonial empire lost in its dream world, the men go their "long, long way." And as the symbol implies, their way in this land is circular and futile, without a destination and with their personal health and safety as their only purpose, a purpose that they will pursue with extraordinary exertions. TRA

QUESTIONS

1. Summarize the events of Sam's marriage to Nova. What kind of person was she? Why might she have wanted their house to be in her name?
2. How does Damson's disappointed life compare to the life lived by her brother Sam? Which of them actually had a more difficult marriage? Why is it so easy for Sam to laugh her out of her moroseness? How has the story prepared the reader for the shock of his vulgarity?
3. The plot of this story has very little action. What conflicts does it display? Does it resolve them?
4. The family's conversations are discussions of "character" rather than storytelling. How is that a clue to the point of this story?
5. Analyze the final paragraph of the story for its developing attitude and for its sensory richness. How is it a fitting conclusion to the concerns raised by Damson and by Sam?

Sam thinks that his "kinfolks never told stories or reminisced when they sat around on a Sunday. Instead, they discussed character." This habit suggests the technique of the story, which minimizes the element of plot and emphasizes character. The story juxtaposes past with present (but does not "reminisce" about that past) in order to show how present character has been developed by the tension between events-as-they-occurred and the hopes and wishes that were frustrated by those events.

The three remaining members of the family in the sixty-year-old photograph Sam and Damson look at are showing the signs of aging. Their ages are nearly 84 (Sam), nearly 78 (Damson), and probably early seventies (Hortense). Hort's cooking is not up to standards, her house smells of fish, and there are weeds in the yard. Damson is "still pretty, still herself in there" despite her "puffed-out old face." Sam is careless and forgetful, troubled with arthritis and a sour stomach, and a source of concern to his two sisters who worry about the way he lives. They are holding up well, for their ages, but their ages are telling on them.

What is telling more, however, is the sense of loss and of a "ruined" life that Damson feels, and the parallel feeling evoked in Sam by her confession and complaint against their father for keeping her from the man she loved and possibly causing his suicide. After her hysteria passed, she married her husband " 'for pure spite,' " a man she " 'never cared a thing about.' " (The story doesn't reveal whether she had children, but that seems more an omission of reporting than anything else: with the constant reflection about grandchildren and great-grandchildren, Damson's not having had a family of her own would certainly be a fact arising in Sam's consciousness.) These ancient events knocked the hope out of her and left her with a lifelong sadness that Sam has always known was there, though the precise nature of her loss has apparently not surfaced until now. Luckily for Damson, when she wishes that her life had been different, Sam has just the right vulgar shock to restore her equilibrium: " 'wish in one hand and shit in the other and see which one fills up the quickest!' '' The coarseness of the remark shows her the idleness of her wish, and also smartly plays upon the euphemistic propriety that has been evinced earlier in the family conversation when "*H*" was substituted for "hell."

But after Damson brightens up and then leaves, Sam looks back on his own disappointments. His "wish" also has to do with love and marriage, but in contrast to his sister, years of disappointment have not soured and saddened his outlook. Throughout the story his mind (and some of the conversation) turns to his wife Nova, now dead eight and a half years. Through scattered glimpses, we learn that she had prevented Sam from keeping his parents' homeplace, had forced him to sell the house he loved to move into town — to a "brick box" that she maintained with such rigor that they had to put towels on the furniture to protect the upholstery. She was a woman of "squirrelly" habits who possessively wanted their house in her name (though perhaps with some reason), contributed to evangelists, and in general was excessively prudential.

But as Sam in his insomnia begins to "replay" his life with her, he reveals deeper discontents than Damson has confessed — several times he wanted to leave Nova and divorce her, for she was not someone he "'never cared a thing about'" but rather the object of resentment and animosity. His life with his spouse was in fact worse than Damson's with hers. Nova took from him those things that he most loved — the old house with its porch and swing, its view of the woods, the "special dog" that he sat with looking out over the tobacco fields. And in his final retrospection, these are the things that he also associates with his first love, Nettie Slade — the old bird dog Obadiah, the woods and fields where they lay together.

The last paragraph of this story is a marvelous evocation of Sam's still young heart and mind. It begins with the distasteful recollection of Nova's death, going "without needing him at all" as he now has no need for her, nor does he blame her. As he surveys the small room in the "brick box" that he has chosen for his own, he sees the spartan cell of a man who has relinquished caring about the things that concerned his wife, a man who now himself needs nothing of the present world. For in his memory of that first lovemaking, he has all the sensuous richness that life affords — the touch of the damp grass, the sweet smell of the new mown hay, the coolness of the air and the warmth of Nettie's breath, the vivid sharpness of the stubble pressing against his back, the beauty and precision of the starry night, and even the unforgotten detail of the pressure of her buttons as they embraced, "hard like seed corn." This conclusion, so full of life and living, is a perfect rejoinder to Damson's wishing for some other life than she has lived. Sam has dispensed with the need to blame or to wish, and can in fact delight in his memories. He can experience in the tranquility of old age a "spontaneous overflow of powerful emotions" that makes wishing things were different insubstantial and empty. The "seed corn" of that experience has grown and flourished through a long life.   TRA

QUESTIONS

1. Identify the protagonist, and define the kinds of conflict that make up the plot.
2. Characterize the staff at the Wall Street office before the arrival of Bartleby. How are they comic? Why does the lawyer not replace them?
3. Track the development of Bartleby's performance in his job at the office. Are there any verifiable reasons for his behavior? Is he a developing character?
4. How does the lawyer feel about Bartleby at the various stages of his story? Are his feelings clear to him? How do you feel about Bartleby as the story develops? Can you say for certain *why* he does what he does (or does not do what he does not)?
5. What kind of man is the lawyer? Is there any reason to disbelieve what he says about Bartleby or about himself and his reactions? Is he a good man? Is he a developing character?
6. What is tragic about Bartleby's story? What is comic about it? How are these emotions complementary?

As a narrative, this is a simple, straightforward story, with little plot complication, with a single external conflict that is fully resolved, and told by an observant and sensitive narrator. It is also profoundly enigmatic, and since the "rediscovery" of Melville early in this century has aroused critical opinion of the widest divergence — not about its excellence, but about its theme. What does the simple story *mean*? To answer that, most have turned to an analysis of the characters of the protagonist/narrator and the antagonist/scrivener.

The interpretations cannot all be summarized or argued here, but this and the following paragraph contain a sampling of their points: the elderly lawyer who tells the tale is smug, obtuse, and unreliable, unable to understand either Bartleby or himself; he is defensive because he feels guilt for what happened to Bartleby; he is an exploitive representation of capitalism and business ethics who warps his clerks and destroys Bartleby; he is an exemplar of Christian forbearance and charity but is too cowardly or weak to act upon these virtues; he is an ordinary man facing an extraordinary test, and does as much as could possibly be expected.

Bartleby is a Thoreauvian dissenter, using "passive resistance" to make a point about capitalist exploitation; he is a martyr whose death condemns the system represented by the lawyer; he is going insane; he is a writer who has learned that art is impossible because communication is impossible; he is a man who cannot cope with the complexity of human interaction, and withdraws into immobility and death.

For this note, two things need to be kept clear as an approach to the story: first, the character of Bartleby *is* enigmatic, and no amount of argument or research can penetrate it, for we can know only what the narrator knows, and Bartleby is an agonizing puzzle to him. Second, the narrator is a man who candidly confesses his puzzlement, who is jolted out of his complacency by the persistent truculence of Bartleby. He does his best to understand both the scrivener and his own reaction to him.

He tries to discern the best course of action in a situation that baffles him, and therefore is constantly examining his possibilities and his motives.

The simple story is this: a pale and melancholy young man is given a job as a copyist in a law office on Wall Street, and gradually refuses to perform his duties. Although he no longer works, he also refuses to leave the office, and takes up residence there. The lawyer who has employed him vainly tries in various ways first to induce him to do his job, then to leave the premises. In frustration, the lawyer moves his establishment to another office, and the clerk is arrested by the new tenant of the Wall Street office, is imprisoned, and refusing to eat, dies.

The complication of the story arises from the lawyer's various attempts to cope with this unusual situation, and to search himself for an understanding of how he is responding and should respond. The lawyer is and remains ambivalent, for there is no way of explaining *why* Bartleby behaves as he does, nor can the lawyer figure out the best thing to do. His last exclamation ("Ah, Bartleby! ah, humanity!") reveals the depth of his anguish over what has happened to this young man, and what may happen to us all.

The story has that tragic dimension, the inexplicable self-destruction of a human being that touches so deeply. At the same time, it has its comic side, and readers are well advised not to overlook that, for the ambiguities of the theme are mirrored in the doubleness of its tone. Before the advent of Bartleby there is a Dickensian description of the other employees of the office, the odd three who have nicknamed each other Turkey, Nippers, and Ginger Nut. The first two of them have split personalities but together form a unity: Turkey is wonderfully efficient in the mornings until he has his lunchtime drinks, after which he is essentially incapable of good, steady work; Nippers is the opposite, except his problem seems not to be drink but perhaps an ulcer that pains him in the mornings until his midday meal. This complementary pair comically anticipate Bartleby's progress in the office, for at first he is marvelously efficient, and then he grows less and less useful. Ginger Nut, the office boy, does his chores with alacrity, and although he is ostensibly learning the law he seems to be only a typical twelve-year-old errand boy.

These caricatures are not however the type of comedy that reinforces the deeper ambivalences of the story. For that, we must look at some of the comic absurdities of the exchanges between Bartleby and the lawyer. Two examples (cited by McCall, below) will suffice. When the lawyer is desperately looking for something for Bartleby to do rather than stay on at the old office doing nothing, he suggests "going as a companion to Europe, to entertain some young gentleman with [his] conversation" (paragraph 208) — a suggestion so incongruous as to be hilarious, for entertaining conversation is what Bartleby lacks altogether. In that same scene, as he approaches his old law office the lawyer comes upon Bartleby:

> Going upstairs to my old haunt, there was Bartleby silently sitting upon the banister at the landing.
> "What are you doing here, Bartleby?" said I.
> "Sitting upon the banister," he mildly replied.

(paragraphs 191–93)

This is deadpan humor, the statement of the literal fact as a response to a figurative question – the lawyer did not mean to ask what he was doing there, but why he was doing it. And Bartleby never answers "why" questions.

The famous "'I would prefer not to'" which becomes Bartleby's only explanation shares in the kind of doubleness that the simultaneously tragic and comic story contains. "Prefer" has positive implications, a term used for those things we like or want or favor; it suggests desire *for* something. What Bartleby desires, however, is negative, "not to" do or have something. The key term thus has its own dimension of preposterousness, a simultaneous mingling of desire and denial, that makes Bartleby so inscrutably baffling.

I will cite only one reference here (the standard bibliographical sources are available and daunting). Dan McCall in *The Silence of Bartleby* (Ithaca, NY: Cornell UP, 1989) presents a most level-headed, sensible, and graceful account of the approaches taken by what he calls "the Bartleby Industry," and offers a sympathetic and sane interpretation of the story. His notes will guide the curious teacher into the labyrinth of other, more partial interpretations.   TRA

Edgar Allan Poe   **The Cask of Amontillado** (page 484)

QUESTIONS

1. Are there any clues to the motivation of Montresor's revenge beyond those in the opening sentence?
2. In carrying out his revenge, how does Montresor take advantage of (a) Fortunato's "one weakness," (b) the carnival season, (c) the catacombs? What similarity is there between the way he handles Fortunato and the way he handles his servants?
3. What kind of man is Montresor? Is he mad or sane? Rational or irrational? Emotional or unemotional? Explain.
4. What symbolic or ironic functions are served by (a) Fortunato's name, (b) his costume, (c) Montresor's name (in French, "my treasure"), (d) Montresor's coat of arms and family motto, (e) the carnival setting, (f) Montresor's account of his pleasure in meeting Fortunato on the street, (g) Montresor's reply to Fortunato's declaration, " I shall not die of a cough," (h) Montresor's drinking "long life" to Fortunato, (i) Montresor's declaration that he too is a mason, (j) Montresor's speech after fettering Fortunato, "Once more let me *implore* you to return"? Do you find any further examples?
5. Why and to whom is Montresor revealing his crime fifty years after he committed it?
6. Does Montresor's revenge satisfy his two criteria for perfect revenge? Why or why not?

Detective fiction and journalistic reportage are often concerned with the concept of "the perfect crime" – a murder or a train robbery so perfectly planned that its perpetrator is never apprehended or even identified. "The Cask of Amontillado" has most often been interpreted as the story of a perfect revenge. Montresor succeeds in making himself known to Fortunato, but to no one else, before taking Fortunato's life, and he plans the crime so successfully that it is still undiscovered after fifty years. Fortunato's death, moreover, is sufficiently lingering that he has time to meditate on his fate; his life is not instantly snuffed out as by a rifle shot. (The phrase *"At length"* in the story's first paragraph is open to two meanings).

Many readers of the story feel, however, that in a psychological and spiritual sense the revenge has failed, that Montresor does not get from it the satisfaction he had anticipated, and that, ironically, Fortunato has in fact been taking revenge on Montresor for fifty years through the agency of Montresor's tormented conscience. The central interpretive issue of the story, then, is whether Montresor's revenge is, as judged by his own criteria, successful or unsuccessful.

When we reread carefully Montresor's two requirements for a successful revenge, we find that each is ambiguous. (1) "I must not only punish, but punish with impunity. A wrong is unredressed when retribution overtakes its redresser." Ambiguously, this statement does not tell us whether retribution by one's own conscience is included or excluded. (2) "[A wrong] is equally unredressed when the avenger fails to make himself felt as such to him who has done the wrong." The victim must know who killed him, and must recognize that the killing is an act of vengeance. Ambiguously, this principle does not tell whether the victim must know *why* he is being avenged, what he has done to provoke vengeance.

Those who view the revenge as unsuccessful state their case somewhat as follows: (1) Fortunato never understands what Montresor is doing, or why, but thinks it only "an excellent jest"; thus Montresor's second condition for a perfect revenge is never fully satisfied. (2) The key sentence of the story is Montresor's assertion "My heart grew sick" in the final paragraph. Montresor's heart-sickness is caused, not as he says by the dampness of the catacombs, but by a sudden nausea of guilt and hypocrisy. Thus Montresor's first condition for a perfect revenge is not satisfied. (3) Poe has taken pains to draw an ironic parallel between Montresor and Fortunato; both are from noble families; both are connoisseurs of wine; their names are similar in meaning; both wear carnival costumes; in different parts of the story each repeats the words of the other. The identification is completed when Montresor re-echoes the screams of Fortunato. (*"Montresor. Fortunato.* Are these not synonymous?" asks one commentator. "Has not Montresor walled up himself in this revenge?"*). (4) The dead Fortunato, buried with Montresor's ancestors, may be said to have taken over the Montresor family motto, *Nemo me impune lacessit*, and to be punishing Montresor for his crime. (5) After fifty years of agonized mental torment, Montresor, very likely on his deathbed, feels compelled to confess his crime to his family priest. (6) Montresor's final words, *"In pace requiescat!"*, are a plea for peace for himself—a peace he has not known for fifty years.

Most of the similarities noted in (3) above can be accounted for as well by the "successful revenge" theory as by the "failed revenge" theory. The similarity of

*The quoted commentator is Daniel Hoffman, in *Poe Poe Poe* (New York: Random House, 1985) 218-19, first published by Doubleday, 1972.

names simply indicates that both are from noble wealthy families. Both wear carnival costumes because it is the carnival season. Montresor imitates Fortunato's screaming to assure himself and to demonstrate to Fortunato that no one else is in hearing range. Only the first two points in (3) need more discussion.

Fortunato knows *who* is murdering him but doesn't know *why*. The evidence, in fact, suggests that he doesn't even know *how* he insulted Montresor, or even that he *has* insulted him; and Montresor is very careful not to let him know. "Neither by word nor deed," he says, "had I given Fortunato cause to doubt my good will." Indeed, Montresor throughout the story refers to Fortunato as his "friend," and, until the very end, treats him like one. Fortunato has no suspicion nor reason for suspicion that Montresor regards him as anything other than a friend.

What *is* the motivation for Montresor's action? Montresor claims that Fortunato has done him a "thousand injuries" and finally has "ventured upon insult." A "thousand" can be dismissed as overstatement, but what puzzles a contemporary American reader is the ranking of "insult" above "injury" as a motive for revenge. This story, written almost a century and a half ago, is set in Italy, where Old World families of noble descent were very much concerned with family "honor." For them an "insult," even a very slight one, might well be considered as worse than an injury, since the insult is aimed at family "honor," whereas an injury is more likely directed against family goods. Though neither the injuries nor the insult is specified in the story (possibly because Poe was after his "single effect" and wanted the reader to concentrate on the revenge and not upon its cause), there are some clues from which we may make inferences.

Shortly after they have entered the catacombs, Montresor proposes that they turn back: "You are rich, respected, admired, beloved; you are happy, as once I was." A short while later, in response to Fortunato's comment on the extensiveness of the vaults, Montresor replies, "The Montresors . . . were a great and numerous family." Fortunato says, "I forget your arms." Montresor replies, "A huge human foot d'or, in a field azure; the foot crushes a serpent rampant whose fangs are imbedded in the heel." "And the motto?" asks Fortunato. "*Nemo me impune lacessit.*" Montresor's use of present and past tenses in the remarks suggests that the Fortunato family is at the height of its power and prestige, while the Montresor family is in decline. That Fortunato has forgotten the Montresor arms reinforces this conclusion (and may constitute another such "insult," unconscious on Fortunato's part but perhaps as keenly felt by Montresor as the one that first provoked him). The family motto, "No one attacks me with impunity," recalls Montresor's first criterion for a successful revenge: "I must not only punish, but punish with impunity." In the coat of arms, as interpreted in this context, Fortunato's family is represented by the human foot and the Montresor family by the serpent. Putting all these considerations together, we may conclude that Montresor's revenge is motivated, not necessarily by some personal insult but by some slight which in Montresor's mind impugns the family honor. Thus Montresor feels that he must perform the role of the snake in the family crest, else the motto will be a lie.

Possibly the most pointed questions one may ask in trying to decide whether Montresor's revenge is successful or unsuccessful concern the *tone* of the story and the identification of the person to whom it is told (addressed in the opening paragraph as "You, who so well know the nature of my soul"). Is this story a confession of guilt made to a father-confessor, by a man perhaps on his deathbed, who has been suffering agonies of conscience for the past fifty years? Or is it an account given to a kinsman or close friend of how the speaker preserved the integrity of the family motto? Although the four words "My heart grew sick" admittedly are a difficulty that interpreters favoring the successful-revenge theory must deal with, they seem to me a slight basis for positing fifty years of moral anguish; and, in fact, they offer an obstacle to the unsuccessful-revenge interpreters as well, for if the story is a "confession," why should Montresor explain this heart-sickness as caused by "the dampness of the catacombs"? As to the *tone* of the story, I cannot find a word that expresses remorse or guilt or a pleading for forgiveness. I find, instead, a prideful voice that says, in effect, See how clever I was in preparing a niche for Fortunato in the catacombs, in assuring that my servants would not be present, in luring my enemy there, and, in fact, in managing the whole affair. The tone is boastful or gloating rather than contrite. And why that half-century between the doing and the telling? It is a good round number. But if Montresor is suffering agonies of conscience, why should he not seek an earlier confession? On the other hand, if he was seeking the perfect revenge, a condition of his definition (the avenger must "punish with impunity. A wrong is unredressed when retribution overtakes its redressor") requires a waiting period before it can be known whether this condition has been met. For this use, a good round number would be expected, and fifty years would seem more than ample. But Montresor is capable of patience, as he showed early on in the interval between the planning of his revenge and his execution of it.

I do not wish to referee this revenge dispute. The critics who have argued for the failed revenge have done so much more persuasively and more fully than I have been able to do for them here. And indeed their interpretation adds one more irony—a crowning one—to the pervasive ironies that any reading of the story must acknowledge. Rather than commit myself firmly to either side, I provide a selected list of critiques "for further reading."

Successful revenge:
Kenneth Kempton, *The Short Story* (Cambridge: Harvard UP, 1947) 86–89. Joseph J. Moldenhauer, "Murder as a Fine Art: Connections Between Poe's Aesthetics, Psychology, and Moral Vision," *PMLA* 83 (1968): 284–97. Marvin Felheim, "The Cask of Amontillado," *Notes & Queries* 199 (1954): 447–48. Terence Martin, "The Imagination at Play," *Kenyon Review* 28 (1966): 195–98.

Unsuccessful revenge:
Robert Foulke and Paul Smith, *An Anatomy of Literature* (New York: Harcourt, 1972) 873, 876–80. James W. Gargano, "'The Cask of Amontillado': Masquerade of Motive and Identity," *Studies in Short Fiction* 4 (1967): 119–26. Charles A. Sweet, Jr., "Recapping Poe's 'Cask of Amontillado,'" *Poe Studies* 7 (June 1974): 10–12. Sam Moon, *Notes & Queries* 199 (1954): 448. Donald Pearce, "'The Cask of Amontillado,'" *Notes & Queries* 199 (1954): 448–49. Richard H. Fossum, "Poe's 'The Cask of Amontillado,'" *Explicator* 17 (1958): item 16. LP

Katherine Anne Porter   **The Jilting of Granny Weatherall** (page 489)

QUESTIONS

1. The narrative technique of this story is called stream-of-consciousness, a subspecies of the limited omniscient point of view. Based on this story, what are the defining characteristics of this technique? What qualities of Ellen Weatherall's mind does it represent? How effectively does it reveal events of the past? How clearly does it reflect the present? What is gained by this lack of precise clarity?
2. The protagonist reveals herself to be in conflict with other persons, and with her physical environment, both in the past and in the present. Identify her antagonists. To what extent has she experienced conflicts within herself? To what extent is she now experiencing such conflicts?
3. What does her memory present as the major turning points in her life? Is it more than a coincidence that one of them occurs every twenty years? Considering the many major events in a woman's life that *might* have been climactic (her marriage, the birth of her first child, and so forth), how do the ones she recalls so vividly define her character?
4. What kind of life has Granny Weatherall made for herself? What have been her characteristic activities and attitudes? Can her "jilting" be seen as a partial cause for these activities and attitudes?
5. What is the significance of Hapsy? What religious symbolism is attached to the vision of her and her infant son on page 494?
6. Most critics understand the title to refer to two "jiltings," the one by her fiancé sixty years earlier, the other by God at the moment of her death. Can you justify this interpretation? Does the story have a determinate or indeterminate ending?

The life of an indomitable matriarch comes to an end in a confused accounting of her fourscore years and an ambiguous prediction of her soul's destiny. Like Emily Dickinson's speaker in "Because I could not stop for Death," Granny Weatherall's busy life ends with an imagined journey "outward" with no clearly defined destination.

The last day of Ellen Weatherall's life registers jaggedly and incoherently on her consciousness, and the narration represents that psychological fact by a skipping chronology, mistaken identities, and a selective memory that expresses in fragments the major events of her long life. This is an example of a stream-of-consciousness narrative, presenting an unedited sequence of thoughts at a critical moment in the character's life—in Granny's case, her dying day. (This technique gives the impression of an "unedited" narration, switching topics, losing and regaining threads of stories, and thus realistically implying the inconsistencies of the way we think and remember; but of course such a narration is highly structured and selected by the author, who is ordering her materials in order to create the sense of a mind in action.) That Ellen's consciousness is represented by disorderly perceptions and recollections is ironic, since she has for sixty years been devoted to neatness, cleanliness, and order. She managed to "weather all" the adversities of a long life by keeping it strictly under control.

Granny Weatherall's life has had three events of major consequence, spaced out at twenty-year intervals. When she was twenty, she was left waiting with the priest for a husband who never turned up; at forty, she bore her last child (Hapsy), suffering greatly from thrombosis in her legs ("milk-leg") and then pneumonia; and at sixty, she made a circuit of her living children to bid them goodbye and ready herself for death, "made her will and came down with a long fever" (page 491)—and then recovered to live twenty more years without any fear or sense of dying. The significance of these events to Ellen is that each of them led to redefinitions of her life and her faith. What the stream-of-consciousness technique permits is emphasis on events in the order of their relative importance to the character, to the exclusion of potentially more significant incidents. In this woman's case, for example, one might have expected some greater importance to be attached to her first childbirth, to the untimely death of her husband, or to the death of her favorite child Hapsy. By her remembering the events that she does instead, those three remembered events are made to be the shaping incidents of her life.

The first, the jilt by her fiancé George, is the most important both in literal and symbolic senses. That was the day when "a whirl of dark smoke rose and covered" the orderliness of her life; "that was hell," and she knows that "remembering him" and "losing her soul in the deep pit of hell" were the same thing (page 493). So she has willed herself, for sixty years, to forget him and to trust in her salvation through the intercession of "a few favorite saints who cleared a straight road to God for her" (page 494). The emotional and spiritual shock of that event (notice that the story is titled after that, not after its central event, the *dying* of Granny Weatherall) has led her to shape her life into the varieties of order and meaning available to a strong-willed woman—working by the sweat of her brow, raising a large family after their father's death, ministering to her livestock and her neighbors, caring for the sick and offering her services to the church. It is an exemplary life, but of course it lacks what it lost at the jilting: a beloved husband, a mate to do those things assigned by her religion to the male, an emotionally full life not only as mother and homemaker but as woman. That jilting was the event that turned her to self-sufficiency and to a smugness about her faith and her destiny that even now, at the time of death, display themselves in querulousness and a wish to be left alone to get ready for "tomorrow" in her own way.

The death of her last-born child, who had herself borne a son, is perhaps the most odd omission from Granny's recollection of climaxes. It is obvious that Hapsy is the child who matters most to her, the only one Granny calls for at the last, the one she mistakes the nurse for, "the one she had truly wanted" (page 494). Her one vivid memory of Hapsy may account for this omission: she recalls "Hapsy standing with a baby on her arm. She [Granny] seemed to herself to be Hapsy also, and the baby on Hapsy's arm was Hapsy and himself and herself, all at once . . ." (page 494). This merging of identities of herself with both a child and his mother symbolically implies her faith in those "favorite" persons of her Catholic religion—

in this case, clearly, her daughter and grandson are to her the Madonna and Christ. Hapsy is *not* dead, then, in Ellen's spiritual life. (What has become of Hapsy's son? The terms of the story and of religion suggest that he, too, is physically dead but divinely immortal.)

At the climax of the story — Granny's death — these symbols are finally focused and the title brought into a new light. What if Hapsy is not to be found, she wonders. That would define death as a bottomless sinking, "down and down . . . into endless darkness," so she pleads for God to give her a sign. With cosmic irony (and grim wit), she realizes: "For the second time there was no sign. Again no bridegroom and the priest in the house" (page 496). Her hope for an earthly paradise ended with the jilting at the altar; are her hopes for heaven equally frustrated? Her consciousness, of course, cannot answer that question.

Much has been written about this story. Among the valuable discussions to which the present remarks are indebted are Joann P. Cobb, "Two Modern Losers" (repr. Harold Bloom, ed., *Katherine Anne Porter* [New York: Chelsea, 1986] 97–106); John Edward Hardy, *Katherine Anne Porter* (New York: Ungar, 1973) 89–96; Darlene Harbour Unrue, *Truth and Vision in Katherine Anne Porter's Fiction* (Athens, GA: U of Georgia P, 1985) 98–101 and passim; and Eudora Welty, "Katherine Anne Porter: The Eye of the Story," *The Eye of the Story: Selected Essays and Reviews* (New York: Vintage, 1979) 307–40. TRA

Jean Rhys **Pioneers, Oh, Pioneers** (page 496)

QUESTIONS

1. From the attitude Irene expresses in the opening exchange with Rosalie, and from the attitudes of both blacks and whites toward Ramage, construct the code of proper behavior that governs this community. On what is the social order modeled? Are there differences between black and white codes?
2. What was Ramage's initial purpose in coming to the island? How does his costume reflect it? What does his nudity imply about a change of purpose? What happens to his relationship to the black community?
3. Characterize Dr. Cox. How does he behave toward Ramage? What is his attitude toward rumors and gossip? In what ways is his daughter Rosalie like him?
4. What qualities and purposes do you associate with "pioneers"? The title of this story duplicates the title of a poem by Walt Whitman. Look it up, and consider the contrasts between his vision of the pioneering spirit and the "pioneers" who live along the Imperial Road.

The title alludes (ironically) to Walt Whitman's paean to the courageous, energetic and hearty people who drove westward across the North American continent subduing the land, the "youthful sinewy" men creating "a newer mightier world" than that inhabited by "the elder races . . . wearied over there beyond the seas." In contrast to this vision, Rhys's British settlers in the Caribbean have come to exploit the native population and re-create the world they've left behind. So we learn "of young Errington, of young Kellaway, who had both bought estates along the Imperial Road [a suitable name] and worked hard. But they had given up after a year or two, sold their land cheap and gone back to England." These pioneers were part of the failure of the "'costly experiment [of] the so-called "Imperial Road" [which] was meant to attract young Englishmen with capital who would buy and develop properties in the interior.'"

The English who do not give up in the face of the "loneliness and melancholy of the forest" establish for themselves a duplicate of the England they have left behind—or rather, brought with them. So Dr. Cox, an admirable and tolerant man who criticizes both the gossiping English women and the natives who won't leave Ramage alone, nevertheless has his English pipe and tobacco and his English weekly *Times* and *Cornhill Magazine* and medical journal. His drawing room is a crowded picture of high Victorian furnishings, incongruously mingling middle-class European furnishings with the spoils of empire:

> comfortably full of rocking chairs, a mahogany table, palm leaf fans, a tigerskin rug, family photographs, views of Betws-y-Coed and a large picture of wounded soldiers in the snow, Napoleon's Retreat from Moscow.

This transplanted society is also a society with strict hierarchical values, a strong sense of what is and is not "done." The opening scene, with the two girls in Market Street commenting on the eccentricities of Mrs. Menzies as she carries her own ice to cool her drinks suggests how thoroughly the island has adopted the values of the colonials: eleven-year-old Irene finds Mrs. Menzies shameful for doing a servant's task, and points out that "the black people laugh at her" too. The exploited have themselves accepted the code of propriety that separates them from the white English, assigning to each their defined roles.

Into this neat and rigid world comes the newest "pioneer," Ramage. Having costumed himself as he supposes the white settler should look, with a white linen suit and red cummerbund and "solar topee" (pith helmet), he cuts a fine colonial figure in his first appearance, much to the amused admiration of a "crowd of little Negro boys" who trail him through the streets. His desire is to find an estate as remote as possible from the English town where he can live in peace and isolation. He begins his transformation almost at once, discarding the sash and hat, then marrying a black woman with a reputation, then "going native" by stalking around his estate in the nude wearing a cutlass, "burnt a deep brown" with his hair and beard untrimmed. As his reputation for strange behavior spreads through the gossiping English and the disapproving natives, and his wife disappears, both the black and white populations turn against him. After a confrontation with a mob he apparently turns his shotgun on himself.

This sad tale of the deterioration of a man is punctuated by Dr. Cox's vain attempts to explain him and to bring him back into sociability, a display of charity and concern, and by the attitude of his daughter Rosalie who "fell in love" with Ramage at her first glimpse of him at dinner. Through the two years of Ramage's short life on the island, Rosalie's interest and infatuation persist, in part, her older sister Irene says, because Rosalie likes "crazy people" (that is, eccentrics and non-conformists). Rosalie in fact is displaying the beginnings of the independence and stubbornness that eccentrics such as Mrs. Menzies and Ramage have, as she sticks out her tongue at Irene's back, and pesters Ramage into singing because her mother's disapproving expression makes her more insistent.

Rosalie attempts to reach out to Ramage in the letter she starts to write after his death, wishing that Protestants like Catholics can receive messages on All Souls Day. She wants to let him know that to at least one of the people on the island he is "dear darling Mr. Ramage," and not a man deserted by his wife and spurned, scorned, and threatened by all. Like her father's letter of advice, Rosalie's cannot really reach him, but the concluding image suggests that the child's letter is what he would have needed: "There was a stiff breeze and [Mrs. Cox] watched it bouncing purposefully down the street [toward the Protestant cemetery]. As if it knew exactly where it was going."

Ramage arrived on the island with some romantic, idealistic notions of himself and his place. The social system into which he thrust himself—and from which he tried to stay aloof—was such that he not only loses those notions but sinks under the pressure to behave as both blacks and whites dictate. Dr. Cox's cynicism about idealistic schemes proves valid: "Nothing lasts in this island. Nothing will come of it. You'll see." While many of the people initially feel some guilt about Ramage's death, they soon close ranks and console themselves: "'He was evidently mad, poor man—sitting in the sun with no clothes on—much worse might have happened.'"   TRA

Leslie Marmon Silko   **Private Property** (page 503)

QUESTIONS

1. Construct a chronology of Etta's life from her orphaned childhood to her return in old age. What are her values, and how have they been formed?
2. Reyna's dispute with Etta is over a piece of land, but also represents a conflict of values. As precisely as you can, determine what constitutes "the old ways" of this Pueblo village.
3. What is the role of women in this society? How does the story of the orphan (paragraph 1) reflect that role? What is the role of men? What kinds of "property" does each hold, and how does that property define their roles?
4. Etta's and Reyna's mother-in-law tells them "to share and love one another." How well is the concept of sharing maintained, not only between the two of them but in the village at large?
5. Etta apparently is defeated in the conflict about the fence. Is this reassertion of "the old ways" presented as a victory? Is there an emotional resolution to this story?

The story presents the conflict of values between the widows of two brothers in a Pueblo Indian village. Ostensibly the women are quarreling about a strip of land that runs between their two houses. In their society, according to "the old ways," the property must be held by the women, but as their mother-in-law told them as she equitably divided the land and houses, "'we only make use of these things as long as we are here. We don't own them. Nobody owns anything.'" Furthermore, although the women hold the houses and fields, they are taught to share and love one another. This teaching does not always govern the actions of the younger people, however, who tend to connive for bigger shares.

The quarrel between Etta and Reyna began when Etta returned from the white world after many years to live in the little stone house, bringing with her the white concept of "private property." The mother-in-law had said that the smaller house got the larger yard, and Etta is now trying to establish that fair settlement by cleaning up and burning off the trash and by restoring the old fallen-down fence between the yards, planting hollyhocks and morning glories along it to mark the boundary between her land and Reyna's. She even has plans to plant a row of tamarisk trees along the fence "so people cannot see her yard or house." Reyna on the other hand wants to make use of the disputed strip of yard for her woodpile.

Etta's desire for privacy has developed from her years of living in Winslow, both because she learned the white attitude toward protecting property and because for much of her life her people have been falsely gossiping about her and the changes that occurred in her from her contact with whites. She believes that "fences tell you where you stand," and she is determined to maintain them.

The course of Etta's life (which must be patched together from scattered details throughout the story) shows that such a position was developed over a long period of time. Etta was an orphan who was taken in by an old clanswoman, according to the traditions of the community. Sent to the Indian School where she boarded through the school year, Etta was befriended by one of the teachers who taught her to love and care for flowers (while the other children were learning to sew and cook). The teacher showed care for her, spent time with her, taught her habits of cleanliness — and thus provoked gossip among the girls about Etta's spending so much time with her.

These initial ruptures between Etta and her people led to a clash between her and her foster mother. The teacher had given Etta some hollyhock seeds which she planted, much to the annoyance of the old clanswoman who berated her for wasting water on something you can't eat — the same rift as between Etta's learning about flowers while the other girls learned cooking. Etta announced that she would be spending her summer working at the school greenhouse, and thus broke her ties with the old woman and the life of the village. When she visited there, her future sister-in-law Reyna repeated the stories that were being told about Etta and the teacher — untrue stories, as the narrator explicitly says.

Somehow — no details are given — after finishing her schooling Etta returned, married, was given the house by her mother-in-law, and was left a childless widow. She had received letters from the teacher "all the years of her marriage," and so accepted a job at the school after her husband's death. She lived there for many years, and nursed her friend the teacher through a long last illness. Then it was she returned to the village, to retire in the old stone house. True to the new values she

81

has developed, she is in conflict with the old ways, and wants to establish her new way by repairing the fence and marking the edge of her "private property."

The dispute between the old women is resolved in a curious way. Three horses that have been wandering at large throughout the story turn up at dawn in Etta's yard. One of them is eating the hollyhock blossoms, and when Etta hurries out in her nightgown to chase them away, the horses knock down the fenceposts and drag away the fence wire, erasing the boundary between the yards. Reyna has apparently won, and the "old ways" have been reasserted by natural as well as communal forces.

The horses thread their way through the narrative, turning up in several places, always being pursued without much vigor by their owner Cheromiah. They provide a contrasting comment on Etta's determination to keep her "private property," for though "the horses belong to Cheromiah, . . . the horses don't know that." So he keeps tracking them down, from river to sand hills and back, always carrying a halter and rope, but he never manages to corral them. The horses' refusal to behave like property extends to their assaults on corrals and fences, and the big white one actually has learned how to knock down a corral by leaning against its planks until they give way.

Symbolically, the horses in the story are associated with men, and with liberty and lawlessness. Only three men appear in the story (and the husbands of Reyna and Etta are not among them): Cheromiah, the owner of the string of horses (the big white one given him by his father-in-law), Reyna's brother Uncle Joe, who has a team of wagon horses that cause his fatal accident, and Ruthie's husband, whose horses haul the wagon he loads with rocks to build a shed or corral. The freedom from ownership that the horses symbolize is like the freedom taken by the adulterous husband — when the opportunity is there, he accepts it, and the blame falls upon the woman who was after him.

According to tradition, the women govern the village and maintain its mores and morals. The diatribe is loosed upon the woman discovered with Ruthie's husband because it was her responsibility to uphold those values (and again, cooking is associated with them, as the women insult the way she makes her chili). The depth of this matriarchal system is reflected in the responsibilities accepted by Juanita who looks after the old folks, who inherits Uncle Joe's house and livestock, and who shares in the female attack on the adulterous woman. Unlike Etta, whom she resembles in being independent of men and capable of making her own way, she has not broken from the traditions, and she sides with Reyna in their disputes even while her communal responsibilities include looking after Etta as well.

The matriarchal power is also reflected in the bit of lore that opens the story — the myth of the orphan girl who is adopted into a family but is treated as a poor dependent, who remains meek and unassertive, quietly listening but never sharing, until she emerges as the savior "who confronts the danger and the village is saved." She is of course contrasted to Etta, who began very early to assert herself and her difference from tribal custom, and who in the end is the advocate of dangerous ideas that the village (and the horses) must confront and defeat.

With its uninvolved, matter-of-fact tone, the story remains ambivalent about Etta's history. There is considerable sympathy for her as she grows into a strong and independent woman, but there is also an inevitability about her defeat, for the forces arrayed against her, both natural and communal, are too great for her revolt to succeed. The matriarchy is collective, not individual, and while it tyrannizes the individual it also offers support and stability. TRA

Eudora Welty **A Worn Path** (page 510)

QUESTIONS

1. What is the purpose of Phoenix Jackson's traveling this "worn path"? When does the reader fully understand her purpose? What is gained by that delay? How does the limited point of view contribute to the effect of the story?
2. As precisely as possible, sum up Phoenix's attitude toward herself and toward her journey. Compare her sense of what she is to the definitions of her by others, and measure her estimation of her trip against the values other people place on it. To what extent does she undervalue herself? What kinds of undervaluation do the other characters reveal?
3. What kinds of adventures befall Phoenix on her trip? What are her feelings about them? Analyze the two daydreams she experiences.
4. Trace the references to birds throughout the story. What symbolic meanings do they have? (What is a phoenix? What further name symbolism does the story employ?)
5. What does it mean that Phoenix momentarily forgets the purpose of her trip?
6. In answer to a student who wrote to ask her "Is the grandson really dead?" Welty responded "my best answer would be: '*Phoenix* is alive.'" What might have led the student to ask that question? How can the author's remark be seen as an answer?

Any discussion of this story should proceed from the author's own essay "Is Phoenix Jackson's Grandson Really Dead?" (*The Eye of the Story* [New York: Vintage, 1979] 158–62). There Welty makes two necessary points: first, the events in a story may have no meaning beyond the literal, or like life they may have multiple meanings (both literal and figurative), but they may not mean *other* than their literal meanings—that is, her story may have symbolic meanings but these do not violate the reality of the events themselves; and second, the subject of the story, expressed through Phoenix's journey, is "the deep-grained habit of love."

Phoenix's journey is not quite allegorical (there is no one-to-one correspondence of event to antecedent meaning), but it is symbolic in the way Eudora Welty's fiction is symbolic: true-life incidents, perfectly comprehensible simply as the things that people do and have done to them, are revelations of human realities beyond the individual example. For Phoenix Jackson, the journey is repeated when necessary, whenever her grandson's throat requires the soothing medicine; its incidents are, as Welty says, passing adventures—some dreams and harassments and a small triumph or two, some jolts to her pride, some flights of fancy to console her, one or two encounters to scare her, a moment that gave her cause to feel ashamed, a moment to dance and preen . . . parts of life's uncertainty.

The story includes name symbolism: "Phoenix," the mythical bird of immortality, repeating in its life cycle the perpetuation of life; "Jackson," the name of two heroes (a general and a President), and the center and capital of the state. These slightly ironic comparisons are reverberative rather than explicitly symbolic, as are the "passing adventures" of Phoenix, the Christmas season, the mission of the journey itself, and the many references to antiquity and age. One would not say that Phoenix Jackson is everyman, that Christian salvation is a topic, that charity is extolled as the greatest of the virtues: these are all implied parts of the texture of the story, but all are supportive to the subject, "the deep-grained habit of love."

It is the word "habit" in the author's definition that sets this story off from allegory and symbol: Welty's point is that Phoenix Jackson is not immortal, not heroic, not even exceptional or special. She even forgets momentarily what the whole arduous trip has been for. She doesn't sentimentalize her invalid grandson, nor perceive anything special about herself besides her age. It is the *habit* of her love that moves her. It is certainly not Phoenix who notices connections and symbols in the various bird images, in the sequence of ordeals and trials she passes, nor in the life-giving sun. Rather, in her simple way, she reveals her unpretentious vision of heaven: in "a pearly cloud of mistletoe" she is offered a slice of marble-cake by a little boy, to whom she modestly says: "That would be acceptable." The understatement of that response captures the emotional tone of the story.

A valuable analysis of the story is Alfred Appel's in *A Season of Dreams: The Fiction of Eudora Welty* (Baton Rouge: LSU Press, 1965) 166–71. TRA

Tobias Wolff **Say Yes** (page 517)

QUESTIONS

1. Explore the contrast between how this couple's marriage looks to their friends, and the conflict displayed in this episode. How can the couple have so much shared mutual knowledge and yet have such intense arguments? How do we know that such arguments between them are not unusual?
2. What is it that they are arguing about? How does the argument move from impersonal to personal? Trace the stages in the development of the argument. Is racism an actual issue in the story?
3. How is the conflict resolved? Why does the wife ask for the lights to be put out, and what will occur next? Is she really "a stranger" as she approaches the bed?
4. What are the symbolic implications of the color changes in the silverware (paragraph 26) and of the play of the two dogs (paragraph 44)? How do those two apparently irrelevant details extend the meaning of the behavior of the man and woman?

5. What does the theme of the story tell us about the nature of the love of long-married people?

This brief but intense domestic quarrel runs its course from apparently trivial annoyance through persistent pestering to vivid anger and finally to amorous reconciliation. It is an example of serious role-playing, partially conscious, and ironically displays the odd kind of cooperation in which a couple may tighten the bond they share by threatening to destroy it.

That theme is made clearest in two symbolic details. The first occurs at the climax of the dishwashing scene. Husband and wife have adopted the habit of taking turns at washing and drying the dishes, an example to the husband and to their friends of how "considerate" he is of her. This night, the apparently irrelevant subject of mixed marriages creates a difference of opinion that builds into outright anger and then the separation of pretended indifference. As the argument builds, the wife becomes hurried and careless in washing the dishes, the husband brusquely dumps the silverware back into the water, and the wife angrily thrusts her hands into the water and punctures her thumb. After ministering to her superficial wound with a great display of concern (for which he thinks his reward should be her dropping the conversation), the husband takes on the task of washing. As he sprays hot rinse water over the silverware, a symbolic process takes place: "The water was so hot that the metal darkened to pale blue, then turned silver again." This visual image captures the form that their evening is taking: the domestic chore of dishwashing, interrupted and resumed with reversed roles, builds to an emotional heat so intense that it discolors them, but by the end of the evening they are restored to themselves, clean and perfectly matched.

The second symbolic detail takes place after the wife has withdrawn from the kitchen in an anger so fierce that she expresses it through studied, cool indifference. The husband matches her pretense by ignoring her, pretending an indifference of his own, and finishing the kitchen chores. He is so diligent that when he has completed the job, the kitchen seems so pristine that it reminds him of the first time they saw it, before it became the arena of their perfectly shared marriage and the wounding quarrels that have occurred there. (We know that this quarrel is not the first, and is in fact part of a pattern, when in the fourth paragraph of the story the husband knows by looking at his wife that "he should keep his mouth shut," but he *never* does that—the look on her face always makes him talk more, and so the quarrels begin.)

Having restored the kitchen to its original perfection, he steps outside with the garbage and meditates on the insignificance of their quarrel. He reminds himself "of the years they had spent together and how close they were and how well they knew each other," and has an upsurge of emotion that is erotic in its sensations. It was this closeness and this knowing that provided some of the material for their conflict, as he smugly assumed these as shared experience, while she sarcastically questioned them.

The second symbolic event then occurs as he sees the two dogs sharing their own deep pleasure playing and foraging in the garbage. The dogs suggest another dimension in the relationship between the man and woman. The male is "rolling around on his back," smearing himself in the filth and stench of the garbage (as some dogs will do on occasion, apparently reverting to an instinctive need to mark their territorial dominion through scent). The female, meanwhile, is playing at capturing prey and worrying it, tossing some trash into the air, leaping up to catch it, growling and shaking it back and forth. Like the dogs, the man and woman are reveling in instinctive behavior that gives to their good and sensible marriage a passionate dimension. They are playing at hatred, creating a conflict of wills, animosity, anger, indifference, and then surrender.

In the last scene the woman demands the right answer—"say yes," the title says, revealing what the woman thinks and what, through her direction, the man commands himself to do. He must agree that he would marry her if they were in love, even if she were black. His reward for that verbal surrender is the lovemaking that is about to take place. In the dark, all color obliterated, she approaches him "as a stranger." They have been able to go back to the beginning of their passion, to revert to an intense and new-found delight, by means of quarreling and role-playing.

How consciously do they play their roles? We cannot tell about the woman, for the point of view is strictly limited to the man. We do know that he is accustomed to these angry displays, and that even knowing how to avoid them he shares in creating them. There is little reason to suppose that their years of closeness and mutual knowledge have not given her the same insights. What we witness in the story is an elaborate and recurrent preparation for sexual delight.   TRA

The Elements of Poetry

CHAPTER ONE

What is Poetry?

1. *Alfred, Lord Tennyson* **The Eagle** (page 525)

The first stanza presents what one sees looking at the eagle, perhaps looking up at him, with the sun above him and the blue sky around him. The second stanza is more concerned with looking down from the eagle's vantage point; it presents what *he* sees. The first stanza is more static (with "clasps," "Close," "stands"), the second stanza more dynamic (with "crawls," "watches," "falls"). These are small points, but they help to organize the poem. The expressions mentioned in the first study question are all figurative. LP

2. *William Shakespeare* **Winter** (page 526)

The words "merry" and "sings" are used *ironically* (see page 624).* LP

3. *Wilfred Owen* **Dulce et Decorum Est** (page 527

The poem makes its bitter protest against the idea that dying for one's country is "sweet and becoming" by describing the agonizing death of one soldier caught

*Unless otherwise specified, all page references in this manual are to the text of *Literature: Structure, Sound, and Sense*, Sixth Edition.

in a gas attack during World War I. (We infer from the last two lines that the soldier is dead; what we witness in the poem is the anguish and horror of his dying.)

The speaker is a fellow-soldier, a member of the same unit, and a witness of the dying. His account is given some time after the event (as measured by weeks or months), for he has re-experienced it in recurrent nightmares ever since (15–16). From our knowledge of World War I and of the poet's own experience, we may infer that the speaker is English, that the gas shells were German, and that the action occurrred in France or Belgium. The speaker has probably been furloughed back to England at the time of his account, for the person he ironically addresses as "My friend" would seem to be an older man who is patriotically recruiting teen-aged boys into the service of their country, or into readiness for such service (the word "children" is undoubtedly an overstatement of their youth).

The simile in line 1 compares the soldiers' packs to sacks carried by beggars. The word "softly" (8) is particularly sinister, for it connotes something gentle but here denotes something deadly. The phrase "sick of sin" (20) means "sick from sin." The most remarkable image in the poem is the simile in lines 13–14. The phosgene gas used in World War I was greenish in color, hence the man caught in it seems "As under a green sea . . . drowning." The under-ocean effect is enhanced by the fact that he is viewed by the other soldiers through the misty panes of their gas masks, which were like the goggles in the helmets used by deep-sea divers at the time. Finally, the man is literally drowning (being suffocated) in that his lungs are being deprived of oxygen; but the phosgene gas also corrodes the lungs, thus leading to the uglier imagery in lines 21–24.

The theme of the poem is obvious: It is NOT sweet and becoming to die for one's country in modern warfare.   LP

4.   *William Shakespeare*   **Spring** (page 530)

Though a light, semihumorous poem, "Spring" beautifully displays Shakespeare's poetic skill. It pivots about a contrast that divides each stanza exactly in the middle. Spring is the time of flowers and birds and delight, and to this traditional aspect of spring Shakespeare yields the first four lines of each stanza. It is also the time of love; but in treating this aspect Shakespeare gives the traditional treatment of spring a wry twist. The cuckoo's call reminds the married man not only that "In the spring a young man's fancy lightly turns to thoughts of love" (as Tennyson points out), but also that in the spring young wives are most likely to prove unfaithful. "Cuckold, cuckold!" the cuckoo seems to say to the husband by way of warning. The poem thus throws the innocent and delightful into contrast with the unpleasing or painful.

The poem twice makes skillful use of *metonymy* (see page 585). The wild flowers, Shakespeare says, "paint the meadows with delight" (4). The metaphor in the verb "paint" prepares for the metonymy in the word "delight." What the flowers actually paint the meadows with is color, but Shakespeare, by substituting the effect for which the color is the cause, makes the line doubly meaningful, for it suggests both *cause* and *effect*. In line 8, by using "word" instead of *notes* for the cuckoo's call, Shakespeare leads us to read a pun into "cuckoo"—for it is indeed the word "cuckold" that the married man fears, not the bird-notes that suggest it. And thus the poet prepares us for the second metonymy—"ear." It is the married *man*, of course, who hears the cuckoo, but Shakespeare, by using the part for the whole, reduces the man imaginatively to the one quivering, sensitive organ that will receive the insult when he is cuckolded.

For flowers to represent the spring, Shakespeare might have chosen from a whole seed catalogue. His daisies and violets are traditional enough, and we are not surprised to find them. But why has Shakespeare chosen lady-smocks and cuckoo-buds? Because they serve double duty. The lady-smocks throw a connecting loop to line 13 in the second stanza, and this loop ties the two stanzas together. The cuckoo-buds prepare us for the cuckoobird and the implied *cuckold*, which are the central subjects of the poem.

The word "tread" (12) deserves special attention. "Turtles" are turtledoves, and the traditional poet, writing of the innocent pleasures of spring, would have said, "When turtles *mate.* . . ." But Shakespeare uses the technical or barnyard term for the copulation of birds, and thus introduces a more earthy note. He continues: "When turtles tread, *and* rooks, *and* daws. . . ." The repeated "and's" are not there simply to fill out the meter. They have the effect of enormously magnifying the activity. The line is not at all the same as "When rooks, daws, and turtles tread." With all this activity going on, no wonder the married man is apprehensive.

Pattern also works effectively in "Spring." The iambic tetrameter pattern with alternating rimes that Shakespeare uses in the first four lines of each stanza is generally a tripping measure, appropriate to light, cheerful, and songlike matters. It is highly appropriate for spring flowers and merry larks and meadows painted with delight. But in the last four lines, the pattern changes, and so does the mood. The change is signaled in the phrase "Mocks married men," where the jammed meter and the heavy alliteration inform us that the subject matter is shifting to something more solemn. The rime pattern also alters, shifting from alternating rimes to riming couplets. The iambic tetrameter continues; but the lines now, instead of tripping along merrily, are broken up. They are broken first by the extrametrical trochaic "Cuckoo," placed on a line by itself, which interrupts the iambs and tetrameters and thus receives a heavy emphasis appropriate to its importance. Second, the pattern is broken in the following line by the ending of the sentence in the middle of the line, thus separating it into two sharply divided parts, the first half trochaic, the second half iambic. We simply *cannot read* these last four lines with the same blithe abandon with which we read the first four lines. The cuckoo's call breaks into the stanza with the same violence with which it breaks in on the married man's peace.

[This commentary is adapted from Laurence Perrine, *The Art of Total Relevance: Papers on Poetry* (Rowley, MA: Newbury, 1976) 7–10.] LP

5. *Robert Hayden* **The Whipping** (page 531)

This narrative poem—in the present tense, with a memory flashback in lines 13–18—strongly suggests that the speaker's assurance that "it is over now, it is over" is true only of this particular whipping of this particular boy. But as the concluding stanza clearly indicates, "hidings" have been the lifelong story of the old woman's experience, were clearly part of the speaker's life, and are and will be the boy's experience. That is, physical punishment and its even more damaging counterpart, "hateful / Words," are persistent conditions of life.

There is little beauty in the experience of the poem, though one could make a case for the beauty of artistic arrangement, the precision of imagery, and the musicality of the language.

For a comparison, Ann Stanford's "The Beating" (page 846) presents a more brutal example of physical abuse from the perspective of the victim.   TRA

6. *John Donne* **The Computation** (page 532)

The speaker is a lover who has been separated from his mistress for a day and, apostrophizing her, strives to express the magnitude of his love for her by exaggerating the length of time she has been gone, leaving him lonely and desolate. (The poem does not indicate *why* she has gone away, but since the speaker does not reproach her, it seems logical to assume that she has not permanently deserted him but has been called away perhaps by family affairs or some similar duty.) The numbers are arranged in an increasing sequence—20, 40, 40, 100, 200, 1000, 1000—to lead to a rhetorical climax. They are chosen to total 2400, thus indicating precisely the scale of the speaker's exaggeration: each hour that she has been gone has seemed to him like 100 years. In the last two lines he counters the possible objection to his statements that by this computation he should be 2400 years old by claiming that he is not alive; he is dead, not of old age, but of a broken heart. This metaphor of the lover's dying because of his mistress' absence or disdain was, of course, a trite one in Donne's time, but Donne revivifies it by giving it a fresh setting and a new twist: the "dead" lover—the mere "ghost" of his former self—has been immortalized by his love: he cannot die, being already dead.

In line 4 the pronoun "they" refers to "favors." In line 7 the verb "divide" means "distinguish": he did not distinguish between thinking and doing, the whole period being "one thought" of the beloved. Line 8 is difficult: it possibly means that the last 1000 years he spent in torpor.

The whole poem may be described as a witty and ingenious love poem, intended by the speaker to make his beloved smile rather than be deeply concerned for his health or his state of mind.   LP

7. *Anonymous* **The Two Ravens** (page 532)

We have used a modernized version of this ballad because beginning readers are often baffled by the queer spelling and unusual syntax of such poems, and are lost to poetry forever. (After all, what can they make of such phrases as "auld fail dyke" and "white-hause bane"?) We have included the original as well so that readers may see what has been sacrificed for the sake of easier reading. In this transfer from Middle English to Modern English what has been lost is brilliantly identified by T. R. Henn (study question 3). There has also been a loss in the change of the title: *raven*, with its *r, v,* and *n,* is a soft word; *corbies,* with its cutting *c* and its explosive *b,* has a hard sound appropriate to the subject of the poem. LP

8. *Dudley Randall* **Ballad of Birmingham** (page 534)

This moving poem displays many of the characteristics of a traditional folk ballad: it is a narrative poem with a large component of dialogue; it presents a contemporary event; it tells its story without overt analysis or explanation; and it employs simple metrical and stanzaic forms.

As in the ballads, the material *not* explicitly reported is significant—chiefly, in this case, the identity of the perpetrators, their motives and the motives of the police and others who suppress freedom, the effect on the city of the bombing outrage, and the precise fate of the child (the poem only refers to the shoe, not to the child, though we might infer from lines 23–24 that the child was among the four who were killed: "that smile was the last smile / To come upon [the mother's] face"). These are the issues that would be included in a newspaper account, along with speculation about future consequences.

Instead, the poem focuses on just two people, the mother and child, and their motives and actions. The child, in a precocious show of social responsibility, wants to help "make our country free" (12). (Notice that the poem does not identify her race until line 19, and that her concern is stated in terms that encompass more than racial injustice in Alabama.) The child is willing to give up her "play" time for the larger cause. The mother, on the other hand, displays protective love and fear for her child's safety, and denies her daughter's twice-requested wish to participate in the Freedom March. In arguing against it, the mother carefully does not excite her daughter's animosity toward the police—their "clubs and hoses, guns and jails," and "fierce and wild" dogs are given an autonomy that makes them sound self-wielding. She does not say, "I am afraid the police will beat you, or set their dogs on you, or shoot you," nor in making her request does the child say, "I want to march so that unjust and brutal people will be forced to give up their power over us." This verbal reticence is part of the ballad tradition, and also serves to create additional sympathy for these two who are not expressing hatred for the government or the police.

The images in the fifth stanza increase sympathy and respect for this child who wants to take on adult cares. We witness her "grown-up" preparation for going into a house of worship, we observe the care she takes with her beautiful "night-dark hair," we smell the sweetness of the scented soap of her bath, and we see the purity and delicacy displayed in her white gloves and white shoes. Given the racial situation, there is some dramatic irony in the contrasts of "night-dark," "brown," and "white" associated with the child (but we must resist reading too much into the child's choice of "white" articles—she is not trying to be like a white child, but is wearing what is appropriate to church). We can be sure that the pronoun "She" (17) refers to the child, since line 21 identifies "the mother" as a contrast to the "She." It is important that the child be the one who bathes and dresses and cares for her hair, for these are further signs of the adult competence that led her to want to join the Freedom March.

The central irony of the poem is of course that the "sacred place" of safety to which the mother guides her child is the place that destroys her. That irony also embodies the theme of the poem, for in this microcosm of mother and child the senseless brutality of the racial bigots is displayed at its worst: the bombing of children at prayer is a symbol of the viciousness and cowardice that lay behind racist suppression. In offering this single personal incident to represent that theme, Randall can achieve more in 32 lines of poetry than an orator might in an hour-long speech denouncing racial injustice.   TRA

9.   *William Carlos Williams*   **The Red Wheelbarrow** (page 536)

The simplicity of this free verse poem inevitably leads students to question "What *does* depend upon these things, and *how* much is 'so much'?" The answer is "human life," both as physical existence and as aesthetic experience.

Momentarily ignoring the visual details—"red," "glazed," and "white"—one might investigate the importance of the objects. A wheelbarrow is a basic farm implement associated with the most primitive stage of human toolmaking, only one step advanced beyond the use of sledges or unwheeled barrows for dragging heavy loads. Rain water is obviously an essential for farming as for all life, and chickens provide two common foodstuffs in their flesh and in their eggs. Thus, the objects can be seen as among the most basic in providing physical sustenance, and much therefore "depends upon" them.

By contrast, the visual imagery is nonutilitarian. Although paint does protect against rot and rust, the color red has no specific usefulness. The glazing of rain (and the potential rotting of wood that it implies) is more potentially harmful than beneficial, and a chicken is an egg-layer and a source of meat whatever its color. These visual references thus run counter to the utilitarian functions of the objects they adorn. But they provide contrasts and harmonies of color, shape, and texture basic to aesthetic enjoyment. White and red are clear contrasts, as are a shiny glaze contrasted to the downy softness of a chicken's feathers. While there is a contrast between the living and nonliving objects, one may also see a vague similarity in the triangular shapes of a wheelbarrow and a pecking chicken. (It helps students to see this if blackboard sketches are provided.)

The poem thus offers two distinct dependences: we depend upon farmers for our food (and they depend upon nature in producing it), and as sensitive observers we depend upon visual perceptions to feed us aesthetically. TRA

10. *A. E. Housman* **Terence, this is stupid stuff** (page 536)

Housman's poem compares the efficacy of three things for helping one lead a satisfactory life: cheerful poetry, liquor, and pessimistic poetry. The first two, by making one "see the world as the world's not," arouse expectations that life can rarely fulfill. The result is disappointment and disillusionment. Pessimistic poetry, by truly picturing a world containing "much less good than ill," prepares one for the troubles that are sure to come. Thus fortified, one can withstand their shock and lead a satisfying life.

In the first verse-paragraph a friend playfully criticizes Terence (Housman) for the kind of poetry he writes and gives a delightful parody of it in the two lines (7–8) about the cow. Reading his poetry, the friend claims in a humorous overstatement, is driving Terence's friends mad and causing them to die before their time. He pleads with Terence to write cheerful poetry instead.

Terence replies that if his friend wants gaiety and cheer, liquor is more efficacious than poetry. It makes the world seem a "lovely" place and oneself a "sterling" lad. The only trouble is that this picture is "all a lie." By implication, cheerful poetry likewise misrepresents the world. Liquor and optimistic poetry are for "fellows whom it hurts to think." Their effect is temporary and ultimately enfeebling. They offer escape, not a solution.

In the first six lines of the third section Terence sums up his philosophy. To train for ill is to prepare oneself for the world as it is. One can do this by reading the kind of poetry Terence writes. It will strengthen "heart and head" and prepare one's soul for adversity. Many students misread the poem at this point. They fail to see that "the stuff I bring for sale" is Terence's poetry, metaphorically compared to a bitter brew that is "not so brisk" (so intoxicating) as the literal ale of the second-verse paragraph. Its "smack is sour" because it was wrung out of bitter experience.   *allusion*

In the final section Terence clinches his point by telling a parable. Mithridates immunized himself to poison by first taking a little and then gradually increasing the dosage. As a result, Mithridates lived a long and satisfactory life. Similarly, Terence implies, one can immunize oneself against the troubles of life by reading the kind of poetry Terence writes. LP

metonomy- pewter pot

93

11. *Archibald MacLeish* **Ars Poetica** (page 538)

The poet's philosophy of his art is summed up in the opening and closing lines of the poem's third section. A poem is concerned with experience, not with propositional statements. When it is successful, it is "equal" to the experience it creates; the reader properly responds to it by imaginatively "living" that experience, not by judging the content of the poem as right or wrong, true or false. To create experience, the rest of the poem tells us (and illustrates in its telling), the poet must rely upon images and symbols.

"Ars Poetica" has three sections, each of which includes what seems a paradox or a violation of common sense. Section one declares that a poem should be "palpable" and "wordless." Yet if we run our fingers over this poem as printed on the page, the only palpable thing is the page; our fingers make no distinction between recipe, advertisement, poem, or blank sheet of paper. And does not MacLeish's statement that a poem should be "wordless" run directly counter to Wallace Stevens's (in "The Noble Rider and the Sound of Words," *The Necessary Angel*) that "Poetry is a revelation in words by means of the words"? No, I think not. What MacLeish means is that the "experience" or "revelation" created is wordless. When we read a poem, we must of course be acutely sensitive to the words, but the result of sensitive reading is that we are drawn into an imaginative experience in which we see "globed" peach or pear, or draw our thumb over an old medallion, or feel the soft moss and worn stone of an ancient casement ledge, or watch a flight of birds crossing the sky.

Section two asserts that a poem "should be motionless in time / As the moon climbs," which seems contradictory in itself, for how can something be "motionless" and yet climb? Yet the moon "climbs" so slowly that its motion is imperceptible except when it can be related to some earthly object, such as the horizon or a "night-entangled tree," and watched for some time. What is this section saying about a poem then? That when we read it, we are so caught up in the experience created that we are unconscious of the passage of time? Or that the experience it creates lingers in the mind and fades from memory slowly and almost imperceptibly? An excellent case for the latter reading is made by Edwin St. Vincent, in *Explicator* 37 (Spring 1979): 14–16, through a detailed analysis of the difficult syntax of this section.

And so we come to the summary third section, which says that a poem should be "equal to: / Not true" and "should not mean / But be." Does this mean that a poem should be meaningless? No, only that its "meaning" (what we have called in Chapter 9 its "total meaning") is an *experience*, not an idea or propositional statement, and is expressed through images and symbols. The symbolic image of "An empty doorway and a maple leaf" (suggesting absence, loneliness, and the transitory quality of life) creates "all the history of grief," and the image of "leaning grasses and two lights above the sea" (suggesting perhaps a summer field where two lovers might lie overlooking the ocean) creates the experience of love. LP

POEMS FOR FURTHER READING

Poems 276, 280, 281, 288, and 298 from Part 2 provide additional illustrations of topics presented in this chapter.

CHAPTER TWO

Reading the Poem

12. *Thomas Hardy* **The Man He Killed** (page 542)

The hesitations and repetitions of stanza 3 beautifully reflect the thought processes of the speaker. The pause after "because" (9) occurs because he is groping for an explanation. When he finds one, he must repeat the "because." He then has to convince himself that this answer is correct and sufficient. He does this (or tries to do it) by telling himself three times emphatically that it is: (1) "Just so"; (2) "my foe of course he was"; (3) "That's clear enough." But despite this triple emphatic effort at self-assurance, we know that the attempt is unsuccessful, as it trails off into "although . . . ." LP

13. *Philip Larkin* **A Study of Reading Habits** (page 543)

Even the slow student should see that neither the language nor the attitudes of the speaker in this poem could possibly be those of a poet. To clinch the case, one can point out that Philip Larkin was by profession a librarian.

The speaker is a weak person, unable to face reality, who as boy and adolescent avoided it by reading "escape" fiction, either in pulp magazines or in paperbacks. As a boy (stanza 1), he identified himself with the virtuous hero, the man who overcomes villainy by physical force. As an adolescent (stanza 2), he vicariously engaged in sex escapades by identifying with the bold villain (Dracula type) or the picaresque hero (James Bond type). As a young man, he has reached a stage at which reading no longer conceals from him his own failures; he now recognizes himself in the weak secondary characters, and he must find escape in alcohol.

Even better than Hardy's "The Man He Killed" (page 542), this poem demonstrates that poetry need not be made out of lofty, dignified, exquisite, or even original language. The language here is vulgar, slangy, and trite; yet it is perfectly chosen to express the intellectual poverty of its speaker. Good poets choose their words not for their beauty or elegance, but for their expressiveness—that is to say, their maximum appropriateness to subject, situation, and speaker. Trite language need not make a trite poem, as this piece effectively demonstrates. And even working within the limitations of deliberately trite language, Larkin achieves striking effects. The word "ripping" (10), for instance, has not only its slang meaning of "exciting" or "great" but also its literal meaning (here) of "ripping the clothes off of"—a doubleness of which the poet was probably aware and the speaker unaware.

96

In "Terence, this is stupid stuff," Housman agrees with the speaker that "ale's the stuff to drink" for "fellows whom it hurts to think" and that one should "Look into the pewter pot / To see the world as the world's not"; but for wiser fellows, Housman recommends reading. However, Housman is recommending quite a different kind of reading from that engaged in by Larkin's speaker; he is recommending a kind in which one can "see the world" as the world *is*. Thus, Housman is in diametrical disagreement with Larkin's speaker, and probably in perfect agreement with Larkin himself. LP

14. *A. E. Housman* Is my team plowing (page 546)

The word "bed" (28) signifies literally the bed that the living man sleeps in, metaphorically the grave that the dead man lies in, and symbolically a lot in life, or condition of existence. The word "sleep" has corresponding meanings: of sleeping, of being dead, and of having a certain lot. In addition, it gathers up from the last stanza the meaning of sleeping with a woman, that is, of making love.

The poem at first seems cynical, suggesting, as it does, the transience of human loyalties. On reflection, however, few people expect a man or woman not to remarry after a first mate has died. (Housman's poem probably doesn't refer to marriage, but the principle is the same.) In general, Housman's poetry is pessimistic about our chances for happiness, but Housman is not cynical about human courage or human virtue. LP

15. *John Donne* Break of Day (page 549)

The situation presents two lovers in bed. The man has just remarked "It's day!" (or something of the sort) and has made a gesture toward getting up. The woman's reply is a protest against his leaving. In the three stanzas of the poem she suggests three reasons why he might be thinking of leaving (because it's light; because he fears to expose their relationship; and because he has business to attend to) and shows each in turn to be invalid. The second of these concerns shows that the lovers are unmarried.

The speaker is conclusively proved to be the woman by her use of the pronoun "him" in line 12. Additional evidence is offered by the following considerations: (a) it was the woman who, under the double standard of morality, risked her reputation ("honor") in an illicit relationship; (b) a man would have been more likely than a woman to be drawn away by "business"; (c) the speaker makes her complaint against "the busied man," not the busied *person*; (d) the speaker compares the offender to a "married man" who woos another, not a married *person*, married *woman,* or *wife.*

Lines 15–16 may be read as meaning either (a) love (personified as a sovereign) can admit the poor man, the foul man, even the false man into her province, but cannot admit "the busied man," or (b) the poor man, the foul man, and the false man can admit love into their lives, but "the busied man" cannot. We do not have to choose between these two readings. Both make sense.

The woman clearly has a scale of values that puts love at the top. She is not ashamed of her relationship with the man (as shown in the second stanza). She has committed herself to him and expects an equal commitment from him. His "business" threatens that commitment, and she is jealous of it as she would be jealous of any rival. Their love is as sacred to her as if legitimatized by marriage; he cannot have *two* mistresses: "business" and her.

Though the arguments of the three stanzas are logically discrete, they are verbally linked. Stanza 1 is connected to stanza 2 by the repeated image of "light"; stanza 2 is connected to stanza 3 by the contrast of her "being well" and his having (possibly) "the worst disease of love." The poem's title not only means *Morning* but suggests the threatened separation ("break") between the lovers.

Students may have to be guided through the figurative legerdemain of stanza 2. Light is personified (as a mute, unable to speak); it is metonymically linked with its source, the sun; and the sun is metaphorically compared to a large eye (which is in turn referred back as the sole anatomical feature of the personified Light). The sun may discover the two lovers in bed together but, having no tongue, it can spread no scandal; *even if it could* (the woman declares), she would not be shamed by anything it could say. LP

16. *Emily Dickinson* **There's been a death in the opposite house** (page 550)

The speaker in this poem has not been informed of the death across the way and apparently does not know who has died. He (his sex is revealed in line 12) is not one of the neighbors who "rustle in and out." Probably he is a visitor in the house from which he watches. But he is no stranger to the ways of country towns: he knows by the signs immediately and intuitively that a death has occurred. He is a sensitive observer, able to report and to interpret precisely and imaginatively what he sees and to enter empathetically into the thoughts and feelings of the children who hurry past.

What he focuses on is the difference that the death makes in the ordinary life of a house. The house itself seems to have a "numb" look, as if stunned by the unusual occurrence. Neighbors—mostly women, for their skirts "rustle"—come and go, offering help and sympathy. The sick room is ventilated, a mattress hung to air across the window sill. The children hurry by, scared, for death to them is mysterious and vaguely terrifying: they can think of the corpse only as "it," not as a person, and they wonder if "it" died on the mattress they see. The minister enters "stiffly," not relaxed: this is a solemn occasion, and he will be the most important person in the funeral ritual. He immediately takes command. The milliner and the undertaker arrive to measure—between them—the corpse for the coffin, the mourners for black veils and other mourning apparel, and the house itself for getting the coffin in and out and perhaps for hanging with crepe bunting. (The word "house" is used, throughout the poem, as a metonymy to indicate, not just the house itself, but the activity and the people around and within it, although the house itself seems to reflect this numbness in the way its window opens. Even the minister reflects it in his stiffness.) The speaker concludes with an account, not of what he sees, but of what he knows will soon be seen—the funeral procession of black coaches hung with tassels that will take the body and the mourners to the cemetery. He then generalizes his opening observation—how easy it is to tell when a death has occurred in a country town.

Some students will have difficulty with the tone of this poem, seeing it or the people in it as regarding death callously, impersonally, or coldly. The mistake may result from misinterpreting the role of the speaker (who is an observer, not a participant), or from misconceiving the "numb" look (which signifies not lack of emotion, but the stunned state following or accompanying too much emotion), or from identifying the attitude of the children toward the corpse with that of the adults or the observer. The poem focuses on the outside of the house, not on the dead person, because that is what the observer sees; but all of the activity he sees results from the presence of the dead person within. The tone of the poem reflects the awesomeness of death and its solemnity. Part of the speaker's attitude is revealed in his reference to the undertaker as the man of the "appalling" trade (in the double sense of "horrifying" and "putting a pall on" a coffin) and to the funeral procession as a "dark" parade (dark literally because of the black badges of mourning but with the additional connotations of mystery and awesomeness).

Though written by a woman, this poem has a male speaker. Donne's "Break of Day," though written by a man, has a female speaker. An instructive point can be made from this juxtaposition. LP

17. *Mari Evans* When in Rome (page 551)

The first speaker is a white woman, the second her black maid. We are given only the unspoken thoughts of the second speaker, hence the inclusion of her words in parentheses.

Though the white employer's words take the outward form of affection and solicitude ("Mattie dear . . . take / whatever you like"), their tone, without her realizing it, is subtly patronizing. The invitation to take "whatever you like" is qualified by "don't / get my anchovies / they cost / too much!" And her utter ignorance of what the black servant likes to eat betrays the essential emptiness of her solicitude. The phrase "take / whatever you like / to eat" functions on two levels: *take whatever you wish to take*, and *take whatever you enjoy eating*. (There is almost nothing in the icebox that the black woman really *likes*.)

The black woman's attitude is one of repressed antagonism. Consciously or unconsciously, she knows she is being patronized, and though she is accustomed to speaking outwardly in terms of respect ("yes'm"), her resentment expresses itself through the use of irony: "what she think, she got— / a bird to feed?" and "yes'm. just the / sight's / enough!" The last phrase can be read in two ways.

The title and the conclusion are an allusion to the familiar saying "When in Rome, do as the Romans do." Rome in the poem serves as a metaphor for the white world, and the speaker is tired of having to eat what whites like to eat rather than what blacks like to eat. LP

18. *Edwin Arlington Robinson* **The Mill** (page 552)

"The Mill" was first published in 1920. Its setting is earlier, sometime during the Industrial Revolution, probably late in the nineteenth century. The miller's remark (5) means that individual millers are no longer able to make a living: they are being replaced by industrialization.

Certainly, Robinson has not been at pains to be perfectly clear about what happens in this poem. The miller's remark (5) is cryptic. We are not told "What else there was" (13) in the mill, or "what was hanging from a beam" (15), or where the miller's wife went (16), or what kind of "way" she is thinking of (19), or what ruffles the water (23). But surely this story of a double suicide gains in power exactly *because* it is not at first perfectly clear. Readers feel a growing horror as its meaning gradually dawns on them, as bewilderment shifts to suspicion and suspicion to certainty. If we change "what was hanging from a beam" to "his body hanging from a beam," the poem is made clearer, but its effect is greatly weakened. We no longer experience the terror of the half-seen.

Obscurity in a poem may arise from various causes, including the poet's ineptitude. It is not always as integral a part of meaning as it is here. But it can be. The point can be driven home by analogy to the person who spoils a joke by explaining it. A joke, too, is a small work of art. It must not be made so clear that its effect is destroyed.

This poem is briefly discussed by Wallace L. Anderson in *Edwin Arlington Robinson: A Critical Introduction* (Boston: Houghton, 1967) 103–104. LP

19. *Sylvia Plath* **Mirror** (page 553)

Although the speaker is the personified mirror, who in the second stanza goes on to personify itself as a lake, the subject of the poem is the woman who looks into the mirror and learns the truth of the changes in her appearance that time brings. Like a person, the mirror looks outward, observing—and meditating about—the objects that come into view. But unlike a person, the mirror has no preconceptions; it does not distort its vision with emotional responses. It is godlike in its detached truthfulness, even if it is a little god with a limited area of observation.

As a lake (and perhaps like the pool into which Narcissus plunged in adoration of his own beauty), the mirror still will give only the truth about the surface of reflections, no matter how the woman might want to find a deeper truth. Candlelight and moonlight, which cast flattering dim gleams of romantic imagination, are by comparison with the mirror's faithful images "liars."

What the searching woman finds in the truthful reflection is the sad fact of aging: the little girl that she was is now dead, and the old woman that she will become lurks in the depths of time, waiting to appear and terrify her.   TRA

20. *William Wordsworth* **I wandered lonely as a cloud** (page 554)

The subject is typically Romantic and Wordsworthian: the speaker in an idle moment, alone in nature and feeling detached from it and from the social world, comes upon a natural event that moves him so deeply that his future life is shaped by it, and the memory of it can spontaneously return to him, to renew the emotion of the original experience. But why *should* a scene of natural beauty have such an effect? Is there more to this than the portrayal of the emotional response of a sensitive person? Does he *do* anything or only passively receive a gift from nature?

First, the speaker's condition before the event: wandering alone, but also "lonely," an emotional state in which he regrets his isolation, and yet in his simile also glories in it—"lonely as a cloud / That floats on high," superior to the valleys and hills of earth. And the simile contains another figure as well, personification, so that the opening situation is an example of poetic perception: the self compared to a cloud, the cloud given two human attributes, loneliness *and* superiority. So the speaker sets out from a point of poetic creativity even while he feels himself to be idly uninvolved.

As soon as the daffodils are visible, the poetic imagination shifts into a higher gear. The first impression, "crowd," is immediately and spontaneously revised into a more reverberative "host," the daffodils are "golden" in more than color, the rhythm takes on a lilt as the tetrameter line is broken in half with "Beside the lake, beneath the trees" ("beside" and "beneath" establishing a different spatial relationship from "high o'er"), and the daffodils are given costume and dance motions. What we might judge to be a serene and dispassionate emotional state in lines 1–2 suddenly leaps into creative energy that continues through line 14.

The major figure of the second stanza is overstatement, revealing the speaker's need to capture the intensity of his excitement—the flowers seemed infinite, heavenly, brilliant, "never-ending"; the speaker's sensitivity enabled him to see "Ten thousand . . . at a glance." They seemed all to be dancing in unison, and the waves seemed to mimic (but of course fell short of) them in dancing.

At line 15, the submerged self-consciousness that has been implied by the spate of poetic devices finally comes to the fore: the "poet" must examine both his response and the external stimulus to it. He discovers that despite his reluctance ("could not but be" implies that he has tried to avoid it—perhaps that's what he was consciously doing by wandering "lonely as a cloud"?), he feels cheerful being in the "jocund company" of the daffodils. Unlike the "sparkling waves," he does not try to dance with them, but only gazes and gazes, storing up the emotion of the moment without knowing or thinking that the "golden daffodils" brought him more wealth than the single experience.

The additional wealth is the ability to relive that experience, not only as a memory but as an emotion, even—what he did not do when he actually saw them—to the extent of letting his heart figuratively dance "with the daffodils." But notice again the emotional straits that he is in when they come to him: alone, lying on his couch, "In vacant or in pensive mood," looking into himself with "bliss" that comes from solitude—then once again, unbidden and unexpected, the merry daffodils "flash upon that inward eye."

But what is really flashing is his own creative power—for, in fact, the daffodils cannot be jocund, cannot feel glee, do not dance. The lively, bright beauty of a surprising natural sight was the starting point for a poet's imaginative creativity; *that* is what can fill his heart with pleasure. TRA

21. *William Wordsworth* The Solitary Reaper (page 555)

The poem relates the awakening of the speaker's imaginative response to an experience of wordless expression and the extended effect of the experience on him. Apparently on a walking tour in the Highlands of Scotland, the speaker sees and hears a girl gathering grain while she sings a native song. Moved by both her solitude and the sorrowful melody, the speaker tries to find correspondences between the unintelligible song and other human experiences, but finally acknowledges that whether he understands it or not, it has moved him deeply enough to live on in his memory.

In accordance with his theories about poetry as the "spontaneous overflow of powerful feelings," a power which he attributes to the singing girl, Wordsworth frequently strives to give his poems both immediacy and the sense of personal experience. In this case, however, his starting point was not at all personal; the poem is based on a passage from a friend's manuscript account of a Scottish tour. Thomas Wilkinson had written: "Passed by a female who was reaping alone, she sung in Erse as she bended over her sickle, the sweetest human voice I ever heard. Her strains were tenderly melancholy, and felt delicious long after they were heard no more." The poem reports this (with direct quotation and verbal echo) as if it had happened to the speaker, achieving immediacy in the first three stanzas by using the present tense.

The opening lines emphatically establish the solitariness of the girl and awaken parallel feelings in the speaker: "single" (1), "solitary" (2), "by herself" (3), "Alone" (5). He has, or imagines, companions whom he exhorts to "Behold" and "listen," demanding excited attention; yet this he balances against the injunction to remain quiet so as not to disturb the girl's song and to preserve her sense of being alone. What strikes him most in the opening stanza are her solitude and the "melancholy" nature of her song, which seems to overflow the deep valley in which she works (the Scottish Highlands are for the most part barren and sparsely inhabited, with arable land restricted to the valleys).

In the second and third stanzas, as he listens to the music in a foreign tongue, the speaker imaginatively searches for corresponding situations that will explain the emotions with which he responds. The second stanza offers two comparisons, both suggesting relief from the hardships of natural surroundings. The singer is like two very different kinds of birds in two contrasted geographical locales, implying the universality of the experience: the nightingale singing in an oasis in the parched Arabian desert, promising cool comfort to exhausted travelers; or the cuckoo signaling the coming of spring to the stark, rocky islands battered by the seas in the northern-most reaches of Scotland. Both scenes are isolated, forbidding, and lonely; both are momentarily relieved; and both imply that the speaker feels himself isolated, wandering in a wholly uncongenial natural setting, momentarily restored by the beauty of the song he hears.

The third stanza moves from geographical extremes to contrasts of time and social rank. The song might be a traditional lament expressing grief for ancient, heroic battlefield defeats or it might refer to the "natural sorrow, loss, or pain" of ordinary daily life in the present. Just as loneliness and weariness were universalized in stanza 2, stanza 3 universalizes melancholy here and everywhere, now and in the past.

The third stanza has asked for intelligible fact: what is she singing about? In the final stanza, the poem suddenly shifts into the past tense, in its first line denying the possibility (or even the necessity) of understanding exactly what the girl was saying. As it turns out, the speaker's inability to understand the meaning of the song has been an advantage. He has found in the melody and in the singer's isolation the occasion for his own imagined creation of the universal themes of loneliness and melancholy. Looking back on this experience, he has discovered that his imagination was revitalized, and that his profound feelings have persisted even after he has mounted up from the scene of her singing.

A full, suggestive reading of this poem is in Geoffrey H. Hartman's *Wordsworth's Poetry, 1787–1814* (New Haven: Yale UP, 1964) 3–18.   TRA

POEMS FOR FURTHER READING

Poems 212, 213, 221, and 250 from Part 2 provide additional illustrations of topics presented in this chapter.

CHAPTER THREE

Denotation and Connotation

22. *Emily Dickinson* **There is no frigate like a book** (page 558)

Miles suggests a measurable and therefore a lesser distance than ''lands''; also, it suggests distance only. ''Lands'' suggests not only distance but difference—not only far lands, but foreign lands, perhaps even fairylands. The connotations of *cheap* are unfavorable; of ''frugal,'' favorable. ''Prancing,'' besides participating in the alliterative sequence of ''a page / Of prancing poetry,'' brings to mind the metrical effects of poetry and the winged horse Pegasus, symbol of poetry in Greek mythology. **LP**

23. *William Shakespeare* **When my love swears that she is made of truth (Sonnet 138)** (page 559)

Because of the pun on *lie*, students frequently misconceive the tone of this sonnet as light. It might better be called dark. The pun is grim, not merry. Trapped in a love affair that he knows to be unworthy of him, too weak to break loose, the speaker cynically resigns himself to continuing it, though he knows his mistress is unfaithful. He cannot leave the honey-pot; it has become a ''habit.''

The attraction of the affair is sensual, as shown by the two meanings of ''lie''—conjunction at the physical level, separateness at the spiritual. Not only do the two lovers lie to each other, the speaker lies to himself, and *knows* that he lies to himself. He *pretends* to believe the woman's lies (2) in the hope that she will think him young and naive (3–4), and he makes himself think in one part of his mind that the deception works (5) though he knows in another part that it does not (6). A no-longer young man—one who is fully learned in ''the world's false subtleties,'' including his own—he has ambivalent feelings toward his mistress and toward himself. Line 11 is not mature wisdom but rationalization. Love's *best* habit is trust, not *seeming* trust. Mature lovers can accept each other's faults without needing to lie to each other about them, and the speaker would not feel insecure about his age if he were confident of his mistress' love for him.

The speaker is a number of years older than the woman and is uneasy about the discrepancy. He cannot be really *old*, else he would have no chance even in his own mind of making her think him young.

''Simply'' (7) carries its older meaning of ''foolishly'' (cf. the nursery rhyme ''Simple Simon met a pieman''), while ''simple'' (8) means ''plain'' or ''unadorned.''

"Vainly" (5) primarily means "futilely" (cf. "in vain") but with overtones of "in such a way as to please one's vanity." "Habit" (1) is a garment or clothing and also a customary practice. "Told" (12) means both "spoken" and "counted."   LP

24. *Robert Graves* **The Naked and the Nude** (page 560)

In "The Naked and the Nude" Graves is concerned with both semantic and human values. Though seemingly he uses differences in human behavior only to illustrate differences in the connotations of two words often regarded as synonyms, actually he is as much concerned with moral as with lexical values. This ambiguity begins in the first stanza. If Graves were talking only about words, his proper beginning would be "For me, *naked* and *nude* . . ." or "For me, the words 'naked' and 'nude' . . . ." By introducing two definite articles and omitting italicization or quotation marks, Graves forces us to take "the naked and the nude" as people. At the same time, by having them "construed / As synonyms," he forces us to consider them as words. This duality of interest persists throughout the poem.

The moral qualities characteristic of the opposed kinds of people connoted by the two words are in part named in the last line of stanza 1 and in part suggested by the kinds of behavior shown in stanzas 2 and 3. In general, the naked are natural, honest, unashamed, unselfconscious, undesigning; they are swayed by some passion (love, truth, or justice) that carries them beyond mere self-concern. The nude, in contrast, are deceptive, sly, and designing; by artifice and trickery they seek to attract attention to themselves and arouse prurient desire for their own pleasure or profit.

But ambiguities and paradoxes abound. In stanza 2 Graves's three examples are lovers, doctors, and a Goddess. The lovers are deeply consumed by physical desire, but reciprocally and unashamedly so; their passion is a natural part of their love. The physicians, on the other hand, in their passion for diagnostic knowledge, are completely beyond physical desire. Notice, however, that, though the physicians illustrate the moral quality concerned, it is their patients who are "naked." Finally, the Goddess, nonhuman and immortal, will not be among those sent to the underworld by death in the final stanza. The shifts of category in the second and third examples are explainable by Graves's dual interest in lexical and moral values.

In stanza 3 the nude both boldly flaunt and slyly conceal their charms, like a dancer with fans or veils, to entice and hold the gaze of onlookers. "Draping by a showman's trick / Their dishabille in rhetoric," they are paradoxically both clothed and unclothed, nude but not naked. Thus arrayed in illusory attire, the nude assume a holier-than-thou attitude and pretend to be more modest than the plainly naked, while actually more seductive. The reference to "rhetoric" keeps the interest focused on semantic as well as moral values; the word "rhetoric" suggests verbal embellishment of the plain and unvarnished, just as "nude" suggests embellishment of the "naked."

Though, in stanza 4, both the naked and the nude tread the "briary pastures of the dead," it is clear that the nude, who in this world defeat the naked in terms of material reward, will get their comeuppance in the underworld. At this point, Graves is clearly talking about people, not about words. But, in this stanza, the poet keeps his interest in words alive by giving the word "naked" a brilliant new twist in connotation: in the last line of the poem it means not just "unclothed," but "unprotected"—cruelly exposed to the lashes of the Gorgon's whips. Though both the naked and the nude may be pursued by the Gorgons (whose "long whips" suggest serpents torn from their hair), it is the nude who will suffer cruelly from their exposure.

[This commentary is adapted and abridged from an item in *Explicator* 39 (Fall 1980): 36–38, by Laurence Perrine and Margaret Morton Blum.]   LP

EXERCISES (pages 562–63)

1. (a) steed, (b) king, (c) Samarkand.
2. (a) mother, (b) children, (c) brother.
3. (a) slender, thin, skinny, gaunt; (b) prosperous, opulent, moneyed, loaded; (c) intelligent, smart, brainy, eggheaded.
4. (a) having acted foolishly.
5. Denotations: fast *runner*: swift; fast *color*: permanent; fast *living*: reckless; fast *day*: abstinent. Connotations: the third is negative, the other three positive.
6. In the first example *white* suggests rare beauty; in the second it suggests extreme fear.

25. *Edwin Arlington Robinson* **The Sheaves** (page 563)

A meditation on natural growth, ripening, and death, this Italian sonnet is strict in its structure and form, employing only four rime sounds (*abbaabba cdcdcd*), dividing its octave in half, and employing the turn from octave to sestet as a time break between the ripening process and the harvest. In the octave, the speaker is drawn to imagine the natural process as a magical one in which the value ("mighty meaning," 7) surpasses both what nature can do and what human understanding can comprehend. The speaker demonstrates thus his desire to think of the naturally explicable, and the materially valuable, in terms of mystery and awe. This desire is reflected in the allusive language that conjures up fairy tales and stories of magic (study question 3). What he is observing is after all commonplace and utilitarian: a ripening wheatfield that is in fact part of the world of things that are bought and sold, a phase in the creation of the staff of life.

In the sestet his imaginative perception grows more intense, as he pictures the wheat sheaves as "a thousand girls with golden hair." But as the final line also indicates, there is an emotional price to be paid for such imagination: what has been transformed into an image of beauty is transitory, and the act of imaginative transformation will result in loss, regret, and nostalgia.

"Gold" and "golden" are color descriptions denotatively, but of course carry their connotations of value. Ironically, the connotation of material value is denied in the poem as the speaker asserts the superiority of the wheatfield's "gold" to anything "bought or sold." The denotative pun in line 8 has a similar irony: the wheat has a meaning that "tells" (speaks, and counts) more by not being "told" (counted, and explained).

The word "fair" in lines 9 and 10 is more complicated. It clearly denotes "sunny" as well as "beautiful"; but when in lines 11–12 the harvested wheat sheaves are "golden" and "Shining," implying full sunlight, the poem draws on another denotation. There is a third kind of day involved—"not fair" (9) means cloudy, "Fair" (10) means sunny, but what is a day that is "another day" (10), sunny and yet different from what has been called "fair"? It is a day in which the quality of the light is not the defining quality, a sunny day that has lost its connotations of beauty and attraction (and perhaps of justice). It is, in fact, another example of the emotional cost of imagination: prizing what is so beautiful may result in a sense of unfairness (injustice) when that beauty passes.

Study question 5: "green wheat" has not only the virtue of its sound, but the freshness connoted by "green," and the greater denotative specificity of "wheat"; "undivined" connotes magical or mystical divination; "land" carries the same connotative force as in Dickinson's "There is no frigate like a book"—romantic, and associated with fairy tales; "thousand" connotes a large but uncounted number (compare it to 997, for example, in terms of emotional meaning), and "girls" connotes innocence and vulnerability.   TRA

26.   *Henry Reed*   Naming of Parts (page 564)

The poem presents a corporal or sergeant giving instruction to a group of army trainees. There are two "voices" in the poem, but their dialogue is conducted within the mind of one person, probably that of a recruit. The first three-and-a-fraction lines of all but the last stanza are the spoken words of the sergeant as heard by the recruit. The last two-and-a-fraction lines of these stanzas, and the whole of the final stanza, are the unspoken thoughts of the recruit. This interpretation can be disputed, for there is some ambiguity about the "speaker" in the poem. Exact determination, however, is unimportant. Whoever the "speaker" is, he is a sensitive person. His unspoken thoughts furnish a comment on the instruction he receives or is compelled to give.

The instruction takes place out-of-doors. It is spring. Not far off are gardens in blossom, with bees flying back and forth, cross-pollinating the flowers. The time apparently is just before or just after the outbreak of a war, during a period of rapid mobilization, for the equipment of the recruits is incomplete. Their rifles have no slings and no piling swivels.

The meaning of the poem grows out of the ironic contrast between the trainees and the gardens, both of which have symbolical value.

Besides lacking slings and piling swivels, the trainees have not got a "point of balance," in one sense the point on the rifle at which it balances on the finger, in another sense a psychological point of balance in their lives. Living in barracks, apart from wives and sweethearts, they are living an unnatural kind of life. Their lives are incomplete, like their equipment. By learning the parts of the rifle, they are preparing to kill and be killed. They are living a regimented life. Being raw recruits, they are awkward. Their lives are tedious, as expressed by the repetition of dull phrases. The rifle is a mechanical instrument, and their lives are likewise mechanical.

The gardens represent the natural, the free, the graceful, the beautiful, the joyous—everything that is missing from the lives of the trainees. The bees, by fertilizing the flowers, are helping to bring about new life. The trainees and the gardens thus symbolically represent a series of opposites: death versus life, incompleteness versus completeness, the mechanical versus the natural, regimentation versus freedom, awkwardness versus grace, drabness versus beauty, tedium versus joy—the list can be extended. Through this ironic juxtaposition, the poet indirectly makes a statement about the kind of life imposed on man by war and preparation for war.

The poem is heavy with sexual implications, and, if handled with tact, discussion of these will open up a further dimension of meaning. If handled clumsily, such discussion will give this aspect of the poem a false emphasis and send students away thinking it a "dirty" poem. Men segregated from women tend to become obsessed with sex and to think of women as sexual objects rather than as persons. The absence of normal contacts between the sexes is one reason for the lack of a "point of balance" in the recruits' lives. Many words and phrases in the poem symbolically or connotatively suggest sexual "parts" or actions: "thumb," "bolt," "breech," "rapidly backwards and forwards," "assaulting and fumbling," "cocking-piece." Instructors must rely on their own discretion as to how explicit to be about these matters, remembering that they are properly overtones and undertones, not the burden of the poem.

The language and rhythm of the poem beautifully support its central contrast. The words of the sergeant are prosy, and their rhythm is a prose rhythm, frequently faltering and clumsy. In the lines about the gardens, the words are beautiful, and the rhythm flows. The abrupt change in rhythm from smooth to halt is especially striking in the middle of line 17.

The poem is discussed by Richard A. Condon in *Explicator* 12 (June 1954): item 54.   LP

27.   *Ellen Kay*   Pathedy of Manners (page 565)

Though it wittily satirizes certain modes of social behavior, this poem does not quite fit the literary category of "comedy of manners," for it has no happy ending; nor does it fit the category of "tragedy," for it does not dramatize the sudden "fall" from high to low estate of a protagonist of heroic stature. It is accurately labeled a

"Pathedy of Manners," for it concerns the pathetic waste of life and talent by a woman whose false values made her prefer appearance to substance and choose manners over merit. Inasmuch as her false values are those of a class, the poem presents a form of social pathology.

Brilliant, beautiful, and wealthy, the woman of the poem wasted her gifts on inauthentic goals. She might have made some great and useful contribution to humanity; instead she chose to shine in fashionable society and expended herself in acquiring the superficial graces to make her successful there. She learned to distinguish authentic pearls from paste (in necklaces or cufflinks) and to tell real Wedgwood from a fraud, but she let fashionable opinion ("cultured jargon") govern her artistic tastes rather than a truly formed and independent judgment. Back home from the obligatory trip abroad, she made an "ideal" marriage (that is, she married a man with impeccable social credentials) and had "ideal" (well-behaved, well-dressed, clean) but lonely children, in an "ideal" (fashionably situated and well-appointed) house. (The thrice-repeated adjective exemplifies verbal irony.)

Now at forty-three, her husband dead and her children grown, she is going through a middle-age crisis, reevaluating her life and regretting that it has not been more meaningful. She "toys" with the idea of taking a new direction, but it is too late. The phrase "kill time" (19) has a double meaning. She would like to destroy the time lost since her college years, but she can only waste time by dreaming of doing so. Her dreams of taking up that lost opportunity are only an illusion, and she can only "re-wed" (another double meaning) these illusions. Unable to pursue an independent course of action, she can only fend off "doubts" (about the value of her present life) with "nimble talk." Though a hundred socially elite acquaintances call her, she is without a single intimate friend. The poem ends with a brilliant combination of pun and paradox: "Her meanings lost in manners, she will walk / Alone in brilliant circles to the end." In terms of true intimacy she will be alone, although she will move in brilliant social circles to the end of her life; in terms of meaningful living she will walk in circles till the end of her life, not advance along a line of significant purpose.

The speaker is probably a college classmate of the protagonist, who has seen her the day before, roughly a quarter-century after their first acquaintance. This meeting has caused the narrator to reflect on the protagonist's life. LP

28. *Langston Hughes* **Cross** (page 566)

The speaker is a "cross" (literal) between black and white, and this is the "cross" (metaphorical) that he has to bear. There is also an overtone of the adjectival meaning "angry" in the title. LP

29. *William Wordsworth* **The world is too much with us** (page 566)

This sonnet juxtaposes nineteenth-century Christian English faith in industrial development and mercantile values with a primitive faith in the pagan deities of nature. As one scholar puts it, it is in the traditional mode of the conflict between Christ and Pan, but the conflict is exacerbated by identifying Christianity with modern materialism and urban insensitivity to nature. Wordsworth places his speaker at a fulcrum: he is forlornly identified with the modern, and his own way of "glimpsing" natural vitality and harmony is by wishing he could be a pagan—though he knows intellectually that the beliefs of ancient Greece are "outworn."

The speaker stands in a grassy meadow on a calm moonlit night, in view of the sea. This placid and unspectacular situation makes him forlorn as he thinks of the worldliness that destroys emotional and imaginative response to natural beauty. "We," including the speaker, have traded away the real power of imagination that we possessed; we "get" wealth, but we "spend" our hearts for it. Nature is no longer ours, nor we hers.

The opening quatrain abstractly generalizes, withholding the motive for the generalizations. It contrasts the presumed power of trade with the internal power of the imagination, and declares that the real cost of a materialistic value system is our hearts.

The second quatrain begins to set the scene, establishing the time and place: it is night, the sea is calm, the moon is bright, and the expected high winds of the seaside are subdued. The speaker poetically personifies sea and winds, an imaginative contrast to the philosophical generalizations of the first quatrain, representing the speaker's attempt to display his own sensitive image-making powers—but his images tend toward triteness, as lines 8-9 suggest by abruptly changing the tone to straightforward colloquialism. The phrase "For this, for everything" reveals a loss of imaginative concreteness, and the cliché "out of tune" emphasizes the speaker's failure either to feel or to create. As a transition from octave to sestet, these lines appear to give up the attempt to counter crass materialism with poetic originality.

Instead, beginning in line 9, the speaker swears (by his Christian God) his preference for a "pagan creed" that would allow him to believe in such mythical nature deities as Proteus and Triton, as antidotes for his forlorness. But in fact he was not "suckled" in such a creed and can summon up only a glimpse of these nature gods, ironically created for him by great Christian English poets of the past. "Pleasant lea" is quoted from Spenser's "Colin Clouts Come Home Again," a description of Colin's first view of England (line 283); the reference to Proteus alludes to Milton's *Paradise Lost* (3.603–604); and line 14 refers again to "Colin Clout": "Triton blowing loud his wreathèd horn" (line 245). Desiring to reach backward to a natural paganism, the speaker must rely on his Christian poetic heritage. Furthermore, he realizes that he cannot actually hold such beliefs, and is wistful about the "outworn" but imaginative mythological personifications of sea and wind, visible Proteus, audible Triton, representing a lost harmony between man and nature.

For further discussion of the mythical and literary allusions, see Douglas Bush, *Mythology and the Romantic Tradition in English Poetry* (Cambridge: Harvard UP, 1937) 58–59. TRA

30. *John Donne* **A Hymn to God the Father** (page 567)

According to Izaak Walton, Donne's first biographer, this poem was written during a severe illness in 1623. It is a *confession* of sin and a *prayer* for forgiveness; but by its acknowledgment of the power and mercy of God, it becomes a *hymn* as well.

The first two lines refer to *original sin*, the sin we are all guilty of, by inheritance from Adam's sin in the Garden. Having "spun / My last thread" means roughly "having reached the end of my life." The image derives from the Greek myth of the three Fates—Clotho, who spun the thread of life; Lachesis, who twisted it; and Atropos, who cut it short—but Donne has effectively simplified the myth. The "shore" is the shore on *this* side of the river or water that one must cross to reach eternal life.

The poet puns on his own name in the penultimate line of each stanza. In the first two stanzas the first "done" means "finished"; the second means both "finished" and "Donne." In the third stanza the first "done" means "performed" (as also in line 2), and the second again means both "finished" and "Donne."

In line 15 "thy Sun" is an obvious pun on "thy Son." It is particularly relevant because Jesus was God's agent to bring mercy to mankind, and this poem is a prayer for forgiveness.

In the final line of each stanza, the word "more" is a pun on the maiden name of Donne's wife. We must not think, however, that Donne regarded his marriage as a mistake or counted it among his sins. Rather, he subscribed to the "Neoplatonic belief that to rise to the love of God one must leave behind the love of 'creatures' "*; thus his continuing love for Anne is an obstacle to his reaching heaven.

It is worthy of notice that this eighteen-line poem involves only two rimes; and that the word "forgive" occurs four times, the word "sin" eight times, and the word "done" seven times. These repetitions, along with the two-line refrain, account for much of the poem's power. LP

*Two worthy articles on this poem, especially as to the pun on *more*, are "John Donne's Terrifying Pun," by Harry Morris, in *Papers on Language and Literature* 9 (Spring 1973): 128–37; and "Donne's 'A Hymn to God the Father': New Dimensions," by David J. Leigh, in *Studies in Philology* 75 (1978): 84–92. My quotation comes from the first of these, p. 132.

31. *Siegfried Sassoon* **Base Details** (page 568)

The poem expresses the resentment of a front-line soldier in World War I, exposed to the constant dangers, discomforts, and deprivations of trench warfare, toward the frequently casual attitudes and soft lives of officers assigned to staff duty at the base, safely located miles behind the front. Although we can't know his rank, the speaker is almost certainly an officer and is perhaps, like the poem's author, a captain. Company commanders (captains) and platoon commanders (subalterns) suffered the highest mortality rates during World War I because they had to lead their men "over the top" on charges across "No Man's Land" against withering enemy fire. The speaker expresses his bitterness through irony; he is really strongly averse to being the kind of person and living the kind of life he describes so deprecatingly.

The title expanded to manifest both its meanings might read "Ignoble Particulars about Officers Detailed for Duty at the Base."

"Fierce" is used ironically (fierce manner, inward timidity). "Scarlet" suggests the red face of someone who is choleric, acts fiercely, is short of breath, and drinks too much, as well as implying the red lapel tabs and cap bands worn by staff officers in the British army. "Puffy" means both short-winded and fat. "Guzzling and gulping" connotes gluttony. "Scrap" minimizes the seriousness and horror of battle by reducing it in importance to a street-corner altercation between kids. "Youth stone dead" has ambiguous reference: it may refer either to the utterly vanished youthfulness of the returning majors or to the young men left literally dead on the battlefields. "Toddle" suggests second childhood and senility.   LP

POEMS FOR FURTHER READING

Poems 218, 245, and 294 from Part 2 provide additional illustrations of topics presented in this chapter.

CHAPTER FOUR

Imagery

32. *Robert Browning* **Meeting at Night** (page 570)

33. *Robert Browning* **Parting at Morning** (page 571)

The auditory imagery of "Meeting at Night" is strongly reinforced by onomatopoetic effects. In lines 5–6 the sound of the boat's hull grating against the wet sand of the beach seems echoed by the series of *sh, ch,* and *s* sounds in "pu*sh*ing . . . quen*ch* . . . *s*peed . . . *sl*u*sh*y *s*and." In line 9 the sharp *p* of the onomatopoetic "ta*p*" is repeated in "*p*ane," and the *-tch* of the onomatopoetic "scra*tch*" is partially anticipated in "*sh*arp" as well as repeated in the rime.

Both meanings suggested for the last line of "Parting at Morning" are applicable. The "world of men" does need the contributions of the male speaker to its daily labors; and the speaker himself—as Browning's answer implies—needs the companionship of men as well as the love of a woman. LP

34. *Richard Wilbur* **A Late Aubade** (page 572)

An *aubade* (from a word meaning "dawn") is a sunrise love song, a morning serenade, a lyric addressed at dawn to one's sweetheart. The word is used whimsically here, for, though the lovers have recently awakened, the time is almost noon. It is a very late aubade indeed. The woman has apparently made some gesture toward rising. ("It's almost noon," she has said. Implication: it's time to get up and go about one's business.) The man is pleading with her to stay in bed with him a while longer, and then to cap their lovemaking with some delicious snacks from the icebox.

Are these lovers unmarried? The question is irrelevant to the theme of the poem, and ought not to be raised. If students insist on bringing in a moral issue, however (and some will), one should be prepared to point out that the poem does not answer the question one way or the other. The lovers might be a recently married couple with no children as yet. They are in a house with two stories, not in a bachelor apartment, and the woman knows her way to the refrigerator.

The poem is a celebration of the delights of the senses. Both the woman, who would rather "lie in bed and kiss / Than anything," and the man, who orders up a connoisseur's menu from the kitchen, know how to savor these delights. The images chosen appeal to touch (kisses, chilled wine), to taste (wine, cheese, crackers, pears), and to sight. (Though white wine and blue cheese refer more to kinds than to colors, they suggest, when combined with "Ruddy-skinned pears," a visual as well as a gustatory treat. The arrangement of items indeed suggests the eye of a painter, a Cézanne or Renoir, as well as the palate of an epicure.) All the images suggest a keen appreciation of such delights by the lovers, not coarse sensuality or gross overindulgence.

The poem belongs to the *carpe diem* tradition, famously exemplified by Herrick's "To the Virgins, to Make Much of Time," with its opening line "Gather ye rosebuds while ye may" (page 607). The theme of such poems is "Time flies; therefore enjoy to the fullest each moment as it passes."

The speaker in the poem is a cultivated person, familiar with "centuries of verse," with Schoenberg's music, with the appearance of old books ("some liver-spotted page"), and with the manner of library research ("sitting . . . in a carrel"). It is clear that he is thoroughly acquainted with the life of the intellect, but has not allowed intellectual interest to dull or dry up his delight in the senses. In listing the activities that the woman might otherwise be engaged in, he manifests a wry wit and describes each in a manner that makes it seem unattractive ("liver-spotted," "cage," "raucous," "screed," "unhappy," "bleak") beside the pleasure he proposes. The woman, we may infer, has qualities of mind and imagination similar to his own. He does not need to explain to her the "rosebuds-theme of centuries of verse"; he knows she will understand his references to "Schoenberg's serial technique" and to carrels and old books. He can apparently count on her for an appreciative response to his quiet humor. There is between them a mutuality of mind and taste.   LP

35. *Robert Frost*   After Apple-Picking (page 573)

Let us be clear from the start about one thing. The speaker in this poem has had a richly satisfying experience. He may be "overtired," but it is that good kind of overtiredness that comes when a man has worked hard and long at a task he loves and does well. There may be two or three apples he has overlooked somewhere, but what is that to the thousands he has harvested? No human task is done perfectly. The love he has felt for his task and the care he has put into doing it well are best expressed in lines 30–31: "There were ten thousand thousand fruit to touch, / Cherish in hand, lift down, and not let fall." His love and the care he takes with each apple are beautifully expressed by the grammatical pauses, which slow down the rhythm and divide line 31 into three infinitive phrases, and seem to divide the action itself into separate phases, emphasizing each. His love for the task shines out radiantly from the word "Cherish." His care and concern are indicated by the paradoxical phrase "lift down." His conscientiousness for the quality of his work is further shown by his sending to the cider-apple heap every apple that falls to the ground, no matter how unblemished it appears on the outside. The whole harvesting experience is symbolized by the ladder which, one end planted firmly on earth, points with the other end "Toward heaven." This speaker can find in his work here on earth an almost heavenly joy.

Repetitive labor brings repetitive dreaming. When the speaker tells what form his dreaming is about to take, his dream continues the labor of the day, but on a larger scale: "Magnified apples appear and disappear, / Stem end and blossom end, / And every fleck of russet showing clear." The dream experience blends into the working experience, so that in the lines that follow he is describing both. A rich use of imagery makes the experience vivid and exact: the visual imagery of the magnified apples; the tactile and kinesthetic image in "My instep arch not only keeps the ache, / It keeps the pressure of a ladder-round"; the kinetic image of "I feel the ladder sway as the boughs bend" (where the rhythm makes the line itself sway); the auditory image of "The rumbling sound / Of load on load of apples coming in." These figures of dream experience are one with the work experience. Earlier in the poem we have the olfactory image of "The scent of apples," together with the visual and tactile images of the thin ice skimmed from the drinking trough.

The time of the poem is the end of the day, the end of a season ("Essence of winter sleep is on the night"), and the end of the harvest. These endings, plus the drowsiness of the speaker and the six-times repeated reference to sleep, inevitably invite the reader to read symbolically. The symbolic implication is that sleep after a day's work represents death after a life's work. Four of the six references to sleep come in the last five lines of the poem where the speaker wonders whether his oncoming sleep ("whatever sleep it is") is like the woodchuck's sleep (hibernation) or "just some human sleep." The speaker does not answer the implied question, but insofar as the poem suggests an answer, it is that, if there is a life after death, it will not differ much from the life lived here on earth, perhaps only as much as his dream differs from his waking life. The speaker has fulfilled his life here, and does not need a future life to complete it. The poem does not *say* that; it suggests it.

The phrase "ten thousand thousand" (30) is overstatement. The phrase "just some human sleep" (42) is understatement. At the literal level, the woodchuck's hibernation lasts much longer than man's winter sleep, but the hibernation is a comatose, torpid, dreamless state. Human sleep is shorter, but dream-filled.

This poem is iambic in meter but with irregular line lengths (ranging from six feet in line 1 to one foot in line 32) and with irregular riming: every line in the poem rimes with some other line, but without a fixed pattern. The longest separation of end-rimes is that of *heap* (35) and *sleep* (42), but internal rimes in between help bridge the gap.

The following discussions of this poem are useful: Robert Penn Warren, "Themes of Robert Frost," *The Writer and His Craft: Hopwood Lectures, 1932–1952* (Ann Arbor: U of Michigan P, 1954) 218–33; Reuben A. Brower, *The Poetry of Robert Frost: Constellations of Intention* (New York: Oxford UP, 1964) 23–27; John Robert Doyle, Jr., *The Poetry of Robert Frost: An Analysis* (Johannesburg: Witwaterstrand UP, 1962) 26–31. LP

The subject of the poem is snakes and the (male) speaker's fear of them, and it is vividly rendered through Dickinson's effective use of visual, tactile, and visceral imagery and through her consistently surprising but precise word-choices.

The word "fellow" (twice used for the snake), when contrasted with nature's "people" (17), suggests someone of inferior class and breeding. The adjective "narrow" is exactly right for a snake, but who ever used it to describe one before? "Rides" suggests effortless motion, without legs. But the characteristic of the snake principally emphasized in the first two stanzas is the suddenness of its appearance. (The departure from normal word order in line 4 not only provides an oblique rime for line 2 but gives unusual emphasis to "instant.") One is not aware of the snake's presence until the grass parts unexpectedly at one's feet and one catches a fleeting glance of "A spotted shaft"; then the grass closes again and opens further on, this time without revealing the snake. (The grass is not that of a mown lawn, but the ankle- or calf-deep grass of a field.)

Stanzas 3–4 indicate how alien to man is the snake's habitat and emphasize the suddenness of the snake's *dis*appearance. Though "Occasionally" snakes come out to forage in a field or enjoy the sun, their preferred habitat is the swamp, land too wet and cool for man to use even for agricultural purposes. Yet the speaker "more than once" when "a boy, and barefoot" (thus vulnerable to snakebite) had come across one basking in the sun and, mistaking it for a discarded whip-lash, had stooped to pick it up, when it suddenly "wrinkled" and vanished.

The first two pairs of stanzas indirectly suggest the power of the snake to startle the speaker, whether by sudden appearance or disappearance. The last two stanzas, partly through effective contrast with each other, reveal the snake's power to inspire deep fear in him. With several of "nature's people" (e.g., squirrels, birds) he has struck up an acquaintance, and he feels for them "a transport / Of cordiality." But he has never met "this fellow" (the snake), either by himself or in the company of friends, "Without a tighter breathing / And zero at the bone." The images in the final two lines strike home with the shock of pure terror. "Tighter breathing," with its unexpected adjective, is precisely accurate for that feeling of constriction in the chest that makes it difficult to breathe. And to contrast with "cordiality" (warmth of heart) in stanza 5, we are given—not just a chill, or cold, or even freezing—but "zero" (the lowest point on the centigrade scale), and not at the heart but at the "bone" (cold piled upon cold).

Many students will have difficulty with the image of the "whip-lash / Unbraiding in the sun," the participle suggesting motion to them. But the basking snake is motionless. A whip-lash of braided leather left out in the sun too long will begin to dry out and disintegrate, its thongs loosening and cracking. The snake, with its mottled leather back, has a similar appearance. When the boy stoops to pick up what he thinks is a whip-lash, it suddenly comes to life and hurries off.   LP

37. *Adrienne Rich* Living in Sin (page 575)

The central contrast of the poem is between glamorous expectation and realistic fulfillment. The central emotion is disillusionment. The woman had thought that "Living in Sin" with an artist in his studio would be romantic and picturesque. The phrase "living in sin" suggests (here) the free, unconventional Bohemian life. The word "studio" connotes something appealing, not just a top-story room in a walk-up flat. The sentence in lines 4–7 gives the picture that had arisen in the woman's mind when he had urged her to come live with him. She had not foreseen that the apartment might be dirty, creaky, and bug-infested, with noises in the plumbing— that furniture would have to be dusted, windows cleaned, beds made, and dishes washed—and that her lover would not be romantic all the time. The irony of the situation is that "living in sin" with an artist in his studio proves not much different from marriage to a workingman in a run-down apartment. LP

38. *Robert Hayden* Those Winter Sundays (page 576)

The central images evoke coldness and heat, and are extended into the emotions reported and experienced by the speaker: his sense of cold indifference to his father in contrast to the emotional warmth expressed in the father's loving care, and in contrast to the warmth the speaker feels for his father now.

The father's actions all imply love: even on Sundays, when he need not rise early to work for his family's sustenance, he is the one who undertakes the task of driving coldness from the house. And he goes beyond the necessity of providing warmth, adding the care of his son's appearance (the "good shoes" that need to be polished for church).

The coldness is made especially vivid in the sensory images which describe it— "blueblack" in the pre-dawn darkness, and so solid and brittle that its retreat from the heat causes it to splinter and break. But the physical warmth of the house cannot dispel the emotional chill: the speaker flatly asserts that "No one ever thanked him," and the household continues to suffer from "chronic angers."

The poem moves from past to present time, and from memory to self-castigation, with the repeated lament "What did I know, what did I know." Thoughtless and indifferent childhood gives way before the mature knowledge "of love's austere and lonely offices," and the poem ends in regret and remorse. TRA

39. *William Carlos Williams* The Widow's Lament in Springtime (page 577)

The most striking imagery in the poem occurs in the first five lines, when the widow is expressing her sorrow directly: "new grass / flames" combines (paradoxically) the color and freshness of springtime's first growth with the visual impression of flickering and leaping upward, and the tactile pain of fire. "The cold fire / that closes round me" compacts the paradox into an oxymoron, combining two contradictory tactile sensations with the suffocating sensation of being closed in. After that point in the poem, the imagery is generalized and flat (in imitation of the widow's lack of responsiveness to what had formerly given her excitement through its visual impressions): the abstractly named colors ("white," "yellow," "red"), the indistinguishable "masses" (denoting quantity, connoting heaviness), even the flatly anonymous "some bushes" have little image-making vividness or specificity.

The widow's choice of her "yard" as the symbol of her grief is appropriate: a fenced, protected, nurtured, cherished space, specially arranged and created for its beauty (and in context, a beauty shared with her husband) has become for her a stifling, heavy, depressing enclosure. A yard, as an artificial arrangement of nature, is contrasted to natural meadows, woods, and marsh. Her son's suggestion is also apt: he wants to entice his mother to go out beyond the yard, to move gradually out of her grief. (The gradualness of the process is beautifully imitated in the periodic sentence structure that draws the attention outward through a series of prepositional phrases in lines 21–23.) For the widow, of course, there would only be one virtue in going out there, a place where she could fall downward into the flowering trees and sink into a literally suffocating marsh.

The tense shift in lines 18–19 is purposeful, though not grammatical or even logical. Now, in her grief, the widow can "notice" in the present tense (without her accustomed joyful response to spring), but even this uninvolved act of noticing feels to her like a past moment to be forgotten, not a present event to be experienced. TRA

40. *Gerard Manley Hopkins* **Spring** (page 578)

Hopkins's poem is an Italian sonnet. The octave is descriptive; the sestet makes a religious application. The abstract statement of the first line is made concrete with rich particularized imagery in the rest of the octave, and this richness of imagery is supported throughout the poem by richness of sound—alliteration, assonance, consonance, interior rime, end rime.

In the sestet spring is compared to the Garden of Eden, and this in turn to childhood. The three things thus compared have at least three things in common: (1) they are characterized by abundant beauty, sweetness, and joy; (2) they each occur at the beginning of something—the year, human existence, individual life; (3) they are innocent, free of sin. But the mention of Eden reminds the poet that human beings were thrust out of paradise through the sin of Adam and Eve. He therefore exhorts Christ, the innocent "maid's child," to capture the minds of girls and boys before they too spoil their lives by sinning. The poem is—or ends in—prayer.

The poem is as rich in associational connections as it is in imagery and sound. For example, blue, the color of thrush's eggs, is the color of the sky (and thus of heaven) and is also the Virgin Mary's color, symbolic of purity. White, the color of lambs and pear blossoms, symbolizes innocence, as do lambs themselves, which also have symbolic association with Christ. Thus religious connotations are already implicit in the octave, ready to be activated by the explicit references in the sestet. LP

41. *John Keats* **To Autumn** (page 578)

Opulently rich in imagery, "To Autumn" is also carefully structured. The first stanza deals with the ripening process, the second with harvesting activities, the third with natural sounds. Although each stanza blends various kinds of imagery, each gives prevalence to one kind. The first stanza is dominated by images of fullness and tension, a kinesthetic-organic imagery apparent in such words as "load," "bend," "fill," "swell," "plump," "budding," and "o'er-brimmed." The second stanza places greatest emphasis on visual imagery. The third stanza stresses auditory images, some of them onomatopoetic (*wailful, bleat, whistles, twitter*).

The poem is also structured in time, the three stanzas presenting a progression both in the season of the year and in the time of day. The first stanza presents early autumn: fruit and nuts are coming to ripeness. The second stanza presents mid-autumn: harvesting is in process. The third stanza presents late autumn: the harvest over, stubble-plains remain, and the swallows gather for their migration southward. In parallel movement, the first stanza presents morning: mists are on the fields and the sun is "maturing" (perhaps in the triple sense of climbing the sky, moving toward the winter solstice, and bringing the fruits to maturity). The second stanza presents midday and afternoon: the reaper, overcome by lassitude and the fume of poppies, sleeps on a "half-reaped" furrow, and the worker at the cider press watches "the last oozings hours by hours." The third stanza presents evening: sunset streaks the clouds and touches the stubble-plains "with rosy hue," crickets and birds resume their songs.

This double movement in time toward endings, plus the question asked at the beginning of stanza 3, points to the theme of the poem—Keats's most persistent theme—that of transience. In this poem, however, Keats does not regard transience with the anguish manifested in "Ode on a Grecian Urn" and "Ode to a Nightingale." Autumn (symbolic of the latter part of life) has its beauty (its "music") as well as spring (symbolic of youth); and the images of the third stanza, though touched with melancholy (the day is "soft-dying," the small gnats "mourn," the light wind "lives or dies," the swallows gather to depart), are as lovely as those in the first (when one thinks "warm days will never cease"). The mildness and beauty of the images throughout the poem, the peacefulness especially of those in the third stanza, and the assurance that Autumn has its music too, all reveal a serene acceptance of passing life.

The poem is a sustained apostrophe, addressed to a personified Autumn. Though this personification is most explicit in the second stanza, where Autumn is pictured in various roles as a harvest worker, it is manifested also in the first stanza (where Autumn is "bosom-friend" of the sun, conspires with him, and blesses the vines) and in the third (where it is exhorted not to "Think" of the songs of spring). The sun is also personified, and the fecundity of nature in stanza 1 results apparently from the union of female Autumn and male sun.   LP

POEMS FOR FURTHER READING

Poems 214, 237, 245, 279, 285, 286, 287, 293, and 304 from Part 2 provide additional illustrations of topics presented in this chapter.

CHAPTER FIVE

Figurative Language 1

Simile, Metaphor, Personification, Apostrophe, Metonymy

42. *Frances Cornford* **The Guitarist Tunes Up** (page 581)

The guitarist is compared negatively with a ''lordly conquerer'' and positively to a lover or husband; but, since all three are men, the figurative element in this simile is slight. It is strong, however, in the other half of the comparison—that of a guitar with ''a loved woman.'' Here there is no question of the essential unlikeness of the things compared. (The similarities exist in the curved shape, in the capacity to utter sweet sounds, in responsiveness to the man's touch, and, most of all, in the way they are approached by the man—with ''attentive courtesy.'')

The literal and figurative terms of the simile come together in the pun on the word ''play''—meaning (1) to perform music and (2) to engage in sexual play. **LP**

43. *Robert Francis* **The Hound** (page 581)

The dual possibilities of the ''hound's intent'' are underscored by the poet's craftsmanship each of the three times they are mentioned: (1) The four-syllable word ''Equivocal'' occupies a whole line of the poem. (2) The opposed possibilities in lines 4–5 are given in a riming couplet (the only one in the poem) and by the exact duplication of the meter in the two lines (the only adjacent lines in the poem that match each other exactly). (3) In line 10 the two possibilities are designated by two alliterating monosyllabic nouns (''teeth,'' ''tongue'') naming parts of the dog that serve as metonymies respectively for a hostile or friendly intent.

The basic meter of the poem is iambic dimeter, though only lines 2, 7, and 10 are perfectly regular. All lines rime, but in an irregular pattern. **LP**

44. *Robert Frost* **Bereft** (page 582)

Time: a fall evening. Place: an isolated house with a wooden front porch (in disrepair) on a hillside overlooking a lake. The speaker has opened the front door to inspect the weather. A storm is coming up. The door tugs at his hand. The wind swirls the leaves up against his knee like a striking snake. There are waves breaking in foam and spray against the shore of the usually placid lake.

There is "Something sinister" in the tone of the poem as well as in the sound of the wind. The title, the imagery, the massed rimes all give the poem such ominousness and weight as to overbear any comfort the speaker may hope to give himself in the last two words.

The sounds of the poem reinforce the oppressive tone. Although the poem is sixteen lines long, it uses only five rime sounds, almost only three. Ten lines end in rimes containing long -o- sounds, reinforcing the onomatopoetic *roar* and the desolation of the twice-repeated *alone* (see discussion of phonetic intensives on page 718). Four lines end in rimes with prominent -s- sounds reinforcing the onomatopoetic *hissed*. The two remaining lines end only in an approximate rime (*abroad-God*), further weakening the force of the last line to reassure the speaker or the reader. The onomatopoeia of *hissed* is supported not only by the rimes, but by the repeated *s*-alliterations in the lines following; it is anticipated in the repeated -s- sounds of the lines preceding.

The wind in line 3 would seem to be compared to a wild beast. The "restive" door is personified—as if it had a will of its own. The speaker's "life" (15) is like some habitation he lives in that is larger than his house—but no stronger.   LP

45.   *Emily Dickinson*   It sifts from leaden sieves (page 583)

The subject of "It sifts from leaden sieves" is snow, though nowhere is this subject named. Instead, it is developed through a series of metaphors in which the literal term is represented by the pronoun "it." Most of these are metaphors of the third form in which only the figurative term is named ("alabaster wool," "fleeces," "celestial veil"). In lines 1–2 and 17–18, however, not even the figurative term is named. In 1–2 it is flour; in 17–18 it is some kind of soft white cloth or lace. These are metaphors of the fourth form.

The "leaden sieves" refer to the darkened sky or clouds from which the snow is falling (a metaphor of the third form). But kitchen sieves were ordinarily (during Emily Dickinson's time) tinware; hence another metaphorical process is involved in the substitution of "leaden," with its connotations of heaviness and darkness in the weather, as opposed to the lighter, shinier connotations of tin. "Wool" as a figurative term for snow suggests softness and whiteness, but the introduction of "alabaster" as an adjective brings in an additional comparison, making the snow whiter and giving it a surface crustiness or hardness.

"Face" is an appropriate metaphor for a natural surface (even a dead metaphor in such phrases as "the face of a cliff"), but faces are seldom "even"—so this is a special face, a face compared to something having a smooth, flat surface. "Unbroken forehead" works in a similar way: this is an unwrinkled or unfurrowed forehead. The harvested field of "stump and stack and stem" is metaphorically compared to a room once inhabited (before the harvest) by a personified "summer"

122

but now "empty" (no longer filled with growing grain). The "artisans" are snowflakes, the ghostlike weavers of the fleeces, veils, ruffles, and laces. At the end of the poem the snowflakes stop falling, but their creation—the variegated designs of snow on the ground—remains. LP

46. *Anonymous* **Joy and Temperance** (page 585)

This couplet may be profitably compared with two similar verses: Benjamin Franklin's epigram, "Early to bed and early to rise / Makes a man healthy, wealthy, and wise" (see page 756), and the one quoted in the study question: "An apple a day / Keeps the doctor away." This last is a neatly worded slogan that passes as folk wisdom (or folk medicine), originating sometime in the nineteenth century. Its eight words, dividing in the center (four words in each line), and its simple language and grammatical correctness make it a highly efficient instrument for its purpose—but the purpose is didactic, not poetic, and we should refer to it as verse, not poetry.

Franklin's couplet is chiefly pleasing to the ear. The first line, with its repetition, balance, and opposition in meaning, pleases both mind and ear; the second pleases by its two alliterations (*Makes a man; wealthy, and wise*), but chiefly by the juxtaposition of its two internal double rimes (*healthy, wealthy*), which slide so gracefully into the completion of the second alliteration.

These two epigrams are literal; "Joy and Temperance" is figurative all the way. The three capitalized nouns in line 1 are personified abstractions. Slamming the door in line 2 is equivalent to never needing to visit the doctor nor be visited by him. The doctor's nose is any aspect of his welfare: his income, his bank account, his feelings, or any loss he may incur as a result of not enjoying the patronage of the healthy inhabitants of his town.

Do we need to be told which of the three epigrams is truest in its content? LP

47. *Anonymous* **Western Wind** (page 585)

"Western Wind" is the oldest lyric poem in this book. Only the two ballads (narratives) "The Two Ravens" and "Edward" may possibly be older. Moreover, we have no authoritative source for this poem. It did not appear in print until 1792, when Joseph Ritson published it in a collection called *Ancient Songs*. We are not told how ancient, but scholars have estimated, on the basis of its language, spelling, and style, and the dating of the other songs in Ritson's collection, that it was probably composed from two to three hundred years before its publication.

The sole manuscript version of the poem was found by Ritson in a collection of papers in the British Museum. It accompanies a musical notation of the song. The four lines of verse, unpunctuated, look like this:

Westron wynde when wyll thow blow
the smalle rayne downe can rayne
Cryst yf my love were in my Armys
And I yn my bed A gayne

This brief history—for which I am chiefly indebted to John Frederick Nims in *The Harper Anthology of Poetry* (New York: Harper, 1981)—will illustrate some of the difficulties scholars and critics have in transcribing and interpreting poetic texts. Modern scholars have disagreed radically on the interpretation of this lyric; but no matter how widely they disagree, they all esteem it as a poem of extraordinary power and intensity.

First, let me give my own sense of the poem, and then comment briefly on other interpretations. The speaker is and has too long been far from home and apart from his beloved (young wife or sweetheart). He pleads with the west wind to bring the "small rain" (gentle showers) needed for crops and flowers. (Like most other commentators I interpolate an understood "so that" between the first and second lines.) Spring has been late this year; but when it comes, it will release the speaker from his exile, allowing him to return to his home and his beloved. His despair is caused by the unnatural delay of these events.

No explanatory details about the speaker's situation are given. Has he been forced by agricultural failures at home to seek work elsewhere to support his family? Has he been taken as a prisoner of war but promised release with the coming of spring? No account of his circumstances is given, only his response to them. The greatness of the poem rests on its powerful expression of loneliness, longing, and despair.

The relationship between the two halves of the poem is not explanatory or logical, but analogical or symbolical. The two situations parallel each other; the first in a sense symbolizes the second. The earth is suffering drought, and the speaker pleads for the fall of a life-giving rain; the speaker is suffering spiritual drought and longs for the return of a life-giving love. The analogous ideas are of drought and refreshment. The parallelism of the two situations makes an immediate emotional impact and sets vibrating a whole register of suggested interconnections.

The most formidable challenge to this interpretation has been that of linguistic historians who assert that the word "can" did not have the same meaning when the poem was written as it has today. One of them (Richard L. Greene, in a personal letter to me dated 5/29/69) writes: "The meaning of 'can' is 'does.' It is raining now; the lover wants the west wind to come and *dry* the country for him to travel." Another (Richard R. Griffith, quoted in *The Case for Poetry*, 2nd edition, ed. Frederick L. Gwynn et al. (Englewood Cliffs NJ: Prentice, 1965) writes:

The original error . . . lay in misreading *can* as its present-day equivalent, and accepting that the west wind would somehow *enable* it to rain. Our modern word *can* . . . was rarely used until recently without a sentient subject. However, in Middle English *can* is a familiar variant of *gan*, . . . usually meaning simply "did," and this is far more likely to be the intent of the sentence. For the British winter is so notoriously damp and unpleasant that a wish for additional drizzle in the spring could occur only to some improbable farmer-poet. . . . Thus the true meaning of the opening lines is the exact opposite of that usually suggested; the speaker, far from requesting rain, declares that showers—the first token of spring—have already appeared, and longs for the warm breezes and fair weather which should follow. Exactly why the two lovers cannot be together cannot be inferred. . . . Perhaps she is dead. . . . LP

EXERCISE (page 588)

1. Personification and metaphor: day = a man; sky = a blue urn; sunlight = fire. ("Ode")
2. Simile: words = sunbeams.
3. Metonymy: pen = literature or persuasive writing; sword = armed might or armies. (*Richelieu*, 2.2)
4. Metaphor: oaths = straw; human desire or impulse = fire in the blood. (*The Tempest*, 4.1)
5. Metaphor: conventional minds or souls = furnished rooms. (Nothing in a furnished room belongs to or is original with its occupant.) ("The Cambridge ladies . . .")
6. Literal.
7. Metaphor: the desert = a lion. ("Sister Songs," 2)
8. and 9. When asked the difference between these two statements, students usually say that the first expresses certainty, the second possibility. The real difference is that the first is metaphorical, the second is literal; that is, it is literally true that we *may* die tomorrow, but it is literally unlikely that we *shall* die tomorrow. Tomorrow = the day of death; the underlying metaphor is a *lifetime = one day*; and the meaning is "Life is very short; therefore we should enjoy it while we can." The imaginative force that shrinks the span of a lifetime to a single day is destroyed, and the statement rendered drab and prosaic, when this passage is misquoted, as it so often is. "Eat and drink," of course, is somewhat more than literal in both 8 and 9. The sense is "Let us be merry and enjoy ourselves" (we are being urged to drink wine, not water). Eating and drinking may be taken as a symbol, or a metonymy, for living the good life.

48. *Richard Wilbur* **Mind** (page 588)

The first two stanzas extend the comparison of a mind at "purest play" to a bat flying alone in a pitch-dark cave. The meaning is that as a bat, by means of a physical faculty (its ability to emit high sounds and guide itself by their echoes), can fly freely in the darkest enclosure, so the human mind, with its intellectual capacity, can move freely through the darkness it inhabits—presumably, ignorance, the unknown, mental spaces not yet explored and understood. The qualifying phrases in this comparison are significant: this is the mind at *play*, not striving or reasoning or employing its trained thought processes. And this play of the mind is compared to "senseless wit" in the bat, a paradoxical phrase of multiple denotations. "Senseless" denotes both deprived of sensory perception (as a bat is unable to see) and mentally lacking, stupid or meaningless. The word "wit" denotes the power of drawing surprising and amusing connections between ideas, and expressing those ideas in clever language—but it also denotes intelligence, sagacity, and understanding. Putting those four denotative implications together yields a number of witty combinations: stupid intelligence, blind cleverness, unconscious insight, and so forth. A "senseless wit" guides the blind bat, for without the sense of sight it flies perfectly and purposefully in its cave; that same kind of wit guides the human mind in playful flights that move as if instinctively, or unconsciously, into new areas of intelligence and understanding.

What the bat and the mind can *do* with this "senseless wit" is also brilliantly laid out in the pun in line 4: they can avoid destruction (physical for the bat, intellectual for the mind). The mind will draw no false conclusions, nor will its thinking processs cease because of some impenetrable obstacle; the bat will not conclude its flight, nor its life, by colliding with a stone wall.

The last stanza turns to examine and evaluate the simile: has the poet been as witty as a bat in making his comparison? Yes, he answers, but (unlike the bat) the mind also can make mistakes, and some of those mistakes may alter the whole intellectual environment. There is another pun in the "happiest intellection," for *happy* means both delighted or pleased, and lucky or fortunate: the freely playing mind may by good luck come up with new insights that are delightful.   TRA

49.   *Emily Dickinson*   I felt a funeral in my brain (page 589)

A strange, powerful, highly original poem, "I felt a funeral in my brain" is also a difficult one. It describes a funeral and burial service from the point of view of the person who is being buried. But is this funeral literal or metaphorical? If figurative, what is the literal term in the metaphor? If literal, where is the speaker? And why does she report her experience through only one of the traditional five senses—why tell us what she hears but not what she sees, smells, tastes, or touches? It is *not* strange that competent critics have disagreed about a proper reading of this poem.

The description of the funeral service is formal and exact. In stanza 1 the mourners view the body, which has been placed in an open coffin at the front of the church. In stanza 2 the mourners have taken their places in their pews while the preacher conducts the service with Bible readings and observations about the life of the departed. In stanza 3 the pallbearers carry the coffin from the church to the graveyard. In stanza 4 (but beginning with line 12) the dead person hears the church bell tolling for her death. Since they are now outside, the bell's tolling seems to fill the whole of space. Silence itself (personified) has been destroyed, along with the speaker, who has been silent throughout the poem. In stanza 5 the coffin is lowered into the grave.

The poem is confined to auditory imagery because the speaker is confined in her coffin. She cannot see through the coffin lid, and in any case her eyelids have been drawn down over her eyes, so she cannot see even in stanza 1 when the coffin is open. After it has been closed, hearing is the only sense available to her. That she *can* hear is one of those fictions that we must accept on poetic faith.

Is the burial metaphorical or literal? The critical consensus is that it is metaphorical. One interpretation sees the funeral service as a metaphor for spiritual suffering and pain. In the words of William H. Shurr (*The Marriage of Emily Dickinson* [Lexington: UP of Kentucky, 1983] 79), the poem expresses the "mental and nervous exhaustion" Dickinson felt during a crucial period of her life.

The majority of critics, however, read the poem as a metaphor for a mental breakdown—a psychotic episode in the speaker's life. The fact that the "funeral" was felt in the speaker's "brain" (not her soul), that she feels her "sense" breaking through and her "mind" going numb, and especially the climactic assertion that "a plank in reason broke," plunging her rapidly down through successively lower states of irrationality until she finally ceases "knowing"—all point toward the funeral's being a metaphor for a progressive case of insanity. But these two interpretations are really not far apart (the second may be seen as including the first), and we need not spend much time debating them. By any standard or by either interpretation, this is a great poem.   LP

50. *Sylvia Plath*   **Metaphors** (page 590)

The speaker is a pregnant woman. The "loaf" is the growing fetus (an allusion to the common euphemism for pregnancy, "she's got a loaf in the oven"). The "fat purse" is her belly, swollen as if she had eaten a bag of green apples. The "red fruit" (like the "yeasty rising" and the "new-minted" money) is the unborn child; "ivory" refers to its skin, "fine timbers" to its delicate bones. The "train" is pregnancy; the "nine syllables" are the nine months of pregnancy. The poem has nine lines. Each line has nine syllables.   LP

51. *Philip Larkin*   **Toads** (page 590)

Toads are squat, cold-blooded, warty creatures, and, though they can be handled quite harmlessly, their warts do contain a poisonous fluid that oozes out when they are attacked and makes the attacking animal sick. The speaker in this poem, no doubt the poet himself, lugubriously but humorously complains that he is encumbered with *two* toads. The first, specifically identified as work, squats *on* his life, binding him down to a repetitive six-day routine, all for the sake of the weekly or monthly paycheck and an old-age pension. The second toad, left unidentified, squats *in* him, and represents those internal qualities that prevent his throwing over his job and using his wits to live a day-by-day existence, choosing the risky, free life over the safe, unfree one.

Why is the second toad not identified? Because it represents no single nameable quality but a combination of qualities that the speaker himself might find difficult to specify with any exactitude: timidity, prudence, middle-class morality, love of material comforts, perhaps even conscience (though the speaker would be slow to claim this last).

In the final stanza the speaker won't go so far as to say that the first toad embodies the second toad's spiritual truth, but neither does he deny it, and pretty clearly it at least comes close to doing so. That is why he will probably never rid himself of either toad. As so often in Larkin's poetry, the speaker finds himself in a dilemma, caught between alternative choices neither one of which is fully attractive to him.

The poem is remarkable for its use of an expressive colloquial diction that can modulate through the plain, the slangy, and the vulgar (*"Stuff your pension!"*) yet gracefully pun on that vulgarity with an allusion to one of Shakespeare's most exquisite passages—Prospero's speech in *The Tempest* that includes the lines ". . . We are such stuff / As dreams are made on, and our little life / Is rounded with a sleep."

The phrasing "Lots of folk . . . Lots of folk" (*not* "Lots of folk . . . These folk") seems to indicate that the people mentioned in stanza 3 are not quite the same as those mentioned in stanzas 4–5. Those in stanza 3 "live on their wits" and probably make a fair go of it, perhaps even blarneying their way to fame or the girl or the money, if not all three. "Lecturers" seldom "live up lanes." The people in stanzas 4–5 are paupers, still they don't actually starve, and the toad *work* doesn't squat on their lives.   LP

52.   *John Donne*   A Valediction: Forbidding Mourning (page 592)

Izaak Walton, Donne's first biographer, tells us that Donne wrote this poem to his wife and gave it to her before leaving on an embassy to the French court, a project that would separate them for two months. His wife, who was with child at the time, had been reluctant to let him go, as she feared some ill during his absence.

Without this biographical information, however, we can know that the speaker in the poem is not dying. In the famous simile that concludes the poem, it is the traveling foot that "comes home" to the fixed foot, not the fixed foot that follows after the traveling foot to join it in some other place (such as heaven). Students often get the wrong notion of this poem, partly because of the title, partly because of the death-image in the first stanza. It should be pointed out to them that the dying "virtuous men" in this stanza belong to the figurative part of a simile, not to the literal referent. The sense is "Let us part from each other as silently and imperceptibly as a dying virtuous man parts from his soul."

The love of the true lovers (members of the "priesthood") is a love of souls and minds rather than primarily of senses; therefore they can never be truly parted, and they do not "carry on" (like "lay" lovers) when they are physically separated. Donne has skillfully managed his meter so as to force an equal accent on both

syllables of "absence" (15), thus bringing out the pun. Absence, for the "laity," is literally *ab + sense*: to be away from sense, to be separated from "eyes, lips, and hands."

Three similes compare the parting of true lovers to the parting of virtuous men from life, to the expansion of gold beaten into gold leaf, and to the separation of the legs of a pair of drawing compasses. A metaphor compares it to the almost imperceptible "trepidation" (trembling) of the spheres (as contrasted to the gross movements of the earth—flood, tempest, and earthquake). LP

53. *Andrew Marvell* **To His Coy Mistress** (page 593)

Perhaps the greatest obstacle to student understanding of this poem is its title. The word "Mistress" has none of its most common modern meanings: the "lady" (2, 19) of the poem is, in fact, a virgin (28). Also, the word "coy" means no more than "modest" or "reluctant," without its usual modern connotations of teasing or playing hard-to-get. The lady is reluctant to accede to her lover's pleas because of "honor" (29), which requires that she preserve her virginity until marriage. But the young man is not proposing marriage. In short, this is a seduction poem. It is also a *carpe diem* poem. The speaker belittles the lady's "honor" as of no importance in the face of the brevity of life and the imminence of death. Life being so short, they must enjoy their pleasures NOW! He puts his argument into syllogistic form: (1) *If* we had time enough, your coyness would not be a crime; (2) *but* time rushes on, death comes quickly, and nothing follows; (3) *therefore* we should make love *now*.

The poetic force of the poem derives, not from the cogency of the syllogism, but from the fancy, wit, and imaginative force with which it is presented. First, the speaker elaborates the temporal with a spatial dimension. If they had "world enough, and time" (he says), not only could they stretch out his courtship from "ten years before the Flood" (an immeasurably distant time in the past) till "the conversion of the Jews [to Christianity]" (an inconceivably remote time in the future), but they could pass their time separated by oceans and continents (she looking for rubies along the river Ganges in India; he complaining, in verse or song, of her coldness by the river Humber in England). He could allow his "vegetable love" to grow "Vaster than empires, and more slow." (The phrase "vegetable love," suggesting a love bloodless and unimpassioned, capable only of growth, subtly makes such a prospect seem undesirable.) He could also spend the amount of time praising her beauty that each of its features deserves, and would end up praising her heart (implying that his love for her is more than physical, as he would be glad to demonstrate if he had time). The tone of this first section is fanciful and playful; it is appropriately the longest of the poem's three sections for it depicts a state of nature in which there is no need to hurry.

At line 21 the tone changes dramatically. It becomes urgent. The speaker constantly feels "Time's wingèd chariot" about to overtake him. Time is at his back;

and ahead (after death) he sees nothing but "Deserts of vast eternity" (eternity is a desert, a vast blank, a place without life). In the grave, she will lose her beauty; he will no longer be able to sing her love songs; she will lose her "long-preserved virginity" ("You're going to lose it anyway," the lover implies; "would you rather lose it to me—or the worms?"); her "quaint honor" will turn to dust (the word "quaint" has a slightly deprecatory connotation here, suggesting something without real importance; and a sexual pun buried beneath the word further trivializes the "honor" it is attached to); and, finally, his "lust" will turn to ashes (the speaker is quite frank here in confessing that his desires are physical). This section ends with a wry irony: the grave would seem a perfect place for making love—dark, quiet, private—but, strangely, no one makes love there.

Therefore, says the speaker, let us make love while we are young and eager, desiring and desirable. Let us love, not with a "vegetable love," but like "amorous birds of prey" (fiercely, like hawks or eagles). Let us devour time before time devours us. Rather than remaining as far apart as the Ganges and the Humber, "Let us roll all our strength and all / Our sweetness up into one ball" (a sphere is the most compact concentration of matter) "And tear our pleasures with rough strife / Thorough the iron gates of life." (There is considerable disagreement about the exact reference of the "gates of life" image, but the tone and meaning of the lines are clear enough. The tone is resolute and determined; the meaning is, Let us love, not passively and delicately, but passionately and actively.) Thus, though we cannot make time stand still (we cannot hold back death), we can make it seem to pass very quickly (excitingly, vitally, rather than dully or monotonously).

The poem concerns time more than love. It is perhaps the intensest, most urgent *carpe diem* poem in English. The poet has chosen love-making as a symbol for any activity that involves living intensely. As an argument for seduction, the poem is certainly specious. The lady, by waiting till she can fulfill her desires honorably, may save herself fifty years of misery. Conceived of, more generally, as an argument for spending one's hours in pleasurable, useful, or rewarding activities, the argument has greater force. The person who has to "kill time" out of boredom is a pitiful failure. The speaker is determined to master time rather than let it master him.   LP

54. *Edmund Waller* **Song: Go, lovely rose!** (page 595)

In comparing the qualities of a rose to those of a beautiful young woman, the poet had several options available, as study question 3 suggests. What does he gain from his choice of apostrophe?

In the first place, there is wittiness (an attractive quality in a would-be lover) in the speaker's sending the rose on an errand with messages for the woman. Second, his indirect means of approaching her—for we must assume that she is intended to overhear or read this set of instructions—makes him seem more lighthearted, less drearily self-centered than the traditional rejected lover. He doesn't seem to be pressing so hard when he says to the rose "now *you* tell her what I've been trying to get her to believe." The rose is thus another character who can attest to his sincerity.

The message he is sending begins grumblingly: she has been wasting her time (presumably her time would be better spent with him) and she has been wasting him (presumably causing him to suffer and waste away). But the rose can bear witness to what he has been saying: she *is* as "sweet and fair" as a rose.

His problem with her behavior is delineated in the two middle stanzas—she refuses him access to her, she will not allow him (or other men, he says) to see her graces, she will not permit herself even to be desired or admired. So he draws his moral for her from the rose: concealed beauty is of little worth; it requires the commendation of men to achieve its greatest value.

The tone of the last stanza switches to disappointed spite, as if the woman had made some gesture (or maintained her silence) indicating that his suit has failed again. The rose's last message to her will be embodied in its dying: all rare, sweet, and fair things share a common fate—a brief life. Therefore (he implies), being young and beautiful, she should emerge from her retirement from society and live her short time to its fullest.

Is this tactic likely to work on a reluctant mistress? Who knows? One can only say that the speaker is trying hard not to seem to be trying hard. TRA

55. *Isabella Gardner* **In the Museum** (page 596)

Sardonic denotes scornful derision, biting, mordant, and contemptuous. Can we know what reply this mummy's laughter is making to this bride? Not in detail, of course, but we can surmise that the questions evoke that bitter laugh, that the mummy feels that they are contemptible. That is, the bride's interest is in being loved, understood, cherished and protected, and her fear is of dying young and (perhaps) gracelessly. The questions define a set of values, and the laughter denies their worth. The gesture in the last line is made vivid by the two denotations of "quick": "rapidly," and "alive." It reaffirms the speaker's vitality as a response to the message from the long-dead mummy, and it also reveals the desperateness of needing reassurrance from her husband—she must very quickly reestablish the life in herself. The husband's staring reveals how strange her reaction to this museum specimen seems to him, and perhaps how vehemently she is showing her need.

Of course the mummy neither hears nor laughs. Apostrophe in this poem is employed as a means of revealing the speaker's thoughts and her responses to her thoughts. These are *her* questions as she confronts the disturbing reality of physical decay, and the sardonic laughter is *her* judgment on what those questions mean. Dramatically, she expresses her desires, judges them worthless in the face of death, and yet desperately reasserts their value. (It is probably worth noting, too, that the apostrophe is not uttered aloud, or the husband would have been less dumbstruck by having his hand so suddenly seized.) TRA

131

56. *A. E. Housman* **Loveliest of Trees** (page 596)

"Loveliest of Trees" (*A Shropshire Lad, 2*) is a *carpe diem* poem expressing the philosophy that life is short and that one should therefore enjoy it fully while one can, wasting no moment that might be filled with pleasure. The pleasure proposed in this poem is the enjoyment of beauty, especially of natural beauty, as symbolized by the blossoming cherry tree.

In assuming that the natural life span of man is seventy years, the speaker *alludes* to the Old Testament (Psalms 90:10): "The days of our years are three-score years and ten." The speaker is twenty. Normally one would think of a young man at that age as having ample time left for pleasure and enjoyment. His "only" and "little" therefore come as small shocks of surprise, emphasizing how little fifty years really are for something so wonderful as the enjoyment of nature. This is not verbal irony (for the speaker means what he says), but irony of situation—a discrepancy between what the reader anticipates and what he actually hears.

"Snow" (line 12) is metaphorical, representing the masses of white bloom with which the cherry trees are hung at Eastertide. The critical argument concerning this point is summarized in Laurence Perrine, "Housman's Snow: Literal or Metaphorical?" *CEA Critic* 35 (1972): 26–27.

The speaker is not Housman but a Shropshire lad (for Housman was older than twenty when he wrote this poem), but he undoubtedly speaks *for* Housman, or one aspect of him. This aspect should be contrasted with other aspects, as expressed, for instance, by the speaker in "To an Athlete Dying Young" (page 812).   LP

57. *Donald Hall* **Names of Horses** (page 597)

The length of this poem and its subtle shift to the plural (and to the past as well as the present) are essential parts of the experience it evokes—for 150 years, "Generation on generation," the horse had performed its needed task. Reflecting exact knowledge of farm procedures and farm life, and of the history of rural America, Hall's poem brilliantly expresses the central importance of the horse: it hauled cut wood for heat and cooking, it contributed its strength to the manifold tasks of an agrarian life, it provided locomotion and played its part in the community of small-town farm country. That the apostrophe is in the singular through line 14 at first implies that only one horse is being addressed, but with the shift at line 15, the meaning becomes clearer: the poem is addressed to *the horse*, that generic animal so intimately involved in all aspects of rural America until the advent of the gasoline engine.

Through line 16, the portrait is of an obedient and even cooperative animal that works hard yet seems to take pleasure in the labor (lines 7–8 particularly convey that feeling, with the tirelessness of "All summer," the variety and extent of "meadow and hayfield," the amusing sound of "the mowing machine / clacketing," while overhead the sun appears proud to be a participant in the horse's pageant).

132

But then there is a shift in tone from the admiring portrait to the matter-of-fact necessity of destroying so good a worker when its working days have passed. Tones of regret mingle with the admiration and yield a new kind of love—the love of the enduring, blending natural process to which each horse has succumbed. The fertile droppings of the living horse (6) give way to perpetual fertility as the carcass produces pine trees and yellow blossoms—as the generations have become "soil makers."

The literalness of the language (except for the exalting metaphor of line 8) and the persistence of apostrophe as it shifts from generic particularity to individuals in a repeating sequence give the poem the solemnity of an anthem of praise and regret. The "Names of Horses" that finally emerge as the last line are surprisingly ordinary and typical, a fittingly realistic conclusion. These were not just animals, and they were more than *the horse*: their individuality will be an enduring memory.   TRA

58. *Langston Hughes* **Dream Deferred** (page 598)

Specifically the "Dream Deferred" is that of full and equal participation of blacks with whites in the political and economic freedoms supposedly guaranteed by the Constitution. Metaphors, because more condensed, are (other things being equal) more "explosive" than similes. The metaphorical comparison of black frustration to a bomb (metonymically representing a race riot or even armed revolution) is therefore appropriately placed in the climactic position.   LP

POEMS FOR FURTHER READING

Poems 205, 247, 252, 253, 259, 266, and 292 from Part 2 provide additional illustrations of topics presented in this chapter.

CHAPTER SIX

Figurative Language 2

Symbol, Allegory

59. *Robert Frost* **The Road Not Taken** (page 599)

Since the publication (1970) of the second volume in Lawrance Thompson's three-volume biography of Frost, there have been an increasing number of different interpretations of "The Road Not Taken." These interpretations see the poem principally as an example of dramatic irony rather than of symbol. They are perhaps best summed up in Elaine Barry's discussion (in *Robert Frost* [New York: Ungar, 1973] 12–13) by her statement that "the poem is a gentle parody of the kind of person whose life in the present is distorted by nostalgic regrets for the possibilities of the past, who is less concerned for the road taken than for the 'road not taken.' " The impetus for these interpretations was provided by Thompson's revelation that Frost himself regarded the poem as a gentle spoof of his English friend Edward Thomas and thought of Thomas rather than of himself as the speaker in the poem (*Robert Frost: The Years of Triumph* [New York: Holt, 1970] 87–89, 544–48). After a careful review of the evidence, both external and internal, I find myself unable to accept these ironic interpretations. (I fall back on D. H. Lawrence's adage, "Never trust the artist. Trust the tale"; and I hope sometime, time permitting, to argue the case in an article.) However, the instructor should know of the existence of these other interpretations, and may wish to raise them for discussion in the classroom. LP

60. *Walt Whitman* **A Noiseless Patient Spider** (page 601)

The situation of a man accepting the energies of a spinning spider as an example to himself should recall the famous story of the fourteenth-century Scottish king Robert the Bruce (Robert I), who in apparent defeat retired into a cave for refuge. There he watched the tireless efforts of a spider that despite repeated failure refused to give up spinning; the king resolved to continue in battle—and was victorious. By the nineteenth century this anecdote had become a moral exemplum of the virtue of pertinacity (a narrative version of "If at first you don't succeed, try, try again!").

In its earliest unprinted version this poem had as its theme the poet's sense of loneliness as he searches for love in a world of "fathomless latent souls of love." [See Gay Wilson Allen, *The Solitary Singer* (New York: New York UP, 1967) 342.]

The present version transforms both the moral tale and the earlier unprinted poem, changing the subject to the soul's yearning for spiritual truth. "In measureless oceans of space," the soul seeks security, an "anchor." Despite the traditional symbolism of an anchor as Christ or as the hope for salvation (see Hebrews 6.19), the poem does not openly suggest that Christianity is the answer to the speaker's problem. In fact, a "ductile anchor" attached to a "gossamer thread" suggests fragility and plasticity, rather than the security of a defined, systematic religion.

In Whitman's image, the spider resembles a fisherman, unreeling his lines as he launches them forth. The vocabulary of the poem tends to corroborate an implicit nautical or fishing context: "promontory," "launched," "unreeling," "oceans," "bridge," "anchor." Though the speaker seems not to be consciously aware of it, the imagery itself suggests a Christian solution to his problem—the anchor of Christian salvation, with the speaker's search evoking the church's role as a "fisher of men."

While the poem draws an explicit comparison between the spider's activity and that of the spiritually questing man, there are clearly implied contrasts as well: the contrast of size and perspective (a spider's promontory is indeed "little," and the area of exploration may seem to it to be a "vacant vast surrounding," but the range of "measureless oceans of space" inhabited by man is considerably grander); the spider's patience is in contrast to the "musing, venturing, throwing, seeking" of the man; the noiselessness of the spider may be contrasted to this verbal outpouring from the human being; and of course the spider's actions must be read literally, the man's metaphorically.

The poem should be examined for examples of alliteration, assonance, and consonance, as poetic devices providing a replacement for regular rhythm and rime. Overstatement, particularly in the spatial references, emphasizes the need to recognize contrasts within the overt comparison.   TRA

61.   *William Blake*   The Sick Rose (page 602)

The "night" and the "howling storm" are part of the symbolic design of the poem: they give it depth and resonance and they *may* be assigned a specific meaning. (The "howling storm" is materialism, say a couple of critics, and I have no objection.) In general, however, there is a danger that the student (and sometimes the professional critic), once the powers of symbolism have been discovered, will want to press down all the buttons, to find an equivalent for every noun in the story or poem. At this point, reading the poem becomes an exercise in ingenuity rather than one in understanding and enjoyment. Symbol-hunting is a practice no less bad, perhaps, than moral-hunting. The symbol-hunter tends to restrict rather than expand the meaning of a poem by converting a symbolic story into an allegory. LP

62. *Archibald MacLeish* **You, Andrew Marvell** (page 604)

The implicit metaphor running throughout the poem compares the coming of darkness to the rising of flood waters. The night comes on steadily, without interruption or pause; the absence of punctuation and the repetition of "and" embody that unceasing, uninterrupted movement in the form of the poem. The substitution of suspension periods for a single period at the end indicates that the movement continues beyond the end of the poem. LP

63. *Robert Herrick* **To the Virgins, to Make Much of Time** (page 607)

The rosebuds in the first stanza symbolize pleasures. The general meaning of the poem is to enjoy life while one can, for life is short, and the capacity for enjoyment is progressively and sharply reduced in middle age and old age. The last stanza specifies one kind of pleasure—but an important kind: sexual fulfillment in marriage. The use of "virgins" instead of *maidens* underscores the sexual significance.

The meaning of a symbol, like the meaning of a word, is largely controlled by context. Herrick's rosebuds are generalized by the author's emphasis on the swift passage of time, and by his use of the plural rather than the singular. *Gathering* rosebuds suggests getting as many as possible, and thus the rosebuds suggest a variety of pleasures—including, of course, the pleasure of gathering rosebuds.

"Smiles" (3) personifies the flower that is dying, thus adding poignance to its death and preparing us for the idea that it is the death of persons, not of flowers, that Herrick is really concerned about. "Race" (7) emphasizes swiftness. "Spent" (11) has the connotation of exhausted or wasted, whereas "use" (13) suggests making a profitable or worthy employment of a resource (in this case, time). LP

64. *George Herbert* **Peace** (page 608)

A mental quest in this poem is allegorically treated as a geographical search; that is, the literal question *How can I achieve peace of mind?* is translated into the figurative question *Where does Peace dwell?*

The "reverend good old man" (19) is a clergyman. The word "reverend" is skillfully used to suggest two meanings: worthy of being revered, and belonging to the clergy. His "garden" (37) is the Church. The "prince" (22) is Christ, "the Prince of Peace"; the "twelve stalks of wheat" (28) are the twelve apostles; the "grain" (37) is the Christian gospel. The first three stanzas have the general meaning of "I searched everywhere." But, more specifically, the secret cave suggests solitude; the rainbow, beauty; and the "gallant flower" (the "Crown Imperial"), the royal court.

The simplicity of language and the narrative plainness of this poem are beautifully supportive of its subject matter. The poem convinces us by its very manner

136

(at least while we read) that the good life is to be found in plain living and a simple Christian faith, shared in a Christian community—not in the excitements or adornments of a life at court, or in straining after beauty, or in withdrawing from the world. Seldom is allegory more simple or more appealing. LP

65. *Robert Frost* **Fire and Ice** (page 610)

Scientists have made various predictions about how the world will end, most of them involving either a fiery or an icy terminus. At the time that Frost published this poem (December, 1920), probably the two leading theories were (1) that, as the earth gradually loses momentum in its orbit, it will be drawn by gravity closer and closer to the sun, until finally it plunges into the sun, and (2) that, as the sun gradually cools, or as the interior of the earth itself cools, the earth will get colder and colder, until finally all life is extinguished in a new ice age. Both theories still have many supporters.

Frost makes symbolic use of these theories. Fire becomes a symbol for desire or passion, ice a symbol for hate, the earth a symbol for human or civilized life (''world'' means both physical and social world). The poet has experienced enough of desire and hate within himself to recognize that both passion (e.g., desire for sensual gratifications, possessions, or power) and hate (e.g., between nations, classes, or races) are forces strong enough to bring an end to mankind.

The last line is understatement. Instead of saying that desire or hate could ruin, wipe out, or annihilate mankind, Frost says only that either would ''suffice.'' LP

66. *John Masefield* **Sea-Fever** (page 610)

The theme of this poem is expressed by the desire of a former seaman to return to the life that he had found so exhilarating in the past. The persistence and urgency of this ''call'' are indicated by its repetition. Literally stated three times, once at the beginning of each stanza, it provides an initial refrain that contributes to the poem's musicality. But literal statement is not enough. The poem comes alive through its sharp imagery and spirited meter. The imagery is *visual* (the ''white sail's shaking,'' ''gray mist,'' ''white clouds flying,'' a ''star''); *auditory* (the ''sea-gulls crying,'' the ''wind's song''); and, especially, *tactile* (the ''wheel's kick,'' the ''flung spray,'' the ''blown spume,'' the wind ''like a whetted knife''). Note that not all of the imagery points to pleasant experience: the sharp cold wind is decidedly unpleasant. What draws the speaker to life on the sea is not a sybaritic softness but a recurrent challenge.

The final line of the poem is symbolic. In nautical parlance a ''trick'' is a tour of duty, and all tricks are of equal length. But Masefield's speaker talks of a ''long'' trick, and puts it in a context that also includes ''quiet sleep'' and a ''sweet dream.'' It thus suggests a lifetime followed by some sort of afterlife that the speaker anticipates will be pleasant but does not attempt to define.

137

The meter of the poem is an extremely varied anapestic heptameter. There are seven feet in each line, and anapests are dominant; but the number of substitute feet— iambic and monosyllabic—is extraordinary. The result is a rhythm which, in its richness and variety (combined with end rime and other musical recurrences—e.g., *star-steer; wheel-white; gray mist-gray dawn; day-spray; gull's way-whale's way; sleep-sweet-dream*, plus a secondary refrain in "And all I ask") gives the poem a musicality that is not only appealing in itself but also concordant with the sameness and variableness of the sea. LP

67. *Alfred, Lord Tennyson* **Ulysses** (page 611)

Ulysses represents and recommends a life of continuous intellectual aspiration; he has an avid thirst for life and experience that finds fulfillment primarily in the life of the mind rather than in the life of the senses (his concluding injunction is "To strive, to seek, to find," not "to taste, to touch, to smell"). Geographical exploration in the poem symbolizes intellectual exploration. The key lines for this interpretation are lines 30–32: "And this gray spirit yearning in desire / To follow *knowledge* like a sinking star / Beyond the utmost bound of human *thought*." But throughout the poem are words and phrases that reinforce this reading. In line 5 Ulysses characterizes Ithacans as a savage race that "hoard, and sleep, and feed, and know not me" (that is, a people who live a materialistic and physical life and know not the excitement of the intellectual life). In line 13 he says, "Much have I seen and *known*." In line 46 he addresses his mariners as souls that "have toiled, and wrought, and *thought* with me."

The westward journey has a double symbolism that is also congruent with this reading. In sailing westward (toward the setting sun), Ulysses is sailing toward death (going west is a traditional symbol for death); he is also sailing from what, for the Greeks, was the *known* world (the Mediterranean world) into what was for them the *unknown* world (the world of the Atlantic, beyond the Strait of Gibraltar). The meaning is that Ulysses will continue to seek new knowledge, new discovery, until his death. The continuing nature of this search is also indicated in the images of following knowledge "like a sinking star" (31) and of sailing "beyond the sunset, and the baths / Of all the western stars" (60–61). One cannot, of course, ever catch up with a sinking star or with the setting sun; no matter how far west one sails, they still set beyond a horizon still farther west. Likewise, no matter how much knowledge one gains, there is still further knowledge to be sought. Thus Ulysses's quest is truly one of continuing aspiration: his thirst for new knowledge will never be satisfied; he will continue to seek new knowledge until he dies. What will become of him *after* death, he does not know (62–64), but his program for life before death is clearly mapped out.

The image in lines 18–21 includes the idea of a horizon that is always to be sought, never to be reached—that is, the idea of knowledge that is never to be exhausted. Lines 26–29 tell us that every hour of life brings new experience, new knowledge. (Grammatically, the subject of "is saved" is probably to be construed as "something more," with "A bringer of new things" in apposition and "every hour" treated as an adverbial modifier; but the ambiguity of the construction suggests the wisdom of saving every hour possible from death, of living as long as possible in order to learn new things.) "Thunder" and "sunshine" (48) are symbols for adversity and good fortune. "Hearts" and "foreheads" (49) are metonymies for wills and minds (the meaning is "We confronted the thunder and the sunshine with free wills and free minds"). The poem celebrates strength of will as much as it does the intellectual quest. The metaphor in line 23 compares a person to a sword or a shield.

In recent years "Ulysses" has been the subject of considerable critical controversy, some of it captious, and some oversubtle. Extreme views are presented by E. J. Chaisson in "Tennyson's 'Ulysses'—A Re-Interpretation," *University of Toronto Quarterly* 22 (1954): 402–409, and by Paul F. Baum in *Tennyson Sixty Years After* (Chapel Hill: U of North Carolina P, 1948) 92–95, 299–303. John Pettigrew, in "Tennyson's 'Ulysses': A Reconciliation of Opposites," *Victorian Poetry* 1 (1963): 27–45, gives an overview and seeks to reconcile conflicting viewpoints; and Charles Mitchell, in "The Undying Will of Tennyson's Ulysses," *Victorian Poetry* 2 (1964): 87–95, adds still another point of view. The critical pendulum continues to swing, however; A. Dwight Culler, in his prize-winning book *The Poetry of Tennyson* (New Haven: Yale UP, 1977), presents persuasive evidence for the traditional (and I think correct) interpretation.

The relation of sound to meaning in the poem is discussed on pages 721–23 of the text.   LP

68.   *Alastair Reid*   **Curiosity** (page 613)

In its own sardonic and humorous fashion, this poem has much the same theme as Tennyson's "Ulysses." Cats and dogs symbolize two different kinds of people: cats, the intellectually curious, the adventurous, and the unconventional; dogs, the incurious, the prudent, and the conventional. Though the parallel is not to be pressed too hard, Ulysses is a cat, Telemachus a dog. The poet's sympathies are with cats. (Tennyson regards Telemachus more favorably, however, than Reid regards dogs.)

The poem utilizes two folk sayings: "Curiosity killed the cat" and "Cats have nine lives." The poem says that curiosity is dangerous, but that one cannot really *live* without it. Curiosity leads to suffering and discomfort; nevertheless, it is the condition of being really alive. Intellectual curiosity is the kind in question.

"Death" in line 3 means literal, physical death. "To die" in line 16 means to die intellectually, emotionally, and spiritually; that is, to exist in a merely physical sense, like Tennyson's Ithacans—or like dogs. "To die" in lines 34–35 means "to suffer," and "dying" in lines 41–42 means "suffering." Thus "to die" has exactly opposite meanings in lines 16 and 34–35, and these two opposite meanings, being both figurative, are in turn both opposite to the literal meaning of "death" in line 3. These contradictory meanings are not a sign of the author's confusion, as they would be in a logical treatise or in any discursive prose; they are what give life and interest to the poem. Manifested in metaphor, and resulting in paradox, they help the poet probe the real significance of living. He is firmly in control; he knows what he is doing. LP

69. *Carter Revard* **Discovery of the New World** (page 614)

The title recalls the Eurocentric assumptions of the explorers who reached the western hemisphere and considered that they had "discovered" what no one had known before, despite the presence of human beings already dwelling there. The allegory extends those assumptions into colonial exploitation and the extermination of the original inhabitants for the sake of their conquerors.

The speaker is the commander of an expedition to earth, and he is reporting to his master, who issues proclamations that the natives cannot comprehend. The natives seem gullible, believing that machines ("oxygen absorbers") are either angels or devils. When the speaker reports on their legends and history and compares himself to General Sherman in his treatment of "Indians," the historical allegory is brought into focus.

The coined words (for example, "asterize," derived presumably from *civilize*, thus meaning that the speaker believes it his duty to bring to this planet the culture of the star from which he came) help to achieve the futuristic science-fictional tone of the poem. These colonizers have come with their own jargon, which seems natural speech to them.

So the poem relies on the historical past of North America, from the fifteenth through the nineteenth centuries, to lend credibility to its reference to some distant future of space invaders. But those two poles of past and future are used to express certain recurring and still prevalent attitudes about exploitation, mastery over inferior races, the destined right of some to conquer or destroy. One classic expression of that right was that of John L. O'Sullivan (1813–1895), who wrote of "our manifest destiny to overspread the continent allotted by Providence for the free development of our yearly multiplying millions" (*United States Magazine and Democratic Review* 17 [July–Aug. 1845]: 5). This poem has a satirical purpose, and offers another example of dramatic irony (see Chapter 7). TRA

70. *John Donne* **Hymn to God My God, in My Sickness** (page 616)

Because of the personal reference to lines 28–30, we may not unfairly take Donne himself as the speaker in this poem. In stanza 1 he is preparing his soul ("I tune the instrument") for his entry into heaven, where he will become part of the holy choir that not only furnishes but *is* God's music.

In stanza 2 the dying poet initiates the extended geographical metaphor that governs the poem's four central stanzas—for which the first stanza and the last provide a frame. Lying flat on his sickbed, with his doctors bent over him trying to make a proper diagnosis and prescribe a suitable treatment, he compares himself to a flat map of the earth stretched out on a table with geographers bent over studying it. The explorers of Donne's day were fervently seeking a "Northwest Passage" or strait that would give merchants easier access to the treasures of the Orient. A strait is of course a narrow and difficult passageway connecting two larger bodies of water, and Donne makes it symbolize the confining, difficult fever through which he must pass in moving from this life to eternal life. In these straits, he sees his "west," a natural and traditional symbol for death (because it is there that the sun sets).

He is not afraid of death, however, for he is confident that it is closely followed or accompanied by resurrection. He illustrates this belief by reference to the map. On a flat map (containing, from left to right, eastern Asia, the Americas, Europe, Africa, the Middle East, and central Asia), if you trace a line *westward* from the righthand edge of the map to the lefthand edge, you arrive finally again at eastern Asia or the Orient, at the same meridian from which you started, demonstrating that west and east are one. In the same way, Donne argues, death and resurrection are one.

Illustrating from the map again, he shows that its three principal straits all lead to places that, in one way or another, may be taken as symbols of heaven, the realm of resurrection. The Anyan (Bering) straits lead ultimately to "the eastern riches" (that is, the precious spices of the East Indies); the straits of Magellan lead from the stormy Atlantic Ocean to the peaceful "Pacific Sea"; and the straits of Gibraltar (entered from the Atlantic) lead through the Mediterranean to the Holy City, "Jerusalem." Moreover, the three straits lead to the three continents that were thought, in the medieval period, to constitute the whole world, and that were peopled (according to Christian legend) by the descendents of the three sons of Noah. The whole world and its riches, material and spiritual, in turn are symbols of the glories of heaven. The symbology here is rich and complex and perhaps needs a chart to clarify it:

Anyan Straits — "eastern riches" — Asia — Shem	Riches	Glories
Straits of Magellan — "Pacific Sea" — Africa — Cham	of the	of
Straits of Gibraltar — "Jerusalem"* — Europe — Japhet	world	Heaven

The biblical names in the last line of this fourth stanza provide a transition to the biblical and Christian geography of the fifth stanza. Speculative Christian writers had proposed that the Garden of Eden has been located at the same spot where Jesus was later crucified, thus giving a neat formal design to the Christian story. The place where Adam had sinned by eating the forbidden fruit was the same as that where Christ had redeemed mankind from the eternal consequences of that sin. Christ's "tree" (the cross) stood in the same place as Adam's tree (the tree of the knowledge of good and evil). This identification endorses the identification of the first Adam and the last Adam (Christ).

*Jerusalem, as part of the Mediterranean world and a "center" for Christianity, was probably considered by Donne more European than Asian. It was certainly not oriental.

141

The last eight lines of the poem are a prayer. The first Adam, because of his sin, had been condemned by God to get his bread by the "sweat" of his face (Genesis 3.19); the last Adam (Christ) had redeemed that sin by shedding his blood on the cross. Donne prays that the Lord will find "both Adams" met in him. The anguish of his fever has brought beads of sweat to his brow, and he prays he may be saved by the blood of the Redeemer. "Purple" (a word that in Donne's day applied to any color between modern purple and crimson) was a metonymy or symbol for royalty (being the color of kings' robes), and was also the color of blood (compare "The Flea," page 674, line 20). Thus the poet wishes to be received by the Lord wrapped in Christ's "purple" (the blood of Christ the Redeemer and the robe of Christ the King). He also wishes to exchange the "crown of thorns" that had mockingly been put on Christ at the crucifixion (and which in Donne's case is a symbol of suffering) for Christ's "other crown"—the golden crown that Christ wears enthroned at the right side of God in heaven (and which for Donne is a symbol for salvation). The last three lines identify the speaker as the Dean of St. Paul's, who preached God's "word" to others' souls and now wishes to preach it to his own. As traditionally all sermons elaborate on a biblical text, he appropriately chooses for his sermon to himself a passage from Psalms, roughly paraphrased in the final line. It is an appropriate choice for Donne, for it repeats one of his favorite themes (compare "Batter my heart, three-personed God," page 629).

For a brilliant and much fuller discussion of this poem, see Clay Hunt, *Donne's Poetry: Essays in Literary Analysis* (New Haven: Yale UP, 1954) 96–117. There is also an excellent but shorter discussion in Charles B. Wheeler, *The Design of Poetry* (New York: Norton, 1966) 192–95.   LP

71. *Emily Dickinson* **Our journey had advanced** (page 618)

One critic would prefer to see this poem as "anti-allegory" because it does not rest on a one-to-one system of traditional meanings, and because—as all commentators agree—the experience that it reports must necessarily be incomplete, as the poem cannot define what "Eternity" will be like.

Put another way, the poem allegorizes the progression of human consciousness up to the point of death, from where there is a vision of possibility but no defined forward motion, only the certainty that despite an awe-struck reluctance to proceed, the journey must continue. The "journey" is certainly the progress of a life, the "road" the sequence of life's experiences, and the literal experience of the poem the coming to the brink of mortal consciousness in confronting death. "The forest of the dead" has been most convincingly explained as the cemetery—those marble or stone monuments through which the corpse is borne and the last place through which a still-living human being can peer toward "Eternity."

Some of the imagery is less easily explicated. There seems no clear explanation of the "fork in Being's road," since *fork* denotes branching into two or more directions, but the poem offers no sense of a choice or option, emphasizing instead that there is only going forward on this road—even if the feet are "reluctant," they continue to lead on. The best sense that can be made is that there is a fork in the progress of the human consciousness when it stops following "Being" and moves toward "Eternity." That is, the "odd fork" is an understated metaphor for dying, as if to say "what a curious road I'm now taking" as one dies.

The final image, developed out of a military metaphor, presents an apparent problem with the "white flag" flying over the cities. Since God is "at every gate," one cannot assume that this is a flag of surrender but rather a flag identifying the place. The whiteness then may very well derive from the repeated use of white to describe the garments and the appearance of the angels, the Lamb of God, the elders, the saints, and the gates of pearl of the heavenly city in Revelation. That is, white signals the perfection of eternity, and God manifests himself—in a gesture of greeting, or of menace?—at all the gates to the city.

Among many discussions of this poem, the following are most helpful: Yvor Winters, *In Defense of Reason* (New York: Swallow, 1947) 289–90; Robert Weisbuch, *Emily Dickinson's Poetry* (Chicago: U of Chicago P, 1972) 50–52; Sharon Cameron, *Lyric Time* (Baltimore: Johns Hopkins UP, 1979) 109–112; Douglas Novich Leonard, *Explicator* 41 (Summer 1983): 29; Greg Johnson, *Emily Dickinson: Perception and the Poet's Quest* (University, AL: U of Alabama P, 1985) 183–85.   TRA

72.   *Robert Frost*   **Dust of Snow**   (page 618)

73.   *William Blake*   **Soft Snow**   (page 619)

"Dust of Snow" describes a literal incident, "Soft Snow," an allegorical incident.

"Dust of Snow," except for the muted metaphor in its title, may be taken quite literally. The beauty of the scene (powdery white snow, black crow), the animation provided by the movement of crow and snow, the suggestions of cheeriness and humor (as if the crow were greeting the speaker or playing a sly practical joke on him)—all combine to give a lift to the speaker's heart and to change his mood from one of sorrow, resentment, frustration, or whatever, to one of delight.

Other readers have read this poem rather differently, seeing sinister connotations in "crow," "dust," and "hemlock." I strongly disagree. If one insists on calling the crow a symbol, it is a life symbol, not a death symbol. In two published notes I have attempted to refute what I consider overingenious and mistaken interpretations of the poem, using my own arguments in one and quoting Frost's remarks on the poem in the other. Those wishing to acquaint themselves with both sides of this controversy should consult the following: Edgar H. Knapp, in *Explicator* 28 (Sept. 1969): item 9; Laurence Perrine, in *Explicator* 29 (Mar. 1971): item 61; Norbert Artz, "The Poetry Lesson," *College English* 32 (1971): 740–42; Laurence Perrine, "Dust of Snow Gets in Our Eyes," *College English* 33 (1972): 589–90. Whatever its symbolical implications, the *incident* in the poem may be taken literally.

143

The last line of Blake's poem cannot be interpreted literally, and it forces us to look for a metaphorical or allegorical interpretation of the whole. (I would myself classify "Soft Snow" as allegory—one of the shortest in existence.) The clues to the allegorical meaning are the personification of the snow as "She"; the possible sexual connotations of such words as "soft," "play," "melt," and "prime"; the fact that the speaker doesn't play *in* the snow but *with* the snow, or, rather, the snow plays with *him*, after he has first *asked* it ("her") to play with him; the moral judgment implied by "dreadful crime." The snow (in her prime) is a maiden. The speaker asks her to "play" (amorously) with him. The maiden consents and "melts" (yields her virginity). Conventional society ("winter") calls it a "dreadful crime."

It is clear that Blake takes an unconventional stance. He regards sexual desire and fulfillment as natural and innocent. By identifying society with "winter" he suggests that its judgment is cold and harsh, and by identifying sex with "play" and the melting of snow he implies that society's judgment is not only harsh but absurd. Blake expressed similar unconventional judgments in a number of poems; for example, "The Garden of Love," "Ah! Sun-flower," "Abstinence sows sand," and "The Lilly."   LP

EXERCISES (page 619)

1. a. simile.   b. literal.   c. metaphor.   d. simile.
2. Shaw's "Shut In" explicitly compares the fly to "us," thus symbolizing a series of human actions and attitudes. Shapiro's "The Fly" introduces several figurative comparisons, but its literal subject is a fly.
3. The symbolism of the tiger is discussed on page 260 of this manual. The "lamb" in this poem is faintly symbolic of meekness, weakness, purity. It might rather be considered an example than a symbol. Whatever symbolic force it has in this poem is allusive, derived from its traditional uses; this poem does not create that force. We would call it more literal than symbolic.
4. The following are symbolic: a, b, e, h, j, k, m; the literal poems are the remainder: c, d, f, g, i, l.

POEMS FOR FURTHER READING

Poems 207, 208, 217, 228, 229, 231, 235, 242, 243, 244, 277, 284, 302, and 303 from Part 2 provide additional illustrations of topics presented in this chapter.

CHAPTER SEVEN

Figurative Language 3

Paradox, Overstatement, Understatement, Irony

74. *Emily Dickinson* **Much madness is divinest sense** (page 621)

Emily Dickinson wrote many poems on madness or mental breakdown, incipient, current, and past; and John Cody, a practicing psychiatrist and a highly competent reader of poetry as well, has written an excellent book—*After Great Pain: The Inner Life of Emily Dickinson* (Cambridge: Harvard UP, 1971)—in which he examines these poems. *This* poem, however, quite properly is not one of them, and, quite properly, is not even listed in his index, for the "madness" here belongs to a different category of meaning. This poem is not actually concerned with the examination of neurotic or psychotic states.

The issue in this poem is the individual versus society, or conformity versus nonconformity; its "madness" is a metaphor for nonconforming genius, a nonconformity of self-reliance as advocated and practiced by Emerson and Thoreau. When a true genius appears among us, with ideas and beliefs quite different from our own, society ("the majority") regards him or her as a dangerous lunatic who should be locked up in bedlam and chained to the wall. Years later we may discover that this person, not the majority, was the one who had sensible ideas. The point may perhaps be illustrated by a brief consideration of the careers of Socrates, Jesus, Columbus, Galileo, and Dickinson herself.

The paradox of the poem is resolved when we see that "madness" is here a metaphor. LP

75. *John Donne* **The Sun Rising** (page 622)

Like many other Donne poems in this text, this presents the dramatic situation of a speaker addressing a second party (in this case, the personified sun) from an easily identified place and time: he is in bed, with his love, at break of day. Like "Batter my heart, three-personed God" (page 629), "The Flea" (page 674), and "Song: Go and catch a falling star" (page 800), the poem has a sense of immediacy arising from the speaker's apparent change of heart or mind as he is speaking, so that these poems have the effect of motivating their own conclusions out of the ideas with which they begin.

In the impertinent and colloquial opening lines, the speaker angrily chides the busybody sun for interrupting the lovers. Let him go elsewhere, remind other people for whom punctuality is a necessity (schoolboys, apprentices, courtiers, farmers) that it is time for them to be up and busy. Lovers, he says, are not governed by the sun with his "rags of time"—seasons, hours, days, months; his peeping through their curtains is improper and rude (as rude as is the speaker in addressing the interloper).

While the first stanza insists that this is neither the time nor the place for the sun to intrude, it does acknowledge the sun's power in keeping the world on time. But in the second stanza the speaker denies that the sun's beams do have the power to control mankind: he can shut them out merely by blinking, though he won't do so because that would mean not looking at his love. With a traditional overstated metaphor, he suggests that his love's eyes are so bright that they might blind the sun himself; but if they have not, then the sun should go off on his daily inspection of the world, and return—tomorrow (as he inevitably will)—to report whether the East and West Indies, sources of spices and gold, haven't left their accustomed places to gather into the person of his love, here in the bed. And if the sun in his journey should ask for all the kings of the world, he will be told that they too have left their kingdoms, and are gathered into the person of the speaker.

The third stanza extends the metaphor of the world contracted into the one bed-chamber. The woman is all the nations, the speaker all their rulers—and there is nothing left out there for the sun to shine upon. All those who call themselves princes are imitations, as are their honor and their wealth. Having reduced the world to that point, the speaker then pityingly tells the weary old sun that he can do his job of warming the world merely by shining on the two lovers, as he invites him to do.

Thus the initial attitude, chasing away the powerful sun, changes to welcoming his warmth and attention. What does the speaker really want, then? (And does he, literally, have any choice in the matter?) Most of all he wants his lady to overhear the extravagance of his praise for her and his claims of the importance of their love. The changes in attitude, from chiding the sun to denigrating his power to welcoming him into the chamber, while they are inconsistent, have in common the theme that he and his love are superior to the whole world, to the sun itself. The intellectual playfulness of his dialogue, the wide-ranging references, even the inconsistencies, mean "this woman means more to me than the whole world." The sprightliness of this "overheard" speech might have his lady laughing at his outrageousness, but she could not help being flattered by it.   TRA

76. *Countee Cullen* **Incident** (page 623)

Good poetry may be simple or complex. This poem relates a simple incident simply, in simple stanza form, without elaboration of metaphor or simile. And yet, in twelve lines, it sums up the poignant tragedy of the black experience in America—friendliness rebuffed, the childish hurt that leaves a scar, happiness turned to ashes.

Simple as the poem is, we should not regard it as artless. Notice how the four mouth-filling syllables *Heart-filled, head-filled* in line 2 are counterpointed against the five skipping syllables of *Baltimorean* in line 3. Because the two hyphenated words are jammed with consonants and separated by a comma, and because they spread two metrical accents evenly over four syllables, they take twice as long to pronounce as the five syllables and three accents of *Baltimorean*. The emphasis is appropriate to their emotional importance and gives them the sense of *fullness* required by the meaning. Notice also how the climactic incident of the poem is set off by the rhythm. The other lines of the poem are all to some degree end-stopped; even line 3 is followed by a natural pause. But lines 7 and 8 break in the middle, and line 7 is the one line in the poem that demands that the voice rush on to the next line without pause. Thus the contemptuous action and the contemptuous epithet are isolated by the rhythm. Finally, notice how the significance of the incident is brought home by understatement. We are not told that the speaker's glee was turned to pain, that the contemptuous epithet went through him like a sword or rankled in his consciousness, or that he felt suddenly crushed and humiliated. We are told only: "Of all the things that happened there / That's all that I remember." Need we be told more?

[Reprinted from Laurence Perrine and James M. Reid, 100 *American Poems of the Twentieth Century* (New York: Harcourt, 1966) 190–91.]   LP

77.   *Phyllis McGinley*   The Adversary (page 625)

In this example of verbal irony the word "Relentlessly" (4) matches the title in its negative connotations. Line 2—presenting the mother's kind motive—defines the irony in the first line: what would lead one to think that such kindness needs to be forgiven? The point, of course, is that loving attention, protectiveness, and tolerance can be as annoying or oppressive as the onslaught of an "adversary" whose motive is one's destruction or captivity.   TRA

78.   *William Blake*   The Chimney Sweeper (page 626)

Blake uses dramatic irony here for sympathetic rather than detractive purposes. In line 3 the boy, too young to articulate clearly, is calling out his trade in the streets— sweep, sweep, sweep, sweep—but the poet is telling us that we should weep over his pitiful plight. In lines 7–8 the innocent boy is genuinely trying to comfort his friend and does not recognize, as the poet does, the ironic discrepancy between the comfort he intends and the lack of comfort he actually offers, for not being able to have one's hair soiled is hardly consolation for having it shaved off! In line 24 the boy's words are an expression of a childlike trust that the poet, with more experience of the world, knows to be unfounded: the poem, in fact, is a protest against the harm that society causes its children by exploiting them for labor of this kind. In each case the dramatic irony arises from the poet's knowing more or seeing more than the child does, but in each case also the boy's ignorance testifies to his good heart and likable innocence.

The dream in lines 11–20 is obviously a wish-fulfillment dream, though Blake would not have been familiar with this Freudian terminology. It is also a miniature allegory, capable of two interpretations, one applying to this world, the other to the next. On the first level—most obviously the wish-fulfillment level—the "coffins of black" are the chimneys the boys work in; the Angel who releases them is a wise legislator or rich benefactor (like Oliver Twist's Mr. Brownlow) who releases them from the bondage of their labor with the key of social legislation or of wealth; the green plains represent a happier future. At this level, the dream represents only a wish or a hope. On the second and perhaps more relevant level, the coffins are real coffins and the Angel is one of God's angels who releases the boys into heaven with the key of death. At this level, the poet is saying that the only release for these boys, under the then existing conditions of society, is through death.   LP

79. *Percy Bysshe Shelley* **Ozymandias** (page 628)

The central theme of "Ozymandias" is the vanity of the claims of human tyrants to enduring glory. It is brilliantly conveyed through irony of situation: the overturn of expectation by fulfillment. After reading the inscription on the pedestal, the second line of which may be paraphrased, "Look on my works, ye mighty (but lesser) kings, and despair of ever equaling them," one expects to look up and see a great imperial city with marble palaces, temples, hanging gardens, monuments, and fortified walls; instead, as far as the eye can reach, one sees only emptiness and sand.

Increasing the irony is the fact that the sole remaining work of this self-proclaimed "king of kings" is a huge broken statue (its hugeness manifesting his megalomania), carved by an artist who saw through the self-deluding egocentrism of the ruler and recorded it in stone, mocking Ozymandias, as it were, to his face. In the "frown, / And wrinkled lip, and sneer of cold command," the sculptor knew that his imperceptive and arrogant master would see only the signs of his awesome authority and power whereas the more perceptive viewer would note the absence of joy, wisdom, compassion, and humility—the marks of true greatness—and see only crude ambition and cruel passions. The insight of the artist has outlasted the power of the conqueror.

The emptiness of Ozymandias's pretensions to everlasting fame is further increased by the fact that this whole account has been related to the speaker by "a traveler from an antique land." That is, the speaker would never have heard of Ozymandias at all had it not been for his chance encounter with a desert explorer. (And most of us, in our turn, would never have heard of Ozymandias had the poet Shelley, another artist, not written a poem about the incident.)

No English reader in 1817 could have read this poem without thinking of Napoleon, who had made himself conqueror and ruler of almost all of Europe before he was defeated at Waterloo in 1815 and exiled on the barren island of St. Helena in 1817. In more recent times we may be reminded of Hitler, Mussolini, Stalin, Mao, or Ceauşescu.

Except for the awkwardness caused by the separation of the transitive verb "survive" (7) and its objects "hand" and "heart" (8), the poem is brilliantly written. In "Nothing beside remains" (12), the word "beside" means both "beside" and "besides." The alliterating *b*'s, *l*'s, and *s*'s of the last two lines put a heavy emphasis on the words that re-create the vast level emptiness, and the final unstopped vowel sound allows the voice to trail off into infinity.

Two pitfalls for the student: (1) The "hand" that mocked the passions of Ozymandias is the sculptor's; the "heart" that fed those passions was Ozymandias's. The passions depicted in the stone visage have outlasted both the artist and the tyrant. (2) The words on the pedestal were not composed by the sculptor. Ozymandias commanded the sculptor to inscribe them there. The sculptor "mocked" Ozymandias by his frank portrayal of the ruler's character in the sculptured visage. LP

EXERCISE (page 629)

1. Paradox.　2. Irony.　3. Overstatement.　4. Understatement.
5. Paradox.　6. Overstatement.　7. Paradox ("immortal" is ironic).
8. Paradox.　9. Paradox.

ADDITIONAL EXERCISE

Follow the instructions for the exercise on page 629, of which this is a continuation.

10. Whoe'er their crimes for interest only quit,
　　　Sin on in virtue, and good deeds *commit.*　　　*Edward Young*

11. No doubt but ye are the people, and wisdom shall die with you.
　　　　　　　　　　　　　　　　　　　　　Book of Job, 12.1

12. One soul was ours, one mind, one heart devoted,
　　　That, wisely doting, asked not why it doted.　　　*Hartley Coleridge*

13. Give me my Romeo: and, when he shall die,
　　　Take him and cut him out in little stars,
　　　And he will make the face of heaven so fine
　　　That all the world will be in love with night,
　　　And pay no worship to the garish sun.　　　*Juliet, in Shakespeare*

14. Have not the Indians been kindly and justly treated? Have not the temporal things, the vain baubles and filthy lucre of this world, which were too apt to engage their worldly and selfish thoughts, been benevolently taken from them? And have they not instead thereof, been taught to set their affections on things above?　　　*Washington Irving*

15. There lives more faith in honest doubt,
　　　Believe me, than in half the creeds.　　　*Alfred, Lord Tennyson*

10. Paradox.   11. Irony.   12. Paradox.   13. Overstatement (containing also metaphor and personification).   14. Irony.   15. Paradox.

80. *John Donne* **Batter my heart, three-personed God** (page 629)

In the first quatrain Donne metaphorically compares God to a tinker who is trying to mend a metal utensil such as a kettle. Donne (the kettle) cries out to God that he needs to be made anew, not just repaired. It is not enough for God to "knock, breathe, shine," He must "break, blow, burn," and batter. The parallel series of verbs reflect the three persons of the Trinity. The verbs "knock" and "break" belong to the Father (representing Power); "breathe" and "blow" belong to the Holy Spirit (the word *spirit* comes originally from a Latin word meaning "to breathe"; cf. *respiration*); "shine" and "burn" belong to the Son, a concealed pun on *sun*.

In the second quatrain Donne compares himself to a town "due" to God but "usurped" by Satan (or sin), who has taken captive God's viceroy, Reason.

The "enemy" (10) again is Satan (or sin).   LP

81. *Elisavietta Ritchie* **Sorting Laundry** (page 630)

The opening stanza metaphorically links the "you" of the poem to clothes and other laundry. The word "Folding" literally describes the speaker's handling of the laundry, and figuratively implies the loving actions that she has performed in making this man part of her life (including the ordinary domestic actions she is now engaged in, which also give her pleasure).

The catalogue of laundry that must be folded (stanzas 2–9) is witty and self-assured. The seams of their pillowcases are strong enough not only to preserve the cases for their ordinary use, but metaphorically also strong enough to preserve the dreams of the people who slept on them. The gaudy towels, bought on an impulse and not in keeping with the style of the household, refuse "to bleach into respectability." Shirts, skirts, and pants, as they go through the cycles of the washing machine, are *re*cycled and recapitulate themselves. Socks that went into the machine two-by-two, like the beasts entering the ark, come out "uncoupled."

The poem turns at line 28 to a different kind of catalogue: objects that have neglectfully been put into the washer (a comment perhaps on the two people who aren't overly fastidious in cleaning out their pockets). The list is again of ordinary objects, until it reaches lines 39–40: "broken necklace of good gold / you brought from Kuwait." This token of love, a gift brought back to her from his distant travel to the wealthiest part of the Middle East, raises other associations for her—in particular, she notices "the strangely tailored shirt / left [behind] by a former lover" of hers (41–42). There may be a small drama in these two articles—perhaps the gold necklace was a courting gift, perhaps it tipped the balance in his favor and led her to dispense with her former lover.

(Because of events that have taken place since this poem was written—the invasion and spoliation of Kuwait by Iraq and the liberation of it by U.S. and allied forces—it will probably be necessary to remind students of what Kuwait represented before the events of 1990–1991: a luxurious, oil-rich kingdom busy with foreign businessmen. It is to *this* Kuwait and what a gold necklace from there would call to mind that the poem makes reference.)

In any case, the rather tidily separated catalogues (first laundry, and then found objects) are mixed together in this stanza, and what follows is a surprising leap. A lover's gift and a recollection of a love affair broken off lead the speaker to the fearful thought: "If you were to leave me" (43). The consequence of such desertion would be shattering loneliness, expressed in a return to the opening metaphor. Folding clothes for two of them was an expression of her love; folding only her own clothes would leave a void so great that "a mountain of unsorted wash / could not fill / the empty side of the [king-sized] bed" (49–51).

The many references to pieces of laundry prepare the reader for the overstatement of the "mountain" of washing, as in its way does the reference to the former lover's shirt. This household is full of clothes and household items and everyday objects, including things that need discarding and clothes left behind by others. Like the constant use of plurals in naming things, less obtrusive overstatements earlier in the poem prepare for the "mountain": "giants" (6), "so many" (7, 16), "All" (19), "Myriad" (22), and "maelstrom" (37). The grammatical structure also contributes to this sense of fullness, as the lists are presented in noun phrases rather than complete sentences. Yet the speaker can be witty about them and enjoy her housekeeping, as long as she can keep her love with her. Her insight into how important her love is to her is the result of her "sorting," not only laundry but her life.

The linking of domestic chores with a lasting, loving relationship may be contrasted with what Judith Wright displays in her "Portrait" of a marriage (page 859)—studies in satisfaction and dissatisfaction.   TRA

82.   *Philip Schultz* **I'm Not Complaining** (page 631)

Among the many understatements in this poem are the following: "who's perfectly happy" (5), "no one ever said city life was easy" (9), "anxiety is good for weight-loss" (12), "almost everyone is insulted daily" (16), "I'm basically / almost happy" (25–26), and of course the title and last line, "I'm really not complaining" (27). What these all understate is the speaker's sense of the miseries and sorrows of life in a modern city—specifically, New York, as identified by line 2.

151

The poem presents an interesting use of dramatic irony. Through his repeated understatement that things are not so bad as they seem, the speaker attempts to deny that he is feeling beleaguered. The portrait is of a pathetic victim desperately trying to convince himself and whoever else might be listening that his situation is no worse than anyone else's, lest he find himself wallowing in self-pity and complaints.

The trite language of the poem implies the widespread nature of the problems he is suffering—these are ready-made phrases implying that many have felt the same thing. They also introduce the possibility that the speaker's feelings are partially derived from the verbal commonplaces, that he has learned to feel what everyone else is complaining about. There is a sense of community created where "almost everyone is insulted daily."

The run-on sentences and use of ampersand create the impression of rushing as the whole catalogue of ills comes tumbling forth.   TRA

83. *W. H. Auden*   The Unknown Citizen (page 632)

The title alludes to the "Unknown Soldier." It is ironic because *everything* is known about the "unknown" citizen—except, apparently, his name. The information about him is filed under a code number. The citizen has been reduced to a set of statistics. The loss of his name symbolizes the loss of his individuality. The unknown soldier's *body* had been blown to bits; the unknown citizen's *soul* has been blown to bits.

In the old sense, a "saint" (4) was a person who served God. In the "modern" sense, he is a person who serves "the Greater Community." The old-fashioned saints, to serve God, often had to defy the world—and in doing so, they found their souls. The modern saint, to serve "the Greater Community," must only do everything he is told to do—and in so doing, he loses his soul. The things "necessary to the Modern Man" are purely materialistic things—"A phonograph, a radio, a car and a frigidaire"—and they are "necessary" not mainly to serve the man but to keep the economy going. The unknown citizen had no opinions of his own but adopted those of the State—that is, he accepted State propaganda. He "never interfered" with the education of his children: what his children really received was indoctrination, not education, and the unknown citizen never questioned the rightness of what his children were taught.

For Auden himself the questions "Was he free? Was he happy?" are the important questions, not absurd ones, and in his eyes *everything* was wrong. The answers to the questions are that the unknown citizen was *not* free, though he never realized his lack of freedom, and that he was neither happy nor unhappy, for it takes a *man*, with a soul, to be happy or unhappy—and to be a man, one must be free, at least in his soul. The unknown citizen did not live; he existed. He was not a man but a statistic, a comfortable conformist, a pliant tool in the hands of the State.

The satire in the poem is against several tendencies of modern life: its increasing demands for conformity, uniformity, and collectivization; its materialism; and its disposition to do everything by statistics, to exalt the "average," and to put life into the hands of social scientists and managers. The old-fashioned saint was an extraordinary man; the modern one is an average man—if he can be called a man.

Be sure to ask students, "*Was* he free? *Was* he happy?" LP

84. *Robert Frost* **Departmental** (page 633)

The poem is a gentle satire—not against mankind or human nature—but against the increasingly departmentalized structure of the modern bureaucratic state, in which all human functions and needs are provided for by the state, with a resultant depersonalization of human relationships, specialization of human interests, and loss of individuality.

The satire is gentle because it is comic, and it is comic partly because the society actually observed is an ant society (we can be amused by behavior in ants that would be unamusing to us in human beings) and partly because of Frost's comic treatment (playful riming, humorous personifications, constant flow of whimsy). But this ant society is symbolic of modern human societies.

"Ants are a curious race" (13): this generalization coming at the conclusion of the first example of ant behavior (the discovery by an ant of a huge dormant moth) and serving as introduction to the second illustration (the discovery of a dead ant by another member of the colony), is literally true in one sense of the word "curious"; but, ironically, what is curious about them is that, in another sense, they are an extremely incurious race: they have no curiosity about matters unrelated to their own assigned duties in the colony. The ant who discovered the moth "showed not the least surprise. / His business wasn't with such." The ant who discovers his dead fellow isn't "given a moment's arrest— / Seems not even impressed." But both ants pass the word along to the proper authorities, and the second illustration concludes with a "solemn mortician" heaving the dead ant "high in air" and carrying him away. "No one stands round to stare. / It is nobody else's affair." It is not that ants are apathetic or lazy (each is extremely busy pursuing his own assignment, and the whole society seems to function fairly efficiently); it is just that they are so extremely specialized. (No provision is made for grief, wonder, or personal relationships in the efficiently organized bureaucracy.) Nor is it that ants are selfish or self-centered. The adjective "selfless" (24) implies just the opposite: they devote their whole energies to serving the welfare of the colony (the "Greater Community" of Auden's poem), but in doing so, they have become selfless in another sense: lacking selfhood. To shift metaphors violently, they are cogs in a machine.

The poem begins with the poet's having just observed the behavior of an ant on his dining table. (The interest shown by the poet in the much smaller ant contrasts with the lack of interest shown by the ant in the much larger moth.) This observation leads him to ruminate about ants in general, and to provide a second illustration of their behavior from past observations. The whimsy in the first observation about "the hive's enquiry squad / Whose work is to find out God / And the nature of

153

time and space'' is perhaps a thrust at the departmentalized university. The whimsy in the second illustration about the state burial is clearly aimed at the bureaucratic nation-state. For further discussion, see John Robert Doyle, Jr., *The Poetry of Robert Frost: An Analysis* (Johannesburg: Witwatersrand UP, 1962) 92–99. LP

85. *Randall Jarrell* The State (page 635)

The paradox in line 18—''I'm dead, and I want to die''—accounts for the strange tone of the poem. The speaker has become emotionally dead (the first phrase is thus figurative), and wants therefore to die, literally. Robbed of all he loved and no longer able to rationalize the losses or restrain his grief over them, he finds nothing to live for. The tone is eerily out of proportion, reflecting a mad or hallucinatory attempt to find what is normal or *right* in the apparently insane actions of ''the State.'' The understatement that finds reasons for the execution of his mother (''she was crazy,'' and beside that her appetite was huge) and a salubrious justification for his sister's being drafted suppresses the normal response to such events, and at the same time the speaker overstates the benefits that these sacrifices bring.

Perhaps strangest of all, it is the loss of his cat, for which he cannot find a consoling rationale, that tips the speaker into despair. The distorted perspective comes into focus, finally: here is an ironic portrait of a man whose emotions can be held in check when the losses are greatest, and who breaks down for the slightest of his sacrifices. *His* sacrifices, of course, are the subject—the poem twice returns to how *he* feels at finding one less person ''sitting there'' where he is accustomed to seeing them, and shows him taking credit to himself for ''helping to win the War'' when his sister is drafted.

The chief difference between Jarrell's satire of the actions of ''the State'' and Auden's and Frost's (''The Unknown Citizen'' and ''Departmental,'' pages 632 and 633) is in the personality or mental state of the speaker. Auden's functionary is fully committed to all the standards and norms of his impersonal bureaucratic nation—he is the butt of the satire in his acceptance of those ideals; Frost's observer is detached and amused at the hyperspecialization of a modern nation; but Jarrell's victim of state policies has been driven over the edge into dementia: he has exhausted his means of approving the actions of the State, and falls into self-absorbed depression and despair.

This ''mad song'' is supported well by its formal arrangement, anapestic tetrameter that sings its way through some of its craziest statements, attempting to lighten their burden:

And she died, after all, in her way, for the State,

and at other moments using the same meter for anguish:

And I cried, and I cried, and I want-ed to die.

154

Jarrell achieves a conversational rhythm as well in the same unlikely meter:

When the neigh- ˘ bors came ˘ in, ˘ as they did, ˘ with my meals. ˘

The rimes are also slightly eccentric and mad. The six-line stanzas rime thus: *xxaabb xababb xaaaaa*, with exact rimes in the first stanza, approximate rimes in the second, and an improbable mixture of identical and approximate rimes in the third (*-ply, mice, die, life, die*).

The theme is a harrowing one: the pressure of seeking normal and rational explanations for arbitrary and irrational state actions can produce insanity.　TRA

86.　*M. Carl Holman*　**Mr. Z**　(page 635)

M. Carl Holman was a black poet, and "Mr. Z" is the ironic portrait of a black man who attains distinction in life by disowning his own racial and cultural heritage and adapting himself to the manners and values of the white world. He is apparently light-skinned, for he is able to do this quite successfully, and he marries a white woman who, out of a similar motivation, has disowned her Jewish heritage and is adapting herself to the manners and values of the gentile world. The marriage is a marriage of convenience for both of them, for through the marriage, they are both enabled to shake off some of the social stigma of their own backgrounds. There is also the suggestion that neither of them could have acquired a purely white gentile mate of respectable social pretensions: they have had to settle for the second best, which is nevertheless better, in their eyes, than marriage within their own cultures.

In giving Mr. Z only an initial, not a name, the poet suggests that Mr. Z has lost personal identity by disclaiming racial identity. In choosing the last letter of the alphabet for that initial, the poet suggests his own low opinion of Mr. Z. The satire of the poem is directed mainly at Mr. Z and the type of person he represents. But the satire also hits, secondarily, at the snob values of a WASP society that make people like Mr. Z and his wife possible. Mr. Z is clearly a person of considerable ability, and in a healthy society he could have remained himself and still have acquired the kind of recognition he needed.

The obituary notices cruelly reflect the false values of this society by making Mr. Z's distinction relative, not absolute. There is subtle though probably unconscious condescension in the statement that Mr. Z was " 'One of the most distinguished members of his race.' " (Implication: He did pretty well for a black person. Further implication: Blacks are inferior.) But the obituary notices are particularly cruel for Mrs. Z, for they implicitly reveal the fact that she and Mr. Z had labored all their lives to conceal. This is irony of situation.

There is muted irony throughout the poem: "perfect part of honor" (2), "Faced up" (7), "exemplary" (9), "profane" (10), "right" (17), "Not one false note" (23). The first ironic note is in the first line, and it might be labeled either verbal or dramatic. The reader realizes, as Mr. Z's "teachers" and Mr. Z do not, that an accident of birth cannot possibly be a "sign of error." (One infers, incidentally, that Mr. Z was lighter skinned than his mother, and that his father may have been white.) LP

87. *Sterling A. Brown* **Southern Cop** (page 636)

Brown's poem is a stinging indictment against racial prejudice, showing how it reduces black men and women to the status of creatures who may be shot dead just because they are running. But it has enough compassion in it, and enough wisdom, to show that whites are also the victims of such prejudice. It proceeds chiefly by means of irony and understatement. Perhaps the most obviously ironical lines in the poem are 7–8 ("The Negro must have been dangerous, / Because he ran"); the most obvious understatement is found in lines 15–16 ("And all we can say for the Negro is / It was unfortunate").

The first lines of the four stanzas, though parallel in form, carry different degrees of irony. The most ironical is that beginning stanza 3. Ty's behavior is in no way to be condoned, let alone approved. The least ironical is that beginning stanza 2. This stanza examines the psychology behind the shooting, and though that psychology is irrational, it is understandable. Verbally, no irony at all may be intended in the first line of stanza 4, for Ty is surely to be pitied, both for his simple-mindedness and for the ordeal of having to suffer the consequences of his mistake; but the situation makes the line ironical, for the dying Negro and those who loved him are the ones most truly deserving of pity. There is also irony in the contrast between Ty's having all the power ("his big gun smoking") and his being psychologically defenseless ("Rabbit-scared"). The irony of the opening line must be weighed in a delicate balance. It is Christian to forgive, and it has been said that "to understand all is to forgive all," but full forgiveness for the brutal exercise of power is humanly difficult (perhaps only God is capable of it), and one doubts that the speaker is in a wholly forgiving mood. His use of irony elsewhere argues against it.

Sterling A. Brown is a black poet. Whether the irony is verbal or dramatic depends on whether one takes the speaker to be the poet or someone quite different from the poet—say, a prejudiced white who truly believes what he says: that Ty's behavior should be condoned and perhaps even rewarded. The evidence supports the first supposition. No real sense of a separate speaker is created by the poem, and if we try to suppose one, we find ourselves involved in contradictions. A white bigot would refer to Ty's victim as a nigger, not a Negro; and the insensitivity of bigotry is difficult to reconcile with the speaker's obvious sensitivity to human behavior. These inconsistencies disappear if we take the speaker to be the poet himself, using verbal irony incisively and skillfully and with varying degrees of weight, able to see the situation both from the black man's point of view and the white man's, but clearly and justifiably angered over the black man's victimization by the racial attitudes that molded Ty Kendricks. LP

The verbal irony is in the first phrase, "Treason doth never prosper," since the poem proceeds to explain what happens if it *does* prosper. One might also find situational irony in the final phrase, since it indicates an outcome contrary to truth or fact: that treason must be called by another name if it succeeds, even though it remains by definition what it is. This final phrase puts irony to the service of satire, pointing an accusing finger at those who for the sake of expedience (or out of fear) will avoid stating the truth.

The word "prosper" is the only equivocal term in the epigram, because it carries with it two relevant meanings—to succeed in an endeavor and to achieve wealth. One might conceive of a successful act of treason that does not bring with it wealth—that of the Minutemen in the American Revolution, for example, who were traitors to the British crown not for personal gain but for an idealistic goal. Harington's epigram, because of the ambiguities of "prosper," seems clearly to suggest a self-interested treason, perhaps the venality of an ambitious usurper.

Harington's wit thus plays with two aspects of language—the ambiguities that allow a single word to radiate meanings and connotations, thus enlarging its application; and the dicta of the powerful, who may suppress the use of a word, thus diminishing its ability to present truth, so that political success determines linguistic limits.   TRA

89. *John Hall Wheelock* **Earth** (page 637)

The Martian astronomer has just witnessed the destruction of the planet Earth by a nuclear bomb. The adverb "drily" is the clue that reveals the Martian astronomer's judgment of humankind as foolish rather than wise. It *does* take a high order of intelligence to create an atom bomb, but it requires an even higher degree of unintelligence to use it. Humankind is brainy but lacking in wisdom.   LP

90. *Robert Browning* **My Last Duchess** (page 638)

Speaker: The Duke of Ferrara. Time: Late Italian Renaissance, probably mid-sixteenth century. Place: An upper room or corridor in the Duke's palace. Audience: An envoy from the Count whose daughter the Duke plans to marry. Occasion: The Duke and the Count's emissary have just concluded negotiations over the terms of the marriage and the dowry that the Duke expects to receive with his bride. (Students need to know that a duke of Ferrara was a supremely powerful figure, equal in status to a king.) On their way to join the company of guests and courtiers in the assembly hall below, they pass a portrait of the Duke's former Duchess, and the Duke pauses to display it for the emissary, engaging him now in what seems purely social talk.

The primary subject of the poem is the character of the Duke, but Browning is interested in his character also as it reflects his period in history (the pride and arrogance of the aristocracy, its system of arranged marriages, its enthusiasm for art and artists). A secondary and pendant point of interest lies in the character of the Duchess.

The Duke is characterized, first, by pride—pride of birth and station. He is a duke—let no one forget it!—and one with a "nine-hundred-years-old name"! His dissatisfaction with his former wife (but he refers to her always as his "Duchess") is that she forgot it. Instead of being lofty and reserved like himself, saving her smile only for him, thus enhancing the eminence of his station, she treated social inferiors as equals, blushed when they complimented her, was too visibly pleased when they did her favors. She did not comport herself like a duchess! And why didn't he try to correct her? Because to have done so would have been to "stoop." Even if she had accepted his tutelage without making excuses or arguing back (the ultimate humiliation)—"E'en then would be some stooping; and I choose / Never to stoop." A proud purchaser doesn't haggle over defects in the merchandise; he simply sends it back and demands replacement.

Second, the Duke is cruel. Were it not for the "stooping," the Duke would not hesitate to tell his wife "this . . . in you disgusts me." But since he wouldn't stoop, he "gave commands; / Then all smiles stopped together." What were the commands? Browning doesn't tell us, and doesn't need to, for the very tone in which the words are uttered sufficiently underlines the Duke's cruelty and arrogance. But probably they were to have the Duchess put to death. In the opening lines, "That's my last Duchess painted on the wall, / Looking as if she were alive," the subjunctive mood implies that she is no longer living—a suggestion repeated in line 47.

Third, the Duke is a connoisseur of art. There is no need to believe that his love of art is not genuine: love of art can coexist comfortably with egotism and cruelty in some natures (read *The Autobiography of Benvenuto Cellini*); and this was a time of great enthusiasm for art and artists. The Duke is a patron and collector of art. He speaks appreciatively of the merits of Fra Pandolf's painting and keeps a protective curtain in front of it, which he allows no one but himself to draw. Nevertheless, his love of art is not pure; it too reflects his pride. He is proud of having commissioned work from painters and sculptors of such eminence as Fra Pandolf and Claus of Innsbruck, and he carefully drops their names into his conversation ("I said / 'Fra Pandolf' by design"). Part of the value of his Neptune taming a sea-horse is that it is "thought a rarity," and that Claus of Innsbruck cast it in bronze "for me!"

Finally, the Duke is shrewd. He knows what he wants, and he knows how to get it. While apparently simply making pleasant conversation about the shortcomings of his former Duchess, he is indirectly informing the envoy what he expects in his new Duchess, knowing that the envoy will report it back to the Count. Primary evidence of the Duke's shrewdness is his skill in speech. His disclaimer of such skill (35–36) is part of the evidence for it, and should remind the reader of a similar disclaimer by Shakespeare's Mark Antony in his oration on Caesar, which serves a similar purpose. It is a rhetorical trick, designed to throw the listener off his guard.

The Duke's momentary gropings after words (21–23, 31–32) by no means support this disclaimer, for the words he eventually comes up with are exactly the right words, and the hesitation in his speech only serves to give them added emphasis. But the conclusive proof of the Duke's skill in speech is the beautifully modulated passage (48–53) in which he couches his demand for dowry. Clearly the dowry is his main motivation in this new marriage (he is driving a hard bargain: his rank and nine-hundred-years-old name for her money), but he is too polished to avow this openly, so he adds, "Though his fair daughter's self, as I avowed / At starting, is my object." The words "I repeat" and "as I avowed / At starting" show that the Duke has mentioned both of these matters before, in reverse order; he is now driving them home in the order of their real importance, making sure he is clearly understood. The passage is a masterpiece of diplomatic circumlocution. Though the nature of the demand is made perfectly clear, it is gloved in a sentence softened by a double negative and by a skillfully tactful and euphemistic choice of diction: not *riches* but "munificence"; not *proves* but "Is ample warrant"; not *my demand* but "no just pretense / Of mine"; not *refused* but "disallowed." The hard bargaining is thus enveloped in an atmosphere of perfect courtesy. The Duke's diplomatic skills are also shown throughout in his treatment of the emissary, which is subtly designed to flatter. After the business conference, he gives the emissary a private showing of his prized portrait and chats in a friendly manner about personal affairs. This courtesy, from the man who is accustomed to give commands and who objected to too much courtesy in his Duchess, is apparent throughout the interview: "Will 't please you sit and look at her? . . . / Will 't please you rise?" And when the envoy, having risen, waits respectfully for the Duke to precede him downstairs, as befits his eminence, the Duke tells him, "Nay, we'll go / Together down, sir." And so the envoy walks side by side down the stairway with the possessor of a nine-hundred-years-old name who has just said, "I choose / Never to stoop." How can he do other than return a favorable report to the Count?

So much for the Duke; what about the Duchess? The Duke paints her as being frivolous, trivial, too free in manner, "too soon made glad." The reader's reaction to her, however, is controlled by the genuine pleasure she takes in compliments; by her graciousness to all, regardless of station; and especially by the simple things she takes delight in: the beauty of a sunset, a gift of a bough of cherries, a ride round the terrace on a white mule. Her response to these indicates a warm, sensitive nature that takes joy in natural things rather than in gauds and baubles or the pomp of position and power that attract the Duke.

The poem is a masterpiece of dramatic irony, a dramatic irony that is manifested chiefly in the whole tone of the poem rather than in specific passages. The Duke speaks all the words. He seeks to give a favorable impression of himself (and no doubt succeeds with the envoy, who belongs to his world and has not our advantage of perceiving him through the lens of art) and an unfavorable impression of his last Duchess. What Browning conveys to the reader is exactly the opposite. LP

CHAPTER EIGHT

Allusion

91. *Robert Frost* **"Out, Out—"** (page 641)

A newspaper account would have given us facts—the boy's name, his age, the exact place and time of the accident. The poet, as omniscient narrator in this poem, is interested in communicating experience. The first six lines provide a vivid sense of the setting through combined images of sight (sawdust, "stove-length sticks of wood, / Five mountain ranges / Under the sunset"), of smell (the resinous scent of new-cut timber), and of sound (the onomatopoetic snarling of the buzz-saw as the timber is pushed through it, its onomatopoetic rattling as it waits for the next load). Vivid visual imagery continues through the poem (the boy holding up his injured hand, the boy under ether puffing his lips out with his breath). The poem also provides dialogue (as a newspaper account wouldn't except in the form of a witness' answers to a reporter's questions) and includes the poet-narrator's own comments ("Call it a day, I wish they might have said . . ."; "the saw, / As if to prove saws knew what supper meant, / Leaped out at the boy's hand . . ."; "No more to build on there").

The role of chance is underscored in the poem in that the boy's death is really a double-accident. The cutting of the hand is caused by a moment of inattention, but moments of inattention rarely have such a dire consequence. The boy's death is caused by shock, but fatal shock infrequently follows such a "minor" accident. The boy does not expect it. The attendants can't believe it. There is indeed a terrible situational irony involved in the swift progression from the boy's first reaction ("a rueful laugh") to his perception that the accident may cost him his hand to the ending that no one anticipates.

The abruptness of the last line-and-a-half misleads some students into thinking the central theme of the poem identical with that of Housman's "Is my team plowing" (page 546): namely, that life goes on without us when we are gone just as it did before. To be sure, these lines do embroider the central theme with the truth that individual death does not bring human life to a halt. But Frost deliberately leaves the antecedent of "they" ambiguous, and he does not say how quickly "they . . . turned to their affairs." We should not assume that the sister returned to the normal course of her life as quickly as did the doctor, or that the unseen parents immediately resumed their lives as if nothing had happened. LP

92. *William Shakespeare* Excerpt from **Macbeth** (page 643)

The importance of recognizing Shakespeare's poetic rhythms is made clear in the punctuation and scansion of the third line of this passage. A prosaic reading, emphasizing the dictionary stresses only, sounds like this: toMORrow and toMOR-row and toMORrow. But the commas fall between the syllables of iambic feet, throwing greater stress on the normally slurred syllable "and," to this effect:

$$\breve{\text{To-mor-}} \,\overline{\text{row,}} \mid \text{and} \,\overline{\text{to-mor-}} \mid \breve{\text{row,}} \,\overline{\text{and}} \mid \text{to-mor-} \,\overline{\text{row.}}$$

That boring, eventless regularity imitates the apathy that has hardened Macbeth's heart and poisoned his mind.   TRA

93. *e. e. cummings* in **Just-** (page 644)

In this little poem about "Just- / spring"—that is, the very first beginning of spring—cummings captures the perennial delight of the children in a world that is "mud- / luscious" and "puddle-wonderful" and in which they can again play outside at marbles and piracies and hop-scotch and jump-rope. The setting is urban, and the whistle of the balloonman advertising his wares in the park or along the sidewalks brings the children running.

The description of the "little / lame balloonman" as "goat-footed" links him (or identifies him) with Pan, half-man, half-goat, the Greek god of nature and legendary inventor of the panpipes. When Pan blew on his pipes in the spring, all the little creatures of the field and wood came running. Thus cummings's city scene reenacts ancient ritual, and "the queer / old balloonman" ushers in the season that begins life anew as he has done each spring since the beginning.

Though the poem is written in free verse, it is organized into alternating four-line and one-line "stanzas" with a floating refrain in the thrice-repeated "balloon-man whistles far and wee" each time preceded by an announcement that it's spring. The hyphenated adjectives "mud- / luscious" and "puddle-wonderful" express exuberance in the assonance of their principal vowel sounds and echoing *d*'s and *l*'s; the hyphenated nouns "hop-scotch" and "jump-rope" display assonance and consonance respectively; the lines "luscious the little / lame balloonman" glide on alliterating *l*'s; and breathless *eddieandbill* and *bettyandisbel* echo each other in both vowel and consonant sounds. The whole builds up a celebration of spring and the children's delight in it. Cummings called it a "Chanson Innocente."   LP

94. *John Milton* **On His Blindness** (page 645)

The three parables grouped together in Chapter 25 of Matthew's Gospel teach the necessity of being prepared for the day of judgment, for the coming of the Lord. They emphasize chiefly two aspects of preparedness: that the Lord's arrival will be

sudden and without warning, and that the actions of the waiting life are an enactment of the judgment to be made (and, as in the third parable, verses 31–46, that
men cannot recognize the meanings of all their actions). The middle parable to which
this poem alludes teaches that the state of being prepared for the Lord's return is
an *active* state, which insofar as possible requires the servants to perform as their
master has performed—even if, to their limited understanding, the master has seemed
a sharp dealer more interested in profit than in justice.

The parable of verses 14–30 contrasts the behavior of servants of a lord who
in his absence are entrusted with sums of money. Two of them employ the money
as their lord had, in trade and usury, and double their sums, while the third buries
the one talent he has been given. When the lord returns from his travels, the two
who have doubled his money are rewarded, but the one who has only the single
talent to surrender back is cast "into outer darkness." The parable has been interpreted to equate the talent with faith, and to mean that one must not merely possess
faith, but employ it in the manner God intends. (Taken literally, of course, it seems
to teach the value of investing and taking risks, and castigates the person who merely
hoards and saves.)

Milton had begun going blind in the late 1640s; this sonnet has been dated variously
from 1652 to 1656, while Milton was actively involved in his duties as Oliver
Cromwell's "Latin Secretary" (a position roughly equivalent to secretary of state),
explaining and justifying Cromwell's Puritan regime to the monarchies of Europe.
In the sonnet he ponders his future life and work, contrasting the possible use of
his literary talent (and his faith) in ways far different from writing public statements
and pamphlets supporting the Cromwellian theocracy. The poem seems to report
a crisis in his life, examining the alternatives for a writer who wants his gift to fulfill
God's plan for him.

In his blindness (both physical and, momentarily, spiritual) Milton laments that
he is not employing his talent, which he supposes useless to do the Lord's work,
and fears that when he is confronted by his Maker and made to render his account,
he will be cast away. He is foolishly about to ask how a man whose sight has been
taken by God can be expected to do the same work as others. But his Patience, personified, forestalls the question, telling him that his affliction is not a heavy burden
and that his service to God may be merely to "stand and wait" rather than to pursue
a life of action.

The word "wait" has several relevant denotative meanings (this poem might be
used as the occasion for students to learn to consult the *Oxford English Dictionary*,
with its full historical definitions). It may mean "to await"—that is, to stand in
readiness for the master's arrival; or "to wait upon"—to attend to less active tasks
than the "thousands" who range over the world carrying out the Lord's commands,
as Milton figuratively is doing for Cromwell. In obsolete meanings current in Milton's
time, it also meant "to hope" or "to expect," or—a definition that returns to line 1
—"to consider." Patience is thus counseling him to accept his less spectacular tasks,
to be ready for whatever God intends, to live in Christian hope and expectation of
his salvation, and to return to the starting point of the sonnet—to consider again.

In the octave, Milton appears to misunderstand the meaning of the parable, thinking it unfair of God to expect "day-labor" from one who has been deprived of eyesight. But like the verbal echoes of the language of trade, the objection to the parable is literal-minded; properly understood, as Patience instructs him, it teaches him to bear what he must, to stand in readiness, and not to believe that only great activities gain God's grace, for the best service is performed by those who accept their limitations and maintain an active faith.

The word "prevent" is the hinge of the sonnet, occurring at the point separating the octave from the sestet. In its sense of "forestall" it reveals that the ideas of the sestet prevent him from voicing the foolish question to which his considerations have led him. In its further reference to the concept of "prevenience," it suggests that the advice of Patience is an action of God predisposing him toward performing God's will. In both senses, it reveals a circularity in the poem: "as I was about to murmur my complaint, Patience counseled me to consider again." This circularity is also suggested in the obsolete meaning of "wait"—"to consider." In effect the poem says that a reading of the parable momentarily led the poet to a misunderstanding of God's purposes, but God's prevenience checked him in time to see what those purposes really are. The half-rebellious mood of the octave never turns into open rebellion.

For further discussion of this sonnet, see Marjorie Nicolson, *A Reader's Guide to John Milton* (New York: Farrar, 1963) 152–55; E. M. W. Tillyard, *Milton* (New York: Collier, 1967) 160–62; and Macon Cheek, "Of Two Sonnets of Milton," reprinted in *Milton: Modern Essays in Criticism*, ed. Arthur E. Barker (New York: Oxford UP, 1965) 125–35.   TRA

95.   *John Donne*   Hero and Leander (page 645)

Greek philosophers believed that the universe is composed of four basic elements: air, earth, fire, and water. Donne uses this scientific concept as a basis for celebrating the legendary love of Hero and Leander, who, separated from each other by the wide waters of the Hellespont and by the opposition of Hero's parents to their union, nevertheless managed to meet secretly every night by Leander's feat of swimming the Hellespont guided by Hero's signal light. On one stormy night, however, Hero's light was blown out by the fierce winds and Leander was drowned by the fierce waves. When Hero saw Leander's body wash ashore, she threw herself into the water and later was buried by his side.

Of the four elements uniting the lovers in the poem, "air," "ground," and "water" are all literal, but "air" is part of a form 2 metaphor that compares it to a commodity or possession of which one can be "robbed." "Fire," on the other hand, is the figurative term in a form 3 metaphor, whose literal term is passion. LP

96. *Edwin Arlington Robinson* **Miniver Cheevy** (page 646)

"Miniver Cheevy" is a portrait etched in irony. Misfit and failure, unable to adjust to the present, Miniver escapes reality by dreaming of a romantic past and by drinking. Miniver longs for "the good old days" (or "bad old days"), which are more highly colored in his imagination than they were in actuality.

"Child of scorn"—this deliberately ambiguous phrase suggests a mythological paternity. Miniver's father was Scorn personified, and Miniver is his father's son. Miniver scorns the present: its art, its warfare, its materialistic aims, its drabness. But Miniver is also the target of scorn. His own scorn of the present is a rationalization of his failure to adjust to it, a defense against the scorn of others. The word "child" points up his essential immaturity.

The triteness of "days of old," "swords . . . bright," "steeds . . . prancing," "warrior bold" signals the superficiality of Miniver's idealization of the past, and its source in romantic literature. The homely word "neighbors" next to "Thebes and Camelot" makes Miniver's dream ludicrous, and the ironic juxtaposition of "grace" with "iron clothing" sounds a clank. That Miniver, if he could have chosen, would have belonged to one of the wealthiest families of history—the Medici—reveals the falsity of his contempt for gold; that then he would have "sinned incessantly" exposes the cheapness of all his values. Notice how the collocation of "ripe" and "renown" makes the first word suggest "overripe" and the second "notoriety." "Fragrant," because it follows, brings to mind not springtime and blossoms but fall and decaying fruit.

Robinson achieves his effect through form as well as diction. The repetition of Miniver's name at the beginning of each stanza reinforces the self-centeredness of his dreams. The short last line and feminine ending of each stanza furnish an anti-climax that jars Miniver's romantic idealization. The hissing *s* sounds in *assailed the seasons* and *sinned incessantly* echo Miniver's scorn and his evil glee in the prospect of sin. Robert Frost has expressed his delight in the second to last stanza: "There is more to it than the number of 'thoughts.' There is the way the last one turns up by surprise around the corner, the way the obstacle of verse is turned to advantage." The last "thought," of course, is the drop that overflows the bucket, emphasizing the futility of Miniver's thinking. In the final stanza the alliteration of key verbs— *kept, coughed, called, kept*—reasserts the continuance of the activity. The last line is brilliant poetic economy. Robinson first tells us that Miniver has been drinking by telling us that he "kept on" drinking. And the parallelism of "kept on drinking" with "kept on thinking" makes us supply a "drank, and drank, and drank, and drank" to match the previous repetitions of "thought."

Born too late? Miniver would have been "born too late" whenever he had been born.

[This discussion is condensed from a much more detailed analysis in the *Colby Library Quarterly* 6 (June 1962): 65–74.] LP

What this sonnet describes is, quite literally, a rape. The action of the rape is indicated precisely through sexual terms and symbols. The first quatrain describes the fierce assault and the foreplay; the second quatrain, the act of intercourse; the first part of the sestet, the sexual climax; the last part, the languor and apathy following the climax. But this is no ordinary rape: it is a rape by a god, by divine power temporarily embodied in the majestic form of a swan. And so it is described in terms that bring out awesomeness, not sordidness. The divinity appears as a "feathered glory" and its assault is a "white rush." It is also a momentous rape: it has large consequences for the future. And so the climax is described in terms that convey not only the experience of orgasm but also its remote consequences: the destruction of Troy, the death of Agamemnon. And then, after the moment of passion is over, and its results indicated, Yeats asks a question about the significance of the act: "Did she put on his knowledge with his power?"

Neither the word *swan* nor the name *Zeus* is mentioned in the body of the poem. We must rely on the title for our cues to the mythological event. Leda was a mortal princess by whose beauty Zeus, king of the gods, was smitten, and with whom he consummated his passion, having taken the form of a swan. There are several versions of this story, but in all of them Helen of Troy was one offspring of this union, and in the version used by Yeats, Clytemnestra was another. (See William Butler Yeats, *A Vision* [New York: Macmillan, 1956] 51.) The later abduction of Helen by the Trojan prince Paris from her husband the Greek king Menelaus led, of course, to the ten-year siege of Troy by Greek forces under the command of Agamemnon and to the ultimate defeat of the Trojans and the burning of Troy by the Greeks. On his return from Troy, Agamemnon was murdered by his wife Clytemnestra and her lover. (It matters little which version of the Leda story we know; the ultimate results are the same.)

In her union with the god, Leda clearly took on some of the power of the godhead, for she bore in her womb the forces that were to shape the future. Did she also take his knowledge? The question can be formulated in different ways. Can human sexual passion ever foresee its consequences? Can power and wisdom coexist in human life? Can man ever combine the vitality and passion of youth with the knowledge and wisdom of age (cf. "The Coming of Wisdom with Time," page 669)?

The question posed is left unanswered. Critics differ over whether an answer is implied. Some say the question is left open: that it is unanswerable. Others claim that it is the third of three rhetorical questions asked in the poem, all implying a negative answer (lines 5–6: "They can't"; lines 7–8: "It can't help but feel"; lines 13–14: "No"). Others suggest that power and knowledge can be combined in moments of artistic inspiration. This is a rich poem. For three provocative discussions, see Arnold Stein, in *Sewanee Review* 57 (1949): 617–20; Hoyt Trowbridge, in *Modern Philology* 51 (1953): 118–29; Leo Spitzer, in *Modern Philology* 51 (1954): 271–76. LP

98. *R. S. Gwynn* **Snow White and the Seven Deadly Sins** (page 647)

Fancifully mingling fairy tale, Christian lore, and modern life, this poem exuberantly lavishes its irony on all three. Its underlying allegory posits a "Good Catholic girl" in bondage to sins, but maintaining her virtue through hard work, prayer, and the instructions of her church. At the end, presented with a fairy-tale possibility of escape into a more acceptable kind of bondage, marriage to a "charming . . . *Male*," she chooses instead to withdraw from both sin and the role assigned to women in scripture, and to immure herself in a convent. There *is* a meaning there, but to state it in this way seems far too ponderous for the delightful wittiness of this poem.

One important twist that Gwynn gives to the "Seven Deadly Sins" rests in the modern setting. These seven are certainly not tempting or alluring (what sin is *supposed* to be), but rather coarse, contemporary versions. Pride is not spiritual pride but narcissism; Lust is into pornography and sadomasochism; Gluttony is a besotted beer-guzzler; Avarice expresses himself in poker games; Envy is cheap but brand-conscious; Sloth is a lazy slob; and Wrath is a physical brute. Allegories of the sins traditionally tend to portray them either as seductive or as monsters; Gwynn's are entirely human portraits, reminding us that the grandeur of evil (Milton's Satan, Shakespeare's Iago) is much less prevalent than debased humanity.

"Impeccably" as an adverb for the charming prince's speech is wonderfully right: from the Latin, he is exempt from the possibility of sinfulness.

Gwynn's poem alludes primarily to the Disney version of the tale, which it employs both for witty contrast and as an ironic butt—such happily-ever-after visions of reality don't contain much human truth apart from our desire for wishes to come true. The Disney dwarfs cannot be identified with these sins except perhaps for Grumpy (Wrath?) and Sleepy (Sloth?); there is no corresponding sin for Doc, Happy, Dopey, Sneezy, or Bashful. Disney's jolly work-song ("Hi ho, hi ho, it's off to work we go") is answered by *"Ho-hum. Ho-hum. It's home from work we come."* And the episode of Snow White's eating of the poisoned apple and being awakened by her Prince Charming is turned upside down as this "Good Catholic girl" wards off both an evil spell and a bridegroom. TRA

99. *Emily Dickinson* **An altered look about the hills** (page 649)

In the first fourteen lines, the poet presents a random list of images that are signs of the return of spring to her small New England town. She *smells* fern odors on roads impassible in winter; she *hears* the sound of an axe cutting away winter's dead wood; but mostly she *sees* the phenomena that accompany her vision. The days are getting longer, the sun is rising sooner, and thus there is an "altered look" on the hills and in the village. "Tyrian purple," named for the city of Tyre on the eastern coast of the Mediterranean, was a dye highly valued in biblical times. The word "purple" in ancient days referred to a color somewhere in the range between our purple and crimson; it was the color chosen for the robes of kings and emperors. The "Tyrian light" in Dickinson's poem is therefore a rich color caused by the early rising sun.

The collection of items in the first fourteen lines is brought together and unified by the biblical allusion in the last two. In the Gospel According to St. John, 3.1–5, Jesus tells a Pharisee named Nicodemus, "Except a man be born again, he cannot see the kingdom of God." Nicodemus then asks, "How can a man be born when he is old? Can he enter the second time into his mother's womb and be born?" This question is "Nicodemus's mystery," and Dickinson's speaker answers by pointing to the annual renewal of nature every spring.

The poem is charming though not deeply serious, for it "plays" off three different meanings of rebirth. Nicodemus is thinking of physical rebirth, Jesus is speaking of spiritual rebirth, and the poem is manifesting nature's annual rebirth. LP

100. *Emily Dickinson* **Abraham to kill him** (page 650)

This poem illustrates a use of allusion in contrast to Milton's in "On His Blindness" (page 645), for while Milton's sonnet applies the meaning of his allusive source to the reality of a modern man's spiritual condition, taking the biblical story "straight," Dickinson re-examines a scriptural story and finds an ironic meaning. She does not expect or require faith in the original meaning of the story, but revises its significance for a less credulous age.

In this poem, Dickinson ironically presents the sovereignty of a testy "mastiff" of a God over a totally compliant servant and his "urchin" son. Abraham was unthinkingly, unhesitatingly obedient to God's pointless command; the heavenly tyrant was flattered, and so withdrew the command, allowing the urchin to grow into maturity and fatherhood. The "Moral," tacked on as if the poet were paraphrasing Aesop rather than Moses, alliteratively jokes about the way God's creatures can learn how to placate Him to their own best interests. One might notice, though, that the speaker keeps her fingers crossed: she refrains from naming God or the Lord, whose orders are cast into the passive voice, and whose metonymous label ("Tyranny") and metaphoric incarnation ("mastiff") carefully sidestep direct delineation. And there is more fun in the poem arising from the elliptical way in which the events are narrated: you really do have to know (or consult) Genesis in order to understand what events are being alluded to—and when you do, you see that the detachment achieved by the cool latinisms of the second stanza (contrasted to the earthiness of lines 3–4 and the cliché of line 10) wryly deflates the incident. Does the poem have a "moral"? Probably "don't take that old Thunderer so seriously—His growl is worse than His bite." TRA

101. *Anonymous* **In the Garden** (page 650)

If the answer to the question is not immediately forthcoming, it should be possible to elicit it from any class by means of a leading question or two. For example, the instructor may ask: Why does the poet say "the garden" instead of "a garden"? Is any garden so famous that one may refer to it as "the garden" and count on being understood?

It is also useful to ask why (besides for rime) the poet compares the maid to "flowers of the morn" instead of to flowers at noon or flowers at evening, for this question points up the difference between ordinary logic and poetic logic. Morning, noon, and evening flowers are equally fair, but there is a symbolic connection between the morning of a day and the morning of human life. Poetic logic calls for as tight a coherence of all details in the poem as possible. Emotional connections are more important than strictly logical ones.

A few students may need to have it explained that Eve was never "born." LP

ADDITIONAL EXERCISE

An allusion may be offered as a comparison or parallel, or it may be used as an ironic contrast. In the following examples, is the poet using allusion positively, to enrich the theme, or ironically, to undercut the speaker's ideas?

1. Evans, "When in Rome," page 551 (allusion to the maxim, "When in Rome, do as the Romans do").
2. Larkin, "A Study of Reading Habits," page 543 (allusions to the types of cheap fiction read by the speaker).
3. Hardy, "Channel Firing," page 807 (lines 35–36, allusions identified in the footnote).
4. Keats, "Ode to a Nightingale," page 817 (line 66, allusion to the Book of Ruth).
5. Machan, "Leda's Sister and the Geese," page 824 (allusion to Yeats's "Leda and the Swan," No. 97).
6. Revard, "Discovery of the New World," page 614 (allusions to events in the history of North America).
7. Ferlinghetti, "Constantly risking absurdity," page 802 (line 29, allusion to Charlie Chaplin).
8. Frost, "Never Again Would Birds' Song Be the Same," page 806 (allusion to events in the Garden of Eden).
9. Lowell, "Watchmaker God," page 822 (line 11, allusions to Descartes and Paley).

ADDITIONAL EXERCISE ANSWERS

1. The speaker is quite clear: she rejects the advice "When in Rome, do as the Romans do"—or at least she rejects the "Roman" diet of her white employer,

as she silently satirizes her mock-generosity. The poet is more harsh than her obsequious speaker, for rather than thinking "yes'm," she displays the white woman's insensitivity and condescension. There are *no* values in this "Rome" that she would adapt to.

2. The types of fiction the speaker read in his "growth" are presented by the poet with dramatic irony. Although the speaker liked to identify himself with the heroes and villains—and regretfully came to recognize himself in the ineffectual cowards—the poet makes it clear that to have found such books satisfying was at least one of the speaker's mistakes: those books are indeed "a load of crap," but not for the reasons the speaker intends.

3. The three allusions that conclude the poem, as the footnote to the poem says, moving "backward in time through the historic, the legendary, and the prehistoric," offer support to the poem's theme: mankind from its earliest traces through its historical glory and in its creative imagination has consistently demonstrated its bellicosity, its tendency "to make / Red war yet redder." The allusions are offered in comparison to the theme, although the fact that the poet is stating what he sees as an irony of our race may momentarily mislead the student.

4. Ruth's sad, forlorn condition—"sick for home, / . . . amid the alien corn," listening to the song of the bird—is offered by the speaker as evidence of the immortality of the nightingale's song, a parallel to himself. That Ruth is also alone, forlorn, and unhappy further reinforces the speaker's situation both before his imaginative transport and after he returns to the reality of his "sole self."

5. Machan's poem alludes to Yeats's in order to set up a deflating complaint: Leda's sister is a down-to-earth, even vulgar girl, whose attitude toward Leda is anything but solemn and reverential. *Her* answer to Yeats's rhetorical questions is uniformly negative.

6. Revard's extraterrestrial invader approvingly cites Sherman and describes the attempted genocide of the native Americans. This is the basis for the dramatic irony of the poem.

7. Charlie Chaplin as a performer was celebrated for his mastery of walk and gesture as an artistic expression of the clumsy, accident-prone tramp. The allusion is to his powers of illusion, and is cited approvingly.

8. The poem uses dramatic irony to express the fullness of Adam's love before the Fall; his assumption that Eve's mission is to add beauty to Creation points toward the concupiscence that made Adam sin.

9. Descartes and Paley represent a limited vision of God's nature as defined by a scientific approach, a "pale romance" based on "the cold light of science," while the speaker asserts that "life is both the fire and fuel."

POEMS FOR FURTHER READING

Poems 204, 220, 225, 249, 251, 255, 270, and 282 from Part 2 provide additional illustrations of topics presented in this chapter.

CHAPTER NINE

Meaning and Idea

102. *Anonymous* **Little Jack Horner** (page 651)

"Little Jack Horner," of course, presents an example of dramatic irony—a boy who sticks his thumb in a pie is *not* a good boy. LP

103. *Sara Teasdale* **Barter** (page 652)

104. *Robert Frost* **Stopping by Woods on a Snowy Evening** (page 653)

The statement that the reader should be able to enjoy both of these poems does not imply that they are of equal poetic value. Frost's poem is by far the richer, more resonant, more tightly structured of the two. Teasdale's poem is unified by its central metaphor of buying and spending. Its first two stanzas, after their opening thematic statement, comprise a brief catalogue of beautiful things, all lovely in themselves, but with no ordering principle beyond that dictated by the rime scheme. Frost's poem has a tight narrative and dramatic, logical, and psychological organization in which no lines or images could be interchanged without loss. There is further discussion of "Stopping by Woods . . ." on page 666. LP

105. *William Cullen Bryant* **To a Waterfowl** (page 654)

106. *Robert Frost* **Design** (page 656)

Bryant's and Frost's poems both begin with an observation from nature and end with an idea about God, but their conclusions are diametrically opposite. Bryant observes the solitary waterfowl at sunset as it flies on its annual spring migration to its summer breeding grounds. Though the air through which it flies is "pathless," empty, and "illimitable," the bird is not lost (Bryant tells us), for there is "a Power [God] whose care" teaches it its way through "the boundless sky" and "Guides" it safely to its destination. The poet concludes optimistically that he can safely entrust his own life to the guidance of the same Power.

The connotations in Frost's poem work in two opposite directions. First, there is a series of words and images suggesting innocence—"dimpled," "heal-all," "morning," "right," "snow-drop," "flower," "blue," "innocent," and the five-times repeated "white." Second, there is an equally impressive sequence suggesting evil—"spider," "death," "blight," "witches' broth," "dead," "night," "darkness," "appall." The collocation of these two kinds of words seems to pose a question.

The design indicated by the title is formed by three things—a white heal-all, a white spider, a white moth. The heal-all, a wild flower with medicinal virtues, is usually blue. Spiders are ordinarily black or brown. What has brought together these three white things, two of them so rarely white? It would seem the work of a conscious artist. But what is the consequence of this artistry? Death. The white moth, lured by the usually protective kindred color of the heal-all, has been trapped by the spider and killed. It is held now "Like a white piece of rigid satin cloth" (the image not only describes a dead moth exactly but suggests the lining of a coffin). The three white things are thus "Like the ingredients of a witches' broth." The suggestion that these ingredients have been mixed "to begin the morning right" (rite?) is ironical. There is irony also in the connection of the innocent color white with this sinister enterprise of death.

In the eighteenth century, a favorite argument for the existence of God was the so-called "argument from design." The intricate construction of the universe, it was held, with all of its stars and planets whirling in mathematically chartable courses regulated by the law of gravity, testified to the existence of an infinitely wise creator, for how could there be design without a designer? As the nineteenth Psalm so eloquently expresses it, "The heavens declare the glory of God, and the firmament showeth his handiwork."

Frost's title alludes to this famous argument in a grimly ironical fashion: the design in nature, Frost points out, is that of "a witches' broth." Thus the poem asks a terrible question: "What brought the kindred spider to that height, / Then steered the white moth thither in the night? / What but design of darkness to appall?—" (11–13). Perhaps the universe is governed, not by infinite goodness, but by infinite evil. The poem does not assert this proposition as an actuality; it merely suggests it as a possibility. And the suggestion is immediately softened, apparently, by the provision of another possibility—that perhaps design does not govern in a thing so small. But the afterthought, tossed in so casually, when examined closely turns out to be not very comforting either. If nature is not governed by design, then it is governed merely by chance, coincidence, anarchy, chaos—certainly not by the traditionally omnipotent, benevolent God who is concerned over the smallest sparrow's fall.

Cast in the sonnet form but confining itself to only three rime sounds (the title might refer to the pattern of the poem as well as the design made by the three white things in nature), Frost's brief poem chillingly poses the problem of evil.

Bryant's use of the verb "guides" (30) and Frost's of "steered" (12) make Frost's poem seem almost a reply to Bryant's. The waterfowl's instinct in Bryant's poem guides it unerringly to its distant destination. Conclusion: a benevolent God presides over the universe and protects His creatures. The white moth's instinct in Frost's poem steers it unerringly into the spider's trap. Conclusion: perhaps the Power that presides over the universe is malevolent rather than benevolent, evil rather than good. Bryant offers reassurance; Frost offers terror. Frost's terror is more authentic than Bryant's reassurance, for Bryant ignores the fact that many waterfowl do *not* escape the fowler (5). (Whooping cranes were almost extinguished in the nineteenth and twentieth centuries to provide feathers for ladies' hats.)

Bryant's poem has been called a "great lyric" by Yvor Winters [*In Defense of Reason* (New York: Swallow, 1947) 239]; it was greatly admired by Matthew Arnold, and was once enthusiastically described by Hartley Coleridge as "the best short poem in the English language" [John Bigelow, *William Cullen Bryant* (Boston: Houghton, 1890) 42–43]. "Design" is surely one of the most powerful sonnets in the language.

[This commentary is partially adapted from Laurence Perrine and James M. Reid, 100 *American Poems of the Twentieth Century* (New York: Harcourt, 1966) 46–47.] LP

107. *John Donne* **The Indifferent** (page 656)

108. *John Donne* **Love's Deity** (page 657)

The irony in "The Indifferent" depends on a simple reversal of what human beings usually call vice and virtue. For the speaker, constancy in love is a vice, promiscuity is a virtue. Love's "sweetest part" is variety, not fidelity. In the speaker's "religion" any woman who is faithful to one mate is a "heretic." The goddess of this religion is Venus (Aphrodite), who in classical mythology was herself unfaithful to her husband Vulcan (Haephestus) through affairs with Mars (Ares), Mercury (Hermes), Bacchus (Dionysus), and others, by one of whom she was mother of Cupid (Eros). When Venus hears the speaker's complaint that modern women are guilty of heresy (that is, of fidelity to one man), she forms herself into a one-person investigating committee and finds that the report is greatly exaggerated—she has found two or three faithful women, but no more, and she will punish them by giving them unfaithful mates.

The speaker in "Love's Deity" suffers from unrequited love and accuses "Love's deity" (Cupid) of having overreached his assigned duties. He wishes he could speak to the ghost of some lover who died before Cupid ("this child") was born, in order to confirm his charges. He believes that the older gods, who put Cupid in office, intended that his duties be restricted to assisting mutual lovers and bringing together young persons who could and would reciprocate each other's love. But, like other ambitious bureaucrats, Cupid has enlarged the powers of his office beyond its intended limits; he has tyrannically seized powers not meant to be his and aspires to powers equal to those of Jove himself. Instead of presiding over and helping to create a realm of harmonious and reciprocated feeling, Cupid has introduced obsession, lust, intrigue, and betrayal into his domain. Worst of all, the speaker seems to feel, Cupid has caused *him* to be in love with someone who does not return his love.

This is the burden of his complaint through the first three stanzas. In the third stanza he becomes openly rebellious and blasphemous, proposing that if humankind were sufficiently aroused "by this tyranny / To ungod this child again, it could not be / I should love her who loves not me."

In the final stanza, however, shocked by the violence to which his thought has risen, he returns to a more moderate dissatisfaction. Addressing himself as "Rebel and atheist" (for wanting to "ungod" the child again), he reproaches himself for complaining; as he realizes, there are two worse fates that Love could have made him suffer. Love could have (a) made him cease loving or (b) made her return his love.

But is this not an almost complete reversal of his previous thought? Indeed it is. Are these worse fates not paradoxically the very solutions he had earlier been desiring for his problem? Indeed they are. How do we explain them then? First, by understanding that the speaker, psychologically, must give vent to his pain (as he does in the first three stanzas) before he can view his situation more calmly and philosophically. Second, by absorbing the new information (withheld until the final stanza) that the woman loved by the speaker is already attached to another man (she is probably a married woman; but at least she is fully committed elsewhere and was so before the speaker fell in love with her).

What, then, are the philosophical beliefs or values which serve to moderate, though not to obliterate, the speaker's suffering? First, that there is value in *all* loving. Although unrequited love involves deep anguish, there is a richness of feeling in this anguish that makes it better to have experienced it than never to have felt at all. Second, that infidelity in love is a grave moral deformity. "Falsehood [infidelity]," the speaker says, "is worse than hate." He would rather endure the pangs of unreciprocated love than enjoy the favors of a faithless woman.

[*Note:* Donne's favorite figurative devices are paradox and overstatement. It is probable that "hate" (27) and "scorn" (4) are both overstatements of her lack of responsiveness to any suit of adulterous love; or perhaps they literally express her feeling toward infidelity itself rather than her feeling toward the speaker.]

But now that we have resolved the contradictions and paradoxes in "Love's Deity," how do we resolve the contradictions between "Love's Deity" and "The Indifferent," both composed by the same poet? The speaker in "Love's Deity" regards fidelity in love as a virtue; the speaker in "The Indifferent" regards it as a "dangerous" vice. The two recommendations are polar opposites.

The easiest and best way of explaining the contradiction is simply to say that the two poems, though written by one poet, have two different speakers, neither one necessarily speaking for Donne himself. Donne in many of his poems seemed to be exploring different ways of regarding love by deliberately expressing disparate views through disparate speakers.

It should be noted that the speakers in these two poems mean different things by the word "love." The speaker in "The Indifferent" consistently uses the word to mean physical love—copulation. Nothing in the poem suggests that he recognizes any further dimensions of meaning for the word. The speaker in "Love's Deity" consistently means something more by the word: something perhaps combining warm affection, admiration, and physical desire. He makes a distinction, as the other speaker does not, between "love" and "lust." LP

109. _Dudley Randall_ **To the Mercy Killers** (page 659)

110. _Edwin Arlington Robinson_ **How Annandale Went Out** (page 659)

Although these two poems (both sonnets) are not diametrical opposites, both are centrally concerned with the subject of euthanasia, one opposed, one in favor.

Randall's is the one opposed. But the important point to notice is that Randall does not raise the question to the level of a universal issue. He does not contend that euthanasia is wrong; he says only that he does not want it for himself. Can we infer any ethical attitude in what he says? He certainly does not impugn the motivations of those who might "conspire" (3) to end his suffering. They are "kindly" (2), and are motivated by mercy. Nevertheless, the word "conspire" has negative connotations, and even more so does the word "murder" in line 1.

The most effective lines in the poem are those in which he lists what he might become. Line 6, a series of monosyllabic nouns (_stub, stump, butt, scab, knob_) preceded by those in line 5 (_clot, clench_) and followed by those in line 7 (_pain, stench_) with their two multisyllabic adjectives (_screaming, putrefying_), all held together by alliteration, assonance, and consonance—like links in a chain or boxcars in a freight train—are a powerful _tour de force_. But there is an important consideration that the speaker has not taken into account: the consequences for other people. He adopts a heroic stance in his determination to experience the full range of human life, but other lives besides his own will also be affected. He will need doctors, nurses, caretakers; and who among them, performing their duties, will find pleasure in attending "a screaming pain, a putrefying stench"?

"How Annandale Went Out" is a dramatic poem involving three characters and an implied dialogue, though we actually hear the voice of but one of the characters. Thus, though both poets use the sonnet form (Robinson the Italian, Randall the English), the difference between the two poems is greater than their similarity. Randall's is more like a speech, Robinson's like a little play.

The speaker in Robinson's poem is Annandale's physician and also his very close friend. He is speaking to another close friend, giving him an account of Annandale's death. While the information supplied in the first study question provides background, the focus of the poem is on the events that follow, and particularly on the moral and ethical issues that faced the narrator. The "given" fact in the poem is that Annandale could not be mended, and that any life remaining to him would be hell until his death. As the doctor sees it, nothing can be done to restore him to recognizably human life or to protect him from unendurable pain.

In the doctor's recollection, Annandale is only an "it" (1), an "apparatus" (6) that cannot be repaired. All the doctor can do is to "flourish" and "find words" (2)—that is, to lie about Annandale's true condition and thus hypocritically to raise

175

false hopes for the possibilities of recovery among Annandale's family and friends. But the doctor "Knew the ruin" (intimately) as he "knew the man" (9) (intimately), and he knows that there is no hope whatever for Annandale's recovery. He repeats "I was there" (1, 8) to emphasize that the full horror of the event could be felt only by someone who had actually been there and seen it as he had seen it. The phrase "on the spot" (12) adds to the meaning of "I was there" the meaning that he (as Annandale's physician) was the one responsible for deciding what to do next. He must face up to the dilemma presented by his legal responsibilities and his professional duties as a physician, complicated by his personal and social duties as a friend. His decision is to take "a slight kind of engine" (13), a hypodermic needle, and make an injection that will quickly take Annandale's life. He illustrates what he has done by mimicking with his thumb and first two fingers the action of giving the shot, bringing his thumb forward between the tips of the outstretched fingers. He hopes and believes he has done the right thing, but cannot keep it a secret all to himself. He needs intelligent moral support to ease his mind from any sense of guilt, so he goes to his and Annandale's friend to make full confession of what he has done. The friend agrees that the physician has done the right thing.

The poet nowhere states his own opinion, but he presents the physician sympathetically as a man willing to apply such words as "Liar" and "hypocrite" (3) to himself and, more importantly, willing to risk his own reputation and perhaps his life (depending on the laws of his state). The word "hang" in the final line may be taken either literally or metonymically as any form of capital punishment.   LP

---

111. *Emily Dickinson* **Alter! When the hills do** (page 660)

112. *Emily Dickinson* **We outgrow love** (page 661)

These two poems have love as their common subject but make contrasting assertions about it. The first makes the traditional claim that true love is permanent and unchanging (compare Shakespeare's sonnet "Let me not to the marriage of true minds," page 840). Love is as unchanging as "the hills," as consistent as the glorious sun moving across the heavens, and as unquenchable in desire as a flower is for life-sustaining (and beautifying) moisture. The speaker addresses her beloved (genders identified in line 7), creating a dramatic situation in which extravagant assertions are not necessarily to be taken for literal truth; by virtue of their figurative language, the three metaphors may seem to underscore the absence of factual truth.

The second poem appears to say the opposite: love can be outgrown, and when we look back at it we see that while it may have been beautiful in its time, it would certainly seem merely quaint and odd now. The central metaphor compares love to an article of clothing that was well-fitted and in fashion at one time, but that was put aside by the wearer when it no longer fit. Taking it out of the drawer some time later, the person now finds that it is both too small (it has been "outgrown") and very much out of fashion. The speaker in this poem is not addressing anyone, and is not even identifiable as to gender; "grandsires" (4) suggests masculine forbears, but the concern for "fashion" and the action of storing clothes away in a drawer have feminine associations. The poem lacks the dramatic situation of the first along with its identifiable personal motivation—and so does not have a need for overstatement. With only a single, developed metaphor and its detached, abstract tone, it may strike the reader as more "true" than the first, but both poems express comprehensible human truths—(1) what love feels like when we are experiencing it, and (2) how we may think about love in the abstract. TRA

113. *Gerard Manley Hopkins* **The Caged Skylark** (page 661)

114. *A. E. Housman* **The Immortal Part** (page 662)

"The Caged Skylark" is an Italian sonnet. The octave concerns the relationship of the spirit and the body in life, the sestet, the relationship of the spirit and the resurrected body in eternity. The basic analogies may be expressed thus:

1. spirit-in-life : mortal body = caged skylark : cage
2. immortal spirit : resurrected body = wild skylark : nest = meadow-down : rainbow.

Both a rainbow and a shadow are perfect images for weightlessness, but a shadow suggests evil, fear, darkness, death, whereas a rainbow suggests hope, joy, beauty, God's compact with man in the Bible. Hopkins's rainbow beautifully demonstrates how a poet gets extra dimensions of meaning out of his words and images. (Experience indicates that students will have difficulty with "meadow-down," because of the unfamiliarity of "down" as a grassy hill or slope, and will try to see an image of downy feathers or foliage.)

Housman's poem divides man into three parts—the flesh, soul, and skeleton. The soul is the perceiving, thinking, and willing portion of the man, concentrated in the brain: it directs the activities of the flesh—tongue, lungs, and thews—as well as of the skeleton. The poem thus parodies Christian belief: where, for Christianity, death may be a rebirth—of the soul—for Housman death is birth for the skeleton. Every human being—male or female—is pregnant with a skeleton, and is delivered of it at death. At death the soul blows away like smoke, the flesh decays, the bones remain. When we search for the remains of former human life on earth, all we find are bones.

In lines 3–16 the personified bones are compared to a slave of the personified flesh and soul. In line 12 the boundaries of the brain are metaphorically compared to a hive in which the thoughts and dreams are bees. In lines 19–27 the living skeleton is compared to a foetus, the grave to a bed in which one simultaneously lies down to die and to give birth, and the dead skeleton to the "fruit" (of the womb), for which "the eternal seed" is a metonymy. In line 43 "night" is a metaphor for the oblivion of death. LP

177

One of the oldest and deepest philosophical problems is that sometimes referred to as the body/soul or the mind/matter problem. Are the body and soul two separate entities, like a paper bag and its contents? Or are they simply two aspects of a single entity, like the two sides of a sheet of paper, and thus inseparable? From this problem hang various contingent problems. How are body and soul related in life (the problem of determinism and free will)? What happens to them at death (the problem of immortality)? These problems are as legitimate a subject for poetry as for religion, science, and philosophy. In literature they especially invite allegorical treatment (see, for instance, *Everyman*).

In an earlier poem, "A Dialogue between the Resolved Soul and Created Pleasure," Marvell, a Puritan poet, pictures the resolved Soul, armed with the shield of faith, the helmet of salvation, and the sword of spirit, as a soldier singly facing a whole army under the command of Pleasure. Pleasure, however, instead of challenging the Soul to combat, invites him to share "Nature's banquet" and therewith offers him a series of earthly temptations (the pleasures of the five senses: taste, touch, smell, sight, and hearing; plus the pleasures of love, wealth, and glory). The Resolved Soul easily rejects each of these in a victory so effortless that the reader gets no sense of conflict.

How much more interesting and complex is the allegory in "A Dialogue between the Soul and Body"! Here, though there is no combat, the conflict is real, and the poet does not betray his sympathy for either side. He even allows Body the last word, though in the earlier poem he was clearly on the side of Soul. Here each participant complains of his bondage to the other. They are not two completely separate forces armed against each other, as in the simplistic concept of the earlier poem. But neither are they one. They are two, so tangled up together that neither can get loose from the other. Their "Dialogue" is a debate, and the object is to see which can make his plight seem more burdensome and himself more oppressed by the other. Which wins? Does anyone have the audacity to judge?

But how wittily the debate is conducted! What a succession of brilliant paradoxes, stunning metaphors, and multidimensional words! The Soul complains of being "fettered" with "bolts of bones" (how does sound here echo sense?), "blinded with an eye" (paradox), and "Deaf with the drumming of an ear" (the paradox enriched with a pun on "drumming"), "hung up, . . . in chains / Of nerves, and arteries, and veins" (metaphor), and being tortured in a "vain" head (useless, hollow, egotistical) and a "double heart" (two-chambered, duplicitous, an organ of the body).

The body, in turn, laments that his soul so "impales" him that he is "[his] own precipice" (in danger of falling off the edge of his own upright self). He concedes that his soul warms and moves him, but declares that a mere fever could do as much, and complains that his feverish soul has never let him rest.

In the third stanza the soul replies, in a series of dazzling paradoxes, that it suffers the pains of the body as well as its own. Being the more compassionate and "sensitive" partner (though without senses), it shares whatever suffering the body undergoes: "I feel, that cannot feel, the pain." Thus the soul is "Constrained not only to endure / Diseases, but, what's worse, the cure; / And ready oft the port to gain, / [Is] shipwrecked into health again." The "port" (29) in this metaphor is heaven; the "cure" (28) is entry into heaven. Thus, when the body is cured from an illness, the soul is deprived of the opportunity to reach its own desired destination and is "shipwrecked into health" again!

But, replies the body, in the final stanza, the ills visited by the soul on the body cannot be cured by any medicine. The "cramp of hope," the "palsy shakes of fear," "the pestilence of love," "hatred's hidden ulcer"—all are maladies of the soul that are imposed upon the body, just as those in stanza 3 were maladies of the body imposed on the soul.

It is evident, in this poem, that the poet believed body and soul to be two entities, not one, for both disputants are confident that they will eventually be separated and relieved of their mutual bondage. The body declares (18) that the spirit "Has made me live to let me die." And the soul complains (29–30), when the body is saved from death, that he (the soul) has been "shipwrecked into health again." But this is a minor theme in the poem; the major theme is the intricate entanglement of the soul and body during life. LP

CHAPTER TEN

Tone

116. *Richard Eberhart* **For a Lamb** (page 667)

117. *Emily Dickinson* **Apparently with no surprise** (page 667)

For a far different poem about a lamb see Blake's "The Lamb" (page 789), one that evokes the positive implications that Eberhart plays upon. In comparing them, note the contrasting poetic stances that contribute to their tones: Blake's speaker is a child who mirrors the innocence of the lamb and symbolically links himself to it; Eberhart's speaker is a mature realist who doesn't apostrophize but is imaginative enough to draw some larger consolation from the fact of universal mortality.

Dickinson's poem may profitably be compared with Frost's "Design" (page 656), for both poems raise similar issues, and both (like Melville in *Moby-Dick*) make the color white, usually associated with purity and innocence, take on exceedingly sinister connotations.   TRA, LP

118. *William Butler Yeats* **The Coming of Wisdom with Time** (page 669)

Yeats associates youth with "leaves," "flowers," and "sun," which are agreeable, and with "lying," which is disagreeable. He associates age with "truth," "wisdom," and oneness, which are agreeable, and with "wither," which is disagreeable. Thus he carefully balances youth and age as to favorable and unfavorable qualities. Yeats is neither exulting over a gain nor lamenting a loss; but he *is* lamenting the fact that one can't have everything at once—beauty, vigor, and enthusiasm, *and* wisdom. Life is never complete: one gains some desirable qualities at the expense of losing others.   LP

119. *Michael Drayton* **Since there's no help** (page 669)

From the first eight lines of this sonnet it seems apparent that the speaker (the male, as we shall see) and his beloved are breaking off their relationship. Does the speaker want to break it off? He asserts quite positively, perhaps too positively, that he does (3–4), but even in these first eight lines this assertion is undercut by the implication that he is acting under constraint ("Since there's no help") and by the suggestion that at any future meetings they may have difficulty disguising their still-existent feelings for each other. If any doubt remains that he does not really want to break off the relationship, it should be dissolved by the sestet, especially the last two lines, where he declares that she could still bring their love back to life, if she only would. He obviously hopes that she will. The rich allegorical and poetic language of the sestet (as opposed to the clipped, prosaic language of the octave) indicates that his true feelings come out here, and that he deliberately falsified the feelings in the octave.

Does *she*, then, want to break off the relationship? Although she is given no words in the poem (he is the speaker throughout), the "Nay" beginning in line 2 is a clear signal that this line is spoken in response to some gesture or word of protest made by her against his pronouncement in line 1. She does not want to "kiss and part." A further clue to her feelings is provided by his including her along with himself in his forecast of the difficulty *both* will have in concealing their feelings at future meetings.

But if neither of them *wants* to break off the relationship, *why* are they breaking it off? To answer this question, we must examine the allegorical death scene depicted in the sestet. When asked how many figures are involved in this scene, students initially answer four. But do we then have two dying figures, two deathbed scenes? Or are not "Love" and "Passion" two different names (suggesting the spiritual and the physical aspects) for one dying figure? Clearly they are one person, most fittingly called "Love/Passion." There is only one deathbed (11), and the dying figure is referred to by a singular pronoun in each of the last four lines ("his," "his," "him," "him"). The masculinity of the pronoun suggests that the dying Love/Passion is *his* (the speaker's). The logic of the situation suggests that the two attendants at the bedside, Faith kneeling in prayer, Innocence pulling down the eyelids of the presumably dead figure, are *hers*. By a subtle associative logic these two attendants, ostensibly present to ease the death, are made to appear the causes of the death. Her innocence is closing up the eyes of his passion; her faith (religious scruple) is assisting at the bedside. Yet, he asserts, if she would, she might at the very moment of death—"Now," in an instant—bring his Love/Passion quite suddenly back to life. Surely, the situation is clear. Though the woman wishes to retain his love, she also values and wishes to preserve her innocence (her purity, her chastity); her faith tells her that fornication is a sin. He claims that, by refusing to satisfy his passion, she is causing both it and his love (they are one and the same) to die.

The relation of sound and sense in this sonnet is discussed on pages 722–23 of the text.   LP

120.   *Emily Dickinson*   **One dignity delays for all** (page 670)

121.   *Emily Dickinson*   **'Twas warm at first like us** (page 671)

The theme of "One dignity delays for all" is that all of us, no matter how humble, will one day be honored and treated like nobility—namely, on the day of our burial. In the second stanza the funeral procession through the streets of the village is compared to the progress of a king, duke, or bishop through his domain. The hearse is a carriage, the casket is the royal chamber, the undertaker and his assistants are footmen, bells toll in the church towers, crowds stop to watch on the sidewalks or follow behind the hearse. In the third stanza the procession stops at the graveside, the officiating clergy (''dignified attendants'') conduct a funeral ceremony (like a coronation ceremony or an official welcome to a visiting prince), and everyone takes off his hat as prayers are read and the casket is lowered into the grave. (The above account may be overspecific in its point-to-point comparisons, but the general meaning is valid.)

''Meek escutcheon'' combines oxymoron and metaphor. Metaphorically it represents our humanity. Just as a coat of arms entitles its bearer to ceremonial treatment on all occasions, so our common humanity entitles us to ceremonial treatment at death. We may all look forward to this moment of grandeur. It ''delays'' (waits) for all.

'''Twas warm at first like us'' describes the changes that take place in a body between death and burial. The poem begins its description at a point a split-second after the instant of death. Though still warm, the body has already become an ''It,'' is no longer a *he* or *she*. Then, in almost clinical detail, are shown the loss of body warmth, the vanishing of expression from face and eyes, the stiffening of rigor mortis, the increasing and finally utter separation between the worlds of the dead and the living. In the final stanza, as it is lowered into the grave, the corpse is a mere thing, a weight, unable by any sign to assent or demur to what is happening. The final word ''adamant'' underscores its stoniness.

Written in Dickinson's characteristic elliptical style, the poem demands for grammatical completeness that we supply an *it* at the end of line 2, an *if* after ''as'' in line 12, and a completing verb (*show? manifest? manage?*) at the end of line 12. But the meaning is clear without these additions. Dickinson's omissions simply compact her meaning.

There may be a latent irony in the fact that the ''dignity'' that ''delays for all'' does not occur till we can no longer be conscious of it, but in the poem this irony is muted. The tone of the poem is generally one of excited anticipation, marked by the exclamatory elation of the last two stanzas, and by words like ''dignity,'' ''mitred,'' ''purple,'' ''crown,'' ''state,'' ''grand,'' ''pomp,'' ''surpassing,'' ''ermine,'' and ''escutcheon.'' Death in this poem is not the great democratizer, leveling all ranks, but the great ''aristocratizer,'' elevating all to the status of nobility.

The tone of '''Twas warm at first like us,'' on the contrary, is one of unrelieved and increasing horror. Concentrating not on the funeral ceremonials but on the physical facts of death, it projects not an elevation in status but a reduction in status, from human being to thing. Its tone is determined by words like ''chill,'' ''frost,'' ''stone,'' ''cold,'' ''congealed,'' ''weight,'' and ''dropped like adamant.'' Instead of ''pomp surpassing ermine,'' it presents us with a dead body crowding ''cold to cold.''   LP

122. *Alfred, Lord Tennyson* **Crossing the Bar** (page 671)

123. *Thomas Hardy* **The Oxen** (page 672)

Despite the fame and popularity of "Crossing the Bar," students often have difficulty with it, and it is well to make sure that they understand it. The two complementary sets of figures used to express approaching death are the coming of night and setting out on an ocean voyage. The moment of death in the first set is the disappearance of the last light of day: the arrival of "the dark." In the second set it is the moment of "crossing the bar": leaving the harbor, which belongs to the land, and setting out on the ocean. As the land represents temporal life, the ocean—"the boundless deep"—represents eternity. "That which drew from out the boundless deep" is the soul: in Tennyson's thought the soul comes from eternity, takes fleshly embodiment during life, and returns to eternity upon death. Tennyson wants no "moaning of the bar"—no lamentation over his death—for his soul is returning "home," is passing on to eternal life, and will see its "Pilot" (God) "face to face" after death. The occasion should therefore be one for joy rather than for sadness.

The whole poem expresses Tennyson's faith in immortality. Despite its popularity, which stems largely from its message, the poem is a good one. An oversubtle cavil about the image of the pilot, raised by Brooks and Warren in their manual for *Understanding Poetry*, 3rd ed. (New York: Holt, 1960), is satisfactorily answered by G. Geoffrey Langsam in *Explicator* 10 (Apr. 1952): item 40. For a debate about the tone of the poem, see James R. Kincaid, "Tennyson's 'Crossing the Bar': A Poem of Frustration," *Victorian Poetry* 3 (1965): 57–61, and Laurence Perrine, "When Does Hope Mean Doubt?: The Tone of 'Crossing the Bar,'" *Victorian Poetry* 4 (1966): 127–31.

"The Oxen" divides exactly in the middle, the first two stanzas presenting a scene from the speaker's childhood, the second two, one from his adult life. If we take the speaker as Hardy himself, or as a contemporary of Hardy, the two scenes are divided by Darwin's *Origin of Species* (1859) and by the dramatic decline of religious faith that it accelerated. In the poem the superstition of the kneeling animals is symbolic of the whole system of Christian belief that Hardy was taught as a boy and that he gave up as a man, but that, like Matthew Arnold (see "Dover Beach," page 675), he never ceased to regret. Though he can no longer subscribe to Christian doctrine or to its world view, he regrets the loss of the emotional security and comfort provided by that world view.

In emotional tone the two halves of the poem differ sharply. In the first two stanzas, there is a sense of warmth, of comfort, and of community. Young and old sit "in a flock / By the embers in hearthside ease," and the speaker uses the plural pronoun "we." In the last two stanzas, there is isolation and darkness. The speaker uses the singular pronoun, refers to the barton as "lonely," and with the word "gloom" describes not only the darkness of the night but also the spirit of the times— the desolation caused by the loss of religious faith. The superstition of the kneeling oxen—along with the divine birth and the resurrection—is dismissed as a "fancy," one that few people any longer accept, but that was nevertheless "fair" (attractive).

The word "hope" in Tennyson's poem and in Hardy's has opposite meanings relative to the expectations involved. Tennyson's *hope* expresses expectation without real doubt; Hardy's expresses a wish without real expectation. Tennyson's poem expresses confident faith that it will be so; Hardy's expresses a wistful yearning that it might be so. Hardy does not say that he would go out to the barton to see the oxen kneel. He says (in effect), "I *feel* I would go *if* someone asked me." But no one will ask him, and it doesn't occur to him to go alone. Moreover, if someone did ask him, he wouldn't really go. The feeling is an ephemeral one that would not survive the invitation. Hardy (or the speaker) is an intellectually sophisticated twentieth-century man who would feel himself a goose to go on such a fool's errand. To put this point across to a class, it might be useful to ask: Would Hardy go if someone asked him? Would *you* go? Today Charlie Brown may wait in the pumpkin patch on Halloween to see the Great Pumpkin, but he won't when he is five years older, and no one of high-school or college age in America today would be caught dead waiting for Santa Claus to come down the chimney. Hardy's "hope" is a wistful yearning, not a hope.

Reading Tennyson's poem aloud, one should read the word *hope* very quietly; without emphasis, for to emphasize it is to express doubt, and the serenity and beauty of the preceding imagery indicate absence of doubt. One need not, in reading Hardy's poem, put artificial emphasis on "hoping": the inversion of accent (a trochee instead of an iamb) forces an emphasis on it. Hardy's poem, in its own way, is as quiet and as beautiful as Tennyson's, but the quietness comes from resignation rather than from faith. (For further comment, see the discussion of "The Darkling Thrush," page 287 of this manual.)   LP

124. *John Donne* **The Apparition** (page 673)

125. *John Donne* **The Flea** (page 674)

"The Apparition" has frequently been misread as an expression of hate and revulsion in which the motive of the speaker, a rejected lover, is revenge. It is, in reality, a poem of thwarted love and unspent desire in which the speaker is making a last desperate effort to obtain his lady's favors. In doing so, he adopts a new strategy. In the past, he has presumably tried and failed with all the usual methods—praising the lady's beauty, flattering her in various ways, declaring the strength and depth of his love for her, and so on. This time he attempts to *frighten* her into his arms. He works on various anxieties he *hopes* she may have. Instead of telling her how much he loves her, he tells her that his love "is spent." (By portraying himself as having slipped the hook, he may make himself seem more valuable in her eyes than when she was assured of his devotion.) He predicts that, if she rejects him, she will in the future have to settle for a much inferior lover. He attempts to frighten her with the prospect of his ghost appearing at her bedside, scaring her to death. Most of all, however, he tries to terrify her by threatening that his ghost will utter some unspecified but awful pronouncement or curse upon her, possibly capable of damning her soul for eternity, the nature and content of which he will not reveal to her now, because (he says) he wants revenge—and if he told her now, she would do anything necessary to avoid it.

But the speaker's assertion that his love (*desire* would be a more accurate term) "is spent" is undermined by the whole tone and intensity of the poem. If he no longer cares about her, why should her "scorn" be killing him? Would it not be more logical for him to say he was "cured"? And why should he send his ghost to her bedside? Obviously he has intense feelings concerning her still.

Most misreadings of the poem misinterpret "feigned vestal" as meaning "feigned virgin." But why should Donne use the fancier term if a simpler one means the same? The speaker, having unsuccessfully solicited the woman many times, has no personal grounds for doubting her virginity. What he accuses her of is not that she has falsely claimed to be a virgin, but that she falsely thinks herself capable of *sustaining* the state of virginity, as the vestal virgins did. Inferentially she has rejected his advances in the past by claiming that she wants to preserve her virginity or that she is by nature virginal. (The word "feigned," spelled *fain'd* in the manuscripts of Donne's poems, is a pun blending the meanings of *feigned* ["pretended"] and *fained* ["wished for"].) The speaker in effect is telling her, "Don't deceive yourself. You have the same strong carnal desires as I have, and if you do not take me, you will eventually settle for someone much less capable than I of satisfying your sexual needs." This "someone," tired out from their earlier lovemaking, will think, when she tries to wake him to protect her from the ghost, that she wants *more* lovemaking, and he will pretend to be asleep. Thus she will have to face the scary ghost alone. Trembling like an aspen tree and bathed in cold sweat, she will be "scared to death." Her "sick" candle will blink out, and she will become hyperbolically a "verier ghost" than her visitant. The "sick taper" is metaphorically her life (see "Out, out, brief candle" from *Macbeth*). It could be taken literally as well if we assume that a couple could go to bed leaving a candle burning by the bedside. It was commonly believed that a candle would dim in the presence of a ghost.

The speaker will not tell her what his ghost would say because, he says, he wants her to "painfully repent" her mistreatment of him, and if she knew *now* what it would say, that knowledge would "preserve" her and keep her "innocent." Innocent of what? Innocent of the one crime that has been alleged against her in the poem—that of being a murderess—of "killing" the speaker by her scorn. She can remain innocent of this crime only by ceasing to "kill" him—that is, by granting him her favors. What could the ghost say that would be terrible enough to accomplish this end? We do not know—nor does the speaker know. If he did, he would say it now. But he is gambling on the psychological principle that an unknown threat is more frightening than a known one. It is the darkness at the top of the stairs which daunts us. It is more frightening to hear a strange cry in the dark than to face five armed men by daylight. Thus the speaker does not reveal what the ghost will say, first because he does not *know*, and second because not telling will be more frightening than telling. In short, he *wants* her to remain "innocent" of the crime of "killing" him. He *wants* her to fulfill his unspent desires.

Donne here uses the cliché of Renaissance poetry which makes a woman "kill" a man by refusing to satisfy his desires, but he gives it an original twist by taking the metaphor literally and developing the whole poem on its literalness. It is important that the speaker accuses the lady of "killing" him, not having "killed" him. He is not *yet* "dead"; therefore there is still time for her to revive him and remain innocent of "murder."

In "The Flea" a young man attempts to seduce a young woman by the use of highly ingenious but highly sophistical reasoning. Basically, his argument is that losing her virginity will be no more damaging to her than a flea bite.

Before the first stanza, a flea has bitten the young man and then has jumped to the young woman and begun to bite her. The young man sees an opportunity and seizes it. He points to the flea and remarks that it has innocently mingled their bloods within itself, which is not more than sexual intercourse does (according to a traditional belief), and yet is more than she will allow to him. (When he says "more than we would do," he means, of course, more than *she* would do, for he is eager enough himself.) His remark that the flea's action cannot be called a "sin" or "shame" or "loss of maidenhead" indicates that she is a virgin and wishes to preserve her virginity until she can surrender it without sin and disgrace.

Between the first and second stanzas the young lady raises her finger to squash the flea. The young man protests, urging her to spare the flea, in which, because of their commingled bloods, they "almost, yea more than married are." With dazzling sleight-of-wit he has parlayed his claim that the mingling of their bloods within the flea is tantamount to a sinless act of sexual intercourse into a claim that it is tantamount to marriage. The flea is their "marriage-bed" and "marriage-temple." If she kills it, he claims, she will be destroying three lives—his, hers, and its—and committing three sins—murder, suicide, and sacrilege. (The line "Though use [habit] makes you apt [habitually disposed] to kill me" indicates that the speaker has already attempted many times to seduce the young woman and has failed. He is metaphorically playing with the poetic lover's traditional complaint that he is "dying" of his unrequited love and therefore that the lady is "killing" him by withholding her favors.)

But the young lady pays no attention to the speaker's protest. Between the second and third stanzas she has cruelly (according to the young man) killed the flea—has "purpled [crimsoned]" her nail with "blood of innocence." The flea's only guilt, the speaker claims, was contained in the drop of blood it sucked from its murderess, and now she declares triumphantly to the young man that neither he nor she has been injured (let alone "killed") by the flea's death. With one quick stroke of her finger she has indeed thoroughly discredited the young man's "logic." But the young man is not for a moment discountenanced. Nimbly, he turns his defeat into a further argument for his original design. Because his fears proved false, he contends, *all* fears are false, including hers that she will lose honor in yielding to him. She will lose no more honor in submitting to his desires, he claims, than she lost life in killing the flea. This argument (a generalization from a single instance) is, of course, as specious as those that have gone before, yet we have to admire the young man's mental agility in turning the tables and putting the young woman on the defensive once again.

Though one cannot make a dogmatic statement about what action follows the conclusion of the poem, evidence favors the inference that this attempt on the young lady's virginity is as unsuccessful as those that have preceded it. We know from lines 2, 9, 14, and 16 (we are given the information four times) that the young lady has previously denied the young man, and not just once but many times. Presumably this young man has also tried with no success the ordinary tactics of seduction—protestations of adoration, lavish compliments to the lady's charm and beauty, and pleas for pity—so he now turns to witty casuistry. We also know on what grounds the young lady has turned him down. She would consider the loss of her chastity a "sin" and a disgrace (line 6); she is concerned for her "honor" (line 26). In addition we see that the young lady is not taken in for a moment by the young man's preposterous "logic" in stanza 2. She calls his bluff, kills the insect, and laughs in his face. True, the young man is undismayed by this refutation and turns it immediately to his advantage. But are we to believe that the girl suddenly turns gullible or loses concern for her honor just because the young man has made a clever answer? If we extrapolate from the evidence given *in* the poem as to her past behavior, her intelligence, and her morality, we must conclude that she is a sensible young lady, not at all deceived by the young man's sophistry, and that she is holding out for honorable marriage, whether with this young man or another. The young man may have "won" this skirmish between the sexes, but only at the verbal level.

In a previous manual I wrote that this poem is "not to be taken too seriously as a reflection of human life, but to be enjoyed for what it is—a virtuoso display of ingenuity and wit." On further reflection I would modify that statement. It may be truer to life than at first appears. We are given a situation where a young man has attempted many times to obtain the woman's favor but has always been refused. Yet the woman by all indications enjoys his company. She has never told him, "Begone, vile seducer. Never darken my doorway again!" And, indeed, why should she not enjoy the company of such a witty and clever young man? Is it not quite possible that the "seduction attempt" has become a little game they play? That after the first rejection or so, the young man has realized that her virtue is unshakable, yet keeps on inventing more and more preposterous reasons why she should yield to him, not expecting her to do so, but for the "fun" of the thing? A student of mine once declared indignantly that no man could ever win *her* heart with an analogy drawn from a *flea*! Exactly. But if we see the seduction attempt as a "game" that neither of its two players takes very seriously, it becomes quite believable.

Both "The Apparition" and "The Flea" present an often-rejected lover taking a new and "far-out" approach to winning a woman's favors. But in tone the two poems are radically different. In tone "The Apparition" is dark and menacing; "The Flea" is light and playful. The speaker in "The Apparition" attempts to attain his goal by threats, the speaker in "The Flea" by obviously specious reasoning. The speaker in "The Apparition" attempts to win his lady's favors by maximizing her fears of what will happen to her if she refuses. The speaker in "The Flea" attempts to win them by minimizing his lady's fears of what will happen if she consents. Fear is the weapon of a rapist. The methods used by the speaker in "The Apparition" are ingenious and sinister. The methods used by the speaker in "The Flea" are ingenious and witty. LP

126. *Matthew Arnold* **Dover Beach** (page 675)

127. *Philip Larkin* **Church Going** (page 677)

"Dover Beach" is Arnold's lament over the decline of religious faith in his time. "The Sea of Faith," he tells us, was once "at the full," but now he only hears "Its melancholy, long, withdrawing roar," like the roar of waves receding or of the tide going out. Certainly, the mid-nineteenth century was a time of religious crisis—a time when vast numbers of thinking people were losing the simple Christian faith of their childhood teaching before the advance of scientific and rationalistic thought. The conflict and the agony are recorded in work after work of literature. Arnold's poem, first published in 1867 but possibly composed some ten or twelve years earlier, is surely one of the most eloquent expressions of despair ever written, combining profound pessimism with imperishable beauty.

The speaker is in a room overlooking the cliffs of Dover. He is so situated—where the cliffs curve—that not only can he look out over the English Channel and occasionally glimpse the coast of France (twenty-two miles away at this point) as it catches a gleam of moonlight, but he can also see, across the bay, the face of the cliffs themselves and the waves breaking on the shingle at their foot. In the room with him is a beloved woman (wife or sweetheart) to whom he unburdens his despair—not over any personal misfortune but about the state of the world.

The poem turns on a series of contrasts, of which the two most important are those (a) between the physical beauty of the world he sees outside his window and its actual spiritual darkness, and (b) between the full tide he sees outside the window and the ebbing "tide" of faith that he feels is responsible for the world's spiritual darkness.

Looking from his window, the speaker is first impressed by the beauty of the moonlit scene before him, and he summons his companion to the window to share its beauty with him. But then he becomes aware of the sound of the breakers crashing on the shingle, and this sound is a sad one. Being a person of broad intellectual culture, he is reminded by the sound of a passage in a Greek drama by Sophocles, who compared the ebb and flow of the sea to the ebb and flow of human misery. Then he thinks of his own time, and he is reminded by the sound of the ebbing of religious faith. This thought is so melancholy to him that he cries out to his beloved, "Ah, love, let us be true / to one another!" for a loving human relationship seems the only value left in a world that has lost every other source of meaning—a world that, despite its illusory physical beauty, has "really neither joy, nor love, nor light, / Nor certitude, nor peace, nor help for pain"—surely two of the most pessimistic lines in English poetry. The simile ending the poem gives concrete embodiment to this abstract statement and is deservedly one of the most famous in English poetry. As an image for complete meaninglessness in human life, it can hardly be surpassed. Words of negative connotation pile up—"darkling," "confused," "alarms," "struggle," "flight," "ignorant," "clash," "night"—to give a picture of utter confusion, blindness, cross-purposes, and uncertainty, in which warring armies cannot tell friend from foe and strike at both alike in the darkness. This uncertainty embodies the lack of "certitude" mentioned in line 34, which in turn stems from the ebbing Sea of Faith. The one remaining consolation—the possibility of a loyal personal relationship between two lovers, because of its positioning, seems a very frail one indeed. Instead of one person lost on a tiny raft at night in mid-ocean, we are left with two people on the raft clinging to each other out of desperation. The poem begins with light and ends in darkness.

Students must be made to see that the image in the last three lines is the figurative, not the literal, term in a simile. This poem is not about war, nor was it written during time of war—it is a poem about the loss of a common religious faith that once linked men together in a belief, hope, and some degree of brotherhood or community—a loss that has resulted in a world where men work only for self-advancement and at cross-purposes with each other.

It is also important to note that the poem was written, not by a believer blaming the rest of the world for its lack of belief, but by a poet who himself can no longer accept the stories and assumptions on which the old faith was based, and who regards its consolations and certainties as no longer possible for thinking men. If he had been himself a believer, he would have cried out, "O Lord! bring these people back to a belief in your eternal truth and loving overlordship!" Instead, his cry is to a human companion, "Ah, love, let us be true / To one another!"

The syntax in lines 7–14 is somewhat involved. The noun "roar" (9) is not the direct object of "hear" but the subject of the infinitives [To] "Begin," "cease," "begin," and "bring" (12–13). The direct object of "hear" is the whole infinitive phrase of which "roar" is the subject. In reading the poem one must reject the temptation to drop one's voice at the end of line 11.

The title "Church Going" may be interpreted in three ways: (1) the habit of church-going, of regularly attending Sunday services, a practice continued by diminishing numbers of people; (2) the visit to an old church by the speaker who is making the visit from motives far different from religious worship, but who ironically speaks of himself as a churgh-goer; (3) the historical decline in importance of the Church in the lives of ordinary people and in affairs of state.

The speaker is taking a bicycle tour of his country. We know this because he takes off his bicycle-clips after entering the church. What an economical way of telling us! Have bicycle-clips ever been mentioned in a poem before? Or since?

The speaker constantly undermines any pretense of self-importance. His motivation seems mostly idle curiosity. He is not an expert in church architecture. Inside

189

the church he wonders "what to look for" (21). Is the roof new, cleaned, or restored? "Someone would know: I don't" (12). He wonders who will be the last to enter the church for what it was. Will it be some fanatic expert on church architecture, or someone addicted to Christmas nostalgia who will not give it up? Or will it be someone like himelf: "Bored, uninformed" (46)?

But though he poses as a non-intellectual, and uses slangy speech, the speaker entertains thoughts and questions about the future of the church (and belief) that would not enter the thoughts of an ordinary man. Will it be kept up as a tourist attraction or will it be turned into grazing ground for sheep? Will it be a place to nourish superstition? Like Matthew Arnold's speaker in "Dover Beach," this speaker believes that Christian belief is waning and will soon be gone; churches will fall "completely out of use" (22). "But superstition, like belief, must die, / And what remains when disbelief has gone?" (34–35). The church will be no more than "Grass, weedy pavement, brambles, buttress, sky" (36).

Though the assessments of the present and the future made in Larkin's poem and in Arnold's are similar in their intellectual components, the two poems differ widely in tone. Arnold's poem sounds the depths of human despair; Larkin's seems inspired more by idle curiosity. LP

128. *Rupert Brooke* **The Dead** (page 679)

"Hearts" (1) is a metonymy for the lives of those young men killed in war—who are referred to by the pronouns listed in the first study question. The metonymy leads to the definition of these men as sensitive, emotional beings whose lives were characteristically full of mixed contradictions—joy, care, sorrow, mirth, dawn and sunset, slumber and waking, friended and alone, and so forth—elements that might seem the whole compendium of experience of the young. Note, however, that they are not given some of the less admirable qualities, such as irresponsibility, careless-ness, selfishness, lust, and other traits equally characteristic of young men. In pay-ing his respects to the fallen, Brooke purposely sets out with the word "hearts," a potentially sentimental approach. (Even though we know about "hard-hearted" people, the unmodified word seems to point connotatively toward the "kindness" that Brooke singles out as the gift of the years: "kind-hearted" would be the modified term in this poem.)

The symbols in the poem are introduced in the sestet with images of water, wind, sunlight, and of frost, stillness, and darkness. The "laughter" of line 9 is a metaphor for the appearance of sunlit waves on a lake, and echoes the "mirth" in line 2. The literal process presented in the sestet is the freezing over of a lake that was bril-liantly active in the sunlight and wind, and now is brilliantly still in the moonlight. The frost that stills the winds and freezes the lake symbolizes death, as does the night that now covers the lake. The metonymies listed in study question 3 are all references to the broad expanse of the shining surface of the frozen lake, and all of them connote the glory of the remembered lives of the men. The sunlit lake is a symbol for the lives of these young soldiers, and the frozen lake a symbol for them in death. They are equally beautiful, though completely opposite.

The tone of the poem is thus poignantly sorrowful, expressing a sense of loss but also admiration for the transforming glory that came to these men.   TRA

129. *Wallace Stevens* **The Death of a Soldier** (page 680)

This poem has both a specific and a general subject, and it might best be read as a symbolic statement: it presents what the title says, but the meaning expands from the specific issue of the death of a soldier on a battlefield to encompass human death in general. The "soldier" is only an extreme example whose death invites certain special responses not always associated with the deaths of ordinary people— chiefly, those traditional attitudes that are so easily evoked by apologists for war, by national holiday commemorators, by politicians and patriots: those who die in war "have not died in vain," but have served some national (or religious, or universal) purpose. Stevens has chosen a soldier so as to excite such stock responses, which he subjects to situational irony: a military death is apparently the most meaningful death in a secular, non-theist society—and it is no more meaningful than the changing of the seasons.

Death in this poem is part of a natural process, linked in simile twice to the change of season in autumn, just another "fall." It is not the occasion for imposing upon survivors the duty of memorials or funereal pomposity. Its apparent uniqueness— that something in particular has stopped, a singular human life—is compared to the momentary cessation of wind, a stillness that is deceptive in the larger context of climatic motion. No human life is important, no human death is important, not even those that a secular, patriotic nation celebrates.

Such nihilism is not pleasant to contemplate, yet this poem has a shapeliness and rhetorical power that make the ideas less repugnant. There is, after all, a kind of beauty in the stark, simple, and unadorned presentation of the idea: an individual human death is no more important than the change of the seasons, and the impersonal physical processes of the world will go on, "nevertheless," in the impassive reality of absolute truth. ("Nevertheless" is a marvelously evocative word, in this context, for in its double negation it emphasizes Stevens's point: mere human life or death can *never* make any *less* the reality of a world of factual truth.)

Formally, the poem reflects its reductive philosophy in its structure. The free verse stanzas have a syllabic pattern made visible by the printing. The norm is an opening line of about 10 syllables, a second line of 8, and a final line of 4 (the last stanza offers this variation: 7 in line 2, 5 in line 3). The stanzas themselves, that is, seem to dwindle down toward immobility and silence, "as in a season of autumn /

When the wind stops . . .'' Yet, as the stanzas repeat the pattern and thus imply continuity, the clouds (and poetry) will ''go, nevertheless.''

The similarities between this poem and Brooke's ''The Dead'' are the ostensible subject matter and the use of natural phenomena as symbols. The differences in tone are, of course, enormous. Here the ongoing natural process lessens the importance and meaning of the subject, making this death insignificant and ''without memorial.'' For Brooke, the process results in an ''Unbroken glory'' and ''gathered radiance.'' Part of the tonal difference may derive from a contrast of ulterior subject: Stevens is concerned with human mortality in general, Brooke with a particular group of young men. But essentially they are at philosophical poles on the value and meaning of life.

In comparing the tones of these two poems with those of the other poems listed in study question 4, it will be of central importance to define the involvement of the speaker and how fully he is characterized. Another poem not listed in that question, Keith Douglas's ''Vergissmeinnicht'' (page 800), might also be considered. TRA

130. *Alexander Pope* **Engraved on the Collar of a Dog Which I Gave to His Royal Highness** (page 680)

The *speaker's* tone is plain enough: it is one of supreme *hauteur*. The *poet's* tone is more complex. Is there a bit of pride expressed in the title at being on such close terms with the King? A bit of flattery for the King in the implication that no higher honor could befall a dog than to belong to him? But surely some irony too in having dogs take pride in the station and birth of their owners. How much more snobbish can a creature get! Yes, a sly dig at snobbery in any station of life. LP

131. *Anonymous* **Love** (page 681)

There is a brief comment on these verses on page 755 of the text. LP

EXERCISE 1 (page 681)

The three *carpe diem* poems differ chiefly in the sense of urgency with which their message is communicated, which in turn develops largely from the differing speaker-audience relationships and situations in the three poems, although other factors (diction, imagery) are also important.

The most urgent—one might almost say desperate—is ''To His Coy Mistress'' (page 593). Here the speaker is a young man addressing a young lady, urging her to make love with him. There is, he claims, no afterlife (''yonder all before us lie / Deserts of vast eternity''), and there is no lovemaking after death (''then worms shall try / That long-preserved virginity, / And your quaint honor turn to dust, / And into ashes all my lust''). They must therefore fulfill their strong physical desire for each other *now*!

In "To the Virgins, to Make Much of Time" (page 607) the speaker is no longer a young man urging his own passionate desire upon his mistress *now*; rather, the speaker seems to be a disinterested older man advising, not a specific young woman, but young women in general. He urges them not to satisfy their senses *now*, in an illicit relationship, but to "go marry," a process which they may set in motion now but which may demand several weeks to consummate.

In "Loveliest of Trees" (page 596) the sense of urgency almost vanishes, disappearing into a tone of serenity and fulfillment, for this time the speaker, a young man of twenty, is not urging anyone, not even himself (and he appears to be addressing only himself) to do something; he is doing it, or preparing to do it. He is simply announcing his intention to do now and his resolve to do in the future what he would undoubtedly advise others to do, if asked. And the desire he is about to fulfill is nothing illicit, like fornication, nor momentous and perhaps irreversible, like marriage; it is an act entirely innocent, one that no one would protest against or advise against, namely, enjoying beauty, in particular natural beauty, while he has the opportunity to do so.

POEMS FOR FURTHER READING

Poems 204, 220, and 270, and the pairs 276/277 and 273/291 from Part 2 provide additional illustrations of topics presented in this chapter.

CHAPTER ELEVEN

Musical Devices

132. *Ogden Nash* **The Turtle** (page 683)

One might also ask why Nash chose to write about a turtle rather than a tortoise. The anatomical problem is the same for each.   LP

133. *W. H. Auden* **That night when joy began** (page 685)

The two people in the poem have been disillusioned by their experiences with love. They have found that it is not lasting and that it ends in disappointment. They have been "burnt" by it. Thus they are deeply skeptical about their present affair. It begins, as have past affairs, in the joy of sexual excitement; they are prepared to find in the morning that their attraction has little or no other basis, but in the morning they are still in love; days pass, then weeks; they begin to realize that they have found a true human relationship, one rooted in something deeper than sexual attraction.

The basic metaphor presents two foot travelers cutting across fields that they hope are the public fields of love, where all may travel, but that they fear may be private lands, where they will be shot or apprehended for trespassing. The metaphor in lines 3–4 beautifully combines the visual image of the sun's horizontal rays awakening them from their dream and the metaphorical idea of the landowner's shooting them for trespassing—that is, destroying their temporary illusion of love. But as they hike for additional miles (days), they outgrow their nervousness and begin to believe in spiritual peace, for they are not reproached for trespassing and they can see in the future (through love's field glasses) nothing that is not genuine and lasting love.

The rime pattern:

Lines 1 and 4 (of each stanza): alliteration and consonance
Lines 2 and 3 (of each stanza): alliteration and consonance
Lines 1 and 3 (of each stanza): assonance
Lines 2 and 4 (of each stanza): assonance

In line 10 the last syllable must be thought of as beginning with *r* rather than with *p* to preserve the integrity of this pattern, and in line 12 the final syllable must be thought of as including the final *s* (really a *z*) of *his*. The whole is ingeniously worked out, along with the extended metaphor; and the poet's pleasure (and ours) lies partly in the working out of this design.   LP

134. *Gerard Manley Hopkins* **God's Grandeur** (page 687)

The theme of the poem might be stated in some such words as these:

The natural world is filled with the beauty and energizing power of its Creator. But men, ignoring God's authority, through their commercial and industrial activities, have despoiled and polluted this beauty and separated themselves from its spiritually regenerating power. Nevertheless, this power is never used up; through God's love for his world, nature's beauty is continuously renewed.

How pale and flat this prose statement is as compared to the poem's "grandeur"!

In line 1 the word "charged," because of its associations with electricity and gunpowder, has many times the force of *filled*. In line 2 the image is of crinkled metallic foil (gold, tin, silver, or lead) being shaken in the sun and flashing light-reflections from each of its multifold creases and facets. In line 4 "rod" is a metaphor or symbol for God's authority and chastening power. In lines 7–8 the soil is "bare" because man has pitted it over with his heaps of coal and iron ore and paved it over with streets and walks; and man cannot feel the grass underfoot anyway because his feet are cased in shoes. (We need not assume that Hopkins denounces the wearing of shoes, though he may indeed think it good sometimes to walk barefoot in the grass.) Pavement and shoe leather serve the poet here as symbols for man's twofold separation from nature. In lines 11–12 the image of the sun's light disappearing in the west, only to reappear next morning in the east, is a symbol for the perpetual renewal of nature. And this renewal springs from the love of the Holy Ghost (third member of the Trinity) in His traditional metaphoric embodiment as a dove (symbol of gentleness and tenderness) brooding over the world (as over a nest) with warm breast and bright wings. The word "bent" means both that the earth is curved (as suggested by the preceding image of the sun's apparent travel around it) and bent out of shape from man's misuse of it.

Just as the world is charged with the grandeur of God, so this sonnet is charged with a rich verbal music appropriate to its subject. In its end-rimes it follows the strictest and most demanding pattern for the Italian sonnet (four rime sounds). Alliteration is apparent in almost every line, perhaps most brilliantly in the three two-word clusters of line 14 (''*W*orld *br*oods-*w*arm *br*east-*br*ight *w*ings''). Assonance is especially apparent in line 11 (''l*a*st-bl*a*ck,'' ''W*e*st-w*e*nt'') and line 13 (''H*o*ly Gh*o*st *o*ver''). Consonance is prominent in line 1, where each stressed syllable ends with a *d* (''worl*d*-charge*d*-gran*d*eur-Go*d*''). In the question in line 4, where nine short monosyllables (all but two of them stressed) are spat out in rapid succession like bullets from a machine gun, there is internal rime (*men-then*), alliteration (*now-not, reck-rod*), and assonance (*not-rod, reck-men-then*); except for the initial ''Why,'' each stressed syllable in the series gets into the act once if not twice. In line 5 the triple repetition of a whole phrase (''have trod'') emphasizes the repetitiousness of the action described. In lines 6–7 two sets of internal rimes (*seared-bleared-smeared; wears-shares*) combined with the three *sm*- alliterations (*smeared-smudge-smell*) put such an emphasis on words of disagreeable meaning as to give one a feeling of

195

almost physical revulsion. But we leave this analysis incomplete; the reader's patience will be "spent" long before the poem's "music" is.

An interesting thematic comparison may be made between this sonnet and Wordsworth's "The world is too much with us" (page 566).   LP

135.   *Gwendolyn Brooks*   **We Real Cool** (page 688)

The placement of the pronouns in this poem gives its rhythm a syncopated effect appropriate to the jazz culture of the speakers.

The critic who called the poem immoral was oblivious to its dramatic irony (its tone). The poet does not share the opinion of the speakers that they are "real cool," nor does any moderately good reader, which obviously the critic was not.
LP

136.   *Dudley Randall*   **Blackberry Sweet** (page 688)

A simple love song addressed to a black girl by a black poet, "Blackberry Sweet" poses no difficulties that need explanation, no coiled ambiguities that demand interpretation. Yet considerable poetic skill was required to achieve its apparent simplicity.

Each stanza has its own unifying scheme. Stanza 1 is devoted to the girl's appearance as metonymically represented by her lips, which in a series of similes are compared to fruits. Cherries express the redness and roundness of the lips, grape bunches their fullness, and blackberries their sweetness. The blackberries furnish the climactic comparison not only because of their sweetness (though they are actually no sweeter than cherries, grapes, or various other fruits), but obviously because the poem is addressed to a black girl, and also because the quality of sweetness would be sensed through the taste of kisses.

Stanza 2 is devoted to motion. When she walks, she is like "a rising bird" or "a falling star." The two motions are in opposite directions, but are magical in their beauty, by day or by night.

Stanza 3 picks up the "magic" of the preceding stanza and speaks of the "spell" cast by the girl on the speaker. The "magic" here is achieved by the three spaced one-syllable verbs. The meter of the poem is varied but consists mainly of three-beat lines (trochaic trimeter). The refrain lines have two beats, but the unstressed syllables are so strong that they nearly convert the line from two trochaic to four monosyllabic feet. No matter how we scan them, however, the refrain lines have a metrical uniqueness that gives them an appropriate emphasis. The greatest uniqueness in the poem is its final line, which reduces the trimeter lines from a norm of six syllables to three. These three monosyllabic feet bring the poem to a particularly emphatic climax. The poem is simple, but not as simple as at first it sounds.
LP

137. *Edna St. Vincent Millay* **Counting-Out Rhyme** (page 689)

A counting-out rhyme, as its name implies, is a verse (usually for children) that involves counting things, often using numbers ("1, 2, Buckle my shoe / 3, 4, Knock at the door . . .), but just as often not ("Eeny, meeny, miny, mo, / Catch a Dutchman by the toe . . ."). They are usually passed down from obscure origins by oral tradition through generations of children and are usually nonsensical in content.

Millay, however, gives the form artistic treatment. First, she gives it unity of content. She counts the parts (bark, leaf, wood, stem, twig), usually distinguished by their color (silver, sallow, yellow, green, pale), of different species of trees (beech, birch, willow, maple, apple, popple, oak, hornbeam, elder). Second, she gives her verse a subtler and more sophisticated form than the usual clunking iambic or trochaic rimed couplets. She invents a three-line stanza with a strict pattern of feminine half-rimes, using trochaic trimeter in the first two lines and dimeter in the third, varying this with a high percentage of run-on lines. Third, obviously enchanted by the sounds of words, Millay enchants the reader with a dense variety of sound-correspondences (alliteration, assonance, consonance, internal rime, feminine half-rime), made more striking by their skillful juxtaposition of euphony (*silver-yellow-willow*) and cacophony (*oak for yoke and barn-beam*).

This poem, all said, may not "say" much, but what it does say, it says enchantingly. It delights by its sheer love of language and sound.   LP

138. *Emily Dickinson* **As imperceptibly as grief** (page 690)

The subject of the poem is ambivalence about seasonal change. The initial simile sets the tone: summer lapsed away imperceptibly, as "grief" lapses imperceptibly; were the diminution of grief consciously perceived, its passing would seem to be a perfidious betrayal of the person for whom we grieve. So, the simile says, the passing of summer evokes an emotion that includes one's love and loyalty, the sadness of loss, and the consciousness of separation. But how can these emotions be identified with summer, the season of richness and growth, the apogee of the year to which spring climbs and from which autumn (in the distinctly American term) falls? If summer is like grief, what are we grieving *for*? "Spring" might be one logical answer—the loss in summertime of the exuberant excitement of that early time—yet the terms of the poem do not invite such a comparison.

The grief, rather, is associated with summer's relationship to us: it is summer that passes so imperceptibly that its betrayal *of us* is almost overlooked. This personification (overtly revealed in the feminine pronouns) and the constant tone of regret imply the imaginative act of the speaker: we long for the personal, permanent love for us of what we love. Why does the summer betray us by leaving us? The two middle stanzas present a series of appositives for the diminution of the season, presenting it in terms of its voluntary withdrawal and increasing alienation yet without showing any ill will toward those it leaves behind. These two stanzas also present a series of attempts to pinpoint or define the precise feelings excited by the imminent departure of summer: Is it like an intensification of quietness? Has nature withdrawn from us as a person might shut herself up for a long, quiet afternoon (the metaphor must be especially poignant when we recall Emily Dickinson's own sequestration)? The factual evidence is that both the coming on and the departure of night, at dusk and daybreak, seem strangely changed—an earlier darkness and a foreign sunrise. The process resembles the ambivalence of a dear guest "who would be gone," whose gracious behavior is both full of courtesy and deeply distressing.

These attempts at definition reveal the ambiguities of feeling already noted in the simile of grief in line 1: the increased beauty of "quietness distilled," the sense of being excluded mixed with an understanding approval of nature's sequestration, and most of all (placed in the climactic position), the paradoxical combination of "A courteous, yet harrowing grace." But this is a poem about the "imperceptible," and it is to that quality that the poem returns for its conclusion. Without any of the "perceptible" (and humanly comprehensible) means of transportation, neither the wing of the bird nor the keel of the boat, two silent means of departing, "summer made her light escape / Into the beautiful." The guest, though gracious, does not live with us, but elsewhere, and finally manages to escape. The final line, "Into the beautiful," has been criticized for its abstract vagueness, but the sense of an ideal, abstract realm of beauty as the proper "home" for this sojourning visitor, this sequestered captive, may be appropriate in its vagueness. If the process of its departure is "imperceptible," so too may be its destination.

The music of this poem is muted, as befits its subject. Approximate rimes, subtle consonant links, delicately unobtrusive alliteration, and the poet's marvelous ear for related vowel sounds all reinforce the elegiac tone. For example, in the last stanza, the phrase *without a wing* alliterates the initial *w* followed by the assonance of short *i*—but the effect is softened by the fact that the syllable *with-* is metrically unstressed, while *wing* is stressed. The preponderant consonant sounds in the stanza are the sibilant *s* of "thu*s*," "*s*ervice," "*s*ummer," and "e*s*cape," the crisp *t* of "withou*t*," "ligh*t*," "in*t*o," and "beau*t*iful," and the *k* of "*k*eel" and "es*c*ape"—consonants that with the *w*'s and *l*'s underscore the quickness and lightness of the action being described.

But perhaps the most interesting example of the use of musicality is to be heard in the key term, *imperceptibly*, a word so proper to its purpose that the poet reiterates a form of it two lines later. The word has the flickering of its consonant sounds— *mp*, sibilant *c, pt,* and *bl*, all rapidly unobtrusive—and the light swiftness of its collection of short vowels. It also has an intrinsic rhythm that finds echoes throughout the poem in words with an elegiac "falling" rhythm: IM-per-*CEP*-ti-BLY and IM-per-*CEP*-ti-BLE both alternate stressed and unstressed syllables, and both occur in perfectly regular iambic lines. The stresses within the words, however, are not equal: in both, the syllable *-cep-* is more heavily stressed than the initial *im-*, and both of those syllables receive greater stress than the final stressed *-bly* or *-ble*. Both words, that is, are rapid in pronounciation (owing to their vowel and consonant combinations) and rise to a central stress before falling off in a final, very lightly stressed syllable. This falling effect in a final light stress can be heard as well in such key words as *PER*-fi-DY and *BEAU*-ti-FUL; the elegiac tone is also reinforced by the high incidence of words that are individually trochaic in rhythm (though they usually function in regular iambic foot patterns): *summer, twilight, nature, spending, earlier, morning, foreign,* and so forth. TRA

139. *John Crowe Ransom* **Parting, without a Sequel** (page 690)

The disappointment of first love bears a slightly comic aspect when viewed from the outside or when looked back on over a perspective of years, but to those who are actually suffering it, it is undiluted tragedy. We may try to talk "wisdom" to the disappointed youngster, but how can she understand? Or how can *we* understand? "She just doesn't realize," the oldsters say; "this will be nothing to her in a few months or years." "They just don't *know*," the youngster thinks; "how can they know what I feel?"

John Crowe Ransom catches both the comedy and the tragedy in this wryly poignant little poem. Observing the termination of a first attachment from a point of view partly inside and partly outside the heartbroken girl, he is able both to *feel* the tumultuous suffering of the girl and to note its theatrical exaggerations and its humorous ambivalences. The comic aspects are reflected in the double and triple rimes, many of them slant; in the melodramatic triteness of the phrase describing the girl's attitude toward her letter "which he so richly has deserved"; in her gloating satisfaction with the letter's crushing language ("And nothing could be better"); in the stagy *hauteur* of her command as she delivers it to the messenger boy—" 'Into his hands' "; in the solemn pretentiousness of the epithet for the messenger boy— "the blue-capped functioner of doom"; in her mixed feelings as she watches the messenger boy ride off (hoping at once that he will deliver the letter promptly, which will put her errant lover in his place, and that it will get lost, allowing one more chance for reconciliation); and in her exaggeration of the episode's significance—"the ruin of her younger years." The comedy is also reflected in the title, where the phrase "without a Sequel" suggests the theatrical component of the affair ("Final Parting" would have been more straightforward).

But if we allow ourselves amusement at the girl's expense, we must also bleed with her. The parting *hurts*. We are moved to pity as the blood drains from her face and she goes to seek comfort from her father. The fourth and fifth stanzas are ambiguous. Is it her father or a tree she goes to? Either reading is possible. The "oak" may be a metaphor for her father, chosen to connote his strength and pride. Or it may be literally an oak, one perhaps that her father has planted by the front door ("lintel") of the house, a tree that embodies his strength and through which his spirit seems to speak. At any rate the father, or the father's presence in the oak, tries to calm the daughter, gently reproaching her for the foolishness of her despair. In vain, of course. His talk is like the sound of leaves as it ceases and begins again. There are several double meanings here. The word "sere" means old and dry, but

199

also suggests wise (seer). Is there something dry and meaningless in the wisdom of the father? The word "vaunting" applied to a tree would mean large and spreading; applied to a man, proud. Combined with "sere-seer" it suggests a gently wry ironic comment on the father's "wisdom." Wisdom comes easily to an old man who is himself past the storms of youth.

The use of figurative language is imperative if we are to be faithful to the full truth and complexity of human feeling. The bitterness of the girl's feeling is summed up in the marvelous metaphor of the last stanza comparing the tread marks of the bicycle tire to the track of a snake (and to the pattern on the back of the snake). Both visually and emotionally the metaphor is exact. The girl has been venomously bitten by her disappointment and hopes that her letter, whose characters are also snakelike, will bite the offending young man. The physical effects of the bite (i.e., of her emotion) are accurately conveyed through the paradox of the last two lines: "she stood there hot as fever / And cold as any icicle." Logically the statement is contradictory and impossible, but in the epistemology of human feeling it is not only true but could be conveyed in no other way.

[This commentary is reprinted, with a slight alteration, from Laurence Perrine and James M. Reid, 100 *American Poems of the Twentieth Century* (New York: Harcourt, 1966) 139–41.] LP

140. *Ted Hughes* Thistles (page 691)

The thistles symbolize the persistence of unyielding, stern, and violent qualities in man and nature—a dogged prickliness that is the dark counterpart of the pertinacity that Marianne Moore celebrates in "Nevertheless" (page 714). Hughes finds this quality both in the ineradicable thistle and in the marauding Viking of old—and links them fancifully by imagining the decayed bodies of the Vikings as the nutrient source of the thistles. He even identifies physical resemblances: the spikes of the thistle are like spears or swords; the fine hairiness of the blossom is like that of the blond Scandinavian, and its redness recalls both a decorated helmet and blood bursting from a head wound; and the autumnal change from green to woody grey is like the greying of hair and of flesh tones.

The opening line invites an investigation of musical devices, starting the poem off with the assonance of *rubber tongues* and the alliteration of *hoeing hands*, but the primary sound effect comes from repeated harsh consonants: *k, sp, st, p, f,* and guttural *g*. Appropriately, these reinforce the spikiness of the central symbol.   TRA

141. *Barton Sutter* Shoe Shop (page 692)

The central contrast of the poem is between "image" (in the public relations sense of the word) and substance; between shoddy work (with a high gloss) and honest craftsmanship. The cobbler is a man who knows and values craftsmanship, and who cares nothing for "image." In his shop there are no "displays"; boots and shoes lie "tumbled" in heaps. There is a smell of real leather; nothing pretends to be what it is not. He himself is without the ingratiating smile and slick manners of a salesman. He gives the work in hand more attention than he does his customer, "as if [he] held a grudge / Against business." There is double meaning here, for he does have a grudge against "business" in the sense of large-scale production, corporate enterprise, "factories," everything brought in by the Industrial Revolution. For him good craftsmanship is hand craftsmanship, not the product of assembly-line techniques, not the creation of advertising. His values are directly opposed to those of much of the modern business world, as seen in his ironical statement of its creed: "'Cut the price. / Advertise! Never mind the merchandise.'" He is, he realizes, an anachronism in this world. His pride is "steeped in bitterness," and he knows that his "guerrilla warfare" (his fuming and bitching) is hopeless. Yet, paradoxically, he derives tremendous satisfaction from his work. He has pride in his own workmanship; but, even more importantly, he can find physical and emotional release from his frustrations by whacking the tacks with his hammer—as if each were one of the enemy!

The poem begins when the speaker closes the door on "the racket / Of rush hour traffic," where the sleek machines of the modern world speed by, and steps into another world: an older world, like a blacksmith's; a more human world, like a barbershop (not a "hairstyling salon"), where the workers (one to a customer) fill the air with talk and sharpen their nonelectric razors on leather strops; a world opposed to modern values, yet not a "front for agitators" (or anything else), for there is no back room. (The word "front" suggests a false appearance, like the "fronts" on a movie lot.) What the speaker finds in the shop is reality, respect for craftsmanship, and contempt for illusion. No wonder that when he steps into the street again, back into a world of illuminated billboards and dancing city lights, the whole city looks as "flimsy" and as false "as a movie set."

Except for the concluding couplet, the poem is written in a series of four-line stanzas with mostly approximate rimes, masculine or feminine, arranged in an *abba* pattern. In the first stanza, however, both sets of rimes contain a *k* sound that helps to magnify the noise of the onomotopoetic first rime *racket*. In the second stanza, similarly, all lines end with a sharp *p*, reinforcing the onomatopoetic *whippersnap*, in which the sound occurs twice. There is also onomatopoetic reinforcement in the riming of *satisfaction* with *whack it* in the final full stanza. In line 27 an almost perfect internal rime, contained in the first and final metrically similar words, is combined with assonance in the middle word, with an alliteration of *m*'s, and with a pair of unstressed *-ver* syllables plus a stressed *mer-*, to make the line sound, ironically enough, like the perfect advertising slogan it almost is.   LP

142. *William Stafford* **Traveling through the dark** (page 694)

Line 3 makes clear that it is not unusual for dead deer to be found on the Wilson River road. The only inference to be drawn is that they are hit by autos as they cross the road on their way to the river, but that most drivers, after the impact, leave the carcass where it falls and drive on. That the speaker stops—even though he was not the one who hit the deer—shows him to be an unusually responsible person. He has carefully driven around in front of the animal, has turned down his headlights—another responsible action—but has left the motor running, hoping to make quick work of pushing the carcass over the edge, not stopping too long on the dangerous unlit road.

That he recognizes an ethical dilemma when he discovers the unborn fawn still living inside the dead doe particularly marks him out as a thoughtful person concerned with the preciousness of all life; and that he hesitates—thinking hard "for us all"—again reveals his deep sense of involvement. Who are the "us all" for whom the speaker thinks? Himself surely, the unborn fawn surely, other motorists traveling the Wilson River road, and, beyond that, all humanity, perhaps all life forms, which need relationships with other forms of life in order to exist.

But what are his options? There is no way he can deliver the unborn fawn: he is hardly equipped to perform a Caesarean in the middle of the road. Nor could he mother the fawn, were it born. He must either take responsibility for killing the fawn by pushing its dead mother over the edge, or walk away and leave the dead doe there, endangering other lives—motorists who might be killed while swerving to miss the body. There is no choice really. The second alternative would be equivalent to washing his hands of moral responsibility—like Pontius Pilate in the Bible. The fact that he hesitates, however—considering the options—makes us like him. That one "swerving" from what should and must be expeditiously done makes him fully human.

Many of the images have symbolic implications, though perhaps not of the kind that benefit from being pinned with a label and spelled with a capital *S*. The image of "Traveling through the dark" (how different in effect from "Driving at night"!) suggests the difficulties of living life and having to make moral decisions with only limited knowledge and with no certain moral guidance. The cold of the doe's body and the warm spot in its side are *signs*, not symbols, of death and life. The car, its steady engine purring, its parking lights "aimed ahead," suggests a kind of automated life that never hesitates, does not make decisions, and is always ready for action. Its purring engine contrasts with the stillness of the wilderness (and of the unborn fawn), which has its own claims on the speaker, and which seems to "listen" (16), as if for his decision. The red tail-light of the car is a conventional symbol of danger, and "the glare of the warm exhaust turning red" in which the speaker stands (15) almost symbolizes his dilemma. He must choose between spilling the warm blood of the unborn fawn over the edge of the canyon or endangering the lives of other human beings.

"Canyon" (3) is the only line-end in the poem without any correspondence in sound to another line-end in its stanza, and even it alliterates with the first line-end in the following stanza, just two lines away.   LP

143. *Robert Frost* **Nothing Gold Can Stay** (page 695)

The paradox in line 1 is to be explained by the fact that, when leaves first bud in the spring, they have a yellow tint, more gold than green, which they lose as the leaves grow larger.

The paradox in line 3 has been explained by Alfred R. Ferguson as referring to much the same thing: "The earliest leaf unfolds its beauty like a flower," but I believe it refers to something different. Some trees and shrubs blossom in the spring before they bear leaves (the plum, for example; also the redbud and some species of peach and cherry). In botanical language, however, the term *leaf*, in its broadest sense, includes all foliar structures of the higher plants, including the sepals, petals, pistil, and stamens of a flower: all parts of the blossom, technically, are modified leaves. For trees like the plum, therefore, it is literally true that the "early leaf's a flower." That it remains so only "an hour" is an overstatement, but the blossoming period of these trees is brief at best; then the flowers drop off and the ordinary leaves begin.

Frost's poem, then, lists four things that have an early but brief period of perfect beauty (or happiness): the foliage of trees; plants that blossom before they bear leaves; the course of human history (as storied in the Eden myth—or other myths of a "golden age"); and a day (which begins with the fresh gold-tinted air of sunrise). It ends with a generalization: "Nothing gold can stay." But by this time Frost's examples have assumed the force of symbols: they remind us as well of the year (which begins with spring), of the individual human life (which blooms in youth), and perhaps of love (most blissful in its early stages). Frost's "gold" is a symbol of perfection, and his theme is that most things reach their moment of perfection early and retain it briefly. His poem is about the transiency of beauty, bliss, youth, spring, and the transport of early love.

For another treatment of this theme in Frost, see his poem "The Oven Bird." For additional perspectives on "Nothing Gold Can Stay," see Lawrance Thompson, *Fire and Ice* (New York: Holt, 1942) 169–70; Charles R. Anderson, *Explicator* 22 (Apr. 1964): item 63; Alfred R. Ferguson, in *Frost: Centennial Essays* (Jackson: UP of Mississippi, 1974) 436–39; and John Robert Doyle, Jr., *The Poetry of Robert Frost* (Johannesburg: Witwatersrand UP, 1962) 174–76. For a possibly fuller analysis than you may want of the musical devices in the poem (and *their* perfection), see John A. Rea, "Language and Form in 'Nothing Gold Can Stay,'" *Robert Frost: Studies of the Poetry*, ed. Kathryn Gibbs Harris (Boston: Hall, 1979) 17–25. LP

POEMS FOR FURTHER READING

Poems 214, 240, 245, and 261 from Part 2 provide additional illustrations of topics presented in this chapter.

CHAPTER TWELVE

Rhythm and Meter

A Note on Scansion

English meter is still a matter of considerable controversy—perhaps it is becoming more so—and I do not expect everyone to agree with my own scheme. In fact, I do not agree with part of it myself. But I believe that *serious* students of poetry need some familiarity with traditional terms. If they don't know what iambic pentameter is, they will be handicapped in reading about poetry.

Many writers, for purposes of scansion, prefer to use *x* for an unstressed syllable and an accent mark (') for stressed syllables. I find this system clumsy for classroom use. The *x*'s take too long to write on the board (two strokes instead of one) and the accent marks get confused with uprights dividing the feet. An additional merit of the horizontal stroke for stressed syllables is that the stroke may be lengthened to indicate heavy stresses or shortened to indicate light stresses.

Some metrists include the pyrrhic (∪ ∪) and the amphibrach (∪ — ∪) among the kinds of feet, but I don't find them necessary or helpful. The notion of a foot without an accent violates my definition of a foot. Where scansion might seem to call for a pyrrhic, one syllable will nearly always be slightly heavier than the other and thus can be regarded as bearing a light stress. As for the amphibrach, one gets it only by dividing the feet in an unusual and unwarranted way. LP

---

144. *George Herbert* **Virtue** (page 698)

Three stanzas presenting sweet things that die are contrasted with a fourth presenting the one thing that does not die. The first three stanzas parallel each other: each is an apostrophe beginning with the word ''Sweet'' and ending with the words ''must die.'' The fourth stanza, which is not an apostrophe, reserves ''sweet'' for the third position in the opening line, and ends with the word ''lives.'' The first three stanzas are interconnected because the ''day'' of the first stanza may be thought of as containing the ''rose'' of the second, while the ''spring'' of the third stanza contains them both. The ordering is also marked by the opening words of the fourth lines: ''For thou . . . ,'' ''And thou . . . ,'' ''And all . . . .''

In stanza 1, the day is presented in an apt metaphor as the ''bridal'' (wedding) of the earth and sky, uniting them in light; the metaphor connotes a beginning, brightness, and hope. The dew is fittingly chosen to mourn the death of the day, for dew is associated with evening. The dew is both a personification and a metaphor, both the weeper and the tears that are wept. The words "to night" function both as an adverb and, because the hyphen has been omitted, as a prepositional phrase in which the noun is a traditional symbol for death.

In stanza 2, through a bold metaphor, the crimson rose is compared in color to the face of an angry man, and, in an even bolder overstatement, is described as so bright that it causes tears in an observer who rashly gazes at it without shielding his eyes (like looking directly at the sun). Yet, despite this dazzling brilliance, it too is doomed to die. Its "root" is ever in its "grave" (a metonymy for earth). The rose's death is a condition of its birth: it dies back into the very soil from which it sprang; its root is "ever" there.

In stanza 3, the spring is compared metaphorically to a box where "sweets" lie compacted. (For the seventeenth-century reader the connotations would suggest, not a box of candy, but a box of perfumes—rose petals, lavender, cedar sprays, etc.) But the poet's "music" shows that the spring also has its "closes" and must die like the rest. The "music" may be read literally as well as metaphorically (Herbert was a musician as well as a poet). The word "closes" has three relevant meanings: the spring ends or terminates, the metaphorical box shuts, and a "close" in music is a cadence or concluding strain.

Stanza 4 presents a contrast. A "sweet and virtuous soul," it declares, is immortal. Like "seasoned timber" it never "gives" (*buckles* or *snaps*). Even should the whole world "turn to coal," it would survive. Spiritual in its origin, and having preserved its purity and strength through virtuous discipline, it will live even more intensely after the destruction of everything physical.

Two thoughtful brief discussions of this poem, by Louis L. Martz and M. M. Mahood, may be found in *Metaphysical Poetry*, ed. by Malcolm Bradbury and David Palmer (London: Arnold, 1970) 109–10 and 143–44. There is an extended discussion in Helen Vendler, *The Poetry of George Herbert* (Cambridge: Harvard UP, 1975) 9–24.   LP

EXERCISE 1 (page 707)

a. Blank verse, with a high incidence of anapestic and trochaic substitutions and run-on lines contributing to the conversational rhythm.
b. Blank verse, approaching the rhythms of free verse in the frequent disparity between what we have called the expected rhythm and the heard rhythm.
c. Blank verse.
d. Rimed iambic pentameter.
e. Blank verse. The first and last lines in this speech are trimeter, but that is explainable by its being an excerpt.
f. Blank verse. Some lines in this poem are rough and almost unscannable (especially line 2), but the majority point to iambic pentameter as the norm.
g. Free verse.

h. Irregularly rimed iambic, with varying line lengths (pentameter predominates, but trimeter and tetrameter are frequent).
i. Free verse.
j. Free verse, with repeating emphatic cadences.

145. *William Blake* **"Introduction"** to *Songs of Innocence* (page 708)

The child upon the cloud substitutes for the traditional Muse. The Lamb symbolizes innocence. The poet is first inspired by an emotion or idea (stanzas 1–2), then finds words to express that experience (stanza 3), then writes down or publishes his poems for all to read (stanzas 4–5). (In the poem he fashions a pen from a hollow reed and dyes water to make ink.) In this "Introduction" Blake indicates the source of inspiration for his poems—childhood; their subject matter—innocence; their intended audience—both children and adults (the last line indicates that "Every child" may joy to hear them; but line 14 indicates that the book is for "all" to read); and their tone—pleasant (2), merry (6), cheerful (6), happy (10), joyous (20). (Actually they are all these and more.)

Lines 1–2 and 9–10 establish a regular tetrameter pattern with accents on both the first and last syllables of the line. In scansion the pressure of the pattern forces us to promote the initial prepositions (*On, In*) and the conjunctions (*And, So, While*) to accented status. *Every* (20) is pronounced essentially as two syllables. Dividing the feet *after* the stressed syllables produces one monosyllabic foot and three iambs in each line. Dividing the feet *before* the stressed syllables produces three trochees and one monosyllabic foot in each line. It is obviously duple meter, but whether one calls it iambic or trochaic is a purely arbitrary decision: it is no more one than the other. LP

146. *Robert Frost* **It takes all sorts** (page 709)

This couplet can be scanned either as iambic:

Ĭt takes | all sorts | of in- | and out- | door school- | ing
Tŏ get | a-dap- | ted to | my kind | of fool- | ing

or as trochaic:

Ĭt | takes all | sorts of | in- and | out-door | school-ing |
Tŏ | get a- | dapt-ed | to my | kind of | fool-ing. |

Scanned as iambic, both lines have an unaccented syllable left over at the end of the line. Scanned as trochaic, both lines have an unaccented syllable left over at

206

the beginning of the line. Both scansions yield an equal number of iambs and trochees. This is a pentameter couplet in duple meter. LP

147. *A. E. Housman* **Epitaph on an Army of Mercenaries** (page 709)

In the essay cited below, Richard Wilbur identifies two important allusions in this poem: first, to *Paradise Lost*, 6.668 ff. and 867 ff., the account of the battle in heaven which includes the phrase "the sum of things" as a term for the universe and refers to the peril applied to its "foundations" by the revolt of Satan, finally averted by God's direct intervention in the person of the Son; and second, to the myth of the mortal hero Heracles temporarily bearing the weight of the heavens on his shoulders. These allusions enrich Housman's poem, but also help to define its complex tone—for he is using the word "mercenary" and its venal connotations ironically, as a rebuttal to the sarcasm with which the German press labeled the British regulars at the Battle of Ypres. Housman adopts the slanderous word, and uses it to pay tribute to men whose professionalism led to their certain death, but who were at the time the only resistance to a force that threatened to destroy the world. We must not misunderstand the tone of this poem: it does not say "dulce et decorum est pro patria mori," claiming selfless idealism for these dead, nor does it deny that these men were in the army as a job for pay; rather, Housman's point is that ordinary men, with ordinary worldly motives, were called upon to perform extraordinary self-sacrifice, and did so, to the salvation of the world—although saving the world was probably not what led them to become professional soldiers.

In Herbert's "Virtue" (page 698), extra-metrical syllables at the ends of lines 9 and 11 are variants to the pattern of the poem; Housman establishes such syllables as part of his pattern, since they occur regularly at the ends of all odd-numbered lines—that is, they are a part of the rhythm, not an exception or syncopation. They contribute a "falling" rhythm to the ends of those lines, which is made more obvious by their feminine rime contrasting to the masculine, monosyllabic rime words of the even-numbered lines. And in scanning the odd-numbered lines, we may detect another pattern, the substitution of a trochaic foot at the beginning of the line:

These, in | the day | when heav'n | was fall- | ing   1

Fol-lowed | their mer- | ce-nar- | y call- | ing   3

Their shoul- | ders held | the sky | sus-pend- | ed   5

Notice that in lines 1 and 3, there can be no dispute about the initial trochee, while that in line 5 might be questioned. Read as prose and out of context, the line might sound like "their SHOULders held the SKY susPENDed," with an iamb at the beginning. But the purpose of the statement is not to point to "shoulders," but to discriminate *these* men from others who did not bear the great burden; it was *their* shoulders, the only ones available. Line 7, on the other hand, provides no such clear-cut interpretive support for reading the first foot as a trochee, and one might rather read it as an iamb—or as a spondee. This departure from the rhythms Housman has established for the odd-numbered lines is of course appropriate to this emphatically blasphemous line, this complete reverse of what God did in *Paradise Lost*. In the absence of divine protection and intervention, the world must rely on its own resources, even if that requires heroic deeds from unheroic men.

For a fuller discussion, see Richard Wilbur's essay, "Round about a Poem of Housman's," in *Response: Prose Pieces, 1953–1976* (New York: Harcourt, 1976) 16–38; also included in *A Celebration of Poets*, ed. Don Cameron Allen (Baltimore: Johns Hopkins UP, 1967) 177–202. TRA

148. *e. e. cummings* **if everything happens that can't be done** (page 710)

The subject is love. The season is spring. The tone is ecstatic. Cummings is a romantic poet for whom, if there is anything more wonderful than being a live individual with a heart and feelings of one's own (a ONE; not a cipher, a blank, a nothing, an emotionally dead person), it is being one of two such individuals (two ONES) who achieve identity through love. But being a ONE is prerequisite, and the poet devotes the first two stanzas to establishing that "there's nothing as something [so important] as one." Being a ONE, for cummings, is a function of feeling, not of intellect. The analytic reason (symbolized throughout the poem by "books" and in stanza 2 by analytic terms such as "why," "because," and "although"), for cummings, deadens and kills, whereas feeling (symbolized by "buds" and "birds" and "trees") enlivens and vitalizes ("buds know better than books" and "books don't grow," to expand cummings's telescoped phrase). The consummation of natural feeling comes with the mutually realized love of two individuals; and the love theme (introduced in the third stanza with "so your is a my") is explicitly stated in the fourth stanza ("now i love you and you love me") and receives its triumphant expression in the fifth (where all the pronouns have changed to "we's"), especially in the poem's final line, which incorporates, with a neat bit of word play, the mathematical equation for this identity ("we're WONderful ONE times ONE"). When such miracles happen (when "everything happens that can't be done"), as they regularly do in the spring, then even "the stupidest teacher" (representing the intellect again) will dimly guess the miraculousness of individuality, feeling, spring, life, and love.

Cummings has constructed his poem on an intricate pattern. Each stanza is linked to the one that follows (like persons holding hands) by the repetition of its last word as the first word in the next. Lines 2–4 of each stanza contain a parenthesis in which life and feelings are contrasted with intellect. Lines 6–8 of each stanza contain a second parenthesis showing the participants in the poem to be engaged in a spontaneous joyous dance. Each stanza is additionally organized by a pattern of approximate and perfect rimes in which lines 1, 4, 9 rime together, and lines 5, 8. The prevailing meter is anapestic (freely mixed with iambic and monosyllabic feet, which give it spontaneity and variety), in which the nine lines of each stanza have four, two, one, one, four, one, one, two, and three feet respectively.

Had cummings printed the two parentheses of each stanza as one-line rather than three-line units, he would have had a simple five-line stanza with all lines riming (anapestic $aabb^4a^3$). But by breaking up the parentheses, he introduces into them two additional rhetorical (line-end) pauses which, without altering the meter or slowing it down, give it additional spontaneity, variety of movement, and a bit of a swirl, reinforcing the dancelike quality of these lines. Indeed the joyous tone of this poem is as much the result of the meter as of the words. Notice, moreover, that line 28, which states the subject of the poem, the cause of its joyousness, consists of four regular iambic feet. Had the poem been printed, as proposed above, in five-line stanzas with the parentheses compacted into one line each, line 28 would be the only one in the poem without a single anapestic foot. This slowing down of line 28, through the use of exclusively duple feet, gives it an emphasis appropriate to its thematic importance in the content of the poem.

[This discussion is adapted from the essay "A Look at Rhythm and Meter" in *The Art of Total Relevance: Papers on Poetry*, by Laurence Perrine (Rowley, MA: Newbury, 1976) 70–73.] LP

149. *A. E. Housman* **Oh who is that young sinner** (page 711)

The poem is a satire against the prejudices that cause men to hate and persecute each other for superficial and accidental differences between them. The color of one's hair, having nothing to do with intrinsic human ability or worth, symbolizes any such difference. When I first read the poem I identified it in my own mind—because of my American experience with racial conflict—with skin color. I have since learned that the poem was occasioned by the conviction and imprisonment of Oscar Wilde for homosexuality. Either reading of the poem is legitimate, and so probably would be such religious or racial differences as presently divide Protestant and Roman Catholic in Northern Ireland and Moslem and Jew in the Middle East.

I would call the irony verbal, for the poem gives me no sense of a dramatic speaker different from the author. LP

150. *William Butler Yeats* **Down by the Salley Gardens** (page 712)

The meter is basically iambic heptameter, but the fourth accent regularly falls on a pause—except that in lines 3 and 7 it *might* be taken as falling lightly on "as." By the former option, the fifth foot in these two lines is anapestic; by the latter, iambic. LP

151. *Walt Whitman*   **Had I the Choice** (page 713)

152. *Robert Frost*   **The Aim Was Song** (page 714)

Walt Whitman defends free verse (in unrimed free verse); Robert Frost defends metrical verse—"measure" (in rimed iambic tetrameter). The verse form, in each case, is perfectly chosen for the subject matter. This may seem elementary, but what would have been the effect if Whitman had defended free verse in meter, and Frost, meter in free verse?

In Whitman's poem even the greatest poetic art is seen as pale and inferior when set beside nature. The implication for poetry is that the most desirable poetry will be that which is most natural, most *like* nature. The further implication is that free verse is natural and that metered, rimed verse is artificial. Still another implication is that metaphors, similes, and contrived paradoxes ("conceits") are artificial.

In Frost's poem successful poetry is seen as an improvement on nature. Though it uses natural materials, it orders them, imposes form on them, and thus gives them a power that they do not have in their natural state. In repeating the words "By measure" in line 13—and placing a period after them—Frost gives the phrase tremendous emphasis. Song, he insists, is "measured"; rather than taking form from nature, it gives form to nature. Thus nature is made humanly meaningful.

Readers must judge the two philosophies by their own standards. But the fact is that great poetry has been written both in meter and in free verse.   LP

153. *Marianne Moore*   **Nevertheless** (page 714)

As the title implies, the subject of the poem is persistence and pertinacity, both physical and moral. The various examples of plant life "overcome" apparent obstacles, from which the poet derives the moral lesson for human beings: "Victory won't come / to me unless I go / to it; . . . The weak overcomes its / menace, the strong over- / comes itself. What is there / like fortitude!"

What looks like random diversity, mingling bizarre examples, has its order, from seed to root to tendril to fruit, an upward growth representing the cycle of vegetable nature. It commences with the "multitude / of seeds" on the surface of a crushed strawberry (transformed, by its "struggle" to maintain its integrity, into the semblance of animal forms); it proceeds to the protected internal seeds of an apple, doubly enclosed in the core. Whether vulnerably superficial or protectively enclosed, these seeds are designed to reach fertile soil and give birth to new growth.

Parallels exist in the root references: there is growth both in the rigid enclosure of frozen soil and in exposed air, and some plants' roots undergo such twisting that they seem to transform themselves into the shapes of animal forms. Even the fragility of grape tendrils and the stems of cherries possess transforming potency, the frail tendril capable of binding what has supported it, the "thread" transmitting the ripening coloration of the cherry. And the poem ends its plant references where it began, with sweet fruits that carry the source of new growth.

Thus what may seem a random collection of "oddities" in nature has a direction, drawing comparisons between the seemingly disconnected examples. The whole plant world illustrates the power of life to maintain and propagate itself—and so the human world should learn to persist, employing its inner moral virtues as well as its outward physical powers. To paraphrase the moral statements: "Real bravery, and true victory, are seen not only in overcoming external dangers but also in self-control."

The poem is written in syllabic verse (only the number of syllables in a line is counted, not accents) rimed *xaa*. The form, which appears like free verse, thus echoes the meaning, since random rhythms (like bizarre subjects) are "locked in" by syllable-count and rime.   TRA

154.   *Alfred, Lord Tennyson*   **Break, break, break** (page 716)

The tone and mood are established in the first two lines, through imagery, sound, and rhythm. In context each word in the image-bearing phrase "cold gray stones" has negative connotations that reinforce each other and give the reader a good notion of how to interpret the opening line with its three carefully spaced repetitions of the one word "break." Good things and bad things can both be broken, but the second line makes it impossible to read a cheerful note into the speaker's apostrophe. The tone will be sorrowful; and the repetitions of the opening line give the tone an emphasis that suggests that the speaker's sorrow may continue forever, as indeed the sea waves do. The sorrowful tone is given additional weight by the assonance of the long *o*'s in "c*o*ld-st*o*nes-*O*" and a lesser but still appreciable effect by the repeated long *a* sounds in "br*ea*k" and "gr*a*y."

We do not learn the source of the speaker's sorrow till halfway through the third stanza. There we learn that it is grief for some very beloved person who is irrevocably gone. The last two lines repeat and make more specific the source of this grief: "But the tender grace of a day that is dead / Will never come back to me" (15–16). This is an elegiac poem. The speaker's beloved is dead.

But if the poem is elegiac in tone, what purpose is served by the intermediate images (lines 5–10)? They symbolize progressive stages in human life. The "fisherman's boy" and his sister represent childhood at its careless innocent play. The "sailor lad" is late adolescence or early manhood singing at his work. The "stately ships" are maturity performing its necessary duties. By their happiness, their joy in their work, or their "stately" missions in life, they provide foils for the sorrow of the speaker. But, under the burden of his grief, their activities are meaningless to him.

Lines 6, 8, and 12 are perfectly regular anapestic trimeter, which I would call the basic meter of the poem despite the existence of two tetrameter lines (11 and 15). This is not free verse: it has a definite metrical beat throughout. The most obvious

211

and most memorable departures from a strictly anapestic form are, of course, the monosyllabic lines that begin the first and last stanzas. What is more grievously broken than a broken heart? What is less likely than sea waves to be influenced in their motions by the bidding of a human voice?   LP

ADDITIONAL EXERCISE

The following passage, a scene in the Garden of Eden, is excerpted from Milton's epic *Paradise Lost*. The poem is written in blank verse, but the *visual* signs of its metrical form (line spacing, capital letters at line beginnings) are here removed. Using your ear and your knowledge of the poem's meter, decide where the line breaks occur, and indicate them with a slash mark. (In the text of the poem as properly printed, "Now came" begins a full line, and "threw" ends one.)

> Now came still evening on, and twilight gray had in her sober livery all things clad; silence accompanied, for beast and bird, they to their grassy couch, these to their nests were slunk, all but the wakeful nightingale; she all night long her amorous descant sung; silence was pleased: now glowed the firmament with living sapphires: Hesperus that led the starry host rode brightest, till the moon rising in clouded majesty, at length apparent queen unveiled her peerless light, and o'er the dark her silver mantle threw.

ADDITIONAL EXERCISE ANSWER

Now came still evening on, and twilight gray
Had in her sober livery all things clad;
Silence accompanied, for beast and bird,
They to their grassy couch, these to their nests
Were slunk, all but the wakeful nightingale;
She all night long her amorous descant sung;
Silence was pleased: now glowed the firmament
With living sapphires: Hesperus that led
The starry host rode brightest, till the moon
Rising in clouded majesty, at length
Apparent queen unveiled her peerless light,
And o'er the dark her silver mantle threw.

PL 4.598–609

CHAPTER THIRTEEN

Sound and Meaning

155. *Anonymous* **Pease porridge hot** (page 717)

This verse has been described as a "clapping game" for children. LP

156. *William Shakespeare* **Song: Come unto these yellow sands** (page 718)

The first six lines of the poem set up the onomatopoetic passage, and make it meaningful. This song is sung by the sprite Ariel as he leads Prince Ferdinand from the supposed dangers of a shipwreck to safety on shore, and the opening lines imply a dance entertainment of sprites celebrating the prince's rescue and the calming of the stormy seas. The song thus concerns reaching safety and security after the threat of danger and death. The "burden" is most appropriate, for it ushers in two harbingers of safety to people in darkness: watch-dogs who warn off nocturnal intruders, and the crowing cock who proclaims the approach of daylight.

Even with onomatopoetic words, we must not assume an *identity* between sound and meaning. The French equivalent of "Cock-a-doodle-doo" is *co co rico*; in German it is *ki-ke-ri-ki*; in Spanish it is *kiriki*. (Asking a class which of these actually sounds more like a crowing cock may increase their sensitivity to the relations between sound and meaning; occasionally a student will be bold enough to try an actual imitation of a rooster, not using verbal syllables.) TRA, LP

157. *Carl Sandburg* **Splinter** (page 719)

Thin and *splinter* (also *cricket*) are phonetic intensives, and in line 4 their effect is reinforced by the short *i*'s in *singing* (and, though their effect on the ear is slight, by those in *It* and *is*). The consonance of *last, first,* and *frost* also adds to the effectiveness of this miniature. LP

158. *Robert Herrick* **Upon Julia's Voice** (page 720)

"Silvery" (literally *like silver*) suggests something precious, beautiful, smooth to the touch, softly gleaming in color. Julia's voice is smooth, soft, agreeable, and precious to the speaker. "Amber" (a fossilized resin) is a translucent substance that glows with soft rich golden-yellow light. Julia is singing and accompanying herself on a lute made of wood but finished with an amber-colored varnish. More importantly, the sound of the lute under her fingers is softly and richly resonant, golden-toned, the perfect complement to her voice. It is as if the melodious words she sings each melted into a purely translucent amber lute. LP

159. *Robert Frost* **The Span of Life** (page 723)

No one who has ever been greeted at the door by an affectionate and enthusiastic puppy can miss the image implicit in the second line, which is all the more effective because of Frost's *understatement* (almost *un*-statement) of it. Frost's title universalizes the subject of the poem, making the dog a symbol of human as well as of animal life. LP

EXERCISE (page 725)

The letter in parentheses indicates the superior version.

1. (a) ("Independence") The linkage in sound of "*guide*" and "*guard*" (alliteration and consonance) emphasizes their syntactical parallelism in an iambic pentameter couplet. Version *b* takes more words (and an extra foot) to make a less forceful connection. (The biblical allusion is to Exodus 13.21.)

2. (b) (*Comus*) The blank verse passage, after the generalization in line 1, calls for harshness in line 2 and musicality in line 3. The three hard consonant sounds of "*crabbed*" crowding around one vowel are much harsher than the soft consonants in "*rough*" (pronounced *ruff*); in addition, two accents coming together on "dull fools" emphasize these words (as does their repetition of *l*'s) and strain the meter (a monosyllabic foot replaces the expected iamb in the fourth position), whereas "foolish men" is pleasant in sound and regular in meter. The name "Apollo," with its final open vowel and its mellifluous *l*'s (picking up *l*'s in "musical" and "lute") is far more melodious than "Phoebus."

3. (b) ("Mid-Winter") The core of each version is "crows croak hoarsely" with its suggestion of raucous cawing. The three sharp *k*-sounds in "crows *croak*" are supported in version *b* in "out-*c*ast" and "a*c*ross"; and the hissing *s* of "hoarsely" is reinforced in "out-ca*s*t" and "acro*ss*," and "whitene*ss*" (with the addition of three sharp *t*'s). In version *a*, "fleeing" and "over the snow" are rather pleasant in sound.

4. (b) (*Tristram*, 6) The gaps in "Your _____ how bells of singing gold / Would sound at _____ over silent water" must be filled with pleasant, musical sounds. In version *b* "low voice" is soft and lovely, "tells" provides an internal rime with "bells," and "twilight" a half-rime with "silent." In version *a* "talk attests" is noisy; "evening" is softly pleasant but provides no rime.

214

5. (b) (*The Princess:* "Come down, O maid") The blank verse of version *a* is metrically regular throughout. In version *b* the superfluity of unstressed syllables in line 1 (MYR-i-ads of RIV-u-lets HUR-ry-ing THROUGH the LAWN) gives the effect of speed; and the onomatopoetic words "moan" and "murmuring" are reinforced by the *m*'s, *n*'s, and *r*'s in "*my*riads," "*im*memo*r*ial," "*el*ms," and "*in*nume*r*able."

6. (a) (*Romeo and Juliet,* 3.5) The effect wanted is a harsh unpleasantness. The nasal "sings so" is less pleasant and less flowing than "warbles." The metrical irregularity of "STRAIN- ing HARSH DIS- cords" strains the meter and puts heavy emphasis on harshness, whereas the smooth regularity of "with HARSH dis-CORD-ant TONES" mutes it. "Unpleasing sharps" lacks the pleasant assonance of "tones" and "doleful."

7. (b) (*Don Juan,* 7.78) The flowing rhythm and euphonious sound of version *a*—its liquid *l*'s, *r*'s, and *m*'s and its soft *f*- and *v*-sounds—make it beautiful to listen to; but this beauty is highly inappropriate to the subject. The sharp monosyllables, the clogged meter, and explosive *b*'s and *d*'s of version *b* make it far superior.

8. (a) ("Reconciliation") The repeated *s*-sounds in "*sis*ters," "in*ces*santly," "*soft*ly," and "*soiled*" provide the repetition called for and perhaps even the sound of hands sloshing repeatedly in sudsy water.

9. (b) ("Elegy Written in a Country Churchyard") In line 1 "tolls," like "knell," is onomatopoetic. In line 2 a spondee appropriately slows down the line by bringing three accents together:

The low- ing herd wind slow- ly o'er the lea.

In line 4 a slight accent on "and" in the fourth foot requires a slight compensatory pause before it (as if there were a comma after "darkness"), thus isolating the final pronoun and preparing for the meditative nature of the poem. (In version *a* lines 3 and 4 are absurdly swift for the solemnity of the subject.)

10. (b) ("Epistle to Dr. Arbuthnot") In line 1 the succession of short monosyllables with sharp endings ("let," "flap," "bug," "wings") spits out the spite of the speaker at the subject of his satire, and line 2 adds another ("child"). But the manifest superiority of version *b* is the superiority of "stinks and stings" to "smells and bites." The alliterating *st*'s, the assonance of the short *i*'s, and the sharp final consonants link these verbs in sound as well as in syntax and give them a force that the soft word "smells" lacks (though "bites" has it).

160. *Alexander Pope* **Sound and Sense** (page 726)

Introducing his topic with the general observation that good writing is the result of art (it looks easy, but mastery is acquired only by long practice), Pope then states the thesis of his passage in line 4: In good writing "The sound must seem an echo to the sense." He elaborates and demonstrates this thesis (simultaneously) through a series of five examples, each included within an iambic pentameter riming couplet. When a poet writes about a gentle west wind and a smooth-flowing stream, Pope begins, the verse should also be soft and smooth. (The following scansions represent my sense, and may be modified to fit yours.)

Soft is the strain when Zeph-yr gent-ly blows,
And the smooth stream in smooth-er num-bers flows.

The reversal of stress in the first foot gives additional emphasis to *Soft*, which is the key word in the first line. Most of the words in the line are soft in sound, especially *Zephyr*, whose *z-f-r* combination of consonants is softer than the *w-st-w-nd* of *West wind*, despite the latter's alliterating *w*'s. The *g* in *gently* is a *j*. The explosive *b* of *blows* is gentled by the following *l* and long vowel sounds. *Soft* and *strain* contain a gentling *f* and *n* respectively. In the second line the key word *smooth*, itself a smooth-sounding word, is emphasized (a) by the meter, which joins it with *stream* (also smooth in its long vowel sound and concluding *m*), and (b) by its repetition in *smoother*. The fourth foot contains the soft consonants *n* and *m*. The fifth combines the soft *fl*- with a long vowel. The repeated *s*'s in these two lines (I suspect) take on the color of their surroundings.

But when loud surg-es lash the sound-ing shore,
The hoarse, rough verse should like the tor-rent roar.

It is arguable whether the key word *loud* is a loud sound (its vowel, of course, is a dipthong, and is the sound we use for a cry of pain—"ow!" or "ouch!"), but it is inarguable that the meter puts a stress on it appropriate to its importance in the sentence, and that its effect is intensified by its near-rime with *sounding*. The onomatopoetic *roar* is emphasized by its anticipation in *shore, hoarse,* and *torrent*. The alliteration of *loud* and *lash* and the consonance of *hoarse* and *verse* give emphasis and linkage to these two pairs of words. Though none of the words in these two lines sounds particularly harsh (the roughness and hoarseness we may imagine in *rough* and *hoarse* disappear from *ruff* and *horse*), by bringing three accents together in *hoarse, rough verse*, the meter puts extraordinary emphasis on words that are hoarse-meaning and rough-meaning, and pushes together three syllables that do not articulate easily. The grammatical pause contributes to this lack of articulation.

When A-jax strives some rock's vast weight to throw,
The line too la-bors and the words move slow.

It is not just the five stressed syllables in a row that slow down the first line and give it such a sense of strain and muscular effort; it is the impossibility of sliding these words easily off the tongue, the muscular effort required in the reading. The mouth has to be reshaped for each word in the series. Even in a single word like *strives*, effort is required, for we must pronounce five distinct consonant sounds (*s-t-r* and *v-s*) with only one vowel sound between them (*v-s* is harder than *s-t-r*). In the second line the two spondees, bringing three stresses together at two points in the line, slow the line down.

Not so, | when swift | Ca-mil- | la scours | the plain,
Flies o'er | the un-bend- | ing corn, | and skims | a-long | the main.

In each of these lines the reader has the choice of stressing the first or the second syllable in the opening foot. I have elected to stress *Not* because (a) it signals the change from the grunting effort of Ajax to lift his rock to the effortless ease of swift Camilla running, (b) the two unstressed syllables following it speed up the line, and (c) the increased distance separating the first two stresses gives added emphasis to the second stress—*swift*—which is the key word in the couplet. The name *Camilla* (like *Zephyr*) fits Pope's purpose perfectly, so easily do the syllables flow together. (Contrast the effort and speed involved in saying the three syllables of *Camilla* and of *rock's vast weight*.) The assonant short *i*'s of *swift, Camilla* and *skims* quicken these words, as well as link them in meaning. In the second line I stress the initial *Flies*, again because the reversed stress gives added emphasis to the more important word, and because the succeeding unstressed syllables add speed to the line. (The three unstressed syllables together were not allowed by the strict rules of Pope's day, however, nor the two consecutive vowel sounds in *the* and *un-*. Pope's unmodernized text—*th' unbending corn*—blends *the* and *un-* together in one syllable.) The notable variation here, however, is the introduction of a six-foot line (called an *Alexandrine*) into the pentameter pattern. The extra foot, making it possible to divide the line into two three-foot segments (separated here by a comma), gives the line additional lightness (see discussion in Exercise 1, page 707).

Hear how | Tim-o- | theus' var- | ied lays | sur-prise,
And bid | al-ter- | nate pas- | sions fall | and rise!

With no other text than that before us, the reader with a sensitive ear can confidently declare that Pope put the accent on the second syllable of *alternate*. With the accent on the first syllable, the meter goes smash. Put on the second syllable, the line perfectly alternates unstressed and stressed syllables (it is the most regular line of the whole fourteen), thus echoing the alternation of passions of which Timotheus sings. (British usage, as opposed to American, even today stresses the second syllable of *alternate* when used adjectivally, as we do with the word *alternative*.)

Pope's passage is a brilliant display of technical virtuosity.   LP

161. *Emily Dickinson* **I like to see it lap the miles** (page 727)

The basic metaphor of the poem compares a train to a horse, though neither train nor horse is named in the poem. The subject is a train because it laps miles and valleys up, feeds itself (takes water) at tanks, peers (with its headlight) into shanties by the sides of roads, hoots (with its whistle), is punctual, and stops "docile and omnipotent" (obedient to the engineer but tremendously powerful) at its stable (station or roundhouse). It is a horse because it laps, licks, feeds, steps, peers, has ribs, crawls, complains, chases itself, neighs, and stops at a stable. It is a whole train rather than just a locomotive because it chases itself downhill.

The most unusual technical feature of the poem is that each of the first three stanzas ends with a run-on line. These run-on lines give the poem, or the train, a continuous forward motion (there are no periods until the end of the poem), a forward motion that finally grinds to an abrupt halt on the word "Stop" (line 16). The stop—it must be a strong one to stop a train—is made strong in a number of ways: first, the word *stop* itself stops suddenly, ending with an explosive consonant; second, though in a normally unstressed position, the word receives a strong metrical stress (with the partial exception of the preceding line, which slows the train down, this is the only line in the poem stressed on the initial syllable); third, it is followed and preceded by grammatical pauses; fourth, it is followed and preceded (on the other side of the grammatical pauses) by stressed syllables, with one of which it has assonance and with the other of which it alliterates. All these features emphasize or isolate the word *stop* in a remarkable way. The phrase that follows—"docile and omnipotent"—is a beautiful expression of power at rest.

But before the train comes to a stop, it makes a variety of motions and sounds. In the first two lines the regular meter and the predominance of *l*'s give the train speed, while at the same time the monosyllabic words ending in *p* or *k*, found throughout the first stanza, give it the clippety-cloppety-clackety sound of iron wheels going over joints in the rails. In line 4 the big word *prodigious*, set off between commas, slows the line down as the train slows down to "step" around a curve—an effect that is repeated in line 6. The division of what would normally be line 9 into two lines, comma-interrupted, again slows the train down, this time to a crawl, as it goes through a tunnel, tooting its whistle each inch of the way. The three trochaic words in succession—*horrid, hooting stanza*—convey the regularity and repetition of the whistle's sound, intensified by the narrow walls of the tunnel. The onomatopoetic word *hooting* sounds like *tooting* but alliterates with *horrid*, thus emphasizing the repetitiveness of the sound while also retaining the metaphoric sense that this is a creature rather than a machine.

This brief analysis by no means exhausts the adaptation of sound to sense in this poem, but it perhaps indicates the chief features.

The poem employs approximate rime (consonance) in even-numbered lines. Lines 8 and 16 contain overstatement. LP

162. *Gerard Manley Hopkins* **Heaven-Haven** (page 728)

The speaker is a nun taking the vows that commit her to the cloistered life of the convent. This life, dedicated to religious meditation and the worship of God, is metonymically represented by "heaven" and metaphorically represented as a "haven" or sheltered place. In the extension of the metaphor, the sea represents life in the outside world and the storms are especially violent commotions in that life—passions, desires, appetites. The "havens" are pictured in the first stanza as gardens or sheltered fields (as inside a convent wall), in the second stanza as harbors protected from the ocean swells. "Springs" (2) refers both to springs of water— sources of pure refreshment—and to the mildest season of the year, free from wintry storms. "Lilies" (4), because of the pure white color of Easter lilies, are a traditional symbol of purity, chastity, religious worship, absence of sexual passion. Be sure your students realize that "blow" (4) here means "blossom," *not* "sway in the wind."

The basic stanza pattern is iambic $a^3b^2b^5a^3$, but there are many variant feet. In the last line the substitution of anapests for iambs in the last two feet gives the line a swinging motion that imitates its meaning. The effect is enhanced by the use of monosyllables, by the extreme lightness of the unstressed syllables, and by the alliteration of *swing* and *sea*. LP

163. *Wilfred Owen* **Anthem for Doomed Youth** (page 728)

The octave has its geographical setting on the battlefield (since this is a World War I poem, in France). The sestet has its geographical setting back home (since Owen was an English poet, in England). The octave concerns the death of soldiers in battle. The sestet concerns the bereavement of friends and families back home. The imagery of the octave is primarily auditory. The imagery of the sestet is primarily visual. The tone of the octave is angry and indignant. The tone of the sestet is tender. (Line 8 is transitional: the "sad shires" are back in England. This line connects the deaths to the bereavement and shifts the geographical locus from battlefield to home.) Both octave and sestet are introduced by questions.

Octave and sestet are unified by the central metaphorical image of an Anglican funeral service. Neither the literal terms of this metaphor (battle and bereavement) nor the figurative term (church funeral service) is named, so this is a metaphor of the fourth form (see page 583). The terms of the central metaphor are arrived at, as it were, by adding up the subsidiary figures and drawing a total. In the octave, at least, the central metaphor emphasizes contrast more than similarity, for the point is that these soldiers will never have a church funeral. Instead of the items in the second column of the list at the top of the next page (the figurative terms), they will have only the items in the first column (the literal terms):

literal	*figurative*
Owen's poem	anthem
monstrous anger of the guns	passing-bells
rapid rifle fire	orisons
wailing shells	choirs singing
bugles calling	voices of mourning
glimmers of good-byes in boys' eyes	candles held by altar boys
pallor of girls' brows	pall-cloth on coffin
tenderness of patient minds	flowers
dusk coming each evening	drawing-down of blinds

The last metaphor on this list does not belong to the funeral service image, but it too is associated with the formal observance of death. (In addition to the metaphors, the octave uses considerable personification: guns are angry, rifles stutter and patter out prayers, shells wail and are demented, bugles call, shires are sad. Words like "monstrous," "stuttering," and "demented" suggest that the noises of battle are like those of a madman.)

Students will have their greatest trouble with lines 10–11. Many will identify the "boys" with the "doomed youth" and read these lines as referring to the gleam in the eyes of the dying soldiers on the battlefield. Candles at a church funeral, however, are not held by the dead man but by attendants (altar boys). The logical organization of the sonnet, moreover, places this scene back home rather than on the battlefield. The boys and girls of the sestet are younger brothers, sisters, sweethearts, or other persons close to the dead.

The main point of the poem is that a church funeral service would be a "mockery" for these dead soldiers. Funeral services are a means of ritualizing or giving dignity to human death. These soldiers, however, did not die a human death; instead, they were slaughtered like "cattle." The dignity of a funeral service would be inappropriate to the indignity of their death. Owen's poem, though a tribute (an "anthem") to the dead soldiers, is mainly a bitter attack on modern war. It expresses horror, indignation, and anger at the senseless slaughter of human beings by mechanical means. Modern warfare, it implies, is mass slaughter: a mockery of human dignity. Death in modern warfare is an animal death, not a human death.

In the octave, sound is adapted to sense chiefly by the use of words and phrases whose sounds imitate meaning. The onomatopoetic series *stuttering-rattle-patter* is reinforced by the *t*'s in "ca*tt*le," "mons*t*rous," and "has*t*y." The onomatopoetic *wailing* is reinforced by the *l*'s in "be*ll*s," "shri*ll*," "she*ll*s," "bug*l*es," "ca*ll*-ing." (*Bells* and *shrill* may perhaps themselves be considered onomatopoetic.) The phrase *rifles' rapid rattle* is given speed by its pronounced trochaic rhythm (the phrasing corresponding with the meter)* and by the alliteration of the liquid *r*'s, but the hard *p* and *d* of *rapid* reinforce the staccato quality of *stuttering-rattle-patter*.

*The basic meter of the poem is iambic pentameter, and in *scansion* line 3 would be divided as follows:

On-ly | the stut- | ter-ing rif- | les' rap- | id rat- | tle.

In *reading* the line, however, we hear "rifles' rapid rattle" as the three trochees.

220

In the sestet, sound is adapted to sense chiefly by the linking together through similarity in sound of words logically connected in meaning, e.g., *candles-hands, glimmers-good-byes, pallor-pall, dusk-drawing-down.* LP

164. *A. E. Housman* **Eight O'Clock** (page 729)

The place of execution is probably the courtyard of the town jail. The clock is one of those that plays a four-note tune at a quarter past the hour, extends it to eight notes at the half hour and twelve at three-quarters past, and then plays a full complement of sixteen notes before beginning the bong, bong that announces the new hour. The young man, strapped and hooded, with a noose around his neck, sees nothing, but he hears the sixteen notes (the four "quarters") of the clock's tune "tossed" down upon the town, then the noises of the clock machinery as it tightens its springs (almost literally collecting its strength) before beginning the series of eight monotone strokes, at the first of which the trap will be sprung beneath him, and he will drop the distance (carefully calculated according to his weight) sufficient to break his neck.

The stanzaic form is iambic $a^3b^5a^5b^2$, with the *a*-rhymes all feminine, but with considerable metrical variation. The second line, for instance, with its initial trochee and its very lightly accented *on* in the third foot, brings together a number of unstressed or lightly stressed syllables that give it a speed consonant with the indifferent brightness of the tune played by the chimes. In contrast, the two internally punctuated spondees that begin line 3 and the internally punctuated first foot of line 5, followed by an initially stressed trochee, slow these two lines dramatically in consonance with the subjective experience of the protagonist. Of particular importance is the series of sharp *k*-sounds beginning in line 6: "*counted-cursed-luck-clock collected-struck*," and the heavy *str*-alliteration of "*Str*apped" (5), "*str*ength," and "*str*uck" (8). The syntactical displacement of "Its strength" from the expected position immediately following the verb places the alliterating monosyllables *strength* and *struck* together in the final line, where the final word *struck* culminates both the *str*- and *k*- series of repetitions. In addition, the heavy metrical regularity of this line, with its internal comma isolating the final verb, gives *struck* enormous force (the result of alliteration, consonance, rime, syntax, meter, and punctuation), thus putting a heavy emphasis on its double meaning. Not only does the clock mechanically strike the hour, but it (or perhaps the whole clock tower), personified as an executioner, brings down its axe with a powerful blow on the neck of the victim, striking out his life.

The use of "morning" and "nighing" as adjectives is unusual enough that one may detect a suggestion of *mourning* and *sighing* behind them. LP

165. *Janet Lewis* **Remembered Morning** (page 730)

The word "stir" (13) draws together three relevant denotations, and thereby focuses the theme of the poem: it denotes a brisk movement, a bustling sound or commotion, and a mental impulse or feeling. The motions of the morning are identified by their sounds, and both the girl and the remembering adult are stirred by them. In a poem about the power of recollected sounds to call up happy, ebullient memories, the word is apt. In addition, the adjective "early" plays upon all three denotations: the stir came early for the woman, who is still moved by that early stir.

The onomatopoetic words are *rings* (1), *murmur* and *hum* (5), *slaps* (7), *crackles* and *snaps* (9), and *slams* (15). Words that might seem to be onomatopoetic but in fact are not imitations of sounds are *axe* (1) and *ripples* (7), in both of which sound reinforces meaning (*axe* rimes with *hacks*, and *ripples* displays phonetic intensives). Together these words, the short riming lines, and the varied anapestic rhythms focus the attention on sound and the memory of sound.

The present tense for a memory-poem makes the experience immediate and enduring—the event "Goes on and on" in the speaker's heart, the memory of the murmuring of the children "goes on as it should . . . forever."

The imagery is predominantly auditory, appropriately enough, but there are significant blendings of auditory and visual, as in *water ripples and slaps* (7), which links true onomatopoeia with phonetic intensives. The most striking example of the mingling of sensations occurs in the last sentence, where a metonymy creates a visual sensation of the wind, and the personified day runs and catches the girl "into its way" (into going in its forward direction and into sharing in its temporal process). The result is a mature adult who early learned to be stirred by sensations, and who can still be stirred by the memory of them. TRA

166. *Maxine Kumin* **The Sound of Night** (page 730)

The metrical form is highly varied iambic tetrameter, with a hexameter line to open each stanza.

The stanzaic form is three rimed tercets (*aaabbbccc*) primarily achieved through approximate rime, most often consonance. Lines 1–3 share only the concluding voiced -*s* preceded by contrasting vowel sounds; 4–6 share -*t*, and 4 and 6 in addition have an unvoiced -*s*; lines 7–9 share -*nk*, while 8 and 9 have exact rime. There are some random links between tercets, as in stanza 2 where the terminal -*k* of the first tercet carries over into the fourth and fifth lines (*blankets, Crickets*), although the rime sound of this tercet is in the terminal -*t*. (Note that a *t*-rime characterizes the middle tercet of each stanza.)

The most striking variations occur in the last stanza. The first three lines are linked by alliterated *s*- while the first and third lines have exact rime as well. The terminal -*t* of the second tercet is repeated in the final tercet at the same time that exact rime joins these tercets together (*light-tight-night*). This last variation of the pattern occurs at the climactic point, for the theme of the poem contrasts light with night, and the final two lines state the theme most directly.

That theme: that "day creatures" may luxuriate in the sounds of night and delight in their variety and vitality, but they will always find these sounds mysterious and a little threatening. TRA

167. *Emily Dickinson* **I heard a fly buzz when I died** (page 731)

Of the more than seventeen hundred poems in Dickinson's collected work, over five hundred are on the subject of death. Over and over she pictures or imagines what the experience of dying is like, and what, if anything, exists beyond it. Her solutions to these problems are as various as Donne's on sexual love. In this poem— one of her greatest—the poet projects her imagination into the future through a speaker who is recollecting the past—a technique she also uses in "Because I could not stop for Death" (page 797).

The poem presents a death-bed scene—a conventional motif in nineteenth-century fiction when people had large families and died more often at home than in hospitals. In these scenes the protagonist is shown on her deathbed, surrounded by relatives, neighbors, and friends, who have gathered to give comfort, to hear any last words, and to say farewell.

Some readers will regard the appearance of the fly as the first event of the poem because it is mentioned first, but the poem does not follow a strictly chronological order. (The answer to question 1 is *b, d, a, c.*) In line 1 the speaker announces her subject and theme, providing the poem's "topic sentence," as it were. She then goes back and relates what led up to it. (It's as if one said, "I shared a sandwich with our president once. Here's how it happened" or "Here's how it was.") Use of the past perfect tense in line 5 indicates that earlier there had been weeping and lamentation, but now the mourners have ceased weeping and are restraining external displays of feeling in preparation for witnessing the solemn moment of actual death. The "stillness" (both of sound and motion) in the room is not a mere *absence* of speech and movement; rather, the atmosphere seems charged, like that lull in a storm when the air takes on a greenish tint and the silence is electric. The first "heave of storm" had been the weeping and mourning of those gathered around the deathbed; the second will presumably accompany or immediately follow "that last onset"—the moment of death itself. In stanza 3 the speaker is not literally making out her will. The formal conveyance of her larger properties (land, house, bank deposits, investments) would have been made, in the presence of a lawyer, long before. In the poem she is disposing of smaller items ("keepsakes"), saying perhaps that she wants Cousin Lizzie to have her blue scarf, her daughter to have her favorite brooch, and her son to have the family Bible. The terms "willed" and "signed away" are metaphorical.

It is at this moment ("and *then* it was"), when everyone is silently awaiting the moment of death, that the fly makes its appearance. Whether it has just arrived or has been present all along but unnoticed is an unanswerable and unimportant question. What *is* important is that the fly now dominates the dying woman's awareness and does so till her actual death in the poem's final line.

What are we to make of this fly—and of the poem?

The poem is structured on an ironic contrast between expectation and fulfillment. The imagery and language of the second stanza ("last onset," "the king," "Be witnessed") indicate a confident expectation among the onlookers, and undoubtedly in the dying woman also, that some solemn and awesome event is about to occur. (Notice how much more formal and solemn is the phrase "Be witnessed" than "be seen.") The *king* will appear to carry off the soul of the dying woman. And who is "the king"? The king may well be Death itself, personified as a majestic figure. Perhaps more likely the king is God, or Christ, or the Angel of Death. But, for the speaker, all that appears is a small and rather nasty domestic insect—a bluebottle or blowfly—trying to make its escape through the windows but continually bumping up against the glass, which it cannot see. It interposes itself between the light from the windows and the speaker. And perhaps the light also represents some special enlightenment the speaker had expected but failed to receive at the moment of death.

Some students will interpret the windows in line 15 as the eyes of the dying woman, but this interpretation is too allegorical. The "room" is not allegorized, why should the windows be? The windows are literal windows, but as the speaker's vision blurs and dims, they become the last thing she can discern; and then they too go dark. It is her eyesight that fails, not the windows; but it fails in the sense that her literal eyes can no longer see the literal windows. In the final line, being dead, she can no longer see at all. She cannot see to see any illumination she might have hoped for from the windows, because of the interposition of the fly, or death.

At one level, the poem may be given a purely psychological interpretation about the experience of dying. One expects it to be a momentous and illuminating experience; but, the poem hypothesizes, death may turn out to be merely the diminution and final cessation of one's sensory and physical powers. Instead of illumination at the end, the dying person's consciousness in the final moments may be unable to focus on anything more significant than the sound and movement of a blowfly.

Most readers, however, will want to give the fly more than a purely literal significance, and, indeed, one can hardly avoid seeing the fly as a symbol of death, coming not in the majestic form of a king but in the trivial and even repulsive aspect of a fly. However, if we stop with the simple assertion that the fly is a symbol of death, we will lose much of the richness of the symbol. For its fuller meanings we must examine all the connotations of the "fly" in this context, especially as they contrast with those of "king." For fuller discussion, see Clark Griffith, *The Long Shadow: Emily Dickinson's Tragic Poetry* (Princeton: Princeton UP, 1964) 134–37; Robert Weisbuch, *Emily Dickinson's Poetry* (Chicago: U of Chicago P, 1975) 99–102; and Charles B. Wheeler, *The Design of Poetry* (New York: Norton, 1966) 188–92.

In addition to the symbolic richness in this poem, we need also to appreciate the marvelous vividness with which the poet brings to life the actual, literal fly, especially in line 13 (one of the most magical lines in English poetry).

The basic rime scheme is *xaxa xbxb xcxc xdxd*, but the rimes are perfect only in the final stanza. The one onomatopoetic word in the poem is *buzz* at the end of line 13. But notice how this buzz is brought into the poem and gradually intensified. In line 11, the final word, *was*, though unrimed in its own stanza, and unrimed in the formal rime scheme, nevertheless rimes perfectly with *buzz* in the first line of the final stanza. In line 12 the word *interposed* continues the buzzing into the final stanza. In line 13 the vowel sound of *buzz* is preceded by the identical vowel sounds in "*u*ncertain" and "st*u*mbling," making three *u* sounds in close succession. Finally, the *b* sound in *buzz* is preceded in line 14 by the *b*'s in "*b*lue" and "stum*b*ling." Thus, *all* the sounds in *buzz*—its initial and final consonants and its medial vowel— are heard at least three times in lines 11–13. This outburst of onomatopoetic effect consummates the aural imagery promised in the opening line, "I *heard* a fly buzz when I died." But line 13 combines images of color, motion, and sound. Though the sound imagery is the most important, the poem concludes with a reference to the speaker's dimming eyesight, and we may infer that she *saw* a blur of the blue-bottle's deep metallic blue as well as hearing its buzz. The images of motion between "blue" and "buzz" belong to both the visual and aural modes of sensing. The speaker hears and imperfectly sees the "uncertain" flight of the fly as it bumbles from one pane of glass to another, its buzzing now louder, now softer. The meter of line 13, if the poem is scanned, is perfectly regular, but the two grammatical pauses help to give it an uncertain, irregular effect. Would it be too fanciful to say that the line itself stumbles over its three *b* sounds?   LP

168. *Herman Melville*   **The Bench of Boors** (page 732)

169. *William Carlos Williams*   **The Dance** (page 733)

The two poems here juxtaposed have much in common. Both are by American poets; both show remarkable skill at fitting sound to sense; both were inspired by oil paintings done by historical Flemish painters, David Teniers the Younger (1610–1690) and Pieter Breughel the Elder (1525–1569). Both men were genre painters of Dutch peasant life (note that the English word *boor* is derived from the Dutch word *boer*, meaning peasant). Breughel is the more famous of the two, and his painting *The Kermess* is well known (it is sometimes called *The Country Dance*). I have so far been unable to locate the specific painting referred to by Melville, but have seen several reproductions of Teniers's work that fit the general description in the poem. The chief difference between the two paintings, of course, is that Teniers pictures the peasants lazily at rest, while Breughel pictures them in lively motion.

In Melville's poem the speaker suffers from insomnia. He is an intellectual who cannot sleep because his active brain will not let loose of the problems and cares and worries that intellectuals are concerned with. He has recently seen an exhibition of Teniers's paintings showing the peasants sitting before the fireplace, drinking their beer, and lazing and yawning and dozing and smoking their pipes, seemingly without a care in the world. It is clear that he envies the boors, and wishes he could fall asleep as easily as they do. It is not clear whether he would like to change places with them. Does he want to be a "slug" or a "losel" too? The poem makes no commitment to either kind of life. It merely suggests that no kind is without its problems or limitations.

The stanza form or shape of the poem reflects its content. The middle two lines of each stanza present the condition of the speaker, characterized by the coldness and brightness of intellectual thought; the first two and the last two lines present the condition of the boors, characterized by the warmth and dim light of their sensual pleasures. The fifth line of each stanza contains a symbolic refrain: the "low doors" of their homes and taverns are literal *and* metaphorical—they symbolize the constricted minds and interests of the boors. But perhaps the most remarkable technical aspect of the poem rests in the sounds made by its words: *muse, Teniers, boors, losels, doors, slugs, laze, doze, dreams, drowsy, hazy, eyes, boozy* (I have listed these words only once for each, but some of them occur several times in the poem). What do they all have in common? They all contain the buzzing, voiced *s* sound, spelled either with *s* or *z*. And how do our cartoonists and comic strip makers represent that a character in their drawing is asleep? With a speech balloon with *z-z-z-z-z-z* inside it.

Williams's poem is equally brilliant in adapting sound to sense, for opposite effects. The repetition of the first line as its last line gives the poem a circularity of form, which is emphasized internally by the repetition of the word *round* (2, 2, 5), *around* (3), and its rimes *impound* (6), *Grounds* (9), *sound* (10), plus the assonant *about* (8). The poem lacks end rime, but is rich in internal rime, exemplified in the above; in *prance as they dance* (11); and in such approximations as *squeal-tweedle-fiddles* (3-4), *tipping-thick-hips* (5-7), *bellies-balance* (7), *about-butts* (8-9), etc. The abundance of participial verb forms—*tipping, Kicking, rolling, swinging, rollicking*—contributes also to the sense of vigorous motion. The triple meter gives this motion speed, but is subject to occasional jolting irregularities (as in 5, 6, 8), which remind us that these are thick-shanked, big-bellied, heavy-butted peasants dancing, not a graceful group of nymphs on Mount Olympus. The great majority of the lines are run-on (only the last ends with a full stop, and 1 and 6 with partial stops), thus giving the poem a sense of continuous motion, especially when the lines end with such traditionally unlikely words as *and, the,* and a hyphenated *thick-,* where the reader is thrown forward into the next line without even a pause to observe the line-ending. This fact is further enhanced by the fact that all but three of the lines (5, 6, 11) have feminine endings, so that the meter as well as the grammatical incompleteness throw the reader forward. A highly unusual feature of this poem is that all but three (*around, impound,* and *about*) of the words of more than one syllable (there are twenty-six of them) are accented on the first syllable; and this also contributes to the sense of continuous motion. The exceptions to the foregoing observations occur just frequently enough to keep the reader a bit off-balance, like the peasants themselves.

Three onomatopoetic words provide the music for all this motion—the *squeal, blare,* and *tweedle* of the bagpipes, bugle, and fiddles. LP

ADDITIONAL EXERCISE

Follow the instructions for the exercise on page 725.

11. a. Like an iron-clanging anvil banged / With hammers.
    b. Like a massive iron anvil hit / With sledges.　　*Alfred, Lord Tennyson*
12. a. I am quiet sand / In an hourglass.
    b. I am soft sift / In an hourglass.　　*Gerard Manley Hopkins*
13. a. Dress! arm! mount!—away!
      Save my castle before the day
      Turns to blue from silver gray.
    b. Boot, saddle, to horse, and away!
      Rescue my castle before the hot day
      Brightens to blue from its silvery gray.　　*Robert Browning*
14. a. The lilies and languors of virtue,
      . . . the roses and raptures of vice.
    b. The lilies and boredom of virtue,
      . . . the roses and pleasures of evil.　　*Algernon Charles Swinburne*
15. a. And still she lulled him asleep.
    b. And yet she conjured him to sleep.　　*Anonymous*

ADDITIONAL EXERCISE ANSWERS

The letter in parentheses indicates the superior version.

11. (a) (*The Princess,* 5) The four short *a*'s in succession ("clanging," "anvil," "banged," "hammer") give the effect of repeated blows. "Clanging" and "banged" are onomatopoetic.
12. (b) ("Wreck of the Deutschland") "Soft sift" is softer and more nearly silent than "quiet sand."
13. (b) ("Boot and Saddle") The basic anapestic meter enhances the speed of the action. The first line, by its meter and punctuation, gives the effect of starting from a standstill and gradually picking up speed:

$$\overline{\text{Boot,}} \mid \overline{\text{sad-}}\breve{\text{dle,}} \mid \breve{\text{to}} \; \overline{\text{horse,}} \mid \breve{\text{and}} \; \breve{\text{a-}}\overline{\text{way!}} \mid$$

14. (a) ("Delores") The poet contrasts virtue and vice unconventionally. The

alliteration of "virtue" and "vice" makes the contrast vivid. Each is described by a symbolic flower and an abstract noun. The flower and noun ("lilies and languors," "roses and raptures") are in each case joined and made parallel by being alliterated, two-syllabled, and trochaic.

15. (a) The soft *l*'s in "still" and "lulled" are more "sleepy" than the sharp sounds in "yet" and "conjured."

CHAPTER FOURTEEN

Pattern

170. *e. e. cummings* **the greedy the people** (page 735)

When read in the two ways suggested, cummings's poem reveals a multiplicity of patterns. First, a rime pattern (*abcbac*), repeated in each stanza, utilizing both approximate and perfect rimes. Second, a metrical pattern, built on an anapestic base (five lines of dimeter and one of monometer), in which the corresponding lines of each stanza match each other exactly. Third, a sound pattern that relates the two chief words of each first line by assonance (*greedy-people*), alliteration (*timid-tender*), or rime (*chary-wary*). Fourth, a syntactical pattern that matches the corresponding lines of the various stanzas, putting identical grammatical structures and parts of speech in corresponding places. (The second line of each stanza, for instance, is always a parenthesis in which the framework "as _____ as can _____" is filled in by words related in form but opposed in meaning.) Fifth, and most important, a structural pattern in which the meaning of the first four lines of each stanza is countered by the meaning of the last two, and within which words of similar or related meaning and form are balanced neatly against each other (such pairings as "sell" and "buy," "don't" and "do," "when" and "how" are obvious).

The cummings trademark comes out in this poem in his imaginative transformation of the parts of speech, particularly in the final word of the fourth line in each stanza, in which conjunctions ("because"), pronouns ("which"), verbs ("seem," "must"), and prepositions ("until") are made to serve as nouns. "Because" (4) for cummings represents the cold sterility of abstract reason as opposed to the warm life of instinct and emotion (Faith asks of materialism, "Why?"). "Which" (10) is a thing rather than a person ("Who"). "Seem" (16) indicates a mere illusion of existence as opposed to real existence ("be"). "Until" (22) represents an indefinite future as contrasted to the living present ("Now"). "Must" (28) represents the restrictive authority of artificial social conventions and rules as opposed to the permissiveness of nature ("May"). Cummings concludes his poem with a triumphant pun, for "May" is not only the auxiliary verb of permission; it is that season of the year that stands for youth, for growth, for nature, and for life.

The two nouns in line 1 of each stanza represent undesirables in cummings's vocabulary ("people" [1] stands for "masses" rather than "individuals"; "tender" [25] is probably meant in the sense of "tender-minded" rather than "tender-hearted"). Of the two variables in line 2 of each stanza, the first always represents something undesirable, the second something desirable ("you're" [14] is a plural as opposed to a singular "i'm"). The activities depicted in lines 3–4 of each stanza

229

are undesirable ("work" [27] represents materialistic drudgery as opposed to creative play; "pray" [27] is directed toward an authoritarian god [a "must"] rather than toward a God of love).

In summary, the poem opposes states of unbeing and being. The first four lines of each stanza pass in review those people who feverishly pursue materialistic goals and whose lives are governed by greed, anxiety, prudence, convention, and conformity. In the last two lines of each stanza, the steeple bell, moon, stars, sun, and earth offer a laconic comment on these people's foolishness.

[This commentary is adapted from Laurence Perrine and James M. Reid, *100 American Poems of the Twentieth Century* (New York: Harcourt, 1966) 156–57.]   LP

---

171.   *Anonymous*   **I sat next the Duchess at tea** (page 737)

The limerick's never averse
To expressing itself in a terse
   Economical style,
   And yet, all the while,
The limerick's *always* a verse.   LP

---

172.   *John Keats*   **On First Looking into Chapman's Homer** (page 738)

The octave is concerned with exploration, the sestet with the experience of discovery.

The octave is an extended metaphor in which travel is the figurative term for reading, and "the realms of gold" the figurative term for literature. The "goodly states and kingdoms" are various kinds of literature, and the "western islands" are specifically poetry, the domain of Apollo, god of poetry and inventor of the lyre (from which the term *lyric* is derived). Though geography should not be pressed too hard, these islands are probably called "western" to associate them with the West Indies, where many of the early English and Spanish explorers sought for gold.

The sestet consists of two similes conveying the thrill of discovery. First, the speaker compares himself to an astronomer looking through his telescope when "a new planet swims into his ken." Anyone who has looked through a good astronomical telescope can testify to the "swimming" or quaking motion that an observed celestial body has as it enters the field of vision. The word "ken" is also beautifully effective here, for it not only means "range of vision" but is associated with knowing or knowledge; and the excitement here is generated by the astronomer's discovering a planet—a whole new world—previously unknown to man.

The second simile partly derives its force from the fact that the early explorers, seeking a shorter route to the East Indies and Cathay, at first thought they had found it and did not realize that what they had actually found was a new continent separated from their destination by another whole sea. Balboa's discovery of the Pacific thus came as a surprise and vastly expanded European ideas about the size of the earth. Keats captures the exact awe-struck moment when the explorer and his men first encounter this vast, shining, and unguessed-at new ocean while crossing the mountains of a land they did not know to be an isthmus.

One would prefer poets to be historically accurate, and it would be folly to pretend that nothing is lost when they are not. Yet Keats's subject is not history but human experience, and when one contemplates the consequences of substituting the three syllables of *bal-BO-a* for the three syllables of "STOUT COR-tez," one may even be glad for the blunder. (The name "Cortez" in Spanish is accented on the second syllable, but common British pronunciation reverses the accents.) The first loss is the adjective "stout," which, along with "eagle-eyed," gives strength and stature to the discoverer. The second loss is one of sound and rhythm, which support his strength. "STOUT COR-tez" with its three *t*'s, sharp *k*-sound, and two stresses, gives the adventurer just that intrepid quality which is needed, while *bal-BO-a* softens its *b*'s with a liquid *l* and trails off into two vowel sounds suggestive more of grace than of strength. The heroic description of the discoverer matches the heroic verse and voice ("loud and bold") of Chapman's translation, which for Keats first captured the heroic qualities of Homer's epic narratives.

But if this poem were only about Keats's discovery of Chapman's translation, it would be of limited interest. What gives it enduring value is Keats's transformation of his discovery into a symbol for all discovery, his magnificent success in conveying the excitement that may attend any discovery, made by any of us, whether it be of universal or only personal significance. LP

173. *William Shakespeare* **That time of year** (page 739)

In this sonnet an aging speaker, constantly aware of his approaching death, addresses a beloved person considerably younger than himself.

The structure of thought in the sonnet is perfectly matched to the formal divisions marked out by its rime scheme. In each of the three quatrains the speaker makes a metaphorical statement of his increasing age and nearness to death, and in the concluding couplet he makes a counterstatement of his beloved's increased love for him. This structure is formally expressed in the language of the poem. Its opening line contains the words "thou mayst in me behold"; the second and third quatrains each begin "In me thou see'st"; the concluding couplet, before making its counterstatement, summarizes what has preceded in its opening words "This thou perceivest."

In the opening quatrain the speaker compares himself to "That time of year" (late autumn or early winter) when "yellow leaves, or none, or few" hang upon the trees. In the second stanza he compares himself to the dusk of day, fading from sunset into night. In the third he compares himself to a sinking fire, whose glowing embers are about to be extinguished by the ashes of the fuel that once "nourished" it. Though the quatrains (each a sentence) make parallel statements, they are arranged in a climactic order and could not be rearranged without loss. First, they are concerned with diminishing periods of time (a year, a day, the length of time that a fire will burn), and thus they bring us metaphorically closer and closer to the thought of death (weeks, hours, minutes). In addition, the first quatrain emphasizes coldness ("bare" boughs "shake against the cold"); the second emphasizes darkness (twilight fading into "black night"); the third combines cold and dark in the image of the sinking fire, which is losing both warmth and light. Finally, the first quatrain looks backward in time to what has been lost, the second looks forward to what will be lost, and the third combines references to past and future.

Each central metaphor is complicated by an additional metaphor or metaphors. In the first, the tree's leafless boughs are called "bare ruined choirs." A choir is that section of a church or chapel containing wooden choir stalls, and the sight of "bare ruined choirs" would have been familiar to every reader of Shakespeare's time because of the confiscation of Roman Catholic monastic properties throughout England by Henry VIII some half-century earlier and the subsequent spoliation of the monasteries by Reformation landowners. Through this association of thought the "sweet birds" become not only the songbirds that have migrated south for the winter, but also the choir singers who once sang in the now-ruined monastery churches. The image of desolation is thus intensified. In the second quatrain, "black night," because of its association with sleep, is called "Death's second self"—a kind of twin or surrogate of Death "that seals up all in rest." In the third quatrain, the ashes of the fire become the deathbed on which the fire's personified youth is expiring, paradoxically "consumed" (in a third metaphor) by the food that once "nourished" it.

Against the three quatrains with their metaphorical statements of declining life and approaching death, the speaker opposes a concluding counterstatement concerning love. He throws human love, as it were, into the teeth of death. That the couplet is a counterstatement is metrically signaled by the inversion of stress in the opening foot. It begins, however, as a summarizing statement—"This thou perceivest"— where "This" refers for its antecedent to all of the images in the preceding quatrains (that is, to the grammatical objects of the verbs indicating seeing or beholding). The speaker then asserts his belief that the friend addressed throughout the sonnet loves the speaker all the more intensely because of the friend's realization that the speaker must soon die. The friend's increased love compensates for the speaker's impending death. Death's negative is countered by an affirmation of love.

Or so it would seem, on a first reading. On a second reading, we may be less sure of the strength of the affirmation. The speaker, we notice, is a person who needs to be loved. He does not conclude: "This thou perceivest, which makes my love more strong, / To love that well which I must leave ere long." That is, he is not primarily concerned with giving love but with receiving it. We may then ask what evidence he has for his final assertion and perhaps question whether he is asserting a belief, expressing a hope, or making a plea. We may also begin to wonder whether he is actually as old as the metaphors in the quatrains suggest, or whether he does not mix considerable overstatement with these metaphors, perhaps as a play

232

for the beloved's sympathy. The poem, seemingly simple on the surface, becomes increasingly complex and ambiguous as we delve into it. Some readers will read it for moral profundity; others will find it more notable for psychological profundity. (The questions raised here are more likely to rise in the mind of a reader who has read more of Shakespeare's sonnets than in that of a beginning student who reads the sonnet out of context. Such a student, however, may be asked to recall Sonnet 138—"When my love swears that she is made of truth" [page 559], where the speaker, surely not far past thirty, also refers to himself as "old" and quite clearly feels insecure in his relationship with a younger beloved.) LP

EXERCISES (page 740)

1. a. Italian, strict in rime scheme but with a run-on in structure as the thought of the octave is not concluded until the middle of line 9.
   b. Italian, strict in rime scheme and structure, with a slight variation in the sestet rime: *ccdccd*.
   c. Italian, strict in rime scheme but with a variant sestet: *cdccdd*. Departs from Italian structure by running-on between the two quatrains of the octave.
   d. English, strict in rime scheme (more strict than usual in repeating the *b* rime as the *d* rime). Structure is broken by allotting portions to the speakers; Shakespeare effectively reinforces the increasing emotionality, when after matching a different speaker to each of the opening quatrains, he has them share the third quatrain and the couplet.
   e. English, strict in rime and structure. Rhetorical break between lines 8 and 9 resembles Italian.
   f. English, strict through two quatrains, then an Italianate structural break signaled by line spacing and by insertion of the couplet at lines 9–10 rather than 13–14: *ababcdcd ee fgfg*.
   g. Italian through line 8, then English: *abbaabba cdcd dd*. Structured as English, with separate metaphors developed in 1–4 and 5–8; then the third metaphor develops in 9–11, and 12–14 draw the last two metaphors together.
   h. Highly varied English, beginning and ending with quatrains: *ababacdcedefef*. Structurally irregular.
   i. Mixed. Two English quatrains followed by Italian sestet: *ababcdcd efgefg*.
   j. Italian, irregular: strictly rimed octave, sestet consisting of a couplet followed by English quatrain.
   k. Mixed. Two English quatrains followed by a variant Italian sestet: *ababcdcd effegg*.
   l. Nonce sonnet: 14 lines of iambic tetrameter couplets. Arguably not enough formal resemblance to be called a sonnet.
2. We first notice that all four of these poems have 19 lines divided into five stanzas of three lines and a final stanza of four. We notice next that they employ only

two rime-sounds, and deploy them in accordance with a fixed system. If we take "Do Not Go Gentle into That Good Night" (page 852) as the "purest" (using "purest" as a descriptive, not an evaluative, term) we see also that there is a pattern of refrain lines entwined with the riming pattern. We can express the pattern thus: A^1bA^2 abA^1 abA^2 abA^1 abA^2 abA^1A^2. In brief, lines 1 and 3 of the first stanza become refrains that are used alternately to end stanzas 2, 3, and 4, and then used together in the concluding quatrain, becoming the last two lines of the poem.

The other three poems take minor liberties with this traditional pattern. In "The Freaks at Spurgin Road Field" (page 813) Hugo uses approximate A rimes (*clap-back*) and discards the *a* and *b* rimes (but creates some approximate rime links between them and the refrains, such as assonance in all three of the first lines, and the incidence of expected *b* rimes ending in *-k* sounds [lines 8, 11, 14]). He also violates the pattern of the concluding quatrain—not abA^1A^2 but xA^2xA^1. His refrain lines are exactly maintained, including end-stopping, until the quatrain.

In "One Art" (page 788) Bishop slightly varies her first refrain in the concluding quatrain, but the only remnant of the second refrain is the terminal word *disaster*. She also uses approximate rimes (*master, fluster, gesture*).

In "The Story We Know" (page 748) Collins has obviously sought for variety rather than uniformity in her refrain lines. No two are alike. Lines 1 and 12 contain the same words in the same order but with different punctuation and syntax. Her first refrain lines, however, all contain the words "way," "begin," and "Hello." Her second refrain lines all contain the words "Good-bye" and "end," and the phrase "story we know."

174. *Anonymous and others* **A Handful of Limericks** (page 741)

The limerick can be useful for giving students personal experience with versification. Give them a first line ("A freshman who snored in his sleep") or part of a first line ("There was a young man from _____") and offer a prize for the best completion, taking into consideration both successful handling of the form and cleverness of the punch line. (Be sure, if you give them the first line, to provide one with ample riming opportunities.) Note that, though the basic meter is anapestic, iambs may be freely substituted in the first foot (but only in the first foot) in any line. Rarely, if ever, are the first feet in a limerick all anapests; but often (as in "There was a young lady of Lynn") they are all iambs. LP

175. *Matsuo Bashō / Moritake* **Two Japanese Haiku** (page 742)

Just as the limerick is a useful form for giving students experience with versification, the haiku is a useful form for initiating them into original *poetic* composition (experiential rather than merely clever). The brevity of the form forces them to practice verbal economy; its nature, by delivering them from the hampering notion that meter and rime are essential to poetry, frees them to concentrate on other dimensions—particularly imagery. The essence of haiku poetry is that it suggests rather than states. It strives to give the reader some unique perception of nature, or some immediate insight into the nature of things, without intervention of the abstracting intellect. It accomplishes this, most frequently, either by presenting a single sharply observed image, or by juxtaposing two images that parallel or contrast with each other in significant and suggestive ways. So essential to the form is brevity that many writers of haiku in English have abandoned the traditional 5-7-5 syllabic pattern and written poems even briefer. The haiku composition assignment may therefore be made in various ways. If you wish to give your students the discipline of working within a prescribed form, insist on their adherence to the 5-7-5 pattern. If you wish to free them from all constraints of form, ask for a poem of not more than three lines. If you want to stress chiefly verbal economy, let them write a poem of any number or arrangement of lines but containing no more than seventeen syllables. The important stipulation should be that the poem purvey its perception through imagery rather than through abstract statement. LP

176. *Dylan Thomas* **Poem in October** (page 743)

In tone this poem is rhapsodic. It begins on a note of delight and anticipation, climbs steadily to joy, leaps into an exalted state of visionary experience and recollection, then lapses slightly back into joy and hope. There are contrasts of tone in the poem, but they are not sharp contrasts. The whole poem is pitched at a high level of exultation. This exultation comes from the poet's relationship with nature, not only its beauty, but a sacredness he senses in it, akin to what Wordsworth found in it a century and a half earlier.

The poet celebrates his birthday by rising early in the morning (he hears the morning beckon him to set forth) and walking beyond the gates of the town and up the mountain that lies behind it. He climbs so high that he gets above the weather. The month is October, and it has been raining in the town, but high on the mountainside the sun is "Summery," birds are singing, and he hears only "the rain wringing / Wind blow cold" in the woods "faraway" under him. From this height the town church seems small as a snail with its "horns" (its two towers) rising through mist. Where he stands, however, "all the gardens / Of spring and summer" seem to be blooming, and it is a fit spot to "marvel" his birthday away—"but the weather turned around." We must be careful not to put too much emphasis on that "but" or to read the following clause literally. The weather does not turn from rainy to sunny or from fall to summery: these changes had already occurred as he climbed the mountainside. The weather metaphorically and psychologically turns "around" in that the poet's mind is carried in vision and in time away from the "blithe" summery scene presently before him where he could "marvel" his birthday away, back to his childhood days when he felt an even intenser and completer identification with the "wonder of summer." He remembers the forgotten mornings when "he walked with his mother / Through the parables / Of sun light / And the legends of the green chapels" (the woods), and "the mystery / Sang alive / Still in the water and singingbirds." In the final stanza the first three lines are a recapitulation of lines 38–40, not a new turning; nevertheless, this final stanza brings him slowly back to the reality of the present with its full recognition that the "true / Joy" of his visionary experience had been that of a "long dead child," that it is now his "thirtieth / Year to heaven" (a recapitulation of the opening line), and that the town below him is wearing its autumn foliage. The poem ends with the poet's prayer that on his next birthday he may still be capable of such visionary experience.

Though less explicitly philosophical, "Poem in October" in several ways resembles Wordsworth's "Tintern Abbey." The adult poet is a lover of nature, responsive to its beauty, and a believer that it somehow embraces the divine (as shown by Thomas's use throughout the poem of "sacramental imagery" and language: "thirtieth year to heaven," "heron / Priested shore," "water praying," "the blue altered sky"—with its concealed pun, "parables / Of sun light," "legends of the green chapels," "mystery"). Yet the poet regrets the loss of the even intenser involvement with nature that he enjoyed as a child when he felt the divinity of nature (his "true / Joy") less consciously in the intellect but more fully through his whole being.

A minor difficulty in this poem is caused by Thomas's omission of the hyphen from such compound adjectives as *mussel-pooled, heron-priested, net-webbed, rain-wringing, lark-full,* and *blue-altered.* The involved syntax of the first stanza has also caused difficulty. Its skeleton is "It was my thirtieth year to heaven [that] woke to my hearing the morning beckon myself to set foot in the town and set forth." Thomas has omitted the relative pronoun between lines 1 and 2. "Woke" is an intransitive verb modified by the prepositional phrase beginning with "to"; the object of the preposition is the long gerund phrase "my hearing the water beckon . . . etc." The object of the gerund is an infinitive phrase with "the morning" as its subject and "[to] beckon" as its verb. For fuller discussion, see *Explicator* 27 (Feb. 1969): item 43.   LP

177. *William Shakespeare* From ***Romeo and Juliet*** (page 745)

Since *Romeo and Juliet*, except for a few brief prose passages, is written throughout in iambic pentameter, and since much of it also rimes (the lines riming sometimes alternately and sometimes in pairs), it is not surprising that 14 lines from a total of almost 3,000 should fall into the rime pattern of an English sonnet. That this excerpt does so from design, rather than from coincidence, however, can be definitively demonstrated.

1. The passage has four kinds of unity: grammatical, situational, metaphorical, and tonal. First, the passage begins at the beginning of a sentence and ends at the end of a sentence. It is grammatically self-contained. Second, the passage covers a

self-contained episode or situation: it begins with the first words of Romeo and Juliet and ends with their first kiss. Third, the passage is unified by a single extended metaphor, one in which a pilgrim, or palmer, is worshiping at the shrine of a saint. Fourth, the religious nature of this metaphor—employing words like "profane," "holy," "shrine," "sin," "pilgrims," "devotion," "saints," "palmers," "prayer," and "faith"—combines with the delicious punning wit of the dialogue to give the passage unity of tone: a tone of earnest delicacy and delightfully charming gravity, which forces us to take seriously an episode we might otherwise take cynically. Romeo, we feel, is not simply a fresh young man on the make and Juliet an easy mark: this is genuine love at first sight. "Dear saint, let lips do what hands do" is tonally a great deal different from "Gimme a little kiss, won'cha?"

2. In structure as in form, the excerpt is organized into three quatrains and a final couplet. In the first quatrain Romeo, initiating the basic metaphor, apologizes for taking Juliet's "holy" hand in his unworthy one, but humbly offers to make up for the offense by giving the hand a gentle kiss. In the second quatrain Juliet reassures Romeo, telling him that he has done no wrong but has only shown mannerly devotion in taking her hand, for pilgrims quite properly touch saints' hands, and pilgrims "kiss" by clasping hands. She thus simultaneously encourages Romeo to hold her hand but with maidenly delicacy indicates that there is no need for him to kiss it. In the third quatrain, however, emboldened by this reassurance, Romeo decides to play the long shot and ask for a kiss on the lips. But he puts the request delicately and charmingly. Do not pilgrims and saints have lips as well as hands? he asks. Translated, this means, why should we not kiss with our lips instead of merely with our hands? Juliet, still modest, yet keeping to the metaphor, replies that pilgrims' lips are for praying with. Then Romeo brilliantly seizes his opening: "let lips do what hands do." The line has two meanings. Hands not only kiss, they also pray. Lips not only pray, they also kiss. So Romeo, shaping his hands into the attitude of prayer, prays also with his lips; but what he prays for is a kiss. In the final couplet Juliet, not unwillingly defeated in this contest of wit (for what can a saint do when a faithful pilgrim prays to her?) gracefully surrenders: she grants the kiss, thus answering Romeo's prayer. The first quatrain is Romeo's apology; the second is Juliet's reassurance; the third is the plea; and the couplet is the plea granted. Structure follows form.

3. In Shakespeare's time the sonnet form was used primarily for the treatment of love. His play concerns a pair of "star-crossed lovers." The episode in the excerpt concerns their first meeting and their first kiss. What more appropriate than that Shakespeare should deliberately cast the episode into the form of an English sonnet?

[This discussion is abridged from the essay "When Form and Content Kiss, / Intention Made the Bliss," in Laurence Perrine, *The Art of Total Relevance: Papers on Poetry* (Rowley, MA: Newbury, 1976) 75–77.] LP

178. *John Donne* **Death, be not proud** (page 746)

This tightly constructed sonnet matches structure to form while producing some surprises for those acquainted with both the English and Italian sonnet forms. There are three quatrains and a couplet (as in the English sonnet), but the riming pattern is not *abab cdcd* etc., but *abba abba cddc aa*: the Italian quatrain is used in the English rhetorical structure, and the English closing couplet returns to the *a*-rime, thus implying circularity.

These formal elements are in harmony with the structure of thought. The sonnet, an extended apostrophe, consists of these rhetorical units: an opening quatrain that makes an assertion (based on faith) denying that death is either mighty or dreadful; a second quatrain offering "proof" that death is not dreadful; a third offering "proof" that it is not mighty; and a couplet that returns to faith and faith alone as a support, and to the riming sound of the opening line. While the speaker attempts to use reason and logical proof to shore up his opening remark, he unwittingly reveals the weakness of his reasoning, the falseness of his premise, and the desperation that would lead a man to such an undertaking: he reveals a man stating a deep wish as if it were easily demonstrable truth.

The opening quatrain, in a tone of forced bravado, uses only two techniques of argument, neither logically admissible: the simple insistence that what "some" have said is not true, and the condescending tone of "poor death." If it is a *fact* that people overthrown by death "die not," then the final phrase of the quatrain is valid, for the syllogism is clear: death cannot kill men; I am a man; therefore, death cannot kill me. What is not established here, of course, is the universality of immortality, so the syllogism, though valid, has been based on an unproved major premise.

It is important to bring formal logic into the discussion of this poem, for the patent illogicality of the speaker is what makes the poem so moving. In his desperate need to reassure himself, the speaker is nevertheless the butt of dramatic irony, an example of the futility of attempting to prove an article of faith by means of reason—and so intensely in need of such proof that he argues fraudulently.

The second quatrain attempts to prove that death is not to be feared. But the two "proofs" are fallacious: lines 5–6 argue by analogy (death is like sleep; sleep gives pleasure; therefore death gives pleasure), while line 7 employs the favorite device of advertisers, the "endorsement" of "our best men." The third quatrain, intended to prove that death is not powerful, opens with two illogical devices: name-calling ("slave," because death is caused by other agents) and the aspersion of dwelling with evil neighbors. It returns to argument by analogy, insisting that drugs or spells induce a better sleep than death does, and then closes with another belittling condescension.

The concluding couplet, in a tone of triumph, asserts that the case has been proved and that eternal life is our universal destiny. It does so in paradox, the death of death, which requires the only possible resolution, the faith of a believer in Christian salvation.

The key to further meaning in the poem may be found in the speaker's apparent unawareness of what he is additionally revealing about himself and his feelings about death. When in the second quatrain he attempts to disprove death's dreadfulness, he inadvertently uses death's might as his evidence: death is *more* powerful than "rest and sleep," and it has the power to deliver the soul from the captivity of the body. When in the third he attempts to disprove death's power, he calls to witness its dreadfulness: in line 9, the frailty of human life makes us subject to a frightening array of powerful killers, and in line 10 the neighbors of death are a catalogue of dread. Perhaps even more telling is the speaker's ambiguity about "sleep," death's analogue. In the second quatrain, rest and sleep are the sources of "much pleasure," though not so much as death can give. Yet in the third, the sleep induced by drugs or charms is "better" than the sleep of death—and in the couplet, what is most desired is eternal wakefulness, not rest or sleep. The great victory is that both sleep and death "shall be no more."

The speaker knows what he wants—the eternal bliss of salvation—but he is vainly trying to prove through logical argument that he can receive it. That attempt is doomed, as theologians and philosophers have long demonstrated, and the speaker's own desperation is vividly shown by his failure. Finally, he rests where he began— and where according to the scriptures he can find his much-desired certitude. He accepts and triumphs in the paradoxes of his faith, which defy logical or rational analysis, but which assure him that "the last enemy that shall be destroyed is death" (1 Cor. 15.56), that "death is swallowed up in victory" (1 Cor. 15.54), and that "death and hell [will be] cast into the lake of fire" (Rev. 20.14). TRA

179. *Linda Pastan* **The Imperfect Paradise** (page 746)

In Genesis 1, on the sixth and last day of creation God made all the beasts of the earth, and man and woman with dominion over all life forms. Genesis 2 presents a "close-up" examination of the sixth day, with details of the Garden of Eden, the naming of the animals, and the creation of Eve; the third chapter relates the fall of Adam and Eve. (The poem ignores the fact that on the fifth day God created marine life and birds, for it posits nothing but vegetation as its starting point.)

The forms of both the English and Italian sonnets are combined here. The rime scheme is English, and the couplet at the end proffers the two contrasting possibilities that make up the theme (without explicit resolution). But the structure more closely resembles the Italian—an octave of "if" clauses, and a sestet of questions that follow from the hypotheses of those clauses.

There are few difficult passages once the central allusion is explained. Lines 7–8 suggest that the wind would have had to make the sounds of lamentation if there were no human beings to express their grief and sorrow in prayer—prayer understated in the phrase "picture postcards of the soul." The last line presents an interpretive difficulty in the "strict contract between love and grief": the contract refers explicitly to God's prohibition of the tree of knowledge, with death as the consequence of breaking that contract. "Love" may refer to God's love of his creature, and "grief" to his grief that his favorite has fallen; equally, these terms may refer to Adam's love for Eve, which led him to accept the forbidden fruit, and to the ensuing grief of mankind.

There is no explicit answer to the final question, which is in fact an unresolved dilemma: which is better, a sinless world devoid of mankind, or a world of fallible human beings? The title leaves the question open, too: is paradise imperfect if the last creation is missing, or is it imperfect because God *did* create mankind?

Wallace Stevens's "The Poems of Our Climate" (page 849) asserts one resolution of the dilemma (and may provide an allusive source for Pastan's poem): "The imperfect is our paradise." That is, the most intense living is comprised of the desire for perfection combined with the knowledge that it is unattainable.   TRA

180.   *Robert Frost*   **Acquainted with the Night** (page 747)

At a purely literal level this poem says merely that the poet has taken many walks at night through the city and is thoroughly familiar with its nighttime aspects. But clearly the poem is meant to be read symbolically. The chief symbol is the night, which suggests the darker aspects of existence. But to grasp anything like its full significance, we must examine the details of the poem. The following discussion does not pretend to exhaust their implications.

That the poet has walked out and back in rain indicates that he has endured physical discomfort. That he has walked beyond "the furthest city light"—beyond the city limits—may suggest that he has "transgressed"—gone beyond legal or moral limits. His having looked down "the saddest city lane" indicates that he has seen the poverty and misery of the city's slum areas. His unwillingness to explain to the watchman what he is doing out so late at night suggests feelings of guilt or embarrassment. The "interrupted cry" across houses from another street—possibly a scream of terror cut short by strangulation—suggests violence and evil. That the cry is not directed toward him suggests his loneliness. The illuminated clock, which seems detached from the earth and at "an unearthly height" (because its tower is blotted out by darkness), may at first seem like something supernatural, but is really only a man-made instrument able to "proclaim the time" but not to judge it. It thus suggests a universe without moral or divine oversight—a universe indifferent to man.

The night in Frost's poem is thus a remarkably subtle and evocative symbol for hardship, guilt, sorrow, loneliness, evil, desolation, and isolation at the personal, social, and cosmic levels. The clock against the sky, man-made but "at an unearthly height," strikingly proclaims the absence of authoritative moral direction, human or superhuman, in an indifferent universe.

And how does the poet respond to this dark perception of the universe? The calm, matter-of-fact tone of voice in the first and final lines counters the dark experience of the intervening lines with a quiet refusal to be daunted. The final line is indeed an understatement. The poet has been more than "acquainted" with the night—he has explored it thoroughly; but his tone of voice says, in effect, "I can take it."

Though the poem resembles a sonnet in containing fourteen lines of iambic pentameter, its rime scheme is that of *terza rima*, made famous by Dante's use of it in *The Divine Comedy*, of which the *Inferno* is the best-known section.

Some critics have read the "luminary clock" as a metaphor for the moon. But (a) one cannot easily tell time by the moon, as one can by the sun; it rises at a different hour every day and is often observable in full daylight; (b) this is a city poem, and its imagery is city imagery; (c) if the clock *were* the moon, then the phrase "at an unearthly height" would be literal, obvious, and uninteresting; (d) Frost has himself identified the clock as a tower clock in Ann Arbor (see *Frost: Centennial Essays* [Jackson: UP of Mississippi, 1974] 521; and *Frost: Centennial Essays III* [1978] 296).

There are excellent discussions of this poem in Reginald L. Cook, *The Dimensions of Robert Frost* (New York: Rinehart, 1958) 107–108; and in Reuben A. Brower, *The Poetry of Robert Frost* (New York: Oxford UP, 1963) 126–29.   LP

181.   *Martha Collins*   **The Story We Know** (page 748)

The poem departs from the strictness of its chosen form by varying the two refrain lines, which should be identical in language (if not in syntactical function or meaning). Its maintenance of the proper rime scheme for a villanelle is emphasized by the high incidence of monosyllables as rime words, seeming to insist that we notice the perfect riming. That kind of self-consciousness about form and its fitness to subject (which is often the tone adopted in lighter verse) is parodied in line 2, which presents a bouncing iambic regularity in the monosyllables of an empty social encounter, mimicking the shallowness of the occasion in the monotony of rhythm. Line 2 is also one of only three perfectly iambic pentameter lines, and is the only one of them to punctuate pauses precisely between all of its feet, to reinforce its sense of empty repetition (the other two, lines 4 and 16, vary the rhythm to avoid such regularity).

The metrical norm in the poem, however, is anapestic pentameter, as determined by the relative frequency of the triple foot, and particularly by the meter of the two refrain lines:

The way | to be-gin | is al- | ways the same. | Hel-lo,   1

and Good-bye | at the end. | That's ev- | er-y sto- | ry we know,   3

This meter is well suited to such society verse as the villanelle, and Collins plays ironically with the expectations aroused by this traditionally light, polite form. In fact, part of the poem's force comes from setting up a shallow, blasé expectation in both reader and speaker, for if we are conditioned to the superficial pleasantries of social verse, so the speaker in her ennui seems to have conditioned herself to expect only superficiality in her relations with other people. She "knows" how all relations begin and end: a social "hello," "and Good-bye at the end," a pattern of uninvolved pairing with all the expected accoutrements of love affairs without love—external things that take the place of feelings. It is, as she says, a boring sequence, "a story we know / so well we don't turn the page." But on this occasion, something more meaningful takes place, not only a mutual dependency but a shared fear of death. The social routine of hello/goodbye comes to symbolize the physical reality of mortal life, "the way we all begin and end" signalled to the speaker by the "cold white sign" of snow obliterating both the air and the pine.

Blasé sophistication, so aptly captured in the form of light verse, turns out to have a darker implication, as the speaker learns that the pattern of her personal social life, full of empty beginnings and endings, is also the pattern of mortal existence. TRA

182. *Anonymous* **Edward** (page 749)

The story told in "Edward"—a dark domestic tragedy of greed, guile, murder, and remorse—is unfolded gradually through dialogue, question, and answer. Not until the third stanza do we learn what Edward has done. Not until the last do we learn why he has done it. The tension of the poem mounts steadily through the first climax to the last.

A man of noble birth and heir to his father's estate, Edward has killed his father because of the "counsels" of his mother, who had hoped to get control of these properties into her own hands. To accomplish this end, she has been willing to subvert her own son. Crafty, manipulative, greedy, and entirely lacking in natural affections, she has somehow worked on her son's feelings through hint, suggestion, and insinuation, until he has felt it his duty or his interest to kill his father. But the psychological dimensions of the story exist largely between the lines.

Why does the mother, if she put him up to it, have to ask why Edward's sword drips with blood? She is perhaps surprised to see Edward "sad" rather than rejoicing, and needs to confirm her hopes. Why does Edward lie about what he has done? Since doing the deed, he has undergone a revulsion of horror and remorse, and is lying more to himself than to his mother. He cannot admit to himself what he has done. The mother calls his bluff, presses her question; Edward lies again, and is again detected; but the mother reveals something about herself. One steed is the same as another to her, and she does not understand that a man might have a peculiar affection for a particular steed, especially an old one (like his father). When Edward finally admits the truth, the mother shows no emotion; it is what she had secretly known and hoped for. In her question about what penance Edward will do for his deed, she cunningly washes her hands of any share in the guilt. Edward, overcome with guilt, sees exile from home and family and all he has loved as the only possible penance. The next question—what will Edward do with his towers and hall?—brings us to the center of the mother's interests. But Edward cares not a whit for the towers and hall: they are the witnesses of his dreadful crime. Failing of the answer she wanted, the mother shrewdly digresses in her next question, disguising her main concern. Edward's reply to what he will leave his wife and children does not indicate that he is uncaring, but only that he is so emotionally overwrought that he feels any provision made for them can only contaminate them with his own guilt. In her final question the mother returns to her main concern: "And what will ye leave to your own mother dear?" In that final phrase we glimpse the mother's manipulative method. Twice in the poem up to this point she has addressed Edward as her "dear son" (12, 28); now she reminds him that she is his own dear mother. But she is totally unprepared for the switch in parental allegiance that Edward has undergone since the killing. Edward uses the word "dear" in the poem only in speaking of his dead father (21, 23).

Edward's final outburst comes with a shock to the reader as well as to the mother. For the reader it is a double shock—that of hearing a son deliver the curse of hell on his mother and of learning that he killed his father at his mother's suggestion. Yet the reader is left, most likely, with a feeling of pity for Edward and of horror for the mother. The emotional Edward suffers torments of horror, guilt, and remorse for what he has done; the crafty and unnatural mother feels nothing but greed.

The narrative kernel of each stanza (lines 1, 4, 5, 8) is in ballad stanza, iambic $a^4b^3a^4b^3$. The two refrains ("Edward, Edward" and "Mother, mother") keep the crucial family relationship constantly before us. The repeated lines prolong the suspense and add immensely to the emotional power. LP

183. *William Burford* A Christmas Tree (page 751)

The pattern of this poem is metrical as well as typographical. The lines have respectively one, two, three, four, five, one, and two feet. The poem's meaning is reinforced visually not only in the Christmas-tree shape but also in the word "huddld," where the omission of the letter *e* huddles four tall-stemmed letters together. The rime scheme is *aabccxb*, the *b* rimes being approximate. LP

EXERCISE (page 751)

1. Rime (riming lines aligned, at margin or indented).
2. Meter (trimeter lines indented).
3. Structure (cadenced phrases moving left to right, possibly in imitation of high-wire artist's short, hurried steps and pauses for balance on the wire).
4. Structure (verse paragraphs allotted to the three parts of the argument).
5. Syllable count.
6. Refrain.

CHAPTER FIFTEEN

Bad Poetry and Good

184. *Anonymous* **God's Will for You and Me** (page 756)

185. *Gerard Manley Hopkins* **Pied Beauty** (page 757)

The poetic deficiencies of "God's Will for You and Me" are not far to seek. Its literal language is trite ("when things go wrong," "God knows best"). Its figurative language is trite ("willing feet," "our daily key"). Its remaining imagery is feeble ("child," "song," "dark or bright"). Eight of the poem's fourteen lines repeat the phrase "Just to" ten times, followed by "be." These three words constitute almost 40 percent of the poem. The rest is mostly a string of abstract adjectives—"tender," "true," "glad," "merciful," "mild," "trustful," "gentle," "kind," "sweet," "helpful," "cheery," "loyal"—strung together in no particular order, and often duplicative or overlapping in meaning (*kind-helpful, glad-cheery, gentle-tender-mild*). Worst of all, the poem's tripping triple meter and childish repetition of "Just to be" make God's will for you and me seem simple, undemanding, and easy to carry out. In truth, no man could do it successfully for one whole day. The poem not only fails to create experience; it falsifies it.

Though both poems concern God, their themes are quite different. "God's Will for You and Me" is didactic verse instructing us how God wishes us to live our lives; "Pied Beauty" is, first, a hymn of praise to God for the variegated, changing beauty of the natural and human worlds, and, second, a contrast between this variegated, changing beauty of the created world and the uniform, unchanging beauty of the Creator. (The theme has its biblical base in James 1.17: "Every good gift and every perfect gift is from above, and cometh down from the Father of lights, with whom is no variableness, neither shadow of turning.")

The first theme is stated in the title and first line of the poem and is developed and exemplified in the next eight. "Glory be to God," the poet exclaims, for the beauty of things that are pied, dappled, couple-colored, brinded, stippled, plotted and pieced, fickle, or freckled. With one exception these terms all apply to things that are of more than one color. The exception, "fickle," referring to variation in time rather than space, ties in with "swift, slow" and reminds us that this various beauty is in constant motion and is constantly changing. The white clouds move and change in shape across a brightening or darkening blue sky; the decoratively rose-mole-stippled trout swim in a changing current. In line 5, which introduces human activities into the poem, farmers alter the landscape by laying it out in plots of grazing, fallow, and plowed land.

The concluding two lines of the poem summarize the first theme and introduce the second. The praise for this diverse, changing beauty is due to a Creator whose beauty is "past [beyond] change." The poem thus brings into contrast multiplicity and unity, constant change and changelessness, plenitude and amplitude, with the implication that the latter are greater. If the wonders of the created world (a world that varies "who knows how?") pass understanding, how much more so must the beauty of their Creator!

The achievement of the poem lies, first, in its packed, vivid imagery. Line 4, for instance, in six words introduces three separate vivid images (two literal, one figurative). There are "finches' wings" (black and gold) and "chestnut-falls" (fallen chestnuts beneath a tree, glowing in mahogany browns), these latter compared by a compound adjective to fresh firecoals glowing golden and umber in a grate. Though the imagery of the poem is chiefly visual, the opposition of "sweet, sour" reminds us that the world is variegated in its appeal to the other senses as well. Second, the poem is remarkable for its rich use of sound: patterned end-rime; paired alliterations linking words parallel or opposed in meaning (*swift, slow*; *sweet, sour*; *adazzle, dim*), or simply the complex orchestration of such a line as 4 (with the alliteration of *Fresh-fire-falls-finches*; the assonance of *fresh-chestnut* and *finches' wings*; the *l*-consonance of *coal-falls*). Third, the poem is remarkable for its concentration. In line 4 every word is image-bearing; in line 9 all words but the initial "With" carry a full freight of meaning (contrast such lines with the slackness of "Just to be tender, just to be true"). Finally, "Pied Beauty" is notable for its freshness of diction. The four adjectives in line 7 are all apposite yet unexpected; the adjectives in "God's Will for You and Me" are as predictable as those in the Boy Scout oath. LP

186. *Emily Dickinson* **If you were coming in the fall** (page 757)

187. *Ivan Leonard Wright* **The Want of You** (page 758)

Wright's vehemently rhetorical poem is characterized by its strained language and by its trite imagery. The verbs chosen to denote what the "want" does are typical: it "smites," "binds," "flashes," "creeps," "hammers," "sighs," "cries," and "leaps," verbs that are variously either violent or swooning, and that create almost no precise imagery (the alliterating second line, for example, at best mixes its metaphor, as it has the "want" smiting with feelings of nausea). The bare statement of the poem is that the longing for an absent love is so extreme that it manifests itself in all kinds of painful experience, until the speaker blasphemously accuses God of injustice or ignorance of what the feeling is.

Dickinson's poem, in contrast, is extremely precise in its sequence of images. In increasing time increments, expressed through simile and metaphor, the speaker expresses a love so strong that it can patiently bear separation for a season, a year, centuries, or until doomsday—if only the speaker could be certain of the hoped-for union with her beloved. The imagery is homely and domestic in stanzas 1, 2, and 4, all denying that waiting would be of much significance. The patient, assured lover would be no more annoyed or anxious than a tidy housekeeper brushing away a fly, or a meticulous needleworker storing away balls of yarn, or a cook discarding the peelings of a piece of fruit. The third stanza has been convincingly explicated as a reference to a child's riddling hand game:

> the riddler holds out his hand, palm down and fingers extended. He then explains that each digit is a person, and then one by one he bends each under his palm and asks, 'Where have all the people gone?' The answer which he gives is, of course, 'To Van Dieman's land—they are all "down under!" '

(Van Dieman's land, as dictionaries will inform students, is an older name for the island of Tasmania, south of Australia.) So this image, too, shares the understating of the others. Even a delay of centuries would be as easy as counting them out on the fingers and then dismissing them.

The last stanza reveals the real depth of feeling that the hypotheses of the first four have been understating: those subjunctive "if" statements do not present belief but hope; the reality is that the speaker cannot know how long before she will see her love, and that uncertainty is like being frightened by a bee that may or may not sting, but will not stop circling around. A fly is easily "spurn[ed]," but a "goblin bee" will not leave her alone. And what might that withheld sting symbolize? A different kind of certainty, perhaps—the certain knowledge that she will never meet her love?

Lee J. Richmond has published a fine, full discussion of this poem, "Emily Dickinson's 'If You Were Coming in the Fall': An Explication," *English Journal* 59 (1970): 771-73. The passage quoted above is from an item by Frederick Keefer and Deborah Vlahos, *Explicator* 29 (Nov. 1970): item 23.   TRA

188. *William Blake*   **A Poison Tree** (page 758)

189. *Granfield Kleiser*   **The Most Vital Thing in Life** (page 759)

One might almost judge these poems from their titles alone. The first title presents an image; the second is an abstract phrase, more suitable for an essay or sermon than for a poem.

The second poem is abstract from beginning to end. It has no dramatic situation. The poet addresses the reader directly. His message—that the most vital thing in life is to control one's feelings—is stated baldly and repeated over and over. The reader is told to "curb resentment," to "maintain a mental peace," to "learn to keep strict silence," to "keep [his] mental balance." The tone is preachy and didactic. There is no development: the good advice simply comes out in a string of platitudes. The poem is without imagery. Its one metaphor is the utterly trite one of a "battle" (13). The poet mixes formal diction ("defrauded") and colloquial diction ("peeved") without purpose and without any sense of impropriety. His meter (iambic-anapestic trimeter, with feminine endings in the odd-numbered lines) is much too swift and bouncy for so serious a theme. A number of words seem included simply to sustain the meter: "quite" (4), "mental" (6), "all" and "simply" (8), "Be assured" (23). This is didactic verse, not poetry; it conveys advice, not experience.

"A Poison Tree" also has a message, but it is conveyed through a parable or extended metaphor rather than explicitly stated. The poem has a beginning, a middle, and an end, and could not be rearranged in its presentation, as could "The Most Vital Thing in Life."

The speaker (who is not the poet) sets up the basic contrast and theme of the poem in the first stanza. To tell one's wrath is to end it. To conceal one's wrath is to cause it to grow and become destructive. The speaker presents two episodes from his life: one in which he was open and candid about his feelings, the other in which he suppressed his feelings. The first episode is presented briefly, for it ended quickly. The second occupies the rest of the poem, for it is of slow development. It is related in a sustained metaphor, which begins in the last phrase of the stanza. The speaker has buried his wrath like a seed, and like a seed it begins to "grow." In the second stanza the speaker nurses his anger. He waters it with fears of his foe and with tears of rage and frustration. He suns it with hypocritical, deceiving smiles. The seed has sprouted. In the third stanza the seed-become-tree bears an apple, poisonous because it is the fruit of wrath, but bright and shiny on the outside because the wrath has been concealed. The speaker's "foe" sees and covets it, and in the final stanza steals and eats it. The speaker finds his foe dead beneath the tree, and is "glad." Thus the consequences of concealed wrath are shown to be horrifyingly destructive, for they include not only the death of the "foe" but the moral perversion of the speaker. The most chilling aspect of the conclusion is released by the word "glad." It touches emotional centers never approached in "The Most Vital Thing in Life." The speaker has destroyed not only his "foe" but himself. (It is here we see that the speaker is not the poet. Where the speaker is "glad" for the death of his foe, the poet is appalled, and makes us feel appalled. Dramatic irony is at work.)

Note the simplicity and economy with which this tale is told. The seed-sprout-sapling-tree development does not need stating; it is implied in the verbs of the poem. The facts that the apple is poison (stanza 3) and that the foe has been killed by eating it (stanza 4) also need no statement; they are implied by the title and the sequence of events.

Blake's message has been embodied in a simple but powerful and moving poem; Kleiser's message remains a versified message.

And what about the messages themselves? Blake's poem advocates expressing one's wrath. Kleiser's recommends suppressing it. Which advice is more valid? One may wish to hedge a little here and to suggest that it depends on circumstances (the occasion for the anger, its intensity, and one's relationship to the person causing it). One can agree with Kleiser that it is unwise to express irritation over every petty annoyance or to tell strangers exactly what one thinks of them. But Blake is talking about "wrath" and about wrath felt toward persons with whom one is in daily association. Kleiser's maxims are tepid, conventional, and often questionable. (Is controlling one's temper really "the most vital thing in life"? More important than love? More important than standing up for justice? Is it really true that "to win a worthwhile battle / Over selfishness and spite, / You must learn to keep strict silence / Though you know you're in the right?") Blake's advice is bold and unconventional and in fact anticipates by over a century some of the insights of Sigmund Freud. In short, Blake's poem presents a poet who is both feeling and thinking deeply; Kleiser's presents a poet who is doing neither.

A further question remains about the interpretation of Blake's poem. Does the speaker *plan* the death of his "foe," or is he merely pleased when it occurs? Is this poem about revenge? The answer, certainly, is that the speaker does not plan the death from the beginning. The central issue of the poem is not between forgiveness and revenge but between the expression and concealment of anger. Suppressed anger, the poet believes, festers and turns poisonous. At some point it turns into hate and the hate *possibly* into planned revenge. The question cannot be answered with certainty and is ultimately unimportant. The speaker's gladness at his foe's death fully reveals his moral perversion whether the death has been plotted or not. A good case can be made, indeed, for the contention that the speaker's "foe" is his foe *because* the speaker conceals his anger from him, rather than vice versa. If "friend" and "foe" were interchanged in the first stanza, would not the "foe" become a friend and the "friend" turn into a foe? LP

190. *Matthew Arnold* **Longing** (page 760)

191. *Matthew Arnold* **To Marguerite** (page 760)

"Longing" is an apostrophe that at first seems addressed to an absent woman whom the speaker loves and who is for some reason permanently gone from him. He asks only for a dream of her that will sustain him through his "hopeless longing."

But this reading is not supported by the details of stanzas 2 and 3, where we find that the woman has in fact never been with him, and that what he desires is not a reunion with a lost love but a visitation of solace and comfort from "a messenger from radiant climes" who will "be / As kind to others as to" the speaker. The implications are more mythical than personal—he is longing for a divine visitor who will resolve the pain and suffering of all, who will come from a world of radiance and create a "new world" here of universal comforting. To the extent that the poem refers to a lost or missing love, then, that situation is a symbol for the absence of God's love.

"To Marguerite" (the poem was given various titles by Arnold) develops a more explicit symbol: human beings are symbolized as single islands forever both linked and separated by a sea that clasps them to itself and estranges them from each other, while they eternally yearn to be merged into "a single continent." This predicament is made more painful because the islands can share and communicate a sense of the beauty of the world (stanza 2), yet that beauty serves only to create "a longing like despair" and the desire for a union that can never be.

The last stanza asks the reasons: why should they be subjected to the "fire" of desire that will be immediately cooled, why should they at the same time feel "deep desire" and yet know it is in vain? The answer is that "a God" has so created them.

Both poems, then, share a common theme: to be human is to be aware of suffering and despair, and to long hopelessly for relief. Both poems express the belief that this predicament is of a divine origin. The major differences between them delineate the superiority of the second. "Longing" is an apostrophe that keeps its focus on the individual speaking, and emphasizes his suffering (only line 8 generalizes his desire to include the relief of others). The imagined scene in lines 11–12 brings out the self-pity that has characterized the poem. But most of all, the theme is muffled by the lack of specificity in the repeated first and last stanzas: the speaker is not "well" (spiritually? physically? emotionally?) and suffers from "hopeless longing" (for what? why is it hopeless?).

These weaknesses verging on sentimentality are absent from "To Marguerite." The speaker is more percipient, and his symbolic expression is both emotionally powerful and intellectually comprehensible. He speaks definitively, in the plural, without pushing his feelings to the front. The imagery is valid (especially in lines 7–14), and the language has freshness and power—who can read the poem carefully and not be haunted by "The unplumbed, salt, estranging sea" of life?

An extended analysis of "To Marguerite," exploring not only its themes but also its debt to tradition, is Kathleen Tillotson's " 'Yes: in the Sea of Life,' " *Review of English Studies* 3 ns (1954): 346–64. TRA

192. *Malcolm Cowley* **The Long Voyage** (page 761)

193. *Sir Walter Scott* **Breathes there the man** (page 761)

"The Long Voyage" arises from a specific situation. The poet, or speaker, is on a ship rapidly taking him away from his native country. As is natural in such a situation, a powerful feeling of nostalgia, even of homesickness, arises in him for the land he loves and is leaving. The emotion is convincing, first, because it is expressed through images, concretely—hills, trees, birds, seasons—not abstractly; second, because it is uttered in a quiet voice—the poet does not rant about the emptiness in his heart, the tears in his eyes, the anguish in his soul; third, because he doesn't make exaggerated claims about his country, which he says is like "almost . . . any country": its pines are no darker, its dogwood no brighter, its birds no swifter. Nevertheless, this is *his* country, and that makes the difference. He knows "its face, its speech." The very water folding back against the prow reminds him of his country's earth breaking against the plow—an excellent simile—and the foam on the water reminds him of his country's dogwood. The emotion is not strained or exaggerated; the poem expresses a universal feeling arising from a specific situation.

"Breathes there the man" does not arise from a specific situation. It talks about no specific man. The poet is expressing not his own feeling for his country but scorn for some other (hypothetical) man who has no such feeling. There are no images in the poem—no sharply defined pictures, sounds, or smells. The language is abstract. It is spoken not quietly but shrilly, at the top of the poet's voice. The tone is oratorical, as established by the diction and the construction of the sentences ("Breathes there the man . . . ," "go, mark him well," "High though his titles . . . ," "foreign strand" [for "shores"], "power, and pelf" [for "money"], "fair renown," and so forth). The poet climbs up the ladder of his own eloquence till he calls his hypothetical victim "a wretch, concentered all in self" who "doubly dying shall go down" to "vile dust." The poet has lashed himself into a frenzy of virtuous indignation, and the sentiment is strained and exaggerated. Surely, if a person lacks a love of country, it is more his misfortune than his crime; he deserves compassion, not consignment to the "vile dust." Love cannot be compelled. Moreover, such a person is not necessarily "a wretch, concentered all in self." Surely men who have voluntarily left the country of their birth and found other places to live that they liked better—whose hearts have not "burned" when they returned to the original country—have lived decent lives, loved their families, been kind to babies, enjoyed life, and been mourned by friends when they died. The poet has exaggerated and oversimplified the facts of life, has whipped himself up by means of words to an artificial state of feeling. The emotion does not well up naturally. The poem rings resoundingly, but it also rings hollowly, like a drum.

Sir Walter Scott was a good man who wrote good novels and some good poetry, but this poem is "rhetorical." It is taken from the opening of Canto 6 of *The Lay of the Last Minstrel*, in which it is sung by the ancient minstrel who tells the story. In context it has a certain dramatic propriety, but it is not clearly distinguished from an utterance that might not be Scott's own—that is, there is no detectable dramatic irony. It is, of course, usually reprinted out of context as a patriotic set piece.   LP

194.   *Robert Frost*   **Happiness Makes Up in Height for What It Lacks in Length** (page 762)

195.   *William L. Stidger*   **A Day** (page 763)

A superficial comparison might conclude that the difference between these two poems is that the first is pessimistic, the second optimistic. More properly, the first displays realistic optimism and the second sentimentality.

Frost's poem begins by conceding that *most* days reflect the "stormy" nature of the world, and by questioning how in the face of that fact one could have "the lasting sense / Of so much warmth and light" (10–11). The answer is given in the title—

happiness is measured by its intensity, not by its duration. "One day's perfect weather" is enough to create that lasting sense of goodness and beauty in life—particularly if on that one day a person can be alone with a loving companion with whom it can be shared.

Stidger, on the other hand, asserts that "love" is the characteristic that makes a day—"A lot of love," he reiterates (2, 20). His catalogue of the types of love oversteps the bounds of credibility—if all of them are required "to make a day," it is highly unlikely that any days will be "made." One would have to experience the love of father, mother, lover (or no doubt wife, in this case), comrade, baby, needy stranger, and—again—mother and baby. But this busy day would also have to include some challenging task that requires the full exertion of mind and limb, attendance at a church service with its hopeful hymns, and a charitable act that affirms a sense of brotherhood. In short, it would take an incredible "lot of love."

Stidger's poem piles on the clichés of sentimental good feeling with no regard for realistic probability, while Frost's understates the importance of a shared love (the word is not used, and the concept is only implied by the plural pronouns in lines 21 and 23).

Finally, Frost's poem has an organic unity that Stidger's poem lacks. Both poems are written in riming couplets, but in Frost's poem not a couplet could be removed or added without damaging the poem; in Stidger's almost any number could be added or subtracted and the reader would never know the difference. Frost develops his idea through a dynamic structure; Stidger repeats his superficial idea over and over, without any necessary order.   TRA

196.   *Eugene Field*   **Little Boy Blue** (page 763)

197.   *Coventry Patmore*   **The Toys** (page 764)

"Little Boy Blue" is an appealing poem. Its melody is pleasing, and so are its rimes. The word order is natural and unforced, and so are the words themselves. The poem makes effective use of alliteration and other musical devices. The picture it presents of the loyal toy soldier and dog awaiting the return of their Little Boy Blue is touching. The poem is skillfully done, and it has been much beloved by the American public. It is nevertheless a sentimental poem, manipulating its materials to draw tears from the reader, subtly falsifying life by dimming the darker colors and brightening up the warmer ones. It aims at being sweetly sad.

Its title is sweet. The boy who dies is not Bobby, or Peter, or Donald; he is "Little Boy Blue"—the name has nursery rime associations. And he has not only a sweet name but a sweet disposition. He played nicely with his toys on the evening of the night he died (though he must have been sick, and most children are short-tempered and hard to manage when sick), and then he toddled sweetly off to bed at the appointed time, without a single protest, quite contrary to ordinary boy-nature. If Boy Blue ever had fits of ill temper or disobedience, they are not mentioned; only his pretty actions, such as kissing his toys, are mentioned. In describing Boy Blue and his possessions, the poet uses the adjective "little" eleven times in twenty-four lines. Not only is Boy Blue "little," his hands are "little," his face is "little," his chair is "little," his toys are "little." Most of these "little's" are quite superfluous; the word is being used only to manipulate the reader's sympathies, to evoke a stock response. Also, instead of telling us that Little Boy Blue *died*, the poet says that he was "awakened by an angel song." It is a sweet way of describing death; the uglier features are avoided, and death becomes a gentle and sweetly sad experience, like a song. (Some students will have difficulty with the "angel song" metaphor and think that Little Boy Blue grew up—apparently rather suddenly—leaving his childish toys behind.) This death occurred many years ago, but the little toys are still true.

But now, three questions. First, how does the poet know that Little Boy Blue "dreamt of the pretty toys" if he died in his sleep? Second, in what sense are the toys "true"? Do they really wonder what has happened to Little Boy Blue "Since he kissed them and put them there"? Or is this not an example of what Ruskin called "the pathetic fallacy"—the fallacy of attributing human emotions to inanimate objects? That is, has not the author sentimentalized not only the little boy but also even his toys? And third, why, after all these years, are the toys still where Little Boy Blue left them? (Here is a question that the poet did not intend us to ask. If the toys are still in the chair where Boy Blue left them, his parents must have closed up his room when he died and resolved to leave everthing just as he left it. People occasionally do such things, to be sure, but only very rarely; and we usually feel that such a reaction to death is excessively sentimental or even morbid, not healthy. Quite understandably, the poet glosses over this aspect of the situation and concentrates our attention instead on the supposed fidelity of the toy dog and the toy soldier, as though this quality was what really kept them there.) In short, the author is not treating death seriously; instead he is playing with us and with our emotions.

"The Toys," at first view, may seem a slightly crude poem beside "Little Boy Blue." The meter is not so lilting, the rime is not so regular, there is no stanza pattern, and even the syntax may at times seem slightly strained.* But the meter is such as to keep our attention focused constantly on the content; it does not set up a separate tune or by a pretty lilt soften and sweeten a pathetic subject matter. Moreover, the treatment of the subject matter is honest. Having once described his son as "little," the poet drops the adjective and does not use it as a spurious means of attaching sympathy to his subject. He does not idealize the behavior of little boys. Though his son is grave, quiet, and thoughtful, he is also, like most boys, sometimes willful and disobedient. The father's behavior, as contrasted with that of the parents of Little Boy Blue, is normally human. He loses his temper, strikes the boy and scolds him, then later feels remorse and worries about what he has done. But the boy, though he has been sobbing, is not so grief-stricken that he cannot sleep, as a

*Actually, the syntax in lines 3–6 is skillfully arranged so that "dismissed" may take either "him" or "His Mother" as its object, both meanings being appropriate. By one construction "His Mother" is the subject of an absolute phrase; by the other it is the object of the verb.

sentimentalist might have made him. He is deep in slumber, and beside his bed, to console himself, he has arranged his treasured collection of toys. These toys are enumerated and described: they include "a red-veined stone," "A piece of glass abraded by the beach," and "two French copper coins." The imagery is fresh and precise. We are not told, moreover, that the boy kissed these toys before going to sleep, or that he is dreaming of them, or that they, on their part, are faithfully waiting for him to wake up. The incident is moving because it has been honestly treated. Moreover, the poet has effectively used the incident to communicate, by analogy, a larger truth about life. We are all children, ultimately, and have our childish ways. We grown-up children have our grown-up toys no less foolish really than the contents of a child's pocket. And we too disobey the Commandments of Our Father and stand equally in need of forgiveness.

In referring to his son's having disobeyed "the seventh time" (3), the poet enriches his meaning by a biblical allusion to Matthew 18.21–22. When Peter asked Jesus how often he should forgive his brother's sinning against him, Jesus answered, not seven times, but "seventy times seven."

[This discussion is abridged from the essay "Are Tears Made of Sugar or of Salt?" in Laurence Perrine, *The Art of Total Relevance: Papers on Poetry* (Rowley, MA: Newbury, 1976) 125–29.] LP

198. *A. E. Housman* **Loitering with a vacant eye** (page 765)

199. *Maltbie D. Babcock* **Be Strong** (page 765)

The speaker in Housman's poem is a lad who has come to the big city from the provinces (Shropshire, as we know from Housman's other poems) and who feels homesick and alone. Who is the speaker in Babcock's? Much of the strength of Housman's poem is that it presents a dramatic situation—a specific speaker and a specific place (the British Museum in London)—whereas Babcock's poem is generalized and unlocalized. The triteness of language and metaphor and the absence of real imagery in Babcock's poem hardly need comment. Of particular note in Housman's poem is his effective use of *st-* alliteration to hammer home the idea of stoutness, sturdiness, strength. The repeated word "still" (lines 4, 5, 11, 20) has three meanings—"motionless" (not fainting or drooping), "silent" (uncomplaining), and "yet" (still standing after all these centuries). Such compressed use of language is beyond the range of Babcock, as is the metrical boldness of line 22. Babcock's poem ends with an optimistic but vague affirmation—"Tomorrow comes the song" (Here? In the afterlife? The result of labor? The reward of labor?)—that, since it grows out of nothing in the poem, seems a sentimental afterthought. Housman's poem promises no reward or result for stoicism beyond the psychological benefit it has for the person himself ("light on me my trouble lay"). Housman's attitude is not necessarily truer or more admirable than Babcock's, but it forms part of a more tightly integrated, deeply imagined, and self-consistent poem, and its meaning is definite, not vague. LP

CHAPTER SIXTEEN

Good Poetry and Great

200. *John Donne* **The Canonization** (page 769)

Useful discussions of this poem may be found in Cleanth Brooks, *The Well Wrought Urn* (New York: Reynal, 1947) 10–17; Clay Hunt, *Donne's Poetry* (New Haven: Yale UP, 1954) 72–93; Doniphan Louthan, *The Poetry of John Donne* (New York: Brookman, 1951) 110–18; Patricia Garland Pinka, *This Dialogue of One* (University AL: U of Alabama P, 1982) 126–32. LP

201. *Robert Frost* **Home Burial** (page 771)

The three critics paraphrased in question 8 are (a) John F. Lynen, *The Pastoral Art of Robert Frost* (New Haven: Yale UP, 1960) 114; (b) George W. Nitchie, *Human Values in the Poetry of Robert Frost* (Durham NC: Duke UP, 1960) 129–30, 166–67, 223; and (c) John C. Kemp, *Robert Frost and New England* (Princeton: Princeton UP, 1979) 118–19, 155–56. Of these, Lynen seems to me furthest from the truth. Against Nitchie it may be argued that on a previous occasion of emotional conflict between them, the young wife *had* left her husband (39), and had either come back to him voluntarily or been persuaded by him to come back, and that her last action in the poem is to open the door wider. The husband accepts the fact that she is leaving ("Where do you mean to go?"), and threatens that *this* time he will bring her home "by force."

The most remarkable critical discussion of this poem is Randall Jarrell's illuminating line-by-line analysis, "Robert Frost's 'Home Burial,'" *The Third Book of Criticism* (New York: Farrar, 1969) 191–231; also in *The Moment of Poetry*, ed. Don Cameron Allen (Baltimore: Johns Hopkins UP, 1962) 99–132. If, after reading Jarrell, you want to read more, the following may be worth your perusal: Elaine Barry, *Robert Frost* (New York: Ungar, 1973) 75–78; Frank Lentricchia, *Robert Frost: Modern Poetries and the Landscape of Self* (Durham NC: Duke UP, 1975) 62–65; and Richard Poirier, *Robert Frost: The Work of Knowing* (New York: Oxford UP, 1977) 124–35. LP

202. *T. S. Eliot* **The Love Song of J. Alfred Prufrock** (page 775)

"Prufrock" is one of the most discussed poems of the twentieth century. Of the mass of commentary that has accumulated concerning it, some of the following may

255

be particularly helpful: Roy P. Basler, *Sex, Symbolism, and Psychology in Literature* (New Brunswick NJ: Rutgers UP, 1948) 203–21; Cleanth Brooks and Robert Penn Warren, *Understanding Poetry*, 3rd ed. (New York: Holt, 1960) 386–99 (also in earlier editions); Elizabeth Drew, *T. S. Eliot: The Design of His Poetry* (New York: Scribner's, 1949) 34–36; Paul Engle and Warren Carrier, *Reading Modern Poetry* rev. ed. (Glenview IL: Scott, 1968) 148–55; Laurence Perrine and James M. Reid, *100 American Poems of the Twentieth Century* (New York: Harcourt, 1966) 110–12; Grover Smith, *T. S. Eliot's Poetry and Plays* (Chicago: U of Chicago P, 1956) 15–20 *et passim*; and Morris Weitz, *Philosophy of the Arts* (Cambridge: Harvard UP, 1950) 94–107, 145. LP

203. *Wallace Stevens* **Sunday Morning** (page 779)

"Sunday Morning" is almost universally celebrated as the great poem of Stevens's early career, and has therefore been very widely analyzed. Among the published essays devoted to it in whole or in major part, the following are useful: R. P. Blackmur, "Wallace Stevens," *Language as Gesture* (New York: Harcourt, 1952); Price Caldwell, " 'Sunday Morning': Stevens' Makeshift Romantic Lyric," *Southern Review* 15 (1979): 933–52; J. V. Cunningham, "Tradition and Modernity," *Tradition and Poetic Structure* (Denver: Swallow, 1960); Frank Lentricchia, "Wallace Stevens: The Ironic Eye," *Yale Review* 56 (1967): 336–53; Carol Kyros Walker, "The Subject as Speaker in 'Sunday Morning,' " *Concerning Poetry* 10 (Spring 1977): 25–31; Yvor Winters, "Wallace Stevens, Or the Hedonist's Progress," *In Defense of Reason* (New York: Swallow, 1947); Michael Zimmerman, "The Pursuit of Pleasure and the Uses of Death: Wallace Stevens' 'Sunday Morning,' " *University Review* 33(1966): 113–23.

Among the many book-length studies of Stevens's poetry, the following have illuminating readings of this poem: Harold Bloom, *Wallace Stevens: The Poems of Our Climate* (Ithaca NY: Cornell UP, 1976) 27–35; Merle E. Brown, *Wallace Stevens: The Poem as Act* (Detroit: Wayne State UP, 1970) 157–63; Joseph Carroll, *Wallace Stevens' Supreme Fiction* (Baton Rouge: Louisiana State UP, 1987) 48–55; David M. LaGuardia, *Advance on Chaos: The Sanctifying Imagination of Wallace Stevens* (Hanover NH: UP of New England, 1983) 45–49; A. Walton Litz, *Introspective Voyager: The Poetic Development of Wallace Stevens* (New York: Oxford UP, 1972) 44–53; Robert Rehder, *The Poetry of Wallace Stevens* (New York: St. Martin's, 1988) 65–86; Herbert J. Stern, *Wallace Stevens: Art of Uncertainty* (Ann Arbor: U of Michigan P, 1966) 87–104; Henry W. Wells, *Introduction to Wallace Stevens* (Bloomington: Indiana UP, 1964) 52–57. TRA

POEMS FOR FURTHER READING

Poems 243, 244, 247, and 302 from Part 2 provide additional illustrations of topics presented in this chapter.

Poems for Further Reading

204. *W. H. Auden* **Musée des Beaux Arts** (page 787)

The poem descriptively alludes to three paintings by Pieter Brueghel the Elder (which might be shown to students): lines 5–8, *The Census* (or *The Numbering at Bethlehem*); lines 10–13, *The Massacre of the Innocents*; and lines 14–21, *Landscape with the Fall of Icarus*. The title of the poem may be derived from the name of the museum in Brussels where the Icarus painting hangs, the Musées Royaux des Beaux Arts, though it simply means "Fine Arts Museum," a title general enough to include all three "Old Master" paintings.

The poem is in free verse and has an irregular rime scheme. In the opening verse paragraph the following lines rime: 1/4, 2/8, 5/7, 6/13, 9/11, 10/12, and there is no rime for line 3. The concluding verse paragraph, while not regular, tightens up the rimes somewhat, in keeping with the single focus of the subject: 14/15, 16/20, 17/21, 18/19. The two sets of rimed couplets begin to suggest some more explicit closure of meaning for the poem, but the last two lines return to the more random pattern, reinforcing the understated meaning—that something as momentous as a boy falling out of the sky does not signal a definitive event, but only a momentary amazement to the men who continue on about their business. The apparently irrelevant or random riming may thus be seen as a reinforcement of the theme, that great events seem irrelevant or not personally significant to the mass of self-involved people.

The sequence of the pictured events may also be seen as reinforcing the theme: they move from the birth of Christ, to the slaughter by Herod of the first-born sons, to the mythical story of Icarus—events that would seem to the modern picture-viewer of decreasing personal significance, even if the last of them did originally symbolize a very human problem, the danger of rashly pursuing a superhuman aspiration. TRA

205. *D. C. Berry* **On Reading Poems to a Senior Class at South High** (page 787)

The poet begins by assuming, from their orderly appearance in rows of chairs, that the students are "frozen" and incapable of a living response to his poetry. But as he reads, planning "to drown them" with his words, the power of poetry floods the room, and the surprised poet and the class metaphorically swim together until the ringing of the school bell, which breaks the enchantment. All of them, students and poet, then go on to other more normal pursuits, back to their ordinary lives. The experience, however, has transported the poet beyond himself, and it takes his domesticated, imaginatively named cat to bring *him* back to normal.

The poet's defensive condescension—his prejudice that these students are cold to poetry, his fear that his poetry may not move them—is washed away by the mutual experience, to the extent that he himself must be restored to his human form. The poem wittily converts the pejorative image of "frozen fish" into the vital image of "thirty tails whacking words," and his plan of drowning his audience converts into the water in which, for the time, the poet and students have a medium they can share. Both "frozen fish" and "drown" are used metaphorically, apparently as the poet's self-conscious device for asserting his superiority, but both come so vitally to life that even after the experience the poet feels fins at the end of his arms. Ironically it is his cat who restores him from his fishy condition. TRA

206. *Elizabeth Bishop* **One Art** (page 788)

With a forced tone of nonchalance, the speaker in this modified villanelle insists that all losses can be faced stoically. She begins with insignificant losses—keys, a little time, memories of places and names—and proceeds to those of greater emotional value—a prized keepsake, loved houses. Hyperbolically, she reports the loss of realms, rivers, and a continent. The climax of the poem occurs in the final stanza, the loss of a beloved person, which too can be mastered—almost. The last line, with its parenthetic command to herself, reveals that the mastery of this loss requires a great exertion of will, if indeed it can be mastered at all.

Whimsically, the poem is presented as a lesson to the reader: "Lose something every day," until practice in mastering the sense of loss will render future losses less disastrous in their effects. The first three stanzas, in the second person, present the lesson; in the last three the speaker offers her own experience as supporting evidence. But with the increasing sense of regret and even pain, the ironic stance of the speaker is made clear: mastering the sense of loss is not "one art" that can be learned through coping with lesser losses.

The word "loss" is used both metaphorically and literally, undercutting the statement that all losses are equal. The inequalities are manifest when one questions whether or not the references to losing keys, losing time, and losing a beloved person employ the term "loss" in the same sense. What the poet achieves, in seeming to believe that the word is single in its meaning, is the statement that not all loss can be mastered. TRA

207. *William Blake* Eternity (page 789)

This succinct epigram paradoxically presents Blake's Romantic conviction that joy, delight, and goodness are only to be found in freedom and change. So to "bind" oneself to *anything*, even "a joy," is to "destroy" one's soaring, angel-like freedom. On the other hand, to accept the fact that all high delights and joys are swiftly passing, and to enjoy what one can of them as they fly, is to experience the most one can expect of life.

The last line presents the paradox central to this idea: eternity (timelessness) is at its most beautiful just as it begins to exist. This is a paradox because it attributes temporal phases to what is without time. The resolution rests in recognizing that "eternity" is not literal but refers to the intensity of experience. In simplest terms, one should always feel that every moment in a lifetime is the beginning of unending joy. TRA

208. *William Blake* The Lamb (page 789)

209. *William Blake* The Tiger (page 789)

"The Lamb" was first published in *Songs of Innocence* (1789) and "The Tiger" in *Songs of Experience* (1794). Blake described the two volumes as "Showing Contrary States of the Human Soul." Though the poems in *Songs of Experience* are generally darker in tone than those in the earlier book, Blake is not necessarily suggesting that innocence is better than experience. Rather, each state shows the incompleteness or the inadequacy of the other.

In the "Introduction" to *Songs of Innocence* (page 708), Blake was bid by his muse to "Pipe a song about a Lamb." This is it. The central question asked in this poem is "Little Lamb, who made thee?" The central question asked in "The Tiger" is "Did he who made the Lamb make thee?" "The Tiger" was obviously written to complement "The Lamb." Together the two poems make a poetic diptych.

In "The Lamb" the speaker is a child, and the chief effect of the poem is a childlike simplicity, produced by the use of a simple vocabulary—mostly monosyllabic, end-stopped lines—one statement to a line, a songlike meter (six four-beat lines in each stanza, framed at beginning and end by a pair of three-beat lines), paired rimes, and frequent repetitions. The situation and content of the poem also express this childlike simplicity. The child talks to a lamb, asks it a question and answers the question himself, and in his answer shows his trustful, unquestioning acceptance of the Christian story he has been taught. The lamb was created by Christ, who in the New Testament is called "the Lamb of God," and who through his incarnation became "a little child." The child and the lamb are thus one with Christ in name as well as in gentleness and love, and the poem appropriately ends, "Little Lamb, God bless thee."

In "The Tiger" the speaker is an adult, possibly the poet; he does not literally speak to the tiger, he apostrophizes it; and the central question of the poem is left unanswered.

The image in the first two lines is one of the most vivid in English poetry. Primarily we are meant to see two eyes glaring in the dark (see line 6); but if we think of the orange and black stripes of the tiger's body, we also have a flamelike image. The tiger is associated with images of fire throughout the poem. He is imagined to have been made in a cosmic smithy ("forged," "hammer," "chain," "furnace," "anvil"), and his creator is personified as a powerful smith. But is this smithy in "distant deeps or skies"—hell or heaven? And was the smith Satan or God? And, having created the tiger, did the smith "smile" to see what he had made? These are the questions urged on the reader, insistently, like the blows of a hammer on an anvil (the interrogative "what" is used thirteen times during the poem), and in a meter whose accents fall also with the force and regularity of hammer blows. The tiger is described as awesome—that is, as arousing both fear and admiration in the beholder. Its "fearful symmetry," the burning brightness of its eyes, its twisted sinewy heart, the "deadly terrors" of its brain—these qualities suggest beauty, strength, fierceness, and violence. But if the tiger is awesome, its creator is even more so. He is "immortal" (3, 23), daring (7, 8, 24) winged (7), strong (9–10), "dread" (12, 15), and an artist (9).

The difficult lines 17–18 have been explained in too many ways to go into here—in terms of astrology, as metaphor for dawn and dewfall, as symbolic of love and pity, as an allusion to the war in heaven between the good and the rebel angels depicted in Milton's *Paradise Lost*, as an allusion to symbols in Blake's private mythology, as an image for showers of sparks sent out from the cosmic forge and of the water used to temper the glowing metal, etc. Perhaps, in their broadest and simplest sense, they can be taken to suggest, "When even the stars wept, did the creator of the tiger smile?"

No answer to its central question is stated in the poem. Is one implied? A survey of Blake criticism produces no consensus. About half of the critics say that the question is rhetorical, intended by Blake to be answered Yes. The creator of the Lamb was also the creator of the Tiger, and He looked on his work and found it "good." The power of the poem is the power with which it expresses this mysterious paradox in the nature of God, creator of both the rainbow and the whirlwind. But another half say that the question is unanswerable, and was not intended by Blake to be answered one way or the other—that Blake's poem is about the mystery and ambiguity of the universe, which is ultimately beyond man's understanding. (And one lonely voice—Kathleen Raine, in *Encounter* 2 [1935]: 48—declares boldly: "The answer is beyond all possible doubt, 'No'; God, who created the lamb, did not create the tiger.")

A greater variety of answers is produced by the question, What do the lamb and the tiger symbolize? But here we welcome a variety of answers, for the symbolism is rich and permits a range of meanings. (The poems obviously call for symbolical reading. We are being asked much more than whether the same god created the aardvark and the camel.) Among the answers suggested are good and evil, God's love and God's wrath, gentle meekness and powerful energy, innocent purity and strong sexuality, peace and war, mercy and justice, pardon and punishment.

Textual note: The text of "The Tiger" used here differs in line 12 from that published by Blake in *Songs of Experience* ("What dread hand? And what dread feet?"). In the original manuscript this line is followed by a discarded stanza of which the first line is "Could fetch it from the furnace deep?" The cancellation of the stanza left line 12 syntactically incomplete, and Blake seems to have been dissatisfied with it, for in a copy later given to a friend he altered the line in ink to "What dread hand formed thy dread feet," and another friend, perhaps on Blake's authority, printed the poem in a book of memoirs with "forged" in the place of "formed." I have used the version that seems to me best, and the one that may have represented Blake's final intention. LP

210. *Philip Booth* **Stefansson Island** (page 790)

Vilhjalmur Stefansson was the last of a breed, an explorer who without the modern support of airplanes or radio mapped a vast area inhabited only by aboriginal natives. Between 1913 and 1918, he led the Canadian Arctic Expedition in making an accurate map of the Beaufort Sea. His preparation for such an exploit included the study of anthropology and archaeology before going to live among the Eskimo people, and he continued to study these people up to the beginning of his work for the Arctic Expedition. In his honor, Canada named an island for him at the coordinates identified in the poem, within 200 miles of the magnetic north pole. "Martin Point" (16) in northeastern Alaska was the starting point of his mapping journey.

In honoring the celebrated explorer, Booth interweaves references to objects and events associated with the Arctic in a blend of literal and figurative descriptions of the man and his accomplishments. He is a "polar man" (26), "a walrus of a man" (1) with the physical strength of "a white bear" that eats "blubber" (8) and "seal meat" (7). His mind is like a "winter island" (5) that possesses "glacial knowledge" (13), his skin as hard and wrinkled as "the ranges of the Yukon" (10).

Through this variety of references, the poem evokes the indomitable, courageous scientist wholly dedicated to his cause. And it also defines the rightness of his purpose—"to tame not barren lands to man, / but man to what is barren" (14–15). His work was to understand whatever life there was in this desolate place, and in recompense even the place itself seems to praise him as the night-long light of "the solstice sun / fires lichen into arctic bloom" (29–30).

The stanzaic pattern consists of four iambic tetrameter lines followed by a concluding line that ranges from pentameter to heptameter, all highly varied (so that

261

regular lines stand out, for example lines 6 and 26). The rime scheme is *abbax*, more often approximately riming; the *x*-rime lines all have some form of sound linkage with some other rime in the stanza (alliteration, assonance, or consonance). TRA

211. *Elizabeth Barrett Browning* **If thou must love me** (page 791)

In its rimes, this is a very strict Italian sonnet, limiting itself to only four rime sounds: *abbaabbacdcdcd* (convention permits the last syllable of *eternity* to rime with *dry*). In contrast, the internal structure of thought is played against the strict form. The first thought-unit comprises the first line and much of the second. The next sentence proceeds to the middle of line 9, running on into the opening line of the sestet, and after another unit of three-and-a-half lines, the sonnet uncharacteristically ends with a two-line sentence—a rhetorical structure that would be more appropriate to the couplet of an English sonnet.

These formal effects support the meaning of the poem, contrasting an abstract and rigid form with a freer structure. The poem proposes a definition of loving that rejects certain commonplaces as too fragile or mutable, offering instead a kind of tautology—"love me for love's sake"—since the abstraction "love" is eternal, while those qualities, habits, or pleasures that might be thought to be justification for loving are all lodged in time.

The concluding overstatement does not, however, make love an abstraction only, for in counseling her beloved about what he should *not* love her for, the speaker does in fact catalogue many of the "lesser" causes of their love: her smile, her way of looking, her speech, the sympathy of thought they share, and his tender pity for her discomfort and unhappiness. In effect, then, the speaker manages to include both the abstract and the concrete in defining the kind of love she hopes for.   TRA

212. *Lucille Clifton* **Good Times** (page 791)

Occasions for joy in the lives of the poor are few and far between, but when they come they are likely to be jollier, more spontaneous, and more festive than the pleasures of the well-to-do. The joyousness of the occasion is in direct proportion to its rarity. Lucille Clifton, a black poet, here presents just such an occasion in the lives of a poor black family. The first stanza states the causes for celebration, the second stanza presents the celebration itself. For once the rent, the insurance premiums, and the electric bill have all been paid, and uncle Brud has "hit / for one dollar straight"—that is, his one-dollar ticket in a lottery or numbers game has won the whole prize: it does not have to be divided among several winners. The result is that the mother has made homemade bread, Grampaw has come to visit, and there is spontaneous dancing and singing in the kitchen, with a bottle of liquor to add to the gaiety.

The speaker is one of the children in the family, possibly the oldest one. She is so deeply impressed by the "good times," which are in such contrast with their usual life of debt and privation, that she ends each stanza with three lines devoted to proclaiming them, and then adds a two-line coda in which she instructs her younger sisters and brothers to "think about the / good times." Lay them up in your memory, for you may not experience many more.

The irony in the poem is that the "good times" being celebrated in this poem are what a middle-classs observer would call hard times.   LP

213.   *Elizabeth Coatsworth*   **Song of the Rabbits outside the Tavern** (page 792)

This charming bit of whimsy raises (but does not answer) some more penetrating questions. As the rabbits sing their superiority to the human beings and scorn the cat and dog, the poem draws a sharp line between artifice and nature, between tame and wild, between restraint and liberty, between lives lived in security and comfort and those subject to hunger and cold.

Some of the pleasure of the poem arises from the exercise of seeing familiar things from a new or strange perspective, in this case from the point of view of wild rabbits. The rabbits see fires as "Suns . . . in a cave" and candles as "stars . . . on a tall white stem," and looking into the tavern dining room think that food is simply "ready at hand."

The poem is metrical, but so freely varied that at times it seems to be controlled only by a three-stress line without regard for pattern. It is what we should call "iambic-anapestic" trimeter (see page 706) with frequent dropping of an initial unstressed syllable. The opening lines may be scanned thus:

```
 _   �‿  ˿  _ | ˿  ˿  _  |
We who play un- der the pines,
 _   ˿  _ |˿  ˿  _ |
We who dance in the snow
 ˿   ˿   _ |˿  ˿  _ |˿  ˿  _ |
That shines blue in the light of the moon
 _ | ˿  _ |˿  ˿  _ |
Some- times halt as we go,
 _ | ˿  ˿  _ |˿  _ |                            5
Stand with our ears e-rect,
 ˿  _ |˿  _ |˿  ˿  _ |
Our nos- es test- ing the air.
```

This free meter makes the simple iambic lines stand out:

```
 ˿  _ | ˿  _ |˿  _ |                            8
Be-hind the win- dows there.
 ˿  _ | ˿  _ |˿  _ |                           16
We lit- tle rab- bits stand.
```

The rime scheme is also loose and seemingly random, though the concluding three lines of each stanza lock into a pattern that reflects the theme. With an intervening line, the first and last lines of these tercets are exact rimes (*air-there, hand-stand, spoon-moon*); and the non-riming middle lines of all three tercets have approximate rime (*world-cold-wild*). In the final tercet the riming *spoon* and *moon* delineate the distance between the two worlds of the poem, and the intervening *wild* tips the balance in the rabbits' favor.   TRA

214. *Samuel Taylor Coleridge*   **Kubla Khan** (page 793)

The first publication of this poem included a lengthy note by Coleridge attributing its inspiration to a combination of having taken a prescribed dose of opium, for an illness he was suffering, and then reading a seventeenth-century travel book about the Chinese ruler; he claims that in his "reverie" he had composed between two and three hundred lines of verse, but as he was beginning to write them down he was interrupted by a visitor, and returning to his work discovered that he had forgotten the rest. (The account is available in any collection of Coleridge's works and need not be quoted here.) Whether this was literally true is less important than the effect Coleridge had in mind in reporting it; the account was written some fifteen years after the poem, and seems to have as its purpose emphasizing the air of magic and mystery of the poem itself, as well as promoting the Romantic ideal of poetry as spontaneous, impulsive, and free of narrowly rational thought.

But as many commentators have shown, the poem itself is highly crafted, not likely the product even of a practiced poet unless he is paying close attention to his effects. Elisabeth Schneider analyzes at length the assonance, consonance, alliteration, and internal and end rimes of just the first five lines, demonstrating the "half-caught echoes, correspondences of sound felt but too complex to be anticipated or to remain tabulated in the mind even after they have been analyzed."

Through line 36 the poet describes the site of Kubla Khan's pleasure-dome: a landscape of contrasts and opposites, with a river bursting forth with great force from a fountain in a "romantic chasm," meandering through a pleasant valley, then sinking once again into a cavern leading to the "sunless sea." The dome itself is built over "caves of ice," and the dome is surrounded by gardens and forests, bounded by walls and towers. The scene combines wildness with gentleness, heights with depths, explosive creative force with calm obliteration, warmth with coldness, holiness with demonism, tumult with lifelessness, artifice with nature, the momentary present with an ancestral past, light with dark, a peaceful scene with prophecies of war. It is, says Harold Bloom, a "vision of creation and destruction, each complete." It presents "the balance of reconciliation of opposites" that for Coleridge was "the mark of the creative imagination."

At line 37 the poem turns to a different scene, a "vision" the poet once had of another distant and exotic moment, of a singing maiden (playing on an antique instrument) whose song seems to him to have corresponded to Kubla Khan's pleasure-dome. If he could revive within himself the feelings aroused by this vision, he too would be able to create "in air" what Kubla did on earth—and his creation would mark him off from the multitudes who would see in him a holy man of magical powers.

His desire is to create poetically the totality that was expressed in Kubla Khan's achievement; as he phrases it, however, this is only a wish, something beyond his powers. Yet as Bloom points out, what the poem "Kubla Khan" does is precisely that.

This intriguing poem has excited much commentary, among the best of it the following: Walter Jackson Bate, *Coleridge* (New York: Macmillan, 1968) 75–84; Harold Bloom, *The Visionary Company* (Garden City NY: Anchor/Doubleday, 1963) 229–33; G. Wilson Knight, *The Starlit Dome* (London: Methuen, 1968) 90–97; Elisabeth Schneider, "Kubla Khan" from *Coleridge, Opium and Kubla Khan*, repr. in *Coleridge: A Collection of Critical Essays*, ed. Kathleen Coburn (Englewood Cliffs NJ: Prentice, 1967) 88–93.   TRA

215.   *Walter de la Mare*   **The Listeners** (page 794)

"The Listeners" is an atmospheric, not a symbolic, poem. Its purpose is to conjure up a sense of mystery, eeriness, and strangeness. It succeeds in doing so through its haunting description, its haunting rhythm, and its apparent presentation of one episode from a long narrative whose beginning and end are left unrecounted and unexplained.

For an excellent refutation of misguided symbolic interpretations, see the note by Frederick L. Gwynn and Ralph W. Condee in *Explicator* 12 (Feb. 1954): item 26.   LP

216.   *James Dickey*   **The Lifeguard** (page 795)

In this deeply imagined poem, James Dickey has embodied the guilt and defeat of a lifeguard who has failed to prevent the death of a child by drowning. There is no need for him to feel guilty: he had tried desperately to rescue the child; but the child's friends had expected a miracle, and he is overwhelmed by his failure to perform one. He feels that he has disappointed the expectations of those who had counted on him. He wishes that he could have been the child's "savior," or that even now, like Christ, he could restore the dead child to life.

The poem has two scenes. The primary scene—that of lines 1–12 and lines 33–60—is a moonlit scene, the night of the day of the drowning. The other scene, presented by flashback (lines 13–32), is a sunlit afternoon scene, the actual scene of the drowning as remembered by the lifeguard. He had seen the child's cropped head go under. He had dived again and again, searching the cold, dark depths without success. Each time he surfaced, his lungs exploding, he had winced from the disappointed and accusing looks in the children's faces. Finally he had swum to the boathouse, with only his own life in his arms.

Now it is night. The children of the village are asleep. The moonlight lies upon the water like a silver skin. The lifeguard lies in "a stable of boats" at the lake's edge, haunted by his failure of the afternoon. In dream or in imagination he steps forth upon the silver skin of water, walks to the lake's center, softly calls for the child, and is answered by the child slowly rising to the surface. But all this is imaginary. The child's head breaks not water but a "surface of stone"—the gravestone, or the stony barrier between death and life. His face is one the lifeguard does not remember having ever seen "in his life" (not "my life"), for the child is dead. In his fancy the lifeguard kneels by the grave, holding the child in his arms, but the child exists only in his imagination, is a child not of earth but of "water, water, water."

The poem is given power from its beginning by a series of Christ-parallels and associations, suggested by the lifeguard's lying "in a stable," by the leap "of a fish" (a traditional symbol of Christ) from the water, by the imagined miracle of walking upon the water, by the wished-for miracle of restoring the dead to life, by the lifeguard's desire to be a "savior," by the association throughout with children. The lifeguard, like Christ, is the children's friend and protector. His love for the children is like Christ's. But the lifeguard is only human. He cannot perform miracles, except in dream or imagination. He has failed in the role of savior. The two settings of the poem symbolically reinforce its inner tension. The sunlit world is the world of actuality. The moonlit world is the world of imagination, of dream, and of unreality. Seldom have feelings of frustrated love and guilt been more powerfully realized.

[Reprinted from Laurence Perrine and James M. Reid, *100 American Poems of the Twentieth Century* (New York: Harcourt, 1966) 278–79.] LP

217. *Emily Dickinson* Because I could not stop for Death (page 797)

Beyond doubt, this is the most discussed of Emily Dickinson's poems, and it has excited a wide array of interpretations. The literal content seems to offer few difficulties: a woman busy with her life is called away from it by a kindly gentleman (Death), who takes her for a carriage ride past the living, pauses at what must be her grave, and proceeds through centuries toward the destination "eternity." There are many fine details characterizing the stages of life in stanza 3; stanza 4 emphasizes both the femininity of the speaker and the chilliness of her ride; stanza 5 mysteriously understates her burial; and the last stanza perpetuates the ride in Death's carriage beyond the human comprehension of time (the concept of eternity, as Keats says in the last stanza of "Ode on a Grecian Urn," teases us "out of thought").

There is little quarrel among the critics about these literal matters. The continuing question is what this little allegory *means*. Does it link death with sexuality (the gentleman come courting)? Does it pretend to render a judgment on posthumous experience? Does it define the values of life as they are discovered in the moment of dying? Does it celebrate the soul's entry into heaven? These suggestions, and several others, have been made by eminent critics and scholars. Furthermore, there is little agreement about the tone of the poem—is it confident? whimsical? terrified? triumphant? uninvolved?

What follows, then, is *one* interpretation that is both plausible and consistent with the poet's ideas. The teacher may wish to use this poem, and the references below, as an introduction to discriminating between critical approaches and interpretations.

Death is remarkably, and surprisingly, characterized in this personification as "kindly," a word that so violates normal expectations as to signal the need for interpretation. Death has traditionally been thought of as "kind" to the extent that it releases a person from a life of suffering or from the limitations imposed by mortality. Such a meaning might be implied by the fact that "Immortality" is included as a personified fellow-passenger in the carriage, but the images of life in the poem do not suggest a life of pain—it contains both labor and leisure, nonchalantly linked by alliteration, which are as easily put away as a basket of sewing; and it is represented by the playing children and the maturing grain. In fact, life and death seem equally attractive, and the speaker, pleased with Death's "civility," apparently accepts his invitation with pleasure. The poem presents Death's visit not as an inevitable and unavoidable event, but as a polite invitation that the speaker finds attractive—an interpretation that divides the speaker from ordinary people.

The tone of the poem is governed by the speaker's willingness to accept Death's kind offer, and the key to the speaker's choice lies in the final stanza. Until then, the poem has been a retrospective recollection of events, reported from the speaker's present situation and colored by her perceptions and attitudes "centuries" later. Although in real terms (calendar terms, sun terms) hundreds of years have passed since the beginning of the ride with Death, to the speaker this whole span of time "*Feels* shorter than the day" she died. Now being dead, the speaker no longer shares the feelings or the ideas of the living. The word "surmised" (line 23) underscores this, for in mid-nineteenth-century America, and in several other poems by Emily Dickinson, the word had decidedly negative connotations; it meant to guess in error, or to guess without personal experience as a basis. The speaker guessed at the destination of her ride—eternity—but has not reached what the living suppose that implies, heaven. Instead, what she is now experiencing is an endless, cool, and detached journey toward an unknown destination. The speaker retains the power to remember her life, and retains her consciousness, but her present situation is undefinable. In this interpretation, the poem presents an allegorical dramatization of posthumous experience: it is neither hellish nor blissful, but only eternally conscious and emotionless.

Among the important critical readings of the poem, the following offer much variety: Richard Chase, *Emily Dickinson* (New York: Sloane, 1951) 249–51; Theodore C. Hoepfner, " 'Because I Could Not Stop for Death,' " *American Literature* 29 (1957): 96; Charles R. Anderson, *Emily Dickinson's Poetry: Stairway of Surprise* (New York: Holt, 1960) 241–46; Clark Griffith, *The Long Shadow: Emily Dickinson's Tragic Poetry* (Princeton: Princeton UP, 1964) 127–34; Richard B. Sewall, *The Life of Emily Dickinson* (New York: Farrar, 1974) 571–72, 717; Robert Weisbuch, *Emily Dickinson's Poetry* (Chicago: U of Chicago P, 1975) 113–17. TRA

218. *Emily Dickinson* **I taste a liquor never brewed** (page 797)

The poet's delight in nature is expressed through an extended metaphor in which ecstasy is likened to intoxication. The liquor on which the poet gets drunk is air and dew and all the beauty of summer. This liquor is natural: it has not been brewed; and "Not all the vats upon the Rhine" (famous for its breweries) yield a comparable liquor. She drinks it from "tankards scooped in pearl" (cumulus clouds in summer skies by my interpretation, but other interpretations are possible). The "inns of molten blue" are summer skies, and "endless" is an overstatement modifying "days" or "summer" or both. Bees and butterflies (both of which take nectar from flowers) are her drinking companions, but the poet declares she will outdrink both—drink them under the table! Indeed she will make such a spectacle of herself and raise such a hullabaloo that seraphs and saints will run to the windows of heaven to investigate, and, looking out, will see the poet leaning drunkenly against the celestial lamppost!

The fancifulness of the poem's metaphors keeps the poem bubbling with high-spirited fun. The alliteration of *debauchee of dew* (6) follows the vowel-alliteration of line 5 (all vowels alliterate with each other), in which *every* syllable except one (*-bri-*) begins with a vowel, so that reading it is like taking continuous small sips of air. The trochaic substitution in the first foot of line 7 not only emphasizes the word *reeling* but introduces a reeling movement into the line. (The basic metrical and rime pattern is iambic $x^4a^3x^4a^3$, but in line 15 a metrical pause replaces the last beat, giving emphasis to the delightful assonantal phrase "little tippler" by which the poet characterizes herself.)   LP

219. *Emily Dickinson* **There's a certain slant of light** (page 798)

Emily Dickinson here treats an irrational psychological phenomenon akin to those recorded by Wordsworth in "Strange fits of passion have I known" ("Down behind the cottage roof, / At once, the bright moon dropp'd. / . . . 'O mercy!' to myself I cried, 'If Lucy should be dead!' ") and by Tennyson in "Mariana" ("But most she loathed the hour / When the thick-moted sunbeam lay / Athwart the chambers, and the day / Was sloping toward his western bower"). A certain external condition of nature induces in her a certain feeling or mood. But the feeling is more complex than Wordsworth's or Mariana's.

The chief characteristic of this feeling is its painful oppressiveness. "Oppresses," "heft," "hurt," "despair," and "affliction" convey this aspect. A large component in it is probably consciousness of the fact of death, though this is probably not the whole of its content nor is this consciousness necessarily fully formulated by the mind. Yet here we see the subtle connection between the hour and the mood. For the season is winter, when the year is approaching its end. And the time is late afternoon (winter afternoons are short at best, and the light slants), when the day is failing. The suggestion of death is caught up by the weighty cathedral tunes (funeral music possibly—but hymns are also much concerned with death—"Dies Irae," etc.) and by "the distance / On the look of death." The stillness of the hour ("the landscape listens, / Shadows hold their breath") is also suggestive of the stillness of death.

But besides the oppressiveness of the feeling, it has a certain impressiveness too. It is weighty, solemn, and majestic, like organ music. This quality is conveyed by "heft / Of cathedral tunes," "Heavenly," "seal" (suggesting the seal on some important official document), and "imperial." This mood may be partly caused by the stillness of the moment, by the richness of the slanting sunlight (soon to be followed by sunset), and by the image of death that it calls up.

The mood gives "Heavenly hurt." "Heavenly" suggests the immateriality of the hurt, which leaves "no scar"; the source of the sunlight—the sky; the ultimate source of both sunlight and death—God. The hurt is given internally "Where the meanings are"—that is, in the soul, the psyche, or the mind—that part of one which assigns "meanings"—consciously or intuitively—to life and to phenomena like this.

"None may teach it any": both the sunlight and the mood it induces are beyond human correction or alleviation; they are final and irrevocable—sealed. There is no lifting this seal—this despair.

"When it goes 'tis like the distance / On the look of death": the lines call up the image of the stare in the eyes of a dead man, not focused, but fixed on the distance. Also, "distance" suggests the awful distance between the living and the dead—part of the implicit content of the mood. Notice that the slanted ray and the mood are still with us here, but are also going. The final remarkable image reiterates the components of the hour and the mood—oppressiveness, solemnity, stillness, death. But it hints also at relief—hopes that there will soon be a "distance" between the poet and her experience.

[This discussion is adapted from an item in *Explicator* 11 (May 1953): item 50.]
LP

220. *John Donne* **The Good-Morrow** (page 798)

As the title announces, this poem is a morning greeting addressed by the speaker to his love. The questions in the opening lines colloquially declare a parallel between this morning's awakening and an awakening to life that took place when they began to love. All time before then was like infancy, or like a miraculous two-century sleep. The conversational quality of these lines continues throughout the poem, producing the kind of syntactical and elliptical problems found in line 5: "but this, all pleasures fancies be" means "with the exception of this (our love), all pleasures are merely imagined ones." The mock innocence of the first three lines is elaborated on in lines 6–7: the speaker has in the past had his share of sexual experiences, but to his innocent sleeping soul they were only prophetic dreams of the love he now shares.

Pursuing his reference to other love exploits, the speaker assures his lady that there can be no cause of jealousy between them. He puns on the words "watch" and "wake," synonyms in Donne's time, to insist that the alertness to each other which this morning has brought is not for fear of loss, because (he logically says) our mutual love rules out the possibility of loving others. Each of them is the whole of the other's society, just as the room they share is equivalent to all other places. The elliptical syntax of lines 11–12 extends this spatial reference. "Let" in these lines means both "let us concede" and "let us ignore." For other people whose sense of the spaciousness of the world derives from traveling, explorers and map-makers are necessary; but these two lovers in themselves contain all worlds. (Line 14 alludes to the Renaissance theory that each individual human being is a microcosm, a little world that parallels the greater universe and contains all its elements. Each of the lovers is thus a world, and being joined by their love, each *has* a world.)

The third stanza further extends the geographical metaphor, but it begins with a Renaissance commonplace, that the face of the lover is mutually mirrored in the eye of the partner, both of them being simultaneously a mirror and the image in the other's mirror. Line 16 momentarily returns to the theme of jealousy, as the speaker assures his love that their mirrored faces reveal the honesty in their hearts. They are themselves like the hemispheres of the newly explored and mapped earth—but better, since they do not have the sharp coldness of the north, nor the sinking sunset of the west. Lines 19–21 employ another Renaissance notion, that mortality and decay are the result of the mixture of unequal or dissimilar elements in the body. Donne concludes that since the two of them are not dissimilar (being "one" in their love), or, at least, since they are completely "alike" in the intensity of their feelings, they need not fear death.

The rich allusiveness of the poem, with its hyperbolic declarations balanced against recurrent denials of any need for jealousy or the fear of infidelity, make this a more complicated poem than its declarative statements suggest. The speaker insists on the perfection and permanence of their mutual love, but this idealism is presented in a context that acknowledges the probability of change. The references to new geographical discoveries attest to the temporal nature of human knowledge, just as the opening stanza shows that individual human beings develop and change. Despite the insistence in the last three lines, death is a certainty for these perfect lovers; and if the real hemispheres of the earth contain "sharp north" and "declining west," the microcosm of the lovers' united being will ultimately be subjected to the same vicissitudes. At the same time that the poem declares the permanence of this love, it alludes to the actual impossibility of it.

The fullest analysis of this poem is by Clay Hunt, in *Donne's Poetry: Essays in Literary Analysis* (Hamden CT: Archon, 1969) 53–69, a repr. of the Yale UP 1954 ed. Other valuable comments may be found in Wilbur Sanders, *John Donne's Poetry* (Cambridge: Cambridge UP, 1971) 64–68, and Judah Stampfer, *John Donne and the Metaphysical Gesture* (New York: Simon, 1970) 142–46.   TRA

The speaker is (a) a poet and (b) a rejected lover. The complaint of a spurned lover was one of the commonest subjects for poetry in Donne's time; but, as so often in his poetry, Donne here takes a thoroughly conventional subject and gives it a thoroughly original treatment. Part of his originality is that, instead of complaining about his lady's coldness, he turns the blame for his unhappiness upon himself, calling himself a "triple fool." Another part of his originality is his exploitation of the modern idea that writing about one's suffering in a structured form has therapeutic value for the poet. But the originality is also manifest in finer details of the poem; for instance, in the choice of the unusual epithet "whining" attached to "poetry" (is he characterizing *all* poetry with this epithet or just the kind that complains about the cruelty of the poet's beloved?), and in the use of a "scientific" analogy for explaining the healing effect of expressing his grief in verse: ocean water (grief), he claims, is purged of its salt (bitterness) in its passage through narrow, crooked, underground ways ("rhyme's vexations") to freshwater lakes and streams (psychological health). (The word "rhyme" may be read literally here but is more profitably taken as a metonymy for verse in general; "rhyme's vexations" are the difficulty of finding words that exactly fit the writer's meaning and at the same time fulfill the requirements of both meter and rime.) But the main power of the comparison lies in the implicit link between the salt of ocean water and the salt of tears. In speaking of grief Donne mentions neither tears nor salt, but he knows that his readers will make the connection. Having admired Donne's analogy, how do we judge it when we learn that Donne's "science" is false? Although Donne used the standard scientific explanation of his time for the difference between salt water and fresh water, we now know that the real explanation is almost the opposite of his: the salt in the ocean is deposited there by streams that dissolve it from the earth on their way from the lakes to the seas. How does this knowledge affect the worth of the poem? The differences between scientific truth, historical truth, and poetic truth must at some time be confronted. They are germane to other poems in our study, such as Donne's "A Valediction: Forbidding Mourning" (page 592) and Keats's "On First Looking into Chapman's Homer" (page 738).

It is important in reading this poem to determine with some accuracy how serious the poet or the speaker (are they the same?) is in calling himself a "triple fool." A careful reading reveals, I think, that the tone of the poem is relatively light. The speaker bears his follies lightly, humorously exaggerating each of his three claims for being a fool. He is not in despair. First, he claims that he is a fool for loving someone who does not return his love: "she" (the beloved woman) denies him; consequently, he asserts, he suffers "pains" and "grief." But he reneges on this assertion before he has finished making it, by saying, in lines 4–5, " But where's the wiseman that would not be I / If she did not deny?" This purely rhetorical question pays extravagant tribute to the beloved, implying that she has so many desirable qualities that nowhere in the world could a wise man be found who would not want to trade positions with the speaker if the woman did not "deny" him. The speaker's folly is thus substantially diminished. He can hardly be thought too great a fool for seeking the love of so desirable a woman.

Second, he claims that he is a fool for expressing his grief in "whining poetry." But nothing he says in the rest of the first stanza supports this initial declaration. He develops the idea of the therapeutic value through a beautifully apt and ingenious comparison. The poet ends the stanza with a direct statement of his belief in the power of poetry to alleviate grief: "Grief brought to numbers cannot be so fierce, / For he tames it that fetters it in verse."

Third, he claims he is a fool because some musician may set his poem to music and sing it in a public concert. This song, while delighting other members of the audience, starts the poet's grief flowing again. But at this point he makes the most illogical statement in the poem. Love and grief are proper subjects for poetry, he claims, but not if it is *good* poetry—not if it pleases when it is heard; for then the triumph of love and grief over him are published abroad, and he becomes a "triple fool": first, for loving a woman who does not return his love; second, for expressing his grief in verse, which alleviates the pain; third, for thus opening the possibility that his poem may be set to music and sung publicly, thereby (a) arousing once more his grief and (b) subjecting him to the embarrassment of letting the whole world know of his "folly."

The poem ends with a generalization: The biggest fools are not congenital idiots, but those who are "a little wise"—wise enough, perhaps, to perceive their folly. The speaker, basing this generalization on his own experience, has been wise enough to choose an extremely attractive and virtuous woman to fall in love with, is gifted enough to write a good poem about his grief, but is unlucky enough to prompt a gifted composer to set his words to music and sing them in public. We must quarrel, however, even with this last assertion. If he really is grieved and embarrassed by this third event (no act of his own), why does he write *this* poem ("The Triple Fool"), which can only make his follies even more widely known? Is he not sucking pleasure out of his grief? LP

222. *John Donne* **Song: Go and catch a falling star** (page 800)

In content this poem expresses an extremely disillusioned and cynical view of human life and particularly of feminine virtue. The speaker, addressing an unidentified interlocutor, bids him in the first six lines to perform a series of tasks that share the common characteristic of being impossible. The implication is that the task he commands in the last three lines of the stanza is equally impossible: to find any condition of life that favors the advancement of "an honest mind." (In modern idiom, "Nice guys finish last.")

In the second stanza the speaker zeroes in on his true target—feminine virtue. If, he tells his companion, you are a person with a gift for seeing miraculous events or things invisible to the ordinary eye, go on a journey, ride "ten thousand days and nights," do not return until you are old; no matter how wide or long your search, even with your gift for seeing wondrous things, you will be unable to find a woman who is both beautiful and faithful in love. (He may perhaps find some faithful ugly ones, but those women with opportunities to be unfaithful will take them.)

In the third stanza the speaker seemingly retreats half a step from this extreme conclusion. *If* you find one, he tells his companion, let me know, for it would be sweet to make a "pilgrimage" to see such a saint. But then he retracts this injunction, showing that he has not really retreated at all. Do not tell me, he says, for even were she still true when I received your letter, still, by the time I could complete my journey, were it only next door, she would have proved unfaithful to two or three lovers. His "pilgrimage," he is convinced, would turn out to be a fool's errand. It is as impossible to find a woman both "true and fair" as to catch a falling star.

How seriously are we to take this poem? Should we imagine the speaker or poet as a man extremely embittered from a series of personal betrayals? Possibly. But it is called a "Song," and was indeed written to an "air" already in existence. Its meter is songlike (tetrameter, except for two monometer lines in each stanza). Its riming is copious (alternating in the first four lines, then a couplet of feminine rimes, then three rimes on one sound). Moreover, its images and overstatements are so extreme, or so witty and charming, and its progress so amusing, that it is hard to take the poem gravely. It seems more playful than disenchanted, more entertaining than sad. The poet, one feels, has adopted a fashionably cynical pose and tried to see how ingeniously and entertainingly he could deal with it. It short, the poem—and its speaker—are too lively to be lugubrious. LP

223. *Keith Douglas* Vergissmeinnicht (page 800)

The setting is probably the North African desert where British forces under General Montgomery fought a prolonged and bitter campaign against German forces under General Rommel ("The Desert Fox") during World War II. The speaker, a British soldier, accompanied by one or more fellow-soldiers, has returned, three weeks afterwards, to the site of a particularly fierce engagement. They find, still sprawled under the barrel of his antitank gun, the body of a German soldier who had made a direct hit on the speaker's tank before being killed. In the gunpit spoil the speaker finds a photograph of the dead German's sweetheart, signed with her name and the German word for "Forget me not." The poem is based on a series of ironies: the inscription "Forget me not" addressed to a soldier incapable now of memory; the fact that the dead soldier's war equipment is still "Hard and good," while its user is "decayed"; the horrible contrast between the living man loved by the girl and the corpse with its burst stomach and dusty eyes; the dual nature of man that makes him capable of both love and killing; the fact that the shot aimed at the soldier "had done the lover mortal hurt" (an ironic understatement). What the speaker discovers in the dead German is a man once much like himself. His tone expresses neither enmity, hate, nor triumph, but only pity and shared humanity. The poem may be usefully compared with Hardy's "The Man He Killed" (page 542).   LP

224.   *Gavin Ewart*   **Ending** (page 801)

This sonnet of lost love calls upon traditional love-sonnet devices—almost every line has at least one example of figurative language, and some have several. But this is not a "traditional love sonnet," in either its theme or its form. It is iambic tetrameter (not pentameter), rimed in couplets rather than in the forms of Italian or English sonnets. In fact, it may be stretching the definition of the form beyond credibility to call this a sonnet, unless one wishes to regard the 14-line length as an ironic allusion to the sonnet and one of its traditional topics.

Here are the figures, by line numbers: 1. overstatement; 2. simile; 3. simile; 4. metaphor; 5. metaphor; 6. simile; 7. metonymy; 8. paradox ("running slow") and metaphorical comparison to a clock, as well as a non-figurative cliché in "running late"; 9. overstatement; 10. metaphor; 11. metaphor; 11–12. metonymy (while the sexual "parts" of the couple had "transmitted joy," it is the two people and not their organs who are "reserved and cold and coy"); 13–14, personification.

Perhaps even more important to the tone and meaning of the poem is the constant use of situational irony to create bathos as exalted or overstated expectations are punctured by the commonplace and trivial. The first two lines set the tone, and it remains throughout.   TRA

225.   *Lawrence Ferlinghetti*   **Constantly risking absurdity** (page 802)

The poem compares the poet to a circus performer and entertainer—high-wire artist, acrobat, and clown ("a little charleychaplin man") who, apparently, will try to catch the leaping form of Beauty while balanced on the high wire of truth—an almost impossible feat. The extended simile (which includes metaphor and personification) emphasizes that the poet must be constantly entertaining (poetry must give pleasure), but that he is also concerned with such higher realities as truth and beauty. It also emphasizes that the poet's task demands the utmost skill and precision and involves constant risk: a false step by the high-wire artist can cause death; a slip by the poet in published work involves public exposure of ineptitude. The sublime and the ridiculous are often narrowly separated, but in their reviews critics are quick to flay the poet who strives for the first and falls into the second. Ferlinghetti shows his own agility as a performer with a constant flow of double meanings and "sleight-of-foot" tricks (the play upon "sleight-of-foot" is appropriate both for the high-wire artist who performs magic with his feet and for the poet who does it with metrical feet). Serious? Yes. Solemn? No.

The arrangement of words on the page mimics the succession of short hurried steps that the acrobat takes across the wire before pausing to balance himself anew.   LP

226. *Carolyn Forché* **The Colonel** (page 802)

The country is El Salvador, as we know from the context in which it appears—Forché's book *The Country Between Us* (New York: Harper, 1981), in which perhaps a third of the poems stem from visits to El Salvador made over a two-year period. Since the students do not have that context, perhaps they should be told beforehand what country is referred to. On the other hand, there may be value in asking them to identify as nearly as possible the locale of the poem. There are sufficient clues to identify the locale as a small Latin American country dominated by American culture and governed by a military regime, against which there is considerable opposition.

The precise date appended at the end suggests that the poem is based on an actual incident. Does this mean that the poem is factual, not fictional? It is written in prose, not verse. How does it differ, then, from a reportorial account? In many ways. No names are named, either of persons or places. The poem is addressed to a particular reader (a "you"), not to a general reader. The poem uses images that would not ordinarily be found in a newspaper account: "The moon swung bare on its black cord over the house." Perhaps most importantly, the last two sentences are surrealistic. They take us into a fantasy world. How distant they are from the first two!

The first two sentences reveal that the poem is a reply to a friend back home. The friend has asked some such question as "Is it true, as I heard on a news report, that you have been to Colonel _____'s home?" The speaker replies, "I was in his house." The failure to give the "his" an antecedent in the poem, plus the fact that the friend knows his name, suggests that the colonel is well known outside his country and is important within it. His name has appeared in the newspapers. He may be the military dictator; he is at least a member of the ruling military junta. What does he mean when he talks of "how difficult it had become to govern"? What would he consider the signs and purposes of good government?

The central point in this poem lies in the shocking contrast between the civility and the brutality implied by the colonel's life style. The tray of coffee and sugar, the daily papers, the pet dogs, the TV set, the good dinner—all suggest a style of civilized and gracious living such as many in our country enjoy. But the pistol on the cushion, the broken bottles embedded in the walls, the bag of human ears, and the colonel's angry outburst against "rights"—all suggest something quite different. LP

227. *Robert Frost* **Birches** (page 803)

Birches have white bark on the trunk and black bark on the branches and on the junctures where the branches join the trunk. They are such slender trees (unlike oaks) that they are easily bent over during ice-storms: sometimes the weight of the ice carries their tops clear to the ground (to "the withered bracken") and freezes them there. When the ice melts, their tops are released, but the trees seldom resume their original straightness: they lean at all angles across the straighter, darker trees.

Though written in continuous form (no stanza or paragraph breaks), the poem may be divided roughly into three equal parts or "movements." The first twenty lines describe the appearance of the trees and their thawing after an ice-storm that bends the birches down "to stay." And what a beautiful and yet accurate description it is! But this is what the speaker calls the "matter-of-fact" about birches.

In the second movement (21–41) the poet moves away from fact into fancy. Although he knows that ice-storms are what bend the birches, he likes to imagine that they were bent down by a farm boy who had no companions and so had to invent his own amusements. He fancies such a boy getting his best play by swinging on birches; that is, by climbing the trees up into their topmost branches where they can no longer bear his weight but bend over gracefully and allow him to drop to the ground. This fancy becomes so vivid in the speaker's imgination that he seems to be describing a real boy—one who played this game with great skill. "He learned all there was / To learn" about doing it well, climbing to exactly the right height and releasing at exactly the right moment for experiencing the maximum thrill. The poet's use of the past tense here abets the feeling of reality. It almost seems to the poet himself that the boy had bent down all the birches on his father's land. We have forgotten the "matter-of-fact" that "swinging doesn't bend them down to stay / As ice-storms do."

If the second movement takes us away from "matter-of-fact" into improbable fancy, the final movement (41–59) takes us even further, into impossible fantasy. The first line of this section ("So was I once myself a swinger of birches") might be taken as literally true, but in the next line the speaker begins to "dream" of becoming one once again. Swinging birches at this point becomes a symbol for getting away from earth (literally, the ground; symbolically, life) for a while and then coming back to it. This wish, of course, is impossible of fulfillment, but the poet likes to indulge himself with it when his life "is too much like a pathless wood" and he is "weary of considerations" (of having to make countless practical and moral decisions about problems in his life). At such points he'd "like to get away from" life for a while, and then come back, and he imagines himself doing it with the same grace and skill as he attributed to his imaginary farm boy. "That would be good both going [getting away from his troubles] and coming back" (returning to the persons and activities that he has loved).

One other symbol must be explicated to get to the whole meaning of the poem. As the speaker climbs his imaginary tree (54), he is pointed "*Toward* heaven"; but he does not want to get there: "Earth's the right place for love: / I don't know where it's likely to go better." Such a statement could hardly be made by anyone with a strong belief in the traditional Christian concept of heaven as the perfect place that the righteous go to after death. "Heaven" here is not a place, but a perfection of life or art that man can aspire to in this life. The imagined farm boy who "learned all there was / To learn" about swinging birches and who

> always kept his poise
> To the top branches, climbing carefully
> With the same pains you use to fill a cup
> Up to the brim, and even above the brim

is appealing because Frost has endowed him with the desire and the ability to do the thing skillfully. Frost always admires the person who has learned to perform a task or a game with conscious skill, whether it be swinging birches, chopping wood, building a load of hay, or writing poetry.

Frost writes poetry well. "Birches" is written in blank verse. The first four lines are perfectly regular, establishing the meter for the reader. After that, though there is no deviation from the pentameter, there is considerable variation in the iambs, principally to enhance the conversational quality of the verse ("But I was going to say . . ."), but also to reinforce meaning. The best example of this is probably to be found in lines 39–40:

> Then he flung, | out- ward, | feet first, | with a swish, |
> Kick- ing his | way down | through the air | to the ground. |

Frost also makes effective use of onomatopoeia (*click, cracks, swish*); of alliteration (*cracks and crazes, climbing carefully*); of consonance (*left and right, feet first*); of assonance (*Shattering and avalanching*); and even of internal rime (*cup, Up*). The figurative language employed in the poem is homely yet highly original—the most important figures: metaphor, *broken glass*; similes, *inner dome of heaven, girls on hands and knees, fill a cup, a pathless wood*; personification, *Truth*; and understatement, *One could do worse than be a swinger of birches*. These open up a whole new area for discussion and exploration; however, an instructor's manual cannot touch all of the bases, even in a poem that mentions baseball.

However, one allusion in the poem demands attention because of its importance to theme: the motif of the half-fulfilled prayer.

> May no fate willfully misunderstand me
> And half grant what I wish and snatch me away
> Not to return.   (50–52)

In the *Iliad*, 16, Achilles prays that his friend Patroclus may recapture the Greek ships from the Trojans and return safe. In Pope's translation:

> Great Jove consents to half the chief's request,
> But heaven's eternal doom denies the rest;
> To free the fleet was granted to his prayer;
> His safe return, the winds dispersed in air.

Patroclus frees the ships, but is slain by Hector in the process. In the *Aeneid*, 11, the Trojan Aruns makes a similar request: he prays to Apollo that he may slay the leader of the foe's cavalry, and return safe home. In Dryden's translation:

> Apollo heard, and granting half his pray'r,
> Shuffled in winds the rest, and toss'd in empty air.

Alexander Pope, in his mock-epic *The Rape of the Lock*, 2, exploits the tradition by giving his hero the ambition to clip a favorite lock of hair from his heroine's head. He prays to the goddess of Love to help him

> Soon to obtain, and long possess the prize.

But the event is now predictable:

> The pow'rs gave ear, and granted half his pray'r,
> The rest, the wind dispers'd in empty air.

Frost makes it very clear that he wants no half-fulfillments of his wish. If he has to choose between climbing birches and staying back, he will choose staying back, because "Earth's the right place for love." The central theme of "Birches," and of Frost's poetry in general, is life's livability. Is life worth living or not? Sometimes he gives a dark answer, sometimes a bright one, but the most characteristic answer gives a slight edge, often a very slight edge, to the affirmative. Check this generalization with the other Frost poems in this book and see if you agree. "Birches" is one of his most popular and most anthologized poems; first, because it is excellent poetry, and second, because it seems more optimistic than it really is. The description of the thawing ice is a beautiful phenomenon beautifully described. The account of the imaginary farm boy swinging birches is appealing in many ways. The assertion that "Earth's the right place for love" is what we'd all like to believe. The sunniness of these passages is so brilliant that we overlook or forget the passage about life's being "like a pathless wood," so terrifying and painful that we would like to get away from it, not by climbing a tree with a "snow-white trunk" but, perhaps, by plunging into a stagnant pool that we cannot climb out of. If "Birches" is a poem of beauty and love, it is also a poem of terror.   LP

228. *Robert Frost* Desert Places (page 804)

Unlike "Stopping by Woods on a Snowy Evening" (page 653), this poem presents a speaker who observes a snow scene but who does not pause to consider his relationship to it; rather, he is "going past" (2), and the first line suggests speed and urgency in doing so. Nevertheless, his observation draws him into a meditation in which the natural phenomenon is an analogue to his state of mind and spirit. The field is about to become smooth and empty as the snow will cover all evidence of growth, both cultivated crops and intrusive weeds, and has already obliterated traces of animal life. Very soon, the snow will also be completely obscured by the darkness.

Despite his sense that this process is not directly related to him, this suggests to the human observer a loneliness of an extreme sort, a loneliness so profound that it implies cosmic emptiness and meaninglessness: the scene will become "A blanker whiteness [etymologically a redundant phrase] of benighted snow / With no expression, nothing to express" (11–12). The blanking out of all distinctions by the snow is to be followed by darkness so profound that it reminds the speaker of total moral or intellectual ignorance, as the double denotation of "benighted" implies.

This extreme vision of nothingness is expressed in rich and impressive diction that creates the rhetorical climax of the poem. It is followed by a deflating drop in tone and diction as the speaker attempts to deflect the seriousness of his insight. The childlike slanginess of "scare" comes at the point where we might anticipate *terrify* or *horrify*, but instead we hear some of the bravado of a frightened child, daring someone to scare him. This deflation of tone is extended by the usually comic double rimes of the last stanza: *spaces-race is-places*. (That Frost intended this comic effect is suggested by his revision of the poem between its first publication in *American Mercury* 31 (1934) and its book publication in 1936. Line 14 originally read "on stars void of human races"; the revised version, by using two monosyllables to create the feminine rime, calls more attention to it.)

The speaker's strategy—to make little of the terror he has induced in himself by his thoughts about the snow scene—has the dismissive air of the endings of "Design" (page 656) and "Bereft" (page 582), and like them, ironically expresses feelings even more terrifying. Why worry about the infinite emptiness of the universe, he says, when one can find that quality of emptiness simply by examining one's own spirit. Understated and even jocular as it is, this concluding stanza is of course even more frightening than the observation of the snowfield.

The poem makes use of two important allusions. The title and concluding phrase are quoted from Hawthorne's *The Scarlet Letter*, chapter 18, where "desert places" are introduced as a simile to describe the "moral wilderness" into which Hester Prynne is free to wander as the result of her expulsion from society. "They" who cannot terrify the speaker (13) have been identified as astronomers, but also as followers of Blaise Pascal, who wrote, "The eternal silence of these infinite spaces terrifies me" (*Pensées*, 206).

This justly famous poem has drawn many interpreters. Among them there is some disagreement (as indeed this manual entry does not agree with all of them). See two essays in *Frost Centennial Essays* (Jackson: UP of Mississippi, 1974): Albert J. von Frank, " 'Nothing That Is': A Study of Frost's 'Desert Places,' " 121–32, and Edward Stone, "Other 'Desert Places': Frost and Hawthorne," 275–87. Other comments may be found in: Brooks and Warren, *Understanding Poetry* (New York: Holt, 1938) 193–94; Reuben A. Brower, *The Poetry of Robert Frost: Constellations of Intention* (New York: Oxford UP, 1963) 108–110; Lewis H. Miller, Jr., "Two Poems of Winter," *College English* 28 (1967): 314–16; Seymour Chatman, *An Introduction to Poetry* (Boston: Houghton, 1968) 11–13; Charles B. Hand, "The Hidden Terror of Robert Frost," *English Journal* 58 (1969): 1166–68; Carol M. Lindner, "Robert Frost: Dark Romantic," *Arizona Quarterly* 29 (1973): 243–44;

Frank Lentricchia, *Robert Frost: Modern Poetics and the Landscapes of Self* (Durham NC: Duke UP, 1975) 95–99 and *passim*. In Norman Friedman and Charles A. McLaughlin, *Poetry: An Introduction to Its Form and Art* (New York: Harper, 1961), this poem is used in nine chapters as the central example for various approaches to analysis of poetry. TRA

229. *Robert Frost* Mending Wall (page 805)

At first reading this poem will seem to be about walls and about two New England farmers who have opposite philosophies concerning them. Each philosophy is stated twice: the speaker's in the first line and in line 35: "Something there is that doesn't love a wall"; the neighboring farmer's in line 27 and in the final line: "'Good fences make good neighbors.'" But as we dig into the poem a little deeper we may conclude that the poem is less about walls and opposed philosophies concerning them than it is about opposed kinds of mental habit. The neighboring farmer's philosophy is clear and definite, and we know exactly where he got it. He got it from his father, who got it from his father, who got it. . . . In short, it is a traditional piece of folk wisdom, a proverbial saying that he has accepted as dogma without questioning its meaning or validity. The speaker, on the other hand, states his philosophy more tentatively: "*Something there is* that doesn't love a wall." He seems not quite certain what that "Something" is, though, as a matter of fact, he knows exactly what "spills the upper boulders in the sun" over the winter months. It is "the frozen-ground-swell" underneath the wall: the expansion of the earth caused by the freezing of the moisture always present in the ground. Nature causes the wall to crumble. But he inclines to think there may be more to it than that: not just nature but something *in* nature or in the-nature-of-things "doesn't love" a wall. He hasn't put a label on it. But not only is he more tentative in his thinking than his neighbor, he is also more reflective, thoughtful, and flexible. He has a questioning habit of mind. Of his neighbor's proverbial saying he asks, "'*Why* do they make good neighbors? Isn't it / Where there are cows?'" ("*Why*" is the kind of question his neighbor has never asked.) But in asking this question, or rather these two questions, he confesses that there is some truth in his neighbor's position, and he identifies exactly the source of that truth. When one or both neighbors own livestock, the wall prevents contention between them by keeping the livestock in their proper fields and keeping one farmer's cows from eating the other's crops. (A "good neighbor," as defined by the proverb, is one whom you can live next to without friction.) The neighbor's attitude toward walls, like most proverbial wisdom, contains a half-truth. ("Look before you leap" and "He who hesitates is lost," though contradictory, both state half-truths; that is, each is true in some situations, neither is true in all situations.) It is now apparent that the speaker's attitude toward walls is not so diametrically opposed to his neighbor's as at first appeared. He recognizes the necessity, the desirability, of *some* walls. Indeed he has all by himself on occasion gone out and "made repair" after hunters have completely torn down part of a wall. Still, the desirability of a wall depends upon the situation, and " 'here there are no cows.' " Before *he* built a wall he'd ask what he " 'was walling in or walling out.' " He continues to think that there is " 'Something' " that " 'doesn't love a wall, / That wants it down,' " but he is not himself opposed to all walls, just unnecessary ones, and especially those that wall in or wall out something that ought not to be walled in or out. However, he is flexible. *He* is the one who contacts his neighbor "at spring mending-time" to let him know when he is available. He knows what his neighbor's attitude toward walls is, and he knows that to stay on neighborly terms with him, he must honor that attitude even while trying to argue him out of it.

But there is much more to the contrast between these two farmers than simply their attitudes toward walls. The speaker is observant: he can tell the difference between the gaps made by the frozen-ground-swell in winter and those made by hunters in other seasons. He knows how handling rocks all day can wear one's fingers "rough." He has imagination, a playful, whimsical turn of mind, and a sense of humor. Some boulders, he observes, are so round that they "have to use a spell to make them balance: / 'Stay where you are until our backs are turned!' " He compares the process of mending wall to "just another . . . game, / One on a side." He anticipates his point about the cows by saying: "My apple trees will never get across / And eat the cones under [your] pines." His perceptiveness is apparent when he thinks about how to explain what the "Something" is that doesn't love a wall. Whatever it is (Love perhaps? Some principle of community or brotherhood?), the speaker knows that, to reach his neighbor's understanding, he must communicate the idea in concrete terms, not in abstractions. He fleetingly thinks of "elves" because his fancy has a fondness for elves and because elves (if one actually believes in them, as the speaker almost surely doesn't) are a physical agency that the neighbor's mind could grasp—and might accept if he were an Irish peasant rather than a New England farmer. But the speaker immediately realizes the absurdity of this explanation and casts it aside, for "it's not elves exactly, and I'd rather / He said it for himself." This last remark shows the speaker's grasp of an important principle of education: that the learner will be much more likely to grasp and accept a concept that he has figured out for himself than one he has merely had *explained* to him (if you want a fancy name for this method of teaching, it's *heuristic*). Thus we find in the speaker a mind that is probing, perceptive, and critical, but also imaginative, whimsical, and playful, though possibly a little indefinite in its inability to define that "Something" even to itself. In the neighbor we see a matter-of-fact, uncritical mind that accepts traditional wisdom unquestioningly and holds on to it dogmatically. It is this contrast of minds that provides the central interest of the poem. In the speaker's perception his neighbor "moves in darkness"—the darkness of ignorance and uncritical acceptance. He sees his neighbor there, "Bringing a stone grasped firmly by the top / In each hand, like an old-stone savage armed." The implications of the simile are two: first, that an unquestioning habit of mind is primitive, like that of paleolithic man; second, that there is something potentially menacing about such a habit of mind. No doubt the speaker and his neighbor will continue to get on

281

amicably enough, and not start throwing rocks at each other: the neighbor is conscientious and hard-working, and both men want to be "good neighbors" in some sense of the term. Nevertheless, it is people shouting slogans, clinging to half-truths dogmatically, who rush into wars against each other and go on "holy crusades." It is this kind of mental set that creates unnecessary "walls" between men, that "Something" (Love? Reason? Brotherhood?) "wants . . . down."

Such, at least, is my reading (a fairly old-fashioned one) of what has become one of Frost's most controversial poems. On one axis, the range of opinion goes from Robert Graves's statement "If anyone asks: 'But what *is* the something that doesn't love a wall?' the answer is, of course, 'frost'—also its open-hearted namesake, Robert Frost," to Elizabeth Jennings's assertion that "Good fences make good neighbors" is the moral of the poem. On another axis, opinion ranges from Carson Gibbs's assessment of the speaker as "witty, tolerant, and reasonable" to Donald Cunningham's that he is "hollow, vain, and foolish." For varying viewpoints, see Elaine Barry, *Robert Frost* (New York: Ungar, 1973) 109–12; Marie Boroff, *Language and the Poet* (Chicago: U of Chicago P, 1979) 24–30; Donald Cunningham, "Mending a Wall," in *Gone Into If Not Explained*, ed. Greg Kuzma (Crete NE: Best Cellar, 1976) 65–73; Carson Gibbs, "Mending Wall," *Explicator* 20 (Feb. 1962): item 48; Robert Graves, "Introduction," *Selected Poems of Robert Frost* (New York: Holt, 1963) xiii; Elizabeth Jennings, *Frost* (New York: Barnes, 1966) 24; John C. Kemp, *Robert Frost and New England* (Princeton: Princeton UP, 1979) 13–26; Frank Lentricchia, *Robert Frost* (Durham NC: Duke UP, 1973) 104–107; John F. Lynen, *The Pastoral Art of Robert Frost* (New Haven: Yale UP, 1960) 27–31; Marion Montgomery, "Robert Frost and His Use of Barriers," *South Atlantic Quarterly* 57 (1958): 349–50; Richard Poirier, *Robert Frost* (New York: Oxford UP, 1977) 104–106; Charles N. Watson Jr., "Frost's Wall: The View from the Other Side," *New England Quarterly* 44 (1971): 653–56. LP

The other editor speaks

" 'Good fences make good neighbors' " may be the most famous phrase in all of Frost's poetry. Like many famous quotations, it is misleading when quoted out of context or when it is offered as Frost's "philosophy."

The poem is narrative, restricting itself to the speaker's attitudes. It poses the narrator against his neighbor, as men of two opposing philosophies, and as can be the case when we report our experiences, the narrator is given the privilege of considering his position the correct one. The neighbor is only permitted to speak his famous line, twice; what *he* thinks of the speaker is altogether missing from the poem. It can be instructive to ask a class to imagine exactly what the neighbor might be thinking about the speaker—what a man who "will not go behind his father's saying" (or so the speaker claims) thinks about a man who first informs him it is time to mend the wall, and then wants to ask what walls are for, and who seems to believe in some vague " 'Something . . . that doesn't love a wall.' "

A proper reading of the poem requires taking into account the limitation and the implicit prejudice that results from one participant's report of a debate, and that naturally renders the resolution suspect: the speaker clearly thinks he has "won" because he is a thinking man who wants "to go behind" rural lore, while his neighbor "moves in darkness" of the mind. The reader also needs to understand the dialectic opposition of the two points of view. The speaker is a man who wants to know the reasons for his actions, who investigates and meditates, who likes to believe (probably thinking himself only whimsical) in the vague "Something," in using spells to balance the stones, even—almost—in elves. That is, he is a compound of rationality and a desire to find something beyond rationality. He is also a man of apple orchards, of domestication, of playing games according to equitable rules, who takes pride in being civil and civilized.

Stripped of the prejudiced reporting of the speaker, the neighbor is a man who accepts traditional teachings, who shares in the responsibility of maintaining private property, and whose land is in its natural state, a pine forest. He also believes in neighborliness and the soundness of workmanship. What the speaker's attitude contributes to the portrait of the neighbor reveals more about the speaker than about his opponent in the game of wall-mending. Because of the neighbor's taciturnity, the speaker thinks him shallow-minded, ignorant, primitive, unable to think or investigate. That is, he interprets the neighbor's attitude as further evidence of his own superiority. The man who is different from him is the man who is inferior to him. Does the neighbor go so far in interpreting the speaker's difference?

John F. Lynen points out that the poem presents an unresolved question: "Should man tear down the barriers which isolate individuals from one another, or should he recognize that distinctions and limitations are necessary to human life?" Attempting to answer this question, many readers have tried to pin the poem down to a simple set of paired opposites—liberal and conservative, rational and instinctive, civilized and primitive, and many more. But although the terms of the poem teasingly invite the search for an easy symbolic reading, and also tease the reader into supposing that the speaker is "right," no easy symbols or easy solutions are available. The poem is memorable for the irresolution that keeps us searching. TRA

230. *Robert Frost* **Never Again Would Birds' Song Be the Same** (page 806)

Time, place, situation: Adam in the Garden of Eden before tasting the forbidden fruit, expressing his love for Eve and drawing conclusions about her effect on the world and about God's purpose in creating her—to add forever some quality of her beauty to nature. There is probably no example of dramatic irony in this book that is more total and central to the meaning of the poem—for Adam has got it completely wrong, and moreover, in his praise for Eve, he is displaying the primacy of his love for his wife that will cause him to join her in tasting the fruit. (The allusions in this poem are to full accounts of Adam's Fall, such as Milton's in *Paradise Lost*, rather than to the bare story in Genesis.)

Several details of the poem are especially ironic in light of the events that followed. The fact that her "eloquence" could only produce its effect on the birds "when *call* or laughter carried it aloft" predicts in part the grief and lamentation, and the harsh recrimination, which move both Adam and Eve after the Fall. That the sound of Eve's voice "never would be lost" from nature may look toward the permanent change of the natural world as well as the human world caused by the Fall, the coming of death into the world. And the confident last line, asserting that the purpose of Eve's creation was to make the world better, makes fullest use of irony, for the opposite was the result.

Yet for all the darker implications, we should not overlook the genuineness of this loving statement, the praise that expresses Adam's nature as well as Eve's beauty. No man can foresee the future, and there is a hint of self-knowledge on that point in the opening line and in the concession to fact implied in such words and phrases as "Admittedly" (6), "Be that as may be" (9), and "probably" (12). Consequently, when Adam declares his conclusions so forcefully, even while he concedes to some uncertainty, he reveals the depth and grandeur of his love. It is a statement of love that wills itself to ignore or push aside contradictory possibilities, a universal human trait.   TRA

The other editor speaks

Senior editor thinks this all wrong.
His feelings about it are strong.
　　Though it seems a bit cruel,
　　They're planning a duel
To determine who's right and who's wrong.   LP

231.   *Christopher Gilbert*   **Pushing** (page 806)

Lines 21–22 generalize the central idea of the poem, though with enough vagueness of specificity to invite a symbolic interpretation. They define two kinds of motive— desire and rebellion against limits or restrictions. The title refers to the second of these, and is exemplified by two of the three events in the poem—the boys' "pushing" beyond the limits of the shop-owner's restrictions (returning to "try his nerve again") and their throwing snowballs at the sun. The shop-owner too pushes, not as a means of going beyond limits but in order to establish them: " 'buy something or else you got to leave.' " The narrator, being pressed by his young brother to explain why they push against the restriction (knowing as they both do that what they "want" is to be warmed), finally comes up with his "guess" about the second kind of motive.

The things that the boys "can't" do include both the naturally and the artificially prohibited: they cannot own the cars they name nor escape the restrictions imposed by the store owner, both examples of limits placed by social and economic forces; nor can they alter the cold weather or hit the sun with their snowballs. The word "can't" nicely represents the two kinds of limits: strictly defined, it refers to absolute impossibility—if you cannot, you cannot; but its colloquial usage, as a substitute for "may not," refers to the prohibitions of social order. What the older boy is learning (and teaching) is that the apparent impossibility of a task should provoke you to try to do it, rather than to accept inability. "Pushing" is an appropriate title, for it does not offer any false promise of achievement, only an attitude toward restriction.

One may infer from line 9 ("a decent White man") that the speaker, like the poet, is black, and that the restrictions presented in the poem symbolize conditions beyond the rules shop-owners make to protect themselves from "big-eyed" boys and what they are "up to" in loitering in the aisles.   TRA

232. *Barnabe Googe* **Of Money** (page 807)

Verbal irony? dramatic irony? or a sincere expression of disenchantment with friendship? It is difficult to determine, but the evidence tends toward dramatic irony. (1) There is an emphasis on the immediacy of the situation—*once* adversity comes, friends take a hasty farewell, and it only takes one "lowering day" to make them invisible. (2) If gold can in fact do what the speaker claims—lift you out of your misery, ease your distress—why has he not been consoled by it? (3) Why all this protest, if he does in fact prefer money over friendship, since he still has his money?

Despite its statement, the poem is not exalting the material over the emotional, but rather is expressing the speaker's emotional need for true friends.

Some sixteenth-century peculiarities may need clarifying: line 5 (with its thundering spondees—"Fair face show friends") is declarative rather than imperative or vocative, despite its syntax. It means "friends show [you] a fair face" when you are rich. Line 6 opens with a subjunctive expressing a hypothetical situation: "should a time come when their friendship is put to the test, farewell is all you'll hear."

These two examples, incidentally, define more clearly what the poem means by "friendship": that is, it is railing against false friends, those who put on a smiling face until there is a need to give genuine proof of their friendship. A less involved and injured speaker might very well say "good riddance" to such, without having to turn to his money as consolation.   TRA

233. *Thomas Hardy* **Channel Firing** (page 807)

Hardy's dating of this poem may make it seem prophetic, since World War I broke out in August, 1914; but it was a prophecy almost anyone could have made, for the event referred to in line 1 was well known: the Royal Navy was conducting gunnery practice in the English Channel, and the guns could be heard many miles inland. (Hardy is reported to have been surprised, in fact, that the war began only a few months afterward.)

The speaker in the poem is one of the dead, presumably a clergyman buried within the chancel of his church where the clergy were usually interred; he is familiar with the altar, chancel windows, and "glebe cow," and seems to be in the habit of having chats with others buried nearby, including "Parson Thirdly." The folklike simplicity of the poem, achieved through its tetrameter quatrains and simple diction, makes the whole experience seem rustic and unsophisticated, the material of a ballad. The dead have been awakened by the great guns ("loud enough to wake the dead," we might say), and at first they suppose that "Judgment-day" has come. The noise has even terrified the hounds, the churchmouse, the worms, and the cow—not because they anticipate the apocalypse, of course, but because they instinctively fear loud sounds.

God, however, sardonic but comforting, tells the dead to return to their sleep: it's only men threatening men, not a divine event. Although many men *deserve* to go to hell, God has not destroyed the world, nor does he seem to want to anytime soon, for he takes pity on mankind's need for "rest eternal."

Parson Thirdly's reaction to this news in the penultimate stanza is pragmatic: if God is not going to separate the sheep from the goats, it might have been more pleasant to have "stuck to pipes and beer" instead of depriving himself for the sake of piety.

The tone of the poem shifts markedly in the last stanza. Instead of the folk narrative of the speaker and the paternal chattiness of God, the last stanza turns to brooding lyricism. Alliteration, consonance, and assonance ("*roaring-r*eadiness"; "*again-guns*"; "*hour-roaring*"; "*readiness-avenge*") pack the first two lines. The last two abound in *st* and *t* sounds: "*Stourton Tower*," "*Camelot*," "*starlit Stonehenge*"; and the last two feet in this iambic poem are trochees, mysteriously trailing off in the mournful music that the theme demands. The bulk of the poem has been whimsical, folksy, and not particularly alarming—ironically, since the subjects have included naval bombardment, skeletons, damnation and piety, and God's potential wrath; but the theme is the persistence among men of aggression, violence, and the recurrence of military conquest to establish and maintain civilization. God (who tends to speak in clichés, the rustic father of his rustic flock) puts it directly: "'The world is as it used to be.'"

A "glebe cow" is pastured in the parcel of land allotted to a clergyman as part of his benefice; like the land and the parsonage, it is provided for his use but is not his private property. The name "Parson Thirdly" may allude to the Holy Trinity; a Parson Thirdly is a character in Hardy's novel *Far from the Madding Crowd*. The spelling "Christès" (line 15) is archaic, in keeping with the ballad style and the time references implicit in the last stanza.

For further discussion see Babette Deutsch, *Poetry in Our Time* (Garden City NY: Anchor/Doubleday, 1963) 9–10; John Crowe Ransom, "Introduction" to *Selected Poems of Thomas Hardy* (New York: Macmillan, 1961) x–xii; Cleanth

286

Brooks and Robert Penn Warren, *Understanding Poetry* (New York: Holt, 1976)
45–48; J. O. Bailey, *The Poetry of Thomas Hardy: A Handbook and Commentary*
(Chapel Hill: U of North Carolina P, 1970) 262–64.   TRA

234.   *Thomas Hardy*   **The Darkling Thrush** (page 809)

The end of the day, the end of the year, and the end of the century symbolically
unite with the bleakness of the imagery in the first two stanzas of this poem to evoke
a mood of utter desolation and hopelessness. The contrast between this desolation
and the apparently unlimited joy of the thrush's song is the pivot on which the poem
turns, and the contrast is so striking that it leads many students to read into this
poem an optimism that is in fact not there. Conditioned by earlier experience with
more cheerful poets and with sentimental cliché, they see in this poem the dark cloud
with a silver lining, the tale of woe with a happy ending, darkness giving way to
light, despair overcome by hope.

What the poem actually presents is subtler and less cheerful. The speaker is overcome with wonderment at the joy of the thrush's song, and momentarily—but only
momentarily—he is prompted to wonder whether the bird may not know of some
"blessed Hope." But, notice, he does not say that the thrush knew of some blessed
Hope. He does not even say, "I thought [did think] . . . he knew," but only, "I
could think. . . ." That is, it's *as if* the bird sang out of some blessed Hope. The
speaker *could*—but didn't—think so. The thought has crossed his mind, but tran-
siently, too swiftly to take up residence there. The speaker, after all, sees no cause
for joy or hope "written" on the world around him. In the last line he flatly states
that he is unaware of any hope. The bird sings, really, out of instinct, not out of
knowledge, and at the bottom of his mind the speaker knows this. The poem concludes, then, not with hope, but only with the wistful wish that there *were* some
reason for hope, and with wonderment at the mystery of the bird's joyous song.
The conclusion of "The Oxen" (page 672) evokes a similar mood and presents a
similar interpretive problem.

Image and mood blend perfectly in this poem. The simile of the "tangled bine-
stems" that score the sky like "strings of broken lyres" is marvelously effective,
both visually and emotionally exact, giving a sense of music destroyed, of something
else come to an end—like the day, the year, the century.   LP

235.   *George Herbert*   **Redemption** (page 809)

The first clue that this sonnet is not merely a dramatic narrative is not a forceful
one: the title ambiguously refers to a business transaction and to a religious concept. Similarly ambiguous, "Lord" at the end of the first line may refer to a land-
lord or to God (the capitalization is retained from the first printing of the poem,
but there was little consistency in the use of capitals in the seventeenth century).
Only in the fifth line does the poem assert the break from superficial meaning,

placing the manor house of the lord "In heaven." Even that phrase could be read as a metaphor (the manor house is so grand that it seems heavenly to the tenant) until the contrast in line 8 makes it clear that heaven and earth must be taken literally.

The poem allegorically presents what Herbert and other Puritans of the period called the "New Covenant," or the "Covenant of Grace," between God and man. The old covenant, the "Covenant of Works," had come into effect with the creation of Adam; it left man wholly responsible, and punishable, for his sins, and at Adam's fall it condemned mankind to death. By the Covenant of Grace, God sent his son to offer redemption of sin, a new contract by which man could be gathered into heaven as an act of God's grace rather than by his own deserts.

This allegorical meaning is made clear in a very early commentary on the poem by George Ryley at the beginning of the eighteenth century, as quoted by Joseph H. Summers, *George Herbert: His Religion and Art* (Cambridge: Harvard UP, 1968) 60–61:

> The first lease this great landlord gave to man, his tenant, was the covenant of works, by which man was bound to yeild all the profits of the land to his landlord's use; the condition being, *he that doth them shall live in them, and the soul that sinneth shall dye.* Man breaking the articles of this once, rendered himself for ever incapable of retrieving that loss, or of keeping them for the future; so by these articles he could never *thrive,* that is, never be *justified. But what the law* (that is, this law of works) could not do, God, sending his own Son, & c. hath wrought for us, that is, our Redemption: making us free from the law of sin and death, and granting us a new *small-rented lease.* This was purchased for us by, and granted to us att, the death of Christ. These premises will lead us into the plain sence of this poem.

The allegorical form permits Herbert to relate the narrative of "history" to the spiritual reality of every person's life. As Summers says, "the speaker is both one man in the present and all mankind from the Fall to the Crucifixion; the search is the search of the Jews until Calvary and it is also the search of every man who wishes to be a Christian; the discovery was made by humanity at one moment in the past, but it is also made by individuals at every moment, present and future" (182).

This explanation helps us to understand the time reference in lines 7–8, "which he had dearly bought / Long since on earth." The event is obviously the Crucifixion, when the lord paid "dearly" (both at great expense, and with great love) to save mankind. As an historical event that occurred in the first century, it was "Long since"; but as a continuing redemption, it occurs over and over in the lives of individual people. As Herbert would have seen it, the Crucifixion is a recurring event manifested to the spiritual life of each person, so the concluding image of the poem is both historical and present, and the "ragged noise and mirth" of the multitude re-enacts the scene of the original Crucifixion.

Students who may not have examined the metaphorical texture of Christian terminology may at first be shocked or affronted by Herbert's handling of the action of redemption in commercial terms; they can be led to see that the concept of heaven as *reward,* of Christ's *payment* for the sins of the world, and many others that they might contribute, rest on similar mercantile phrasing, justified by the need to express metaphysical truth in physical terms comprehensible to mankind.   TRA

236.   *William Heyen*   **Riddle** (page 810)

The "riddle" of this angry, pained poem is not really a riddle—that is, it takes no effort to answer the question literally. What is riddling about the extermination of a population because of its race or religion is the denial of responsibility—that is, all of them "killed the Jews," but none of them acknowledges guilt. But the real riddle, of course, is not *who* but *why*, focused in the question "Were they human?" (28). The catalogue of "some" beginning in line 16 emphasizes what has been called the ordinariness of these atrocities, listing through line 20 the activities that went into the mass executions, and then in 21–24, listing *other* ordinary activities of the working world.

The first and last stanzas refer to some of the more heartless, inhumane deeds of the extermination camps—removing and collecting the gold teeth and the shoes of victims for their value or usefulness, or making lampshades from human skin. Notice that these, too, are atrocities that are linked to ordinary life, valuable or useful possessions gleaned from people as if they were not fellow human beings.

The form of this poem is deeply ironic, since it has the insistent sing-song rhythms and repetitious structures of a children's song or story—"Who killed cock-robin?" or "Who will tell the king the sky is falling?"   TRA

237.   *A. E. Housman*   **Bredon Hill** (page 811)

The poem is dominated by the imagery of bells, their chiming partly conveyed by the three rimes in each stanza. But the bells have a different meaning for the speaker at different times in the poem, and in this difference the drama of the poem lies.

In stanzas 1–4 the speaker recalls summer Sunday mornings spent with his sweetheart on Bredon Hill. They heard the bells ringing for church service in "steeples far and near." Though heedless of the summons, they found the ringing a "happy noise," for it formed a background to their delight in each other. That she preferred his company over going to church probably made the bells even sweeter to the speaker, and he would call back to them, "Oh, peal upon our wedding" and we will come "in time."

In stanzas 5–6, however, we learn that the girl went to church that winter, not for a wedding but for a funeral service—her own. "Unbeknown" to her lover, she had died and gone to church (was carried there in her coffin) without him. Only one bell was tolled—a bell in only one church, and only one bell of its set of bells—the funeral bell.

In the final stanza the lover again hears the bells ringing on Bredon as he had that summer. But they no longer make a "happy noise"; they only remind him more keenly of his lost happiness. In accents of extreme bitterness he cries out (futilely) to bid them "be dumb," and with almost surly resignation adds, "I hear you, I will come." He will come when he is ready, either to mourn at his sweetheart's grave or to be buried himself.

Bredon Hill is in Worcestershire close to the Shropshire border: these are the two shires mentioned in line 3. From the top of Bredon on a clear day one can see three additional counties—Herefordshire, Warwickshire, and Gloucestershire. The image of "colored counties" (8) conflates that of farmland laid out in plots of different colored crops with a map showing the counties in different colors.   LP

238. *A. E. Housman* **To an Athlete Dying Young** (page 812)

The speaker is a fellow townsman of the dead athlete, possibly (though not necessarily) one of the pallbearers carrying his coffin to the cemetery for burial. The athlete had died within months of winning the annual race for his town. The poem is an extended apostrophe addressed by the speaker to the athlete.

The parallelism of action and language between the first two stanzas beautifully underscores the ironic contrast in situation. After his victory in the race, the towns-people had "chaired" him (borne him in triumph on their shoulders) through the market-place to his home. Now, less than a year later, they bring him "home" again, again "Shoulder-high." But the meaning of "home" has changed between the two stanzas. In the second it is a metaphor for the grave. The "road all runners come" is death, and the youth is being borne "Shoulder-high" in his coffin. The "town" to which he now belongs ("stiller"—an understatement—than that which noisily "cheered" just a few months ago) is the cemetery or necropolis (city of the dead).

The chief ironic shock of the poem, however, comes in the third stanza. Most people would consider the death of a young athlete at the peak of his ability an occasion for lamentation; the speaker considers it one for congratulation. "Smart lad," he says (not "Poor lad,") and proceeds to praise the young athlete for dying "betimes." Except for his hyperbolic use of the word "Smart" when he literally means "fortunate" (the athlete did not commit suicide), the speaker is perfectly serious, and speaks for the poet; that is, the irony involved here is neither verbal nor dramatic but situational. Both speaker and poet regard the athlete as fortunate; the irony lies in the discrepancy between our expectation (initiated by the title and sustained through the first two stanzas) that the athlete's death will be regarded by the poet as pathetic or "tragic" and our discovery that it is regarded quite otherwise.

In the rest of the poem the speaker supports this attitude and is not undercut by the poet. The athlete has slipped away from "fields where glory does not stay." It is better, the speaker feels, to die when everyone is singing your praises than to die in obscurity years later (as so many once-celebrated athletes do). The "fields where glory does not stay" are literally athletic fields, symbolically earth or life in general; "glory" is fame and the pride of triumph. The "laurel" is the symbol, not just of victory (the ancient Greeks awarded a laurel wreath or "crown" to victors in the Pythian games) but of fame. The "rose" is traditionally a symbol for a girl's beauty. Though athletic fame is won by young men at an early age, the speaker declares, its duration is even shorter than a young woman's beauty. This runner, who set a new record for the course he ran, will not be alive to see his record broken; the silence that would have greeted his future athletic decline will sound "no worse than cheers" (an ironical understatement: he will be aware of neither) now that he is dead. In stanza 5 the speaker praises the athlete for having won (metaphorically) one more race: he has raced his fame to the grave and has arrived there first (has died while his name is still unforgotten). In stanza 6 the speaker again speaks to the athlete as if he had some choice in the matter, and urges him to set his "fleet foot on the sill of shade, / And hold to the low lintel up / The still-defended challenge-cup." The "sill of shade" is the threshold of the door to the tomb, the "low lintel" is the crosspiece over it. The "still-defended challenge cup" (his trophy) is the kind that has the winner's name inscribed on it each year. The winner is allowed to keep the cup until he is defeated, when it passes into the hands of the new winner. This athlete has died with the challenge-cup still in his possession.

The last stanza contains a sophisticated literary allusion that supports some identification of the speaker with the poet (Housman was a celebrated classical scholar). In Book 11 of the *Odyssey*, when Odysseus visits the Greek underworld (Hades), he is surrounded by shades of the "strengthless" dead. Since these shades are depicted as peculiarly impotent—strengthless and senseless—Housman is not predicting here some kind of immortality for the dead athlete, but simply making one more contrast between what he was in life and what he will become in death, "strengthless" and senseless. Nevertheless, these shades will find "unwithered" on his head the laurel garland (fame) "briefer than a girl's" rose garland (beauty). The last two lines of the poem allude to the symbols of stanza 3.

Housman in this poem dwells on the transience of youth, fame, and beauty, and on the desirability of dying while one still has them rather than after they are lost. It is a theme that appears elsewhere in his poetry (see especially *A Shropshire Lad*, 23 and 44—"The lads in their hundreds" and "Shot? so quick, so clean an ending?"). It reflects one part of Housman's mind but not the whole of it, as can be seen from "Terence, this is stupid stuff" (page 536) and "Loveliest of Trees" (page 596).   LP

239. *Richard Hugo* **The Freaks at Spurgin Road Field** (page 813)

Moving from a present to isolated moments of memory, the poem is elusive in its reference. The present moment is a baseball game at which a "dim boy," "handicapped," claps not for what is happening in the game but because others in the audience are applauding. His mental handicap presumably makes it impossible for him really to understand what is happening on the field, so his applause is a social act expressing his wish to be a member of the group sitting in the stands.

This disjunction between the way the individual and the crowd perceive, and the boy's need to belong to what is normal, trigger the speaker's memories, since he seems to see in the boy parallels to himself. The first memory (4–5) is of a rueful day he spent in a railroad station, dirty and hung over, a type of social outcast, apparently living the life of a homeless vagrant who drinks cheap wine. The second (10–11) is of the speaker's shame and guilt at not offering to help an abused child but rather laughing at her screams. The memories then lead to pessimistic generalizations of self-blame—life's baseball games are "always close" and hopes are cut short, the speaker's life has been full of destruction, and he and the other "afflicted," like the "dim boy," have never found themselves "in unison" with the rest of the world. This is followed by his recalling a life of frustrated hopes, of "stammering pastures where the picnic should have worked" but never did.

It is a joyless expression of guilt, regret, and remorse, and the refrains of the *villanelle* contribute much to its tone. The first refrain ("The dim boy claps because the others clap") uncomfortably links the speaker to the boy's handicap, and the second ("Isn't it wrong, the way the mind moves back") expresses a sense of the injustice of having to remember a lifetime of incidents that make the speaker feel his handicaps.

The second refrain, though phrased as a question, is a statement that requests the hearer's agreement. The only true question is in line 8, a central issue: is there justice or fairness in a life where some are physically handicapped and others are not? Or to put it in the terms of the incidents in the poem, which is the true handicap— that of the boy who is unaware of what he is cheering about, or that of the man who laughed at a "girl beaten to scream"?

The poet's use of the villanelle as a poetic form is discussed briefly on page 234 of this manual.   TRA

240.   *Randall Jarrell*   **The Death of the Ball Turret Gunner** (page 813)

The poem captures both the terror and the ironic humor of its subject in the phrase "washed me out," which takes literally the euphemism for the failure to qualify for military duty. Rather than failing to measure up to training standards, the speaker has been so mutilated that his body must be flushed from his turret by a water hose.

The poem refers explicitly to the U.S. Army Air Corps in World War II. The B-17 "Flying Fortress" bombers had a gunner's glass turret on the belly of the fuselage, and airmen wore fur-lined leather jackets; anti-aircraft shells were called "flak" as an acronym for the German word "Fliegerabwehrkanone," though the shorter word sounds like an onomatopoetic imitation of the noise of the explosion; and the bombers were attacked by squadrons of fighter planes.

The first three lines of the poem abound with musical devices, chiefly alliteration (*sleep-State, loosed-life, feel-fur-froze*) and assonance (*mother's-hunched, fell-belly-wet, sleep-dream*). These culminate in the internal rime *black flak,* whose flat *a* and harsh *k* sharply bring to a halt such devices. After this rime, the only musical device is the concluding and horrifying rime *froze-hose*. This pattern of sounds reinforces the irony of the poem's conclusion.

The metaphors of the first two lines create a parallel between the position of the unborn child in his mother's womb and the man's position in the "belly" of the bomber. The movement from one to the other is ominously referred to as falling, and the animal processes of generation and birth are obliquely implied in "my wet fur." The speaker seems to pass directly from the moment of birth to his place in the gun turret, and his existence is governed by the dreams of his mother (for her child's success, happiness, and safety) and the subsequent dream of the "State" (for its own safety and its national ideals). These dreams are both shattered when, flying above 30,000 feet, he is shocked by the shells of anti-aircraft guns to the opposite kind of dream, the nightmare of attacking fighter planes. He awakens from idealistic dreams to discover that reality is a nightmare, but his wakefulness lasts only a moment.   TRA

241.   *Ben Jonson*   **Song: To Celia** (page 814)

A courting song of desire, praise, and flattery, this lyric both understates and overstates. In the first stanza, it understates the speaker's desire—he "only" wants a look, or a kiss—and it overstates the effect of such attention: in exchange for a kind look, he will offer a pledge; he would give up his desire for divine blessing if she would favor him. This stanza develops a symbol comparing the woman's kindness and attention to wine that would serve for a pledge (of love) and be sweeter than "Jove's nectar." In the comparisons, her "wine" and "nectar" surpass earthly and heavenly varieties, symbolizing the effect on him if she were to grant his desire.

The second stanza turns from desire to overstated flattery. The speaker's only purpose in sending her "a rosy wreath" (so he claims) was her magical charm to preserve its beauty, but she graciously transformed it into an immortal reminder of herself merely by breathing on it, and returned it to him.   TRA

242.   *John Keats*   **La Belle Dame sans Merci** (page 814)

Vocabulary: *sedge* (3), *haggard* (6), *meads* (13), *zone* (18), *manna* (26), *grot* (29), *thrall* (40), *starved* (41), *gloam* (41).

Even with full explication, this literary ballad retains its air of melancholy mystery, because the meaning of the encounter between the knight and the faery lady is never made explicit. This sense of an unresolved riddle is characteristic of many folk ballads, and it may be that Keats was after no more in the poem than a narration of fairyland and dream omens. When the knight concludes "this is why I sojourn here," the reader might very well reiterate the narrator's opening question, for the events reported by the knight don't seem to account for his despair, his physical debility and suffering, which are what the narrator has asked about.

The three opening stanzas ask the question—"what can ail thee?"—and describe the landscape and the knight. Both are incongruous, the speaker reports: knights should be hearty, purposeful, strong, not pale and feverish; they should be in quest of adventure, not "loitering" beside the dried marsh grass at a lakeside; it is early winter, and the natural creatures have withdrawn either to more congenial climates or to their stored-up winter hoards. This is no place for a knight, nor despite his armor does this man seem heroic.

The tale of the knight's encounter with the faery connects her with the fullness of nature: like an animal, light-footed and wild-eyed, she is met in a meadow, and the knight bedecks her with nature's flowers, and as if rescuing a lost maiden sets her on his horse, rapt with her beauty and her song. (But lines 19–20 ambiguously report her initial response to him: does "as" mean "while," or does it mean "as if"?) Like a goddess of nature, the lady repays his adoration with nature's plenty, and speaks to him an unknown language; surely, he supposes, she is saying she loves him. Strangely, once she has taken him to her cave, her "sweet moan" becomes weeping and sighing, and he must tame her by kissing her "wild wild eyes"; again, as if in repayment, she lulls him to sleep, but that sleep turns to nightmare with a dream that began in the cave and continues to be repeated here on the "cold hill side" where he awakens and the narrator finds him. The dream is apparently of his precursors, vigorous kings, princes and knights, now in the paleness of death as he will be, warning him that he has been enslaved by "La Belle Dame sans Merci."

Obviously, what a reader wants to know is "who *is* this beautiful woman without pity, and why has she done this to the man?" Does what happened to the knight have any relevance to our lives? Does the poem do more than warn us against sexual indulgence? One plausible (but by no means the only or inevitable) interpretation links the poem with the processes of nature and human attitudes toward them. The first three stanzas establish a sense of appropriate behavior as the seasons change, and of appropriate actions for people: in winter, squirrels, birds, even grasses retreat before the coldness and dryness, and wandering knights with their manly strength should be leading their active lives where they can perform their heroic deeds. But this man has fallen in love with the beauty and wildness of nature, and supposes that she loves him, and that he can tame her and live with her. What his horrid dream discloses is that this is illusion, and that by loving her he has become her thrall. His fate is the fate of all men—death—but he must also languish in despair because he has set his heart on what must always be changing.   TRA

243. *John Keats* **Ode on a Grecian Urn** (page 815)

Like other poems by Keats (e.g., "Ode to a Nightingale"), this ode explores the human desire to escape the inevitable effects of living in a temporal world, expressing this desire in response to the permanence of an art object. The poem is a meditation on the continuing beauty of a painted vase from classical Greece and what it seems to communicate to a man who knows his time on earth is brief by comparison. The structure is a dramatic enactment of the stages of the speaker's emotion and imaginative projection.

The poem opens with the speaker praising the urn's calm stillness and its freedom from the ravages of time. Punning on the word "still," Keats encapsulates his attitude: the urn is both silent and unmoving, and it still exists in time. Like the maidens painted on its surface, it has retained its virginal beauty as well as the freshness of a bride. In the paintings on the vase he sees a similarly tantalizing doubleness: they seem to have narrative meaning, displaying figures (human or divine) in a state of motion, yet as paintings they cannot move. He asks, in the last six lines of the first stanza, a sequence of increasingly insistent questions: to what narrative events do the paintings refer?

In the second stanza, however, he changes his attitude, presumably in the light of his not receiving answers to his questions. (In Keats's odes there is a skillful manipulation of psychological transitions that occur *between* the stanzas, where changes of thought and feeling are only implied by what precedes and follows the break.) The speaker moves from the excited forcefulness of his questions to a calm denial of the validity of answers. He now prefers *not* to hear the narrative facts that the urn will not reveal, and relishes instead the "unheard melodies" of feelings without explicit meanings. In lines 15–20, he turns to one of the scenes on the urn: a pastoral scene in which one youth makes music, a tune played on pipes, while another, a "bold lover," is about to capture a maiden he pursues. The speaker celebrates the fact that this amorous pursuit will never end—neither in "winning" the woman nor in losing her. Since they are permanently frozen in a painting, the youth will continue to exist in his state of anticipation just as her beauty will never fade.

The third stanza extends the speaker's delight in the image of time stopped at the height of anticipated bliss: the pictured trees will never be subject to seasonal change, the piper will never tire of playing, and the unfulfilled lover will be forever young and forever in the excitement of desire. This is contrasted with the state of "breathing human passion," which is subject not only to the debility of time but also, more emphatically, to the certainty that continued intensity of feeling would finally exhaust and sicken a mortal human being. Human passion such as the speaker is capable of feeling would ultimately become cloying or feverish, a fact previously implied in the excessiveness of the line the speaker devised to describe the permanence of bliss: "More happy love! more happy, happy love!"

Perhaps because he has exhausted his own capacity to respond to the scene of the piper and the lover, or perhaps because he recognizes that his ecstatic description has become "cloyed," or perhaps because his celebration of the lover's happiness has led him to think of the reality of the human condition—that is, for a number of psychological reasons implied between the stanzas—the speaker in stanza 4 turns to a second scene, on the other side of the urn. A priest ("mysterious," because he is an initiate in secret rituals, and because he is himself a mystery to the speaker) is leading a heifer bedecked for ritual sacrifice, and a crowd of worshippers follows. Like the end of the first stanza, the beginning of the fourth presents the speaker asking for information: who are the people? what or where is the altar? The priest's mystery extends beyond his religious rites to envelop the whole scene. Imaginatively stepping beyond the pictured scene, the speaker asks further: if these people are here, what has happened to the place they have come from? Line 38 is a turning point in the poem, for the speaker for the first time projects his imagination to a place not actually portrayed on the urn—he tries to create an image to answer his question, the image of an empty, abandoned town.

The psychological space between the fourth and fifth stanzas is the most striking in the poem. In his desire to penetrate beyond the pictured events, the speaker had created an image of desolation, an emotional contrast to the permanent anticipation of the lover or of the priest and worshippers. He discovers that such permanence as he has been praising implies other "still" moments of opposite emotional meanings. While some people are frozen in their state of desire (both lover and worshipper), he can imagine other scenes of permanent desolation.

In the fifth stanza the speaker recoils from what his imagination has produced. The urn is no longer a "Sylvan historian," a source of feeling and meaning—it is now, as he willfully distances himself from his projected feelings, a "shape" covered with "marble men and maidens," a "silent form." It has tantalized him into expressing his own desires for permanence (ideas that "thought" could not support, any more than thought can encompass "eternity"). He has been tempted in the course of his meditation to celebrate a pastoral world of idealized love and perfection, but he now recognizes that it is not the warm, sunny world he wanted, but a world gone cold with the realization that the stoppage of time necessary for its perfection implies the permanence not only of love's anticipation but also of loneliness and desolation.

The last five lines, with their famous simplifying tautology that "beauty is truth, truth beauty," comment ironically on the value of the urn as a source of wisdom or feeling. It will outlive the generations of humanity, and will retain its beauty while human beauty fades. Though its beauty makes it seem friendly, its philosophical advice can never satisify someone in quest of the meaning of change and transience. The urn can only say "is," not "will be," and thus though it will outlast the life of a human being, it cannot give any information that will make the passage through a lifetime any more meaningful. The urn beautifully exists beyond time (as the speaker had said in the first stanza), and cannot teach the meaning of living *in* time.   TRA

244.   *John Keats*   **Ode to a Nightingale** (page 817)

The thematic elements of this great poem are at the heart of Keats's work: poetry, human misery, time and change, and the power of sensations. The speaker, moved by the beauty of a nightingale singing, wishes he could join with the bird and escape "The weariness, the fever, and the fret" of human existence. At first he supposes that wine might be the vehicle, but then decides that the poetic imagination will serve him better; and no sooner has he said so than he feels himself transported on "viewless wings of Poesy" to be with the bird. Unable to see in the darkness, he can only guess by scent at the richness of nature, all of it partaking of the "Fast fading" intensity of growth and decay. Still listening in the dark, he recalls his repeated wish to escape the world through death, and that desire seems even more intense as he is ravished by the beauty of the bird's song.

But the nightingale is a bird of life, not of death—it is immortal in the sense that nightingales have flourished in ancient days, in biblical days, and even in legends and fairy tales. Yet through all the past and in fiction, the word "forlorn" has existed, as the speaker discovers to his chagrin when his imagination leads him to re-create an image out of fairy land. He discovers as well that though the imagination can cheat us out of our grasp of reality for a time, the power to think and understand will once again intrude. To use the word "forlorn" in imagining a fairy world is to invite the analytic mind to see that one is not in fact "with" the bird, but alone, a "sole self." Returning to one's own reality also leads to the recognition that the song of a nightingale is the creation of a living thing, and it too will fade, move away, and finally die away, "buried deep" in another valley.

The poem ends in a state of puzzlement: was the experience a "vision" (revealing a supernatural reality) or a "waking dream" of what can never be? Without the actual stimulus of the singing bird, without its music, the speaker is left to ask which is the true state of awareness—this present, grasping the literal reality of existence, or that moment of poetic transport?

This brief outline of the poem does not pretend to exhaust its richness, nor even to touch upon all its complex concerns. Many valuable comments have been written, of which the following are recommended. The most helpful single volume for study of this poem is *Twentieth-Century Interpretation of Keats's Odes*, ed. Jack Stillinger (Englewood Cliffs NJ: Prentice, 1968). Besides Stillinger's excellent introductory essay, the book contains the essays by Brooks and Fogle separately listed below and a note by Anthony Hecht. Additional useful references include Harold Bloom, *The Visionary Company* (New York: Anchor, 1961) 427–32; Cleanth Brooks and Robert Penn Warren, *Understanding Poetry*, 3rd ed. (New York: Holt, 1960) 44–47; Douglas Bush, *John Keats: His Life and Writing* (New York: Macmillan, 1966) 132–38; Morris Dickstein, *Keats and His Poetry* (Chicago: U of Chicago P, 1971) 205–21; Richard Harter Fogle, "Keats's Ode to a Nightingale," *PMLA* 68 (1953): 211–22; F. R. Leavis, *Revaluation* (New York: Norton, 1963) 244–52; H. M. McLuhan, "Aesthetic Pattern in Keats's Odes," *University of Toronto Quarterly* 12 (1943): 175–79; David Perkins, "The Ode to a Nightingale" in *Keats: A Collection of Critical Essays*, ed. Walter Jackson Bate (Englewood Cliffs NJ: Prentice, 1964) 103–11, repr. from David Perkins, *The Quest for Permanence* (Cambridge: Harvard UP, 1959) 244–57; Stuart M. Sperry, *Keats the Poet* (Princeton: Princeton UP, 1973) 262–67; and Helen Vendler, *The Odes of John Keats* (Cambridge: Harvard UP, 1983) 77–109.   TRA

245. *Galway Kinnell* **Blackberry Eating** (page 819)

In this brief poem Galway Kinnell uses gustatory imagery with gusto. The taste of those "fat, overripe, icy, black blackberries" is conveyed from the speaker's tongue to the reader's imagination so vividly as almost to make the reader's mouth water. The vivid gustatory image is compounded with visual imagery ("fat," "black") and tactile imagery ("icy"). There is tactile imagery also in "the stalks very prickly" where the repeated *k*-sound (which also picks up the *k*'s of "black" and "breakfast" in the preceding line) reinforces the prickliness. Then, since the speaker is a poet as well as a blackberry-eater, he notes that the "ripest" berries "fall almost unbidden to [his] tongue, / as words sometimes do." The poet slyly uses the word "tongue" in two senses here, first as an organ of taste and then as an articulator of speech. Notice that blackberries (like raspberries, dewberries, and loganberries; unlike blueberries, cherries, and grapes) are composed of many smaller parts (called drupelets). The words that he especially loves, like the blackberries, come in "fat" little lumps: they are "one-syllabled" but "many-lettered." The words *"strengths"* and *"squinched,"* both containing nine letters, are according to authorities the longest monosyllabic words in the language (*squinch*, to be found only in an unabridged dictionary, is a dialect word meaning "to twist"). But notice that the speaker demonstrates his love for such words not only by his two examples but by choosing three seven-lettered monosyllabic words ("squeeze," "squinch," and "splurge") for his verbs in the final clause of the poem.

The speaker's favorite word in this poem, however, is "black." It occurs three times by itself and four more times as part of "blackberries." We may profitably examine its three solo appearances. In its initial use, "black blackberries" (2), it may at first seem a redundant, but it is not, for unripe blackberries are green, and the speaker is emphasizing that these berries are ripe or overripe. The poet must have chuckled to himself when the next phrase fell "almost unbidden" to his tongue. He was so charmed that he invented a whimsical myth to go with it. The blackberry stalks were given their prickles as a penalty for knowing "the black art" (5) of blackberry-making! This myth obviously lacks the magnitude of the myth of Adam and Eve in the garden, which inspired Milton to write *Paradise Lost* (the prickles are a "penalty," not a punishment), but it is perfectly sized for the brief poem Kinnell puts it in, and is a delightful spin-off from the phrase "the black art." The black arts are ordinarily the arts practiced by witches and conjurors for unauthorized and wicked purposes, but in Kinnell's poem the phrase is stripped of all of its negative implications. The art of making blackberries is a black art only in that it produces black berries; the word is placed in a context where it means only good, not bad. Finally, in its last two lines, the poem gives us a "black language" of "blackberry-eating," thus completing the metaphorical comparison between blackberries and words—both of them good. The image of "black language" may summon up for the reader the image of black words printed on white paper; but in any form it calls up an experience of pleasure and delight.   LP

246. *Etheridge Knight* **The warden said to me** (page 819)

As an example of verbal irony, this poem requires the reader to recognize the distance between the speaker's expressed attitude and his real intention. The repeated parenthetical phrase "(innocently, I think)" has two distinct meanings. In line 2, it pretends to allow the possibility that the warden's bigotry is merely ignorant and therefore excusable; in line 6, it indicates that the speaker intends to seem obsequious and ignorant, to please the warden. These phrases are verbally ironic, since the speaker does not accept the warden's mock ignorance as a sufficient excuse for his bigotry, nor is the speaker sincerely innocent in his rejoinder.

The warden's purpose in asking the question is also verbal irony used in the service of sarcasm: he does not want to know *why* his black prisoners don't attempt to escape, but rather is taunting the black speaker with the charge that they are more stupid, obedient, and passive than white prisoners. It is that taunt which the speaker answers with stereotyped gesture and statement: "yes, sir, we cast our eyes down and scratch our heads when we have to answer hard questions, and we finally come up with the simple fact that you already know—there's no place for a black man in this world."

What the speaker means, of course, is that a society constructed on the lines approved by the warden, in which color defines attitude and ability, excludes *all* thoughtful and sensitive people. TRA

247. *Philip Larkin* **Aubade** (page 820)

While the irony in Richard Wilbur's title "A Late Aubade" (page 572) merely overturns a reader's expectation of a poignant dawn parting of lovers, Larkin's irony reaches deeper: his dawn song is not wistful about separating from a mistress, but terror stricken at the prospect of the inevitable parting from life itself.

Larkin does not make that life attractive, but tedious and mundane. It is a life of work, offices, and telephones, with only drink and "People" to relieve the boredom or the lurking fears of death. The emphasis is not on beauty or pleasure or love, all to be lost in the obliteration of death, but on the fear of nothingness. The images associated with life provide the only defense against the thoughts of death, and they are images of social connection, culminating in the last line: "Postmen like doctors go from house to house." All of us, that is, share in the disease of fearing death, and the cure comes in links with other people. But communication is a temporary cure, an alleviation of the *fear*, but certainly no defense against death itself or the knowledge of its inevitability.

The time of the poem, four o'clock in the predawn morning, is a time of total darkness and silence. Staring into "soundless dark" is like staring at death, for the two primary senses of hearing and sight have been lost. Deprived of physical sense, the speaker must "see" what his mind knows, "the total emptiness for ever, / The sure extinction."

Neither the rich, elaborate fabric of religion—now tattered and "moth-eaten"—nor the fallacious plausibility of the plainer fabrics of rationalism is sufficient to hide the naked fact of fearfulness; rich or plain, these are mere covers or garments, incapable of disguising the reality at such a time as this.

And "Courage is no good" at such times, because it cannot alter the fact the speaker is staring at. Since he defines life in its social connections, "to love or link," courage seems only a matter of social behavior that has value in the impressions one gives to other people. "It means not scaring others" with the horrifying truth that the speaker understands and faces. He does display another kind of courage, though—the courage to acknowledge to himself his fears and to look into the darkness with honesty.

The final stanza, in which the dawn slowly comes, restores the speaker's physical senses, and leads him to project the resumption of daylight activities. The terror subsides and the fact of "what we know," though it is as plain and as familiarly unremarkable as a piece of furniture, may be ignored in the workaday world. The knowledge that he has faced when alone can be put aside; the dilemma of knowing that "we can't escape" death and "Yet can't accept" it can be postponed another day.

The poem carries the additional richness of its verbal echoes of two well-known passages from Shakespeare, Hamlet's soliloquy beginning "To be, or not to be" (3.1.55–89) and the conclusion of Jaques's speech on the seven ages of man (*As You Like It*, 2.7.162–65). The allusions to Hamlet's speech occur in lines 8, 17, 18–19, and 30, and to Jaques's in lines 27–28. These allusions in effect reopen the questions raised in Hamlet's meditation, and in several other themes in that play—courage, friendship, even drink—as if Larkin's speaker were being forced to reexamine Hamlet's condition for himself. What he finds, in his modern (and more squalid) experience is a similar dilemma: although being alive is fraught with pain and misery, chiefly because of fear and loneliness, the alternative "not to be" is worse, and so like Hamlet he will have to live with his "indecision."

Because these allusions are only faintly signalled, by little more than a single word or phrase, Larkin is relying on a reader's thorough recall of the Hamlet soliloquy and of the whole play, and most students are not likely to make the connection for themselves. If the instructor wishes to use the poem for a further lesson in allusion, the class should probably be supplied in advance with copies of the Shakespeare passages, and asked to find the verbal echoes.   TRA

248. *Philip Levine* **The Fox** (page 821)

The speaker gives few clues to explain his identity with a fox. There is an ingrained "loathing for those on horseback . . . mounted ladies and their gentlemen" (13, 47), and a sense of being "the small creature menaced / by the many and larger" (30–31). But the poem leaves these emotional reactions unexplained, so the reader is put in the position of wondering whether the speaker is indeed "demented" (20).

What is clear is the speaker's total commitment to his antipathy toward the class represented by "ladies and gentlemen on horseback," as instinctive to him as is the enmity between fox and hunter. He luxuriates in the feeling that in a previous life as a fox, he was able to wreak his indignation on them in secretive acts of impudence, taking glee in his insults, and exulting in an animal beauty and grace that suits "a creature who must proclaim / not ever ever ever" (45–46) to his human foes.

The appeal of the poem is in part its strangeness, its open-ended symbolism, which invites an interpretation without surrendering its secret center. The fox is something within us that is wild, resentful, uncontrollably repulsed by class pretensions, a natural impulsiveness totally at odds with social artifice. TRA

249. *Robert Lowell* Watchmaker God (page 822)

This blank verse sonnet wryly takes up the dilemma presented by scientific rationalism: a mechanistic universe created by a "tinker," a "watchmaker," that can be examined in "the cold light of science," contrasted to our passionate desire to feel that a loving God cares for us and has created a heaven as our destiny. It is a dilemma of cold and hot, reminding the reader of two Frost poems, "Design" (page 686) and "Fire and Ice" (page 610). Lowell's focus here is on the question of personal immortality, which science and all human experience reject as being contrary to fact. This is posed against the perception that "life is both the fire and fuel," that while we are consumed in the process of living, it is that process that produces our vital heat and leads us to desire its prolongation.

Passionate desire, on the one hand, but "pale romance" on the other. The last five lines sardonically imply that a mechanistic universe satisfies neither man nor God. God "loved to tinker" (an allusion to Donne's "Batter my heart, three-personed God," page 629?), but that kind of love leaves him lonely and distant, and leaves his creature unsatisfied. TRA

250. *George MacBeth* Bedtime Story (page 823)

"Bedtime Story" is science fiction in poetic form. The speaker is a parent (mother or father) telling a "bedtime story" to a child of its species; but this story is supposed to be true—a chapter from history (19), not a "fairy tale." It concerns the accidental killing of the last man, "the penultimate primate" (the ultimate primate being the monkey or ape that the man was stalking), the extinction of the human race as a species. The time of the telling of this story is, from our point of view, in a far far distant future; and the time of the incident which it concerns is, from our point of view, still a distant future; but from the teller's point of view it is in a remote past—not "Once upon a time," but "Long long ago when the world was a wild place. . . ."

The speaker is a huge ant, evolved in size and intelligence from presently existing species. Because of the Queen and the sting, students may suggest a bee. But ants too have queens and stings, and these insects "march" rather than fly through the forest; they are organized in a military fashion (in "brigades"); they forage for greenfly (a kind of aphid that some ants keep like cows and "milk"); and their jaws cut through bark. Ants, moreover, have developed a high degree of social organization and cooperation and are thought by many to be the nearest competitors to man in the struggle for existence. In the poem they have become the dominant species, are larger than men, have developed a language and a recorded history, and have an ethical sense superior to man's.

Although this "bedtime story" tells how the last man was inadvertently killed by a soldier ant, the point of the poem is that man has destroyed himself—or, since the poem is set in the future, may destroy himself. Two facts are stated about man: that he exterminates other species of animals "for pleasure," and that he kills his own kind in wars that "extinguished the cities." The poem is thus an indictment of man's passion for killing and a prediction that unless he acquires the power to govern himself by peaceable methods and becomes as "humane" to other species as the ants in the poem, he will be replaced by another form of life.

The conclusion of the poem links the fate of man with that of the dodo. Dodos are a presently extinct species with a reputation for foolishness. "Dumb as a dodo" is a familiar expression.

The poem is written in dactylic lines of four feet in the first three lines of each stanza and two feet in the last. The phrasing and run-on lines make it difficult to read trippingly, however, and it should not be read so. LP

251. *Katharyn Howd Machan* Leda's Sister and the Geese (page 824)

For the mythological background, see the commentary on Yeats's "Leda and the Swan" (page 166 of this manual). Then add the following: Leda, wife of the King of Sparta, was the mother of Helen, Castor and Pollux (the famous twin brothers), and Clytemnestra, all four conceived on the same day. The rape by Zeus in the form of a swan produced Helen and Pollux; the other two were begot by Leda's lawful husband. (Helen grew up to be, in the eyes of many, the most beautiful woman in the world. Over her the Trojan War was fought.)

The humor of the poem derives essentially from two sources: first, from its point of view. The story of Leda's rape by Zeus has been told many times, but not to my knowledge by a disgruntled sister. The speaker clearly has suffered deeply from "sibling rivalry," as it is now called. She is jealous of Leda's good luck and resentful of the additional chores her sister's pregnancy will throw upon *her*.

Second, the humor of the poem arises from the disparity between the ancient story and the contemporary, colloquial idioms that the sister uses in telling it. We are amused when she says "Hera forbid" rather than "God forbid" or wishes the geese she feeds (as one of her "chores") "to Hades" rather than "to Hell." Slangy idioms such as "stuck at home," the "kid," and "ratty" golden hair clash with the dignity of language we have come to expect in a mythological tale.

The quoted words " 'sore afraid' " (10) add a further tonal contrast. They are from Luke 2.9, where the shepherds are told of the birth of Jesus: "And, lo, the angel of the Lord came upon them, and the glory of the Lord shone round about them: and they were sore afraid." The sister's comment on " 'Sore' " points up the contrast and also adds some vulgar humor to the poem. LP

252. *Naomi Long Madgett* **Offspring** (page 825)

The central metaphor extends and vivifies the adage "As the twig is bent, so grows the tree" (a commonplace derived from Alexander Pope: " 'Tis education forms the common mind: / Just as the twig is bent the tree's inclined," *Moral Essay I*, line 149). The mother sees herself as trunk, roots, and branches, firmly based and striving upward in a natural process. She sees her daughter as a duplicate, but stronger, version of herself, potentially able to reach into a higher atmosphere that the mother had only dreamed of. In the first two sections, the poem presents the mother's attempt to "bend" her offspring in that upward direction.

What she learns, and learns to admire, is that her efforts to direct her daughter's life have failed. The daughter walks an "unfamiliar street" (different from the familial one her mother had planned), but to her own greater gain: she is not "trunk . . . roots / . . . branches," but "feet" and "smiling" face, not an expression in cliché of her mother's hopes but an individual human being. The world the daughter has moved into is not ideal—she may be free and individual, but that sky which had defined the mother's aspirations is "threatening," and the young woman has become "unpliable." To strike out into the unknown and define one's own goals presents risks that tradition might avoid, but individuality is prized over unimaginative conformity, even by a mother who feels the separation from her child. TRA

253. *Cleopatra Mathis* **Getting Out** (page 826)

The most striking detail of this failed marriage is "our matching eyes and hair," for it establishes the identical nature of the two people, as well as the sort of immaturity that would lead a wife and husband to share a matching hairstyle. But if they are such a "match," what caused their marriage to fail? The poem seems to suggest that it was their very closeness, the resemblance they had to one another. With one exception, the statements in the first two stanzas are first-person plural, relating that the stages in the break-up were mutually achieved: "we hardly slept," "we gave up; escaped," "we paced," "we cried," and then the final sentence, "We held on tight, and let go." The exception is in lines 10–12, when the husband "tried / to pack up and go"—but failed.

The extended metaphor in the poem, begun in the title, reinforces the idea of mutuality, for they together were "like inmates" wanting to escape, "Finally locked into" blaming each other as the last mutual act before the divorce. Their marriage was a prison, increasingly more restricted and confining to them both, until—*finally*—they began to find things to accuse each other of. This looks ironic, that they shared the increasing sense of imprisonment as if they together had been locked up by someone else, until they finished with what we would expect at the beginning of the process, turning against each other.

The poem embodies in the person of the lawyer the reader's proper response: bewilderment. Clearly from her tone, the speaker still loves her former husband, and his reassuring annual message implies that he cares for her. How can so much love cause a divorce? Yet it can. The concluding image expresses best the tone: love and regret. TRA

254. *Phyllis McGinley* Trinity Place (page 826)

Trinity Place in lower Manhattan is the western boundary of Trinity Churchyard, the cemetery surrounding one of the oldest churches in the city, situated at the corner of Broadway and Wall Street in the very center of the financial district. Thus the title and the locale disclose the ironic situation of the men who occupy the park benches. This contrast between prosperity and destitution is intensified by the fact that the poem was published in 1937, at the depths of the Great Depression.

In the refrain-like sentence in the last lines of each stanza, this sharply observed poem contrasts the "lean . . . idle . . . hungry" men listlessly passing their days on park benches with the pigeons that forage in the park. The chief figure in the poem is personification, as the pigeons are given the attributes of "industrious" and "prosperous" men—presumably the very sort of men these once were, before the economic crash led them to their sorry fate. In the poem, pigeons and bankers have exchanged roles.

The personification extends to the attitudes of the pigeons as they judge themselves and the men, and touches of dramatic irony are directed at them: they are "pompous," smug, "plump," and "sleek," too self-satisfied to be accepted as disinterested judges; incongruously, their "dignified search of their proper, their daily bread" (10) is conducted in a "waddle." As stand-ins for the men, the pigeons thus display characteristics that may have contributed to their financial collapse. Reality also provides some irony, as we realize that what the pigeons are feeding upon is most probably refuse, their "daily bread" the discarded and dirty trash that the men would not eat no matter how "lean" and "hungry" they are.

The anapestic pentameter of the poem is suitably overdone, supporting the pomposity of the pigeons and their waddling, particularly in the high incidence of extrametrical syllables that end a majority of the lines. One might say, impressionistically, that this poem seems to peck and waddle with the strutting awkwardness of a pigeon. TRA

255. *Alice Meynell* **Summer in England, 1914** (page 827)

Some students will need to be told that World War I broke out in the summer of 1914; Britain entered the war in August. Meynell's poem exploits the irony of such a catastrophe occurring just as a particularly clear and fruitful summer seemed to be blessing the country with natural abundance and fresh beauty. Nature, with loving caresses and strokes, seemed to bode only happiness, as sunlight bathed the capital in clarity and beauty, while beautiful moonlight illuminated the grain fields and orchards. As the allusion in line 5 states, even a street associated with death and grief—London's Wimpole Street, the home of Tennyson's dead friend Arthur Hallam, which had moved the poet to the despair expressed in the poem to which Meynell alludes—even such a famous example of ugliness was burnished into beauty by that summer's light.

Then, as the third stanza shockingly reports, while this ''rose'' of England blossomed in perfection, on the Continent ''armies died convulsed,'' and while the sun ''Softly'' shone at home, the indistinguishable corpses ''heaped the plain'' in Europe. In the fourth stanza, the irony is compacted—three lines given to the natural fecundity of summer, then three to its opposite, the human atrocity of war. The image of ''men shot through the eyes'' focuses on the organ of sight that had perceived and created the happy imagery of the peacetime summer. The truncated twenty-third line reinforces the emotional power of the concluding apostrophe in which the natural power that had blessed the nation, ''Love,'' is asked to avert its face from the race of men who have brought on such destruction. TRA

256. *Josephine Miles* **Oedipus** (page 827)

The speaker might be taken for a modern-day representative of the Chorus in Sophocles's tragedy. As one of ''The gang'' (colloquial, informal), the speaker wants to do the right thing by giving the former king a going-away present, but since ''he had everything,'' the members of ''the gang'' are stymied about what would be an appropriate gift. The gift they eventually give, a ''traveling case,'' fitted perhaps with such toilet articles as brush, comb, and nail clippers, sounds sensible enough, and it seems an even more thoughtful choice since it's what they would ''have liked to receive.''

What the poem leaves out, of course, and what allusion supplies, is the majestic pity and terror of the tragedy, as the self-mutilated, blind king, the incestuous patricide, banished to perpetual exile, is treated as an ordinary mortal going on a little trip. Understatement here creates dramatic irony, as ''The gang,'' like Sophocles's Chorus, is unable to grasp the immense dimensions of the tragedy. (There might be a wry echo of Sophoclean irony in the trite statement that Oedipus was a man who ''had everything,'' though it seems here more comic than tragic, since the speaker is trying to figure out what further *thing* he could want.) TRA

This is another example of Moore's use of rimed syllabic verse (compare "Nevertheless," page 714). The stanza consists of lines containing the following number of syllables: 6, 6, 7, 9, 5, 10, 7, 6, 6; they rime *axaxxxxbb* (though there are some unpatterned rimes of the *x* lines). If one wanted to "visualize" the stanzaic form, its symmetrical shape would be more obvious had the poet indented the first two lines but not the third, and indented the fifth line deeply: the stanza would be seen to broaden outward to its long fourth line, then constrict tightly, and after the fifth line to mirror its first half.

The point is that Moore has used a strict but arbitrary form of rimed syllabics, while apparently allowing the rhetorical and grammatical structure to flow freely. But that is not really how the structure works. The first stanza, with its sequence of abstract questions that are based on its one indicative statement ("All are / naked, none is safe"), is the most freely structured, even running on into the second stanza. Then once the poem begins to answer its questions, both of the stanzas offer a figurative example to support their abstract statements, and both of them move to closure in their final couplets.

Stanza 2 compares the best of mankind to "the sea in a chasm" in continuous rising and falling as waves that are driven in rise up the walls that "imprison" them, fall back, and then rise again. "Mortality" is metaphorically a prison, and to "accede" to its reality gives the soul strength.

Stanza 3 extols a person "who strongly feels," comparing him to a personified caged bird who gains strength from his own singing. The bird defines the theme (and answers the questions of the opening stanza): mere "satisfaction is a lowly / thing," but those (a person, the sea, a bird) who rise up and gain strength from exerting themselves within their limits will experience pure joy. The concluding paradox (echoing the paradoxical couplet of stanza 2)—mortality is eternity—may be resolved by seeing that "eternity" is figurative. A life lived to its fullest capacity will seem to be eternity enough to those who feel strongly.   TRA

258. *Howard Nemerov* **The Amateurs of Heaven** (page 828)

Amateur denotes a person who is unskilled or inexperienced at some particular activity, as well as one who is a lover or devotee; both denotations are functioning in this poem. The two lovers who lie down in a meadow to watch and wonder at the stars above them are clearly not *professionals* as astronomers, nor as investigators of philosophical and anthropological meanings. In part their lack of skill is imparted by such language as "idiot majesty" (5) and "other stuff that dangled" (18), phrases that suggest a lack of serious interest.

But they are "lovers" in the other sense of the word: they are devoted—to each other, and to sharing experiences. In another sense of "heaven," they are devoted to the bliss of their relationship.

As they lie on the ground, they identify the constellations that circle the North Star and express wonder at such phenomena as the darkness of night that allows us to see starlight, and at the "ancestral eyes and the dark mind" (15) of those primitive people who imagined "farm / And forest things and even kitchen things" (10–11) pictured in the star patterns.

The "humbling" of the stars to human "things" imposes our imaginative will on the majestic (but "idiot"—meaningless) splendor of the heavens. Does it make a difference that those prehistoric "amateurs" devised that kind of imaginative link between their lives and the stars? Was that an act of love and devotion, or an act of ignorant self-reference? And was that act somehow parallel to what these two lovers are doing as they lie there and watch the stars?

The lovers may reach for self-knowledge in lines 19–20, though it is not clear whether they do ask if wondering about the stars involves an act of self-examination, or if it is only the speaker who makes that connection. In any case, as they rise—too quickly, since they are made dizzy by the blood rushing from their heads—it is the speaker who evaluates their experience: "the spell of earth had moved them so, / Hallucinating that the heavens moved" (23–24). The "movement" of the stars in the heavens is illusion, the result of the earth's motion (as that professional astronomer Galileo determined, to his peril). The "spell" that these lovers are under is related both to the observation of the heavens, and to their mutual love. Although they are limited in their perspective to this planet (and these lovers may also be limited by the inability to probe deeply into questions), for the human being, that perspective can include both outward and inward vision.   TRA

---

259.   *Howard Nemerov*   **Grace to Be Said at the Supermarket** (page 829)

Superficially the butt of Nemerov's satire seems to be the application of technology to the presentation of food, the complaint of a man who is disturbed by standardized, hygienic market methods. But this commonplace of modern social critics is given a sharper edge when the speaker pretends to be praying not to technology, but to geometry. His target is more ancient and more universal, the very source of these modern effects: our intellectualizing tendencies that we express not merely in the uniform packaging of meats but in the packaging of ideas in language.

The diction of this seriously witty, ironic poem is highly varied, ranging from plain colloquialism to scientific and mathematical terms, from the language of religion to that of literary criticism. Such wide linguistic reference punctures the pretensions of all these mis-users of language: advertisers ("streamlined . . . for greater speed," "like a philosopher should"), casual conversationalists ("if you want to put it that way," "maybe"), literary critics ("aesthetic distance," "significant form"), philosophers ("the greatest good"), preachers and theologians ("our birthright," "the mystical body"), and—the metaphorical center of the poem—mathematicians ("cubes," "cylinder," "ellipsoid," and the rest).

All of these display what Nemerov regards as a linguistic replacement of the honest, natural expression of human nature with inflated—or deflated—terminology. The subject of the poem is the human being as a carnivore, and the variety of dodges we employ to avoid acknowledging the fact. Line 15 represents the only honest expression of it: both we and the "brutes" we consume lead "bulging and blood-swollen lives," though we would prefer to think and speak otherwise. TRA

260. *Sharon Olds* **The Victims** (page 830)

The title becomes ambiguous in its reference as the poem proceeds. At the outset it clearly refers to the mother and all "her / kids" (among them, the speaker) who for years "took it" from the father until she "kicked [him] out." But the sequence of losses suffered by the husband, which fill his ex-wife and children with glee, gradually transform him into a victim, both of their hatred and vengefulness, and of his business circumstances. The "bums in doorways" constitute yet another set of victims, arousing the pity of the speaker and an implicit revaluation of her father as victimizer. And we may see the speaker herself as the final victim—of her mother who taught her to hate and "take it" until revenge became possible.

This last victimization expresses the central theme of the poem, which recalls that of Blake's "A Poison Tree" (page 758). The sequence of abuse, acceptance, revenge, and spiteful pleasure at the father's suffering now haunts the speaker as she observes other men whose lives may have been blighted in similar ways. She comes, at the end, to question the implications of the slangy phrase with which the poem opens: if the family "took it" (referring to some sort of abuse or perceived affront), then the father must have "given it"—but what was he giving? What kinds of giving and taking are fundamentally at stake here? The bums who now have "nothing / left" but their pitiable destitution arouse these questions. What was the family taking from the father—his abuse, or his humanity, or both?

The language of the first ten lines is casual, colloquial, and realistic. The question that begins in line 11 introduces the first figures—the metaphors of dark suits hanging like "carcasses" and of the toes of shoes like noses "with their large pores" (like an alcoholic's nose?). These grotesque comparisons have the effect of representing the distorting hatreds of the speaker. The second set of figures arouses disgust and pity, implying a changed perception on the part of the speaker. The description of the bums, their bodies metaphorically transmuted into "white / slugs," their torn suits so filthy that they appear to be constructed from "compressed silt," their hands like the flippers of marine mammals, and in particular their eyes paradoxically looking like fire underwater, moves the speaker to begin "wondering" about men so transformed and abused, and about their families and associates who might share the responsibility for their dehumanization. TRA

261. *Mary Oliver* **Through Ruddy Orchards** (page 830)

The poem focuses on an autumnal phenomenon: most ripe fruit (when not picked by us) will naturally fall to earth, as part of the reseeding process, but some few specimens will hang on boughs until frost and late autumn winds blow them down.

The first sort are celebrated for their brightness and "health" ("ruddy" connotes health and freshness) as compounded both of the earth from which they drew nourishment and the sun which ripened them "With flavors of the light." Their falling is evidence of the sweet beneficence of the natural process.

The apples that fail to fall, on the other hand, will wilt, lose their bright luster, wrinkle, and turn brown and black, as they hang uselessly. The second paragraph connotes wastefulness and a distortion of the process. The phrase "wry and wrinkled" captures the feeling well—although it may be taken literally, it suggests a personification of apples with twisted, wrinkled faces.

The third paragraph then tells of their fate: once the deep wind strikes these gnarled specimens, they too will fall, either to be "cracked on rocks and bruised to brown"—or to be hidden away in the tall grass, keeping their rich sweetness in secrecy. But at the last, *all* will come down and return back to the earth.

Formally the poem is written in iambics, with little pattern except that each paragraph begins with pentameter lines and ends with shorter (either trimeter or tetrameter) lines. The rimes are random, but when they occur they are usually exact or even identical. The only pattern of rimes also occurs at the ends of the paragraphs, where the last three lines rime *axa*, joining with the shortening of lines at those points to bring the paragraphs to closure. The poem contains varieties of sound effects that reinforce its emotional tone, from euphonious to cacophonous. **TRA**

262. *Simon J. Ortiz* **Speaking** (page 831)

The conclusion is an ironic reversal of the speaker's assumptions and expectations. The father thinks that as the possessor of language, he must interpret and introduce his son to the natural world and its eons of time passed. It is revealed to him that the "infant words" (presumably not actually words) murmured by the boy, and particularly the "small laughter" of delight that "bubbles from him" are more expressive than his learned language. Nature listens to the infant, they being more closely akin than the man and "the millions of years."

The poem gives vitality to a Romantic assumption that the intuitive "wise child" is closer to nature than the adult with his defining, discriminating intellect. The ironies (dramatic in the first stanza, situational in the second) and the underlying condescension of the father that leads to his delighted surprise at the end bring life to the idea.

The poem is structured as two parallel moments linked by rhetorical repetition, and in form consists of two ten-line free verse stanzas. **TRA**

263. *Grace Paley* **The Sad Children's Song** (page 831)

What at first seems a grown children's complaint about their mother's sloppy housekeeping and careless disregard of her appearance becomes a complaint about the failed stewardship of those who have ruled the planet. The mother is thus a symbol for what has gone wrong in world politics and economics in the last half of the twentieth century. The rivalry of nations has led to "bombs all over the place," while unrestrained exploitation of the ecology has destroyed the sources of fresh water and poisoned fields with pesticides and other chemical agents. The three concluding questions may be paraphrased: why did your generation create such danger and destruction for us to inherit? With the planet in such a condition, where can mankind find safety and happiness? What kind of explanation can we offer to the helpless ones who will have to live in this world?

The bluntness and naivete of the statements, the neglect of punctuation, and the triad of opening refrain lines in each stanza help to create the childlike tone of this song. Who but a child would say to its mother "Your face is a wreck" or "Why did you let yourself go"? As far as that is concerned, who but a child would be so ready to find fault and to magnify that fault so universally, making credible the symbolic representation of a single parent as the cause of all the world's problems? TRA

264. *Linda Pastan* **The Hat Lady** (page 832)

The "Hat Lady" appears in line 11 as a realistic milliner whose visit is signalled by the coming of spring, when the trees themselves seem to put on their spring-hat finery as a "turban of leaves." The milliner keeps her pins handy, some pressed between her lips, some stuck in her sleeves, reminding the speaker of portraits of the martyred Saint Sebastian shot full of arrows.

The concluding stanza transforms the literal milliner into the mother's guide into immortality; this time her advent is signalled by the mother's wearing a towel as a turban to cover her chemically induced baldness, in contrast to the flourishing of natural growth in the leaf-turbans of springtime.

The first stanza catalogues the headgear of the men the speaker remembers from childhood, and the third lists some of the memorable hats worn by her mother. By repetition, hats come to symbolize identity (making the hatlessness of the father an odd exception—has he no remembered identity, or did his identity transcend both adornment and seasonal fashion?). The hats of the first stanza have connotative power from their links with place, usage, and etymological origin: soft felt "homburgs" are named for the town of their origin in Germany; stiff, narrow-brimmed "derbies" are named for a nineteenth-century English earl who established the Derby races outside London; Fred Astaire's "high black silk" hat was a trademark of his suave, debonair grace, established particularly by his film *Top Hat* (1935); and a "yarmulke," the Judaic ritual skullcap, is etymologically Turkish in origin. The turban, too, has exotic origins, a word from the Persian used to name the headgear worn by Muslims and Hindus, especially Sikh Hindus whose religion requires their wearing.

The poem rests upon these associations and others to establish hats as identifying parts of personality, so that the fantastic reappearance of the Hat Lady at the end seems a natural extension of meaning: as the speaker's mother was formerly associated with spring, trees, birds, fruits, and the glamour of Myrna Loy, so at the end she moves in her towel-turban to rejoin the dead family members who have gone before. There, Death gives her a familiar wink of greeting, and as a final touch tips his cap at her with a hat-gesture of respect.

The tone of this poem is elusive: there is nostalgia and amusement attached to the memories, whimsy in the association of the milliner with Saint Sebastian, and detachment in the concluding fantasy that returns to the gentle wit and light tone of the opening stanza. TRA

265. *Sylvia Plath* **Spinster** (page 833)

The "plot" of this narrative poem involves a "particular girl"—meaning both "specific" and "fastidious"—who is "afflicted" by the random disorder of a "burgeoning" spring, feels a nostalgia for the exactness and precision of winter's austerity, and chooses to withdraw from both springtime and love into spinsterhood.

The poem establishes two contrasting sets of values through the symbols of spring and winter. To use the diction of the poem, spring is irregular, tumultuous, unbalanced, uneven, rank, slovenly, unruly, vulgar, treasonous, giddy, insane, mutinous. Winter is scrupulous, austere, orderly, disciplined, exact. Connotatively, the terms used for spring are negative, those for winter are positive—but we must look behind the language to determine the poem's central purpose, for it displays an ambivalence that must be taken into account. To the "particular girl," whose sense of threat and danger results in a series of overstatements, all the negative terms seem appropriate; to the poet, the matter is not so simple—as the pejorative title might lead us to see.

What develops is a portrait of a woman "who protests too much," whose rejection of all that disorder brought on by April betrays an unacknowledged desire and fascination. The point is made clearest at the end, where the link between springtime and a man's dangerous desire is brought into final focus. The second stanza had shown him as part of the slovenliness of spring; lines 28–30 transform him and his love into a violent threat—a man trying to break through her "barricade" by means of "curse, fist, threat"—or, what she really fears most, "love." To see love only as the driving force felt by men is to be limited by more than a "frosty discipline." The poem suggests that *love*, if she could allow herself to feel it, might lead her to new perceptions and a fuller life. TRA

266. *Sir Walter Ralegh* **What is our life?** (page 834)

This brief poem is based on a sixteenth-century commonplace comparing a human life to the performance of a role on stage. Famous examples include Jaques's set-piece beginning "All the world's a stage" (*As You Like It*, 2.7) and the passage quoted from *Macbeth* on page 643.

Ralegh's extended metaphor might properly be called a very brief allegory, since the comparison is extended by defining various details of a human career, from pre-natal to post mortem. A few more words might be glossed, considering their usage in the Renaissance: "passion" (1) denoted not just high emotion, but suffering and agony; it also denoted a poem or literary work marked by deep feeling; "latest" (9) means "last"; and "jest" (10) carries a range of relevant denotations, from "joke" to tale of adventure to dramatic pageant or masque.

These more resonant (and now archaic) meanings sharpen the allegory, for they make explicit the more general terms that we would recognize. The *OED* even offers one definition of "jest" that appears to be derived from the last line: "a thing that is not serious or earnest." TRA

---

267. *John Crowe Ransom* **Bells for John Whiteside's Daughter** (page 834)

A child's death is a dangerous subject for a poet. It invites sentimentality. Though the occasion is one for genuine grief, there is always a temptation to "hoke" it up a bit, to sweeten it, to picture the child as a little angel and to soften the harsher contours.

In this poem, the speaker is an adult attending the funeral of a dead child. He is specifically a friend and neighbor of the child's father, named in the title. This title has a double meaning. The "Bells" refer to the church bells that ring for the funeral in the final stanza; they also suggest that the poem itself is a tribute, a chiming of rimes, composed in the dead girl's memory.

The poet-speaker finds it difficult to believe that the child he knew is dead. She was so rapid in her movements, so fleet of foot, so loud and boisterous in her play, that her stillness now is almost beyond belief. Rather than pretend that she is merely playing, however, he speaks of her as being in a "brown study" (a state of somber, abstracted brooding). But such a state is so uncharacteristic of the child that it "Astonishes" the speaker and the other adults gathered for her funeral.

The child in this poem is clearly not a "little rose" but a real child—active, noisy, and often vexatious in her play. Indeed, her games are metaphorically described as "wars," whose clamor reached the adults in their "high window," and whose tyrannies disturbed the geese whom she woke from their "noon apple-dreams" and harried into the pond. The term "little / Lady" applied to her is ironical rather than sentimental in intention and effect (her "rod" is both scepter and prod). The one long sentence comprising the three central stanzas has a freshness of imagery and imagination, and gives us a vivid impression of the child at her play. The geese—lazy, sleepy, proud—serve both as victims of the child's play and as a character-contrast to the child herself; yet the poet's whimsy of having them speak "in goose" is appropriate to the kind of imaginative play that a child might engage in.

In the last stanza, however, the speaker is brought back to the present reality. The bells ring for the funeral service, and the adults who have been "sternly stopped" by the child's death are "vexed at her brown study, / Lying so primly propped." If they had been sometimes "vexed" by her play in life, they are more "vexed" to see her here, lying so "prim" (who was never prim in life), "propped" rigidly in her coffin (who had such "speed" in her body and such a "tireless heart" in life). "Vexed" is an inspired word here; while pointing up ironical contrasts, it expresses genuine grief through understatement. For additional comment on Ransom's poem, see Robert Heilman, in *The Pacific Spectator* 5 (1951): 458–60; Thornton H. Parsons, *John Crowe Ransom* (New York: Twayne, 1969) 53–55; and Robert Penn Warren, "Pure and Impure Poetry," *Kenyon Review* 5 (1943): 237–40. LP

268. *Ishmael Reed* **Turning Pro** (page 835)

At first glance this poem seems a literal description of a baseball player who late in his amateur career effects a heroic victory and is hired into major league ball. But the details finally are too diverse and even contradictory for a literal reading— and not just the overstatement of lines 28–29, where celebratory fireworks are said to scorch a jumbo jet flying overhead. For example, "amateur baseball" does not have a "front office" with an accountant who complains about a "has-been on his last leg" on the payroll—there *is* no payroll in amateur baseball. The reference to "slowness in making / the line-up" implies the manager of a team, not a player. "Runners . . . always faking / you out" indicates either a catcher or a pitcher who cannot throw out a stealing baserunner. Neither of those two positions is likely to be filled by someone with the "ability to steal bases."

In effect, although the poem seems addressed to a single amateur "turning pro," it refers to various team members both amateur and semi-pro, all of them having in common the status of encroaching age and the fading of those skills required for various positions on the team. The triumphant victory scene at the end has therefore the character of a dream or fantasy—for it is usually teammates, not fans, who carry the hero on their shoulders, and the procession only figuratively can lead "into the majors." In real life, one heroic deed does not erase the fact of diminishing capabilities. "Turning Pro" is a fantasy in which a dream of baseball success becomes a symbol for the last-minute reversal of fortune at a time when things seemed most dismal. TRA

269. *Alberto Ríos* Nani (page 835)

The *sestina*, of which this is the only example in this book, is a highly contrived fixed form making use of the patterned repetition of six end words through six stanzas, followed by a three-line *envoi* in which the six words are repeated in the middles and at the ends of lines. Ríos has slightly disguised the fact that his poem is a sestina by not providing stanza breaks except between what the pattern defines as the third and fourth stanzas, and before the envoi.

But even if we do not recognize the form for what it is, the poem becomes hypnotic in the repetition of end-words that in themselves are emblematic of the poem's theme: *serve, me, her, words, more,* and *speak* (to list them in the order of the first stanza). These words display a variety of sound links, including the assonance of *serves-her-words* and *me-speak* and the alliteration of *serves-speak* and *me-more,* which increase the feeling of repetition and reinforce their significance in the poem. Essentially Ríos presents a small domestic scene in which a man is being served food by his grandmother, "the absolute *mamá* (*nana* and *nani* are diminutive nicknames for a grandmother in the Spanish of America). Her serving, and then her smiles, and climactically her wrinkles, are her means of communication, and they speak wordlessly about her love for the speaker and for her dead husband, and finally about her children and all the ties of love. The speaker has lost two-thirds of his ability to speak or understand Spanish, so even when his grandmother speaks, it is to him as if her words dribble down her chin; but mostly she does not speak words, only gestures, looks, wrinkles, though she is so eloquent in these that when she cooks something at the stove it is as if she were doing "something with words." The "me-her" relationship is tenuous, not held by language but by a deep sense of closeness. As "the absolute *mamá*," nani speaks by serving, loves by feeding, and expresses the rich heritage of the family by the accumulated wrinkles of a long life of service and love. To the grandson who has lost the spoken language, the question is how much of this heritage he will be able to maintain: "I wonder just how much of me / will die with her, what were the words / I could have been, was." Yet the nani goes on serving, serving love.   TRA

270. *Edwin Arlington Robinson* Mr. Flood's Party (page 836)

Few poems balance so precisely on the point between comedy and pathos, tears and laughter, as "Mr. Flood's Party." For the poet to have poised it so was a triumph in the management of tone.

The drunk has always been a figure of comedy, and Mr. Flood, as he drinks and sings with himself, "with only two moons listening," is richly comic. The similes enhance the humor. Mr. Flood with a jug at his lips and the ghost of a warrior with a horn at his lips may be visually similar, but the discrepancy between their emotional contexts makes the comparison ludicrous. Mr. Flood setting his jug down may resemble a mother laying down her sleeping child, but the incongruity between the drunk's solicitude for his jug and a mother's solicitude for her baby again is ludicrous. But the fun is not supplied entirely by the poet; it is supplied also by Mr. Flood himself. The grave solemnity, the punctilious courtesy, with which Mr. Flood goes through the social ritual of greeting himself, inviting himself to drink, welcoming himself home, and cautioning himself against a refill ("No more, sir; that will do")—all show a rich vein of humor that makes us laugh with Mr. Flood as well as at him. This is a lovable drunk—though he is not loved. With two Mr. Floods, and two moons, we are almost prepared ourselves to believe that "the whole harmonious landscape rang" (it takes two people to create harmony) until we realize that this is only the heightened sense of appreciation that every drunk has for the beauty of his own singing.

But the things that make Mr. Flood ludicrous also make him pathetic. The allusion to Roland winding his horn calls up one of the most famous and moving episodes in all literature, in *The Song of Roland*, and the comparison, though ludicrous, is also plangent and moves us with emotions more profound than comedy. Roland was sending out a call for help, and Mr. Flood needs help too; but we know that no help came for Roland in time to save him. The comparison to the mother and her sleeping child, in much the same way, reminds us of the familial relationships and gentleness and love that are missing from Mr. Flood's life. These two images, with the help of the silver moon, lay a veil of tenderness and soft emotion over the poem, which moves us to compassion as well as laughter. Mr. Flood, after all, is not a mere ne'er-do-well. He has a delightful sense of humor and an old-fashioned courtesy. He was once honored in the town below and had many friends there. He has an educated man's acquaintance with literature: in speaking of the fleetingness of time, he can quote from *The Rubáiyát of Omar Kháyyám* ("The Bird of Time has but a little way / To flutter—and the Bird is on the Wing") and then use the quotation wittily and gracefully to propose a toast. The reference to *The Song of Roland*, though made by the poet, reinforces our sense of Mr. Flood as a sensitive and educated man. The song he sings—"'For auld lang syne'"—has added force because Mr. Flood can look only backward for better times; he can't look for them in the present or the future. Mr. Flood is old: the husky voice that wavers out, and the trembling care with which he sets down the jug are signs of age as well as of drink. His loneliness is stressed throughout the poem: he climbs the hill "Alone" (1), there is "not a native near" (6), he speaks "For no man else in Tilbury Town to hear" (8), he must drink with himself (9–16), he stands "Alone" (17), the moonlight makes a "silver loneliness" (45), he is "again alone" (52), he has no friends in the town below (54–56). A ghost in the moonlight, Mr. Flood sends out his call for help, and he is answered only by other ghosts—"A phantom salutation of the dead"—old memories.

We are not told why Mr. Flood has been cast out from the town below, why he is no longer honored, for what social sin or error he has lost his place in society. We know only that he is old, alone, friendless, dishonored, deserving of compassion but getting none. The "strangers" who would have shut their doors to him in the town below are probably many of them literal strangers, but some are former friends from whom he has been estranged. The final note of the poem is not one of laughter, but of heartbreak.

[Reprinted from Laurence Perrine and James M. Reid, *100 American Poems of the Twentieth Century* (New York: Harcourt, 1966) 7–8.] LP

271. *Edwin Arlington Robinson* **Richard Cory** (page 838)

Despite the popularity and apparent simplicity of this poem, it is often badly mis-read by students, who reduce it to the platitude that "great wealth does not guarantee happiness." Such a reading ignores nine-tenths of the poem. What the poem actually says is much more terrifying: that good birth, good looks, good breeding, good taste, humanity, *and* wealth do not guarantee happiness. The poem establishes all these qualities as being Cory's, and the "people on the pavement" thought that Cory "*was* everything" (not "*had* everything") to make them wish that they were in his place. This larger meaning must be insisted on. "Richard Cory" may not be as great a poem as, say, Robinson's "Mr. Flood's Party," but it is a genuine poem, neither superficial nor cheap.

The word "gentleman" is used both in its modern sense of one who is well behaved and considerate of others and in its older sense of one who is well born. The first meaning is established by Cory's courteous and uncondescending "Good-morning" to the "people on the pavement" and by his being "admirably schooled in every grace." The second meaning is established by a constellation of words that, by their primary or secondary meanings, suggest aristocratic or royal privilege: "crown," "favored," "imperially," "arrayed," "glittered," "king," "grace," "fine" ("crown" here means "top of the head," but is also a symbol of royalty; "Clean favored" means "clean-featured," but "favored" is also "privileged"; "grace" means a "social nicety," but it is also the term used for addressing a duke; "in fine" means "in sum," but "fine" implies also a quality of character and dress. Notice how the adjective "quietly" before "arrayed" imbues Cory with good taste: he dresses finely but unostentatiously).

Cory's first name has as its first syllable the word *rich* and is the name of several English kings, including the gallant Richard Coeur de Lion. His last name has a sonorous sound and is a good English name such as might belong to the New England landed gentry. It is in addition suggestive of such French words as *cor*, hunting horn; *coeur*, heart; and *cour*, royal court.

"Pavement" is an appropriate word not only because it alliterates with "people." A pavement is lower than a sidewalk; it establishes the commonness of the "people" in contrast with the higher status of Cory; it has the "people" looking up at him.

The surprise ending is not there for its own sake. By setting up an ironic contrast, it suggests a number of truths about life: that we cannot tell from outside appearance what may be going on inside a person; that often the people we envy have as many troubles as we, or more; that, as has been said above, birth, wealth, breeding, taste, and humanity do not ensure a happy life.

There is an excellent discussion of this poem in Norman C. Stageberg and Wallace L. Anderson, *Poetry as Experience* (New York: American Book, 1952) 188–92. I expand slightly on the present discussion in *The Art of Total Relevance: Papers on Poetry* (Rowley, MA: Newbury, 1976) 97–99. LP

272. *Theodore Roethke* **I knew a woman** (page 839)

This poem is a tribute of praise and gratitude from a middle-aged poet to a younger woman whose eager sexual genius taught him in fullest measure the delights of sensual love. The verb in the title may be understood in both its ordinary and its biblical sense. The imagery of the poem throughout emphasizes physical movement and the attractions of the body. The woman was "lovely in her bones," and "when she moved, she moved more ways than one." The "bright container" (4) is her skin. The tribute paid in lines 6–7 is both humorous and deeply meant, for "English poets who grew up on Greek" would include such favorites of Roethke's as Sir John Davies, Ben Jonson, and Andrew Marvell. In stanza 2 the terms "Turn," "Counter-turn," and "Stand" are the English equivalents of the Greek words *strophe, antistrophe*, and *epode*, indicating the movements made by the chorus in Greek drama while chanting a choral ode. The metaphor in lines 12–14 compares the woman to the curving sickle that cuts the grass in harvesting and the speaker to the straight rake that gathers it up. Moving in synchronism they produce a "prodigious mowing." Although the metaphor hardly needs further explanation, it is not irrelevant that the verb "to mow," in Scottish dialect, means to have sexual intercourse, and that the noun "rake" refers not only to the harvesting tool but to a sexually oriented male. Stanza 3 continues the poem's tribute to the sexual talents of the woman. The "mobile nose" in the whimsical mixed metaphor of line 20 suggests that of a rabbit (or other animal) sniffing the air.

Stanza 4 is difficult, for the poet here turns philosophical, and his transitions are abrupt. But if the precise meanings are puzzling, the tone is not. Clearly the poet sees no contradiction between "eternity" and enjoyment of the sensual life. He swears his lady cast a "white" shadow, not a dark one. Perhaps such pleasure as she afforded him is a foretaste of eternity. If he is a "martyr to a motion not [his] own" but hers, he has been a willing martyr, and his old bones still "live to learn her wanton ways." "To know eternity" is the important thing, "But who would count eternity in days?" The question is rhetorical; the answer is, No one but a fool; eternity may be tasted in a minute. The poet himself measures time "by how a body sways." The first line of the stanza seems to refer to the natural process of the human life-cycle from conception to death, but also to glance back at the sexual metaphor in lines 12–14. The simile "white as stone" calls up the image of a white marble gravestone, a marker separating life from eternity. The use of the past tense in the first three stanzas and the switch to the present in the fourth may indicate that the woman is dead (and the poet himself is certainly older). But the last two lines indicate that he has not forgotten the lessons she taught him. The poem ends, as it began, as a celebration of sensual love.

For additional suggestions, see discussions in *Explicator* by Virginia L. Peck, 22 (Apr. 1964): item 66; Helen T. Buttel, 24 (May 1966): item 78; Nat Henry, 27 (Jan. 1969): item 31; and Jenijoy LaBelle, 32 (Oct. 1973): item 15.   LP

273.   *William Shakespeare*   **Fear no more** (page 839)

Both the tone of this dirge from the fourth act of *Cymbeline* and the dramatic situation which is its occasion are characteristic of the late romances of Shakespeare. This is sung or spoken by two young men who suppose their adopted stepbrother is dead; but not only is the stepbrother only in a drugged sleep, "he" is really a princess who has had to flee the tyranny of the court—and the two singers who have been raised as Welsh shepherds are in actuality her long-lost princely brothers. These plot details contribute little to interpreting this song as a poem. But they make it, in its place in the play, a reinforcement of the mysterious powers of goodness that defeat the malevolent plotting of the villains in Shakespeare's last plays. Since everything works out for the best, despite all odds, a funeral lament like this emphasizes escaping life's pains and fears, not the grief of the mourners. Their love is expressed not in joy that the dead person has gone to heavenly bliss (the play is set in pre-Christian Britain), but in the consolation that he is now safe from danger and is sharing in a universal fate.

The "fears" that beset the living are of two kinds: natural (summer heat, winter cold, lightning and thunder) and social, with the greater emphasis on the latter. Although they personally know nothing of court life, these young men describe the conditions of a capital city, where ordinary people have to work for food and clothing, and where social disparities (chimney-sweepers with their gruelling and miserable lives contrasted to "Golden lads and girls") subject people to the frowns of their superiors and the cruelty of tyrants as well as to slander and rash censure. There is some "joy" in such a life, however slight: there is love, momentarily alluded to in line 17. But the preponderance of experience has been "moan," and death's release is to that extent to be welcomed.

The universality of death, encapsulated in the repeated rime "must . . . come to dust," contrasts the equality of the dead to the social hierarchies and injustices that govern the living. Rich and poor, mighty and weak, learned and ignorant, all "must . . . come to dust," and the inequities of society will be obliterated. Death is the great deliverer and equalizer. TRA

274. *William Shakespeare* **Let me not to the marriage of true minds** (page 840)

This sonnet makes an interesting contrast to "My mistress' eyes," poem No. 275. The subject here is a union of minds, while "My mistress' eyes" is a poem about physical attraction; this sonnet is idealistic, the other realistic. The opening sentence refers to the marriage ceremony in the Anglican *Book of Common Prayer*: ". . . if either of you do know any impediment why ye may not be lawfully joined together in matrimony . . . confess it." This reference is made emphatic by the extreme metrical irregularity of the first line, and made more vivid by the regularity of the first three feet of the second line.

The first quatrain proceeds negatively: I do not admit impediments; love is not love if it alters or bends. The second quatrain reverses the rhetoric, insisting that love is permanent and fixed; and the third returns to the negative, "Love's not Time's fool" and again, "Love alters not." In effect, the three quatrains describe what intellectual love is not, what it is, and again what it is not. (One scholar discovers in this, and in other details of the poem, that this sonnet is "protesting too much," and that it must be seen as ironic overstatement. While the poem may seem too hyperbolic when laid beside "My mistress' eyes," there really is little within this poem to suggest less than sincerity.)

The examination of the three quatrains as rhetorical parallels reveals a frequent pattern of Shakespeare's sonnets: they are repetitive, offering three different contexts to make the same statement. In the first quatrain, the context resembles a courtroom or public debate, as the echo from the marriage ceremony implies question and response. Here, the response is suitably intellectualized, a matter of defining terms that is appropriate to the subject of "minds." The diction reinforces the effect, being rational and legalistic ("Let me not," "Admit impediments," "alters . . . alteration," "remover to remove").

The second quatrain develops two two-line images, the "ever-fixèd mark" of a beacon or lighthouse unshaken by storms, and the pole star by which navigators steer, both images sharing the context of nautical travel, its dangers and its safeguards. Line 8 states our inability to know the exact value of the star, even though we can make use of our instruments to steer by its steadfastness, and it contrasts the "wandering" of human life with the star's immobility. True intellectual love preserves us in danger, and guides us when we wander.

The third quatrain continues to develop single images in two-line statements linked together in a common context. "Time's fool" is the toy or plaything of personified time, having no value to him. This is "Father Time," who dispassionately destroys the "rosy lips and cheeks" of the young (this is the only reference to physical beauty in the poem—*it* is "Time's fool"). Time with his sickle is linked to the "grim reaper" who at the day of "doom" will finally destroy all life, and only then will the "marriage of the true minds" be dissolved.

The couplet returns the poem to the courtroom of the opening quatrain. The poet invites disproof of his testimony, and employs as his witnesses two incontrovertible facts: since I have written (this poem proves that), and since certainly at least one man has loved, then my statements must be true. The couplet seems irrefutable, except that its conclusion is not necessarily valid: while it claims that these self-evident facts prove that the argument of his sonnet is also self-evident, there is no real connection. The "proof" is rhetorical rather than logical (and like the opening quatrain, couched in negative rhetoric).

This justly popular poem has been much analyzed. Among the most interesting commentaries are the following: Edward Hubler, *The Sense of Shakespeare's Sonnets* (Princeton: Princeton UP, 1952) 92–93; Kenneth Muir, *Shakespeare's Sonnets* (London: Allen, 1979) 107–108; Paul Ramsey, *The Fickle Glass: A Study of Shakespeare's Sonnets* (New York: AMS, 1979) 157–58; Katharine M. Wilson, *Shakespeare's Sugared Sonnets* (London: Allen, 1974) 301–303. TRA

275. *William Shakespeare* **My mistress' eyes** (page 840)

This witty sonnet might serve as a model of courtship, if a lady were to be won by realistic honesty. The speaker at length rejects the customary (lying) praise of hyperbolic lovers, insisting that his lady is only a woman, not a "goddess," and yet she is "as rare" as any woman who has been praised with overstated comparisons. In other words, he loves her for what she is, and does not think she wishes to be lied to about qualities she does not possess. It is a different kind of praise he offers, a high estimate of her common sense and her delight in wit.

The object of his satire is the "false compare" of the Petrarchan sonnet tradition. The formalities of the tradition required that the poet begin by praising the lady's hair (usually as fine and bright as spun golden wire), proceed to her ivory or alabaster forehead, her eyebrows arched like Cupid's bow, her pearly teeth, cherry-red lips, and so on, moving down the various parts of her body (generally rather coyly below the waist) to her delicate light feet. But Shakespeare seems realistically to present the order in which a man might look at a woman whose inner worth is also important to him, moving from eyes to lips to breasts, then to hair, cheeks, breath, voice, and gait, and at each stop he realistically claims her to be less than ideal. To the modern ear, the least complimentary word in the poem is "reeks," but the word was not used to mean "stinks" until the eighteenth century, and Shakespeare's meaning is much less offensive—it means "exhales." His tactic throughout the poem is not to substitute some other quality for the traditional over-statement, but just to say "she is not like *that*." What she *is* like is a woman, and for that he loves her. TRA

276. *Karl Shapiro* **The Fly** (page 841)

This extended apostrophe is very nearly a literal portrait of this most-loathed insect. The few instances where the fly is given human qualities or attitudes stand out—its "comic mood" that leads it to a mid-air sex act (7), its surprising coyness (10), its courageous and chivalrous hand-kissing (19), its begging to be freed from flypaper (30).

In the first three stanzas, the fly is placed in its environment: in the decaying flesh of cat or man, on a plate of food, in a compost heap, crawling on a hand. All of these descriptions (beginning with the metaphor and comparison of the first line) use witty language to present disgusting and abhorrent actions. Stanzas 4–6 place the fly in juxtaposition to those humans who directly assault it: children, who for fun try to capture and hold buzzing flies in their hands; "wives" who employ pesticides and flypapers to keep them out of the house; and "a man" who feels he must resort to physical violence of various sorts in order to kill, crush, disembowel, and tear the pest, and in his gigantic superiority to the minute corpses strides triumphantly through them.

Unlike other insect poems in this book, Shapiro's is most nearly simply a portrait-sketch, with the secondary purpose of describing how we treat its subject. For contrasting uses of insects as subjects, see Donne's "The Flea" (page 674) and Shaw's "Shut In" (page 842). TRA

277. *Robert B. Shaw* Shut In (page 842)

This is the third of the poems in this book featuring the most familiar insect intruder into our houses, the common housefly, and each of the poets makes a distinct use of it. Dickinson in "I heard a fly buzz when I died" (page 731) uses it as an ironic symbol of death; Shapiro in "The Fly" (page 841) presents an extended description of a literal fly, and catalogues and evokes a number of human responses to it; and Shaw in this poem develops the fly as a personified symbol of the human condition.

Shaw's fly, "Like many of us, born too late" (an echo of Robinson's self-deluded Miniver Cheevy, page 646?), is specifically placed indoors away from the chill of autumn, a situation symbolizing the protected artificiality of most human experience, a *house*fly removed from its natural habitat of "carrion or cow manure." The symbolic comparison is made explicit in lines 29–34—he lives "a life of limits, like our own / enclosed within a temperate zone." Like us, his life is neither "harsh" nor "insecure," without any real challenge, and in its trivial concerns slowly "running out of speed." Finally, the poem is an ironic satire pointed at the "easeful habitat" (13) that we choose to live in, with double-edged irony: it is demeaning enough to find ourselves compared to *Musca domestica*, but a little worse to be shown his superiority to us in his visual and evasive capabilities.

The verse form is suitable to the light tone of the poem. The four-line stanzas consist of iambic tetrameter and trimeter couplets whose exact rimes are insistent (so that the riming of *not* and *swat*, contrasted spellings, adds further wit), while the sentence structures sprawl across lines and stanzas. The departures from strict form and loose structure are therefore striking: lines 19–20 exactly fit line to sentence, underscoring the centrality of their idea: "Outside, the air is chill. / Inside, he's hard to kill"; and lines 35–36 contain the only two approximate rimes (*gone-on*) as well as fitting sentence to line, as the poem concludes climactically with premonitions of death for fly and man. TRA

278. *W. D. Snodgrass* **Powwow** (page 843)

The pathos of a dead or dying culture and the mockery of traditional rites carried on purely for commercial gain are brilliantly expressed in this poem. What has been lost is a sense of tribal identity, and with that loss have been lost enthusiasm and individuality. The Indians have been drawn into the modern American culture of movies, hot-dog stands, bleachers and loudspeakers, automobiles and trailers, filling stations, building contracts, and mechanized war. They wear clothes furnished by the government. They are all alike. This is the reality of their lives; their dances and Indian costumes are the pretense. Thus they shuffle through their dances without spirit, and the dances have all become alike. Continuity with the past has been broken; there is a suggestion that they have learned the dances from the movies rather than from their fathers. The dances no longer have meaning, and the tourists, for whom they are performed, are disappointed. There is lack of meaning on both sides, for the dances are performed for money rather than out of belief (for worship, rain, or war), and the motivation of the tourists is idle amusement rather than genuine interest or participation. Only one old tribesman carries on the tradition out of conviction: he does it for the children rather than for gain; but his great age—his shrunken figure and the toothless jaw—make him forlorn and pitiable, a symbol of a lost past. The children do not pay much attention, and, ironically, he carries on his performance by an electric light. His cause is lost.

All aspects of the poem contribute to its effectiveness. The rhythm of the poem, and the way it is printed on the page, themselves give the effect of a shuffling dance. The diction is unerring. In line 10, for instance, where the Indians are "tricked out in the various braveries," the word "tricked" means fancifully dressed or adorned, but it also suggests falsity or deceit—these costumes are no longer their true ones; the word "braveries" means showy dress or display, but here it suggests also something appropriate to an Indian brave—and a note of irony is sounded. The simile in lines 14–18, of the Indians dancing with their eyes turned inward like a woman nursing a child she knows will die, precisely describes the attitude of the Indians toward their ancient culture, which they know is dying, but which they spiritlessly carry on a little longer. Finally, the concluding image of the broken grasshoppers and butterflies symbolically condenses the entire content of the poem. The garish and beautifully red and yellow splatterings are like the colorfully feathered costumes the Indians don for their dances, but they are the remains of dead creatures "That go with us, that do not live again." The Indians are now submerged in our culture; their traditional way of life is dead forever.

[Reprinted from Laurence Perrine and James M. Reid, *100 American Poems of the Twentieth Century* (New York: Harcourt, 1966) 269–70.] LP

279. *Gary Soto* **Small Town with One Road** (page 844)

The speaker, now a man whose "easy" job is "only words" (poet? professor?), has returned to the cotton farming valley where he was raised. He is accompanied by his small daughter, and as they "suck roadside / Snowcones in the shade," he meditates on his beginnings. He recalls being a barefoot kid, leaping across the black asphalt highway to spend dimes for red candies, and a home life busy with dogs, cats, chickens, beans for supper: "It's a hard life where the sun looks," for "Okie or Mexican, Jew that got lost." The memories are of a life of manual labor, sweating in the hot sun, dreaming "the money dream" of relief from "shovel, / Hoe, broom."

And yet there is a vividly sensuous side to this reminiscence, a richness captured in images of sight, sound, feeling, taste—captured particularly well in the sixth line— "Sweetness on their tongues, red stain of laughter"—where the color of candy or snowcone is transferred to the tongue in a synesthetic mingling of taste and color, so that the pleasure of the taste is transferred to the color, and that in turn is the color of laughter. Soto intensifies what might be a prosaic description (open-mouthed laughing kids reveal the candy's red dye stain on their tongues) through the concentration of metonymy and metaphor. The leaps of meaning in this phrase are like the leaping kids themselves.

The tone of the poem is thus complex: the speaker is pleased that he is no longer trapped in the "hard life," fearful that the success he has had in escaping it might disappear, and concerned for his worrying, serious daughter. Yet as he recalls himself (and then sees himself in the "brown kid" standing and then leaping as he had done), he feels nostalgia for the rich exuberance that he has lost—and probably a little regret that his daughter will not experience it for herself. TRA

280. *Alicia Ann Spottiswood ("Lady John Scott")* **Ettrick** (page 845)

This "literary ballad" (an imitation of the folk ballad) contains an artful array of ballad characteristics—local dialect, songlike rhythms and rimes, a narrative that withholds definitive explanation of causes, and a close emotional linkage of nature with human mood and emotion.

The story it tells is of love in its first joys, fearful premonitions of the loss of love, and the heartbreak of lost love. There are no explicit clues about the reason that the love fades, nor about what has become of the lover. But there is also no clue about how the love was born in the first place—these shifts in emotion are treated as "given," as natural through the course of time as the changes of season that express them. The tight linkage between human response and natural change seems to express just that point: seasonal change is inevitable, and so is emotional change. Life moves from joy to fear to sorrow, as a year moves from summer to autumn to winter.

Metrically the poem is anapestic tetrameter, with dimeter opening and closing refrain lines in each stanza; the stanzaic pattern is $A^2bbcc^4A^2$. An additional songlike music is added by the internal riming of the fourth words in lines 2–3 of each stanza, all of them preceding a grammatical pause. Every line, including the refrains, ends in an extra-metrical unstressed syllable, an effect particularly noticeable in the second and third lines of each stanza where the participles that end the lines echo the riming participles within the lines. These rhythms reinforce the melancholy tone, and the shortened refrain lines contribute to this as well. TRA

281. *Ann Stanford* The Beating (page 846)

This horrific poem captures in imagery and literal language the pain and hallucination caused by a severe beating. What is missing from the poem is what the last stanza focuses on: what the police or hospital attendants want to know, the cause or purpose of the beating. This is compared to a glaring light within the "black ball of [the speaker's] mind" (23–24), implying that to frame that "one white thought" in words would be like another "blow." Perhaps the vicious beating was a revelation of a meaning even more horrid than the physical abuse, an awareness perhaps of the cruelty in someone the speaker loves—or, on the other hand, a new awareness of the random and meaningless violence of modern life as the victim is beaten without cause.

The poem, however, focuses primarily on the sensations of the victim, catalogued in images that grow in intensity through the first ten lines, then seem to subside as the beating ends, only to be followed by the paradox of "My eyes burst closed" (11), as the speaker falls. There follow silence and the sensation of floating, the attempt to cry for help that only issues in a groan, and then the rescue by police or paramedics, and the recovery of full consciousness in a hospital room that resembles another sort of physical torture. Certainly the speaker seems to be pleading to be rescued from this attention as if it were another set of blows, as she connects the "white thought" in her darkened mind to the painful whiteness of the room. The brightness of the concluding metaphor links together the interior enlightenment with the "lights" that went out as the beating ceased (12–13).

The poem is in free verse, though there is a high incidence of alternating stresses that suggests a variant of iambic. The lines range in length from 8 to 11 syllables, and there is a norm of four beats per line until the end of the fifth stanza. There (20) and in the opening and closing lines of the final stanza the lines are reduced to four syllables. TRA

282. *Maura Stanton* **Comfort** (page 847)

Through its matter-of-fact narration, the poem enacts its initial subject: the loss of emotional tones, a topic that runs through the poem and emerges as its thematic concern.

The first reference is simple—the limited frequency response of telephone receivers eliminates the "high and low notes" of speech, thus depriving the listener of the nuances of sound that express tone in verbal communication. The speaker knows that her mother must be inflecting her speech, and could be attempting either to share or repress her worries about her father's health. But the speaker refrains from explicit investigation, fearing to know what the emotional meanings are, avoiding what tone might reveal.

In the second half of the poem (13–25) the speaker turns to speculating about her father's physical and emotional state, focusing on his commitment to the *Meditations* of Marcus Aurelius and what that might now imply. The emperor's Stoicism, summarized in the italicized phrases, recommends "mildness . . . / cheerfulness . . . sobriety" in the face of pain and adversity, qualities for which Aurelius was himself famous. He was remembered by Roman historians as the ideal emperor, both for his success in holding together a vast empire under threat of disintegration and dismemberment and for his generosity, justice, and equanimity. The "low moan, rising from the Emperor's lips, / which the black letters sternly hide" is what she imagines her father now can hear: the private pain and loneliness that an act of will may hold in check—if one cannot hear the tone of voice.

The title itself is another example of uninflected speech: one may take comfort in not knowing or hearing the worst, as well as in hearing comforting news. Comfort may reflect or conceal. TRA

283. *Will D. Stanton* **Dandelions** (page 847)

An unassuming poem about an unassuming flower; on the surface simply a gathering of information about dandelions as if for an informal article in a dictionary of weeds and wild flowers. The poem classifies the plant ("Dandelions fall in this category"), describes its appearance ("More like the sun than sunflowers, / Only smaller"), names its habitats (they thrive "In areas where nothing else will grow"), discusses its uses (wine, salad, money, small comedians' curls), and adds an etymological note about its name (from the French *dents de lion*). The poem does all this with pleasant humor. In describing the dandelion's reproductive capacity, for instance, it tells us that "They seem to propagate about as fast / As a middle-aged gardener can run" (36–37). The wild incongruity of the comparison between frequency and speed is counteracted by the statement's triumphant truth in a different dimension.

In addition, the folklore of dandelions is presented (little girls "hold them under their chins to see if they like butter"). In fact, upon examination the poem turns out to be as much about social science as natural science. Of dandelions themselves it tells us that they inhabit "low-rent sections" and "hang around street corners" and "vacant lots and alleys." And, in telling us about dandelions, it also tells us about the social elite, suburbanites, farmers, kids, little girls, golfers, and gardeners— in fact, about America.

But the poem not only presents information, it also conveys an attitude. Though dandelions are presented as "undesired plants" that people swear at and try to get rid of, the poet classifies them in a category that includes kids, firecrackers, snowballs, and bed-time stories. In an opposite category are "places where society goes," perfume, corsages, weedless lawns, planned parenthood—in short, the "modern social scheme." Obviously the characterization of the former as "Things that don't pertain to public good" is ironic. The poet prefers the unsophisticated and old-fashioned to the fashionable and ultramodern. And he likes dandelions.

This poem is light verse at its best. Neither profound nor passionate, it exhibits a quiet but delicious sense of humor and says more than it seems to on the surface.

[Reprinted from Laurence Perrine and James M. Reid, *100 American Poems of the Twentieth Century* (New York: Harcourt, 1966) 283–84.] LP

284. *Wallace Stevens* **Disillusionment of Ten O'Clock** (page 848)

At first glance, this seems a zany and extravagant collection of images, a surreal poem with little but emotional effect. It is in fact social satire directed at pallid people who have neither overt nor secret excitements in their lives. Like ghosts of the truly living, they haunt their own houses (which, in double meaning, are their only haunts). They do not dress imaginatively, nor do they even possess subconscious dreams of things odd or exotic. They don't "dream of baboons," nor of "periwinkles" (another double denotation: the word "periwinkle" means both a garden ivy and a sea snail; the wild diversity of the word emphasizes the extravagance that they *don't* dream about). And they are already in their nightgowns and in bed at ten o'clock: dull, unimaginative, unexciting, plain people.

All that relieves this vision of domestic drabness is an occasional sailor, passed out drunk in the street or barroom, whose dream reveals a vital, over-imaginative psyche. But the poem doesn't even say he's dreaming: although he is "drunk and asleep in his boots" (13), his imagination is so lively that he actually "*Catches* tigers / In red weather" (14–15). The tigers and the weather are as "strange" (7) as the sleepers are ordinary. TRA

285. *Wallace Stevens* **The Poems of Our Climate** (page 849)

The poem opens with five-and-a-half lines of pure imagery, a still-life painting in words, presented in noun phrases without predication. The images are cool, clear, beautiful—the water is "clear," the bowl is "brilliant" white porcelain, and it contains "Pink and white carnations." The light in the room is lucid and bright without glaring, "like a snowy air, / Reflecting snow," a late winter snow when the days are lengthening and afternoons do not quickly subside into evening gloom. The imagery creates a sense of beautiful, "complete simplicity," a fulfilling sense of unchanging artistic perfection.

But such perfection is nevertheless lacking: "one desires / So much more than that." Even if this vision of perfection had the power to erase the "torments" and the vitality of being "evilly compounded" as a living human being, there would still be a desire for more than perfection, because the "never-resting" human mind cannot exist without striving for more experience, and for change.

So the poem makes its bitter assertion: "The imperfect is our paradise"; beauty and perfection and the unchanging contentment they might yield are never enough. As against the cool vision of artistic perfection, there is the heat of desire. But paradoxically, there is delight to be found in "flawed words and stubborn sounds," in the human striving that can never actually create perfection.

The paradox is resolved when we recognize that the poem is concerned with "poems" (that is, the artistic creation of the restless human mind) in contrast to the still-life perfection of carnations, clear water, and the light of "snowy air." Poetry is "of our climate" in the sense that we exist in a world of changing seasons, perceptions, desires, and delights, not in perfect stillness and complete simplicity. There is a great attraction in such simplicity, but the mind cannot rest in it: it will always "come back / To what had been so long composed," and revise and re-create it. So what seems to be our curse—that we must create out of "flawed words and stubborn sounds"—is in fact "our paradise," for we will not reach stasis but remain "vital" by striving.

A still-life painting, in all its perfection, is finished and complete (the French term for such painting might be in Stevens's mind here—"nature morte," dead nature). A poem can be revised, recomposed, returned to over and over again so long as the poet lives. TRA

286. *Wallace Stevens* The Snow Man (page 850)

The single sentence constituting this poem is ambiguously framed, either offering advice or a definition: in its barest statement, it can be paraphrased, "only a person as cold-minded as a snow man would not think such a cold place implies misery." Is the speaker advocating such emotionlessness as appropriate to the surroundings and as a defense against despair? Or is he lamenting the inhumanity that would be necessary to escape such emotions? The last two lines provide a partial answer: the reality of the situation is that this observable landscape contains "the nothing that is," and that it has no further dimensions of meaning beyond its mere physical existence. To "think of misery" therefore is to add a false meaning, one derived not from reality but from an observer's emotional reaction.

These last two lines may echo *Hamlet*, 3.4, when the Ghost appears to Hamlet in Gertrude's closet but remains invisible to her. Hamlet asks his mother, "Do you see nothing there?" and she replies "Nothing at all; yet all that is I see" (131–32). Stevens's snow man is an unemotional, practical realist, unable to see anything but actuality, and able to see that the actuality implies nothing beyond itself. Neither ghosts nor implications of meaning are available to him.

The only way a person can avoid thinking of misery in such a barren place is to be, like the snow man, "nothing himself," a person without feeling. The first three stanzas create the visual scene, in details that seem quite forbidding. The trees have been subjected to wintry transformations, "crusted" and "shagged" and made "rough" in appearance by the weakness of the distant sun. Stanzas 3 and 4 add the effect of the "sound of the wind," which to an emotional observer would imply misery. The defense against such feeling is "a mind of winter," coldly unemotional and in total harmony with the surroundings.

While this is the overt statement of the poem, there remains a third alternative to either misery or emotional coldness: the visual imagery implies the possibility of perceiving beauty in the chiaroscura of shapes and textures. The three types of evergreen trees have distinctly different shapes, and the winter has given them three distinct textures. The crusted pines tower above with their foliage at the tops of their tall trunks; the shaggy junipers sprawl flat and disorderly in their low branching; and the conical Christmas-tree-shaped spruces are roughened but glittering. Although the scene is not inviting, it nevertheless possesses stark beauty. The snow man's coldly analytical philosophy is a defense against misery and a definition of reality, but it does not comprehend esthetic responses.

For two slightly different interpretations of this much-discussed poem, see A. Walton Litz, *Introspective Voyager: The Poetic Development of Wallace Stevens* (New York: Oxford UP, 1972) 99–100, and Daniel Fuchs, *The Comic Spirit of Wallace Stevens* (Durham NC: Duke UP, 1963) 69–70. TRA

287. *May Swenson* On Its Way (page 850)

"It is death / that tints the leaves," this imagistic poem concludes, providing a definition for what the collection of images has implied. The poem is a description of autumn, of nature "on its way" to winter death, of "Ripeness / on its way to frost." It consists entirely of noun phrases until the concluding sentence, a catalogue of impressions (primarily visual) with occasional interpretive comparisons. A paraphrase would need to supply the verbals that are omitted, as for example: "An orange-colored thing that is in the process of becoming ashen (or a blaze that is subsiding into ashes) is like anger that will pass after a night of sleep. It is also like a sweet, passionate desire that grows and ripens, like a plump pumpkin, before it decays," and so forth. The poem repetitively points to a variety of vivid, living things that in the natural course of time will die, but that ironically achieve their greatest vibrancy just before they come to that end.

There is considerable musicality in the poem (with the striking exception of the last, defining sentence)—alliteration, consonance, assonance—suited to the appreciation of the beauty of the season and the vividness of its colors. Some of it may not be obvious in a hasty reading, such as the assonance of "h*o*ney-p*u*mpkin-pl*u*mp" or the consonant repetition of "a*sh*-quen*ch*-Pa*ss*ion." TRA

288. *Jonathan Swift* **A Description of the Morning** (page 851)

There is a long tradition, stretching back to ancient Greece, of poetic descriptions of morning, idealized and romantic treatments of the joys of the beginning of a new day. One of the most famous in English is Romeo's description of dawn in 3.5:

> Look, love, what envious streaks
> Do lace the severing clouds in yonder east.
> Night's candles are burnt out, and jocund day
> Stands tiptoe on the misty mountain tops.

Swift's poem plays with the tradition in two witty ways: it is a city morning, not a rustic or natural one; and it presents details of realistic ugliness rather than idealized beauty. One critic compares the poem to a drawing of Swift's younger contemporary William Hogarth, whose "Morning" shows such social types as "the Begging Crone, the Loose Girl, the Persistent Rake, the Shivering Page, and the Old Maid" in a snowy street scene with dark buildings and a darker sky (Johnson, p. 11, cited below).

The first two lines of this poem are parodic, indicating their literary target in the "poetic" phrase "showed the ruddy morn's approach." What signals this morning, however, is not sunlight on a misty mountain top, but the beginning of urban bustle as the traffic begins to appear. Lines 3–4 lead us to anticipate a satire on sexual behavior between the upper and lower classes, as the servant girl sneaks back to her bedroom from her master's, to muss up her own bed to make it look slept in. But Swift is not really in one of his satiric moods in this poem; the only other direct references to the injustice of social rank occur at line 13 (the nobility can live in debt, and must be pestered by bill collectors) and lines 15–16 (the prison system requires the convicts to pay for their keep, and thus they are permitted to roam the streets at night to "steal for fees").

What the poem mostly catalogues are ordinary working-class people energetically starting their daily pursuits. They are not particularly attractive, but they are not grotesques: the apprentice in his worn-out shoes cleans the grimy shop front and sprinkles water on the floor to keep down the dust; Moll (a lower-class nickname for Mary), ruddier than the morn with her flaming face (perhaps from drink), flourishes her mop ostentatiously as she prepares to scrub; the scavenger pokes in the gutters for objects to sell; the dealer in "small-coal" (either charcoal, or small lumps of coal, for domestic heating) boomingly announces his wares, while his counterpart, the truly small boy who cleans chimneys, chimes in with his shrill soprano voice. The town is busy, and most of the business of these people is concerned with putting the street back into some semblance of cleanliness. (The "small-coal man" is by contrast a source of grime, both from the smoky fires he supplies and from the coal dust that must coat his clothes and trail behind him as he walks.) The filth that came with the night must now be removed (both dirt and thieves), so along with the cleaners come the turnkey and the "watchful bailiffs."

The last two couplets put an end to the busy activities—the prison doors are locked up, the bailiffs stand silently, and finally (late?) some schoolboys shuffle slowly to *their* form of imprisonment. The scene subsides into a relatively calm day.

Useful analyses of the poem are F. W. Bateson, *English Poetry: A Critical Introduction* (London: Longmans, 1950) 175–80, and Maurice Johnson, *The Sin of Wit: Jonathan Swift as a Poet* (Syracuse NY: Syracuse UP, 1950) 10–15.   TRA

289.   *Alfred, Lord Tennyson,*   **from *IN MEMORIAM A. H. H.,*** Dark house, by which once more I stand (page 851)

290.   *Alfred, Lord Tennyson,*   **from *IN MEMORIAM A.H.H.,*** The time draws near the birth of Christ (page 852)

The 133 sections of *In Memoriam* are all written in the same stanza pattern—iambic tetrameter quatrains riming *abba*; but Tennyson is a master of the local variations that adapt rhythm and music in each section to its unique mood. This mastery is dramatically illustrated in the last lines of sections 7 ("Dark house") and 28 ("The time draws near"). The bleak mood of 7, perfectly imaged in the "drizzling rain," the empty street, and the gray day, is forcibly underscored in the last line by the clogged meter, the long vowels, and the succession of explosive (and hissing) consonants at both the beginning and end of the stressed monosyllables: "On the *bald street breaks* the *blank day.*" The meter of the line violently wrenches the metrical pattern, without breaking it. I scan it thus: a tetrameter line, eight syllables, but with five syllables stressed, and without a single regular foot.

On the bald ǀ street ǀ breaks the ǀ blank day. ǀ

How different is the last line of section 28! Here the regular meter, the short vowels, and the preponderance of liquid consonants (*m*'s, *r*'s, and *l*'s) make the line slip smoothly and easily off the tongue. The one explosive consonant in the line gives a tap to the bell that it sets in motion.

But the adaptation of sound to sense is subtly apparent throughout the two poems. The placement of grammatical pauses in section 7, for instance, is varied—after the first foot in line 1, after the first syllable in line 3, after the first foot and a half in lines 4 and 6, after two feet in line 9. The result is to keep the reader off balance and to prevent the lines from becoming too rhythmical. In section 28, on the other hand, *all* the grammatical pauses come in the exact middle of the line, thus

330

supporting the rhythmical regularity of tolling bells. In lines 6–7, moreover, and even more conspicuously in lines 11–12, the phrasing breaks the lines into four equal parts concordant with the idea of four sets of bells.

Also noteworthy: in section 7, the way the consonance of *heart* and *beat* in line 3 reinforces the sound of the beat; the way the meter in line 11 throws its two heaviest stresses on the cacophonous syllables *ghast-* and *drizz-*; in section 28, the way the consonance of *still, bells, hill, hill* in lines 2–3, of *swell* and *fail* in line 7, and of thrice-repeated *goodwill* in lines 11–12, reinforces the sound of the bells.   LP

291.   *Dylan Thomas*   Do Not Go Gentle into That Good Night (page 852)

In form this poem is a *villanelle*. Its nineteen lines utilize only two rime sounds (based on *night* and *day*); its alternating refrains rime *night* and *light*. Most villanelles are charming, graceful, light poems, characteristic of society verse. Thomas here gives the villanelle a force and intensity it had never had before—though many poets have tried to match it since. ("Do Not Go Gentle into That Good Night" is perhaps a turning point in the history of the villanelle.)

As shown by the concluding section, the poem is addressed to the poet's father. In some respects a fierce militant most of his life, the elder Thomas in his eighties went blind, became ill, and showed a tendency to turn soft and gentle. The son was dismayed by this change. He wanted his father to die as he had lived, to maintain his salty individuality to the last. Though the poet was something of a pantheist in his religious belief and felt that death was "good," he still considered it right and natural that men should resist death, put up a struggle against it, not die placidly. "Wise men . . . Good men . . . Wild men . . . Grave men," he tells his father in separate stanzas (punning on the word "grave"), have all for good reasons raged against their approaching deaths. In the last section (where his tenderness toward his father is manifest), he prays his father (paradoxically) to "Curse" and "bless" him with his "fierce tears" and to "not go gentle into that good night." ("Good night" is both a metaphor for death and a pun for farewell.)   LP

292.   *Dylan Thomas*   Fern Hill (page 853)

"Fern Hill" is Dylan Thomas's evocation of the delight, the wonder, the long carefree rapture of boyhood summers spent on a farm in Wales. The reader is made to share his pleasure in the barns and fields and orchards, in the farmhouse itself, in the animals both wild and domestic, in afternoon and night and morning. In the fourth stanza the poet compares this boyhood experience to the experience of Adam and Eve in Eden. Like theirs, its chief characteristics were joy and innocence and a feeling of timelessness. Like theirs, his experience came at the beginning of life, and, like them, he felt it would last forever. But the theme of the poem is the transience of youthful joy and carefree innocence. All the time that he is heedless of time, he is bound by its chains, which hold him "green and dying." Just as Adam and Eve were thrust out of Eden, so the boy is to be thrust out of the garden of childhood.

The boy is the protagonist of the poem. Time is the antagonist—unseen, unfelt, and unheeded by the boy, but comprehended clearly by the mature poet looking back. The boy, "happy as the grass was green," feels that he has forever. But, inexorably, in its alternation of afternoon and night and morning, Time is carrying him out of the enchanted realm, "out of grace," toward age and death. The boy who is "prince of the apple towns" (6)—and described with such aristocratically connotative adjectives as "golden" (5), "honored" (6), "lordly" (7), and "famous" (10), who feels himself master of all he surveys—is at the same time, though unaware of it, a slave, held by Time in "chains" (54).

Thomas has a talent for refurbishing clichés and getting new or double meaning out of them, both the old and the new. "Happy as the grass was green" (2) and "Happy as the heart was long" (38) both remind us of the commoner expression "Happy as the day is long" and gather its meaning into fresher expressions. "Once below a time" (7) gathers up the meaning of "Once upon a time" and bends it to the use of the poem's theme—that the boy is really a slave of time, not master of it. In "All the sun long" (19) and "All the moon long" (25) the poet freshens the familiar phrases by substituting metonymies for the expected "day" and "night." In "Adam and maiden" (30) Thomas substitutes for "Eve" a noun that represents her in her innocence and at the same time sounds like "Eden," thus tripling its significance.

If you have to beg, borrow, or steal, get a tape or record of Thomas reading this poem and play it for your class. Thomas's voice is as "golden" as his poetry. Mary C. Davidow in the *English Journal* 58 (Jan. 1969): 78–81, and Sister M. Laurentia, in *Explicator* 14 (Oct. 1955): item 1, offer further interesting and useful observations about this poem.   LP

293.   *Jean Toomer*   **Reapers** (page 854)

The plural title ambiguously captures the central contrast of this brief lyric: there are two sets of reapers, both identified as "black"—men, in the first line, and then "horses" in the fifth. The contrast is developed between the human reapers with their sense of completeness (as well as their sense of tradition—"as a thing that's done" refers both to their satisfaction with the accomplishment of a sharpened scythe, and to their sense that this is the way the job is to be done), and the machinelike horses drawing the mechanical mower, insensitive to what they destroy, cutting both "weeds and shade," and slaughtering animals in their path.

There is of course a distortion in this contrast, since it does not pit the human reapers against the human driver of the mowing machine. Instead it pretends that the inhuman horses are the voluntary force in the use of the machine. The focus moves from the observed and admired human mowers of lines 1–4 to the observed and detested effects of mechanical mowing in lines 5–8. But do not human reapers *also* cut both weeds and "shade," and do they not kill field rats? Contrasting the effect of the mechanical mower to the attitudes of the human mowers is in its way unfair, thematically, for it compares not the acts of mowing, human or machine, but the feelings of the observer. He sees in the reapers a collective humanity that nevertheless maintains its individuality—although they act in unison, and in a traditional, inherited fashion, they start "one by one" (4). On the other hand, he does not see the driver of the horses drawing the mower; in fact, he credits the horses with driving.

It is tempting to see here a racial suggestion: to the white owners of the fields, black men and black horses are synonymous. But there is the further suggestion that the sensitive observer, pitying the bleeding rat, cannot *see* the driver of the mowing machine. Is he white? Is he driving horses now, as he drove black men formerly? And is the speaker of the poem black (as the poet was)?

However we answer such questions, we must at least recognize that the poem is clear in its preference for "black reapers" over "black horses," even to the extent of glossing over the distorted comparison that results from such a preference. The sound qualities of the poem reinforce the preference: in the first quatrain, the frequent alliteration of *s* and *st*, the assonance of long *e* sounds, and the lilting repetition of "one by one" create a musicality that harmonizes with the speaker's approving tone; in the second quatrain the *s*- alliteration serves to emphasize not *silent swinging* (4) but *startled-stained* violence, and *b*- and hard *c*- alliteration lend weightiness and abruptness, while the long *e*- assonance turns up in words of negative connotation: *weeds, field, squealing, bleeds.* TRA

294. *Derek Walcott* The Virgins (page 855)

Derek Walcott, a native Caribbean poet, is disturbed by what American commercial exploitation (the "American dream" of a better life for all achieved through abundant material goods) has done to the once simple life and unspoiled natural beauty of the American Virgin Islands. He expresses his distress through his observation of (and observations on) Frederiksted, the chief seaport of one of these islands, while walking through its streets. His observations are sharpened by his skillful use of irony and of words and phrases of double meaning.

The irony begins with the title, for clearly these islands (originally named after Elizabeth, the virgin queen) are no longer virgins. They have been prostituted to, or raped by, American materialism. The "dead" (deserted) streets down which the poet walks are deserted probably because of the midday heat, but the adjective leads the poet to the reflection that the town is "dead" in another sense, having lost its soul to tourism. (The phrase "the first free port to die for tourism" ironically reverses a more familiar pattern of words often found on local monuments: the first citizen of this town to die for freedom.) Continuing his metaphor, the poet describes himself as walking at a "funeral" pace (slowly). One suspects a pun in the adjective "sun-stoned" (built of stones heated by the sun; drunk or drugged by the sun's heat). There is a complex verbal irony in the poet's use of "civilized" and "the good life" and a situational irony in the conjoining of "the good life" and "the American dream" with a rising crime rate. The empty condominium (paradoxically drowning in vacancy) gives evidence of a building boom in which the developers's eager anticipations miscalculated the actual demand. The roulettes spinning "rustily to the wind" evidence the same kind of overdevelopment at the same time that they testify to what "tourism," "the American dream," and "the good life" actually substitute for the speaker's "small-islander's simplicities": not only a rising crime rate, but cheap dreams of quick wealth made at the gambling casinos. In line 16 "trade" has the double meaning of trade wind and commerce. The spinning of the roulette wheels is related both by circular motion and monetary motivation to the "revving up" of motorboats and yachts headed for the "banks" (fishing banks and money banks) of "silver" (silver-sided fish and silver coins). And if "silver" is related to coinage, perhaps "green" is associated with dollar bills.   LP

295.   C. Webster Wheelock   Divorcée (page 855)

Strict adherence to the form of the English sonnet is counterpointed to a loose narrative structure that nowhere matches its syntax to the pattern of quatrains and a couplet, a use of the form that reinforces the theme. A divorced woman now sentenced to "Life without a prison," measuring the length of her life by trivial, irritating sounds rather than by the vicissitudes of an emotional need, is a person whose time is told not by the tolling and ticking of a clock but by random sounds. What was regular (sonnet form, clock time) can no longer provide structure.

From the first reference to a term in jail to the metaphor of the woman's life as a clock (13), the poem poses *felt* time against *measured* time, to indicate that once the emotional life is lost time itself is meaningless. The most moving figure is the metaphor that substitutes the annoying noises of a life lived in silent loneliness (dripping faucets, clamorous radiators) for the regular sounds of a clock ticking and sounding the hours, and compares the ebbing vitality of the woman to a watch-spring in need of rewinding.   TRA

296.   Walt Whitman   When I Heard the Learn'd Astronomer (page 856)

This poem expresses a conflict that may seem even more cogent today than when Whitman wrote it: precise scientific knowledge is an assault on the cherished mysteries of the universe. Feelings similar to Whitman's were voiced in the wake of man's first steps on the surface of the moon on July 20, 1969; as the cameras of rocket probes send back close-up photographs of the more distant planets in our solar system, the skies may seem to lose their appealing wonder.

Whitman's ironic contrasts are readily perceived because of their directness and abundance, and though it may be a violation of his attitude toward "charts" and "columns," they may be indicated as paired lists:

crowd in lecture room	individual man
much applause	silence
mathematical counting	"unaccountable" feeling
lighted room	dark night
indoors	outdoors
approving audience	tired and sick poet
sitting	rising and gliding, wandering
scientific precision	random looking, "from time to time"
scientific thought	poetic feeling

These ironic contrasts make the speaker's decision seem more natural, more attractive, more human. The initial repetition of "When" in the first four lines has a hypnotic sameness, imitating the poet's boredom with the regularity of scientific proofs; and the redundancy of "proofs, figures, columns, charts, diagrams" and "add, divide, measure" reinforces the sense of repetitiousness and—for the speaker—the meaninglessness of such data about the universe. The phrase "perfect silence" in the last line ironically comments on the supposed perfection of scientific knowledge: genuine perfection is not mathematical or measurable, but is the harmonious response of perfect feeling to perfect stars.

The poem presents Whitman's distaste for precise, rational knowledge and his love of emotional, instinctive wonder at the mysteries of nature. His choice of the word "mystical" rather than "mysterious" extends his preference into a claim that his experience surpasses the astronomer's knowledge in a religious sense as well. His insight into the wonders of heaven seems to him to penetrate the merely mysterious and to reach to supernatural wisdom.   TRA

297. *Richard Wilbur* **The Writer** (page 856)

The poem has a double subject, as the ambiguous reference of the title suggests. It concerns the speaker's daughter and the beginning of her career as a writer, and it concerns the speaker-as-writer, creating his poem about her. This situation is made clear at line 11, when the speaker hears in his daughter's pause in her typing her rejection of his "easy figure," so that he must find a more suitable figure of speech to express his wish for her future.

His first figure, elaborated through the first three stanzas, is in fact traditional, a metaphor comparing her life to a voyage. He makes it more vivid and particular by specifying a sea voyage, and by propounding a variety of explicit comparisons: the house is her ship, and the light breaking over the house at the place where her room is located is like the water breaking at the prow of a ship. Her typewriter sounds to him "like a chain hauled over a gunwale" as she weighs anchor for her trip. The "stuff / Of her life"—the weight of her past experiences that she must carry along as cargo (including perhaps his own fame as a writer)—is heavy. He brings the metaphor to a close by wishing her "a lucky passage."

Then it is that he interprets her pause as a dismissal of his comparison, and she and he and the whole house then wait in stillness for his next attempt. His replacement springs to him out of his memory. It is not another metaphor, but a symbol, that of a starling trapped in her room that after many exhausting attempts to escape, managed finally to find "a smooth course for the right window" and flew from the "world" of the house to its own free world.

As a symbol for the girl attempting to become a writer, this is very apt: good writing takes hard work and many arduous attempts; it entails failures and battering. The writer may be able to *see* the goal but may be blocked, as by a window pane, from flying to it. When success finally comes it is like soaring into another world, and the "spirits" of readers will rise with the writer's. So, as he concludes, writing "is always a matter . . . / Of life or death," not a simple forward progression through time and space like a sea voyage but hard work, frustration, and pain, which may be rewarded not with reaching a destination but with transcending the ordinary world.

The poem enacts this process, trying and rejecting a trite metaphor, and from that failure discovering in a memory an original and heartfelt symbol. The girl *may* become a writer; the speaker *is* one.   TRA

298.   *William Carlos Williams*   **Poem: As the cat** (page 857)

This famous gem is not as rich in theme as "The Red Wheelbarrow" (page 536), but it is a fine example of the poet's control of form and structure in a minimal space. The event reported is simple, domestic, familiar: a cat in its curious prowl around the house, apparently going nowhere in particular, is observed in its graceful and delicate movement. But with situational irony, the animal for all its care and precision winds up with its two right feet in an "empty / flowerpot," leaving the observer with an amused smile: cats will go *anywhere*, no matter how inexplicable or incongruous the result. The irony is an anticlimactic revelation of a cat-truth and a false human expectation, contrasting the personifying assumptions behind the word "carefully" and the humor of the final picture.

The structure and form of the poem seem to imitate those careful steps, one precise and measured stanza for each movement (but we must be careful not to be too literal about this: four stanzas, four paws, but the moving paws are the focus only of the two middle stanzas). The normal line length is three syllables, with variations, and the slight pauses required for line ends provide just the right hesitation, particularly in the lines ending in prepositions (2, 3, and especially 10). In the book cited below, Henry M. Sayre calls our attention to the "careful manipulation of certain consonants

. . . c, f, t, and *p.''* Every line but the eighth contains one or more of these sounds, and as Sayre says they occur in the stressed words in a line: *"cat," "climbed," "top," "jamcloset,"* and so forth. It is in the climactic last stanza that these sounds flourish (except for the *c* as in *"cat,"* a sound that disappears after *"carefully"*): *"pit," "empty,"* and especially the piling on of these aspirated consonants in *"flowerpot."*

Is it too fanciful to point out that "pfft" is a sound made by angry cats in comic strips? or that "pfft" came into the American language in the first half of this century as a slang term to indicate an abrupt ending? Perhaps.

This poem receives a slightly different reading in Sayre's *The Visual Text of William Carlos Williams* (Urbana and Chicago: U of Illinois P, 1983) 79.   TRA

299.   *William Carlos Williams*   **To Waken an Old Lady** (page 858)

The poem consists of a single extended metaphor interrupted and turned by the interjection "But what?" at its precise center. The metaphor explicitly compares old age to a flock of birds in winter, in the first half "cheeping" and "skimming," "Gaining" and "failing" as they fly against a "dark wind" in their search for food. As a metaphor for old age, the images suggest weakness but pertinacity, the reduction of natural strength but a continuing effort to keep going in a life beset with increasing difficulties. The metaphor moves from "flight" and the modest "cheeping" to the ominous submission to a "dark wind" that presages death. The literal reference may be to sparrows, nonmigratory flocking "small" birds.

After the interjection, the metaphor shows the birds at rest, having discovered and eaten the seeds on "harsh weedstalks," and with their "shrill / piping of plenty" moderating the effect of the cold wind. That is, what little is left to them, the birds have made use of, and can even in their way celebrate their accomplishment. So, says the poem, old age does not yield to its afflictions and losses, but finds where it can the bare sustenance that it needs to maintain life and vitality.

The interjection has been variously interpreted. Here is one suggestion:

> The line is really external to the images; it suggests at once the old lady's voice, querulous and confused; the poet wondering what to say next; and the covert comment that there is no meaningful end to the whole process of age. It conveys the unfinished in a way no image alone could, as if the artist's hand had withdrawn but left a thumbprint showing.

What it certainly does is bring a human voice into the imagery; and it is also the only point in the poem that can refer to the action of the title, "to *waken* an old lady," for the statement of the poem is concerned with a metaphorical definition of age, not with awakening or arousing someone from sleep. In this function, one might hear it as the voice of the lady, waking up and asking what the metaphor is leading to, or the voice of the speaker calling her attention to facts about old age that the first half of the poem has omitted.

The passage quoted is from Neil Myers, "Sentimentalism in the Early Poetry of William Carlos Williams," *American Literature* 37 (1966): 463. Two other insightful readings are those of Willis D. Jacobs, *Explicator* 29 (Sept. 1970): item 6, and Nat Henry, *Explicator* 30 (May 1972): item 80. TRA

300. *Susan Wood* **Eggs** (page 858)

Through varieties of literal and figurative statements about eggs, the poem explores feelings about the conjunction of the "flawed" and the "beautiful." It begins with a simile—morning breaking is like an egg breaking, both of them "hated" by the speaker because they too quickly show that beauty conceals what is essentially flawed. The contents of the eggshell are thus compared to what daylight will disclose, both of them "staining."

The disclosures of daylight focus chiefly on two personal conflicts—with the speaker's father whose domineering manner ("the one cock / in the henhouse") resulted in a repeated scene of nausea, weeping, surrender, and hunger, and later with the speaker's daughter, whom she beats with a belt. Both of these episodes end in the speaker's self-hatred.

Beginning in line 16, the speaker tries to discover the origins of her hating eggs. She begins with another overbearing male, Freud, and his explanation of the female's subconscious hatred of her sexuality; then she turns to another possibility, that she hates eggs because they always repeat the same "perfect / oval," implying that there can be no change or improvement either in eggs or in human behavior. But neither of these is sufficient, for they do not take into account another human habit, the tendency to nurture our real resentments in secret and to substitute other subjects for them in our conflicts—we fight "our battles over eggs" rather than over the actual causes for animosity.

The poem concludes with a solution for such battles: rather than fight over eggs, we might fight *with* them. We might thus break "the spell" of our fascination with perfection, since it is the source of disillusionment causing us to conclude that any beauty is only an external facade disguising internal flaws. We might instead, in a kind of joyous mayhem, accept the fact that there is no perfection, that we are all *both* "beautiful *and* flawed." TRA

301. *Judith Wright* **Portrait** (page 859)

The poem consists of two iambic pentameter stanzas, each five lines in length, and each having four lines with end rime, either perfect or approximate. The two stanzas are balanced against each other by similarity and contrast. The stanzas are separated in time by the break between them.

The first stanza is dominated by present-tense verbs, the second by past-tense verbs. The first line in the first stanza and the last line in the second stanza both contain the word "game" and the phrase "when it began." These are the two non-riming lines in their two stanzas, but some critics would say that they rime with each other (inventing a category called *identical rime*). Certainly their singularity in their own stanzas and their resemblance to each other, plus the fact that they are the first and last lines in the poem, give them special emphasis in the formulation of theme.

Put together, the poem is the "Portrait" of an ordinary housewife at two stages in her life. In the first stanza, soon after her marriage, she performed her routine duties (cooking, cleaning, mending) cheerfully. Because she was motivated by love, she regarded these chores as permanencies and performed them without complaint. In the second stanza she performs them out of "old habit," cleaning the house that *looks* "like home" and dressing herself for the periodic visits of her grown children in a way that *looks* "like love." We may now notice that the rimes in the first stanza are both perfect rimes, while those in the second are both approximate rimes. The latter are spelled so that they *look* like perfect rimes, but in fact are pronounced differently.

The speaker blames no one for these losses; she merely reports sadly that too often what starts out with the eager enthusiasm of a child's game ends up as sterile ritual in which the real warmth of marriage and family life is absent.   LP

302.   *William Butler Yeats*   **Sailing to Byzantium** (page 860)

In his book *A Vision*, Yeats wrote that if he could be given a month of antiquity and leave to spend it where he chose, he would spend it in Byzantium about the year A.D. 525. Byzantium (later known as Constantinople and presently as Istanbul), the eastern capital of the Holy Roman Empire, was in that period notable for the flowering of its art: painting, architecture, mosaic-work, gold and silver metalcraft, book illumination, etc. For this reason, it represented for Yeats a holy city of the imagination.

The title "Sailing to Byzantium" would seem to indicate that the poem is about a voyage; but line 1 ("*That* [not *This*] is no country for old men") together with lines 15–16 (". . . therefore I have sailed the seas and come / To the holy city of Byzantium") indicate that the voyage has already been completed. It is an imaginary voyage, of course, for it has been made not just across space, from Ireland to Byzantium, but backwards through time, from the twentieth century to the sixth. The important considerations, therefore, are not the voyage itself, but why the poet made it; and not Ireland and Byzantium, but what they represent.

The poem deals with the antitheses of the physical and sensual world versus the world of intellect and imagination, the mortal versus the eternal, nature versus art. Modern Ireland represents the first term in these oppositions, Byzantium the second. The poet, growing old (he was 63 when this poem was published) can no longer engage fully and unreflectively in the life of the senses, and longs for something beyond the life of the senses, for the life of the senses is mortal and dies. He finds what he is looking for in works of art ("Monuments of unaging intellect"), which are eternal. The poem may be looked on as a kind of prayer: Let me leave this country of the young, the unreflective, the sensual, and the dying, and sail to the city of imagination and unaging intellect. There let my next incarnation be as an artificial gold-and-enamel singing bird that cannot decay as my body is decaying now but that will exist eternally. Let me be a work of art rather than a man!

Yeats thus seems to be elevating art above nature, the eternal above the mortal. But there is a catch here. What will this gold-enameled bird sing about? It will sing of "what is past, or passing, or to come"—a line that echoes line 6: "Whatever is begotten, born, and dies." Art celebrates the mortal world—the world of process, change, decay, and death. The poem thus has a circular movement in which the last line returns us to its beginning. The poet presents us, not with a preference but with a dilemma. He wishes to escape from life into art, but as a work of art he will celebrate life. Art is both superior and inferior to life. Though not subject to decay, it is an "artifice," without life. The dilemma is comparable to that presented by Keats in "Ode on a Grecian Urn" (page 815).   LP

303.   *William Butler Yeats*   The Second Coming (page 861)

In 1919, the year this poem was published, Ireland was in the midst of a bloody civil war; World War I had only recently ended (November 1918); and Russia was engaged in civil war following its Revolution of 1917. All these events portended for Yeats the approaching end of the Christian era, the historical cycle begun almost two thousand years earlier with the birth of Christ. In Yeats's historical theory the transition from one historical era to another was always marked by an epoch of violence and disorder.

The poem is divided into two sections. The first gives the poet's impression of the present. The second presents an apocalyptic vision of the future.

His description of the present is terrifying. The opening two lines present a symbol of a world out of control. In the ancient art of falconry the falcon was trained always to return upon a signal to the wrist of the falconer. But in Yeats's image the falcon has flown beyond the hearing of his master's signal. The adjective "Mere" (4) here retains its obsolete meaning of absolute, entire, sheer. "Ceremony" (6) had for Yeats particular value as connected with orderly and civilized living (see "A Prayer for My Daughter," which follows immediately after "The Second Coming" in Yeats's *Collected Poems*). The closing lines of this section describe a familiar crisis situation where good people, by nature moderate and tolerant, are uncertain what should be done, while the bigots, the terrorists, and the assassination squads are full of "passionate intensity"—all too certain in their ignorant minds that they know exactly what is needed.

The opening lines of the second section seem to sound a note of hope. "Surely," the poet declares, "some revelation is at hand"—the word "revelation" suggesting a divine manifestation; "Surely the Second Coming is at hand"—the words "Second

Coming" reminding us of the Second Coming of Christ prophesied in the Bible. Things can hardly get much worse; therefore these violent actions must be auspices of change, signs of the shifting from one historical era to another. No sooner has the poet uttered the words "Second Coming" than he has a vision. An image arises to consciousness (not just from his own unconscious but from the racial unconscious underlying it) of the stone sphinx in the Egyptian desert slowly coming to life and "moving its slow thighs." The vision is vivid. Yeats depicts not only its gaze "blank and pitiless as the sun," but the reactions of the desert birds to this amazing phenomenon. In indignant clamor they "Reel" in circles above the slowly awakening sphinx; but Yeats with marvelous poetic economy depicts them only through their shadows (thus giving us in one picture the shadows, the birds that cast them, and the bright desert sun that causes them). The vision is brief, but now Yeats knows (or claims to know) that twenty centuries of "stony sleep" (the sphinx's) "Were vexed to nightmare by a rocking cradle" (a metonymy for the infant Christ), and he also knows what "rough beast, its hour come round at last, / Slouches toward Bethlehem to be born." The vision is a vision of horror. The new era, its time come to replace the old one, is symbolized by a "rough beast." (The question asked in the last two lines is rhetorical, as shown by the ambiguous syntax of the sentence, in which "And" indicates the presence of parallelism but in which "what" can logically be linked only with "That" (19) ["I know that . . . and what . . ."], making "what" not an interrogative but a relative pronoun calling logically for a period at the end of the sentence. But when was logic ever the most direct way to poetic power?)

Our expectation, set up by the title and by lines 9–10, that the poem would concern the Second Coming of Christ is shattered by the last two lines of the poem. It is the coming of Antichrist that is prophesied. Legends tell us that Antichrist will be born in Bethlehem, and Antichrist is referred to recurrently in the New Testament as the "beast." It is Yeats, however, whose genius has assimilated Antichrist with the desert sphinx and given him new dimensions of horror and evil by his use of the adjective "rough" and the verb "slouches."

Surely, this poem derives its greatness from the feeling of evil and horror it so powerfully evokes. Yet the most controversial critical question regarding the poem occurs just here. Scholars familiar with Yeats's historical theories (expressed most fully in his book *A Vision*) have pointd out that the era Yeats expected to follow the Christian one was more amenable to him than the Christian era, and that therefore the advent of the "rough beast" is to be welcomed. As Marjorie Perloff has pointed out, "The basic argument is whether the poem should be read in the light of *A Vision*, in which case one may argue, as Helen Vendler does, that 'Yeats approves intellectually, if not emotionally of the Second Coming. . . . The Beast is a world-restorer.' " LP

Both his theory and his practice point to the need to read an individual poem by Yeats in the context of the rest of his poetry and of his life. A full understanding of this poem requires at least a reading of Donald A. Stauffer's analysis in *The Golden Nightingale* (New York: Macmillan, 1949) 48–79. But even without the richness of the Yeatsian context, the poem has beauty and power that are available to the sensitive reader.

Both actually and superficially it is a meditation on nature and on the passage of time, which alters the human observer but leaves nature essentially unchanged; it thus resembles Wordsworth's "Tintern Abbey" and Keats's "Ode to a Nightingale" (page 817), poems in which the response of the man is both intensely present and also intensely subjective and retrospective. External natural facts elicit feelings and memories and desires, and time present is contrasted with time past, human and natural. Nature undergoes cyclical changes and keeps returning to its same condition; the human being undergoes progressive changes that include decay and death, but also memories of earlier states. Nature is permanent and always in the present, man is transient but contains his own past, his sensitive present, and his predictions of the future.

The elegiac tone of this poem is established in the first stanza—autumn, dryness, twilight, stillness. But paradoxically the poem also contains terms that contrast with these: beauty, mirror-like clarity, brimming water, clamorous wings. Yeats maintains the tone, and also the contrasts, throughout the poem, summing up his inability to understand the swans in the simple declaration that they are "mysterious, beautiful" (26). Although he attributes much to them, they cannot be wholly captured in his language or his imagination, justifying the recurring Yeatsian strategy of the conclusion—a rhetorical question (for other examples, see "Leda and the Swan," page 647, "The Second Coming," page 861, and "Among School Children.") The questions in these poems are not really questions, for the poem has implied the answer, as it does here. The speaker does not really wonder where the swans will be (in fact, they will most probably be where they are now, in the streams and lake of Coole Park, and if not these particular swans then their indistinguishable offspring). Nor does the question really mean "what other men will be delighted by them," for any man who sees them will be delighted; nor does it mean "where will *I* be when 'I awake some day / To find they have flown away,' " for the answer to that is implicit too: since the swans represent to him the continuity and permanence of the natural world, any awakening that discovers them gone will be an awakening out of nature, into death.

The number "nine-and-fifty," phrased archaically and with an implied hint of magic, first introduces the "mystery" of the swans: although they seem paired "lover by lover," the number is odd. The mystery of this number is augmented by the other one, nineteen; both of them are prime numbers, both end in nine, and both sound so very precise that a reader inevitably asks their significance. Is there a meaningful link between 59 and 19? The speaker has carefully kept track of the number of years he has been returning to this spot, and has carefully counted the swans, year after year—and yet, as he reports, even on that first count he had not finished counting before they flew up off the water. How can he know their precise number? As they suddenly mounted into the air, perhaps disturbed by his presence, perhaps even reluctant to be numbered, they scattered (suggesting random motion) yet wheeled; they flew in rings but the rings were "broken." What this succession of images suggests is a precise but uncountable number, a patterned movement that remained incompleted: a contrast between the human desire to discover number and geometric shape, and nature's reluctance to be comprehended in such intellectual undertakings.

From this perspective, we can see that the qualities attributed to the swans in the remainder of the poem are human interpretations: their wings beat like bells (tolling the passage of time, to the observer?), they are lovers, the water is "Companionable," they are "Unwearied," their hearts do not grow old, and—a clear indication that the qualities are not inherent in the swans—"Passion or conquest" *attend* them. They are therefore genuinely mysterious, for the poem has not penetrated their mysteries, but seen in them parallels and contrasts to the human condition, revealing the impossibility of understanding them for what they are.

The natural world, then, is impenetrable to the human observer. What remains in the poem is the situation in which this places him—seeing the swans in their continuity, recognizing in himself the changes that time brings, confessing the pain that these changes have caused, and projecting further loss in the future. As the final question indicates, there will be other men to fill his place (as in fact there have been other swans to replenish the flock), but there is no consolation for the man in that fact, nor does his verbal tactic of thinking of his future as an awakening lessen the sense of loss.   TRA

343

The Elements of Drama

CHAPTER ONE

The Nature of Drama

Susan Glaspell **Trifles** (page 870)

See the commentary on "A Jury of Her Peers" on page 43 of this manual.

The main difference between the texts of the play and the short story is that the story more explicitly defines the emotions of the characters—and in particular, of Mrs. Hale (given the name "Martha" in the story but not in the play). Mrs. Hale is the point-of-view character in a limited omniscient story. Her feelings and her motives are explored, and she is more clearly presented as a person with internal conflicts having to do with her sense of guilt for the lonely life of Minnie Wright and complicity in the crime she committed. She is initially mistrustful of Mrs. Peters, a woman who has not known Minnie and who by definition is "married to the law." She must therefore be more hesitant in working up her defense of the woman who committed the murder.

In the play, the women approach their task more as "peers" than as characters with a personal conflict. This is shown most clearly in one passage in which Glaspell reverses the roles of these women. The story (page 342) assigns to Mrs. Peters a discovery that Mrs. Hale made in the play (page 876). In the story, Mrs. Peters finds the clumsily sewn quilt piece (an indication of Mrs. Wright's "nervous" lack of concentration on her sewing, and thus evidence of a state of mind that could be linked to the murder of her husband). In both play and story, Mrs. Hale begins to pull out the bad sewing, to Mrs. Peters's consternation. Again, reversing their roles, in the story it is Mrs. Peters who wonders what made Mrs. Wright nervous, and

Mrs. Hale who defends her: "I don't know as she was nervous. I sometimes sew awful queer when I'm just tired." In rewriting the play as a story, Glaspell decided to make the case that Mrs. Peters discovers this evidence, and that Mrs. Hale not only destroys it by pulling out the bad stitches (as she had done in the play) but also denies that the sewing is a sign of distress. Mrs. Peters in the story is at this point like her husband—investigating and analyzing clues—while Mrs. Hale is attempting to cover up for her old girlhood friend. In the play, they were mutually engaged in detection and defense.

Mrs. Peters also does not display "timid acquiescence" in her "thin voice," does not have a "frightened look" and "a voice that seem[s] to shrink away from the subject," "a flurried voice" when she first confronts her husband after the discovery of the dead canary. These are all qualities in her that are added or emphasized in the story, that change its focus from that of the play. In "Trifles," Mrs. Peters and Mrs. Hale mutually arrive at the same position, helping each other determine that although Minnie Wright is legally guilty of murder, she is not to be convicted on the evidence they have found. In "A Jury of Her Peers" Mrs. Hale is the indubitable protagonist, helping and directing Mrs. Peters to share that position.

In the play, the two women are joint protagonists, one more experienced than the other, but no more contrasted than they are in the initial stage direction: Mrs. Peters "is a slight wiry woman, with a thin nervous face. Mrs. Hale is larger and would ordinarily be called more comfortable looking, but she is disturbed now and looks fearfully about as she enters." They are different, but neither of them dominates their growing relationship. As if to emphasize this, Glaspell concludes that stage direction: "The women have come in slowly, and stand close together near the door." They are "close together," not far apart.

This aspect of the play more clearly focuses one of the themes that both works share, the conflict between the men and the women. There are differences of personality but not of philosophy or purpose between the women in the play. They are aligned against the men in two ways, one trifling, the other immediately consequential. They are concerned with what Sheriff Peters laughs at, "the insignificance of kitchen things" (story), the manifold cares of women in a rural life, particularly the sewing, the cleaning, the cooking, the constant labor that to their husbands seems not labor but play. This the women wryly allow the men to condescend to them about, knowing better but not challenging the patronizing jokes. These are the "trifles" of the play and the story. The title of the story points to the other, more significant alignment of the women against the men: they will undercut the attempt to bring the law of the male-dominated society to bear upon Minnie Wright. They will judge her—and on the evidence they have, they find her guilty of justifiable homicide, and they pardon her. Thus with a diminished area of conflict between the two women, the play more directly focuses on the conflict between the sexes and its two expressions, minor and major in nature. The women will allow the men to patronize them; that is the price they pay for their sympathetic forgiveness of Minnie Wright's crime.

There are other differences between play and story that exploit the strengths of both genres. In the story, the author freely interprets Mrs. Hale's feelings and ideas, and allows her to interpret those of the other characters. This too strengthens the position of this character as protagonist, for she emerges as the most sensitive, and the one most open to self-examination and the resolution of inner conflicts. As the point-of-view character in the story she is also the most perceptive, so that we easily trust her interpretations—Mr. Hale is not vicious in belittling the women but speaks "with good-natured superiority" (page 337), the county attorney is "disdainful" when he pushes at the dirty pans under the sink (page 339), she notices the "flurried voice" of Mrs. Peters when the attorney is "too preoccupied to notice" it (page 345), and so forth. Mrs. Hale's perspective controls our reading and directs our sympathies.

In the play, without such interpretive remarks, the characters are more immediate and direct in presenting themselves. They are not filtered through Mrs. Hale's consciousness, but stand alone, unique and believable human beings. The playwright offers stage directions to assist the actors in their interpretations (and the written text thus allows readers some insight by that means), but much of the effect of the play will depend on the abilities of the acting ensemble to feel their way into these characters, to sense the conflicts and congruences of them as integral individuals working together to create the totality of dramatic effect. There is a great burden upon the actors, and an even greater one on the reader who does not see a staged presentation, to interpret and intuit the reality of these people. But if we are competent in doing so, we are more immediately in touch with them, and if the play is staged effectively, we will be able to achieve that sense of reality without the moderating imposition of an author's definitions and descriptions.   TRA

August Strindberg   **The Stronger** (page 881)

The primary question confronting a reader of Strindberg's *The Stronger* is obvious: Who *is* the stronger, Miss Y or Mrs. X? At first reading Miss Y may seem the stronger. Considerable evidence supports such a conclusion. In the first place we are conditioned to believe that a person who is capable of remaining wordless in the face of an uncontrolled spate of words is both strong and wise. A babbler, especially a female babbler, is supposed inevitably to wind herself into a cocoon of her own words and become entrapped. Thus preconditioned, we need only reflect that Mrs. X, however unwittingly, has remade herself in imitation of her rival to become convinced that Miss Y, the rival, is somehow victorious, even though she has lost both her fiance' and the man who formed the apex of the love triangle. When we document the evidence, Miss Y's position as the true victor—the stronger— seems even more convincing. Mrs. X embroiders tulips (which she hates but which are Miss Y's favorite flowers) on her husband's slippers; she accompanies her husband to Lake Mälarn (Miss Y hates salt water); her son is named Eskil (the name of Miss Y's father); she wears Miss Y's colors, reads *her* favorite authors, eats *her* favorite foods, drinks *her* favorite drinks.

Many a woman, realizing, as Mrs. X does in a sudden flash of insight, how powerful Miss Y's influence has been on her and her life would acknowledge the superior strength of her adversary. Indeed, for a few moments Mrs. X seems to be making just such an acknowledgment. "I hate you, hate you, hate you!" she cries, after a passionate speech revealing her recognition of the true meaning of past circumstances.

"I hate you . . . ," however, does not express Mrs. X's final position. Her character, indeed, changes and grows before our eyes. Her angry outburst is followed by scornful vituperation: "You only sit there . . . as quiet as a stork by a rat hole . . . and read the papers . . . to see if someone hasn't been given notice at the theater." This gives place to pity: "You are unhappy, unhappy like one who has been wounded." And pity gives place to triumph: "Thank you, Amelia, for all your good lessons. Thanks for teaching my husband how to love. Now I'm going home to love him."

At one point during this swift dénouement, Mrs. X says of Miss Y, "You come out the weaker one"; at another point, "I am . . . the stronger one." But a bald assertion is not necessarily a statement of fact. (Mrs. X has earlier made several statements that were patently not statements of fact; for example, "And you see he's true to me.") The question, then, presents itself: do we, upon consideration, have to concede that Mrs. X is, in truth, "the stronger"? An affirmative answer to this question is supported by Mrs. X's ability to accommodate to her discovery. After the point of recognition has been reached, Mrs. X, rapidly progressing from one psychologically feasible point of view to another and then another, reveals that her strength lies in the acceptance of what is valid in her marriage and the rejection of what is invalid. In other words, she becomes aware of the change in herself and its importance in her relationship with her husband, and she also recognizes that the delusions of fidelity with which she has comforted herself in the past are only delusions.

Strindberg himself, writing to his wife, Siri, who was to play Mrs. X in the opening performance, instructed her to play Mrs. X as the "stronger; that is to say, the softer. For," he continued, "the rigid person breaks while the supple person bends—and rises again." LP

Samuel Beckett **Krapp's Last Tape** (page 885)

The play has a simple plot: Krapp at 69 observes his birthday as he has for more than forty years, by making an annual tape-recorded report on the year just past. He prepares for this by taking out a previous tape (Krapp at 39) and listening to key passages of it, talking back to it and commenting on the man that he used to be. On the tape, Krapp at 39 has just listened to Krapp of ten or twelve years earlier, so the time perspective is tripled, and we have the opportunity to hear a man recapturing and defining his life at three stages, the third one to be the last. Beckett thus brilliantly exploits modern technology to create dialogue and interaction in a one-character play. Whether Krapp literally dies before his next birthday is irrelevant, since in this "last tape" he renounces life and is prepared to leave it; on the climactic tape he listens to he recorded the decisions that have led to the failure he has become, and a literal death would only lend emphasis to his failure.

Krapp carefully selects the tape he will monitor, looking in his written ledger for the year in which three memorable events occurred: his mother died, he had a vision of the meaning of his life and work, and he renounced love. When he finds the spool of tape he wants (relishing as a writer might the deliciousness of the word "spool"), he listens first to his earlier self commenting on the self in his late twenties. That youngest man had just ended a year in which his father died, and he resolved to drink less, to have a "less . . . engrossing sexual life," and to get to work on his writing. The young man suffered from the chronic constipation that remains with Krapp throughout his life—a condition that he believes is worsened by his addiction to bananas (there seems to be no medical or nutritional validity to that belief). Krapp at 39 laughs derisively at the "young whelp" he had been—and Krapp at 69 joins in the ironic laughter.

The tape then turns to the material of his thirty-ninth year. First he recalls the day his mother died while he waited and watched from a park bench, wishing her misery would soon end, playing ball with a little white dog, flirting with a nursemaid and being rebuffed. At the moment of his mother's death, he lets the dog have the ball and it takes it from him, "gently, gently," a relinquishment that seems to symbolize letting his mother pass out of his life. This remembered scene is rife with images in black and white—the black ball, the white dog, the "dark" nursemaid in her starched white uniform pushing a "funereal" black perambulator.

The light and dark mingle again in the next event, the visionary experience on the night of the vernal equinox (when daylight and darkness equally share the day). In the howling wind at the end of a jetty, with waves crashing on "great granite rocks" and white foam flashing in the light of the lighthouse, Krapp sees "the whole thing . . . the vision at last," and finds in himself "the light of the understanding and the fire" that he juxtaposes to "the dark [he had] always struggled to keep under." The precise terms of his vision are not presented—Krapp at 69 keeps switching forward, so as to avoid them and to get on to the final scene—but we can safely infer that it revealed to him that his beliefs until that day were mistaken, and that his struggle to overcome the darker side of himself was a part of that mistake. The imagery mingling the black and white suggests that for him the chosen road to his great work should combine the light and fire of aspiration and intensity with the darker impulses that he will not be able to rise above.

This idea is also present in the third and, to Krapp at 69, most important of his experiences in that memorable year. On a bright and sunny day he goes with a woman to a lake where after a swim they lie in a punt and drift with the current. It is a scene that marks the end of an affair: "I said again I thought it was hopeless and no good going on, and she agreed." Yet what occurs is a scene of gentle lovemaking in which the waves and the current seem to provide the movement of their copulation—*seem to*, because the man and woman lie "without moving," and their union may or may not be literally sexual. The text is particularly ambiguous: because of the bright sunlight, when he asks her to look at him she can only squint until he shades her with his body: "the eyes just slits, because of the glare. I bent over her to get them in the shadow and they opened. (*Pause. Low*) Let me in." As Beckett's French translation of his play makes clear, her *eyes* let me in, but the sexual implication is certainly there. As a scene of "farewell to love" (as his ledger called it), the event merges two opposing impulses, to accept love and to reject it, for while they intellectually and spiritually agree that their affair is "hopeless and no good," the natural movement of the world urges them to go on.

In the intervening thirty years since that remarkable year Krapp has deteriorated physically and failed in his vocation, as is shown both in the stage actions and in the tape that he tries to make as a record of this year. The description of his costume and the banana-eating pantomime reveal a clownish man. The pallor of skin that rarely goes outdoors and the broken capillaries of an alcoholic's nose give him the face of a clown: "white face, purple nose." His costume is that of a Chaplinesque tramp, though age has made his walk "laborious" rather than comic. In eating his banana, he almost performs the classic banana-peel trip of a clown. His drinking, like his bananas, has now become a constant addiction, as he repeatedly goes into the darkness at the back of the stage where the pop of corks and the sound of a bottle against the edge of a glass signal his tippling.* His great life's work has sold only seventeen copies. His sexuality is now limited to fantasizing about the heroine of a novel and bouts with a "bony old ghost of a whore." And he has given up on his life. What he was thirty years ago is now "all done with," he wants to "let that go," and in answer to his nostalgic wish to "be again, be again" what he once was, he ironically says "once wasn't enough for you."

At 39, he made the decision that ruined his life—to dedicate himself to his writing ("homework," he now ironically calls it) and to cut himself off from love. In sacrificing his life to his art—that high romantic ideal—he destroyed his chance for happiness, though at the time he anticipated a greater happiness through art. But he failed as a writer, and the sacrifice of his humanity has turned out to be pointless.

However, rather than ending his play on this note of fatalism and the desire for death, Beckett allows Krapp to return yet again to his highest point, the scene in the punt. This time, he plays to the end of the tape, when the 39-year-old responds to the same kind of question, would he want to live his life over again: "Perhaps my best years are gone. When there was a chance of happiness. But I wouldn't want them back. Not with the fire in me now. No, I wouldn't want them back." The "fire" of course has not remained, the vision was never fulfilled, but unlike most of us, Krapp can recapture with his tapes the life that still had hope in it.

Beckett's works, like those of his mentor James Joyce, may contain a wealth of esoteric symbolic meanings. While directing the play for the 1969 Berlin production,

---

*I have not found a wholly satisfactory explanation of the popping corks that occur at ten-second intervals, for that specific time period seems to rule out wine or beer (which was sold in corked bottles). The sound of whiskey and soda and the pouring of neat whiskey from the bottle into a glass late in the play are literal and comprehensible, but emptying a corked bottle and then two others in ten seconds each seems impossible unless Krapp has a collection of one-swig corked drinks. I am inclined to think that he may be taking some sort of laxative for his constipation, but there's no evidence for that either. At any rate, in the Berlin production that Beckett directed in 1969, the popping corks are eliminated in favor of a silhouetted pouring of drinks from a whiskey bottle.

350

the playwright prepared a "director's notebook" that elaborates on the meanings of the many references to black and white, dark and light. These are based on Manichean ethics, which promote an ascetic renunciation of worldliness and which represent the world as a dichotomy between flesh and the spirit, associating flesh with darkness, spirit with light. Such a symbolic subtext is not readily available in witnessing a performance of the play, but the sensitive viewer will not miss the images (and the staging, if it follows Beckett's stage directions, will reinforce the sense of a dark/light dichotomy). One specific example may suffice here: as 39-year-old Krapp sits on the park bench watching the window of his dying mother's room, waiting for its blind to be lowered to signify her death, he plays with a white dog, tossing a black rubber ball for it to fetch. When the death-signal is given, he pauses in his game, and then gives the ball to the dog. He says: "A small, old, black, hard, solid rubber ball. . . . I shall feel it, in my hand, until my dying day. . . . I might have kept it. . . . But I gave it to the dog." The ball (like "this old muckball" the earth which the 69-year-old later relinquishes) is a symbol of the world of the flesh which his mother has just left, and after hesitating Krapp delivers it up to the whiteness (spirituality) of the dog, a surrendering that haunts him forever. This action, with its ambivalence and hesitancy, pervades the play, as in one form or another Krapp tries to give up on the world and its pleasures to devote himself to the spiritual light that he wants to capture in his art—tries to, and keeps failing to. Even one passing remark in an arcane allusion touches on this mingling. Krapp at 39 begins his report on Krapp in his twenties thus: "At that time I think I was still living on and off with Bianca in Kedar Street." The name "Bianca" means "white"; "Kedar" (no such street name exists in Dublin) is the Hebrew word for "black," and the name has also been interpreted as an anagram of "darke." The critical interpretations listed below will provide further material for those wanting to pursue the underlying symbolism.

Among the many critical discussions of the play, this note is most indebted to the following: Ruby Cohn, *Back to Beckett* (Princeton NJ: Princeton UP, 1973) 165–72; Vivian Mercier, *Beckett/Beckett* (Oxford: Oxford UP, 1977) *passim*; Beryl S. Fletcher and John Fletcher, *A Student's Guide to the Plays of Samuel Beckett* (London: Faber, 1978) 119–33; and Dougald McMillan and Martha Fehsenfeld, *Beckett in the Theatre: The Author as Practical Playwright and Director*, Vol. I. (London: Calder, 1988) 241–311.

In 1988 a television version of the play was recorded for the Public Broadcasting System under the general title "Beckett Directs Beckett." It was based on a production directed by Samuel Beckett in Berlin in 1977, and stars Beckett's Krapp, Rick Cluchey. There are a number of departures from the printed text, as often occurs in a staged production, but as the playwright was the director who made the changes, they may be regarded as authorized. At this writing, the production is not yet publicly available, but PBS may at some future date issue it on videotape; if so, it will be a valuable teaching aid as well as an important record of the playwright's interpretation of his play.   TRA

CHAPTER TWO

Realistic and Nonrealistic Drama

Henrik Ibsen **A Doll House** (page 898)

It may be difficult, both for the instructor and for students, to look at so famous and influential a play without being dazzled and misled by what it represented in its own time (''the door slam heard round the world'') in the cause of women's rights and by what contemporary readers and producers do to keep it relevant to ''women's issues.'' Perhaps the most important corrective that can be applied is Ibsen's own statement twenty years after the play opened, when he was saluted by the Norwegian Association for Women's Rights as ''the creator of Nora'':

> . . . I have been more of a poet and less of a social philosopher than most people have been inclined to believe. . . . I can't claim the honor of ever having worked consciously for women's rights. I'm not even sure I know what they are. To me it has seemed a matter of human rights.
>
> (Quoted in Shafer, 61)

This disclaimer is important because it broadens the theme rather than denying that Nora's situation makes a statement on the position of women. Nora is certainly the protagonist, but as Ibsen implies, that does not mean that she alone carries the themes of the play. Study questions 3 and 9 may be used to open up this issue. The title: with the permission of the translator, I have used the title that scholars now generally agree is most appropriate, although it is not the one Professor Reinert used nor the traditional ones used for most English translations, *A Doll's House* and *The Doll's House*. *A Doll House*, referring to a child's miniature model of a home complete with furnishings, is the literal meaning of Ibsen's words, and more accurately reflects the situation in which Nora, Torvald, their children and servants, and to some extent their visitors exist: a prettified imitation of a home and a marriage. Of the options offered in study question 3, *A Doll's House* seems to imply that Nora is alone the creator and possessor of the falseness of this home. While her noble, criminal act and the lies it necessitated have presumably made it possible for Torvald to survive and even thrive, not even Nora supposes that she is the possessor of the home (clearly, when she departs, she wants to take nothing of Torvald's with her).

As to who is responsible for the doll-house condition of their marriage, we must recognize that it is a mutual creation. After criticizing her financial irresponsibility, Torvald insists ''I don't want you any different from just what you are—my own sweet little songbird'' (901); Nora is no less conscious of the pretenses required to maintain their play family when she tells Mrs. Linde that she might tell Torvald of her life-saving act ''when I'm no longer young and pretty . . . I mean when

Torvald no longer feels about me the way he does now, when he no longer thinks it's fun when I dance for him and put on costumes and recite for him'' (907). They are both aware that their marriage is founded on childish role-playing, but at the opening of the play neither wants to change that—and it seems, with Torvald's business success, they will never need to do so. But there are stirrings in Nora as she tells Mrs. Linde that someday she would like to tell Torvald of her sacrifice for him, and as she tells her and Dr. Rank that like a mischievous child she wants Torvald to hear her say a naughty word. These are the stirrings toward growing out of her child's world that provide the impetus for the plot.

That plot gets underway as a consequence of one of the many ironies that fill the play: Torvald's promotion, which promises the happpiness that money is presumed by the Helmers to buy, motivates both Krogstad and Mrs. Linde to become involved in the life of this house, and these two influential outsiders precipitate Nora's self-examination and her final decision. Both of them enter the action with good intentions and with financial difficulties, paralleling Nora's situation of years before: Krogstad needs to improve his position in the bank and rehabilitate his name for the sake of his blowing children, and Mrs. Linde needs a job and a sense of being useful to others. Krogstad's villainy develops as he is thwarted and then scorned, while Mrs. Linde's desire to help leads her to push Nora toward the full revelation of the past so that their marriage can be re-established on firm ground—until both characters contribute to the fall of the house, and then, by marrying, resolve their own situations and remove themselves from the life of the Helmers.

Much of the action of the play involves Nora's efforts to maintain her secret, putting herself in conflict with Mrs. Linde's principle of honesty and at the mercy of Krogstad's blackmail. She thus creates a dilemma for herself out of her two desires (to outgrow her child-bride role and show that she has been mature and responsible, and to maintain her presumed innocence and mask the crime). The role of Dr. Rank in this action is to shed light on the dilemma Nora faces. As friend and confidant he is a pillar of the household, both Torvald's best friend and the person with whom Nora can talk of her hopes and affections. But under the pressure of Krogstad's demands, Nora desperately but playfully turns to Dr. Rank for financial help—and her coquetry leads him to declare his love, which makes it impossible for her to pursue their intimacy. On the other hand, the doctor's fatal illness cuts him off from further friendship with Torvald (Rank knows that his friend is too immature to stand up to the ordeal of watching death). With their only friend gone, the Helmers are forced into the intimacy of the final scene.

Is Nora's transformation from child to adult too sudden to be plausible? In one sense, as suggested by the second study question for *Othello* (page 1147), the question is impertinent: we should ask instead, does her change represent a vital, human truth? Her change occurs in the space of three hours in a theatrical performance, in the space of about 36 hours of elapsed time in the dramatized action, and at a rather late point in the life of a woman with three children—but those three ''clocks'' by which we measure this dramatic event all have in common a literalism about the relationship of personality to action. They ask, that is, for an examination of literal psychological causalities rather than for an analysis of a realistic drama. For we must not confuse "realistic" with "real" or "literal." In a realistic play, the pertinent questions should be: Do people make self-discoveries that change the course of their actions? Is Nora sufficiently characterized to explain how the events that are dramatized (and those from the past that are called into the present action as influences) can account for a change in her? Does her change result in an effective dramatic climax? Does her change embody Ibsen's themes? The answer to *these* questions is "yes."

And what does the future hold for Nora and Torvald? This, too, is an impertinent question, for of course there is no "future" after the final curtain. We should ask, rather, with what feelings Ibsen leaves the audience. Do we want Torvald to discover himself and the errors that have led him to his isolation? Do we believe that Nora has the courage to seek out the meaning of her life without the comfortable hypocrisies she deserts? Does this play sadden or exhilarate us? Or both? Does it achieve anything of the double emotion of a tragic ending?

Much has been written about this play, but the indispensable source for any teacher of the play, to be used more or less extensively depending on the amount of time one has, is Yvonne Shafer, ed., *Approaches to Teaching Ibsen's* A Doll's House (New York: MLA, 1985).

Two excellent film versions (both made in 1973) starring Claire Bloom and Jane Fonda are available on videocassette, and a BBC television production with Juliet Stevenson was made in 1991. Claire Bloom also appears on an audio recording of 1971. TRA

Tennessee Williams **The Glass Menagerie** (page 955)

On a realistic-nonrealistic scale, *The Glass Menagerie* lies perhaps midway between *A Doll House* and *The Sandbox*. Its principal (though not only) nonrealistic elements lie in the use made of (1) a narrator, (2) lighting, and (3) music.

1. Tom combines the roles of narrator, stage manager, and character. As narrator he tells us, "The play is memory." He clearly means his own memory, and the play may be said to assimilate the first person and dramatic points of view. It is not realistically consistent, however, for in some scenes (2, 6, 7) Tom is not present, and these scenes could not logically come from his memory.

2. "Being a memory play," Tom informs us, "it is dimly lighted, it is sentimental, it is not realistic." Lighting is indeed used for emotional and sentimental effects. At the climax of the quarrel between Tom and Amanda in scene 3, the upstage area is "lit with a turgid smoky red glow," while in scene 7 the new floor lamp, with its rose colored silk shade, throws a soft light on Laura's face, bringing out "its fragile, unearthly beauty." Williams skillfully handles his plot so that the inopportune-opportune electrical failure in scene 6 not only underlines Tom's preparations for leaving home by using the light bill money to pay dues to the Merchant Seamen's Union but also requires the final romantic scene, between Laura and Jim, to be played out by candlelight. Laura's final blowing out of these candles both ends the play

and symbolizes the extinction for her of any hope for a fulfilling life. Lighting is also used for ironical effects, as when the outsize photograph of Tom's father suddenly lights up in scene 4.

3. "In memory everything seems to happen to music," says Tom. The "fiddle in the wings" playing the Glass Menagerie theme adds poignance and delicate beauty to the scenes featuring Laura. The music from the Dance Hall turns ominous when some cruel revelation is about to be made. But the music, like the lighting, is also used for ironical effects, as when in scene 5 the music from the Dance Hall—"All the World Is Waiting for the Sunrise"—is counterpointed against Tom's remarks about the thirties, when "All the world was waiting for bombardments," or as when, later in that scene, Tom tells his mother they are going to have "a gentleman caller," and this "annunciation" is "celebrated with music."

Williams's original script called for a fourth nonrealistic feature, the "Screen Device," by means of which magic-lantern slides were to be projected on one wall bearing titles and images such as *Où sont les neiges d'antan* when Amanda talks about her former beaux in scene 1, or a picture of blue roses to introduce scene 2, in which Laura tells about her high-school crush on Jim O'Connor. The screen device was not used in the immensely successful first Broadway production of the play, and critics have found it distracting and gimmicky, seemingly designed "to reduce all the scenes—even the tenderest—to ludicrous parodies" (Gerald Weales, *Tennessee Williams* [Minneapolis: U of Minnesota P, 1965] 33). Of the two available editions of the play—the Library Edition (New Directions) and the Acting Edition (Dramatists Play Service), the former includes the "Screen Device," but the latter does not. The text of the play here used is that of the Library Edition with the screen device omitted.

Williams also makes an impressionistic use of time. The domestic drama and the illusions of the "American dream" are played off by Tom against the social realities of the thirties throughout the play; yet we get into trouble if we try to be precise in dating it. In the last scene Jim speaks of having visited the Chicago World's Fair (1933–1934) "summer before last," but Tom in his narration refers to the bombing of Guernica (1937) and the Munich Pact (1938), and in scene 5 he reads a newspaper with the enormous headline "Franco Triumphs" (1939).

Whatever its nonrealistic features, which include the poetic prose spoken by Tom as narrator, the dialogue of the play is completely realistic, and real as granite, and the characters rendered through it are solid and unforgettable.

Whose play is it?—Tom's, Laura's, or Amanda's? A strong case can be made for each. Tom is both the narrator and the trapped young artist struggling to break away from a stultifying environment. Of the three main characters he is the one who takes positive action to break out of illusion and pursue his goal, though apparently to no effect, for in his first appearance he is still dressed as a merchant sailor, and his final narration indicates he has done little but travel a great deal. The negative imagery ("The cities swept about me like dead leaves") enforces a feeling of futility. Instead of pursuing, he is "pursued"—by the memory of his sister Laura.—Is it then Laura's play? The play's title refers to her; she is the focus of the action, which, according to Williams's opening notes, consists of two parts—

preparation for the gentleman caller, and appearance of the gentleman caller; it is she who brings the curtain down by blowing out the candles. Yet Laura is almost entirely a passive character, a figure of pathos, acted upon rather than acting. She has her brief moment of hope and disappointment, and at the end is the same wistful, pathetic creature she was at the beginning. —Is it then Amanda's play? Certainly, Amanda is the most rounded, fully developed character in the play; her role would demand the most talent from a player taking her part; and the actress taking her part would receive top billing on the theater marquee. She is all that Williams says she is in his opening note—heroic, foolish, tender, unwittingly cruel, lovable, laughable, pitiable, and, above all, vital—a unique dramatic creation.

The chief symbol of the play is the glass menagerie, the dream world which Laura retreats to and which, in its delicate and fragile beauty, is a symbol for Laura herself. When Tom, in scene 3, quarrels violently with his mother, tries to leave, has trouble with his coat, and hurls it across the room shattering several of the figurines and drawing a cry of wounded pain from Laura, we see his dilemma. His quarrels with his mother distress Laura, and he cannot leave without damaging her. Of all the figurines in the collection, the glass unicorn most symbolizes Laura, because its horn, like her shyness, separates it from the normal world and makes it unique. When Jim, during the dancing, temporarily overcomes her shyness, and breaks off the horn, Laura is not distressed. "It doesn't matter. Maybe it's a blessing in disguise." But when, after kissing her, Jim draws himself up short and reveals his previous commitment, Laura gives the broken figurine to him to keep as a souvenir, and withdraws forever from the world of normality.

The principal primary sources for investigation of the biographical backgrounds of the play are *Remember Me to Tom* by Edwina Dakin Williams (the playwright's mother) as told to Lucy Freeman (New York: Putnam's, 1963) and Tennessee Williams's *Memoirs* (New York: Doubleday, 1975). The former reveals how much Edwina had in common with Amanda beyond a liking for jonquils. The latter, weaving back and forth in time, mingles family recollections with a very explicit history of Williams's sexual experiences and homosexual activities; it is not recommended for incautious assignment.

A film production starring Joanne Woodward and John Malkovich is available on MCA Home Video.   LP

Edward Albee   **The Sandbox** (page 1003)

In an introduction to his play *The American Dream*, Edward Albee writes, "The play is an examination of the American Scene, an attack on the substitution of artificial for real values in our society, a condemnation of complacency, cruelty, emasculation and vacuity; it is a stand against the fiction that everything in this slipping land of ours is peachy-keen." Elsewhere he tells us that in writing *The Sandbox* he extracted several characters from *The American Dream*, which he was working on at the time, and "placed them in a situation different than, but related to, their predicament in the longer play." We may assume, therefore, that his dramatic purposes in *The Sandbox* are similar to, though not identical with, his purposes in *The American Dream*.

The play belongs, of course, to the "Theater of the Absurd," a contemporary dramatic genre in which the logical absurdity and meaninglessness of the events presented on the stage reflect an absurdity and meaninglessness which the playwright sees in life. But the meaninglessness of the events presented does not mean that the play is meaningless. *The Sandbox*, indeed, is a brief summation of a life and a death; a dramatic synecdoche. What it shows is a life emptied of content and value. Life, as presented here, is vapid, barren, and sterile, and death is without dignity.

The play works largely by means of symbols, many of them multiple symbols. The sandbox itself, for instance, represents (1) a beach; (2) Grandma's second childhood (she plays in it with a toy pail and shovel); (3) the grave (she buries herself in it); and (4) the barrenness of modern civilization, which T. S. Eliot presented as a desert in "The Waste Land." The bareness of the stage reinforces the symbolism of emptiness and sterility. The toy shovel, like the sandbox, is a childhood symbol, but simultaneously a gravedigger's spade.

The Young Man, too, is a multiple symbol. Young, athletic, and a movie actor, he embodies those three popular idols of American life: youth, sports, and Hollywood. More comprehensively, he represents illusion. Handsome and friendly on the outside, he is empty on the inside. Though he greets everyone with a "Hi!" and a smile, he doesn't know what his name is, he forgets his lines, and his smile is vacuous. As a movie actor, his trade is illusion. The worship of such illusions is equivalent to spiritual death; and the Young Man is also the Angel of Death. But the death he brings is as empty and meaningless as the life he represents.

Mommy and Daddy have a marital relationship all too common in modern life, though exaggerated in the play. They call each other by pet names, but there is no affection between them. Mommy is the emasculating female: dominant, scornful, mocking, reproving, impatient, sarcastic. She gives the orders. Daddy, though he has fulfilled his social function by getting rich, is humanly a cipher, completely subjugated by Mommy. Toward Grandma they observe all the proprieties: they give her a place in their house, they give her a "decent" burial with music and the appearance of mourning. In life, however, they really buried her alive, and on stage they literally do so. Beneath conventional expressions of grief ("the time has come for poor Grandma . . . and I can't bear it!"), Mommy is eager to get Grandma out of the way and be done with her.

Grandma is the most authentic character in the play: she says what she thinks, doesn't wrap her feelings in pious ceremonial. She is also the most perceptive character: she knows what's going on, sees through the Young Man's imbecility, is capable of using metaphor. But Grandma has been soured by her life, rendered disagreeable, cranky, difficult, and even subhuman ("Graaa!").

The life that Albee has depicted in *The Sandbox* is absurd and meaningless, and so, he implies, is much of American life today. LP

CHAPTER THREE

Tragedy and Comedy

Sophocles   **Oedipus Rex** (page 1016)

For the beginning student of drama, this play is of course made more difficult by the conventions of classical tragedy—the use of choruses, the nonrealistic set speeches, the "static" stage action, the (translated) poetry, the reporting of off-stage actions by messengers. But this particular example of Greek tragedy is made even more difficult by the apparent importance to the story of incidents that precede the play. Almost without exception, students asked to recount the plot will begin not at the beginning of the play, but at the beginning of Oedipus's career or even at the point of the first oracle to Laïos predicting a parricidal, incestuous son. The distinction between the action *on stage* and antecedent events must be made very clear if the nature of this play is to be properly understood.

A city wracked by plague turns to its king for relief, trusting that his almost superhuman wisdom will save them. Oedipus, however, has already begun the task, for he is awaiting the return of Kreon from the oracle; the message is that the murderer of the former king, living unpunished in the city, is the cause of the plague. Oedipus lays a curse on the murderer ("that that man's life be consumed in evil and wretchedness," l. 234) and begins his search for the identity of the guilty person. At Kreon's suggestion he consults the blind seer Teiresias and forces him to divulge what he is reluctant to reveal: that Oedipus is the pollution in the city, the murderer of Laïos, and is living "in hideous shame with those / Most dear" (ll. 351–52). Enraged at what seems an incredible lie, Oedipus accuses Teiresias of plotting with Kreon so that the latter may gain the crown. Teiresias leaves, pronouncing further that Oedipus is "to her / Who bore him, son and husband" (ll. 443–44).

Kreon's denial of a plot against Oedipus is logical and prudent: since he already has the rights and powers of the kingship, why would he want to add the anxieties and responsibilities of the crown? When Queen Iokastê tries to patch up the quarrel between her husband and her brother, Oedipus reports to her Teiresias's accusation of murder, and to dispel his anger she skeptically offers him proof that soothsayers and oracles are not trustworthy: she and Laïos had been told that her son would kill his father and marry his mother—yet as everyone knows, Laïos was murdered by a band of marauders at a place where three highways meet. Oedipus uneasily recalls that he had received a similar prophecy, and fleeing from the home of his supposed parents to avoid such guilty acts, he had killed a man at just such a place. He begins to realize that he may indeed have been Laïos's murderer—that his own curse may alight on himself. But he takes hope from the report that the king had been killed not single-handedly but by a group. He sends for a shepherd, the lone survivor of Laïos's party, to hear the true circumstances of the murder.

A messenger from Corinth arrives to announce that Oedipus's presumed father Polybos has died of age and illness, thus apparently disproving the oracle's prophecy that Oedipus would kill him, but Oedipus is unwilling to return as king of Corinth because his mother Meropê still lives. When he tells the messenger of the prophecy that had driven him from home, the messenger offers him the good news: he need not fear, for he was not in fact the son of Polybos and Meropê. Tending his flock near Mount Kithairon, this very messenger had received from a Theban shepherd an infant who had been exposed to die on the mountain, and had taken him to Polybos, who raised him as his son. Iokastê tries to dissuade Oedipus from further questioning, having deduced from this news the whole horrid truth: she is the mother of her husband, who had killed his father.

The shepherd appears who had been with Laïos at his death, and is recognized by the Corinthian as the man who had given him the infant. He reveals that the baby was said to be a son of Laïos, and was sent to be exposed on the mountain for fear of the prophecies. Now Oedipus possesses the whole truth, and rushes into the palace, from which another messenger emerges to report that the queen has hanged herself, and that Oedipus has stabbed himself in the eyes with her brooches to blind himself to all the horror and misery he had unknowingly created. Being led forth from the palace, he acknowledges that although Apollo brought his "sick, sick fate" upon him, "the blinding hand was my own!" (ll. 1287–88). He summarizes his life in a powerful lament, asks Kreon to care for his children, bids his daughters farewell, and begs for the fulfillment of the curse he had pronounced on Laïos's murderer, banishment from Thebes.

This rehearsal of the actions of the play demonstrates several important dramatic points: the only causal effect of the oracle in the action is Oedipus's vow to discover and punish the murderer; the whole movement of the plot is toward knowledge, first the discovery of the identity of the murderer, and then the discovery of Oedipus's true parentage. Confusing discussions of the causal role of the gods and oracles are not necesssary, even though they are tempting: we are presented with what Oedipus *is*, not with what he was; we share with him his quest for the truth, not his flight from Corinth to avoid a prophecy, not his defensive murder, not his glorious achievement of the throne nor the early years of his marriage. All those come forth as he searches for the truth of his past, but it is important to accept what the king is at the beginning of the play ("not one of the immortal gods, . . . [but] the man surest in mortal ways / And wisest in the ways of God," ll.35–38). In the justified pride of his position, he undertakes the actions that will save the country, and then unflinchingly goes on when others beg him to stop. The search for enlightenment is rewarded with knowledge of the most horrid kind, too horrid for a mere mortal to look upon, and yet he presses for the execution of the sentence he has pronounced upon himself.

Recognizing the boundaries of the action within the time of the play also clarifies the question of Oedipus's tragic flaw. It is not the rashness of having killed a group of men who attacked him on the highway, nor is it the arrogance of supposing he could avoid the prophecy by fleeing from Corinth. The pride he displays within the action is justified: as a wise king, he must take the responsibility of ridding the city of its pollution; in undertaking the search for the murderer, he is following the instructions of the oracle. His rage at Teiresias and his suspicion of Kreon's plot are motivated by his certainty that he did *not* kill the king, and an intelligent inference based on the fact that Kreon had recommended consulting the soothsayer. His flaw—the traditional term is an unfortunate one—is his insistence on learning the truth, extending his knowledge to discover himself fully. The sight/blindness, light/dark ironies that abound in the play point in this direction, toward an enlightenment too great for a man to bear.

The chorus has several important functions in this drama: it comments, in a slightly obtuse, conservatively pious way on the actions it has witnessed, acting in part as a surrogate for the audience; and its songs (and dances) reinforce the moods created by the actions. By interrupting the action, it also makes the passage of time between events more dramatically credible. The links between the choral songs and the preceding actions are not always immediately clear, and students usually need to have them pointed out. The Párodos is a prayer for divine intervention in the plague, springing directly from the news that the oracle is being consulted. Ode 1 comments on the oracle's warning that Laïos's murderer is still in the city, but rejects as impossible Teiresias's pronouncements against Oedipus—the chorus is thus torn between belief and disbelief in the messages from the gods. Ode 2 is a shocked response to Iokastê's protective and impious skepticism about oracles. Ode 3, after the revelation that Oedipus had been rescued from exposure on the mountain, ignores Iokastê's newfound awareness that her husband will discover himself to be the most miserable of men, and instead is a hymm to Kithairon and the gods who attended Oedipus's rescue, as if the chorus cannot bring itself to face the situation being revealed. Ode 4, after the full revelation of Oedipus's past, grieves for the fall of so great a man, "Majestic Oedipus! . . . now of all men ever known / Most pitiful is this man's story" (ll. 1147–51). In the Exodos, the chorus joins with Oedipus in a "commos," a responsive song or chant, as an introduction to the lament in which he looks back on his life; and it concludes the play with a moral which is not exactly the central theme of the action but is appropriate to the insight of the chorus.

Are the gods just to Oedipus? Has he deserved his catastrophic fate? Too much has been written on this subject already, but we might well remember that these are not the questions we usually ask about great interpretive literature—they mean "has poetic justice been served, have the good been rewarded and the wicked punished?" We might as well also ask "does suffering always bring wisdom?" and "does wisdom always bring happiness?" Perhaps rather than asking for poetic justic or for philosophic truisms, we need to bear always in mind that although Oedipus is *almost* godlike in wisdom, he is human, and that although his sufferings are terrifying, he bears them with courage and determination that are themselves *almost* godlike (for which, in another play about the end of his life, he is rewarded with elevation to an immortal demi-god). Sophocles is not writing a play about the acts of the gods—just or unjust—or about an intrinsic relationship between suffering, wisdom, and happiness. Rather, his subject is a great man who loyally does his duty to others and to his own need to know himself. Such men are not always happy.

Just as this note cannot even mention most of the topics the play includes, so the following brief bibliography should be regarded as only introductory: S. M. Adams, *Sophocles the Playwright* (Toronto: U of Toronto P, 1957); C. M. Bowra, *Sophoclean Tragedy* (Oxford: Clarendon, 1944); Bernard M. W. Knox, *Oedipus at Thebes* (New Haven: Yale UP, 1957); Richmond Lattimore, *The Poetry of Greek Tragedy* (Baltimore: Johns Hopkins UP, 1958); A. J. A. Waldock, *Sophocles the Dramatist* (Cambridge: Cambridge UP, 1951); and Cedric H. Whitman, *Sophocles: A Study of Heroic Humanism* (Cambridge: Harvard UP, 1951). A convenient selection of essays and excerpts from full-length studies is included in *Oedipus Tyrannus*, eds. Luci Berkowitz and Theodore F. Brunner (New York: Norton, 1970).

A faithful videotape production is available in the Films for the Humanities series. It is called *Oedipus the King* and stars Michael Pennington as Oedipus, Claire Bloom as Jocasta, and John Gielgud as Teiresias. TRA

William Shakespeare **Othello, the Moor of Venice** (page 1060)

Of the many "problems" that have been analyzed in the extensive criticism of this play, the one that most intrigues beginning students is explicitly voiced by Othello when he asks about Iago in act 5, "Why he hath thus ensnared my soul and body," to which Iago retorts "What you know, you know," and vows silence. Iago's motivation is a central issue because he himself so often talks about it, and no doubt also because Coleridge famously pronounced that the soliloquy that concludes act 1 reveals "the motive-hunting of motiveless malignity," a fiendish lack of human motivation in a character who continually attempts to find in himself the motives that other men do have. At one point or another, Iago credits himself with ambition, spiteful envy of Cassio's promotion, sexual jealousy because Othello has cuckolded him, profit from robbing Roderigo, the pleasure of deceiving Roderigo and Othello, jealousy that Cassio too has slept with Emilia, love for Desdemona, hatred of Cassio's handsomeness, and mere hatred of Othello; and the careful critic will have not difficulty in finding other implied but not stated motives. That these do not sufficiently define Iago may be seen in disparities between stated motives and action: why, if he loves Desdemona, does he conspire in her death? Why, if he wants the lieutenancy, does he destroy the man who could give it to him? Why, since Roderigo can so easily be robbed of cash, does he kill him? Why, if he is so jealous of his wife, does he malign and finally kill her? While the changing circumstances of the play may answer some of these questions, it is this sort of arithmetic of motive and action that makes Coleridge's conclusion so attractive. Intelligent, cunning, capable of tempting and controlling the characters around him, Iago nevertheless does not use his powers to achieve his stated goals, but in fact renders those goals unattainable.

Like Milton's Satan, Shakespeare's antagonist fascinates, drawing the attention of the reader to himself and in part robbing the protagonist of the attention due him. The more we notice Iago, the less we notice Othello, whose commanding presence in any stage performance may, by contrast, be reduced in reading and analyzing the play. The result is what Shakespeare certainly does not intend, that Othello is read merely as Iago's victim, as passively susceptible as are Roderigo, Desdemona, and Cassio. If only Coleridge's word could be taken, we might more easily focus our interest not on Iago and what makes him tick, but on the great central figure, the tragic hero.

Othello's greatness is nearly a definition of the Shakespearean tragic hero: his weaknesses or "flaws" are virtues carried to excess. He loves, but "too well," too intensely and totally; he trusts, but too much, and too indiscriminately; he has so great a sense of moral virtue and of his own honorable responsibility that he makes of himself an agent of divine justice to extirpate sin; his sensitive, poetic imagination leads him to vivid, pictorial fantasies of his wife and her lover. Iago in his soliloquies provides a partial catalogue, though of course he sneers at the general's virtues: "The Moor is of a free and open nature / That thinks men honest that but seem to be so"; "The Moor, howbeit that I endure him not, / Is of a constant, loving, noble nature." And Lodovico, spokesman for the Venetian government, can only grieve to witness Othello's abuse of Desdemona: "Is this the noble Moor whom our full Senate / Call all in all sufficient? Is this the nature / Whom passion could not shake? whose solid virtue / The shot of accident nor dart of chance / Could neither graze nor pierce?"

The thematic center of the play is the perversion of Othello's goodness by the evil workings of his mind, and the chief concern is Othello's fall from greatness, not as victim but as the agent of his own destruction. By insinuation and apparent reluctance to speak, Iago forces Othello to draw from him his suspicions, and excites Othello's visual imagination into picturing scenes of Desdemona's lustful acts; and then, once he has administered this small dose of poison, Iago urges Othello onward into a deeper conviction by pretending to argue against the certainty of Desdemona's guilt. The growth of Othello's jealousy is the result of his own energies, the strength of his love and his desire for perfection driving him to take up the sword of divine justice.

Is Othello gullible? Does he succumb too quickly, too easily to Iago's temptation? While these questions may arise from an inappropriately realistic approach to the play, what they mean is "How wrong is it to be honest and frank, and to believe that your old friends are too?" Do we admire cynical suspiciousness, or vulnerable trust? Shakespeare created Roderigo (not a character in Cinthio's novella "Tale of the Moor of Venice," the source of the play) to provide a parallel whose gullibility answers these questions. Roderigo is indeed what Othello calls himself in act 5 after he has learned of Desdemona's innocence: fool, dolt, a man without honor. Roderigo's willingness to wait his turn to enjoy the woman he "loves," the ease with which Iago can manipulate him into the cowardly attempt on Cassio's life, the whining stupidity which makes him so easy a prey—these are explicitly contrasted to Othello's true love and noble nature. Iago marks the contrast in his first soliloquy when he apologizes to himself for wasting time gulling such a "snipe" as Roderigo ("sport and profit" excuse the waste), and sets as his real target a man of "free and open nature" to be led (he hopes) as easily as such "asses" as Roderigo. Like Satan's, Iago's cunning is in leading people into self-destruction, not merely in duping them—and his skill is great, for no one in the play has the least suspicion of him (until Roderigo in act 4), not even the two people who must know him best, his wife Emilia and his battlefield companion Othello. If Othello is vulnerable to him, so are Cassio, Desdemona, and Roderigo, and even Montano and Lodovico: everyone to whom he lies believes him (a statistical demonstration that Othello is not to be considered especially susceptible), and ironically almost everyone turns to him for advice.

Structurally, *Othello* moves toward its catastrophe inexorably, with an increasing narrowing of focus. The first act, in Venice, has the breadth of three parallel situations—the gulling of Roderigo, the military danger of the invasion of Cyprus, and the private conflict between Brabantio and the newly married general and his wife. The subplot of Roderigo is maintained right up to the fifth act, repeating again and again Iago's ability to manipulate the young man's sensual ambitions for his own profit and the pleasure of watching him squirm. In terms of development, the Iago-Roderigo action is less a subplot than a recurring situation, a reminder of what Iago can do to lesser men whose "love" is only lust. The great public issue of a Turkish invasion, which in act 1 vies in importance with the private affair of the "unnatural" marriage, is removed at the opening of act 2 when the enemy fleet is "banged" and dispersed by the storm (no doubt Shakespeare's audience would recall the similar fate of the grand Armada), constricting the action to Iago-Othello-Desdemona. The last we hear of the Turks is the proclamation in act 2 that links their loss with the celebration of Othello's nuptials as the double occasion for general holiday. The cashiering of Cassio raises Roderigo's false hopes and sets up Iago's plan to make Othello suspect the motives of his wife as she generously pleads for the lieutenant's reinstatement.

Othello's downfall commences in act 3, after the play has amply established the many virtues in his character. As the poisonous suspicion grows in him, we witness a deterioration of his free, open, and trusting nature, as he commits himself to one act after another that undercuts his greatness: he sets Emilia to spy on Desdemona, he deputizes Iago to take vengeance on Cassio, he stoops to eavesdropping as Iago interviews Cassio, he subjects Desdemona to verbal and then to physical abuse, he lurks in the darkness observing the ambush of Cassio, and then finally murders his innocent wife. But this deterioration is all the while accompanied by the perplexing and paradoxical constancy of his love, for although he is convinced of Desdemona's guilt, he cannot refrain from loving her. This is shown clearly in 4.1, when he exclaims on the "pity of it" after Iago draws him back from thoughts of her sweetness, delicacy, gentleness, and beauty. As he approaches the murder in the last scene, he has managed to subdue whatever hatred he had displayed in abusing her, and thinks of himself as the abstract agent of divine justice—but simultaneously, he is drawn by the beauty of her skin, her balmy breath, the "cunning'st pattern of excelling nature," to kiss her again and again, even to wish that he could preserve her physical perfection and love it after her death. Like the loving God who must punish his beloved creature for her sin, he must strike the one he loves and pities.

363

After the murder, as the unwinding mysteries reveal to him the extent of his injustice, Othello's character sinks lower. For a moment he is willing to hide his crime behind Desdemona's dying words (5.2.121–26), but then pulls himself up to denounce her lie (5.2.128–29). His lowest moral point comes in the speech at 5.2.258, in which he gives way to self-pity, blames his act on "fate" and the stars, and cries out for punishments of hell to remove him from the sight of what he has done—all without acknowledging that he has been personally responsible. This is counterbalanced by his final speech, when once again he resumes his noble, moral character: he yields up his pride as a great commander, asks only for an honest, plain report of his character, and then reorienting himself in the wide geographical world he had inhabited, he accepts both his guilt and his responsibility to the state. Recalling his defense of Venice against her enemies, he identifies himself both with the Turk who "beat a Venetian and traduced the state," and with the hero who brought him to justice. He began the last scene in ignorant usurpation of the role of divine justicer; he ends his life in an enlightened act of human justice and a final farewell to his beloved.

Of the plethora of critical works dealing with the play, the following may be noted: John Bayley, *The Characters of Love* (New York: Basic Books, 1961); A. C. Bradley, *Shakespearean Tragedy* (1904, repr. New York: St. Martin's, 1964); G. R. Elliott, *Flaming Minister: A Study of* Othello *as Tragedy of Love and Hate* (Durham NC: Duke UP, 1953); Helen Gardner, *The Noble Moor* (London: Oxford UP, 1956) and *"Othello*: A Retrospect, 1900–1967," *Shakespeare Survey 21*, ed. Kenneth Muir (Cambridge: Cambridge UP, 1968); Harley Granville-Barker, "Preface to *Othello*," *Prefaces to Shakespeare*, Vol. II (Princeton: Princeton UP, 1947); Robert B. Heilman, *Magic in the Web: Action and Language in Othello* (Lexington KY: U of Kentucky P, 1956); G. Wilson Knight, *The Wheel of Fire*, 5th rev. ed. (New York: Meridian, 1957); Marvin Rosenberg, *The Masks of Othello* (Berkeley: U of California P, 1961); Arthur Sewell, *Character and Society in Shakespeare* (New York: Oxford UP, 1951); E. E. Stoll, *From Shakespeare to Joyce* (New York: Doubleday, 1944); and *Othello: An Historical and Comparative Study* (Minneapolis: U of Minnesota P, 1964). Convenient collections of articles and excerpts from books are Leonard F. Dean, ed., *A Casebook on Othello* (New York: Crowell, 1961), and *Shakespeare: Modern Essays in Criticism* (New York: Oxford UP, 1961).

There is no wholly satisfactory film or video version of the play available, though several have their strong points. A Royal Shakespeare Company production directed by Trevor Nunn featured Willard White, Ian McKellen, and Imogen Stubbs, and was broadcast on BBC. If it should be made available on American videotape it would be worth presenting to a class.

A note on Othello's blackness

There can be no serious question about Othello's race. Iago, Brabantio, and Roderigo all refer disparagingly to it ("thick-lips," "sooty bosom"), and Othello himself states plainly "I am black." The word "moor" was used in Shakespeare's time to identify black Africans as well as practitioners of Mohammedanism. But Othello is black and, insofar as his religion is identified, a Christian.

His race is thematically important, particularly as it would have provided a prejudiced point of departure for Shakespeare's audiences. Brabantio's attitude toward it may be taken to represent the common attitude: his daughter is "unnatural" in loving a black, her action so extreme as to make him suppose that magic or witchcraft is the cause (and Desdemona herself acknowledges that her elopement was "downright violence and storm of fortunes"). Common prejudices of the time would have presumed the black man to be less rational, more passionate and lustful, less civilized, and—at the extreme—inherently evil (as the play indicates, the devil himself was thought to be black in hue). Against these assumptions Shakespeare creates a noble, Christian, virtuous man of great imagination, calm self-control, frankness, and honesty, and he bestows on white Iago the qualities of a devil. An audience perceives not only the literal color contrast between the protagonist and antagonist, but the contrasting inversion of the moral qualities symbolically associated with their colors. As he so often does, Shakespeare achieves intense dramatic effects by demonstrating that common prejudices are opposite to the truth.

A note on teaching Shakespeare

For the inexperienced student, reading a Shakespeare play can be a most difficult task, for the conventions of Elizabethan drama are polar opposites of those of the realistic drama for which such students have had most of their training (chiefly through television and film). Not only do Shakespeare's characters speak verse, in an older vocabulary and syntax, with such conventions as the soliloquy and aside, but the plots present unrealistic patterning of action and feeling, great emotional sweeps from pathos to terror to low comedy, extremes that could not even be considered in a realistic drama. There are few stage directions to aid the visual imagination, and students toiling through unfamiliar speech patterns and vocabulary will find it extremely difficult to visualize the scene or "hear" the dialogue. Such aids as are available on film, videocassette, and sound recordings, while often tending to pull the plays toward more realistic conventions, should be employed to help students imagine the sights and sounds of drama that are implied in the script they are reading. Even a brief sampling of recorded dialogue can encourage students in the necessary exercise of the imagination.

Perhaps most difficult of all lessons is the distinction between action and character, because Shakespeare's characters may seem so psychologically alive that students will be drawn to the assumption that the intention of the plays is to present fully rounded personalities. But as E. E. Stoll rightly points out, a Shakespeare play is not "what we call drama as it is ordinarily practiced today. It is as in Aristotle—situation first and motivation or psychology afterwards, if at all. The effect is emotional, with which psychology or even simple narrative coherence often considerably interferes" ("Source and Motive in *Macbeth* and *Othello*" from his *From*

Shakespeare to Joyce, 1944, reprinted in *Shakespeare: Modern Essays in Criticism*, cited above). It can be useful to offer students an analogy to a dramatic form that is familiar to many of them—musical comedy. There they will find parallels in nonrealistic plotting, appreciation of musical effects analogous to the poetic effects of Shakespeare's verse, versions of the soliloquy represented in musical solos, the acceptance of an emotional effect at the expense of realistic "psychology or even simple narrative coherence," and in general an appreciation by the audience of nonrealistic conventions. Students familiar with opera, of course, will have an even tighter analogy available to them. (I have found that merely playing for them a recording of the concluding duet of the second act of Verdi's *Otello*, derived from *Othello*, 3.2.434–69, excitingly impresses this point upon students.) TRA

Molière Tartuffe, or The Impostor (page 1149)

Like Molière's other masterpiece of the same period, *The Misanthrope* (1666), *Tartuffe* is a comedy with dark overtones. In the later play, the protagonist Alceste is a man with an obsession for honesty and plain speaking that nearly destroys him. His excessive insistence on that virtue in himself and in others brings him to the brink of losing his love and his liberty. In the earlier, Orgon too is obsessed, but the object of his passion is not so clearly a virtue. His religious zeal makes him the dupe of a hypocritical con-artist, so that what might be considered adherence to a valuable belief system is distorted into a feverish adoration of the embodiment of his beliefs. He is thus doubly obsessed, with his religion and with a pretended purveyor of the faith. When the play opens he already seems to have completed transferring his confidence from Christ to Tartuffe.

Orgon's first scene (1.4) occurs as he returns from a two-day visit to his country estate. He brushes aside the friendly greeting of his brother-in-law Cléante to ask about the family—and about Tartuffe, his live-in spiritual adviser. The maid Dorine reports that his wife Elmire was badly stricken with headaches, chills, and fever, and was unable to eat. But Orgon ignores this news, and continually presses Dorine to tell him about Tartuffe, who in contrast was "bursting with health, and excellently fed," devouring pheasant and mutton, downing beakers of port, and snoring away in his bed while others watched over Elmire's sickbed. Because Orgon has not responded to anything she has told him about Elmire, Dorine concludes the scene with sarcastic verbal irony: "I'll go and tell *Madame* that you've expressed / Keen sympathy and anxious interest" (1.4.35–36). But the scene displays more than the fact that Orgon's infatuation with Tartuffe has displaced his affection for his young wife. It has also created in him a kind of blindness to reality. For one thing, he has not even noticed what Cléante has to tell him in the opening line of the next scene (1.5), that Dorine was "laughing in [his] face" with her irony. Even more blindly, he was not hearing what she had said about Tartuffe, the only object of his interest! As she is describing the luxuriant pleasures of Tartuffe's bed and table, Orgon repeatedly interjects "Poor fellow!" His first encounter with the man has so possessed him that he cannot see or hear what Tartuffe is actually doing. That blindness is the basis of the plot, and is the key to Orgon's character. Tartuffe does not actually have to deceive him, because Orgon is bent on self-deception.

The play opens with a scene displaying another representation of that kind of blindness. Orgon's mother Madame Pernelle is denouncing all the members of the household who have not been "Tartuffified." All of them in the house, she declares, "break in and chatter on and on" (1.1.11), a remark that sets up the comedy of her own refusal to allow any of them to speak or defend themselves until Damis introduces the name of Tartuffe. Her complaints are that no one will take her "good advice," that Dorine is too "saucy" for her position as lady's-maid, that Damis is a "foolish . . . dunce," that Mariane's demureness is a sign of secretive hypocrisy, that Elmire is an overdressed spendthrift, and that Cléante indecently counsels them all in their worldly ways. Most of all, of course, they do not obey Orgon and love Tartuffe. When they are allowed to proffer their arguments—that Tartuffe is a hypocrite, bigot, and fraud—she accuses them of lying because Tartuffe has wounded them by the truth of his condemnation. As she departs from the house, she displays the shallowness of her own Christian beliefs, slapping her maid Flipote for moving too slowly.

These two scenes, which I've summarized in reverse order, typify the seriocomic tone of much of the play. In both, we see traditional comic behaviors carried to the point where they cause a shudder of fear. Madame Pernelle is a railing termagant whose verbal abusiveness and intolerance of other points of view are comic. She is rigid and automatic in her thoughts and feelings, and probably should be played for the laughs that such a shrew can elicit—and then her verbal assaults become physical as she arbitrarily and pointlessly takes out her frustration on a defenseless person. She is a petty tyrant who departs from her son's domain because it is too loosely controlled. At home with Flipote as her subject, there is no doubt how total her control will be.

In the case of Orgon's first scene, the comedy resides in the inappropriateness of his concern for his gluttonous mentor as he is being told of his wife's illness. That this is represented by mechanical repetition ("Ah. And Tartuffe? . . . Poor fellow!" repeated four times) drives the satiric joke home. We cannot miss it, any more than we could miss Madame Pernelle's heavy-handedness in cutting off other people's speaking. It is not only the incongruity of Orgon's concern for Tartuffe at such a time, but also the rigid and mechanical means of displaying it, that makes these actions comic. What is seriously threatening in this scene is what Madame Pernelle's made overt and obvious: this obsession can extend to physical danger. (We have a comic version of maid-slapping in 2.2, when Orgon threatens and then vainly tries to slap Dorine, who is too agile and clever to suffer his blows.)

The first act also makes it clear that the members of the family arrayed against Tartuffe are correct in their judgment of him. It is Orgon who unwittingly reveals that zealot's hypocritical conniving when he tries to describe to Cléante the fervent piety of the man as he first saw him, impoverished but devout, in church. The clues are there, but Orgon missed them: Tartuffe would

humbly kneel *nearby*, and start to pray.
He'd *draw* the eyes of everybody there
By the deep fervor of his heartfelt prayer;
He'd sigh and weep, and sometimes *with a sound
Of rapture* he would bend and kiss the ground.

(1.5.26–30)

The ostentatiousness of this performance is obvious to all but Orgon (he's certainly told this story before, as Dorine hints when she defends Valère's presumed apostasy: "Would you have him go [to church] at the same hours as you, / And kneel nearby, to be sure of being seen?" [2.2.71–72]). Cléante correctly judges what has happened to Orgon—he has lost his common sense, his ability to make clear-eyed judgments. How far Orgon has gone down that road he himself defines in paraphrasing the text that Tartuffe has no doubt been preaching to him:

Under his tutelage my soul's been freed
From earthly loves, and every human tie:
My mother, children, brother, and wife could die,
And I'd not feel a single moment's pain.

(1.5.18–21)

Tartuffe's texts have been Matthew 10.35–37 and the harsher version of that teaching, Luke 14.26 ("If any man come to me, and hate not his father, and mother, and wife, and children, and brethren, and sisters, yea, and his own life also, he cannot be my disciple"), which also counsels taking in beggars from the street.

The denial of family ties and adoration of his model are already ingrained in Orgon at the outset of the play, and all that follows is built upon them. The attempt to marry Mariane to Tartuffe, the disinheriting of Damis, and the flat refusal to believe that Tartuffe propositioned Elmire are all of a piece: the truth is with Tartuffe, and all others are plotting against him. His mind having been overpowered, Orgon surrenders everything to the "poor fellow." Once Tartuffe has Orgon completely in his control, he readily gives up his imposture, for there is no more to be obtained from him. In his triumph Tartuffe does suffer two losses—the hand of Mariane, and the body of Elmire—but that they are lost to him seems to be inconsequential to his delight. He has been in quest of power and property, and believes he has achieved them.

Ironically, Orgon's motives have also been for power and control. Like his tyrannizing mother, he wants to direct the lives of his household. He is, luckily, less adept at the power game than Tartuffe, for though Mariane's timidity and spinelessness make her seem an apt subject for his commands, his plan unravels when Tartuffe drops his mask. Disinheriting Damis is another tyranny that almost suceeds, and Elmire manages finally to overcome his incredulous denial of her. In going for control over this family, Orgon has given himself into the control of Tartuffe, but the power game concludes most fortunately with the highest earthly power prevailing through the agency of the king's officer.

Power and authority, in fact, have the sway in this comedy, not good sense and good intentions. Cléante argues cogently, points out Orgon's mistakes, counsels moderation both when Orgon is in his pious fits and when his disappointment with Tartuffe leads him to denounce all religion, but Cléante has no effect whatever. It is good for the audience to have a mouthpiece for rationality and kindness, but it is not so comforting for him to be impotent. Dorine also makes a stab at reining in Orgon, and while she can adroitly avoid being slapped, and can get away with many ironic jabs, her plan to save Mariane's marriage is not working. Audiences also like to see witty servants who can manipulate their masters into doing the right things, but Dorine only reminds us that in *some* plays there are such rescuers, although not in this one.

The fact is that Orgon's disease—the uncontrollable obsession that makes him so easy a prize for Tartuffe—is not curable by the pat methods of comic drama. Only the intervention of what one critic calls *rex ex machina* (an appropriate pun, since the king is given the godlike ability to see into men's hearts) can rescue Orgon from the consequences of his folly. In many plays, the unmasking of the villain is sufficient to produce the comic resolution when he is stripped of his power. But Tartuffe's power over Orgon is increased when he shows his plain face because he now has the motive of revenge added to his desire to acquire Orgon's property, and both civil and criminal law are on his side: he has a deed of property and he has evidence that Orgon is a traitor to the king.

The subtitle "The Impostor" is in fact more appropriate than the title Molière used in the lost earlier version of the play, "the hypocrite." Tartuffe's villainy is not pretended piety; he only employs that as one of his weapons. As the Officer explains, the all-seeing

> King soon recognized Tartuffe as one
> Notorious by another name, who'd done
> So many vicious crimes that one could fill
> Ten volumes with them, and be writing still.
>   (5.7.63–65)

He is a manifold criminal, an impostor whose sins extend far beyond hypocrisy (we actually hear of sins enough—lechery, gluttony, envy, pride, to name a few). Such men do more than dupe the gullible, and more than good sense and judgment is required to fend them off.

For further discussion, see the following: Percy A. Chapman, *The Spirit of Molière* (Princeton: Princeton UP, 1940); Lionel Gossman, *Men and Masks: A Study of Molière* (Baltimore: Johns Hopkins UP, 1963); W. D. Howarth, *Molière: A Playwright and His Audience* (Cambridge: Cambridge UP, 1982); Gertrud Mander, *Molière* (New York: Ungar, 1973); Martin Turnell, *The Classical Moment* (New York: New Directions, 1948).

An English-language version of the play (unfortunately, not the Richard Wilbur translation) is available on videotape. It was recorded by the Royal Shakespeare Company and the BBC in 1984 with Antony Sher and Nigel Hawthorne in the leading roles. Despite some questionable interpretive adaptations, it can be useful for classroom discussions. TRA

Plays for Further Reading

Anton Chekhov **The Cherry Orchard** (page 1204)

QUESTIONS

1. Trace Mme. Ranyevskaya's background: her marriage, her children, the death of her husband, and the events of the years immediately preceding act 1. Why has she returned to Russia? Why is the old nursery an appropriate setting for acts 1 and 4?
2. Characterize the following, taking note of the contradictions within each character as revealed in speech and actions: Gayev, Lopakhin, Anya, Varya, Trofimov, Yepikhodov, Yasha, Dunyasha, Simeonov-Pishchik, Charlotta, Firs.
3. What does the cherry orchard represent to the various characters? What does it symbolize in the play?
4. What is signaled by the sound of the breaking string in act 2? Why is it an appropriate sound, combined with the sound of axes, at the curtain of act 4?
5. In what seasons of the year are the four acts placed? What ordinary expectations are associated with these seasons? How are the actual weather conditions in contrast to the expectations?
6. Each of the acts is constructed around a social occasion. Identify each, and consider how they form a meaningful sequence of events. What ironies undercut the normal expectations about such social events?
7. Many comedies resort to implausible events to produce a happy ending. Is the ending of this play plausible? Is there any sense in which it might be called happy?
8. What elements of farce does the play contain?
9. Is the play a "laughing comedy" or a "smiling comedy"? What aspects of "human folly" does it illustrate?

Despite Chekhov's designation of the play as "A Comedy in Four Acts," and his correspondence with the Moscow Art Theatre during the preparation for the first production in 1904 reaffirming that designation (it is "not a drama but a comedy, . . . in places even a farce''; ''the last act will be merry, and indeed the whole play will be merry and frivolous'' [see Styan, cited below, p. 239]), the serious interpretation used in that production has generally prevailed—the play has most often been performed as pathetic drama or even tragedy. It is not difficult to understand why this contradiction of the author's intention should have taken hold among producers and critics, for the subjects of the play are depressingly serious: the loss of an ancestral estate; the rise of a semiliterate, ambitious middle class to replace the aristocrats; the dispossession and scattering of an entire family; the guilt and remorse of a woman who cannot resist her attachment to an unworthy man; the utter ineffectuality of an entire household. The play is concerned with loss, the failure to comprehend and communicate, and the destruction of an old order.

The Cherry Orchard presents a dilemma: the family faces two unacceptable alternatives, either to lose the estate by auction because of the unpaid mortgage (an experience Chekhov's own family suffered during his childhood), or to destroy it by chopping down its unique distinctive feature and razing its house to replace it with summer cottages. The second alternative (which is finally taken by the man who buys it at auction) offers a ''sordid'' economic solution at the expense of the old values; the first alternative preserves the sense of values, at the cost of everything. In this impossible situation, where the choice of either action is insupportable, Mme. Ranyevskaya chooses not to act (the play has been criticized for its lack of action, a curious charge since the subject is inaction).

But before we lament the losses presented in the play, it is well to understand precisely what is being lost—and whether it was really ever possessed by the characters in the play. The cherry orchard is the central symbol, representing to the characters various things: to Mme. Ranyevskaya and her brother Gayev, the orchard represents childhood innocence, the stability of generations, the beauty of the past, and their own identity as landowners; to Lopakhin, the self-made man who is sentimental about the past but is creating his own future, the orchard (and the estate and its owner) is a reminder of serfdom and the generous condescension of the landed class, though it is now nonproductive and useless, remarkable only for the acreage it covers; to Trofimov, the idealist pressing for a utopian socialist future, it is a remnant of oppression and injustice; to the half-deaf old servant Firs (who preferred to remain with his former owners at the emancipation of the serfs), it is a relic of the days of order when the cherries were abundant, sweet, and profitable. But in this variety of attitudes, Chekhov also presents a number of undercutting realities. Mme. Ranyevskaya is not, nor has she been for a long time, an innocent girl living in a beautiful world (it is to recapture the lost past that she has come back to Russia); the days of serfdom which both Firs and Trofimov link to the orchard were neither as sweet as Firs claims (Lopakhin reminds him, though Firs does not hear it, that those were the days of flogging) nor as vicious as Trofimov declares (since both Firs and Lopakhin recall their early lives sentimentally). What is being lost is not in fact an old order of stability, family love and unity, innocence, and usefulness—these are already long gone. The destruction of the orchard and the estate is the destruction of illusions, a symbolic double negative which the play explores at many levels of action, characterization, and theme.

Throughout, this comedy relies for its comic effect on the linking of contraries, the ambivalence of opposite extremes united in single persons and actions. To take an obvious example from the opening of act 2, the governess Charlotta soliloquizes about her rootlessness, the emptiness of a life without purpose, her lack of identity ("where I come from and who I am, I don't know")—and then, even before she has finished, she pulls a cucumber out of her pocket and chomps on it, muffling her words ("I haven't got anyone") with a ludicrous action. She combines her pathetic self-evaluation with clownishness and, in her magic tricks, exuberance. Her very first line, during the tearfully joyous entry of the family in act 1, is "My dog can eat nuts," an hilarious irrelevancy that punctures the sentiment of the scene. All of the other characters, and many of the scenes of emotion, follow this pattern: sentiment, pathos, joy, idealism are suddenly or simultaneously juxtaposed with ludicrousness, pomposity, slapstick clumsiness. Chastising herself for being a spend-thrift, Mme. Ranyevskaya gives a gold coin to a beggar. Apparently insensible to the beauty of the orchard, Lopakhin recalls "when my poppy was in bloom, what a picture!" Like Charlotta with her cucumber, Gayev pops a candy in his mouth as he is vowing, "I swear, upon my honor, . . . that the estate will not be sold."

This device is not merely ironic undercutting or the satirizing of people whose actions do not match their words or whose words are inconsistent. It is based on Chekhov's honest observation of human nature and the human predicament: we are all mixtures of opposites (a religious writer like Tolstoy would see this as the condition of mankind after the fall of Adam), and the ending of the play does not falsify this fact by providing or promising any implausible conversions. Mme. Ranyevskaya will return to Paris, squander the little money that she has borrowed to pay the mortgage, and then—who knows? Varya will continue to yearn for the two opposite types of existence (wife, nun) which she duplicates in her life as a housekeeper in someone else's family. Anya's naive innocence will no doubt ultimately give way, probably to imitate her mother whose childhood she represents. Gayev, the victim of mortgage holders, is not likely to last long working in a bank. And so on—nothing will really change these people, since they are genuine human beings for whom miraculous changes are not possible. Having been stripped of the illusions of stability and beauty, they may not be so easily duped in the future, but there is not even any certainty that this has been a "learning experience" for them. They have had to face their reality, but in life that does not mean they will not again succumb to an unrealistic vision of themselves.

The ambivalent structure of the play reinforces this evaluation of character. Act 1 takes place at dawn in springtime, with the orchard in full bloom—but the weather is freezing; the family has come together for a joyous homecoming, yet the progression of the act is toward sleep and silence (Simeonov-Pishchik even dozes off in the middle of speaking, and Anya falls asleep while Varya is telling her of the household problems); only the idealist Trofimov is awake at the end, looking forward to sunshine and springtime and love. Symbolically throughout this act of reunion and family solidarity, very little of the dialogue is actual conversation: each character speaks from within, without responding to the remarks of others. The spring is not spring, the dawn is not the beginning, the family reunion is a collection of separate, self-involved people—and, as Lopakhin keeps reminding them, they are in the process of losing the symbol of their identity and unity.

Act 2 is a midsummer sunset scene, out of doors, with the future in the modern world implied by the distant town and the telegraph poles leading toward it, the past represented by decaying relics of religion. The family group assembles after a meal in town, but we do not have the idyllic fulfillment of familial closeness that was forestalled by travel weariness in act 1. Rather, lassitude predominates, topics for conversation have to be concocted, and the act is full of pensiveness, pauses, and long silences. Lopakhin and Trofimov press for their two very different versions of the future, but silence overcomes them all as they "sit lost in thought," together but isolated as the action winds down to a standstill. And then the sound of the breaking string propels them into various responses—fear, confusion, prophecy—and the beggar shows them another version of the future, a frightening vision of poverty and wandering.

While the first two acts seem to be moving into lethargic disunity, an ironic contrast to the seasons and to the desire to reaffirm community and stability, the last two acts are bursting with life though the occasions are dismal. Mme. Ranyevskaya has scheduled her party on the day of the auction, and alternately gives way to anxiety and bursts forth with gaiety. Slapstick and clowning are at their height: Charlotta's tricks delight them all, while Yepikhodov's clumsiness seems to have infected Trofimov (falling down the stairs), Lopakhin (knocking over a table), and Varya (swinging the pool cue). Gayev enters with grief in his heart, and anchovies and herrings in his hand.

Act 4 is in almost every way an inverted mirror image of act 1: in the same room, now denuded of its nostalgic reminders of childhood, it is afternoon (not morning) in October (not springtime)—and the uncharacteristic frostiness of the spring has been replaced by an autumn that is warm and sunny. The family is preparing to disperse to various destinations, to carry out separate, individual lives, in contrast to their coming together to reunite in shared community. There is the same amount of hustle and bustle, a lavish amount of sentimentality, but at the end the only one to doze off (perhaps, according to some critics, to die) is the ancient servant Firs. The gaiety of Anya and Trofimov, looking to the future, is balanced against the despair of Gayev and Mme. Ranyevskaya as they grieve for "life, youth, happiness."

This is not, on the face of it, a "happy ending," with the still form of Firs alone on the stage while the breaking string again sounds and the axes destroy the orchard and all the past. It is, however, a "real" ending, and it holds some promise. Old Firs is the embodiment of the last illusion, dressed as always in his formal jacket and white waistcoat as if there were still a prosperous, aristocratic world to be served. Anya, Varya, and Mme. Ranyevskaya have all voiced concern that he was to be sent to the hospital, but this sincere emotion has not been put to practical results. And so, like the nonproducing but beautiful orchard, the deaf old man has been left behind, a memory of loyal and efficient service in a life now past.

Two full and valuable analyses of the play may be found in Beverly Hahn,

373

Chekhov: A Study of the Major Stories and Plays (Cambridge: Cambridge UP, 1977), 12–36, and J. L. Styan, *Chekhov in Performance* (Cambridge: Cambridge UP, 1971), 239–337.   TRA

Arthur Miller   **Death of a Salesman** (page 1245)

QUESTIONS

1. Critics have disagreed as to whether *Death of a Salesman* can be called a tragedy. Most of the debate centers on whether or not Willy Loman has the stature of a tragic hero. How would you answer this question? What admirable characteristics does Willy have? Could any of his desires or motivations be called noble? Consider particularly Willy's motivations in committing suicide. In what respect are they to be admired? In what respect are they mistaken? Does Willy make any "discovery" before his death? If so, does it involve an increased self-knowledge?

   Miller himself has said that he did not set out to "write a tragedy" in this play, but "to show the truth" as he saw it. It is nevertheless clear from his various comments about the play that he regards it as a tragedy, with Willy as its hero. In his article "Tragedy and the Common Man" he has written that "the tragic feeling is evoked in us when we are in the presence of a character who is ready to lay down his life, if need be, to secure one thing—his sense of personal dignity." Is this remark applicable to Willy Loman?

2. Regardless of your answers to question 1, there can be little doubt that Willy Loman is the victim of a "tragic flaw." Can you isolate that flaw? Is it Willy's own tragic flaw that causes his downfall? Is it society's? Is it a combination of both?

3. Willy is generally assumed to be the protagonist of *Death of a Salesman*, but a case can also be made for its being Biff's play. Consider the play in terms of both interpretations. If Willy is the protagonist, who or what constitutes the antagonistic force? Is the antagonist the same if one considers Biff as protagonist? Explain.

4. Which characters change during the course of the play? In what respects?

5. Some critics have viewed *Death of a Salesman* entirely as a social commentary. To what extent do you consider this evaluation valid or invalid?

6. Discuss the interaction of the characters in *Death of a Salesman* one upon another. What effect has Willy had upon his sons' lives? They on his? Linda has been described as "the perfect wife." Do you find her so? What has been her effect on the lives of her husband and children? Willy's brother Ben is in many ways a character foil to Willy. To what extent, if any, has Ben's "success" contributed to Willie's failure? What is Ben's role in the play? What function do Charley and Bernard serve in the play?

7. What purposes are served by the Requiem? What ironies does it contain? What would be lost by its omission from the play?

8. To what extent is *Death of a Salesman* a realistic play? To what extent is it nonrealistic? Describe as precisely as you can the nonrealistic devices used by Miller in the play, and comment on their purpose.

Miller's play perches between realistic and nonrealistic drama, with stage directions that call for visual changes as lights focus on different playing areas, walls, appear and disappear, surrounding apartment buildings emerge or give way to leafy greenness; musical motifs punctuate and interpret the actions. The scene changes often coincide with movements into the past or with imaginary entrances of the dead brother Ben, or with movements into scenes not observable by the protagonist, Willy Loman. Such fluidity of time and place is more characteristic of the novel than of the drama, and, except for Ben's entrance into the "present" when the dead man appears to urge Willy to suicide, could easily be accommodated to the most realistic cinema techniques. The lack of dramatic realism in the staging is almost entirely due to what in a novel would pass for psychological realism, the author's ability to enter into the mind of the character so as to bring memories or imagining vividly into the present.

Death of a Salesman shares with *The Glass Menagerie* the sense of being largely "a memory play," but without so obvious a device as a narrator, and with a stricter sense of the present time from which to view the past. And it shares with *Oedipus Rex* the sense of the present as the culmination of past actions, and the revelation to the audience of the past as it comes to light in the present. But the differences between Miller's play and these others are great. In Williams's play, the device of Tom's narration is less rigid in its focus, particularly insofar as it suggests that Tom is the center of attention (see the discussion on page 355 of this manual). The memory scenes in Miller's play are restricted to Willy's recollections. Willy's rival for the role of central character, Biff, has no scenes dependent on his memory—even the scene in the Boston hotel, revealing the major conflict between father and son as Biff discovers Willy's adultery, is presented through Willy's point of view when he suffers his breakdown in the restroom of the restaurant.

Miller provides a realistic motivation for these memory journeys: Willy's feverish desperation, his "exhaustion," has slightly unhinged his brain, a condition familiar to Linda and Happy, but news to the visiting Biff. The sequence of flashbacks begins as present thoughts of the car lead Willy to begin a car-polishing conversation with the boy Biff, and then the boys appear as a literal, visual representation of Willy's memory; the past comes to life in the present. In the course of the play, we learn much about Biff's development, but chiefly as a manifestation of Willy's influence on him. Both sons are Willy's spiritual heirs, dividing his attributes between them. Like Willy, Biff is a petty thief, is manually adroit, and is full of restless hopes for the great accomplishment that will mark him a success; Happy has inherited Willy's charm and his habitual mendacity. But neither of them shows any sign of the goodness that Linda sees in her husband (her judgment in that matter may be questioned, of course: she says to her sons, "You're both good boys, just act that way, that's all," suggesting that the goodness she sees in Willy may also be a matter of loving faith rather than an ethical or moral fact).

Unlike Williams, Miller is concerned with a realistic motivation for the memories, and with their direct relevance to the protagonist. Unlike Sophocles, Miller does not imply that the incidents of the past are newly discovered by the protagonist. Willy has known these things, and has evaded their implications and lied to himself and others about their truth. Willy is not searching the past to explain the present; rather, in the misery and mental confusion that afflict him from the first scene, the past seems to be forcing itself into his consciousness, as if to offer him the chance to revalue his life. But his final imaginary conversation with his lucky brother Ben implies no alteration in his values: the world is still a dark jungle; there are diamonds there for the bold man's taking, and defrauding an insurance company is a proper and courageous means to obtain them. Willy's sacrifice of his life is an act of love—for Biff, not for Linda, who is absent from his last speeches—but it is guided by the same principles that governed his life. He wants Biff to be "magnificent," to be a hero by making an impression on "all kinds of people." The voyage into memory has not shown Willy the hollowness of his values.

Biff's claim to be the protagonist of the play rests mainly on two things: his return to New York opens his eyes to his father's deterioration under the pressures of his failures; and this experience leads him to some self-awareness, for in the Requiem he judges Willy ("He had the wrong dreams. All, all, wrong. . . . He never knew who he was") and asserts to Happy, "I know who I am, kid." Though this seems a positive development, especially in contrast with Happy's reaffirmation of Willy's dream, it is difficult to know what genuine gain Biff has made. Presumably he will return to his wandering life in the West, sustaining himself by manual toil, following the self-reliant dream of his pioneer grandfather who deserted wife and sons to fulfill his own dream. Except for the rural setting, which Willy himself had sought in buying a house that was later swamped by apartment development, this self-reliant notion is merely an older, more idealistic (and more selfish) version of the dream that Willy followed. It may be that Biff will be more honest with himself and others in the future, which would certainly be an improvement; but a different setting, with the wife he hankers for, doesn't necessarily imply a different set of values.

Willy's values are all based on the "American dream" of success, and some critics have seen them as the twentieth-century debasement of Emerson's doctrine of self-reliance—a term that Willy himself uses, but in a sense far different from Emerson's meaning. For Willy, the dream has been of fame, one's name in the paper, riches. His father seems to embody an earlier version of the dream—the free-spirited wanderer, the pioneer in the wilderness carving his way (literally), the success through "Yankee ingenuity," an irresponsible Ben Franklin. That nineteenth-century flute maker and flute player (Thoreau played the flute in his cabin at Walden pond) provides the recurring musical motif that opens and closes the play "telling of grass and trees and the horizon," the old simplicities of rural America where possibilities were limitless. In Willy's case, however, the dream has taken on the sentimental falseness of Horatio Alger, and has been used to mask ethical and moral shortcomings. The center of Willy's philosophy is to be "well liked," to achieve success as a salesman through charismatic personality. The measure of success is material possession, and Willy has allowed himself to believe in advertisements, to buy "brand name" cars, a washing machine, a vacuum cleaner (his mistake with the refrigerator was in buying an off-brand). He has always looked to the future to bring fulfillment and happiness (he's "never so happy as when he's looking forward to something"), not only to his hopes for Biff but even to his own funeral. The past he tries to remember with nostalgia about the rustic setting of the house; the future has always seemed ready to open up on those horizons of possibility. But these dreams have assumed such importance in his life that they have justified the petty deceits employed in trying to achieve them—the lies about his sales records, the pilfering of sand and lumber to improve the house, the encouragement of Biff's cheating for the sake of a college scholarship, as well as the not-so-petty adultery that destroyed his son's respect for him, and the suicide made to look accidental to defraud the insurance company. Success at any cost was Willy's program for himself and Biff, but the wages of his sins is self-destruction.

As the comparison with Sophocles suggests, I am not among those who classify this play as a tragedy—but it is not necessary that a play satisfy the definition of tragedy to be great. Miller's achievement is genuine and important, embodying a serious theme and defining a serious flaw in a modern, materialistic world. For Willy Loman, modest hopes and minor dishonesties became a way of life, and Miller shows how understandably they arose, how temperamentally they persisted, and how pathetically they concluded.

Useful articles on Miller and the play are contained in the following: Robert W. Corrigan, ed., *Arthur Miller: A Collection of Critical Essays* (Englewood Cliffs NJ: Prentice, 1969); Robert A. Martin, ed., *Arthur Miller: New Perspectives* (Englewood Cliffs NJ: Prentice, 1982); James J. Martine, ed., *Critical Essays on Arthur Miller* (Boston: Hall, 1979); and Gerald Weales, ed., *Death of a Salesman: Text and Criticism* (New York: Viking, 1967).

Dustin Hoffman, Kate Reid, and John Malkovich star in a television production available on videotape. TRA

August Wilson **Fences** (page 1317)

QUESTIONS

1. Construct a chronological biography of Troy Maxson. How naturally do the expository materials figure into the conversations where they are revealed (that is, what reasons does Troy have for summarizing his past at various points in the play)?
2. Describe the condition of the marriage of Rose and Troy at the opening of the play. What are their habits? How well-meshed are they? What about their marriage has made Troy discontented?
3. What are Troy's relationships to the other characters—Bono, Lyons, Gabriel? Show how these are compounded of both conflict and congruence of feelings.
4. Define the conflicts between Cory and Troy, showing how they develop. In what ways do they resemble those between Troy and his father? What does Troy

377

want to protect Cory from, and what direction does he want him to take? What unspoken dangers does Cory face as a Marine in 1965?

5. Explore the various meanings of the title, from the literal fence Troy is building (why is he? what purpose will it serve?) to the more figurative fences, the obstacles that Troy has faced and overcome. What does the title have to do with Troy's career as a baseball player? How are Troy's victories ironic? (For example, he achieves his wish to become a driver, but what effect does that have on his relationship with Bono? Does it bring him happiness?)

6. What similarities and contrasts exist between this play and *Death of a Salesman*? How is Troy like and unlike Willy Loman, in his situations and in his temperament? What is his attitude toward the importance of being "liked"? Does Troy lie to himself or to others?

7. What aspects of this play make it convincingly realistic in its conventions? What qualities of African-American urban life in the late fifties does it capture? What universal themes are conveyed within this restricted, specific milieu?

At the beginning of the play, Troy has been hardened by his experiences, and has hardened himself against further pain and injury. He doesn't want Cory to be like him, to suffer as he has suffered from the prejudice of the white world, and so he refuses to let his son think of sports as a means of succeeding since he was not allowed to succeed in that way. The world has changed, but Troy cannot see it. His hard life has left him few pleasures—Friday night drinking with Bono, and sex with Rose. He feels stagnant in his "clean . . . hard . . . . useful life," a man who was "born with two strikes" against him who has found a loving wife, a son, and a "halfway decent job" (page 1352). He is, at the outset, "safe." How he reached this impasse is disclosed by a summary of his life to this point reconstructed from realistically scattered conversational remarks:

In 1904, Troy Maxson was born in rural Alabama, the son of a cotton sharecropper and one of eleven children, including his brother Gabriel who was born in 1911. Like Troy in 1957, his father was trapped by his situation and could only concern himself with "getting them bales of cotton in to Mr. Lubin," the owner of the farm. He accepted his responsibility to his family, but he was a hard man, "just as evil as he could be" (page 1343), and when Troy was eight his mother deserted the family; she promised to return for Troy but she never did. His father then lived with a succession of women, all of them deserting him sooner or later. In 1918 when Troy was fourteen, his father found him "fooling around" with a girl when he was supposed to be plowing, and whipped him. Then the father in turn commenced to enjoy the girl, and in his turn Troy began whipping his father. The result was that he was severely beaten, so he left home, walked the 200 miles to Mobile, and then joined a group heading north.

He arrived in Pittsburgh, but couldn't find a job and lived in a shack along the river. For about five years he lived by stealing, then met and married Lyons's mother. When the baby came (1923), he tried to accept his responsibility by stealing more. One day, a man he was robbing shot him and Troy killed him with his knife, and spent fifteen years (1923–38) in the penitentiary.

There he met his best friend, Jim Bono, and learned to play baseball. When he was released in 1938 Lyons's mother had left him and taken their son. Troy felt himself a reformed man, and in 1939 met and married Rose, who bore their son Cory in 1940. Troy played ball in the Negro League, one season batting .432 and hitting 37 home runs facing such legendary opponents as Satchel Paige. By the time that Jackie Robinson became the first black player in the major leagues, Troy was 43 years old. He claims that the color ban still kept him from being accepted, but Bono and Rose insist that it was his age.

Troy nearly died from pneumonia in the summer of 1941. At 37, he was too old to be drafted when the Second World War began later that year, though his younger brother Gabriel served and was severely wounded and mentally disabled. Troy had Gabriel move into their house (using his $3000 veteran's bonus to purchase it), where he lived for more than ten years until renting his own rooms in 1957.

When his baseball career ended at some time in the early forties, Troy found work as a municipal garbage collector. He and his friend Bono still work as pick-up men at the back of a truck driven by a white driver.

As the play opens Troy has created a crisis in his job: he has requested to be made a driver, and has been told to report to the Commissioner's office. His future is uncertain, though he claims to be confident that they cannot fire him for simply asking. In fact, he is given the promotion (though as Bono points out, he has no driver's license) and moves up to the front of his truck. In the course of the play, his promotion leads to his being assigned to a white part of the city and being separated from Bono. The solitude of his assignment makes his advancement less appealing, and not working beside Bono leads to their gradually drifting apart. Their customary Friday evening drinking sessions come to an end, and Bono finds other ways to relax. But more than that, a rift grows between them, because Troy has begun an affair with a woman named Alberta. Bono disapproves, and tells him so; and Troy begins spending all his evenings with Alberta, having no time either for Bono or for his wife Rose.

Troy at length tells Rose of his affair, and of Alberta's pregnancy, for he feels he must accept responsibility for her and her child as well as continue to maintain Rose and their son Cory. Rose is deeply hurt and angered—this is, in fact, the first time that Troy has been unfaithful to her, and she had assumed that they would grow old together in a stable and unchanging life. When he tries to explain to her that Alberta offers him a new sense of himself, a man who has laughter in his soul, Rose can only remind him of how much she has submerged her own identity in him. Alberta's death in childbirth leads to a new accommodation in the relationship of Troy and Rose: she will help him by rearing the child and so fulfilling his obligation, but she will never be intimate with him again.

Troy's other climactic conflict occurs between him and Cory, who is being recruited for a football scholarship for a college in North Carolina. Troy's frustration with his own career in sports, having been barred from the success he should have had in the major leagues because of his color, makes him cynically reject the chance that seems to be opening up for Cory. Troy does not believe that the whites will really accept and reward Cory for his athletic ability, and concludes that the boy will only be hurt and rejected as he himself was: "the white man ain't gonna let you get nowhere with that football noway" (page 1336). His ambition for Cory does not include a college education but what he thinks is more realistic, training and hard work that will lead to slow but gradual advancement—working as an auto mechanic or as a builder, some trade that will surpass such a service job as his own.

When Cory lies to him about a job arrangement at the A & P supermarket that will permit him to practice football and keep his job part-time, Troy has him removed from the football team. In their confrontation, Cory asks him why he doesn't "like" his son, and Troy defines for him his sense of paternal duties: he fully accepts his responsibility for the boy's physical well-being, but "I ain't got to like you." Troy's position is that a man who thinks he can get what he wants by being "liked" is a fool—"Don't you try and go through life worrying about if somebody like you or not" (page 1337); rather insist that you are paid what you earn. Life, Troy has come to believe, is a sequence of debts to be paid when you incur them, and of obligations to be returned by those who owe you. His code is keep your word to others and require others to keep theirs to you.

In his baseball metaphor, Troy counts the strikes against his son. Cory's first strike is when he lies to Troy about the job and football. His second comes when Troy is hurting Rose as they quarrel about Alberta and Cory knocks Troy down trying to protect his mother from abuse. The third strike, and the end of their relationship, occurs when Cory denounces his father for his betrayal of Rose and for taking Gabriel's money and then getting rid of him. When Troy advances on his son, Cory grabs his baseball bat and threatens Troy with it, then loses it as they struggle over it. Troy checks himself and does not strike Cory with it, but throws him out of the house. Cory enlists in the Marines, and does not see his father alive again.

So in the years 1957–58, Troy Maxson sees his life fall apart as he confronts his major conflicts. He breaks through a color barrier at work, but the success cuts him off from his best friend. He finds another kind of love in his life, and through it loses both of the women who satisfy his needs. He confronts his son and tries to force him into a way of life that will be safe and secure, but loses him forever. And he boldly confronts death, and loses.

The title provides a recurring thematic comment. It refers first of all to the little wooden fence that Rose wants Troy to build around their front yard. As Bono says, "Some people build fences to keep people out . . . and other people build fences to keep people in. Rose wants to hold on to you all. She loves you" (page 1348). Rose also sings her prayer to Jesus, "be a fence around me every day . . . protect me as I travel on my way" (page 1328). As the representative of stability, Rose wants a fence to function in both of Bono's definitions, to ward off outside dangers as well as to keep her loved ones within. It is ironic that the literal fence is completed for her after her safe haven has disintegrated through Troy's infidelity, and now functions as the boundary of the yard from which Troy banishes Cory.

In addition to the literal fence there are a number of fencelike barriers, literal and figurative, in the play. Troy has overcome two of them, the outfield fence over which he hit his 37 home runs and the fence that kept him from a promotion in the white man's hierarchy. Unfortunately, both of these triumphs turn to ashes for him, for his baseball career ended in frustration and his work as a driver has made him lonely and unhappy. Troy's life has been filled with obstacles, and more often than not overcoming them creates equivocal victories. Beginning fenced in by the economic system in Alabama, his escape led to criminality in the oppressive system he found in Pittsburgh. Within prison walls, he found a good friend and a new opportunity with baseball, but both are lost to him over time once he is outside the bars. His need to establish a stable home life and to help his disabled brother led to using Gabriel's pension for a house payment for which he is haunted by guilt and taunted by his son. He tries to break free of the constrictions of his domestic obligation and to find "a different understanding" of himself: "I done locked myself into a pattern trying to take care of [Rose and Cory, and] I forgot about myself" (page 1352). His experience with Alberta does give him a new sense of himself as a man taking risks and living more fully—but the consequences are catastrophic.

Troy Maxson is a tragic figure, for his mistakes arise from attempts to overcome barriers to a better, fuller life, and they destroy what he has achieved. It is instructive to compare him to Willy Loman, a man with parallel conflicts with his children, his wife, and the terms of his life, and at whose death the survivors present a concluding "epilogue" evaluating him. Willy does his best to avoid looking straight at his situation—he's evasive, self-deceptive, and incapable. Troy strives to help and support, to understand and to enlarge his life, to overcome both external and internal barriers.

Fences is perhaps the most realistic play in this collection. Its structure is linear, each scene building on the results of the preceding one, and its expository method is wholly naturalistic. The facts we learn about Troy's past are revealed at times when such facts would reasonably come out (for example, he speaks of his boyhood and early manhood to his son Lyons, as a way of telling him about obligations between fathers and sons when Lyons attempts to defend Cory). The passage of time is conventionally established as occurring between scenes, so that what we witness is a sequence of episodes each with its own naturalistic duration. And most emphatically, the life we glimpse is an entirely credible world of a defined social and intellectual nature, honest and true to the experience of its people and its place, captured in vigorous and beautiful dialect.

August Wilson has said this about his play:

> At the end of *Fences* every person, with the exception of Raynell, is institutionalized. Rose is in a church. Lyons is in a penitentiary; Gabriel's in a mental hospital and Cory's in the marines. The only free person is the girl, Troy's daughter, the hope for the future. That was conscious on my part because in '57 that's what I saw.

(Quoted in David Savran, *In Their Own Words: Contemporary American Playwrights* [New York: Theatre Communications Group, 1988] 301.)

In a televised interview with Bill Moyers (available on PBS video), Wilson makes the important point: although this play is directly concerned with the experience of African-Americans at the time and in the place in which it is set, its themes are not restricted to those specifics. It is about relationships between a father and his sons,

THEMATIC TABLE OF CONTENTS

The selections in the first part of each genre in *Literature: Structure, Sound, and Sense* were chosen to illustrate the elements of fiction, poetry, and drama as well as for their interest and literary value. However, instructors sometimes find that a thematic approach works best with their students; in such circumstances, the following thematic contents may be helpful. Since much good literature defies classification into any one category, these lists are only suggestions, not rigid classifications. Not all of the selections in the book are included, and, of those which are, several are listed in more than one category.

YOUTH AND AGE

Fiction

Poetry

384

Drama

THE CONDUCT AND MEANING OF LIFE

Fiction

Poetry

391

FORMS OF VIOLENCE

397